HUMANIORA

ESSAYS IN LITERATURE · FOLKLORE · BIBLIOGRAPHY

ARCHER TAYLOR

HUMANIORA

ESSAYS IN LITERATURE · FOLKLORE · BIBLIOGRAPHY

HONORING ARCHER TAYLOR
ON HIS SEVENTIETH BIRTHDAY

Editors

WAYLAND D. HAND
GUSTAVE O. ARLT

J. J. AUGUSTIN PUBLISHER · LOCUST VALLEY, NEW YORK
1960

Library of Congress Catalog Card Number: 60-13574

PRINTED IN GERMANY
AT J. J. AUGUSTIN, GLÜCKSTADT

DEDICATED TO

ARCHER TAYLOR'S STUDENTS

TABLE OF CONTENTS

ILLUSTRATIONS

TABULA GRATULATORIA

BRYNJULF ALVER, SKEDAMO · WALTER ANDERSON, KIEL · GUSTAVE O. ARLT, LOS ANGELES · ISAAC BACON, NEW YORK · A. A. BAKE, LONDON · HAROLD A. BASILIUS, DETROIT · FRANZ H. BAUML, LOS ANGELES · CARL F. BAYERSCHMIDT, NEW YORK · THEODORE BESTERMAN, GENEVA · JUDITH BINKELE, PEORIA · LAURITS BØDKER, NIVAA · HERMANN BOESCHENSTEIN, TORONTO · R. S. BOGGS, MIAMI · DONALD F. BOND, CHICAGO · LEICESTER BRADNER, PROVIDENCE · SYTVAN AND ELIZABETH BRANDON, HOUSTON · MARGARET M. BRYANT, BROOKLYN · CURT F. BUHLER, NEW YORK · T. MOODY CAMPBELL, LYNCHBURG · FRANCIS J. CARMODY, BERKELEY · REIDAR TH. CHRISTIANSEN, BLOMMENHOLM · CALVIN CLAUDEL, CHALMETTE · CARL COLDITZ, DETROIT · EDWARD CRAY, LOS ANGELES · MICHELE DE FILIPPIS, BERKELEY · HUGH G. DICK, PACIFIC PALISADES · RICHARD AND PEGGY DOREMUS, THOUSAND OAKS · RICHARD M. DORSON, BLOOMINGTON · WOLFRAM EBERHARD, BERKELEY · M. B. EMENEAU, BERKELEY · CURT VON FABER DU FAUR, NEW HAVEN · WILLARD FARNHAM, BERKELEY · ALBERT B. FRIEDMAN, CAMBRIDGE · BEATRICE GALBRETH, PINOLE · HELENA M. GAMER, CHICAGO · FRIEDMAR GEISSLER, BERLIN · IVAN GRAFENAUER, LJUBLJANA · ERIK F. GRAUBART, RIVERSIDE · HERBERT HALPERT, CARLINVILLE · L. L. HAMMERICH, COPENHAGEN · WAYLAND D. HAND, LOS ANGELES · JOUKO HAUTALA, HELSINKI · PROF. DR. HEILFURTH, MARBURG · HUGO HEPDING †, GIESSEN · ARCHIBALD A. HILL, AUSTIN · RUDOLF HIRSCH, SWARTHMORE · WINFRIED HOFMANN, BONN · CARLTON L. IIAMS, OBERLIN · HIROKO IKEDA, HONOLULU · DANICA S. JANKOVIĆ † AND LJUBICA JANKOVIĆ, BELGRADE · ASSAR JANZÉN, BERKELEY · SEARS R. JAYNE, CLAREMONT · GEORGE F. JONES, BALTIMORE · RICHARD F. JONES, MENLO PARK · EDWARD KAHN, SANTA MONICA · WALTER C. KRAFT, CORVALLIS · JULIAN KRZYŻANOWSKI, WARSAW · JOHN G. KUNSTMANN, CHAPEL HILL · MATTI KUUSI, HELSINKI · HENNING LARSEN, URBANA, ILLINOIS · G. MALCOLM LAWS, JR., NARBERTH · HECTOR LEE, CHICO · W. P. LEHMANN, AUSTIN · C. GRANT LOOMIS, BERKELEY · MAX LUTHI, ZÜRICH · GORDON MCKENZIE, BERKELEY · YAKOV AND MARIA ROSA LIDA MALKIEL, BERKELEY · KEMP MALONE, BALTIMORE · GEORGIOS A. MEGAS, ATHENS · WILLIAM W. MELNITZ, LOS ANGELES · GEORGE J. METCALF, CHICAGO · HEINRICH MEYER, EMMOUS · ROBERT T. MEYER, WASHINGTON · MRS. BARRINGTON MOORE, JR., CAMBRIDGE · HANS AND ELFRIEDE MOSER, MUNICH · SIEGFRIED NEUMANN, ROSTOCK · HELAINE NEWSTEAD, NEW YORK · FRED O. NOLTE, SAINT LOUIS · CLAIR C. OLSON, STOCKTON · NILS WILLIAM OLSSON, WASHINGTON · STANLEY PARGELLIS, CHICAGO · HOWARD R. PATCH, WELLESLEY · MRS. LEE PERKAL, VAN NUYS · B. E. PERRY, URBANA · WILLERICH PEUCKERT, GÖTTINGEN · RAUL PIMENTEL, HOUSTON · ROGER PINON, LIÈGE · ROBERT A. PRATT, URBANA · VANCE RANDOLPH, EUREKA SPRINGS · KURT RANKE, KIEL · WILLIAM F. ROERTGEN, LOS ANGELES · LUTZ RÖHRICH, MAINZ · ANNA BIRGITTA ROOTH, LUND · HEDWIG V. ROQUES, ASCONA · JOSEPH RUBINSTEIN, LAWRENCE · INGRID SCHELLBACH, FYVASKLA · THOMAS A. SEBEOK, PALO ALTO · ERICH SEEMANN, FREIBURG · KARL LUDWIG SELIG, CHAPEL HILL · ALFRED SENN, PHILADELPHIA · WALTER SILZ, PRINCETON · GWLADYS H. SIMON, BARSTOW · ELI SOBEL, LOS ANGELES · CHARLES SPERONI, LOS ANGELES · TAYLOR STARCK, CAMBRIDGE · HENRI

STEGEMEIER, URBANA · DAG STRÖMBÄCK, UPPSALA · F. W. STROTHMANN, STANFORD · RANSOM T. TAYLOR, CHAPEL HILL · MARIE-LOUISE TENÈZE, PARIS · LAWRENCE S. THOMPSON, LEXINGTON · STITH THOMPSON, BLOOMINGTON · CARL-HERMAN TILLHAGEN, STOCKHOLM · FRANCIS LEE UTLEY, COLUMBUS · JORMA VALLINKOSKI, HELSINKI · FRANCIS G. VERY, BERKELEY · DONALD J. WARD, LOS ANGELES · WALDEMAR WESTERGAARD, LOS ANGELES · BARTLETT JERE WHITING, CAMBRIDGE · ROBERT WILDHABER, BASEL · ERNEST H. WILKINS, NEWTON CENTRE · E. O. WOOLEY, BLOOMINGTON ·

AMERICAN PHILOSOPHICAL SOCIETY · AMHERST COLLEGE · DET KGL. BIBLIOTEK, COPEN-HAGEN · BIBLIOTHÈQUE DE L'UNIVERSITÉ, LOUVAIN · BOSTON UNIVERSITY · BRIGHAM YOUNG UNIVERSITY · BROWN UNIVERSITY · BUFFALO AND ERIE COUNTY PUBLIC LIBRARY · JOHN CARROLL UNIVERSITY · JOHN G. WHITE COLLECTION OF FOLKLORE AND ORIENTALIA, CLEVELAND PUBLIC LIBRARY · COLGATE UNIVERSITY · COLUMBIA UNIVERSITY · CONNECTICUT COLLEGE · CORNELL UNIVERSITY · DEUTSCHES VOLKSLIEDARCHIV, FREIBURG · DUKE UNIVERSITY · THE FOLGER SHAKESPEARE LIBRARY · GOUCHER COLLEGE · HARVARD UNIVERSITY · INDIANA UNIVERSITY · IRISH FOLKLORE COMMISSION · JOHNS HOPKINS UNIVERSITY · KANSAS STATE UNIVERSITY · LANDSMÅLS-OCH FOLKMINNESARKIVET, UPPSALA · LAVAL UNIVERSITY · LIBRARY OF CONGRESS · LOUISIANA STATE UNIVERSITY · ÖSTERREICHISCHES MUSEUM FÜR VOLKSKUNDE · PIERPONT MORGAN LIBRARY · BIBLIOTHÈQUE NATIONALE, OTTAWA · THE NEWBERRY LIBRARY · NEW YORK PUBLIC LIBRARY · NORDISKA MUSEET · NORTHWESTERN UNIVERSITY · OHIO STATE UNIVERSITY · KANSALLIS OSAKE PANKKI, HELSINKI · PENNSYLVANIA STATE COLLEGE · PRINCETON UNIVERSITY · THE ROYAL LIBRARY, COPENHAGEN · RUTGERS UNIVERSITY · STANFORD UNIVERSITY · SWARTHMORE COLLEGE · SYRACUSE UNIVERSITY · TEXAS WESTERN COLLEGE · UNIVERSITY OF ARIZONA · UNIVERSITY OF ATHENS · UNIVERSITY OF BRITISH COLUMBIA · UNIVERSITY OF BUFFALO · UNIVERSITY OF CALIFORNIA, BERKELEY · UNIVERSITY OF CALIFORNIA, LOS ANGELES · UNIVERSITY OF CALIFORNIA ARCHIVES, BERKELEY · FOLKLORE GROUP, UNIVERSITY OF CALIFORNIA, LOS ANGELES · UNIVERSITY OF CHICAGO · UNIVERSITY OF CINCINNATI · UNIVERSITY COLLEGE, LONDON · UNIVERSITY OF COLORADO · UNIVERSITY OF DENVER · UNIVERSITY OF DETROIT · SCHOOL OF SCOTTISH STUDIES, UNIVERSITY UNIVERSITY OF CINCINNATI · UNIVERSITY COLLEGE, LONDON · UNIVERSITY OF COLORADO · UNIVERSITY OF DENVER · UNIVERSITY OF DETROIT · SCHOOL OF SCOTTISH STUDIES, UNIVERSITY OF EDINBURGH · UNIVERSITY OF FLORIDA · UNIVERSITY OF HAWAII · DEPARTMENT OF ENGLISH, UNIVERSITY OF ILLINOIS · DEPARTMENT OF GERMAN, UNIVERSITY OF ILLINOIS · UNIVERSITY OF IOWA · UNIVERSITY OF KANSAS · THE UNIVERSITY OF KENTUCKY · UNIVERSITY OF LONDON · UNIVERSITY OF MAINE · UNIVERSITY OF MASSACHUSETTS · UNIVERSITY OF MICHIGAN · UNIVER-SITY OF MINNESOTA · UNIVERSITY OF MISSOURI · UNIVERSITY OF NEBRASKA · UNIVERSITY OF NEW MEXICO · UNIVERSITY OF NORTH CAROLINA · UNIVERSITY OF NOTRE DAME · UNIVERSITY OF OREGON · UNIVERSITY OF PENNSYLVANIA · UNIVERSITY OF SOUTHERN CALIFORNIA · UNIVERSITY OF TENNESSEE · THE UNIVERSITY OF TEXAS · DEPARTMENT OF ENGLISH, UNIVER-SITY OF TEXAS · DEPT. OF GERMANIC LANGUAGES, UNIVERSITY OF TEXAS · UNIVERSITY OF TORONTO · UNIVERSITY OF UTAH · UNIVERSITY OF WASHINGTON · WESTDEUTSCHE BIBLIOTHEK · UNIVERSITY OF WISCONSIN · UTAH STATE UNIVERSITY · WAYNE STATE UNIVERSITY · WESTERN RESERVE UNIVERSITY · YALE UNIVERSITY

ARCHER TAYLOR

There is an old cliché that likens a simple, straightforward, and honorable life to an open book. Within the restricted sense of that cliché, Archer Taylor's life is indeed an open book. But in another and much wider sense, his life is not just *an* open book but an enormous number of open books, vast libraries of open books— books that he read and books that he wrote, books that he acquired and collected, books that he induced others to acquire and collect, books that he reviewed, books that he resurrected from oblivion. There are scholars whose lives are identified with laboratories, with formulas, with statistical recordings, but Archer Taylor's life is surrounded with books. Books have determined his career—or, perhaps, it is more accurate to say that he has built his career on books. Twenty years ago, in 1940, he collaborated in the preparation and publication of a little book called *Printing and Progress*; it is so unimportant to him that it is not even listed in his lifetime bibliography. But in this little book he pays tribute to the contribution that the printed book has made to Western culture and, indirectly, to his own life and to his career. And, as we briefly review the course of his life, we shall see that the books that he read and the books that he wrote represent the framework, the skeleton of the career of the man whom intellectual history will probably designate as the greatest humanistic scholar of our era.

Archer Taylor was born on August 1, 1890, in Philadelphia, the son of Lowndes and Florence York Taylor. His was a sturdy, strict Quaker family, and his early training was in the unbending tradition of the descendants of William Penn and of the Philadelphia Old Main Line. It was a foregone conclusion that he would attend Swarthmore College. There he received his Bachelor's degree at the age of nineteen, when most of his contemporaries were only entering college. His under-graduate majors and minors were in languages and literatures, with emphasis on German. A year later, in 1910, he took his Master's degree in German at the University of Pennsylvania. From 1910 to 1912 he marked time as Instructor of German at Pennsylvania State College and then he embarked upon his true academic career.

It began in the traditional manner with the Grand Tour of Europe, but not with capital letters but rather in the manner of a humble and ambitious American student who worked his way over and back. The memories of that first pilgrimage to the shrines of his later studies have remained with Archer Taylor through his life. Upon his return he entered Harvard Graduate School. Those were the last days of Harvard's humanistic splendor: Kuno Francke was still there and George Lyman Kittredge, and John Albrecht Walz was in his youthful prime. Here, for the next three years, "he girded his spirits and deepened the streams that make glad the fair City of God." And here he received the first strong impetus in the direction of folklore that remained the major interest of his life, no matter how involved he became with Sixteenth-Century literature, with Meistergesang, with Jungdeutschland, and eventually with bibliography. His doctoral dissertation on the Wolfdietrich epics, though not directly concerned with folklore, leaned heavily in that direction.

In the fall of 1915 young Doctor Archer Taylor left the charmed precincts of Cambridge for the more prosaic environs of Washington University in St. Louis. But on the way he lingered long enough in Pennsylvania to marry—on September 9, 1915—his childhood sweetheart, Alice Jones, and to take her with him to the metropolis of the Mississippi Valley. In the course of their ten years at Washington University she gave him three children—Margaret, Richard, and Cynthia, all now married and engaged upon careers of their own.

Archer Taylor's phenomenal scholarly productivity began as soon as he arrived at Washington University. In 1916 he made his first small contribution to *Modern Language Notes* and in 1917 he published his first substantial articles in the two journals with which he was later to become intimately connected, *Modern Philology* and the *Journal of American Folklore*. Throughout the ten years at St. Louis, there was probably very little connection between the young scholar's research and his teaching. His classroom activities were largely confined to elementary and intermediate German with an occasional excursion into an upper division course in literature while his research was concentrated almost exclusively on folklore. During this period, also, he began to build his international bridges and to cultivate the acquaintance of folklorists in virtually all countries where such studies flourished. Many of these acquaintances eventually developed into close, lifelong friendships. Somehow also, during this period he found time to interest himself in the post-war plight of the library of the University of Gießen and to render such substantial service that the University honored him by electing him *Ehrensenator*.

Probably the most important change in Archer Taylor's career came in 1923 when the University of Chicago invited him to teach in the Summer Quarter. Chicago was then at the height of its humanistic glory; its departments of Classics, Germanic Languages, and Romance Languages were models of distinction; its library, already great, was rapidly expanding. This was the proper environment in which Archer Taylor's scholarly gifts could unfold and come to full fruition. This was his first opportunity to share the wealth of his erudition and of his research with students advanced enough to profit by it. This was his first opportunity to rub elbows and match wits daily with distinguished scholars in fields related to his own.

In the summer of 1925 Archer Taylor joined the company of scholars at the University of Chicago as Professor of German Literature and two years later he was appointed head of the Department of Germanic Languages and Literatures. His fourteen years at the University of Chicago were in some ways the most satisfying of his entire career. He was in a lively, active department in a dynamic university. His growing reputation brought him excellent graduate students from all parts of the country. Best of all, he was given a very free hand to build the Germanics and folklore library to meet his needs and those of his students. Of this freedom he took full advantage. He combed the book catalogues and the antiquarian stores, and gradually the library in Wiebold Hall became a show place for scholars from America and Europe. Along with the great linguistic scholar, Leonard Bloomfield, he built an incomparable Middle High German collection. The folklore section soon was second only to Harvard. The Reformation and Renaissance sections acquired such rarities as the complete works— thirty-seven volumes—of Geiler von Kaisersberg, not to be found together in any other library in the world. As the resources in these fields of his special interests became adequate and more than adequate, he turned to other areas. He bought the Linke Rental Library, a unique collection of German sub-literary fiction of the late eighteenth and early nineteenth centuries, 16,000-odd volumes. And toward the end of his stay at Chicago he began to build a relatively small but very choice collection of the Jungdeutschland period.

His scholarly output during those years attained astonishing proportions. His appointment as head of the department was marked by the appearance of his first major monograph, *The Black Ox*, published in "FF Communications" in Helsinki, Finland. The year 1931 brought the publication of two distinguished books, *Edward and Sven i Rosengård*, a ballad study, and *The Proverb*, a beautifully written, thorough-going, and at the time definitive study of that genre. In addition to

1*

these major works there were scores upon scores of articles in various journals, reviews without number, and by special assignment, many sections of the two great compendiums that were then appearing in Europe, *Handwörterbuch des deutschen Aberglaubens*, and *Handwörterbuch des deutschen Märchens*.

In his personal life, the years at Chicago brought two events of deep consequence to Archer Taylor. On June 16, 1930, Alice Jones Taylor died, leaving him with their three young children. The months and years immediately following were difficult indeed for the widowed father, trying to provide a home for his motherless children. But two years later, on June 17, 1932, he married Hasseltine Byrd, who, since then, not only provided a home for him and his children, but also presented him with two more daughters, Mary Constance and Ann Byrd. Hasseltine Taylor brought to their union the very qualities which the now mature scholar needed—the personal and social graces of her fine Southern background and the academic training of her doctoral degree in the University of Chicago School of Social Welfare. The achievements of the latter twenty-five years of Archer Taylor's career he owes in large part to the devoted and intelligent care that Hasseltine Byrd Taylor lavished upon him.

The last few years at Chicago saw a remarkable broadening of Archer Taylor's scholarly interests. Early in 1935 he published an article entitled "The überlange Töne in Meistergesang," the first indication of his involvement with the literature and sub-literature of the Reformation period, followed in 1936 by a brief note on Benedict von Watt. Then, almost unheralded, in 1937, appeared his brilliant book, *The Literary History of Meistergesang*, published by the Modern Language Association, and followed almost immediately by *A Bibliography of Meistergesang*. With these two publications Archer Taylor broke sharply out of the restricted area of folklore and established himself as a scholar in late mediaeval studies and, in fact, as the *Polyhistor* he has now become.

. . .

I have tried, up to this point, to keep this account of Archer Taylor's life as objective and as impersonal as possible, in spite of the fact that since 1923 our lives and our careers have undoubtedly had a close interrelation. It has been difficult, as I wrote the foregoing paragraphs, to keep the pronoun of the first person singular entirely out of them, for sometimes it might properly have been there. I can never say, and I certainly shall not try to say it here and now, what I owe to Archer Taylor as my teacher, my Mentor, and my almost lifelong friend. But I must admit—or claim—for better or for worse, some degree of responsibility for his decision to leave the University of Chicago and to come for the last two decades of his career to the University of California. My own dedication to the University of California and to the Pacific Coast and three—for me—unforgettable weeks that Archer Taylor and I spent together in a cabin on the North Rim of the Grand Canyon in 1938 probably helped him to make up his mind. I hope he has never regretted it.

• • •

In the fall of 1939 Archer Taylor joined the faculty of the University of California, Berkeley, as Professor of German Literature. The upheaval of the move from Chicago to Berkeley and the added burden of the chairmanship of the Department of German which was soon thrust upon him brought no interruption to his productivity. In the year of his arrival two new books appeared: *A Bibliography of Riddles*, in "FF Communications," and the distinguished volume entitled *Problems in German Literary History of the Fifteenth and Sixteenth Centuries*. Within a year of his arrival, in 1940, a number of colleagues from two campuses of the University gathered at his house and founded the California Folklore Society and its organ, the *California Folklore Quarterly*, with Archer Taylor as its editor. Today, twenty years later, the Society flourishes and its journal, now called *Western Folklore*, is one of the most highly regarded folklore journals in the United States.

The years from 1940 to 1950 may well be called Archer Taylor's "Riddle Decade." Beginning in 1939 with *A Bibliography of Riddles* he devoted a large part of his time to this genre, producing an incredible number of articles and editing a number of riddle collections. These range from brief items, like "Twenty-three Telugu Riddles from Nellore" through the substantial *Collection of Welsh Riddles*, climaxing in 1951 with the weighty tome, *English Riddles from Oral Tradition*, running to almost a thousand pages.

At the same time, however, Archer Taylor was quietly becoming interested in another, almost untouched field, the history of bibliography. His year, in 1945, as Fellow of the Newberry Library at Chicago helped to establish him firmly in this field of study. His judicious purchases eventually built up his own library until today he owns probably the most complete and most distinguished collection of bibliographical works in private hands. In 1945, also, he began to publish on the subject, first "A Historical Sketch of German Bibliography to 1700," then the *Renaissance Guides to Books*. In 1951 there followed (with F. J. Mosher) *The Bibliographical History of Anonyma and Pseudonyma* and, more recently, *A*

History of Bibliographies of Bibliographies and *Book Catalogues: Their Varieties and Uses.*

In recent years Archer Taylor has returned to one of his old loves, the Proverb in its various forms. Now he concerns himself with proverbial comparisons and similes, proverbial and conventional phrases, clichés and other idiomatic expressions. A number of articles and several substantial annotated collections have already resulted from this revived interest and he has a very large volume of proverbial phrases from California in preparation.

Over the years many honors came to Archer Taylor which he accepted with characteristic modesty. He is a Fellow of the Medieval Academy of America, of the American Academy of Arts and Sciences, of the American Philosophical Society. He was President of the American Folklore Society from 1935 to 1937 and of the Modern Language Association of America in 1951. He is an honorary member of the folklore societies of Switzerland, Finland, Argentina, Sweden, Ireland, and Mexico and of the Academies of Sciences of Finland and Norway.

It comes almost as a surprise to find that this man of unparalleled literary productivity has also found time for leisurely and gracious living. He and Hasseltine Taylor enjoy entertaining their friends in their charming home in the Berkeley hills and their hospitable house is always open for overnight guests from out of town. Early in the 1940s they bought a large tract of hilly and wooded land in Napa County and since then they have spent most of their week-ends and summers there. About 1950 they began to build—with their own hands—a huge, rambling stone house on a hilltop looking down into the Sacramento Valley. The basic materials for this castle all came from their own land—they quarried their own rock and cut their own sugar pines for timber. For anyone who knew Archer Taylor only from his books it would have been an incongruous sight to see the great scholar in overalls, setting a charge of dynamite, affixing a percussion cap and fuse, and running pell-mell for cover behind a tree as the blast went off. Or, on another day, Hasseltine Taylor driving the jeep, they would snake pine trunks from the grove to their sawmill and cut them into joists, beams, studs, and planks. And before the massive walls were finished Archer Taylor had probably wheeled as many barrows full of concrete as he had published scholarly articles.

Today the house is finished and it is as characteristic of Archer Taylor as his office at the University and his study in Berkeley—it is full of books. A portion of his library is permanently installed there and other portions of it travel back and forth between Berkeley and Napa as he needs them. Some day, perhaps, the Squire of the Napa Hills will actually retire to his wooded retreat and devote himself exclusively to his books—those which he reads and those which he writes. But so far his retirement from active teaching in the University of California has meant only more active life, an additional year at Berkeley, a semester at the University of Texas, a semester at the Newberry. If he wanted to do it, he could probably go on indefinitely, teaching at a different university each year. But his remaining years should belong not to a few students in seminar or classroom—students to whom he gave richly and without stint—but to posterity, and the rich heritage which he will pass on to coming generations should be further enriched by the products of his coming leisure years.

University of California, Los Angeles   GUSTAVE O. ARLT

SIR RICHARD BAKER'S
CATO VARIEGATUS (1636)

BARTLETT JERE WHITING

The list of men of letters for whom prison has afforded both opportunity and inspiration for composition is long, even though we look no farther back than Boethius, and contains authors of varying degrees of ability and reputation. From this mixed bag the present paper extracts, if but briefly, Sir Richard Baker, who entered the Fleet prison apparently in 1635 and remained there until his death in 1645.[1] It was in the Fleet that he began to write for publication, his chief and most popular work being his *Chronicle of the Kings of England*, first printed in 1643 and subsequently appearing in many editions. If the casual reader knows of Baker at all it is from references made to his *Chronicle* by Addison and Fielding, references not such as to suggest that either author took Baker too seriously as an historian. Sir Roger de Coverly "had drawn many observations together out of his reading in Baker's *Chronicle*, and other authors, who always lie in his hall window" (*Spectator* 269, Jan. 8, 1712), and again, when Sir Roger visited Westminster Abbey, "The glorious names of Henry the Fifth and queen Elizabeth gave the knight great opportunities of shining, and of doing justice to Sir Richard Baker, who, as our knight observed with some surprise, had a great many kings in him, whose monuments he had not seen in the abbey" (*Spectator* 329, March 18, 1712).

---

[1] For an account of Baker's life, see Sir Sidney Lee in DNB I, 934 ff. He was born about 1568, entered Oxford in 1584 and, though he left without a degree, was made Master of Arts in 1594. In 1593 he had become a member of Parliament and was knighted by James in 1603. By 1620 he was high sheriff of Oxfordshire, but soon after debts, some of them come to him with his wife, piled up and eventually led to financial ruin and prison.

8

In Sir Thomas Booby's house, Joseph Andrews "had read the Bible, the Whole Duty of Man, and Thomas à Kempis; and that as often as he could, without being perceived, he had studied a great good book which lay open in the hall window, where he had read 'as how the devil carried away half a church in sermon time, without hurting one of the congregation; and as how a field of corn ran away down a hill with all the trees upon it, and covered another man's meadow.' This sufficiently assured Mr. Adams that the good book meant could be no other than Baker's Chronicle" (*The History of the Adventures of Joseph Andrews*, bk. i, ch. 3). Sir Thomas may well have owned a copy of the edition of 1679, and if so Joseph's reading had ranged at least from page 165 to page 399, though Mr. Adams, if himself letter perfect in Baker, might have observed that Joseph's versions of the "casualties" in question were somewhat free. Though Joseph (and Fielding) had clearly consulted Baker at first hand, the fact that both Sir Roger and Sir Thomas kept the book in the hall window is probably not pure coincidence.

Our immediate concern, however, is not with the *Chronicle* or with Baker's not inconsiderable number of religious works, but with the first fruits of his imprisonment, his *Cato Variegatus, or Catoes Morall Distichs: Translated and Paraphras'd, with variations of Expressing, in English verse*, entered in the Stationers' Register in November, 1635, and printed by Anne Griffin to be sold by Anne Bowler, in 1636. Of this work Lee writes (p. 935), "It gives for each of Cato's Latin distichs five different English couplets of very mediocre quality, and is only interesting as the work of the old man's enforced leisure."[2] The statement is more precise than accurate, since while the first distich of the first book is represented by five English versions, the second distich appears in eighteen, and only in perhaps a dozen instances scattered through the work did Baker happen to hit upon five.

Baker, in his preface, speaks of a translation of the *Distichs* made by "A Lover of Learning... some twelve years since,"[3] who, by adhering too closely to the original, "could not alwaies, either so fully, or so gracefully, express the mening: for indeed, the words of one language, cannot alwaies be reached, by the very same words of another." This led Baker to attempt his versions, of which he said, "And if many of these, seeme rather Paraphrases, or rather Collateral Conceits then translations: yet seeing they tend all to the same sence: and that the direct translations are sent before, as set always next the latine: they are but after the

<hr />

[2] This passage doubtless led Max Förster (*Archiv*, CXLV [1923] 210) to describe the book as "die metrische Version des Parlamentariers Sir Richard Baker...die zu jedem Distichon fünf (allerdings recht mäßige) englische Verspaare bietet, die der alte Mann in Fleet-Gefängnis, das er schuldenhalber beziehen mußte, geschrieben hatte."

[3] Sig. A 3[r]. This "Lover of Learning" is doubtless John Penkethman, whose *Handful of Honesty, or, Cato in English Verse* (1623) apparently survives in one copy only.

fashion of young men, who weare thin cloaths, in cold winter, but haue good warm wast-cotes vnder them, and some men, may bee of that disposition, to take as much delight, in the conceit of the Expressing as in the expressing of the conceit'' (Sig. A 3r–v). He does not feel the necessity of too much apology for his efforts, "Howsoever it be; the worke I am sure, is such, as need not repent me, of one moneth spent in writing it: Nor thee, whosoever thou art of one houre spent in reading it'' (Sig. A 4r).

An example of Baker's method may be given by citing his translation of III, 19 (pp. 69–70):

Multa legas facito: Perlectis, perlege multa:
Nam Mirranda canunt, sed non Credenda Poeta.

Read much, and much read; Read much more; In briefe:
Poets are all for wonder, not beleefe.

Or thus:

Read much; and much read; Read it againe: Indeed
Poets speake strange things, but not alwayes Creed.

Or thus:

Read more and more: and still Reade more: and know,
Poets tel wonders, but not Gospell though.

Or thus:

Never give over Reading by thy will:
Poets sing sweet; but above Ela still.

Or thus:

Never give over Reading, nor forbeare it.
Though Poets tell thee wonders, Doe not sweare it.

Or thus:

Be Reading still; and never shut thine eyes;
Poets tel Tales, are neither Truth nor lies.

Or thus:

Be Reading still: Poets can give a passe,
To that shall never be, nor ever was.

Or thus:

Thy Bookes and thee, let nothing part a sunder:
In Poets mouthes, A miracle is no wonder.

Some of his verses are original enough and show that he was by no means unaware of the kind of poetry that was being written about him, as the following quotations may serve to indicate:

> Much Opium doth the sences overcome:
> And what is sleepe, but Natures Opium?   (I 2, p. 3)

> Feare not the time, that life shall end her taske:
> The Feare of Dying is Deaths Antimaske.   (I 22, p. 19)

> Gods secrets, Riddles are; for which a man,
> Is no fit Oedypus, Doe what he can   (II 2, p. 34)

> Would any Pedlers, if they were not Typsies:
> Open their Packs amongst a sort of Gipsies?   (II 18, p. 46)

> Set not thy rest up; on things base and meane:
> Who ever knew a Sexton, made a Deane?   (IV 7, p. 79)

> Where may we goe, to finde a faithfull Friend?
> Whither? but to Vtopia or worlds End.   (IV 15, p. 83)

> The streame runs smooth where deepe; and such is one,
> That saeis not much; and lookes like Fryer *Iohn*.   (IV 31, p. 95)

Not unnaturally, Baker often finds it convenient to use proverbs in spinning out his paraphrases, and because these have not been collected in any of the dictionaries of English proverbs, it may be of use to bring them together here. The proverbs are arranged alphabetically under the italicized key words, and references wherever possible are given to the major collections of English proverbs.[4]

What man but meanly read in wisdomes Grammer,
Would be an *Anvile*, that maybe a Hammer? (II 10, p. 40). *The Frank C. Brown
     Collection of North Carolina Folklore* (Durham, N. C., 1952), I, 419.
So *Art* is mockt with Art (I 26, p. 22). Cf. Apperson 16; Tilley A335.
This you shall finde, if to mens lives attend:
The most are starke nought; and the *best* may mend (I 5, p. 5). Tilley B321.
Is like a foolish *Bird*: clips her owne wing (I 25, p. 22). Cf. *Oxford* 97 Clip; Tilley
     W498.
A little *Blowing*, kindles a great Fire (II 11, p. 41).
Blaze not abroad to others, thine owne Evill:

[4] G. L. Apperson, *English Proverbs and Proverbial Phrases* (London, 1929); W. G. Smith and Janet Heseltine, *The Oxford Dictionary of English Proverbs* (2d ed., Oxford, 1948); Morris P. Tilley, *A Dictionary of the Proverbs in England in the Sixteenth and Seventeenth Centuries* (Ann Arbor, 1950).

This were to light a *candle*, to the Devill (II 7, p. 37). Apperson 79 hold; *Oxford* 298, quot. 1649; Tilley C42.

Running Wilde-goose *Chaces* (IV 17, p. 86). Apperson 686; *Oxford* 709; Tilley W390.

In keeping *Christmas*, something must be spent;

But not to make the whole yeare after Lent (I 40, p. 32). Cf. *Oxford* 4; Tilley C367.

Then cut thy *coat*, according to thy cloth (III 12, p. 64). Apperson 131; *Oxford* 126; Tilley C472.

Hard *Commons* make sound sheepe (II 28, p. 55).

'Tis greene fruit, *Death* loves best (I 19, p. 16). B. J. Whiting, *Proverbs in the Earlier English Drama* (Cambridge, Mass., 1938), 289.

Doe not *Dogges* barke at Moone-shine in the water? (III 3, p. 59). Apperson 426 Moonshine; *Oxford* 432; Tilley M1128, quot. [c1633].

Poets sing sweet; but above *Ela* still (III 19, p. 69). NED Ela.

Evils foreseene, grow lesser then they were (II 24, p. 51). Cf. Tilley D29.

Every *Extreme* breeds some extreme Disease (IV 24, p. 90). Cf. Tilley E224.

His Humour may be *Flaxe*, if thine be Fire (II 11, p. 41). Apperson 213; *Oxford* 202; Tilley F268.

Ther's *Flud*: and then an Ebbe in every Tide (I 18, p. 14). Apperson 220 Flow; *Oxford* 211; Tilley F378.

All other things, like *Flowers*, are fading seene (IV 19, p. 87). Tilley F386.

The kinde *Foole*, of all kindes of Fooles, is worst (I 11, p. 10).

A *Foole* sometimes, sees more then one thats wiser (III 11, p. 64). Cf. Tilley F469.

The wheele of *Fortune*, brings the worst about (I 18, p. 14). Apperson 231; *Oxford* 221; Tilley F617.

You must not count a *Friend* untill you trie (IV 28, p. 94). Cf. Tilley T595.

Though lose a *Game*, yet thou mayst win the set (II 10, p. 39).

Looke on the *Givers* minde, not on the Gift (I 20, p. 17). Tilley G97.

Doe thou the like to him; such *Hare*; such Hound (I 26, p. 22).

'Tis not said in vaine;

The lesser *Head*, the better is the Braine (II 9, p. 38). Tilley H261.

And we goe out againe, as poore as *Iob* (I 21, p. 18). Apperson 505; *Oxford* 510; Tilley J60.

Least thou be faine

To turne in at the Signe of Labour in vaine (III 15, p. 67). Apperson 348; Tilley L3, V5.

Learning is like the *Laurell*, alwaies greene (IV 19, p. 87). Tilley L95.

Thy bounty may have leave, sometimes to roame:

But still remember, *Love* beginnes at Home (I 40, p. 32). Apperson 91–92 Charity, quot. 1509; *Oxford* 88; Tilley C251.

You cannot count one (*man*) happy, till he die (IV 28, p. 94). Tilley M333.

Hope not on dead *mens* shooes, that may out live thee (I 19, p. 15). Apperson 138; *Oxford* 132; Tilley M619.

Manners maketh man (I 38, p. 30; IV 15, p. 83. Not Mannours make the man, but manners do). Apperson 398; *Oxford* 404; Tilley M629.

No Meanes can serve, where no *Meane* is observd (II 17, p. 45). Cf. Tilley M793; B. J. Whiting, "Proverbs and Proverbial Sayings from Scottish Writings Before 1600," *Mediaeval Studies* 13 (1951) 97.

Least others thee, in thy owne *mony* pay (III 8, p. 62). Apperson 487 coin; *Oxford* 491; Tilley C507, quots. 1599, 1622.

    Goods are as *Oakes*:

Longtime in growing; Cut downe with few strokes (II 17, p. 45). Cf. *Oxford* 627 Strokes; Tilley S941.

    And *Old folks* are more:

Twice Children, They; Once now; and once before (IV 18, p. 87). Apperson 464–465; *Oxford* 472; Tilley M570.

    Hast not thou

Good Cause to welcome that, brings th' *Olive bough*? (III 23, p. 72). NED Olive-branch.

Where *paines* retaines no Gaines; want comes at last (I 39, p. 31). Cf. Apperson 242 No gains; *Oxford* 457–458; Tilley P24.

Least it be said; Two *Parrats* are well met (I 10, p. 9).

And in as poore a *pickle* we goe out (I 21, p. 18). Tilley P276.

That *Promise* is a due Debt; make no doubt (I 25, p. 22). Apperson 513; *Oxford* 520; Tilley P603.

A crooked *Rule*, can never make streight line (I 4, p. 5).

Doth not our owne *sand* runne, as fast as Theirs? (I 19, p. 15). NED Sand sb.^{2} 5.

Love equally thy Father, and thy Mother:

And doe not *scratch* the one; to claw the other (III 25, p. 73). Cf. Apperson 554; NED Claw v. 4; *Oxford* 567; Tilley B643.

Silence consents (III 16, p. 67). Apperson 571; *Oxford* 589; Tilley S446.

The odds thou mak'st, betweene thy *skinne* and cloak:

Make that, betweene thy selfe, and other folke (I 40, p. 32). Cf. Apperson 437–438; *Oxford* 444; Tilley S356.

The still *Sow* alwaies eats up all the swill (IV 31, p. 95). Apperson 602; *Oxford* 620–621; Tilley S681.

A *sparke* not look't to, may set House a fire (IV 9, p. 80). Tilley S714, quot. 1631. Cf. Apperson 593.

What may not a *sparke* doe, if light on Powder? (II 11, p. 41).

Tis an old saying; *spend*, and God will send;

But what? Beggery, and Barenesse, in the end (I 39, p. 32). Apperson 595; *Oxford* 613; Tilley G247, quots. 1573, 1611.

Strive not above thy *strength* (IV 33, p. 96).

No *Text* so cleare; but that a Glosse may marre (I 12, p. 11). Cf. NED Gloss sb.^{1} la, quot. 1695.

Time is as proud, as Tide: in this much one:

That must be waited on; This waytes for none (II 26, p. 53). Apperson 634; *Oxford* 658; Tilley T323.

Let not thy *Tongue*, speake all thine Eares doe heare (I 12, p. 11).

Two can agree, if one be out o' th way (I 4, p. 5). Cf. Apperson 655. Two may keep counsel if one be away; *Oxford* 330; Tilley T257.

Want makes the Old wife trott, the Young wife trippe (III 22, p. 71). Apperson 439 Need; *Oxford* 446; Tilley N79.

Use that thou hast, but make no wilfull *waste*:

All gone; men turne to Cannyballs at last (III 22, p. 71). Cf. Apperson 687 Wilful waste; *Oxford* 694; Tilley W81.

Is not hee, that feares this, *white liverd*? (III 23, p. 72). A. Taylor, "Proverbial Phrases in the Plays of Beaumont and Fletcher," *Tennessee Folklore Society Bulletin*, XXIII (1957), 58.

Evils are like a *wolfe*; seene, ere they come:

Doe little hurt; Not seene, they strike us dumbe (II 24, p. 51). *Oxford* 722; Tilley W621.

Words are but wind (I 13, p. 12). Apperson 710–711; *Oxford* 729; Tilley W833.

To eate thy *words* (IV 28, p. 94). Apperson 177; *Oxford* 166; Tilley W825.

Although *Cato Variegatus* appeared in only one edition, it had a high rate of survival, certainly in comparison with Penkethman's translation, as William A. Jackson kindly informs me that his revision of the *Short-Title Catalogue* will list at least eighteen copies. Neglect may lead to survival, but even so there were many readers in the century and a half after Baker's death who made use of parts of his translation without being aware of the fact. In 1659 Charles Hoole (1610–1667), a schoolmaster, writer on educational matters, and clergyman, issued a text and translation of the *Distichs* along with *Dicta insignia septem Sapientum Graeciae* and *Mimi Publiani, sive, Senecae Proverbia* in a volume which ran through many editions in the later seventeenth and early eighteenth centuries. The Latin text of the *Distichs* and their English translation face each on pages 4–21 in the edition of 1701, which has been used for this study. Hoole followed this (pp. 52–70) with a literal and interlinear translation for the aid of students.

However valuable Hoole's translation may have been for beginners in Latin, the only remarkable thing about it is the surprisingly large part which he borrowed from Baker, whom he mentions in passing in his preface sig. B 2ᵛ), but without any acknowledgement of debt. In a few cases he takes over couplets verbatim, or nearly so. For example, one of Baker's versions of I 19 (p. 15) reads:

Since God a fraile, vncertane life doth give thee;
Hope not on dead mens shooes, that may out live thee.

In Hoole we find:

> Sith God a frail uncertain Life doth give thee,
> Hope not for dead mens-shoes that may out-live thee (p. 6).

Again, Baker renders I 22 (p. 18) by

> Feare not that Ende of life, which Nature gives:
> He that feares Death; looseth, even that he lives.

Hoole has,

> Fear not that end of life which nature gives,
> He that fears death, loseth even that he lives (p. 6).

Baker translates III 23 (p. 71) [Hoole III 21],

> Resolve: of Death, no feare is to be had:
> Which, though not good; yet Ends all that is bad.

And Hoole repeats it with minor changes:

> Resolve, of death no fear is to be had;
> Which though not good it self, ends all that's bad (p. 14).

A majority of cases do not present such complete examples of borrowing as do those just quoted, but there are many in which it is obvious that Hoole's translation was inspired by Baker's.[5]

Hoole translated I 10 (p. 4):

> To strive in words with men of words, despise;
> All men can speak, but few are truly wise.

The first line duplicates that of one of Baker's versions (p. 9), and the second seems based on a line from another of Baker's (p. 8), 'All men can speake, but wisely speake, skarce any.' I 11 is based on Baker (p. 9), with but the change of *so* to *well* in the first line. I 17 owes the second line to Baker without change, while the first lines are, 'When men be whispering softly; Never care (Baker, p. 13), and 'If one do whisper softly, do not care (Hoole). I 24 takes over Baker's first line exactly, and the second lines are, 'That save thou mayst; Thinke, that thou hast it not (Baker, p. 21), and 'And that thou mayst save, think thou hast it not.' In I 25 the first lines also coincide, and the second lines are, 'Least thou instead of kinde, be counted light (Baker, p. 21), and 'Lest, whilst thou wouldst seem kind, thou dost prove light.' In I 26 the first lines are similar, and the second lines are, 'Be thou so too: so Art is mockt with Art,' (Baker p. 22) and 'Do thou the like;

[5] In selecting these examples I have given Hoole the benefit of every possible chance of coincidence.

thus Art is mock'd by Art.' In I 27 the second lines correspond, with the exception of *whilst* in Hoole for *while* in Baker, and the first lines run, 'Trust not to men, for their faire speeches making;' (Baker, p. 23, misnumbered 15) and 'Think not too well of men for fair words making.' In I 30 the first lines are the same, and the second lines run, 'A Teacher, to need Teaching, is a shame' (Baker, p. 24) and 'When his faults checks him, 'tis the Teacher's shame.' Hoole's version of I 31 is, 'Ask what is just, or what seems good to the eye; / It's fond to ask what 'tis just to deny,' which seems based on Baker's 'Aske that is iust; at least, iust to the Eye / 'Tis shame to aske, what tis iust to deny.' (p. 24)

These examples, nearly all taken from Book I, show the nature and extent of Hoole's pilferings, and it would be pointless to pursue his course to the end. Hoole's successful career as a schoolmaster suggests that it was indolence rather than lack of Latin which led him to a wholesale appropriation which he would perhaps not have set as a scholarly model for his students. To Hoole's credit it may be said that he modernized some of Baker's conservative spellings and corrected his eccentric punctuation. In any case, whatever we may think of Hoole's conduct, he was, in good time, the victim of freebootery more absolute than his own. In 1759, just a century after Hoole's book had appeared, Christian Gottlieb König published in Amsterdam his *Dionysii Catonis Disticha De Moribus ad Filium... Interpretatione Quincuplice*, in which the English version, quite without suggestion of origin, is Hoole's, the only difference being an increased use of capitals. Conclusions, melancholy or otherwise, could no doubt be drawn from these proverbial instances of failure to distinguish between *meum* and *tuum*, but it is enough to observe that the *Distichs* themselves are not by a Cato, whether Marcus or Dionysius.

Harvard University,
Cambridge, Massachusetts

DAS RÖMISCHE BILD DES TODES
IM *ACKERMANN AUS BÖHMEN*

L. L. HAMMERICH

Der Verfasser des berühmten Streitgesprächs zwischen dem „Ackermann" und dem Tod, Johannes von Saaz, hat in seinem Werk bisweilen Selbsterlebtes berichtet oder vielmehr unter Verhüllung angedeutet; die zusammengehörigen Kapitel 16, 17 und 18 sind in dieser Beziehung besonders rätselreich. Am meisten umstritten ist ein Passus, der uns wie in einem Blitz den Renaissancemenschen, der er war, als ersten deutschen Archäologen in Rom sehen läßt.

Es spricht im 16. Kapitel der Tod:

> 16, 18. *Du fragest, wie Wir weren. Unbescheidenlich sei Wir. Pictagoras gleichet Uns zu eines mannes schein, wandelend in allen enden der werlt, der hat basiliskes augen, von des gesicht sterben must alle lebendige creatur. Doch vande du Unser figure zu Rom in einem tempel an einer want gemalt als ein man auf einem ochsen,*
> 5 *dem die augen verbunden waren *netzweis. Der selbe man furet ein hauen in seiner rechten hant und ein schaufel in seiner linken hant; damit do vacht er auf dem ochsen. Gegen im slugen, wurfen und striten ein michel menig volkes, allerlei leut, jeglichs mensch mit seins handwerks gezeug... da was auch die nunne mit dem psalter. Die slugen und wurfen den man auf dem ochsen in Unser bedeutnusz: be-*
> 10 *streit sie der Tod und begrub sie alle.*

„Du fragtest, wie Wir seien. Wir sind nicht zu erkennen. Pythagoras verglich Uns mit dem Schemen eines Mannes, der Augen eines Basilisken hatte, der überall in der Welt herumwanderte und bei dessen Anblick jedes lebendige Geschöpf sterben mußte. Dennoch fandest du Unser Abbild in Rom, in einem Tempel, an der Wand dargestellt als einen Mann auf einem Ochsen, dem die Augen wie mit einem Netz verbunden waren. Dieser Mann trug eine Hacke in seiner rechten und eine Schaufel in seiner linken Hand. Damit focht er auf dem Ochsen. Gegen ihn kämpfte, schlagend und werfend, eine große Volksmenge, allerlei Leute, jeder mit dem Werkzeug seines Handwerks... da war auch die Nonne mit dem Psalterium. Sie schlugen und bewarfen den Mann, der Uns bezeichnet, auf dem Ochsen: der Tod aber besiegte sie alle und begrub sie.''

Der Ackermann-Text ist bekanntlich sehr schwer herzustellen. Ich folge hier im Allgemeinen der Rezension von G. Jungbluth und mir in der Kopenhagener Ausgabe (*Der Ackermann aus Böhmen*. I. = Det Kgl. Danske Videnskabernes Selskabs Historisk-filologiske Meddelelser XXXII, 4. Kopenhagen 1951), jedoch mit einigen, z. T. nicht unbedeutenden Änderungen.

Mit Krogmann[1] und älteren Herausgebern schreibe ich wiederum 1 *wie* (1951 *wo*), *unbescheidenlich* (1951 **unbestetelich*), 10 *bedeutnusz* (1951 16,27 **beteubnusz*). Die große Unsicherheit in der Überlieferung des Satzes 4 = 16,20 *Doch — gemalt* und entsprechend bei den Herausgebern (vgl. die Kopenhagener Ausgabe und Krogmann) wird darauf beruhen, daß die Form *vande*, 2. sg. prt. (klassisch mittelhochdeutsch *fünde / funde*, frühneuhochdeutsch *fundest / fandest*, auch *vandest*), auf die die handschriftlichen Lesarten führen und die ich in den Text stelle, von den Abschreibern z. T. als die Konjunktion *wande* aufgefaßt wurde. Was *vande du* geschrieben wurde, ist wahrscheinlich *vanddu* gesprochen worden. Mit Arnošt Kraus nehme ich jetzt wiederum nach *handwerks gezeug* eine Lücke an. Kleinigkeiten der Textgestaltung bleiben unerwähnt. Das Wort *psalter* konnte damals zweierlei bezeichnen: 1. das biblische Buch der Psalmen, 2. das ,,Psalterium'' genannte Saiteninstrument, oder — ohne technische Genauigkeit — ein anderes Saiteninstrument ähnlicher Verwendung. Der Tkadlec hat es in der ersteren Bedeutung (Krogmann); die zweite Bedeutung ist aber im 15. wie im 16. Jahrhundert die verbreitetere. Und sachlich ist wahrscheinlicher, daß eine Nonne ein Saiteninstrument trägt, als daß sie mit einer Handschrift des Buches der Psalmen herumliefe. Daß eine Nonne genannt wird, beweist übrigens nicht, daß das Bild, das der Dichter gesehen haben will, ein mittelalterliches christliches Bild sein müsse; es beweist aber, daß es eine Figur enthalten hat, die der Dichter als Nonne interpretieren konnte. Aus 4 = 16,21 *gemalt* darf man nicht folgern, daß das vom Dichter beschriebene Bild ein farbiges Gemälde sein müsse (ein solches an der Wand einer Tempelruine zu finden, wäre übrigens höchst erstaunlich), denn *malen* bezeichnet in älterer Zeit nicht nur ,,mit Farben herstellen'' u. ä., sondern auch, wie lat. *depingere*, das es glossiert, im Allgemeinen ,,abbilden, entwerfen, darstellen''; vgl. die Wörterbücher.

---

[1] Johannes von Tepl, Der Ackermann, hrsg. Willy Krogmann (Wiesbaden 1954), die wichtigste neuere kommentierte Ausgabe.

Der Pictagoras-Satz (1–4 = 16, 28–30) steht in allen Handschriften zuletzt (nach *begrub sie alle*) und hat die Reihenfolge ... *der hat basiliskes augen *wandelend (wandelten (wandeln* γ*) HBL* γ *wanderten (die wanderten* α*) A* α*) in allen enden der werlt*. Bis 1951 haben alle Herausgeber (einschließlich Walshe und Spalding) diesen Satz ohne wesentliche Änderungen an seinem überlieferten Platz belassen; so auch die Kopenhagener Ausgabe, in der jedoch das Satzstück *wandernd an allen enden der werlt* herausgehoben und hinter 16,19 versetzt wurde. Krogmann beläßt ebenfalls den Pictagoras-Satz an seinem überlieferten Platz, jedoch ohne das fragliche Satzstück, das er für eingeschoben erklärt. Ich vermute jetzt, daß im Archetypus eine etwa am Rande geforderte Umstellung der unzweifelhaft falschen Reihenfolge der beiden Satzstücke *der hat basiliskes augen, wandelend in allen enden der werlt* dahin mißverstanden worden ist, daß statt dessen der ganze Satz versetzt wurde. Wenn, wie im jetzt vorgeschlagenen Text der doppelte Umstellungsfehler[2] verbessert wird, erhalten wir endlich einen befriedigenden Text: der Pictagoras-Satz hinkt nicht mehr in auffälliger Weise nach; das *Doch* (4 = 16,20) bekommt das bisher vermißte Gegengewicht; und *wandelend* erhält die notwendige Beziehung zu *mannes*.

Schon die Kopenhagener Ausgabe enthält die Konjektur **netzeweis* (5 = 16,22), die jetzt begründet werden soll. Der Befund der Handschriften und Ausgaben ist der folgende: *als ein man auf einem ochsen dem die augen verbunden waren sitzend* ABL und danach Hübner und Spalding. Diese Lesart ist wahrscheinlich die des Archetypus gewesen; allein die ungefällige Wortstellung ist dem Dichter nicht zuzutrauen. *Als ein man sitzend auf einem ochsen dem die augen verbunden waren* H und danach Gierach, Hammerich 1944 und Krogmann. Diese Lesart ist stilgemäß; allein es besteht der Verdacht, daß sie eine der wohlüberlegten Korrekturen in H vertreten könnte. *Als ein man auf einem ochsen sitzend, dem die augen verbunden waren* α und danach Bernt sowie neuerdings Walshe; allein der α-Über-

---

[2] Das ist ein nicht seltener Fehlertypus. Eine deutliche Parallele bietet das althochdeutsche Memento mori (Braune, *Althochdeutsches Lesebuch, Nr.* XXXII), Strophe 11; der ursprüngliche Text muß der folgende gewesen sein:

> *taz eina hant ir iu selben,*   *daz ander gebent ir dien armen;*
> *von diu so ne mugen ir drin gen,*   *ir muozint iemer dervor sten.*

Ein Abschreiber schreibt fälschlich... *gen drin*... Er selbst oder ein Korrektor entdeckt den Fehler und versieht den Text mit einem Umstellungszeichen (etwa am Rande). Dieses wird aber durch einen folgenden Abschreiber mißverstanden, der nicht die beiden Worte, sondern zwei Verse umstellt, woraus dann der überlieferte Text entsteht:

> *taz eina hant ir iu selben,*   *von diu so ne mugen ir gen drin,*
> *taz ander gebent ir dien armen*   *ir muozint iemer dervor sten*

also mit zweimaliger falscher Reihenfolge. Vgl. auch *Neophilologus*, 34, 82–86.

lieferung ist nur in Ausnahmefällen zu trauen; wahrscheinlich haben wir auch
hier eine der bekannten willkürlichen Korrekturen in α; sie legt die Auffassung
nahe, daß nicht dem Ochsen, sondern dem Mann die Augen verbunden gewesen
seien; dieses hat Burdach im Kommentar tatsächlich angenommen. Und schließlich: *als ein man dem die augen verbunden waren auf einem ochsen sitzend* γ; die
anerkannt unzuverlässige γ-Überlieferung erreicht inhaltlich dasselbe Resultat
wie α, wahrscheinlich einfach durch Umstellung der Lesart von L, da die γ-Gruppe
bekanntlich der Handschrift L nahesteht.

Wenn der Philologe diesen Befund betrachtet, wird er gegen das Wort *sitzend*
Verdacht schöpfen. Dieser wird verstärkt, wenn man bedenkt, wie unedel das
Bild des auf einem Ochsen sitzenden, nach allen Seiten fuchtelnden Todes ist.
Wie besonders Zatočil und Krogmann nachgewiesen haben, hat der Tscheche, der
nach dem Muster des „Ackermann" seinen Tkadlec gestaltete, eine gute deutsche
Handschrift als Vorlage gehabt. Es liegt deshalb nahe, den Tkadlec aufzuschlagen,
um hier etwa Auskunft zu finden. Unsere Stelle ist glücklicherweise im Tkadlec
verarbeitet, allein es fehlt ein dem verdächtigen *sitzend* entsprechendes Wort!
Dafür hat der Tkadlec etwas, was in keiner der auf uns gekommenen deutschen
Handschriften steht: „diesem Ochsen war statt eines Sackes ein Jägernetz um-
gebunden" — *na tom wolu bylo gest miest tlumoka uwazano sietne teneto.* Das hat
Sinn: man bindet einem Zugtier einen Sack um den Kopf, um es gefügig zu
machen. In Spanien habe ich solches gesehen: einem Esel oder einem Ochsen, der
im Göpel die Wasserpumpe ziehen soll, werden in dieser Weise die Augen verbunden; nach einem Hieb oder Stich tritt das Tier seinen Rundgang an und setzt
diesen, durch keine äußeren Eindrücke gestört, unentwegt fort, bis die Müdigkeit
es übermannt. Wollen wir dem Tkadlec hier Zutrauen schenken, werden wir nach
einem ochsen dem die augen verbunden waren ein Wort der Bedeutung „nach der
Art eines Netzes" erwarten. Das müßte im Ackermann *netzeweis / netzweis* oder
in netzweis heißen: vgl. 11,3 *gaukelweis*; 27,15 *in gesworens eides weis*; 18,23 *in
wefelsweis*; 25,26 *in spiegelsweis*. Die genaue Form können wir kaum bestimmen,
besonders weil die Endung *-en* vorhergeht, so daß ein *in* leicht abspringen könnte;
vgl. die Lesarten zu 18,23 und 25,26! Graphisch liegt es recht nahe, daß sich
hinter dem überlieferten *sitzend* ein *netz(e)weis* verbergen könnte.

Allein, obschon der Tkadlec eine sehr gute deutsche Vorlage voraussetzt, ist
die tschechische Bearbeitung dennoch so voll von willkürlichen Zusätzen, daß
man — wie besonders Jungbluth unterstrichen hat — mit einer philologischen
Auswertung des Tkadlec für die deutsche Textgestaltung sehr vorsichtig sein
sollte. Das heißt in diesem Fall, daß die vielleicht methodisch aufgebaute, aber
immerhin sehr kühne Konjektur *netz(e)weis* einer Unterstützung außerhalb des
Tkadlec bedarf. Wir müssen ein Bild nachweisen, das der Ackermann-Dichter

gesehen haben kann und auf dem er etwas entdeckt hat, was er als einen mit einem Netz umgebundenen Ochsenkopf deuten konnte.

Konrad Burdach hat mit ungeheurer Energie nach einem Todesbild gefahndet, das dem Ackermann-Dichter hätte vorschweben können, und hat in seinem Exkurs zu 16,16–28 („Das römische Bild des Todes und die bildhaften Elemente der Todesvorstellungen im 'Ackermann'") die Ergebnisse mitgeteilt.

Diese Abhandlung ist höchst lesenswert, bringt sehr viel Neues und Wichtiges zu den mittelalterlichen Darstellungen der Todesgestalt, zum Totentanz, zum Trionfo della Morte. Allein sie führt nicht zum Ziel. Burdach hat unter den Dutzenden von Bildern, die er untersucht hat, kein einziges gefunden, das er irgendwie als „Vorbild" hätte beanspruchen können. Z. T. leidet seine Untersuchung darunter, daß er der schlechteren Überlieferung (die dem Mann, nicht dem Ochsen die Augen verbindet) zu sehr traut und deshalb Darstellungen des Todes mit Augenbinde, die meistens von vorne herein ausscheiden könnten, viel zu stark berücksichtigt; gegen *sitzend* hat er keinen Verdacht geschöpft. Beides gilt teilweise auch für Helmut Rosenfeld, der (*Zeitschrift für deutsches Altertum* 72,241 ff.) behauptet, daß der Dichter an gar kein bestimmtes Bild gedacht habe und daß die verwendeten Bildmotive eher nördlich als südlich der Alpen zu finden seien; dem schließt sich Krogmann an, indem er damit auszukommen glaubt, daß der Dichter einem Typus gelehrter deutscher Dichtung gefolgt sei. Allein die herangezogenen bildlichen und literarischen Darstellungen sind entweder so verschwommen oder so andersartig, daß sich das — mit oder ohne Netz! — scharf umrissene Bild im „Ackermann" ganz davon abhebt.

Seltsamerweise ist die einleuchtend richtige Erklärung schon vom allerersten Kommentator gegeben, nämlich von Benndorf in J. Kniescheks Ackermann-Ausgabe (Prag 1877), S. 61: eine kriegerische Gestalt auf einem Ochsen — damit müsse der Juppiter Dolichenus gemeint sein. Nicht angenommen wurde diese Erklärung nur, weil man an dem im Text vorhandenen Wort *sitzend* festhalten zu müssen wohl glaubte.

In der antiken syrischen Landschaft Commagene lag eine Doliche genannte (im Dorfe Tell-Dülük noch erkennbare) Stadt, nach welcher der Juppiter Dolichenus seinen Namen hat. So heißt in der interpretatio romana der syrische Wetter- und Kriegsgott *Hadad* (Χαδαδός), churritisch *Teshub*, hittitisch *Washawa* genannt. Wie so viele andere orientalische Götter kam auch er in der Kaiserzeit nach Rom: die älteste römische Inschrift mit seinem Namen ist aus dem Jahre 138. Wenig später wurde auf dem Aventin der bedeutende Tempel des Juppiter Dolichenus erbaut. Sein Kult hat unter dem Einfluß von Julia Domna, der tatkräftigen Gemahlin des Septimius Severus (193–211), die aus Hemesa in Syrien war, einen großen Aufschwung genommen und noch Dezennien nach ihrem Tode (217) in

Rom eine Rolle gespielt: die letzte datierbare römische Inschrift mit seinem Namen ist 253 verfertigt. Allein außerhalb Roms blieb der Juppiter Dolichenus ein Lieblingsgott der Legionäre, und in vielen römischen Kastellen, von Britannien bis Dacien wie in Asien und Afrika, sind seine Weihbilder gefunden.

Abgebildet wird der Juppiter Dolichenus als eine stehende bärtige Mannesgestalt, mit der hohen hittitischen Mütze auf dem Kopf, schwertumgegürtet; in einer Hand trägt er die Doppelaxt, in der anderen den Donnerkeil (oder den Dreizack); er steht auf einem Stier (seltener auf überwundenen Feinden). Bisweilen steht ihm gegenüber, auf einem anderen Tier, seine Gattin, die Juno Regina, die ihm eine Kraft und Ewigkeit bezeichnende hittitische Hieroglyphe — von den Römern als Spiegel dargestellt — überreicht. Bisweilen ist er von andern huldigenden Gottheiten umgeben.[3]

Wir geben die Abbildung eines im Capitolinischen Museum aufbewahrten, in den Ruinen vom Tempel des Juppiter Dolichenus auf dem Aventin gefundenen Reliefs.[4]

Man sieht in der linken Seite des Bildes den großen typischen Juppiter Dolichenus auf dem Stier, in der Tracht eines römischen Legionärs, schwertumgürtet, bärtig, mit der hohen Mütze; das Gesicht ist drohend. In seiner hoch erhobenen rechten Hand trägt er die Doppelaxt; nur eine Hälfte des Blattes, die Breitaxt, ist gegenwärtig bewahrt; auf einem gleichzeitigen Relief desselben Typus aus demselben Tempel sieht man auch die zweite Hälfte, die Spitzaxt. Von dem, was er in der linken Hand trägt, ist nur noch der Stiel bewahrt; auf dem genannten gleichzeitigen Relief ist der Donnerkeil als ein Zweizack abgebildet. In der rechten Seite des Bildes steht auf einem unbestimmbaren Huftier die kleinere Juno Regina, in faltiger Tracht, auf einen Stab in ihrer linken Hand gestützt; in der rechten, hoch erhobenen Hand hält sie ihrem Gatten den Spiegel entgegen. In der oberen linken Ecke des Bildes sieht man die Büste des Sol mit Strahlenkranz, in der oberen rechten Ecke die Luna mit der Mondsichel, zwischen ihnen die Dioskuren mit ihren Rossen und den lenkenden Stachelstöcken. Zwischen Juppiter und Juno stehen Serapis und Isis; Serapis streckt die rechte erhobene offene Hand nach Juppiter hinauf; auf dem Kopf hat er den *modius*, das Symbol der chthonischen Götter; der linke Arm umfaßt den Thyrsusstab mit dem Fichten-

---

[3] Der holländische Forscher A. H. Kan hat das Thema 1901 in einer Groninger Dissertation *De Jovis Dolicheni cultu* aufgegriffen und mit der sehr bedeutenden Arbeit ,,Juppiter Dolichenus. Sammlung der Inschriften und Bildwerke" (Leiden 1943) abgeschlossen. Mittlerweile hatte der türkische Forscher Halil Demircioğlu in einem kleineren Werk *Der Gott auf dem Stier* (Berlin 1939) eine anerkennungswerte Behandlung gegeben.

[4] Dem Entgegenkommen von Professor Giuseppe Lugli, Direktor der Musei comunali di Roma, verdanke ich wertvolle Auskünfte und die Photographie des Reliefs.

zapfen. Diesen berührt die danebenstehende Isis mit ihrer rechten Hand; auf dem Kopf hat sie die ihren Namen darstellende Hieroglyphe. Die am oberen und unteren Rande angebrachte Inschrift, *Iovi optimo dolicheno d(onum) d(edit) P Ecnatius Fructus*, gibt uns also den Namen des Stifters an. Schließlich ist auf die Stirn des Stieres aufmerksam zu machen. Sie ist mit auffallend vielen kleineren und etwas größeren Löchern versehen; die meisten sollen — das erhellt auch aus anderen Bildern — die buschige Stirnlocke darstellen; einige waren aber zur Anbringung von astrologischen Zeichen bestimmt; Löcher dieser Art sind vereinzelt auch anderswo auf dem Bilde zu erkennen, z. B. auf den Beinen des Stieres.

Die ganze Darstellung ist sehr lebhaft und wird letzten Endes wohl auf gute Vorbilder zurückgehen; allein die Ausführung ist plump, volkstümliche Kunst des 3. Jahrhunderts.

Ich glaube, daß wir an diesem Relief eben das Bild haben, das der Ackermann-Dichter im 16. Kapitel beschreibt; wir müssen nur versuchen, es mit seinen Augen zu sehen.

Als der kunstverständige kläräugige Johannes von Saaz etwa im Jahre 1401 in Rom war, hat er ohne Zweifel die *mirabilia Romae* aufgesucht, soweit das beim damaligen traurigen Zustand der Stadt möglich war. Neben einer Hauptsehenswürdigkeit, der hochheiligen Basilica S. Sabina, in einer Tempelruine, hat er unser Relief sehen können. Er hat die dominierende furchterregende Gestalt als den Tod, die Doppelaxt als Hacke, den Zweizack als Schaufel, die Haltung des gepanzerten Todes als im Streit begriffen gedeutet. Gegen wen kämpft er? Gegen die ihn umgebenden menschlichen Gestalten, die ihrerseits, jede mit ihrer Waffe, den Tod bekämpfen. Denn Waffen haben sie alle: die oben herbeieilenden Reiterknechte haben, wie sich gehört, ihre Speere; links oben, hinter dem „Riesen,“ entdeckt Johannes die für einen Riesen typische Waffe des Streitkolbens, und zwar die mit Stachelspitzen sternförmig besetzte Abart, die man Morgenstern nennt; rechts oben, hinter der „Riesin,“ gewahrt man eben die Sichel, auch eine bukolische Waffe. Von den beiden unteren Figuren hat die vordere soeben einen Stein geworfen (die Hand ist noch offen), die hintere pflückt etwas vom Baum, um es gegen den Tod zu werfen; beide haben auf dem Kopf große Wurfsteine, die der Tod vielleicht mit der Schaufel geworfen hat. Die Nonne ganz rechts, mit der Kopfbinde und der faltigen Tracht, schickt sich sogar an, ihr Saiteninstrument, das sie am Stiel faßt, gegen den Tod zu schleudern. Das Ganze entspricht der primitiven Wut einer damaligen Schlacht, wie sie Johannes selbst vor kurzem gesehen hat (vgl. Kap. 17). Eine Einzelheit fällt ihm auf: dem Tier, auf dem der Tod steht, ist anscheinend ein Netz um den Kopf gebunden; es muß also wohl ein Zugtier, ein Ochse, sein.

JUPPITER DOLICHENUS

Wenn man das eingangs gegebene Textstück jetzt nochmals lesen will, wird man, glaube ich, bewundern, wie genau das Relief, mit mittelalterlichen Augen gesehen, beschrieben ist.

Sollte man das Wunder, daß gerade das von Johannes von Saaz beschriebene Bildwerk zum Vorschein gekommen wäre, bezweifeln, dann müßte das von ihm gesehene Bild ein ganz ähnliches, sozusagen eine Replica, gewesen sein — welches wohl eigentlich ein noch größeres Wunder wäre.

Lange Jahre nach der Zeit des Johannes von Saaz lag die Ruine des Tempels des Juppiter Dolichenus auf dem Aventin noch am Tage, wahrscheinlich aber immer mehr verdeckt: vollständig verschüttet wurde sie erst beim Umbau der benachbarten Basilica S. Alessio durch Papst Paul V (1605–21). Bei Straßen-arbeiten im Jahre 1935 kamen Überreste des Tempels zum Vorschein, u. a. unser Relief.[5]

Wie und warum Johannes von Saaz nach Rom gekommen war, welche über-haupt seine Beziehungen zu Italien waren — das ist eine andere lange Geschichte, auf die jetzt nicht eingegangen werden kann.

Universität Copenhagen

Unter den mittelalterlichen Beschreibungen von Rom war eine der verbreitetsten die Mirabilia Romae, die (fälschlich) dem William von Malmesbury zugeschrieben wurden; im 28. Kapitel, das vom Aventin handelt, wird das Templum Jovis ausdrücklich erwähnt. Vgl. H. Jordan — Ch. Hül-sen, *Topographie der Stadt Rom im Altertum* I,3 (Berlin 1907), 313ff. Die mittelalterlichen Stadt-beschreibungen. A. Merlin, *L'Aventin dans l'Antiquité* (Paris 1906), 448ff. Aperçu sommaire des principales découvertes faites sur l'Aventin du XVIᵉ siècle à nos jours. — Bollettino della Com-missione archeologica comunale di Roma LXIII (1936), 145–159: A. M. Colini, La scoperta del santuario delle divinità Dolichene sull'Aventino (Hauptbericht über die Entdeckung des Reliefs). Vgl. Giuseppe Lugli, I Monumenti Antichi di Roma e Suburbio III (Roma 1938), 590ff. Juppiter Dolichenus.

SAMUEL PATERSON
CATALOGUER EXTRAORDINARY

Hugh G. Dick

Archer Taylor concludes his *Renaissance Guides to Books* with a rewarding chapter entitled "The Break in the Bibliographical and Cultural Tradition."[1] He shows that by the beginning of the eighteenth century "fundamental alterations in the affairs of the spirit and the world" entailed major changes in the traditions of scholarship, including the discipline of bibliography. The Renaissance bibliographies of bibliographies went by the board, as did also the universal bibliographies and the massive universal subject indexes. The eighteenth century, foundering in an ever-widening sea of printed materials, could hardly call on any one person to undertake, single-handed, such universal bibliographical enterprises as those of Gesner, Labbé, and Lipenius in the preceding two centuries. Rescue came (allowing for various national differences) from publishers' and dealers' catalogues, from the slow rise of institutional catalogues, and perhaps most notably from the catalogues of large private collections, whether specialized or polymathic in character.[2] In this world of eighteenth-century bibliography, at once more fragmented and more specialized, the expert cataloguer supplanted the widely foraging bibliographer. It was an age of catalogues rather than of bibliographies.

[1] (Berkeley and Los Angeles: University of California Press, 1945), pp. 64–82.
[2] The history of these developments belongs to Archer Taylor, *Book Catalogues: Their Varieties and Uses* (Chicago: The Newberry Library, 1957).

> By the Means of Catalogues only can it be known, what has been written on every Part of Learning, and the Hazard avoided of encountering Difficulties which have already been cleared, discussing Questions which have already been decided and digging in Mines of Literature which former Ages have exhausted.

So wrote Samuel Johnson, who toiled for the bookseller Thomas Osborne in cataloguing the Harleian collection.[3] The faithful cataloguer, with an expert knowledge of books and some method to apply to large collections of materials, was a useful citizen in the society of the learned. It is therefore appropriate to examine the work of the British cataloguer Samuel Paterson (1725/26–1802), into whose career Professor Taylor himself has suggested the need for investigation, no doubt recalling Dibdin's tribute to Paterson as "this renowned champion of catalogue-makers."[4]

Then as now, the cataloguer as opposed to the bibliographer labored under several restrictions. The bibliographer was a scholar working for scholars: his aim was the preservation and advancement of learning. In general he was not under complusions of time, and he was a free agent inasmuch as he could collect his materials wherever he found them. But the cataloguer in eighteenth-century England was almost invariably a tradesman concerned with the sale of books by auction: his aims were of necessity economic. He seldom enjoyed any privilege of leisure and, on the contrary, was usually under severe pressure to dispose of a library as rapidly as possible. And of course his activities were almost wholly dictated by the actual collection before him. If the books were of a commonplace nature, so inevitably was the catalogue. The eighteenth-century norm for an auction sale catalogue (not unknown in our own day) was a hasty and perfunctory list in which books were grouped by format and, beneath format, by a rough alphabetical arrangement. Many of Paterson's own catalogues were of this nature for obvious economic reasons.

But several circumstances combined to lead Paterson into the preparation of a number of catalogues of more than common interest. To begin with, Paterson had a genuine, even a consuming interest in books. One of his intimate friends declared:

> Mr. Paterson's reading was so extensive, that I firmly believe he had read most of the works he offered for sale in the English language; and I was induced to believe so from the following circumstance. I happened to be with him one evening, after three cart-loads of books had been brought into the auction-room, to be catalogued for sale; when, upon his taking up one, which he declared to me he had never seen, he

---

[3] *Catalogus Bibliotheca Harleiana*, I (1753), 3.

[4] Taylor, *Book Catalogues*, p. 157; and Thomas Frognall Dibdin, *Bibliomania* (1876), p. 396.

called to the boy who attended him to bring another candle and throw some coals upon the fire, observing, that he meant to sit up to read it.[5]

And another of his contemporaries confirms the testimony:

> Few men of this country had so much bibliographical knowledge; and perhaps we never had a book-seller who knew so much of the contents of books generally; and he was particularly well acquainted with our English poets. If, in his employment of taking catalogues, he met with a book he had not seen before, which excited his curiosity, or interested his feelings, they must be gratified, and his attendant might amuse himself as he chose. The consequence was, that, on many occasions, catalogues could be procured only a few hours before the sale commenced.[6]

Indeed Paterson's apologies for deferral of sale because catalogues were not ready in time were common enough to suggest why he was in financial trouble through most of his life and on at least one occasion bankrupt. But his devouring curiosity about books, however uncontrolled, helps account for the esteem in which he was held by such figures as the Tory Samuel Johnson and the Radical publisher Joseph Johnson, to name only two among his many friends and supporters.

Another force that led Paterson to produce catalogues of scholarly value was his desire to rival the subject cataloguing of the Parisian bookseller Gabriel Martin (1679–1761). Martin's influence on Paterson was that of a general rather than of a precise model. Paterson did not adopt Martin's exact classification scheme: indeed Paterson was opposed to any fixed, more or less immutable system such as that to which Martin was committed. "He was," we are told, "an enemy to those systems of Bibliography which are now generally practised on the Continent."[7] What he took from his French predecessor was the general ideal of the "digested" catalogue—i.e., the practice of carefully grouping books by subject matter (whatever the pattern of subjects might be) and of furnishing more accurate and much fuller information about them than the common sale catalogues did. As a result, the term "digested" was a hallmark of Paterson's catalogues in the later eighteenth century just as Martin's *digestus* had been his trademark in the first half of the century.

Paterson's knowledge of books and his ambition of producing catalogues to serve the needs of collectors and scholars—not as auction-room lumber stacked by folio, octavo, and quarto sizes—won him the privilege of cataloguing great private libraries in England and thus of producing printed catalogues that can be put to scholarly use today.

[5] John Thomas Smith, *Nollekens and His Times* (1828), II, 279.
[6] *The Gentleman's Magazine*, LXII (1802), 1075.
[7] John Nichols, *Literary Anecdotes of the Eighteenth Century*, III (1812), 734.

Paterson was born in the year 1725–26 and died in 1802.[8] Orphaned early and educated abroad, he entered the booktrade sometime in the 1740's as bookseller, book importer, and publisher on a modest scale. As a bookseller he seems to have issued no trade catalogues, and as a book importer he ran, almost predictably, into problems with agents executing his commissions abroad. In 1747 he published, from his shop at the sign of Shakespeare's Head, opposite Durham Yard in the Strand, Charlotte Ramsay's first book, *Poems on Several Occasions*. But apart from this volume he appears to have published only a tiny handful of other books, all of them seemingly issued at the authors' expense.

He therefore turned general auctioneer. Plomer's *Dictionary of Printers and Booksellers, 1726–1775* says that he did so in 1753, but I find no certain record before 1757. In that year an apothecary friend told Paterson of a mass of old papers about to be sold to a cheesemonger for wrappings.[9] These proved to be the papers of Sir Julius Caesar (1558–1636), the holder of numerous and important Crown offices under Elizabeth I and the first two Stuarts. Paterson acquired the collection for £10, put the manuscripts on display, and issued a hurried catalogue. But when antiquarians and prospective buyers came to view the collection prior to sale, they made it plain to Paterson that his catalogue was a useless fiasco, whereupon he postponed the sale for three weeks, grouped the most important manuscripts into 187 related lots, and issued a new catalogue that sold for a shilling. The sale occurred December 14–16, 1757, at St. Paul's Coffee House, St. Paul's Churchyard, and realized £356.[10] Along with his profit on the sale Paterson doubtless learned the value of informative cataloguing where the importance of the materials warranted due pains.

As it happened, however, no challenging collections came Paterson's way for a number of years, although a possible exception might be made for the "curious" English library of John Hutton, which Paterson catalogued and sold in 1764 and which was unusual for its scarce English magic, medicine, novels, criminal tracts, and erotica.

Actually it was not until 1771 that the really notable series of Paterson's catalogues began with the 42–day sale of an impressive collection catalogued as

---

[8] The record of his christening and burial are in *The Registers of St. Paul's Church, Covent Garden, London* (Harleian Society, 1906–09), I, 208; and V, 205.

[9] Nichols, *Literary Anecdotes*, III, 734.

[10] A copy of this catalogue containing prices and purchasers, now in the library of the University of California, Los Angeles, belonged earlier to the collectors James Bindley and Edward Jolly; and it may have been one of Paterson's own copies used at the sale, because the manuscript prices record what is here called "earnest" or "Advance-Money" paid down for the lots through the first day's sale and part of the second.

the *Bibliotheca Anglica Curiosa.* Since no collector is named in connection with this interesting and important library, it is fair to assume that Paterson himself had brought these books together. The subtitle of the catalogue is revealing:

> *A Catalogue of Several Thousand Printed Books and Tracts, (chiefly English) In every Branch of Knowledge; Many of which are exceedingly Scarce. Collected Principally with a View to a History of English Literature. The Catalogue is so digested as to render it useful to Collectors, and of General Entertainment.*

Many features of this collection and of the catalogue (for which, surprisingly, no charge was made) were remarkable at this date. First, this was for its time an extraordinarily extensive collection of materials in the English language (8,844 lots), and its national character was pointed up by the title-page allusion to a history of English literature. That Paterson himself had the hope of writing such a history, at least covering the later eighteenth century, we know on good authority.[11] In modern terms, however, "a history of English literature and learning" would give a better clue to the character of this collection.

Furthermore, this catalogue was the earliest of Paterson's attempts to "digest" a library. The books are arranged in three main groups, although these are not formally labelled:(1) language and letters, (2) theology, philosophy, and the sciences, (3) history, law, and topography. Within each of these main groups stand numerous sections and subsections, although these smaller divisions are not always arranged on a wholly predictable system. For example, the first main group contains a section called "Poetry and Miscellanies" running to about 1,200 lots; and within this section we find such subsections as "Novels," "Writers for and against the Stage," and "Anonymous English Dramatic Poets," these last distinct from the following day's sale devoting a full section to "English Dramatic Poets." Again, in Part II we find a long section of "Divinity and Controversy," which is basically an author list, but inserted amid the author entries are such subsections as those on "Catechism," "Ceremonies," "Eucharist," "Fanaticism," and "Free thinkers." Sometimes the categories are astonishingly capacious, such as that on "Prae-Existence, Prae-Adamites, of the Soul, the Human Mind, Understanding, Faculties, Passions, &c." At other times the sequence of sections is surprising, as when the books on "Love, Marriage, Polygamy, Adultery, Divorce" are followed by a group devoted to "Exercises, Horsemanship, Archery, Fencing—Recreations. Angling, Fowling, Dancing, Swimming, Chess-play, Gaming." These in turn are succeeded by a group of books on "Penmanship, Shorthand, &c."

---

[11] Nichols, *Literary Anecdotes*, III, 736.

This kind of subject arrangement, though never really illogical, is unpredictable enough to make the *Bibliotheca Anglica Curiosa* a little troublesome to use at first. But the fact that these thousands of English books were all arranged under subject headings, often of a highly specialized character, gave this catalogue an evident utility in its time; and even today it would be an excellent starting point for any scholar interested in determining the literature available in the English language on any one of a host of topics down to 1771.

A third distinctive feature of the *Bibliotheca Anglica Curiosa* was the care given to identifying editions of English writers. The offerings of Bacon's *Essays*, which appears under the Walpolian heading of "Royal and Noble Authors," is characteristic:

3156. Essays, 1st, large-paper, 8vo, Windet, 1597
3157. ,, 2nd imp., 12mo, 1598
3158. ,, 2 parts, 12mo, Jaggard, 1612
3159. ,, larger-paper, Beale, 1612
3160. ,, 1613
3161. ,, large-paper, port., 1625.

Set this beside R. W. Gibson's recent bibliography of Bacon (1950), and we see that Paterson, considering the rudimentary state of bibliographical knowledge in his day, was exercising unusual care. He names the printers, at least for the earlier offerings, and he correctly identifies the first edition. He did not know of the second edition (1597), but neither did the compilers of the *Short-Title Catalogue* (1926). Beyond this point he was wisely unwilling to specify edition numbers. He errs in placing Jaggard's 1612 edition before Beale's in the same year, but until the Register of the Stationers' Company was made available to scholars in the nineteenth century no one knew that Jaggard's edition was a piracy. And although Paterson seems to err in calling the Jaggard 1612 a duodecimo instead of an octavo, we cannot be sure that he was in error because he may have been describing a copy since lost, just as the 1597 duodecimo was unknown until fairly recently. On all counts, then, the *Bibliotheca Anglica Curiosa* was a noteworthy performance, and today this catalogue retains more interest and potential use than does Paterson's *Bibliotheca Universalis Selecta* (1786), which drew more overt comment from his contemporaries.

Apparently, however, the *Bibliotheca Anglica* did not pass unnoticed in the booktrade, for Paterson's next "digested" catalogue, the *Bibliotheca Westiana* (1773) was prepared not for a sale conducted by himself but by the bookseller Langford. The library was the polymathic collection of James West (1704?–1772), President of the Royal Society, and was rich in early English printed materials.

But although the catalogue, which sold for 2s., was "digested" by Paterson, it was not well digested. Instead books were grouped first by format (the traditional auction system), then loosely by subject, and within subjects even more loosely by careless alphabetical arrangement. The interest here lies today in occasional notes on individual books, such as that on Hall's *Virgidemarium* (1599–1602), "Mr. Pope's copy who presented it to Mr. West, telling him that he esteemed them the best Poetry and truest Satire in the English Language; and that he had an Intention of modernizing them, as he had done some of Donne's satires"; or that on a copy of Puttenham's *Art of English Poesy*, "with a Catalogue of Puttenham's Books by Ben Jonson, MS."

In 1774 Paterson catalogued and sold two libraries of some note. The first was that of the learned coin dealer Thomas Snelling (1712–1773), a collection rich not only in numismatic and economic materials but also, surprisingly, in its very large number of books and tracts on war and military matters. The second was an 18-day sale catalogued as the *Bibliotheca Monastica-Fletewodiana*. This had originally been the conventual library of Missenden Abbey in Buckinghamshire that had become the property of Sergeant William Fletewood, Recorder of London in the time of Elizabeth I. A manuscript note by William Upcott in one copy of this catalogue furnishes an appraisal of the catalogue, the library, and the sale:

> This is one of the most curious collections ever sold of old English literature. The catalogue, like all Patersons, is carefully drawn up—& may be relied upon for names and dates.... Every thing seems to have gone excessively cheap. Bl[ack] l[etter] & old Poetry had not yet become the fashion. Neither does the relative rarity of the different articles (except in the Caxtons) appear to have been attended to—books of every-day occurrence bringing as high prices, as those of extreme rarity & curiosity.[12]

This collection was notable for its early English printed books and for its sixteenth- and seventeenth-century English literature and drama. Neither this catalogue nor the *Bibliotheca Snellingiana* claimed to be "digested" by Paterson, probably because each collection was a specialized rather than truly polymathic library, yet both were actually subject catalogues. The *Bibliotheca Monastica* offered unusually full information about its sixteenth-century English books: author, short title, editor or translator, place of publication if other than London, publisher, date, and the person to whom the book was dedicated. Books in black-

---

[12] Cited from the copy in the library of the University of California, Los Angeles, which seems to have belonged to William Herbert, Richard Heber, William Upcott, and Thomas Dibdin, and which is almost certainly the copy alluded to in Dibdin's *Bibliomania*, p. 37. It includes some interesting phonetic spellings of eighteenth-century collectors' names including, consistently, "Beauclare" for "Beauclerk."

letter or with illustrations were noted as such, and occasional informative notes were made on different items, as with a 1605 edition of Bacon's *Advancement of Learning*, where Paterson observes: "This copy is corrected by an Amanuensis of Lord Bacon's"[13] But how dismayingly low the prices were is evidenced by the fact that this copy sold for 2*s*. 6*d*., while a first edition of Bacon's *Essays* combined with the first two editions of King James I's *Basilike Doron* brought only 6*d*. Such prices were a dismaying reward for the cataloguer's time and toil.

Since this lamentable state of affairs persisted for some time, Paterson was forced to the wall. *The London Chronicle* of March 11–14, 1775, lists him as a bankrupt; and in August of 1776 Samuel Johnson referred to him as "a Man for whom I have long had a kindness, who is now abroad in distress."[14]

Sometime prior to 1781, and very probably through the good offices of Samuel Johnson, Paterson must have been hired to catalogue the enormous library of Topham Beauclerk, which came to fully 10,000 volumes. This was a polymathic library with particular emphasis, however, on literature and history. The books were predominantly English with about a third of the titles before 1700 and the remainder of the eighteenth century. The library was offered for sale *en bloc* to the Russian Ambassador,[15] but this offer failing, the catalogue was printed for purposes of auction sale, the first volume being announced in *The London Chronicle* of March 8–10, 1781, the day before Beauclerk's death on March 11. The two-volume catalogue, running to just under 400 pages, sold for 3*s*., and the 50-day sale brought over £5,000. The catalogue is, as Dibdin says, "a fair specimen of the analytico-bibliographical powers of Paterson."[16] It gives more abundant details than were then common, including the first names of authors. The books are grouped according to their subjects, and, as an added feature, a summary index of subjects is furnished. By means of it one can readily find the books on such representative topics as freethinkers and their opponents, Provençal poetry, collections of *Ana*, the philosophic and literary transactions of the academies; and on Danish, Swiss, Russian, and Polish history. The *Bibliotheca Beauclerkiana* was a useful tool for collectors and scholars, and the frequency with which it appears in the catalogues of their private libraries (as well as on the market today) argues that it was widely esteemed.

The success of the Beauclerk catalogue and sale in 1781 must have led to Paterson's being entrusted with the cataloguing and sale in 1783 of the truly "Curious and Distinguished Library" of Thomas Crofts (1722–1781). Like Beau-

---

[13] Lot 2139. A MS note identifies this amanuensis as a "Mr. Locker of Leather Sellers Hall."
[14] Johnson, *Letters*, ed. R. W. Chapman (Oxford: Clarendon Press, 1952), II, 148–49.
[15] *Ibid.*, II, 336.
[16] *Bibliomania*, p. 396.

clerk's, this was a library on a grand scale (43-day sale of 8,380 lots, realizing just over £3,450, the catalogue running to 436 pages), but in several respects this was the more choice collection. Both were polymathic libraries, but Crofts' holdings in European books were richer, and his collection of Italian literature and drama was incomparable. Paterson's catalogue was in every way worthy of the library. Indeed Dibdin does not err when he says "that this renowned champion of catalogue-makers shines with greater, and nearly perfect, splendour, in the collection of the Rev. Thomas Crofts—a collection which, taking it 'for all in all,' I know not whether it be exceeded by any which this country has recorded in the shape of a private catalogue." And Dibdin adds (though probably apocryphally, since Paterson detested profanity) that Paterson "used, in his latter days, to hit his knee hard with his open hand, and exclaim—'By G—, Croft's Catalogue is my chef d'oeuvre, out and out.'"[17]

The basic plan of the catalogue is an arrangement by subject except for a concluding section devoted to manuscripts. The twenty-one subjects begin with (1) the origin of letters with grammars and dictionaries, and (2) bibliography; and they end with (20) voyages and travels, and (21) American history and travels. Within each main section are abundant subsections, although these smaller subject groups are not labelled as such. The section on the origin of letters, for example, actually contains three subsections: 8 lots on education, followed by 10 lots on the origins of language and on primitive tongues, and then 14 lots on the diversity and resemblances of alphabets and languages. But what is remarkable here, as elsewhere in the catalogue, is the chronological arrangement of material within these subsections. This chronological arrangement, although it is not faultlessly done, has the great advantage of showing at a glance the earliest and most recent book on a given topic and thus, potentially, the progress of scholarship in a particular field—often a very specialized field—of learning. This system is familiar today in scientific bibliographies and from its use also in *The Cambridge Bibliography of English Literature*, but I know of no catalogue prior to Paterson's *Croftsiana*—certainly of no English catalogue—that employed this kind of arrangement.

Moreover, the specific entries are much fuller than those in common eighteenth-century use. They included such material as the full names of authors, reasonably full titles, illustrations if any, format, binding when notable, place, publisher or printer of pre-1600 books and of post-1600 books where notable, and date. There are occasional notes of bibliographic or other interest, such as that on the *Sermoni* of Leo III, translated by Philippo di Bartholomeo Corsini (Florence, 1490): "There are no *Signatures* to this Book; in lieu of which it is paged in *Numerals* at the

[17] *Ibid.*

Bottom of each Leaf, a singularity rarely to be met with among the early Printers''
(lot 745).

The interest aroused by the *Croftsiana* was substantial. Joseph Johnson's
Critical Review found room for an encomium of the catalogue: "...what will
render it more particularly valuable to men of letters is, the accuracy with which
it is compiled, the full and satisfactory description of every article, and the excellent arrangement of the whole under distinct and regular classes." There was
issued a printed list of the prices brought, possibly the earliest example of such a
procedure in England; and Peignot tells us that in the nineteenth century copies
of the *Bibliotheca Croftsiana* brought a guinea or more in London.[18]

Following the *Croftsiana* of 1783 there is a hiatus of nearly twenty years before
Paterson's next important catalogue.[19] This was the *Bibliotheca Strangeiana* (1802).
The library that it represents (though John Strange, who amassed it, finds no
place in De Ricci's *English Collectors of Books and Manuscripts*) was probably
without a parallel in England. It was polymathic in character but with two very
distinctive features. Of its more than 12,000 volumes, the overwhelming majority
were books of the eighteenth century alone, so that from its sheer size it covered
the learning of that age as few (if any other) English libraries could have covered
it. And although all fields of learning were copiously represented, the great
richness of this library was in science. So vast were the materials in science through
the eighteenth century that even scattered random samples are impressive: 30
lots on electricity, 59 lots on earthquakes and volcanoes, 49 lots on conchology,
and 15 lots on military medicine, to name only a few. Yet the enormous strength
of this library in eighteenth-century science should not obscure its power across
a wide diversity of fields. Again to sample, British poetry and *belles lettres* from
provincial presses (Edinburgh, Glasgow, Perth, Bath, York, Newscastle, Chester,
etc.) were widely represented; the section on Grey's *Elegy* with its Continental
translations down to 1788, remains impressive; and it is doubtful whether any
other library contained just short of two hundred books on Venice published up
to the 1790's.

18 Nichols, *Literary Anecdotes*, VIII (1814), 482; Dibdin, *Bibliomania*, p. 398 note; and Gabriel
Peignot, *Répertoire Bibliographique Universel* (1812), p. 93.

19 During part of these years Paterson served as private librarian to the Marquis of Lansdowne. His
services in cataloguing the Lansdowne manuscripts have somehow, I fear, been obscured, not to
say obliterated, by Sir Henry Ellis's preface to *A Catalogue of the Lansdowne Manuscripts in the
British Museum* (1819), but that would be a story in itself. Here as elsewhere I ignore other large-
scale catalogues that Paterson prepared where their inherent interest does not now seem to
me to warrant analysis, such as the *Bibliotheca Pinelliana* (1789), which, as Paterson himself
points out, was merely a one-volume abridgement of Morelli's original six-volume catalogue of
the library.

3*

Such sampling of the wealth of the Strangeiana is made possible only because Paterson's catalogue of it is a subject catalogue. Whether one turns from agriculture to Venice, or from English literature to medicine, the catalogue is so arranged as to fulfill the abiding needs of scholars. It offers detailed bibliographies of continuing historic value on a host of subjects.

Still other features of the catalogue deserve mention, along with one limitation. The limitation is that the dates do not seem to be as reliable always as those in other Paterson catalogues, but some of this may have been due to an old man's failing hand or to careless printing. On the other hand, Paterson supplied far more annotations on individual books than he commonly did, and these often display the kind of knowledge of eighteenth-century books and writers for which his contemporaries admired him. But his best contribution came in his classification of the books, such groupings, for example, as the publications of the academies arranged by nations or the publications of specialized academies arranged by field of research. Under *Societates Georgicae* (lots 4731–42), for instance, one finds a list of the Swiss, Italian, French, English, Irish, and Russian agricultural society proceedings of the time. Wherever one turns in the *Bibliotheca Strangeiana*, one finds broad bibliographical light on the eighteenth century that can be found, surely, in few places more readily than here. The *Strangeiana*, in the last year of Paterson's life, fittingly rounded out his contribution to learning.

Archer Taylor, in his *Book Catalogues: Their Varieties and Uses* (p. 16), has commented on the infrequent use of older British private library catalogues except to settle questions of provenance or sporadically to determine what books an historic figure has owned or read. In the light of Paterson's toils to develop useful subject catalogues, one may express a regret that this has been so. But the season is late for sentiment, and if the foregoing account of Paterson's chief catalogues is to serve a modern end, it is to suggest that his work can be used as it was intended to be used. Subject catalogues are neither so numerous nor so complete that we can afford to ignore rich and useful ones; nor are catalogues of eighteenth-century English books, such as *The London Catalogue*, so satisfactory that we need recourse to no other sources. Scholars concerned with aspects of eighteenth-century culture, from the history of literature to the history of science, or those in search of subject bibliographies before 1800 will not pass empty-handed from time spent with such catalogues as the *Beauclerkiana*, the *Croftsiana*, and the *Strangeiana*. These were designed to serve the continuing interest of scholars.

University of California,
Los Angeles, California

DIE WAHL DES KIRCHENBAUPLATZES IN DER SAGE UND IM VOLKSGLAUBEN MIT BESONDERER RÜCKSICHT AUF SCHWEDEN

Dag Strömbäck

I.

In schwedischen Gegenden trifft man oft Volksüberlieferungen um den Platz der Gemeindekirche im Dorf an, wie sie gerade dort zu liegen gekommen ist und welche Schwierigkeiten mit ihrem ersten Aufbau verbunden waren. Manchmal kann es auch vorkommen, daß man in einer solchen Gegend auf den ersten Platz hinweist, an dem der Kirchenbau begonnen, jedoch nicht vollendet, sondern aufgegeben wurde, worauf man sich nach einem neuen und glücklicheren Platz umgesehen hat. Die Überlieferung hat da an eine alte Ruine oder Hausfundament angeknüpft, und man hat dann gesagt, daß ein solcher Gebäudeüberrest von einem ersten Kirchenbauunternehmen herstamme, das infolge des Widerstandes von übelgesinnten Mächten nicht weitergeführt werden konnte, weshalb ein neuer Kirchenbauplatz gewählt werden mußte. Bisweilen hat allein die eigentümliche Lage einer Gemeindekirche — weit draußen auf einer Landzunge im See oder Fluß oder dicht an der Grenze zu einer Nachbargemeinde und somit weit vom Dorfmittelpunkt — die Phantasie des Volkes anregen können, und man hat zu erklären versucht, warum, aller menschlichen Vernunft zuwider, die Kirche einen so sonderbaren Platz erhalten hat.[1]

[1] Meine früheren Studien hinsichtlich der Kirchenbauplatzsagen befinden sich in *Gammal Hälsingekultur*, 1931, S. 44ff., in *Västerås stift i ord och bild*, 1951, S. 317ff. sowie in *Norden och kontinenten. Föredrag och diskussioner vid trettonde nordiska folklivs- och folkminnesforskarmötet i Lund 1957*, 1958

Man sollte sich nun denken können, daß diese Erklärungen der Volksdichtung, diese örtlichen Überlieferungen einen historischen Kern, eine tatsächliche Grundlage enthielten, die diese zu wichtigen Bestandteilen der Geschichte eines Kirchspiels oder einer Gegend machen würden. Aus den mittelalterlichen Landschaftsgesetzen wissen wir ja ziemlich gut, nach welchen Bestimmungen eine Pfarrkirche errichtet werden sollte, und es konnte von vornherein angenommen werden, daß die Sagen etwas von Mühen und Enttäuschungen der ersten Bauzeit widerspiegeln würden. So heißt es z. B. in dem Abschnitt des Dalagesetzes, der von der Kirche handelt: ,,Bauern brachten Stämme und Steine herbei, gruben Fundament und bauten Kirche", und aus anderen Gesetzen erfahren wir Verschiedenes über die Erlaubnis zum Kirchenbau und über die Beisteuerung von Boden für den Kirchenbauplatz u. a. m. Aber die Sagen lassen uns hier im Stich. Sie drehen sich in der Regel ziemlich monoton um gewisse Motive der Volksdichtung, und sehr selten erheben sie sich zum Niveau der historischen Sagen. In Wirklichkeit haben wir es — wie ich gleich zeigen werde — hinsichtlich dieser Kirchenbauplatzsagen zum allergrößten Teil mit einer festländischen Motivflora zu tun, aber es gibt innerhalb dieser eine Gruppe, die ein klares nordisches Verbreitungsgebiet und vermutlich auch nordischen Ursprung hat.

Schematisch gesehen kann der Inhalt dieser Kirchenbauplatzsagen folgendermaßen angegeben werden:

Man beginnt die Kirche an einem, wie man glaubt, geeigneten Platz zu bauen, aber der Bau wird durch übernatürliche Mächte (oder durch andere Umstände) verhindert oder erschwert; da überläßt man es der Vorsehung, den richtigen Platz anzuweisen und nimmt dabei junge Zugtiere in Anspruch: Junge Ochsen, Färsen oder Fohlen, die vor einen mit Stämmen oder Steinen beladenen Schlitten oder Schleife gespannt werden und gehen dürfen, wohin sie wollen; wo sie stehen bleiben, wird die Kirche gebaut. Die jungen Ochsen oder Fohlen können auch völlig frei gelassen werden (und nicht vor einen Wagen oder Schleife o. ä. gespannt werden). Sie dürfen frei umherschweifen, und wo sie stehen bleiben, ist der richtige Bauplatz. Neben diesen Sagen, in denen Tiere die ausschlaggebende Rolle als Werkzeuge der Vorsehung spielen, gibt es auch eine Mehrzahl anderer Sagentypen. Eine der gewöhnlichsten ist die, daß man, wenn der erste Kirchenbau mißglückt, einen Baumstamm in einen See oder Fluß hinausstößt und ihn treiben läßt. Wo er an Land treibt, liegt der richtige Kirchenbauplatz. Eine dritte große Gruppe von Sagen wiederum hat als Hauptmotiv, daß das Baumaterial selbst durch übernatürliches Eingreifen von dem Platz, an dem man zu bauen angefangen hat,

S. 161 ff. Das schwedische Überlieferungsmaterial wird im einzelnen in dem bald erscheinenden folkloristischen Teil des *Atlas över svensk folkkultur* der Königlichen Gustav Adolfs Akademie dargelegt werden.

an den Platz, der der Vorsehung gemäß der richtige sein soll, verrückt wird. Der letztere wird dann der endgültige Bauplatz.

Ich will ein paar Typenbeispiele geben. Von der Kirche zu Fellingsbro in der Provinz Västmanland wird berichtet, daß man sich nicht über den Bauplatz einigen konnte. Da befragte man einen weisen Mann des Ortes, und er forderte das Bauvolk auf, ein Paar Zwillingsochsen zu nehmen und sie vor einen Wagen zu spannen, auf den der erste Stein der Kirche gelegt wurde. Sie sollten den Stein fortziehen dürfen, wohin sie wollten, aber wo sie zuletzt stehen blieben, sollte die Kirche gebaut werden. Das Bauvolk handelte auch so, wie sie der Mann angewiesen hatte, und auf diese Weise bekam man den richtigen Bauplatz für die Kirche. Mit kleineren Varianten und gewöhnlich mit einer Einleitung darüber, daß boshafte Mächte ihr Spiel treiben und verhindern, daß die Kirche auf dem zuerst beabsichtigten Platz gebaut wird, kommt dieser Sagentyp hinsichtlich etwa 270 Kirchen in Schweden vor. In der Provinz Uppland betrifft dieser Sagentyp z. B. die Kirchen zu Rasbo, Alunda, Länna, Närtuna, Enåker und Riala, in der Provinz Dalarna z. B. Hedemora, Husby, Gagnef und Svärdsjö, in der Provinz Gästrikland Torsåker und in der Provinz Hälsingland Bollnäs. In einigen dieser Sagen handelt es sich um Färsen oder Kühe an Stelle von jungen Ochsen als Anweiser für den richtigen Kirchenbauplatz, eine — wie wir später sehen werden — recht interessante Variante.

Wie ich eben erwähnte, können in diesen Sagen die Tiere auch völlig frei gelassen werden, und gewöhnlich betrifft es auch dann Jungtiere. Wo sie stehen bleiben, wird die Kirche gebaut. Von der Kirche zu Alfta in der Provinz Hälsingland wird berichtet, daß sie nicht ,,stehen'' wollte, als sie zuerst gebaut werden sollte. Was am Tage gebaut wurde, wurde während der Nacht niedergerissen. Man hatte also nicht den richtigen Kirchenbauplatz gewählt! Da nahm man ein junges Pferd, das nicht eingefahren war, ließ es los und ließ es laufen, wohin es wollte. Wo es zuletzt stehen blieb, baute man die Kirche. Von Järvsö in der Provinz Hälsingland und ebenso von Mattmar in der Provinz Jämtland wird eine ähnliche Sage erzählt. In diesen Sagen über die frei umherlaufenden jungen Tiere (Fohlen, junge Ochsen usw.) als Anweiser für den richtigen Kirchenbauplatz gibt es auch Angaben darüber, daß man eine Schwelle oder einen Stein (oder einen anderen Gegenstand, der für den Kirchenbau von Bedeutung war) auf ihren Rücken legte. Zu dieser Gruppe gehört auch die bekannte Sage von der Gründung der Kirche zu Norrala auf dem Platz, wo das Pferd des Hälsinge-Apostels Staffan mit dem toten Missionar auf seinem Rücken stehen blieb, der von den Heiden im Walde Ödmorden umgebracht worden war.

In diesen Sagen handelt es sich also darum, daß man die Haustiere — und meistens die Jungtiere — den geeignetsten und sichersten Platz für den Kirchenbau anweisen läßt. Und diese Sagen mit Tieren als Handelnde in dem wichtigen Unternehmen bilden zusammen einen großen Komplex mit vielen Varianten, auf die ich hier nicht näher eingehen kann.

Eine von diesen völlig getrennte Sagengruppe bilden diejenigen Überlieferungen, die berichten, daß der richtige Kirchenbauplatz widerspenstigen oder übelgesinnten Mächten dadurch abgewonnen wurde, daß man einen in einen See oder Fluß hinausgestoßenen Baumstamm anweisen ließ, wo die Kirche gebaut werden sollte. Als Typenbeispiel kann die Sage von der Kirche zu Söderbärke im südlichen Teil der Provinz Dalarna angeführt werden. Die Kirche sollte zuerst auf einer Landzunge bei dem Dorf Sörbo gebaut werden. Aber alles, was am Tage gebaut wurde, wurde im Laufe der Nacht niedergerissen. Der Platz war nicht der richtige. Das Bauvolk nahm da einen Baumstamm, hieb seine Äxte in den Stamm hinein und stieß ihn in den See Barken hinaus. Wo der Stamm später an Land trieb — etwa 5 km am See hinauf — wurde die Kirche gebaut. Etwa dieselbe Sage wird von der Kirche zu Rättvik in der Provinz Dalarna berichtet, die zuerst bei dem Dorf Tina liegen sollte, jedoch von den Unterirdischen während der Nacht niedergerissen wurde. Dieses veranlaßte, daß ein Baumstamm in die Bucht Rättviken geworfen wurde, dem man es überließ, den richtigen Kirchenbauplatz anzuweisen. Es gibt eine ganze Reihe von diesen Baumstammsagen von den Provinzen Jämtland und Medelpad bis hinunter nach Närke und Värmland, ja, es gibt sogar einen vereinzelten Beleg so weit südlich wie im südlichen Teil der Provinz Östergötland. Ich kehre gleich zu dem — wie ich glaube — nordischen Ursprung dieses Motivs zurück!

Im folgenden will ich einige Worte über die dritte Hauptgruppe sagen: diejenigen, welche man die Verrückungssagen nennen kann. Baumaterial und Gerät werden während der Nacht von unsichtbaren Händen vom ersten Bauplatz an einen anderen Platz, der dann der endgültige Kirchenbauplatz wird, verrückt. So wird z. B. von der Kirche zu Film in der Provinz Uppland erzählt, daß dort, wo sie zuerst gebaut wurde, der angefangene Bau immer geschliffen wurde und die Werkzeuge verschwanden. Man schaffte neue Werkzeuge an und begann von neuem mit der Arbeit, aber damit ging es ebenso. Schließlich fand man die benutzten Geräte an einem Platz in der Nähe; dort begann man mit dem Bau, und nun ging alles ohne Schwierigkeiten. Ähnliches wird von den Kirchen zu Harg und Skuttunge erzählt. Sonst ist dieser Sagentyp am reichlichsten in den Provinzen Skåne und Västergötland vertreten und scheint im ganzen eine mehr südliche und westliche Verbreitung in unserem Land zu haben.

Es gibt auch viele andere Sagenmotive in diesem reichen Sagenmaterial um den ersten Kirchenbauplatz (z. B. eine Stimme, die aus der Höhe ertönt und den Kirchenbauplatz anweist, ein Vogel, der durch einen fallengelassenen Ast oder

Feder o. ä. anzeigt, wo man bauen soll, Kirchenglocken, die den richtigen Platz anweisen usw.) Aber die großen Hauptgruppen sind die eben genannten, und am größten unter ihnen ist diejenige Gruppe, die von jungen Ochsen oder Kühen oder Färsen oder jungen Pferden handelt, die dazu bestimmt werden, den rechten Kirchenbauplatz anzuweisen.

II.

Man kann sich nun die Frage stellen, ob dieses Material, das zum größten Teil in den letzten Jahrzehnten wesentlich durch die Mitwirkung der Pfarrämter gesammelt wurde, in unserem Land alt ist.

In aller Kürze soll hier gesagt werden, daß damals, als in der Großmachtszeit das Interesse für unsere einheimischen Volksüberlieferungen zu erwachen begann und in verschiedenen Teilen unseres Landes Aufzeichnungen gemacht wurden, wurde man auch auf dieses Material, das die Kirchen betrifft, aufmerksam. Es wurde teilweise aufgezeichnet, und in solchen Fällen, in denen spätere Aufzeichnungen aus einer gewissen Gegend mit Notizen aus dem 17. und 18. Jahrhundert verglichen werden können, herrscht eine bemerkenswerte Übereinstimmung sowohl die Form wie den Inhalt betreffend. Die Überlieferung kann demnach in einer Gegend während 300 Jahren ziemlich unverändert bewahrt werden. Vor allem sind hier die sogenannten Antiquitätsuntersuchungen von grundlegender Bedeutung, Sammlungen von handschriftlichem Material aus der Zeit um 1670 und 1680, entstanden durch einen Erlaß der Königlichen Majestät, wobei ,,Überlieferungen und Märchen... aus früheren Zeiten'' beachtet werden sollten. Aber wir haben auch ein ziemlich reichhaltiges Material von alten lateinischen Dissertationen über gewisse Kirchspiele und von allerhand topographischer Literatur aus dem 17. und 18. Jahrhundert. Ich will dieses Material hier nicht näher darlegen, sondern nur hervorheben, daß es oft nur die Einleitung zu der betreffenden Kirchenbauplatzsage angibt, diese Einleitung, die in dem späteren Material mit fast ermüdender Einförmigkeit wiederkehrt. Die Sagen fangen ja bekanntlich mit dem Mißlingen auf dem für den Kirchenbau zuerst ausersehenen Platz an, und dann wird als Erklärung für das Mißlingen hinzugesetzt: ,,Denn was am Tage gebaut wurde, wurde während der Nacht niedergerissen.'' Man kann sagen, daß dies eine Art feste epische Formel in der Sage ist, und sie kann in der Tat auf mittelalterliche Legenden zurückgeführt werden. Selbst habe ich sie in der Kölbigk-Legende vom Anfang des 11. Jahrhunderts, die im 12. Jahrhundert aufgezeichnet wurde, gefunden: *quia quidquid in die edificabatur in nocte penitus evertebatur*[2], aber Prof.

---

[2] Siehe weiter meine Studie *"Den underbara årsdansen" in Arkiv för nord. filol.* 59, 1944, S. 111 ff.

C. M. Edsman hat mich auf eine Mehrzahl noch älterer Textstellen aufmerksam gemacht, die vielleicht die Zurückführung des Motivs bis in das 4. oder 5. Jahrhundert n. Chr. möglich machen.[3]

Von besonderem Interesse in dem älteren schwedischen Material ist ein Bericht aus dem 17. Jahrhundert, der sich auf die Kirche zu Stenbrohult bezieht und das Patronatsrecht über die Gemeinde betrifft. Der Inhalt ist in Kürze der folgende:

Der Richter Germund Palm Cederhielm auf dem Hof Möckelsnäs ersucht um 1690 König Karl XI. um das Patronatsrecht über die Gemeinde zu Stenbrohult. Als Begründung seines Gesuches beruft er sich auf den Umstand, daß die Kirche zu Stenbrohult von einem Ritter, der auf dem Hof Möckelsnäs wohnte, errichtet wurde — welches er durch ein bemerkenswertes Zeugnis der ältesten Bauern der Gemeinde beweist, die berichten, was sie in dieser Angelegenheit von ihren Vätern und Vorfahren gehört haben. In diesem Zeugnis aus dem Ende des 17. Jahrhunderts heißt es unter anderem folgendermaßen:

> „Wie wir, die unterzeichneten Bauern von der Gemeinde zu Stenbrohult in der Provinz Småland vormals auf Anfrage unsere Bescheinigung und Zeugnis gegeben haben, inwiefern uns kund ist, daß *Jus Patronatus* dem hochgeehrten und wohlgeborenen Herrn Richter Cederhielm auf dem Hof Möckelsnäs zukommen soll, so erklären wir zur Beglaubigung wahrheitsgetreu, nun im Beisein des Herrn Richters, was wir von unseren alten Vätern und Vorfahren darüber haben erzählen und sagen hören, nämlich folgendes:
>
> Daß auf Möckelsnäs in alten Zeiten und vor mehr als 100 Jahren ein Rittersmann mit Namen Karl Tokason gewohnt habe, welcher am Weihnachtsmorgen, als er nach Virestad reisen wollte, mit seinem Pferd durch das Eis gebrochen sei und da gelobt habe, daß, wenn Gott ihm wieder hinauf und nach Hause hülfe, er eine Kirche bauen lassen wolle — welchem Gelöbnis er auch nachkam. Und weil damals die Männer der Gemeinde zu Göteryd sich eine Kirche aus Stein bauen wollten, erwarb er von ihnen ihre Holzkirche, die er dann bei Sandåker (in Stenbrohult) errichten ließ, aber da das, was am Tage gebaut wurde, während der Nacht niedergerissen wurde, baten sie Gott, daß er einen Platz anweisen möge, wo er seinen Heiligen Tempel haben wolle, und also haben sie auf Veranlassung irgendeines Mannes ein Paar ungezähmte junge Ochsen vor einen Baumstamm gespannt, ließen diese dann gehen, wohin sie wollten, welche dann an dem Platz stehen blieben, an dem jetzt die Kirche zu Stenbrohult gebaut und aufgestellt ist."

Das Dokument schließt mit einem Verzeichnis über die Bauern in Stenbrohult, die diese Überlieferung kennen und deren Richtigkeit bezeugen wollen. Und hier hat man ein Verfahren, Gewährsmänner anzugeben, benutzt, das an das genaue Verfahren unserer Tage erinnert, wenn es musterhaft ist. Von jedem Bauern, der

---

[3] Siehe nunmehr *Norden och kontinenten*, S. 189f.

diese Sage kennt, wird teils sein eigenes Alter, teils dasjenige, das sein Vater (der auch diese Überlieferung kannte) erreichte, angegeben. Bei einem der Unterzeichneten ist vermerkt, daß sein Vater 105 Jahre alt war. Damit werden wir hinsichtlich dieser Überlieferung in das 16. Jahrhundert zurückgeführt. Dies ist meines Wissens der älteste Beleg schwedischer Volksüberlieferung über die nunmehr so außerordentlich gewöhnliche Sage von den jungen Ochsen, die den richtigen Kirchenbauplatz anweisen. Gotthard Virdestam, der diese Urkunde behandelt hat,[4] mißt dieser Sage einen gewissen historischen Wert bei und findet unter Zuhilfenahme anderer Quellen, daß die Angaben der Sage über Karl Tokason im wesentlichen richtig gewesen sind und kommt zu der Schlußfolgerung, daß der Kirchenbau „irgendwann im Zeitraum zwischen 1310 und 1377" stattgefunden hat. Hier kann man sagen, daß eine Kirchenplatzsage ausnahmsweise einmal eine historische von Vater zu Sohn weitergetragene Überlieferung berührt hat.

Wenn wir die Aufmerksamkeit auf das ältere schwedische Überlieferungsmaterial richten, wagen wir auf jeden Fall mit Gewißheit auszusprechen, daß im 16. und 17. Jahrhundert diese Kirchenbauplatzsagen in Schweden in der Volksüberlieferung lebten und daß sie später lebendig erhalten wurden und sich vermutlich im Laufe der folgenden Jahrhunderte bis in unsere Tage hinein vermehrt haben. Daß sie, nachdem sie von einigen Kirchen erzählt worden waren, sich auch zu anderen verbreiten konnten, ist nur das, was man erwarten kann, und betrachtet man auf der Karte die jetzige Verbreitung der Sagen, so findet man, daß der Schwerpunkt für die Sagen von den Zugtieren (junge Ochsen, Färsen, Kühe usw.) als Anweiser für den richtigen Kirchenbauplatz im Landesteil Götaland liegt, jedoch gewisse Verbreitungswege hinauf nach den Landesteilen Svealand und Norrland hat, während dagegen diejenigen Sagen, welche von dem treibenden Baumstamm als Mittel zur Anweisung des richtigen Kirchenbauplatzes erzählen, ihr wesentliches Verbreitungsgebiet im mittleren und südlichen Norrland und in den Provinzen Dalarna und Värmland haben. Das Verrückungsmotiv schließlich ist im wesentlichen im südlichen und südwestlichen Schweden beheimatet, kann aber auch stellenweise in anderen Teilen des Landes nachgewiesen werden.

Diese Verteilung stimmt auch ziemlich gut mit den Verhältnissen in unseren Nachbarländern überein. Wir haben in Dänemark eine Menge von Sagen um Kirchenbauplätze, die durch die Anweisung von Zugtieren bestimmt worden sind, und wir haben dort gleichfalls eine ganze Gruppe von Sagen mit dem sogenannten Verrückungsmotiv. Diese großen Sagenkomplexe hängen ihrerseits mit fast identischen Entsprechungen in Norddeutschland, Süddeutschland und der

---

[4] *Hyltén-Cavallius-Föreningens årsbok* 1922, S. 144ff.

Schweiz zusammen. Mit Ausnahme der Baumstammsagen sind nämlich alle diese nordischen Kirchenbauplatzsagen europäischen Ursprungs. Es gibt Kirchenbau-platzsagen auf dem europäischen Festland, die aufs Haar mit vielen von unseren Kirchenbauplatzsagen übereinstimmen, und es gibt ebenfalls in England Sagen-typen von mißlungenen Kirchenbauten, die verblüffende Ähnlichkeit mit ent-sprechenden schwedischen Überlieferungen haben.

III.

Wenn man nun ein solch großes Motivkomplex wie dieses behandelt, kann man es schematisch und geographisch tun und sich hauptsächlich den verschiedenen Motiven oder Typen von Überlieferungen widmen, sie auf großen Karten ein-zeichnen und Verbreitungswege und im Zusammenhang damit vielleicht auch kulturhistorische Verbindungslinien ermitteln. Aber eine andere Frage scheint mir fast dieselbe Wichtigkeit zu haben: Liegt hinter diesen ziemlich stereotypen und unpersönlichen Berichten etwas Reales, etwas, was sich auf wirklichen Glau-ben und Sitte gründet? Sind die Wanderungen und Verbreitungen der Motive von irgendwelchen inneren Voraussetzungen begünstigt worden?

Dies ist eine ziemlich umfangreiche Frage, die eingehend zu behandeln ich im Augenblick nicht bereit bin. Einige Linien glaube ich immerhin schon jetzt ent-werfen zu können, wobei ich mich teilweise auf ein paar frühere Studien des Materials stütze, die ich 1931 und 1951 veröffentlicht habe.[5]

Wenn auch der Zusammenhang der meisten Sagen, die die Wahl des Kirchen-bauplatzes betreffen, mit festländischen Motiven gezeigt werden konnte, so scheint doch für die Sagengruppe, die von dem Baumstamm als Wegweiser für den richtigen Bauplatz handelt, eine einheimische Grundlage vorzuliegen, die Verbindungen mit alter nordischer Sitte und Glauben hat. Für uns alle ist es ja wohlbekannt, wie die ersten Ansiedler auf Island am Ende des 9. und zu Beginn des 10. Jahrhunderts — die sogenannten Landnahmsmänner — sich ihre neuen Wohnsitze auswählten. Sie folgten bemerkenswert streng der Regel, daß sie sich dort, wo einer der Pfosten des Hochsitzes (oder ein anderer der zum Wohnhaus gehörenden Stämme) an Land trieb, niederließen. Manchmal konnte es lange dauern, bevor der Einwanderer seinen Stamm fand, aber da mußte er sich eine vorläufige Behausung einrichten und dann umziehen, wenn der Baumstamm ge-funden worden war. Und dort, wo der Stamm war, dort war auch sein Glück! Ich glaube nicht, daß man an dem tatsächlichen Vorkommen dieses Brauches zweifeln muß. Und wenn man dies nicht tut, muß man feststellen, daß der Brauch begreif-licherweise nicht einzig und allein für Islands Besiedlung erdacht worden war,

[5] Siehe Fußnote 1.

sondern einen Brauch mit alten Ahnen im Mutterland Norwegen widerspiegeln
muß.

In Schweden haben wir soweit bekannt den Brauch hinsichtlich der Wahl des
Wohnplatzes für ältere Zeit nicht klar bezeugt, aber als ein Ableger davon muß
man wohl die alte Erzählung von Stockholms Gründung auf dem Platz, wo ein
Baumstamm von Sigtuna an Land trieb, ansehen. Dort hat man allerdings auch
mit dem Namen selbst als ein für die Sagenbildung stark wirkendes Ferment zu
rechnen. Der früheste Beleg für die Sage bildet das Zeugnis von Johannes Mes-
senius aus dem Beginn des 17. Jahrhunderts; er sagt, daß man auf ,,alte Art und
Weise" prüfen wollte, wo die Stadt liegen sollte. Von einem sehr viel späteren Zeitpunkt haben wir einen — wie ich glaube — ziemlich zuverlässigen Beleg. Die beiden Ansiedler, die sich 1830 am See Sjouten im Kirchspiel Frostviken im nördlichen Teil der Provinz Jämtland niederlassen wollten, schlugen gemäß vertrauens-
würdigen Gemeindeüberlieferungen ihre Äxte in einen ,,Baumstumpf", stießen
ihn in den See hinaus und ließen ihn während der Nacht treiben. Wo er an Land
trieb, bauten sie. Als am Ende des 18. Jahrhunderts die kleine hübsche Kapelle zu
Viken in dem Kirchspiel von Frostviken bei dem See Kvarnbergsvattnet gebaut
werden sollte, schlug man ebenfalls die Äxte in einen Baumstamm und ließ ihn,
nachdem man ihn in den See hinausgestoßen hatte, den rechten Platz anweisen.
Wenn man den kurzen Zeitabstand und die festen Ansiedlertraditionen in Frostviken betrachtet, fragt man sich, ob die Sage hier nicht ein tatsächliches, über-
liefertes Verfahren widerspiegelt.

Meiner Ansicht nach gibt es viel, was dafür spricht, daß ,,der treibende Baumstamm" — der auch von Norwegen und Finnland bezeugt ist — ein altes ein-
heimisches nordisches Motiv ist, das zu den alten Siedlungsriten gehört, jedoch
übertragen worden ist und nunmehr fast ausschließlich hinsichtlich der Wahl von
Kirchenbauplätzen bekannt ist. Den ,,rechten Platz" für die Kirche zu finden,
hat man immer für schwer gehalten, sei es, daß man diesen letztgenannten Umstand mit widersprechenden Meinungen, sei es, daß man ihn mit Vorstellungen
von unterirdischen Mächten, ,,Herrschenden" o. ä. verband.

Hinsichtlich der Anwendung von Tieren bei der Wahl von Wohnplätzen oder
einem anderen wichtigen Platz kann man viele Parallelen aus verschiedenen
Zeiten und Gebieten finden. Aus der altnordischen Literatur kann daran erinnert
werden, wie — laut Islands Landnámabók — Tore Grimsson erfährt, wo er
bauen und wohnen soll. Ein ,,Meermann" weissagt ihm, daß er sich an dem Ort in
Island niederlassen soll, wo sich seine Mähre unter ihrer Saumlast niederlegt. Er
und seine Mutter folgen unter langen Wanderungen der Mähre, bis sie sich
schließlich niederlegt. Dort wählt Tore seinen Wohnsitz und wird ein großer
Häuptling in der Gegend.

Auf ähnliche Weise wurde gemäß der Sage das Schloß Neundorf in Sachsen gegründet. Zwei Ritter vereinbarten, daß sie ihren Packeseln folgen wollten, und wo diese sich mit ihren Lasten niederlegen würden, wollten sie bauen und wohnen. Es wurde eine ziemlich lange Wanderung, aber schließlich blieben die Esel an einem Platz mit üppigem Gras stehen, wo sie weideten und sich schließlich niederlegten. Schon am nächsten Tag riefen die Ritter Leute an den Platz, und der Bau wurde genau an dieser Stelle begonnen.[6]

Auch aus der Antike und dem frühen Mittelalter gibt es viele Sagen über die Rolle des Tieres als verläßlicher Wegweiser, wenn es die Gründung einer Stadt oder einer Siedlung galt. Oft handelt es sich um Hirsche, Kühe, Stiere oder Pferde. Von dem sagenhaften Gründer Thebens, Kadmos, wird erzählt, daß ihn das Orakel in Delphi anwies, eine Kuh Wegweiser für sich werden zu lassen und eine Stadt an dem Platz zu gründen, wo sie sich zur Ruhe niederlegen würde. Kadmos folgt dem Rat und gründet somit die Stadt Theben. Jordanes (*Getica* XXIV, 123–124) erzählt, daß laut einer alten Stammessage die Hunnen dadurch, daß sie einer Hindin folgten, die sie über Sumpfboden führte, den sie vorher nicht zu betreten gewagt hatten, neue Landgebiete entdeckt hätten (vgl. auch Prokopios *Goth.* IV,5). Auch die Sage von Konstantinopels Gründung gehört hierher. Konstantin der Große hat einen Traum, daß er sich auf sein Pferd setzen, ihm freie Zügel lassen und es gehen lassen soll, wohin es will. Während des Rittes soll er seinen Stock auf der Erde schleifen lassen und auf der Spur, die dadurch entsteht, soll er die Stadtmauer aufführen lassen (Wilhelm von Malmsbury, Guntherus Cisterciensis u. a.). Gewissen Tieren überließ man es auch, den Platz für Gräber und Klöster anzugeben. Der irische Missionar Gallus, der in der ersten Hälfte des 7. Jahrhunderts das Evangelium in der Gegend des Bodensees verkündete, sollte laut *Vita St. Galli* an dem Platz begraben werden, wo ein ungezähmtes Pferd stehen blieb. Ähnliches wird in späteren mittelalterlichen Überlieferungen von dem bekannten Papst Sylvester II. (999–1003) berichtet. Er hatte selbst bei Lebzeiten bestimmt, daß seine Leiche von zwei ungezähmten Lasttieren gezogen werden sollte, und dort, wo diese stehen blieben, sollte er begraben werden. Von einem Kloster unter der Regierungszeit Herzog Aethelwins in Ostangeln (d. h. in der zweiten Hälfte des 10. Jahrhunderts) wird in angelsächsischen Quellen berichtet, daß es an den Platz gegründet wurde, an dem ein Ochs stehen geblieben war.[7]

Auch von den Gebieten der finnisch-ugrischen Völker könnten Beispiele für die Anwendung der Haustiere bei der Wahl von „richtigem Platz" angeführt werden, wenn es sich um einen kultischen Zweck oder nur um Umsiedlung zu neuen Wohngebieten handelte. Uno Holmberg-Harva berichtet von den Votjaken

---

[6] A. Meiche, *Sagenbuch des Königreichs Sachsen*, S. 813 f.
[7] J. M. Kemble, *The Saxons in England* I, S. 429 f.

im östlichen Rußland (um die Flüsse Kama und Vjatka herum), daß diese bei der Wahl von neuem *lud* (eine Art heiliger Hain) einen ihrer Zauberer die Sache besorgen lassen, wobei dieser sich auf ein junges Pferd setzt, das vorher noch nie geritten worden ist; der Zauberer reitet ohne Zaumzeug in den Wald hinein, und wo das Fohlen zuletzt stehen bleibt, ist der heilige Ort.[8]

Wenn wir nun die Kirchenbauplatzsagen beurteilen, in denen die Haustiere in so vielen Fällen eine außerordentlich hervorragende Rolle spielen, müssen wir selbstverständlich auch mit jenem tief verwurzelten und weit verbreiteten Glauben rechnen, daß gewisse Tiere (und insbesondere Haustiere) die Fähigkeit hätten, Menschen in vielen schwierigen Unternehmen wie Niederlassung in unbekanntem Gebiet, Auswahl von heiligen Orten u. a. m. leiten zu können. Man kann ja auch daran erinnern, daß im Volksglauben vielen Tieren eine besondere Eigenschaft zugeteilt wird, nämlich die Fähigkeit, allerhand Unwesen und „Teufelszeug" in der Natur sehen und erkennen zu können, die dem Menschen verborgen sind. Es ist auch Grund dazu vorhanden, zu beachten, daß es sich oft in diesen Sagen über die Wahl von heiligen oder profanen Plätzen um ein junges Haustier (Fohlen, Färse) handelt. Das junge, unschuldige Tier hatte die Fähigkeit, das Gefährliche und Feindliche zu meiden oder es abzuwehren und das Friedliche und Glückbringende zu weisen.

IV.

Wir müssen somit damit rechnen, daß gewisse allgemeine Volksglaubenselemente als eine Art Substrat in mehreren der hervortretendsten Kirchenbauplatzsagen enthalten sind. Und begreiflicherweise gilt es, auch diese näher zu bestimmen und zu analysieren. Diesbezüglich konnte hier nur eine Andeutung gemacht werden. Will man dagegen das Material vorzugsweise unter motivhistorischen Gesichtspunkten betrachten, so glaube ich, daß man einen klaren und konkreten Hintergrund zu der größten Gruppe der hier in Frage kommenden Kirchenbauplatzsagen finden kann, nämlich zu der Gruppe, die das betrifft, was ich das Zug-Motiv genannt habe: junge Ochsen oder Färsen oder Kühe werden vor einen (Schlitten oder Schleife mit einem) Baustein oder Baumstamm gespannt und dürfen gehen, wohin sie wollen; wo sie stehen bleiben, kann man ohne Gefahr das Heiligtum bauen.

Wir können hier an gewisse Typenbeispiele erinnern und wählen das erste aus Deutschland. In Schleswig-Holstein gibt es eine Sage, aufgezeichnet in der ersten Hälfte des 19. Jahrhunderts, darüber, wie die Kirche zu Brecklum ihren Platz erhalten hat.[9] Drei fromme, adlige Jungfrauen wollten eine Kirche bauen und

[8] J. A. Mac Culloch, *The Mythology of all Races*, IV, S. 145.

begannen mit dem Bau auf einer Anhöhe. Aber was an einem Tag errichtet wurde, traf man niedergerissen an, als der nächste Tag graute. Da, so heißt es, beschlossen die frommen Jungfrauen, Baumaterial auf einen Wagen zu laden und zwei säugende Kühe davor zu spannen und sie mit ihrer Last gehen zu lassen, wohin sie wollten. Sie blieben an dem Platz stehen, an dem Brecklum jetzt liegt, und dort wurde die Kirche gebaut. J. J. Lagergren legt in seinen Aufzeichnungen aus Småland (erste Hälfte des 19. Jahrhunderts) eine ähnliche Sage darüber dar, wie St. Siegfried die Kirche zu Ås im Kreis Västbo gründete. „Nachdem St. Siegfried einen großen Stein geweiht hatte", heißt es in der Legende, „der auf einem Wagen von zwei trächtigen schneeweißen Zwillingskühen gezogen wurde, welche von Zwangsmitteln frei waren und aus eigenem Antriebe stehen blieben, wo die Kirche jetzt steht, legte er mit eigenen Händen den ersten Grundstein."

Doch diese beiden Versionen haben eine unverkennbare Ähnlichkeit mit dem Bericht der Bibel darüber, wie die Bundeslade zu den Israeliten zurückgeführt wurde. Im 1. Buch Samuels im 5. und 6. Kapitel wird erzählt, wie das heiligste Kleinod der Israeliten, die Bundeslade, von den Philistern erobert und in den Tempel Dagons gestellt worden war. Die Lade richtete jedoch bei den Philistern viel Schaden an und brachte eine Menge Unglück über sie, sodaß sie diese schleunigst in angrenzende Orte hinüberbrachten, wo sie auch viel Unglück verursachte. Niemand wagte es, sie bei sich aufzustellen. Sie mußte zu den Israeliten zurückgeführt werden, und dorthin wurde dieser heilige Gegenstand unter besonderen Zeremonien gebracht. Man spannte zwei noch säugende Kühe vor einen besonderen Wagen, auf den die Bundeslade gestellt wurde. Die Kühe konnten gehen, wohin sie wollten. „Und", so heißt es in 6,12, „die Kühe gingen strackes Weges auf Beth-Semes zu, auf einer Straße, und gingen und blöketen und wichen nicht weder zur Rechten noch zur Linken." Sie hielten schließlich auf dem Acker des Beth-Semiters Josuas an, und dort wurde die Lade auf einen großen Stein gesetzt. Die Schilderung hat auch andere Bestandteile, auf die ich hier nicht eingehen kann. Es erscheint mir sehr wahrscheinlich, daß dieser berühmte und eigentümliche Transport der Bundeslade die größte Gruppe innerhalb der Kirchenbauplatzsagen beeinflußt hat. Wir haben ja in unseren schwedischen Sagen auch ein Motivkomplex mit Kühen und Färsen als Zugtiere, und in Dänemark und Deutschland kommt diese Variante häufig vor. Daß die Bibel das Muster für diese Volkslegenden oder legendenhaften Sagen geworden ist, ist ja auch nur das, was man erwarten kann.

Universität Uppsala

⁹ K. Müllenhoff, *Sagen, Märchen und Lieder der Herzogtümer Schleswig Holstein und Lauenburg*, Nr. CXXXIX.

FIFTY YEARS OF FOLKTALE INDEXING

Stith Thompson

It is just a half century since the first systematic attempt to classify and index folktales. Beginning shortly after the publication of the Grimms' *Kinder und Hausmärchen* there appeared continually throughout the nineteenth century notices of comparisons between versions of folktales, especially in the European collections. The Grimm's themselves made many such observations, and as collectors of *Märchen* and *Sagen* in Europe expanded their activities and issued new collections from every country of the continent and the British Isles, such comparative references multiplied and began to form a considerable literature. Especially in the time of Theodor Benfey, in the 1860's and the 1870's, he and those more or less under his influence became interested in the history of European folktales and began to study them with considerable intensity. Thus Reinhold Köhler[1] wrote reviews of a large number of folktale collections in which he pointed out the parallels between these collections. For this rather unsystematic type of study, reference to well-known collections such as those of Grimm or Asbjørnsen and Moe[2] were reasonably satisfactory. But the need of at least a small checklist of folktales was even then felt.

In his *Griechische und albanesische Märchen*, J. G. von Hahn,[3] impressed with resemblances of certain folktales to ancient Greek myths, went to the extreme of arranging all his folktales according to the ancient myths to which he conceived them to be related. This was not very useful to other scholars, not only because of the doubtful validity of his theory but also because of the limited number of tale-types that he considered. An entirely different kind of listing was developed

[1] R. Köhler, *Kleinere Schriften* (ed., Bolte). 3 vols. Weimar, 1898–1900.
[2] P. Chr. Asbjørnsen og J. Moe, *Norske Folke-eventyr*. 2 vols. Kristiania, 1842, 1871.
[3] J. G. von Hahn, *Griechische und albanesische Märchen*. 2 vols. Leipzig, 1864.

by Joseph Jacobs, the English folklorist.[4] As we see it now, the difficulty with
Jacobs' list comes from his failure to make any distinction between a complete
tale-type and the smaller motifs which often appear in these types but do not
themselves constitute complete tales. Moreover, Jacobs's list is extremely short
and entirely inadequate for indexing complete collections of stories.

By the end of the century, therefore, some definite method of referring to folktales, whether *Märchen* or *Sagen*, was beginning to be urgent if an adequate study
of the expanding materials available was to be made possible. For there had grown
up since the 1830's, when the Finnish Literary Society began its great collecting
program, and especially in the 1870's and '80's in the Scandinavian countries and
Germany, not only a large amount of published material but even more in manuscript. The latter were being arranged in archives, official or private, and there
was a real need for some kind of coordinating system. One had indeed been worked
out for the Danish Archive in Copenhagen,[5] but for a number of reasons it was
not satisfactory when applied to other countries.

The impetus for the development of a comprehensive system for indexing folktales came primarily from Finland. Here existed an extremely extensive mass of
manuscript brought in from all parts of Finland, and often in difficult dialects.
The material was, to say the least, unavailable to the foreign scholar, who seldom
had a command of even standard Finnish. A great work of coordinating the efforts
of folktale scholars in all the world was carried out by Professor Kaarle Krohn in
the last decade of the 19th century. He established FF, or Folklore Fellows, and
initiated a considerable correspondence between scholars of various countries.
Eventually his disciple Antti Aarne undertook a systematic arrangement of all the
folktales of Finland, and, from this point of departure and with the help of colleagues in the other Scandinavian countries and in Germany, he issued his
Verzeichnis der Märchentypen in 1910.[6] This consisted of a systematic arrangement of some 550 different independent tales. Since the classification was based
in the first instance upon the Finnish material, with considerable additions from
northern Europe, it was naturally more nearly adequate when applied to those
countries than for other parts of the world.

The first practical use of the index was Aarne's own survey of the folktales of
Finland.[7] In this he arranged all of the thousands of versions even then present
in the Finnish Archives. For every type he gave bibliographical references to the
published collections and then, arranged by areas in Finland, also to the manu-

---

[4] J. Jacobs in the Papers and Transactions of the International Folklore Congress. London, 1891.
[5] For an account of this see FFC, No. 2.
[6] Antti Aarne, *Verzeichnis der Märchentypen*. FFC, No. 3, Helsinki, 1910.
[7] A. Aarne. FFC, Nos. 5 and 33.

script material. He made no attempt at detailed analysis of each of the versions. But he did make it possible for the foreign scholar to obtain access to the Finnish Archives and to study any item in which he was interested.

Aarne's system furnished the model for most of the surveys that appeared in the next twenty years. Within a decade there were published, mostly in the "FF Communications," surveys for the Swedes in Finland, for the Estonians, the Lapps, the Flemish, and the Livonians.[8] Though all of these followed Aarne's system and attempted no analysis, they all indicated by asterisks a large number of new types for addition to any subsequent classfication.

A new departure in regional indexes came with the appearance of R. Th. Christiansen's Norwegian study.[9] In this he analyzed every individual version in his collection and fitted it into a kind of a master analysis of the type concerned. This work of Christiansen's looked forward in two respects to the surveys that would be made in future years, the detailed analysis of the types and the appearance of the surveys in the language of the country concerned. Help for those who do not read Norwegian was indeed furnished by an English summary, though for the full analysis one must go to his Norwegian text.

By 1924 it had become clear that a new edition of Aarne's classification needed to be made. Many new types had been suggested and it was felt that more analysis of the tales in the classification was to be desired. When I undertook the revision of the classification after the untimely death of Aarne, the analysis of the various types was greatly facilitated by the use of Bolte and Polívka's notes to Grimm's folktales[10] and of Christiansen's Norwegian Survey. For the bibliographical guidance furnished for every type, the preparation had already been made by Bolte and Polívka and by various scholars who had written monographs on tales in the preceding years. The classification was expanded so as to be more useful for Western and Southern Europe, but it is clear now that Southeastern Europe and Western Asia were too much neglected.

Almost simultaneously with the appearance of *The Types of the Folk-Tale* in 1928,[11] Andrejev issued his study of the published Russian tales.[12] This work

---

[8] O. Hackman, *Katalog der Märchen der finländischen Schweden* (FFC, No. 6); A. Aarne, *Estnische Märchen- und Sagenvarianten* (FFC, No. 25); J. Qvigstad, *Lappische Märchen- und Sagenvarianten* (FFC, No. 60); M. de Meyer, *Les Contes Populaires de la Flandre* (FFC, No. 37); O. Loorits, *Livische Märchen- und Sagenvarianten* (FFC, No. 66).

[9] R. Th. Christiansen. *Norske Eventyr*. Kristiania, 1921. Summarized in: *The Norwegian Fairy Tales, a Short Summary* (FFC, No. 46).

[10] J. Bolte und G. Polívka. *Anmerkungen zu den Kinder- und Hausmärchen der Brüder Grimm*, 5 vols. Leipzig, 1913–32.

[11] A. Aarne and S. Thompson. *The Types of the Folk-Tale* (FFC, No. 74). Helsinki, 1928.

[12] A. N. Andrejev. *Ukazatel' Skazočnich Sjuzhetov po Systeme Aarne*. Leningrad, 1929.

4*

demonstrated the fact that the Aarne classification was applicable to the Russian area, though it was necessary to add many types. This survey came out too early for the author to make much use of the revised classification, but he prepared a list of all places in which he differed from this revision.

After the appearance of *The Types of the Folk-Tale*, a considerable number of regional surveys have been published and a number of archives have been arranged in accordance with the system. Some of these call for no special comment, for they use without any marked change the same technique that Aarne had employed in his Finnish list. Each of them do indeed propose a large number of new types. They all appear in French, English, or German, and are easily used. Such are the Rumanian, Hungarian, Walloon, and Netherlands studies,[13] and such is the general plan for the forthcoming survey of Irish folktales.[14]

The application of the revised classification to the tales of Spain showed clearly that the general analyses in the classification were not adequate for that country. R. S. Boggs[15] therefore adapted the analyses by adding supplementary motifs at appropriate places and analyzed his individual versions accordingly. This plan makes for an accurate analysis, though it is somewhat hard to follow. The same system was recently used by Hansen in his study of the tales of the West Indies and of Spanish South America.[16] To some extent it is also employed in the forthcoming list of the types of the oral tales of India,[17] though some of the difficulties just mentioned have been eliminated.

A special problem appeared in the survey of Icelandic tales by Sveinsson.[18] These stories are frequently so different from the typical European form that they are hard to fit into the same index. For that reason the author has frequently given a summary of the tales without attempting to make this summary correspond to the analysis in *The Types of the Folk-Tale*. It seems inevitable that a country on the periphery of a tradition area will develop large individual differences, as in Icelandic, and indeed for one that is so far removed from the center of the tradition as India.

All of the earliest catalogues of folktales, with the exception of the Norwegian and the Russian, had been in languages easily read by most international

[13] A. Schullerus. *Verzeichnis der rumänischen Märchen* (FFC, No. 78); H. Honti. *Verzeichnis der publizierten ungarischen Märchen* (FFC, No. 81); G. Laport. *Les Contes populaires Wallons* (FFC, No. 101); J. R. W. Sinninghe. *Katalog der niederländischen Märchen* (FFC, No. 132).
[14] Being prepared by the Irish Folklore Commission.
[15] R. S. Boggs. *Index of Spanish Folktales* (FFC, No 90).
[16] T. L. Hansen. *The Types of the Folktale in Cuba, Puerto Rico, the Dominican Republic and Spanish South America*. Berkeley and Los Angeles, 1957.
[17] W. E. Roberts and S. Thompson. *Types of Indic Folktales* (in press).
[18] E. Ol. Sveinsson. *Verzeichnis isländischer Märchenvarianten* (FFC, No. 83).

scholars. But this ease of communication was not to be maintained. With the appearance of the Lithuanian survey[19] this change became manifest. Here all of the tales which correspond closely to those in the Aarne Index were listed in Lithuanian without much analysis, but for the new types suggested an English translation was furnished. The scholar unacquainted with Lithuanian, however, often wishes that he knew exactly what the text of the Lithuanian description contains. The index undoubtedly gives an adequate account of the contents of the Lithuanian archives, and such seems to have been its main purpose, rather than the international use to which it might have been put.

The same thing is true of a number of recent regional folktale lists. They appear in the language of the country and are not primarily concerned with making themselves valuable internationally. It will be noticed that in order to make good use of the more recent indexes it is necessary to read Polish, Lettish,[20] Russian, Hungarian, Czech and Swedish, not to speak of Italian and Spanish.

The appearance of the surveys in the language of the country indicates a certain change in point of view. The purpose seems chiefly to make as complete and accurate description of the content of the tradition as possible and not primarily to relate it to that of other regions. There has therefore been a considerable increase in detailed analysis of individual versions, but for such analysis no absolutely satisfactory system has emerged. Perhaps the most elaborate account of the tales of any country is that made by Liungman of the Swedish collections.[21] In this work he has given a text *in extenso* for each of the Swedish types available, and then has made comments as to how other versions differ. Though this system is undoubtedly of great value, it is rather expensive both in time and money. The recent Hungarian index of Berge Nagy[22] has most detailed analyses of every type. The usual scholar is inhibited from making proper use of it because of its appearance in Hungarian. It was a life work and is a noble effort, though one feels that the author has broken his types up into many insignificant and useless divisions. He has not related his index very closely to the analyses in *The Types of the Folk-Tale*.

Unfortunately, the Polish survey[23] has never been completed though the third and last volume is now promised. The special criticism that the international

---

[19] J. Balys. *Motif-Index of Lithuanian Folktales*. Kaunas, 1936.

[20] Alma Medne. *Latviešu dzivnicku pasakas*. Riga, 1940. The other indexes referred to will be mentioned below.

[21] W. Liungman. *Sveriges Samtliga Folksagor*. 3 vols. Djursholm (Sweden), 1949–1952.

[22] J. Berge Nagy. *Magyar Nepmesetipusok*. 2 vols. Pecz, 1957. A new Hungarian Index has been begun by Agnes Kovács. The first number is: *Magyar Állatmesék Tipusmotatoja*, Budapest, 1958.

[23] J. Krzyżanowski. *Polska Bajka Ludowa w Układzie Systematzcnym*. 2 vols. Warszawa, 1947.

scholar can make of the Polish material, outside of its appearance in a difficult language, is the failure to distinguish between folktale (*Märchen*) and tradition (*Sage*). In spite of the fact that it is a simple list and has little analysis, it is most valuable for bringing the corpus of Polish folktales into the easy compass of a single index.

The Russian folktale material is now rather accessible to the scholar who can read Russian. In addition to the index of Andrejev, already mentioned, there have been two editions of the basic collection of Russian tales, that of Afanasief, one twenty-five years ago and one much more recently. For the use of the folklorist the recent edition prepared by Propp is excellent.[24] It is however, confined to those tales which appear in the Afanasief collection, and is therefore supplementary to the Andrejev list. Tales are unanalysed, but a great many additions to the Aarne index are suggested.

In recent years three surveys of Italian tales have appeared, all of them in Italian.[25] The Index of Tuscan tales employs a system so complicated that the user of it is often discouraged, and the mistakes of classification have subjected the author to some severe criticism. His more detailed study of the Italian versions of a few specific types is much more thorough and accurate. Lo Nigro's recent study of Sicilian tales is thorough and useful, but one has to work hard to understand his system.

Two elaborate surveys of folktales are now in the process of publication, one covering Germany and the other France. Two volumes have now appeared of Ranke's important work on the tales of Schleswig-Holstein.[26] The arrangement of *The Types of the Folk-Tale* has been retained, and for each type all of the available versions from Schleswig-Holstein have been given, usually *in extenso*. Frequently there appears an informal discussion of the variations of the story in the different versions. Of especial interest to the general scholar is the detailed bibliography of each of the types for the whole German-speaking area. Thus, eventually the rich materials in the folktale archive at Marburg will have a relatively complete published index. Two volumes of this large work have now appeared. It is hoped that the succeeding volumes can follow within a reasonable time.

Of the masterly study of the French folktale by Paul Delarue,[27] only the first volume has been issued, but notes for the rest of the work were left by him and are being prepared according to the same method by Madame Tenèze, who has worked

[24] A. N. Afanasief. *Narodnye Russkie Skazki* (ed. V. Y. Propp). 3 vols. Moskwa, 1957.
[25] G. D'Aronco. *Indice Fiabe toscane*. Firenze, 1953. G. D'Aronco. *Le Fiabe di Magia in Italia*. Udine, 1957; S. Lo Nigro. *Racconti Popolari Siciliani*. Firenze, 1958.
[26] K. Ranke. *Schleswig-Holsteinische Volksmärchen*. Vols. 1, 2. Kiel, 1955, 1957.
[27] P. Delarue. *Le Conte Populaire Français*. Vol. 1. Paris, 1957.

closely with him. Delarue's early death was a great loss to the study of the folktale, both in France and in the rest of the world. The method used in this index is reminiscent of that employed by Christiansen in his Norwegian survey. On the basis of all the French versions available, Delarue has made a detailed analysis of every type, and then has listed all the versions, analyzing each accordingly. This gives an excellent account of all of the tales available in France, both published and unpublished; and in many respects it is a model for all future indexes. I am told that the forthcoming survey of the tales of the French in America will use the same system.[28]

The regional indexes for Czechoslovakia and Turkey have made little or no use of the Aarne classification. In the belief that the Turkish tales[29] were far removed from Europe, the authors have devised an entirely new system. They have, to be sure, made a concordance, but this is quite incomplete. Fortunately, Professor Walter Anderson has, in a very elaborate review, indexed this whole material according to the Aarne system[30] and has shown that it actually fits rather well into the international classification.

The most difficult of the large surveys for the student of the folktale are those of Czechoslovakia. The first one, which appeared in the early numbers of "FF Communications"[31] had its own system, with a very vague and sometimes misleading set of references to the Aarne index. This work was superseded by the same author in a very extensive index of Czech tales[32] arranged alphabetically by a Czech title. Aside from the fact that it is written in Czech, this work is most difficult for the general scholar. Many of the tales, to be sure, have references to the Grimm tale-numbers, but for many there are no such guides. Again Professor Walter Anderson has been most helpful, since in his review he has furnished the Aarne numbers for these tales.[33] This review had escaped my notice, so that it was necessary for me to engage the help of a Czech student in order to make use of this work. It is hoped that with Professor Anderson's analysis, and with my own study of this text, this material can be made more available to general scholars.

The elaborate and detailed reviews furnished over the years by scholars such as Professor Anderson have resulted in bringing together a large amount of folktale material from many sources, all arranged within the framework of the Aarne

[28] A Survey of the French folktale in America is being prepared by Luc Lacourcière of Quebec.
[29] W. Eberhard and P. N. Boratav. *Typen türkischer Volksmärchen*. Wiesbaden, 1953.
[30] W. Anderson. *Hessische Blätter für Volkskunde*, XLIV (1953), 111.
[31] V. Tille. *Verzeichnis der böhmischen Märchen* (FFC, No. 34).
[32] V. Tille, *Soupis Českych Pohadek*. 2 vols. Praha, 1929–37.
[33] *Zeitschrift für slavische Philologie* IX, 509 ff., XIV 227 ff., XVIII 245 ff.

index. In this way such huge folktale collections are those made by Amades for Catalonia[34] as well as Czech and Turkish material already mentioned, and the large Hungarian collection of Berge Nagy,[35] are available to those who cannot read the original. Recently with the appearance of *Fabula*, such reviews and indexes have increased greatly and have eased the work of all investigators of the international tale. Undoubtedly the important international congress for the study of the folktale held at Kiel in the summer of 1959 will stimulate the preparation of many regional indexes of folktales in the future.

In the past thirty years it has become almost standard practice to annotate published collections of folktales according to the Aarne system, and indexes of learned journals have also begun to follow the practice.[36] Authors of tale collections are spared the necessity of making detailed comments about the tales when they can briefly refer by number to the international classification.

Passing mention has been made of a large number of archives[37] in which folktales are systematically stored and arranged. As a part of my labors in preparing the second revision of the Aarne classification, I have visited nearly all of these institutions. It is always possible very quickly to find how many of each type they have and to secure access to the manuscripts or the published books. One of their great difficulties has been the handling of the types which are not in the Aarne classification. I have been successful in securing an account of all of these types and am attempting to fit them in to the revised classification. In this way the work of the archivist should eventually become somewhat easier.

As one looks to the future of the indexing of folktales, he can see that the problems have changed considerably in the course of fifty years. Certain things have been accomplished. Practically all of Europe is now covered by regional folktale archives, and similarly the French in America are well handled by the excellent archive at Quebec. As for the rest of America, on the other hand, efforts at archiving tales have been feeble indeed. Perhaps some centers now possessing small archives may develop so as to serve large regions of the United States. For South America, except in Venezuela, there is nothing of the kind. For Japan

[34] *Schweizerisches Archiv für Volkskunde* L, 37 ff.

[35] *Fabula*, II, 281 ff.

[36] Examples are the recent indexes of *Fabula* by W. Anderson, and of the *Journal of American Folklore* by T. P. Coffin.

[37] Regional folktale archives which I have recently visited are in Quebec, Edinburgh, Dublin, Paris, Marburg, Copenhagen, Lund, Uppsala, Stockholm, Göteborg, Helsinki, Oslo, Paris, Ljubljana, Zagreb, Sarejevo, Athens, and Haifa. There are a number of others, notably in Budapest, Reykjavik, and Ankara. I have little information as to the state of the archives in Lithuania, Latvia, Estonia, Czechoslovakia, Rumania, Bulgaria, or Russia.

I am told a very large collection of manuscript tales is well arranged in Tokyo. There are plans for making this available to the western student.[38]

Since the appearance of my *Motif-Index of Folk-Literature*[39] I have been much interested in the possiblity of coordinating the two indexes in some way. Motif-analysis of tales has an importance for showing the anatomy of stories and especially for displaying similarities or differences in detail. For that reason in the new revision of the Aarne classification I am preparing as complete a motif analysis of each type as possible.

Some rather unsuccessful attempts have been made to extend the Aarne classification to distant parts of the world. It is clear that this index is valid only for a particular tradition area, that from Ireland to India and to places influenced or settled by those countries. There arises the question as to how valuable similar indexes would be for other large tradition areas. For my own experience I should guess that the North American Indians would form such an area. I am not sufficiently competent in the field to know whether Africa, south of the Sahara, or Oceania or the South American Indians would be field favorable for such indexes of tale-types, but they would be worth trying.

A basic international index of traditions (*Sagen*) still awaits any general acceptance. Archivists are usually skeptical of any such international index, but I am inclined to believe that the difficulties are not so great as they think. Certainly the recent classification of international *Sagen* made by Professor Christiansen[40] is susceptible of very considerable expansion and adaptation. But the indexing of regional *Sagen* on any large international scale seems to be a task for the future.

As far as the folktale is concerned, the last fifty years has seen a remarkable advance, and with the work of classifiers and indexers being so busily carried on, that corps of future scholars who may be interested in the history of the folktale, whether in one country or in all, will find their work not only much easier but much more efficient because of the greater accessibility of their material.

Indiana University,

Bloomington, Indiana

[38] Hiroko Ikeda of Honolulu is preparing a study of this material.
[39] S. Thompson. *Motif-Index of Folk-Literature.* 6 vols. Copenhagen and Bloomington, Indiana, 1955–58.
[40] R. Th. Christiansen. *The Migratory Legend* (FFC, No. 175).

VOLKSERZÄHLUNGEN IN TAGESZEITUNGEN UND WOCHENBLÄTTERN

WALTER ANDERSON

Während heute fast überall versucht wird, sämtliche in einem Staate oder bei einem Volke erschienenen Bücher ohne Rücksicht auf ihren Inhalt oder inneren Wert wenigstens in einem oder ein paar Exemplaren für die Zukunft aufzubewahren, bleiben die Tageszeitungen und die meisten Wochenblätter ein Stiefkind der öffentlichen Bibliotheken. Fast niemals macht sich ein Bibliothekar oder ein Privatmann die Mühe, sämtliche Nummern einer von ihm abonnierten Zeitung sorgfältig aufzubewaren und mit beträchtlichen Kosten einbinden zu lassen: was darin steht, geht eben den Weg aller Makulatur und ist damit für die Zukunft unwiederbringlich verloren.

Mancher Journalist und mancher Politiker wird sich im stillen darüber freuen, daß vieles von ihm Geschriebene und Gesagte auf diese Weise in den Lethestrom versinkt und daß seine journalistische Vergangenheit nichts als eine allgemein zugängliche Schreckenskammer stehen bleibt, in der jeder Besucher ihm seine einstigen unsinnigen Behauptungen und seine durch die Tatsachen widerlegten Prophezeiungen nachweisen kann. Aber für die Wissenschaft ist dies ein schwerer Verlust — nicht nur für die Geschichte der öffentlichen Meinung und überhaupt die politische Geschichte, sondern auch für die Wirtschaftsgeschichte, die Sozialgeschichte, die Kulturgeschichte mit allen ihren Zweigen, die Kunstgeschichte, die Literaturgeschichte und so weiter.

Nun werden in öffentlichen Bibliotheken tatsächlich vollständige Jahrgangsreihen einiger Tageszeitungen von besonderer allgemeiner oder lokaler Bedeutung aufbewahrt, sie bilden aber nur einigen winzigen Bruchteil der tatsächlichen

Presseproduktion; alles übrige fällt schon aus Raummangel der Vernichtung anheim.

Nur kleine Staaten und kleine Nationen dürfen es wagen, auf diesem Gebiete Vollständigkeit anzustreben — oder gar zu erreichen. Ein glänzendes Beispiel dafür ist die Bibliothek des Estnischen Nationalmuseums (Eesti Rahva Muuseum) in Dorpat (Tartu): sie enthält vollständige Reihen aller in Estland erschienenen oder außerhalb Estlands in estnischer Sprache gedruckten Zeitungen und Zeitschriften von der Entstehung der estnischen Presse an. Ich selbst bin dort oft umhergegangen und habe mit staunender Hochachtung die endlosen Reihen einfach, aber dauerhaft gebundener Zeitungsbände bewundert — ein wahres Pompei der estnischen Vergangenheit. Ich möchte nur hoffen, daß es nicht in der letzten Phase des zweiten Weltkriegs zugrunde gegangen ist — der Verlust wäre unersetzlich!

Welchen Umfang würde wohl eine ebenso vollständige deutsche, englische oder amerikanische Zeitungsbibliothek aufweisen?

Aber in Estland hat man sich nicht mit der bloßen Anhäufung des toten Materials begnügt, sondern auch versucht, es der Forschung leichter zugänglich zu machen. Es wurde damit begonnen, alles in den älteren und jüngeren Zeitungen vorhandene inhaltlich wertvolle Material zu verzetteln — ein riesiges Unternehmen, das beim Ausbruch des zweiten Weltkriegs in den Anfängen stecken blieb, jedoch auch als bescheidener Torso von großem Nutzen ist.

Daneben faßte aber die Dorpater Gelehrte Estnische Gesellschaft den Plan, einen *Jahresbericht der estnischen Philologie und Geschichte* herauszugeben, der alles verzeichnen und nach Möglichkeit referieren sollte, was im Laufe des Berichtsjahrs auf dem Gebiete der estnischen Sprache, Literatur, Sach- und Wortvolkskunde, Urgeschichte und Geschichte (mit Einschluß sämtlicher Hilfsdisziplinen, aller Biographien und Nekrologe) erschienen war — *unter besonderer Berücksichtigung der gesamten Zeitungs- und Zeitschriftenpresse.*

Der Plan war von Prof. Dr. Max Vasmer ausgegangen; ich selbst habe die ersten vier Berichtsjahre (1918–1921) redigiert; später erschienen (in etwas beschränkterem Umfang) noch die Berichtsjahre 1922/23 und 1929–1931; dann blieb aus äußeren Gründen (hauptsächlich infolge des Krieges) das ganze Unternehmen stecken.

Bei der Durchsicht der estnischen Zeitungen und Zeitschriften überzeugte ich mich davon, wieviel volkskundliches (meist primäres) Material an zufälligen Notizen und längeren Textpublikationen sie enthielten.[1] Ein besonderes Interesse

[1] Meines wissens ist *Western Folklore* die einzige volkskundliche Zeitschrift, die regelmäßig Tagesnotizen von volkskundlichem Interesse in ihren Spalten als "Folklore in the News" nachdrucken läßt. — WDH.

flößten mir die *Volkserzählungen* ein, die ja mein wissenschaftliches Spezialgebiet sind. Immer wieder stieß ich auf Stoffe, die mir von früher her als traditionell bekannt waren. An wirklichen Volksmärchen und Legenden war freilich nicht allzuviel vorhanden, schon mehr an Sagen, vor allem aber eine riesige Menge von *Schwänken*. Nur selten waren diese ausdrücklich als dem Volksmunde entnommen bezeichnet: meistens standen sie bescheiden in Feuilletonwinkeln herum, aber trotzdem konnte ich in ihnen oft genug alte Bekannte begrüßen, die sich seit Jahrzehnten, Jahrhunderten oder Jahrtausenden auf unserem Erdball von Mund zu Mund fortpflanzen.

Ich machte mir nun zur Regel, in dem Jahresbericht *jeden von mir als traditionell erkannten Schwank (oder sonstige Volkserzählung) kurz wiederzugeben,* und ich hoffe, damit manchem Forscher gelegentlich von Nutzen gewesen zu sein. Da ich aber leider nicht universal belesen bin, werde ich sicher manches traditionelle Geschichtchen übersehen haben.

Was von den estnischen Zeitungen und Zeitschriften gilt, das gilt auch von denjenigen der übrigen Völker. Täglich erscheinen in Zeitungen und Unterhaltungszeitschriften zahllose Texte, an denen ein Folklorist seine helle Freude haben würde — und verschwinden dann ins Nichts „als in daz mer ein slac". *Veröffentlicht — und doch nicht veröffentlicht*!

Ein gutes Werk an der Wissenschaft tut daher jeder Leser, der einen in einer Zeitung oder sonst an versteckter Stelle gedruckten volkskundlichen Text in einer wissenschaftlichen Zeitschrift (wenn auch nur als kurzen Auszug) publiziert — oder auch nur für seine Privatbibliothek ausschneidet oder abschreibt, oder einen solchen Ausschnitt oder Abschrift einem Folkloristen übergibt.

Ich selbst erlaube mir, hier eine kleine Blütenlese solcher von mir zufällig erhaschter Geschichtchen folgen zu lassen — allerdings meistens stark kondensiert, denn der Raum ist sehr beschränkt. Aus demselben Grunde kann ich hier nur einen kleinen Bruchteil des bei mir angesammelten Textmaterials darbieten.

* * *

1. *Kieler Nachrichten*, 12. Sept. 1957 (Nr. 212), S. 11, Sp. 4f. (mit Bild): Annegret Oslislo (Kiel), *Der Kobold in der Mühle.*

> In einer einsamen Wassermühle im Havellande wohnt ein Müller. An einem stürmischen Abend klopft ein Bärenführer ans Fenster und bittet um Nachtquartier. Er selbst findet in der Stube Unterkunft, sein Tier dagegen legt er in der Mühle an die Kette, obgleich der Müller ihm sagt, daß dort seit Jahren ein Kobold Unfug treibe. Mitten in der Nacht erwachen die beiden Männer von einem furchtbaren Lärm in der Mühle. Am Morgen finden sie den Bären wohlbehalten vor, und der Bärenführer zieht ab. Ein Jahr lang läßt der Kobold sich nicht in der Mühle sehen; dann steckt

er eines Abends seinen unförmigen Kopf in die Stube und sagt: „Müller, Müller, lebt Euer großer schwarzer Kater noch?" Der Müller ruft: „Ja, der lebt noch und hat zwei Junge!" Der Kobold schlägt entsetzt die Tür zu und kommt nicht wieder.

Aarne-Thompson 1161; Thompson, *Motif-Index* K 1728; A. Taylor, *Modern Philology*, 17, 305 ff.

2. *Kieler Nachrichten*, 29./30. August 1953 (Nr. 201), S. 7, Sp. 2 f.: *Aus krummer Rippe.*

„Sie war ein Querkopf, und die meisten ihrer Handlungen sprachen aller Logik Hohn. Einmal fuhr sie mit ihrem Mann an den großen Fluß. Nachdem die mitgebrachten Würstchen verzehrt waren, beschloß sie zu baden.

„Aber doch nicht mit vollem Magen," wagte der Mann schüchtern einzuwenden.

„Willst du mir schon wieder Vorschriften machen?" fragte sie zurück.

„Dann kühl dich wenigstens langsam ab," rief er.

Sie lachte verächtlich und verschwand mit einem Kopfsprung in den Fluten.

Eine Minute verstrich, aber sie tauchte nicht wieder auf. Der Mann sprang auf und lief zum Fluß. Auch andere, die in der Nähe lagen, wurden aufmerksam. „Ich muß sie suchen," rief der Mann und lief stromauf.

„Aber doch nicht in der Richtung," rief ihm ein anderer nach, „das ist völlig widersinnig. Stromab müssen Sie suchen."

„Na," sagte der Mann, „kennen Sie meine Frau!""

Aarne-Thompson 1365A; Thompson, *Motif-Index* T 255.2.

3. *Die Welt am Sonntag*, 26. Juni 1949, Nr. 26, S. 6: Sc., *Die Katze.*

„Mohamed Avdibegowitsch schickt von einer Geschäftsreise seiner Frau ein großes Stück Fleisch. Die Frau kann nicht widerstehen, brät das Fleisch und ißt es mit zwei Freundinnen auf. Als der Mann zurückkehrt, behauptet die Frau, das habe die Katze gefressen. Darüber gibt es einen langen Streit, und die Eheleute gehen endlich zum Kadi. Der fragt: „Wieviel hat das Fleisch gewogen?"

„Zwei Kilo," sagt der Mann.

„Bringt mir die Katze," sagt der Kadi, „und bringt mir eine Waage!"

Man legte die Katze auf die Waage und siehe, sie wiegt genau zwei Kilo. Da neigt der Kadi nachdenklich seinen Kopf und sagt: „Jetzt wissen wir, wo das Fleisch ist. Aber wo ist die Katze?""

Aarne-Thompson 1373; Thompson, *Motif-Index* J 1611.

4. *Die Welt*, 1. Sept. 1953 (Nr. 203), S. 5, Sp. 3 f.: Wilhelm Auffermann, *Schwäbische Knopfsuppe.*

Abraham a Santa Clara kommt in seiner Jugend als fahrender Schüler an das Haus einer geizigen alten Jungfrau und bittet wenigstens um einen Löffel Suppe, der ihm aber auch verweigert wird: es sei nichts mehr da. Da fragt er, ob nicht ein paar alte Knöpfe im Hause seien: ein Knopfsüppchen sei ein gar wohlschmeckendes Gericht in seiner Heimat Schwaben. Aus Neugier setzt die Jungfer wirklich einen Topf mit Wasser auf den Herd und rührt eine Handvoll alter Knöpfe hinein; auf Bitten des Schülers tut sie als Zutaten noch ein Stück Butter, einige Eier, eine Prise Salz und etwas Mehl in den Topf. Die Brühe schmeckt dem Jüngling großartig. „Die schweren Knöpfe lagen ganz unten im Topf und hätten noch zur Speisung von mindestens zehntausend braven Christen gereicht."

Aarne-Thompson 1548; Thompson, *Motif-Index* K 1122.

5. *Die Welt*, 12. Febr. 1954 (Nr. 36), S. 5, Sp. 3f.: Martha Solmar, *Es war auf einem Hügel.*

Ein chinesischer Tempeldiener trägt einen fetten Hammel, der geopfert werden soll. Die hungrigen drei Räuber Ming, Mong und Mung beschließen, sich des Tieres zu bemächtigen. Mung tritt allein hervor und fragt den Tempeldiener, warum er ein unreines Tier — nämlich einen Hund — mit sich trage. Der Tempeldiener sagt ihm ärgerlich, er sei blind, und geht seines Weges. Ein Stück weiter stellt an ihn Mong dieselbe Frage und bekommt zu hören, er sei verrückt. Bald darauf wiederholt sich dieselbe Szene mit Ming. Der Tempeldiener beginnt zu zittern und denkt: „Vielleicht bin *ich* blind oder verrückt. Es ist gewiß ein Hund. Wenn drei es sagen..." Er wirft das Tier ins Gebüsch und läuft davon.

Aarne-Thompson 1551; Thompson, *Motif-Index* K 451.2.

6. *Kieler Nachrichten*, 26. März 1957 (Nr. 72), S. 7, Sp. 4f.: Lew Lehr, *Der Farmer in Neuyork* (deutsch von Walter Oettel).

Der Farmer Phil Barker kommt nach New York und bleibt vor einem Wolkenkratzer an der Ecke der 34th Street und der Fifth Avenue staunend stehen. Plötzlich klopft ihm ein Einheimischer auf die Schulter und fragt ihn barsch:
— „Was tun Sie hier?"
— „Ich sehe mir dieses Gebäude an."
— „Das dürfen Sie nicht tun! Es ist eine gesetzwidrige Handlung. Auf welches Stockwerk schauen Sie denn?"
— „Auf das zweiundzwanzigste!"
— „So, so! Das kostet einen Dollar pro Stockwerk — macht also zweiundzwanzig Dollar Strafe!"
Der Farmer gibt ihm die 22 Dollar und erzählt später lachend seinen Bekannten, wie er den hochnäsigen Kerl hinters Licht geführt habe: „Ich habe nämlich nicht auf das 22., sondern auf das 46. Stockwerk geschaut!"

In Rußland gut bekannt: ein Bauer kommt nach Moskau und beginnt, die Dohlen auf den Kirchenkreuzen zu zählen; ein Soldat verlangt von ihm als Strafe 10 Kopeken pro Dohle; der Bauer freut sich hinterher, ihm eine viel zu niedrige Dohlenzahl genannt zu haben. N. P. Andrejev, *Ukazatel' skazočnych sjužetov po sisteme Aarne*, Nr. *1683; Afanaśjev, Nr. 249t.

7. *Die Welt*, 28. Dez. 1956 (Nr. 303), S. 3, Sp. 1: W. W. (Berlin), *Auf die Minute*.

Es wird erwähnt „die Geschichte des zum Tode verurteilten Mannes, der seinem König um den Preis der Verschiebung seiner Hinrichtung um ein Jahr versprach, dem Pferd Seiner Majestät in dieser Zeit das Fliegen beizubringen. Wenn es ihm nicht gelinge, wolle er sich gern den Strick um den Hals legen lassen. Er mag sich dabei gedacht haben: Vielleicht stirbt in diesem Jahr der König, vielleicht stirbt das Pferd, vielleicht sterbe ich auf natürliche Weise oder — wer weiß — vielleicht lernt das Pferd wirklich fliegen."

Thompson, *Motif-Index* H 1024.4. In des Strickers *Pfaffe Âmîs* stellt der Bischof dem Pfaffen die Aufgabe, einen Esel lesen zu lehren; Âmîs erbietet sich dazu, verlangt aber eine Frist von 30 Jahren, denn er denkt (Vers 221–226):

> „wir'n geleben nimmer drîzec jâr
> alle drî, daz ist wâr,
> der esel sterbe oder ich,
> ode der bischof. swaz er sich
> vermizzet ûf mînen schaden,
> des mac mich wol der tôt entladen."

Daraus entlehnt im hochdeutschen *Eulenspiegel* (Kap. 29).

8. *Kieler Nachrichten*, 4./5. Mai 1957, Nr. 103, S. 8, Sp. 2: *Erklärlich*.

„Woher kommt es, daß das Meerwasser salzig ist?" — „Von den Salzheringen, Herr Lehrer."

Eine uralte Scherzfrage, deren Erwähnung ich in Thompson's *Motif-Index* unter A 1115 vermisse.

9. *Kieler Nachrichten*, 16. Juli 1954, Nr. 163, S. 7, Sp. 1–4: Lucia Fels, *Ein richtiges Affentheater*.

Ein arabischer Teppichhändler erzählt, was er einmal an der Elfenbeinküste erlebt hat. Damals handelte er nicht mit Teppichen, sondern mit Hüten und Mützen. Einmal kam er durch einen Wald, der von Affen bewohnt war. Von Müdigkeit übermannt, machte er sich ein Lager zurecht, zog aus seinem großen Bündel einen breitrandigen Hut und legte ihn sich aufs Gesicht. Wieder aufgewacht, sah er, daß die Hülle seines

Warenpakets leer war: die auf den Baumzweigen sitzenden oder darunter hängenden
Affen hatten sich alle seine Hüte und Mützen auf die Köpfe gesetzt. Da er nicht klet-
tern konnte, vermochte er ihnen ihre Beute nicht abzujagen — weder durch Dro-
hungen noch durch Steinwürfe. In seiner Verzweiflung und Hilflosigkeit riß er sich
seinen Hut vom Kopfe und warf ihn zornig zu Boden. Alle Affen folgten sofort seinem Beispiel, und er brauchte seine Waren nur aufzusammeln.

Dies ist eine alte Anekdote, die nicht selten in Kinder- und Schulbüchern er-
scheint und mir seit meiner Kindheit bekannt ist. Unter anderem wurde sie im
Jahre 1920 in der estnischen Kinderzeitschrift *Lasteleht* abgedruckt (Bd. 20,
S. 79f.): *Jahresbericht d. estn. Philol. u. Gesch.*, 3, 92 Nr. III 69b.

10. *Kieler Nachrichten*, 1./2. März 1952 (Nr. 52), S. 7, Sp. 4f. (mit Bild): Wilhelm
Reuter, *Billas Rache*.

Der alte Gleim, ein blinder Bänkelsänger, zieht mit seiner Frau Billa von Dorf
zu Dorf. Diese verwaltet auch die Kasse und erklärt ihrem Manne an jedem Abend,
daß es nur für Brot, Handkäs und ein Kümmelschnäpschen reiche. Eines Abends
schnuppert er aber und stellt fest, daß Billa Speckeier ißt. Als er ebenfalls davon haben will, bekommt er von ihr bloß einen Rippenstoß. Am nächsten Tage marschieren
sie querfeldein; obgleich sie ihm sonst vor jedem Graben oder anderen Hindernis
zuruft: „Hannes hipp!", bleibt sie diesmal einsilbig und warnt ihn nicht einmal
vor einem ansehnlichen Graben, an dessen anderem Rande ein Baum steht. Der
Mann zerbeult sich an diesem Baume seinen Kopf, aber Billa entgegnet ihm auf
seinen Vorwurf: „Kannste rieche, wenn ich Speckeier iß — dann kannste auch rieche, wann ein Baum kommt."

Dieser Schwank ist auch in Rußland bekannt. Es handelt sich dort um zwei
Bettler, von denen der eine blind ist; der letztere riecht den Speck, von dem sein
Führer ißt, und besteht darauf, ein Stück davon zu bekommen; nachher ruft
der Führer ihm, wie sonst vor einem Graben, vor einem Wasser zu: „Spring!"
Der Blinde plumpt hinein und bekommt von seinem Genossen zu hören: „Hast
du den Speck gerochen, so wirst du auch das Wasser riechen."

11. *Kieler Nachrichten*, 1. Juni 1954, Nr. 126, S. 7, Sp. 1: *Die Erstbesteigung*.

Der betrunkene Henke-Bauer bemüht sich vergebens, den breiten Rücken des
soeben gekauften Gaules zu erklimmen. „Nach zehn Minuten zähen Bemühens ver-
suchte es der Henke-Bauer mit Gewalt. Aber so oft er auch sprang, so oft verfehlte
er den glattgestriegelten Sitzplatz. Da hob der Unglücksrabe den Blick und bat leise,
aber inständig: „Alle Heiligen, helft!" Dann lief er noch einmal und sprang. Und
siehe da, er flog förmlich auf den Rücken des Tieres, ja, noch mehr, der Schwung

war so groß, daß der Henke-Bauer an der anderen Seite wieder zu Boden rutschte. Da stand er nun, zitterbeinig, und schlug sich den Staub vom Anzug. Dann warf er abermals den Blick nach oben und sagte: „Verrückt! Erst helfen sie gar nicht, und dann alle auf einmal!""

In Rußland bekannt; der Bauer spricht zuerst ein langes Gebet: „Heiliger Nikolaus der Wundertäter, hilf mir! Heiliger Georg der Siegreiche, hilf mir!" usw. Von der anderen Seite hinuntergefallen, ruft er ärgerlich: „Da ne vse srazu, čerti!" („Aber doch nicht alle auf einmal, ihr Teufel!").

12. *Kieler Nachrichten*, 17. Nov. 1953, Nr. 269, S. 7, Sp. 2f.: K. B. L., *Tünnes, Fietje und die andern...*

„Graf Bobby saß im Theater, in der ersten Reihe des ersten Ranges. Man gab den *Freischütz*. Die Wolfsschluchtszene kam. Es blitzte und donnerte. Das Wildschwein raste schnaubend und feuerspeiend...

In diesem Augenblick passierte es. Ein Knistern im Gebälk, und schon stürzte der erste Rang krachend in die Tiefe. Staub, Lärm, Schreien — aber o Wunder: außer ein paar Knochenbrüchen und Schrammen war den Zuschauern nichts geschehen.

Graf Bobby erhob sich kopfschüttelnd aus Stuhlreihen- und Steingewirr, klopfte sich den Staub vom Abendanzug und sagte: „So an bleedes Stück!""

Dieselbe Anekdote hat Fritz Reuter in „De Reis' nah Belligen", Kap. 14 (siehe auch Kap. 36), sehr lebendig erzählt, *und zwar handelt es sich da ebenfalls um eine Freischütz-Vorstellung*; hinterher heißt es:

„Ja", seggt oll Swart, „dat kann dat sin,
Dat hürt in de Kemedi 'rin".

Ich habe diese Geschichte vor Jahren auch irgendwo in einer anderen deutschen Fassung gelesen: das Unglück ereignet sich da bei einer Taschenspielervorstellung, und einer von den Zuschauern sagt zu seinen Leidensgenossen: „So schreit doch nicht so — gleich sitzen wir alle wieder oben" (er hält das Ganze nämlich für ein Blendwerk).

13. *Die Welt am Sonntag*, 26. Juni 1949, Nr. 26, S. 6: *Ein salomonischer Spruch.*

„Ein Vater hinterließ nach seinem Tode seinen beiden Söhnen ein großes Vermögen an Häusern, Grundbesitz und andern Sachwerten. Die Beiden konnten sich über die Verteilung des Besitzes nicht einigen, und da sie eine gerichtliche Auseinandersetzung nicht wünschten, baten sie einen Freund ihres verstorbenen Vaters um Rat. Der alte Herr gab ihnen daraufhin einen — den einzig möglichen — Rat, wie sie zu einer beide Teile gleichermaßen befriedigenden Aufteilung des Besitzes kommen könnten. Wie lautete der Rat?"

Dazu die Antwort in Nr. 27 (3. Juli), S. 6: „Einer sollte nach bestem Wissen und Gewissen teilen, der andere dann seinen Anteil nehmen."

Kieler Nachrichten, 21. Jan. 1957, Nr. 17, S. 11, Sp. 3: *Weiser Schiedsspruch.*

„Der alte Schotte war gestorben und hatte sein Vermögen zu gleichen Teilen seinen beiden Söhnen Donald und Hamish hinterlassen. Da sie sich über die Teilung nicht einigen konnten, baten sie den Dorfältesten um seinen Schiedsspruch. „Die Teilung ist ganz einfach," erklärte der Dorfälteste: „Du Donald teilst das Erbe, so wie du es für das beste hältst —" Donalds Gesicht glänzte vor Freude, Hamishs Kinn wurde sehr lang. „Und du, Hamish," fuhr der weise Schiedsrichter fort, „du suchst dir deine Hälfte aus.""

Dieselbe salomonische Entscheidung erzählten die Zeitungen während des Burenkrieges von Paul Krüger, den zwei Brüder bei ihrer Erbteilung angeblich um seinen Schiedsspruch gebeten hatten. Dieses Teilungsprinzip wird aber auch in Wirklichkeit im täglichen Leben vielerorts angewendet, z. B. im Gouvernement Minsk (vor der Bolschewikenzeit) hinsichtlich der sogenannten Halbkörner (polovinščiki): der Pächter teilte den Ernteertrag genau in zwei Hälften, der Gutsbesitzer wählte sich die eine davon.

14. *Kieler Nachrichten*, 28./29. Juli 1956 (Nr. 175), S. 9, Sp. 4f.: RS, *He kreeg jümmers de Schuld.*

Einem Schuljungen wird immer die Schuld an allen dummen Streichen seiner Kameraden in die Schuhe geschoben, und er hat sich damit längst abgefunden. Eines Morgens fragt der Schulmeister: „Liebe Kinder, sagt mir einmal, wer hat diese wunderbare Natur, die uns heute morgen ihre Herrlichkeit so großartig offenbarte, geschaffen?" Karl springt auf und legt los: „Dat warr ik wull wedder dahn hem, ik krieg doch jümmers de Schuld!"

Vgl. das Gedicht von Theodor Körner „Der Weltschöpfer": der Pfarrer fragt Gottlieb, wer die Welt erschaffen habe; Gottlieb antwortet:

"Ich will's ja gestehen, ich bin es gewesen,
Und will es auch nimmermehr wieder tun."

15. *Die Welt*, 1. Sept. 1953, Nr. 203, S. 6, Sp. 5f.: Jobu Zozzo, *Je zwei kleine Löcher.*

„Virchow beauftragte einmal seinen Diener, eine Katze für das Laboratorium zu beschaffen, um zu verhindern, daß dort Ratten und Mäuse Schaden anrichteten. Damit die Katze aber auch alle Räume ungehindert durchstreifen konnte, mußte in jede Verbindungstür unten ein Loch gesägt werden.

Eines Morgens stürzte der Diener erregt in das Arbeitszimmer seines Chefs: die Katze habe soeben vier Junge geworfen! Gedankenversunken nickte der Geheimrat und murmelte: „Ja — dann machen Sie mal gleich links und rechts von den Löchern in den Türen je zwei kleine Löcher!"‟

Dieselbe Anekdote erzählte mir 1897 oder 1898 mein Vater von Isaac Newton (dort sägte der Gelehrte die Löcher im Katzenkasten eigenhändig aus).
Vgl. auch das Schulbuch: Kurt Zeidler u. Hans Reimers, *Fundamental English*, Bd. I, Braunschweig–Berlin–Hamburg 1946, S. 28 Nr. 19 "The Two Holes" (Mrs. Clever besucht Mrs. Foolish und sieht in ihrer Tür zwei Löcher — ein großes für die Katze, ein kleines für das Kätzchen).

16. *Münstersche Zeitung*, 23. Sept. 1956, S. 24, Sp. 1: *Schwieriges Unternehmen.*

 „Ein irischer Soldat behauptete in einer Schlacht, er habe einen Gefangenen gemacht. „Er will mir nicht folgen!", schrie er und rief einen Kameraden zu Hilfe. „So laß ihn laufen," antwortete dieser. „Aber er läßt mich nicht los," kam es zurück."

In Rußland gut bekannt: entweder handelt es sich um einen Soldaten, der einen Türken, oder um einen Jäger, der einen Bären gefangen haben will; zum Schluß heißt es: „Tak sam idi sjuda!" („Dann komm selber her!") — „Da on ne puskajet!" („Aber er läßt mich nicht los!")

17. *Neue Post*, 22. Aug. 1953, Nr. 34, S. 8, Sp. 3.
 (Ein Bild: der Gefängniswärter verliest vor dem Sträfling ein Dokument.) „Ihre Hinrichtung ist am Montag." — „Die Woche fängt ja gut an!"

 K. F. W. Wander, *Deutsches Sprichwörter-Lexikon*, V (Leipzig, 1880), S. 328, Nr. 10 und 11: „Die Woche fängt gut an, sagte der Dieb, als er Montag zum Galgen geführt wurde." Vgl. auch *Jahresbericht d. estn. Philol. u. Gesch.* 3, 94, Nr. III 80.

18. *Kieler Nachrichten*, 4./5. Jan. 1958, Nr. 3, S. 21, Sp. 5: *Kinderlogik.*

 „Das Söhnchen eines Flußdampferkapitäns spielt auf der Kommandobrücke. Nach einer Weile ruft der Knabe: „Papa, ist ein Ding verloren, von dem man weiß, wo es ist?" — „Keinesfalls." — „Um so besser. Ich habe nämlich eben deine Uhr ins Wasser fallen lassen.""

Diese Anekdote wurde mir um 1890 von meiner Mutter erzählt. Der Schiffsjunge sagt zum Kapitän: „Dann ist auch unsere Teekanne nicht verloren, denn sie liegt auf dem Grunde des Meeres."

5*

19. *Die Post*, 5. Nov. 1939, Nr. 32, S. 16: H. L. in U. (in der Rubrik: „Der Leser hat das Wort").

> „Einem Menageriebesitzer war während des Jahrmarktes sein einziger Löwe eingegangen. Da es aber ohne Löwen nicht ging, überredete er einen Handwerksgehilfen, gegen Bezahlung in das Löwenfell zu schlüpfen und sich so im Käfig zu zeigen. Als dieser nun möglichst majestätisch im Käfig lag und sich an das Gitter lehnte, gab dieses plötzlich nach und er fiel in den Nachbarkäfig hinüber, in dem ein Tiger lag. In seiner Todesangst rief er: „Alle guten Geister...," worauf der Tiger prompt antwortete: „...loben Gott den Herrn." "

Diese prächtige Geschichte (in der es sich gewöhnlich um zwei Löwen in einem Zirkus handelt) ist mindestens ein halbes Jahrhundert alt. Ich habe sie mehrfach gelesen und gehört — auch als amerikanische und als jüdische Anekdote. Eine zeitgeschichtlich gefärbte Variante hat mir der unvergeßliche Johannes Bolte zwei Tage vor seinem Tode erzählt, als ich ihn am 23. Juli 1937 im Berliner Bethanien-Krankenhause besuchte: Bei dem großen Beamtenabbau in Deutschland nach dem ersten Weltkrieg wird auch ein kleiner, schmächtiger Beamter entlassen; da macht der Direktor eines Zoo ihm den Vorschlag, sich in das Fell eines soeben krepierten Schimpanse einnähen zu lassen und dessen Rolle weiterzuspielen. Der stellenlose Beamte greift bereitwillig zu und turnt fröhlich als Affe auf den Ästen eines über dem Bärenzwinger stehenden Baumes herum. Plötzlich stürzt er ab und kommt neben dem Bären zu liegen; in seiner Todesangst stammelt er: „Ach du mein lieber Gott... Ach du mein lieber Gott..." Doch der Bär brummt beruhigend: „Sei man nicht bange — ich bin ja auch nur ein abgebauter Beamter."

Christian-Albrechts-Universität, Kiel

THE FATE OF OLD LOW GERMAN PRINTINGS: A PRELIMINARY REPORT

Taylor Starck

Archer Taylor has covered many fields in his busy career and is as much at home in bibliography as in folklore. Still the following pages, that deal with a specialized topic in bibliography, may be of interest to him.

Borchling-Claussen's great *Niederdeutsche Bibliographie*[1] undertook not only to describe every printing known to them but also to record the location of every known copy. Only in the case of a few fairly common books did they content themselves with listing a half-dozen or so and adding: "und in vielen anderen Bibliotheken." Since the number of preserved copies is relatively small, perhaps thirty thousand, this task, though great, was perfectly feasible and, in view of the extraordinary rarity of most of the printings, it was an undertaking of great importance to Low German scholars. Of the total number, 4920, of printings listed in the NDB, 2905 were known in single copies, 700 were preserved in only two copies. In addition to these there were 439 printings known only through old bibliographical sources which were definitely lost or could not be located in the libraries that listed them in their catalogues. And, finally, 107 printings have been preserved only in a fragmentary state. There were therefore only 769 printings in complete condition which were preserved in three or more copies. These figures will have to be altered with the help of Claussen's supplementary volume and the unpublished data I have collected. But though there will be additions to the number of

[1] Conrad Borchling und Bruno Claussen, Niederdeutsche Bibliographie. Gesamtverzeichnis der Niederdeutschen Drucke bis zum Jahre 1800, 2 vols., Karl Wachholtz Verlag, Neumünster, 1931–1936. A third volume in 1957.

printings and of known copies there will have to be very considerable subtractions because of war losses so that the number of printings and copies will in the end turn out to be less than those known to BC.

At the close of the War I undertook to survey the extent of damage to the collections of old LG printings, first reversing the BC index, listing the libraries alphabetically according to the name of the city, and their holdings by the numbers in the NDB. Extensive correspondence in the years 1949 and 1950 with all the libraries that had been exposed to war damage was supplemented by visits to the principal libraries for consultation and check-ups on the books themselves, where they were available, during 1951 and annually from 1955 to 1959. This would not have been possible without the hearty and generous cooperation of many librarians and custodians. I am particularly grateful to Dr. Wieland Schmidt, now librarian of the Free University in Berlin, who went to a great deal of trouble to find assistants to check the holdings of the Öffentliche Wissenschaftliche Bibliothek in Berlin and to supervise their work. The many others who took part shall be mentioned in the final report.

In the course of this work a great many inaccuracies in the NDB appeared: omissions, listings of books that were never in the libraries for which BC reported them, references to libraries which no longer exist (as the University of Altdorf), misprints and some bibliographical inaccuracies. I do not wish these remarks to be understood as a stricture on the work of Professor Borchling and Dr. Claussen. The collection of the material began before the first World War and the notes were at first a by-product of Dr. Borchling's famous survey of LG manuscripts. He could not later revisit all these libraries and he lacked the means to recheck all of his entries. Many corrections were made in the addenda and in Dr. Claussen's supplementary third volume. For such a vast and detailed undertaking the NDB is on the whole a marvellous piece of work.

The history of Low German printings, beginning with the Psalter printed by Lucas Brandis in Lübeck, ca. 1473, of which a number of copies have survived, is closely linked with the history of the Hanseatic cities. There had been the beginnings of an LG literary language, described by Agathe Lasch, Conrad Borchling and others, which began to decline with the crumbling of Hanseatic power and the progress of the Reformation. After 1700 the number of literary works, never great, sank to nearly zero and the vernacular came to be used only for limited purposes. Belles-lettres never really figured. Even *Reinke de Vos* is primarily a didactic work. Bibles, psalters, catechisms, mystical works and theological tracts, collections of laws, chronicles,—these make up the great mass of Low German literature. In the 18th century, indeed, purely ephemeral wedding poems (Gelegenheitsgedichte) make up a large part of the printed texts. It was not until the

Romantic period that interest in Plattdeutsch was revived and the number of printed works of literary nature became appreciable. With the decline of interest in the Low German, as High German took its place in church services, schools, and chanceries, the interest in the older works waned and few took the trouble to preserve them. Consequently enormous numbers of books were lost before the antiquarians of the 19th century took steps to preserve them. The great majority of the works listed in the NDB have never been reprinted, almost none of the longer ones, and we are thus for literary, historical, cultural and linguistic studies dependent upon the preserved old printings. The importance of BC's bibliography is thus readily apparent, and it is no less important to bring their work up to date, correct errors and indicate what the effect of the recent hostilities has been.

The NDB contains various indices, but the authors had not made, or at least had not published, lists of the books contained in the various libraries. This I did toward the end of World War II, writing to all librarians, libraries, churches, schools and institutes that might have suffered war damage, listing the books by the NDB numbers and inquiring whether they were still in the library and whether they had other LG printings up to 1800 not included by BC. In some cases the libraries reported that their copy of the NDB had been destroyed or that they had never owned one. Thereupon I wrote out the titles of the books and repeated the inquiry. Even so this was a great deal to ask in the troublesome post-war years when help was scarce, funds still scarcer. All the more cheering was the hearty, in nearly all cases prompt, response of the custodians. They went to much trouble to answer my questions and often reported LG printings unknown to BC. The result has been a relatively complete record of what happened to the Low German books in war zones. I did not circularize any libraries outside Germany since only three, the Royal Library in Copenhagen, the University Library in Uppsala, and the British Museum had any considerable number. These books, as also those in Holland, the Bibliothèque Nationale in Paris and the State Library in Vienna are presumably intact. From only a few libraries in the Soviet Zone in Germany and from none in territories now occupied by Soviet Russia did I receive an answer. Repeated inquiries of the State Library in Leningrad went unanswered. An attempt to get the desired information through our Embassy in Moscow was equally unsuccessful, though our State Department was interested and helpful. It may be that with the revival of cultural exchanges with Russia this information will be forthcoming. In the past year I renewed the inquiries in East Germany but have not yet pushed them. I hope by late 1960 to have the most important missing facts in hand.

It is not my intention to give more than a preliminary survey of the most important collections. The detailed account of the fate of each book and the description of new printings and list of newly found copies will be ultimately printed as a supplement to the NDB. I list the libraries alphabetically by cities.

AACHEN. The Stadtbibliothek had only ten works. On my last visit to the library in 1957 the librarian said that it is extremely unlikely that any of these had survived. It is unfortunate that these books were lost since the damage to the library as a whole, though bad, was not great. By an extraordinary chance a bomb entered a window, blew out the walls laterally and the heavy bomb-proof concrete roof collapsed on the books. Retrieving them was a difficult and time-consuming job and before it was completed many books were also water-damaged.

ALTDORF, Sammlung Schwarz. Thus the entry in BC. They copied their information from Panzer's *Annalen*, 1788–1802. The University of Altdorf was closed in 1814 and most of the library transferred to Erlangen, all except the Collection Schwarz. This was sold at auction to an English collector whose collection was in turn sold about fifteen years later at a number of auctions in London, Brussels, and Paris. The catalogue of the Paris sale shows that the Schwarz books must have been housed in the French capital. The catalogue, in French, makes no pretense of describing the books or even of giving title or date. It is therefore impossible to determine whether the Bible "en Bas-Allemand" is BC 647, which is not a Bible, or some other book from the Schwarz Collection that had not been listed by Panzer, for this collection was the greatest of Reformation books existing at the time. The catalogue of sale in the Folger Library has many annotations of prices but does not indicate the purchasers.

ALTENBURG, Landesbibliothek. This library was dissolved after 1949 and its copy of No. 197 is now probably with the rest of the library's books at the University of Jena.

ALTENKIRCHEN AUF RÜGEN, Kirchenbibliothek, had only No. 3180, Luther's hymnal in the edition of 1626. It is no longer there, which is unfortunate as it was a unique copy. As in the Nazi period a concerted effort was made to assemble small church collections in large provincial libraries, this book may eventually turn up. This remark applies also to some other collections. So the Stadtbibliothek of ALTONA, after the incorporation of Altona with Hamburg, was dissolved, the valuable books being sent to the Universitäts- und Staatsbibliothek or divided between the Staatsarchiv and Stadtbücherei. Since all these suffered severely during the war it is still not clear whether the three items from Altona have been preserved. All three were *Reinke de Vos* editions of which other copies exist.

AUGSBURG. Stadtbibliothek. All eight printings listed by BC have been preserved. All but two of them are incunabula and all excessively rare.

AURICH. The small but important collection of the Staatsarchiv is intact. Unhappily the librarian could not in September, 1949, locate the two oldest items.

No. 862 was reported as "unauffindbar" by BC. So also No. 1147, a unique copy. This may mean that BC's source was mistaken, which is unlikely, or that these two books were lost or stolen since the publication of Wiarda's *Ostfriesische Geschichte*.

BARTH (POMMERN), Bibliothek der Marienkirche. This important collection was not listed in *Minerva*. All my efforts to get information about the fate of this church library have proved vain. Possibly this, like some other church libraries, was incorporated with a large central library. Stettin? If not, it may have been taken by the Poles, as were private collections and some evacuated public collections, assembled and then taken to Breslau, where they were kept in storage at least as recently as 1951. Whether this assemblage of millions of books has been disposed of to antiquarian dealers, or distributed to public libraries, I do not know. According to Swedish reports some did get on the market. It is likely that some of the presumably lost books of the Breslau University library were evacuated and picked up with other private or supposedly private collections.

BERLIN. There were many libraries in Berlin, small as well as large, for which BC listed LG items. The large private library of Albert Lübke, that contained some books from the great Wernigerode collection, was scattered after his death, a few years before the beginning of World War II. The University library contains a considerable number of LG books. But the Preussische Staatsbibliothek had the largest collection of pre-1801 LG books in existence, about 1000 items. Both the University and State libraries were in the same building which received only one serious hit that destroyed the reading room with its reference collection. The massive building in the main survived the bombing, as did also the older part of the University building next to it. Consequently the loss to books in the building was relatively slight. The LG books which the University library lost seem to have been the few in the reference collection. They lost a total of twelve books.

The State Library (now known as the Öffentliche Wissenschaftliche Bibliothek) had evacuated all manuscripts and the greater part of the books. A large part of these were found in the railroad yards of Marburg when the American army moved in. They were kept there and set up in the building of the archives as the Westdeutsche Bibliothek. A small part of the State Library found its way to the University of Tübingen library. Among the latter are about eighty of the Low German books. Consequently the collection of the great Berlin library is today divided among three libraries and will no doubt remain divided until the vexing problem of Berlin itself is settled. A considerable number of the Berlin books were evacuated to safe places now in East Germany. These have not been returned and it is not positively known where they are. Among the latter were a considerable number of LG books, chiefly of the Reformation period, Bibles, catechisms, tracts, and hymnals.

BONN, Universitätsbibliothek. On this there is still no report and will be none for at least a year. The library was housed in the main University building that was burned out. A good part of it had been evacuated, but catalogues and reference books were destroyed and there is still no adequate housing for the University's library pending the completion of a large modern building on the bank of the Rhine. It is not probable that many of the ca. 100 LG items, many of them scarce and even unique, have been lost.

BRAUNSCHWEIG, Stadtbibliothek. This collection was smaller than the one in Bonn, also suffered somewhat, but a complete report will not be ready for a year.

BREMEN, Staatsbibliothek. If the collection had been left in the building it would have suffered no damage at all. But a large part of the library was evacuated to a salt mine and was carried off by the Russian army. Some fifty of the LG books were thus lost.

BRESLAU, Stadtbibliothek, had only five LG items of which the only incunabulum, No. 241, is lost. It was evacuated and need not have been destroyed. However, this would not be a serious loss as it is the Lübeck Bible of 1494, of which many copies are extant, about a dozen of them in the U.S.A.

The Universitätsbibliothek is a different matter. This had a considerable collection with many rare items such as No. 205, a Plenarium from the famous Mohnkopfdrucker in Lübeck. The three copies listed by BC have all, temporarily at least, disappeared. There is now a copy in the Morgan Library. The Polish librarian of the two libraries (they have been combined) thought that the books of the UB had probably been destroyed with the building. As I have indicated in connection with the Barth books, I do not believe this to be the case as they seem to have been evacuated and may well reappear.

DANZIG, Stadtbibliothek, had 43 old LG items concerning which I have not yet obtained any information.

The collections in DARMSTADT (Landesbibliothek), DORTMUND (Stadt- und Landesbibliothek, now combined), DÜSSELDORF (several libraries), EMDEN (four libraries), FRANKFURT (city and university libraries, now combined), have all survived with inconsiderable losses to the LG items.

GÖTTINGEN, Universitätsbibliothek (now Niedersächsische Landesbibliothek) is an example of a large and important LG library that survived the War intact.

GREIFSWALD, Universitätsbibliothek. The first reports were that the entire collection had been carried off ("verschleppt") but some books have reappeared and as there was no bombing damage they may all find their way back to Greifswald as was the case with the Gotha library that was returned by the Russians intact, without ever having been unpacked, in the Spring of 1957.

HAMBURG. The first reports on the various libraries were very discouraging. The bombing of Hamburg had begun early in the war before much had been done about evacuating libraries. As catalogues were also destroyed it was years before the librarians could assess the damage. The Staatsbibliothek and University library (now combined) have made a survey of holdings. Somewhere near half seem to be missing. This does not mean that they are destroyed, but only that they have not been located. However, the loss is very considerable and is not compensated for by the dozen or two of printings and copies not known to BC that have appeared in the course of the check-up.

The loss of the Staatsarchiv was much heavier and I have not yet had a complete report from them. All told the losses in Hamburg were heavier by far than in Berlin.

HANNOVER had in its various libraries many important LG books. Here also the first report in 1950 was that the losses were very heavy. The main damage to the collections of the Archiv, stored in the cellars, came from flood waters and not from fire. The situation was similar to that in Dresden where the great collection in the Japanisches Palais was evacuated, survived the bombing, but was prematurely brought back and stored in the cellars of the destroyed building only to be seriously damaged by water. Fortunately the first reports were exaggerated and I found in 1951 this to have been the case in Hannover. Still there were considerable losses.

HELMSTEDT, Universitätsbibliothek. The University was dissolved in 1810 and the library assigned to the Ducal Library in Wolfenbüttel, but the books are still in large part in Helmstedt, inadequately housed and shelved. Professor Heinrich Schneider, formerly librarian in Wolfenbüttel, assured me that it was during his term of service always a difficult matter to lay hands on any specific book in Helmstedt. It is by no means certain that BC have given a complete list or that the books they have listed for Helmstedt are actually there and in good condition. In any case there was no war damage in Helmstedt or in WOLFEN-BÜTTEL, so that the third largest LG collection is in perfect condition.

HILDESHEIM, with several libraries, KIEL, University library and KÖLN with several libraries all had serious damage which has not been accurately assessed. Perhaps one half of the LG books in the three cities were destroyed by fire. Fortunately the total is not great as regards early LG holdings.

KÖNIGSBERG, Universitätsbibliothek. This was an important collection, especially for the 18th Century. It has been impossible to get any accurate information or, of course, to visit Königsberg. According to most reports the University library was completely destroyed.

LÜBECK, Stadtbibliothek. It had one of the finest collections of LG incunabula. The library was neither bombed nor burned and all the books that remained in the building are still there. The more valuable books and manuscripts like those of the Archiv were evacuated and never returned. Their exact location is unknown.

The losses to MARBURG, Universitätsbibliothek, MÜNCHEN, Staatsbibliothek and Universitätsbibliothek, were small. But the important collection of the Universitätsbibliothek in MÜNSTER was almost entirely destroyed. In NÜRNBERG, on the other hand, in spite of the great destruction in the city, apparently none of the valuable books were lost and the small group of LG items is safe.

In OLDENBURG one wall of the Landesbibliothek was ripped open by a bomb and the books cascaded into the street. I was there four or five times but cannot be sure that I saw all the LG books that survived since great quantities were still piled in rooms of the new quarters for lack of money for shelving. There are probably some losses, perhaps a dozen books.

The small but choice collection in the Gräflich Bismarcksche Bibliothek in SCHLOSS PLATHE, Pommern, seems to have disappeared. It may have been confiscated as private property and merged with some Communist library.

My letters to REVAL, Esthonia, and RIGA, Livonia, where there were small collections with extraordinarily rare LG books, all went unanswered. Whether these have remained there or, since the annexation of the Baltic States by Soviet Russia, were moved to the State Library in Moscow, the future will tell.

The large important collections in the Ratsarchiv and the University library in ROSTOCK, on which Dr. Claussen has reported, are in the main preserved. Nor have I a report of any loss to the collections in SCHWERIN, either the Archives or the Landesbibliothek. From STETTIN, now Polish, however, there has been no report. The collections were small and they must have been intact at the end of the War.

The Landesbibliothek in STUTTGART had the largest Low German collection in southern Germany. Though the building was destroyed and the catalogues burned the books were in the main preserved.

WERNIGERODE, Fürstlich Stolbergische Bibliothek. As is well known this library was sold in 1936 to satisfy the pension claims of the employees of the bankrupt princely house. At that time the NDB was already in type. BC made such corrections as they could in the Addenda but it was of course impossible for them to identify all the purchasers of the 125 LG books in the great library. Many of these were bought by the Berlin, Bremen and Hamburg libraries and by Albert Lübke in Berlin. These last were again resold at Lübke's death. I was able to ascertain that Nos. 902A, 1349, 2159, 2391, 2632 were destroyed or lost in the new locations. The first of these, a unique copy, was sold to the Bremen Staatsbibliothek and was subsequently carried off to Russia. It will take years before all of the Wernigerode books can be relocated.

In this survey I have indicated all the major losses though I have not mentioned some losses small in number, as that of the Theological Seminary in Herborn that lost four books (1987, 1990, 2006, 2045, all destroyed) of which the first three were unique and the fourth was the only perfect copy. Indeed the imperfect copy in Danzig may also have been destroyed. As these were all choice Reformation items their loss means more than that of a considerable number of books that are available in many libraries. On the other hand, I did not list the many collections, some very large, like those in Copenhagen and the British Museum, the preservation of which in some measure compensates for the losses elsewhere. Also, BC by no means gave a complete survey of the libraries outside Germany, especially not of those in America. For instance, they listed only a handful of books for the Harvard library though there are three or four times as many on its shelves. Still, since the total number of copies of the 4920 printings listed by BC was hardly more than thirty thousand, each and every loss was a regrettable one. This is especially true when we consider that a very considerable number of these copies are imperfect, some lacking several signatures, a great many lacking the title page. Comparatively few of the texts had ever been reprinted and only the most important had been studied. Of the 2905 printings existing in unique copies very many have now disappeared for good and all. The most important *Unikum*, the first printing of *Reinke de Vos*, is still on the shelf in Wolfenbüttel. Very few indeed of the incunabula, perhaps none, have been lost to us for the incunabula are for the most part preserved in a number of copies, the Cologne Chronicle of 1499 in dozens, about twenty of them in the U.S.A. Those items that are gone are in considerable measure such things as the wedding poems, interesting but of little or no value to the literary historian, and rarely to the philologist; or books that appeared in many editions so that little if any of the text is lost. Of the total number of books as many as 3500, perhaps, have been definitely destroyed, misplaced or are in unknown repositories. Hardly more than 1500 have been actually destroyed unless the new owners have not taken care of the books. That is about the percentage loss to German libraries as a whole. We can take comfort from the realization that many books will reappear though it may take years. As I expect to make a detailed report of every copy in another year I would be grateful if readers of this survey report to me any items not listed in BC that come to their knowledge.

Harvard University

DER SCHWANK VON DER SCHRECKLICHEN DROHUNG

Kurt Ranke

Stith Thompson vermerkt in seinem *Motif-Index* unter der Signatur K 1771.2 und 3 zwei kurze Anekdoten, die er dem Kommentar Albert Wesselskis zu dessem *Hodscha Nasreddin*-Ausgabe (Vol. 2, Weimar 1911, p. 217 Nr. 450) entnommen hat. Die Fabeln sind zwar jeweils verschieden, die Grundidee ist jedoch gleich: immer handelt es sich um die fürchterliche Drohung: „Entweder...oder...!", die von einem verschmitzten Prahlhans gegen einen anderen ausgestoßen wird, um ihn einzuschüchtern und dem eigenen Willen gefügig zu machen. Die Reaktion ist in fast allen Fällen Angst und Eingehen auf die unverschämten Forderungen. Doch siegt die Neugier des Düpierten, und auf seine Frage, was denn nun eigentlich geschehen wäre, wenn er nicht nachgegeben hätte, erfolgt die verblüffende Aufklärung, daß nichts passiert wäre.

Von dieser einfachen Form: „Entweder...oder...!" sind mir bislang rund ein halbes Dutzend kompliziertere Redaktionen bekannt geworden, deren Analyse und Geschichte vielleicht selbst Ihnen, lieber Archer Taylor, trotz Ihrer meisterhaften Kenntnisse auf dem Gebiete des universalen Schwankgutes, ein willkommenes Novum sein mögen.

I. Das gestohlene Pferd.

Die älteste Fassung dieser ersten Redaktion war schon Wesselski bekannt. Sie steht im dritten Buche der *Carmina* des Theodulf von Orleans, der 794 von Karl dem Großen zum Bischof dieser Stadt inthronisiert wurde. Der Wortlaut ist folgender:

Saepe dat ingenium quod vis conferre negabat,
   Compos et arte est qui viribus impos erat.
Ereptum furto castrensi in turbine quidam
   Accipe qua miles arte recepit equum.
Orbus equo fit praeco, cietque ad compita voce,
   Quisquis habet nostrum reddere certet equum.
Sin alias, tanta faciam ratione coactus,
   Quod noster Roma fecit in urbe pater.
Res movet haec omnes, et equum fur sivit abire,
   Dum sua vel populi damna pavenda timet.
Hunc herus ut reperit, gaudet, potiturque reperto,
   Gratanturque illi quis metus ante fuit.
Inde rogant quid equo fuerat facturus adempto,
   Vel quid in urbe suus egerit ante pater.
Sellae, ait, adjunctis collo revehendo lupatis
   Sarcinulisque aliis, ibat onustus inops.
Nil quod pungat habens, calcaria calce reportans,
   Olim eques, inde redit ad sua tecta pedes.
Hunc imitatus egi fecissem talia tristis,
   Ne foret iste mihi, crede, repertus equus.

Die Anekdote ist leider nicht ganz klar und logisch aufgebaut. Man vermißt den Hinweis, daß dem Pferd Sattel und Zaumzeug abgenommen waren, als es gestohlen wurde, sonst hätte der Soldat sie ja nicht wie sein Vater auf dem Rücken tragen müssen, falls ihm das Pferd nicht wieder zurückgegeben worden wäre. Trotz dieses Mangels wirkt die Pointe überraschend und witzig, und man mag sogar so etwas wie eine ironisierende Psychologie in ihr suchen. Es ist daher merkwürdig, daß rund 850 Jahre vergehen mußten, ehe die Anekdote wieder entweder aus mündlicher oder (uns bis auf Theodulfs Elaborat unbekannter) literarischer Tradition aufgezeichnet wurde. Im *Exilium Melancholiae, das ist Vnlust-Vertreiber* (Straßburg, 1643, p. 96, Nr. 57) finden wir eine etwas modifizierte Fassung:

Ein Soldat zu Pferd kam in eine Statt, daselbst er etliche Excesz begieng, deszwegen die Bürger sich seines Pferdes bemächtigten, vnd jhme den Sattel ließen. Dieses Despects halber war der Reiter sehr erzürnet, dräwete allen in der Statt, vnd schwur, daß sie deren gerewen wolte, vnd dasz er wol wüste, was er zu thun hätte. Nun ausz Rath der Vornehmsten in der Statt wird jhm sein Pferd wider gegeben, vnd er zugleich gefragt, was er wol hätte thun wollen? Was wolt ich gethan haben, antwortete er, ich hätte eben den Sattel verkauft. Hierausz verstunden die guten Bürgersleute, dasz er kein solcher großer Teuffel were, als er schwartz gewesen ist.

Die gleiche Version finden wir rund 80 Jahre später in Helmhacks *Neuvermehrtem, lustigem und curiösem Fabelhannsz* (Hall 1729, p. 122 Nr. 113) und wiederum etwa 40 Jahre danach in Nicolais *Vademecum für lustige Leute* (Vol. 6, Berlin, 1772, p. 32, Nr. 33).

Die neue Fassung unterscheidet sich etwas von der älteren. Die Unklarheit ist ausgemerzt: das Pferd wird nicht gestohlen, sondern die Bürger behalten es wegen des Unfugs, den der Reiter anstellt, ein, lassen diesem jedoch den Sattel. Der Soldat beruft sich bei seiner Drohung nicht auf seinen Vater. Der Witz ist jetzt, daß er den Sattel verkauft hätte.

Ganz offensichtlich liegt also eine Korrektur vor, und ebenso offensichtlich ist ein Verlust an stofflicher und geistiger Substanz eingetreten. Die Korrektur führt nicht zu der alten Form zurück, denn in dieser muß, das zeigen die weiteren Fassungen, der Diebstahl des Pferdes primärer Zug gewesen sein. Der Substanzverlust liegt auf der Hand: die Geschichte ist einfacher geworden, sie entbehrt nun der gehobeneren Spannungselemente des Modellfalls (Beispiel des Vaters) wie des pointierteren Endeffektes (den Sattel tragen zu müssen statt ihn verkaufen zu wollen). Die Anekdote hat also trotz Verbesserung verloren, und es ist schade, daß wir in Westeuropa bislang keine neuen Fassungen gefunden haben, die uns über ihr weiteres Schicksal ebendort belehren könnten.

Jedoch sind in Osteuropa, im Orient und in Nordafrika in den letzten 100 Jahren ein paar Varianten aufgetaucht, die in Struktur und Habitus recht interessant sind und uns vielleicht die Möglichkeit geben, trotz des geringen Materials das „Kulturgefälle" dieser kleinen Geschichte zu erkennen.

Vuc Vrčević hat in den 80er Jahren des vorigen Jahrhunderts eine dalmatinische Variante publiziert:

> Einem Zigeuner wird in Dubrovnik der Zaum seines Pferdes gestohlen. Er droht, man solle ihm denselben zurückgeben oder bezahlen, sonst würde er ausführen, was er sich vorgenommen habe. Die Leute erschrecken und wollen jedermanns Bündel untersuchen. Auf diese Aussicht hin bringt der Dieb den Halfter selber herbei und fragt, was der Zigeuner vorgehabt habe. Antwort: Er hätte sich einen neuen gekauft (Vuc Vrčević, *Srpske narodne pripovijetke*, Dubrovnik, 1882 = Fr. S. Krauss, *Zigeunerhumor*, Leipzig, 1906, p. 143).

Der Zusammenhang mit den neueren westeuropäischen Fassungen (ohne Modellfall) ist zwar evident, jedoch hat sich die alte Diebstahlsversion wieder durchgesetzt. Offenbar muß es also auch Überlieferungen mit diesem Zug gegeben haben. Die kontinuierliche Zersetzung der alten Fabel setzt gleich zu Anfang ein: jetzt wird nicht mehr das Pferd sondern, wahrscheinlich durch den Endeffekt vom Sattel und Zaum herbeigeführt, nur noch der letztere gestohlen. Noch weiter geht die Entstellung in einer Version aus der unfern gelegenen Crna Gora:

Hier will ein Christ von einem türkischen Händler einen Halfter für seinen Esel geschenkt haben und bedroht ihn: Bei Gott, Türke, wenn du ihn mir nicht gibst, tue
ich, was ich mir vorgenommen habe. Um Unannehmlichkeiten zu vermeiden, schenkt
der Türke ihm den Zaum und fragt, was er getan hätte. Antwort: Ich hätte meinen
Esel an meinen Gürtel binden und ihn so nach Hause führen müssen (*Srbsko-dalmatinski magazin*, 1864, p. 96f.).

Charakteristich an all diesen späten Varianten ist das Fehlen des Modellfalles.
Dieser kehrt jedoch merkwürdigerweise in polnischen, litauischen und ukrainischen
Fassungen wieder. J. L. Cahan bringt in seiner *Jewish Folklore* (= *Publ. of the
Yiddish Scient. Inst. Vol. IX, Phil. Ser. Vol. V*, Wilna 1938, p. 199 Nr. 14) folgende Geschichte:

Motke (ein Wilnaer Witzbold) kaufte mit einem anderen zusammen ein Pferd und
einen Wagen. Bald fuhr der eine, bald der andere. Einst kam Motke in ein Städtchen,
hielt vor einem Wirtshaus, ging hinein und ließ das Pferd allein stehen. Als er wieder
herauskam, war das Pferd nicht mehr da. Da ruft Motke: „Das Pferd ist zwar ein
alter Lappen, aber ich werde das tun, was mein Vater zu tun pflegte". Die Leute
dachten ganz verängstigt: Wer weiß, was Motkes Vater einst tat? Sie legten das
Geld zusammen und kauften für Motke ein gutes Pferd. Als Motke nun wieder im
Wagen saß, fragte man ihn: „Motke, was hat denn nun eigentlich dein Vater gemacht?" „Was mein Vater tat? Als ihm das Pferd gestohlen wurde, ging er eben
zu Fuß nach Haus."

Eine sehr ähnliche Fassung finden wir bei Immanuel Olsvanger, *Rosinkess mit
Mandlen. Aus der Volksliteratur der Ostjuden* (Basel, 1931, p. 113 Nr. 195). Die
meisten der in diesem Buche veröffentlichten Geschichten stammen aus Litauen.
    In einer ukrainischen Variante aus Podolien tritt die oben bei den serbischen
Beispielen festgestellte Zersetzung wiederum auf:

Statt des Pferdes wird einem Mann nur der Sattel gestohlen. Er droht: „Ich werde
das tun, was mein Vater einst tat, als man ihm seinen Sattel stahl!" Auf die Rückfrage erklärt er, er hätte sich einen neuen Sattel kaufen müssen (Mykola Levčenko,
Kazky ta opovidannja z Podillja, Kyjiv, 1928, p. 552, Nr. 608).

Überblicken wir an Hand des belegmäßig natürlich nicht gerade üppigen
Materials die Entwicklung und Verbreitung dieser Redaktion in Europa, so ist
wohl doch einigermaßen deutlich, daß sie von Westen nach Osten, d. h. präziser
gesagt, nach Südosten gewandert ist. Wie erklärt sich aber die eigentümliche
Regeneration der nordöstlichen Fassungen? Vielleicht geben uns die noch weiter
östlich und südlich in der Türkei und in Nordafrika gefundenen Versionen, die
der alten Geschichte bei Theodulf von Orleans und den neueren bei den Juden des

Wilnaer Gebietes sehr viel näher stehen als die übrigen europäischen, den Aufschluß über diese Frage.

P. Gentizon teilt in seinem Buche *L'Esprit d'Orient* (Paris 1930 p. 92, Nr. 78) folgende hübsche türkische Anekdote mit:

> Le derviche, son père et l'âne.
> Un derviche monté sur un âne arriva à la nuit tombante dans un village. Il attacha l'animal à un pieu et, s'étant fait un coussin du bât, s'endormit du sommeil du juste. Le lendemain, à son réveil, il s'aperçut que l'âne avait disparu. Baudet par-ci, baudet par-là... pas l'ombre d'une bête. Mais bientôt une idée lumineuse lui traversa l'esprit. Il fit appeler le crieur public: "Ecoute moi bien", lui dit-il. "Va, annonce partout le vol de mon âne et n'oublie pas d'ajouter que si celui qui me l'a pris ne me le rend pas, je ferai ... ce qu'a fait mon père dix ans auparavant". Aussitôt, les villageois se réunirent effrayés. Et, pensant que le derviche pourrait bien leur nuire, ils décidèrent de se mettre eux-mêmes à la recherche de l'âne. Quelques heures plus tard, l'animal était rendu à son propriétaire. Les villageois demandèrent alors au derviche ce qu'il aurait fait, imitant son père, si l'âne n'avait pas été retrouvé. "Mon père perdit comme moi son âne dans votre village", répondit le derviche. "Il s'adressa alors au crieur qui s'égosilla en vain. Et l'espoir l'ayant quitté, il mit le bât sur son dos et s'en alla".

Das ist natürlich ganz und gar das Pendant, ja es ist sogar mehr, es ist die verbesserte Auflage zu Theodulfs Geschichte, denn hier erscheint die Pointe „il mit le bât sur son dos" motiviert. Vielleicht könnte man trotzdem im Zweifel sein, ob diese Ähnlichkeit, die tausend Jahre ebenso wie die in ihnen stattgehabte Entwicklung einfach negiert, nicht doch aus einer literarischen Abhängigkeit der türkischen von der altfränkischen Fassung resultiert. Korrekturen, die die Kausalität zwischen Geschehen und Pointe wieder herstellen, finden wir ja auch in den deutschen Varianten des 17. und 18. Jahrhunderts. Aber da haben wir ein Kabylenmärchen, das Frobenius in seinem großartigen Werke *Atlantis* (Vol. 3, 196ff.) aufgezeichnet hat. In ihm, das uns hier nicht weiter interessiert, taucht plötzlich unsere Anekdote wieder auf:

> Einem jungen Mann sind in einem Bade Schmucksachen gestohlen worden. Der Inhaber des Bades bringt ihn zum Richter (der verkleideten Frau des Burschen). Das verkleidete Mädchen sah den Burschen und wußte nun, daß es ihr Mann war. Der Bursche sagte: „Der Inhaber des Bades hat mir, während ich badete, aus meinem Kleid einen Schmuck genommen und will mir nun dafür ein Kleid geben. Ich will aber meinen Schmuck wiederhaben und kein neues Kleid, denn der Schmuck gehört nicht mir. Wenn der Inhaber des Bades nicht sogleich meinen Schmuck hierher bringt, so werde ich das machen, was mein Vater einmal tat, als man ihm seinen Esel unterwegs stahl". Der Inhaber des Bades wurde von Angst befallen und brachte

den Schmuck herbei... Am Abend (nach der Wiedervereinigung) sagte die junge, schöne Frau zu ihrem Mann, dem Burschen: „Sage mir doch, was dein Vater tat, als ihm unterwegs einmal der Esel gestohlen wurde". Der Bursche sagte: „Er ging zu Fuß weiter".

Diese Fassung entspricht nur im zweiten Teil, in der Exemplifizierung, der alten Anekdote; der erste Teil ist den neuen Verhältnissen des Märchens angepaßt. Ganz ohne Zweifel muß aber den Kabylen die ganze Geschichte bekannt gewesen sein, denn hier in der Märchenkontamination ist der integrierend zur Anekdote gehörende kausale Zusammenhang, eben die Aequivalenz von Fall und Modellfall, zerstört. Der zweite Teil weist aber ebenso eindeutig auf einen Zusammenhang wiederum mit der altfränkischen und der türkischen Fassung hin.

Dürfen wir eine tausendjährige orale Tradition unseres Schwankes im orientalisch-nordafrikanischen Kulturraum annehmen, die zufällig einmal im 9. Jahrhundert in Westeuropa zu schriftlicher Fixierung gelangte, um dann dort ein eigenes Leben zu führen? Ich glaube, daß dieser Annahme nichts im Wege steht. Um 700 p. Chr. n. wird das alte spanische Westgotenreich von den Arabern erobert. Die Goten bleiben natürlich im Lande. Um 800 beruft Karl der Große den spanischen Westgoten Theodulf als Bischof nach Orleans. Was liegt näher, als daß er eine spanisch-maurische Anekdote mitgebracht und sie in etwas derangierter Form seiner Sammlung einverleibt hat? Der umgekehrte Fall, daß Germanen ihr Erzählgut nach Nordafrika mitgeschleppt hätten (das sich von hier aus in der arabischen Welt verbreitet hätte), ist zwar ebenfalls nicht von der Hand zu weisen (ich hoffe später einmal nachweisen zu können, daß es tatsächlich solche Fälle germanischer Völkerwanderungsmärchen gibt). Jedoch sprechen hiergegen zwei Fakten: zum ersten sind die orientalischen Fassungen logischer, zum andern scheint aber das Motiv von der Berufung auf einen schon dem Vater begegneten äquivalenten Fall tatsächlich orientalisch zu sein. Das zeigen einmal die Belege aus den jüdischen Siedlungsgebieten Polens und Litauens, die ganz eindeutig den alten Typus repräsentieren, dessen Tradition und ethno-geographische Isoliertheit hier im östlichen Mitteleuropa sich wohl am ehesten aus Autogenese erklären läßt (wenn auch für die angesprochene Isolation, nicht aber für die Existenz und die Kontinuität dieser archaischen Formen, der äußerst geringe Kulturaustausch zwischen den Juden und den Nichtjuden dieser Länder in Rechnung gestellt werden muß, s. dazu auch Olsvanger, l. c. p. XIII f.). Diese Annahme wird durch die Tatsache erhärtet, daß das Motiv vom Modellfall noch heute im Orient und, wie es scheint, vornehmlich dort durchaus lebendig ist. Als Beispiel führe ich folgende, unserem Schwanke aufs engste verwandte Geschichte an, die von Goha, dem arabischen Gegenhelden des türkischen Hodscha Nasreddin, erzählt wird:

6*

Dem Goha werden einst, als er in der Moschee wie vorgeschrieben barfüßig betet, die Schuhe gestohlen. Laut ruft er, daß er das tun werde, was sein Vater einst im gleichen Falle getan habe, falls ihm der Dieb nicht sofort seine Schuhe zurückbringe. Ein Mann gibt ihm zitternd vor Furcht die Schuhe und fragt, was sein Vater getan habe. „Er kaufte sich ein anderes Paar Schuhe". (Elian J. Finbert, *Les contes de Goha*, Paris, 1929, p. 14f.).

Mir scheint der Fall jetzt klar. Die Anekdote ist arabisch-semitischen Ursprungs. Theodulf hat sie aus dem maurischen Spanien mitgebracht. In Westeuropa entwickelte sie sich mit Verbreitungsgefälle nach Osten zu einer etwas verwässerten Geschichte. Im östlichen Mitteleuropa (Polen, Litauen) behielt sie dagegen auf Grund der ethnischen Isolation die alte autochthone Form, die seit etwa dem 11. oder 12. Jahrhundert p. Chr. n. mit der Einwanderung der aus dem Kaukasus über die Ukraine und Ruthenien nordwestwärts vordringenden jüdischen Bevölkerungsteile mitgekommen war. Im östlichen und südlichen Mittelmeerraum (Türkei, Ägypten, Nordwestafrika) ist die alte Fassung bis in unsere Tage hinein in der mündlichen Überlieferung konstant erhalten geblieben.

Das eigentlich Interessante an dieser kleinen und etwas komplizierten Geschichte ist aber die Tatsache, daß hispano-arabisch-westeuropäische Kulturbeziehungen und damit der Austausch von Erzählgut schon im achten Jahrhundert anzusetzen sind, weit früher also als wir gemeinhin anzunehmen pflegen. Dafür ist die Historie unseres Schwankes ein ganz eklatantes Beispiel.

II. Die beiden Fuhrleute.

Diese Redaktion hat Thompson mit K 1771.2 bezeichnet, und J. Balys hat ihr in seinem *Motif-Index of Lithuanian Narrative Folklore* (Kaunas, 1936) die Nummer 1564* gegeben. Die erste mir bekannt gewordene Fassung erscheint bei Melander-Ketzel, *Joco Seria* (Lich, 1605, Vol. 1, p. 12, Nr. 10). Der Inhalt ist kurz folgender:

Ein lustiger junger Wandergeselle trifft an einer engen Wegstelle mit einem seinesgleichen zusammen. Keiner macht Anstalten auszuweichen. Da ruft er ihm zu: „Du Schelmhalsz geh nur ausz dem Weg, oder ich will dich tractieren, inmaszen ich den gestrigen entpfangen vnd tractirt habe". Der andere denkt, er habe jenen umgebracht und weicht ihm scheu aus dem Wege. Als sie kurz auseinander sind, trifft der, der nachgegeben hat, einen zweiten Wanderer. Ermutigt ruft er den Prahlhans zurück und fragt ihn, was er vergangenen Tages mit jenem gemacht habe. Antwort: „Der gestern wolt mir nit weichen, derwegen so wich ich jhm".

Diese Fassung begegnet völlig identisch zu Anfang des 19. Jahrhunderts noch einmal in Warmunds *Sassischen Döneken-Bok* (Hamburg, 1829, p. 298, Nr. 189).

Sie hat jedoch im 17. Jahrhundert in England eine bemerkenswerte, allerdings singulär gebliebene Änderung erfahren. In *Englands Jests Refin'd and Improv'd*, deren 3. Ausgabe (London, 1693) Ashton in seinem Buch *Humor, Wit and Satire of the 17th Century* (1883) veröffentlicht hat, begegnet folgende Version (Ashton, p. 200):

> A Scholar meeting a Countreyman upon the Road rid up very briskly to him; but the Countreyman, out of respect to him was turning off his Horse to give him the Road, when the Scholar, laying his Hand upon his Sword, said: "'Tis well you gave me the Way, or I'd..." "What wou'd you have done?" said the Countreyman, holding up his Club at him. "Given it to you, Sir," says he, pulling off his Hat to him.

Das ist das einzige Mal innerhalb dieser Redaktion, daß der Bedrohte nicht nachgibt, und wie man sieht, hat die Pointe unter dieser typisch angelsächsischen Änderung keineswegs gelitten.

Weitaus häufiger wird jedoch die Begegnung zwischen zwei Fuhrleuten geschildert. Auch hier kann man zwei wenig differenzierte Formen unterscheiden. In der ersten, einfachen, droht der Prahlhans nur, der andere solle schon sehen, was er tun werde. In der zweiten, die zuweilen in Italien lokalisiert wird, beruft sich der Aufschneider in seiner Drohung genau wie der eine der beiden Wanderer in der älteren Fassung bei Melander auf das, was er vor kurzem einem anderen angetan habe.

Die früheste Fassung der ersten Form scheinen Zinkgref-Weidner, *Teutsche Apophtegmata* (Vol. 1, Amsterdam, 1653, p. 242) zu bringen:

> Ein Fuhrman begegnete einem andern Fuhrman auff der Strasz, ruffte ihm zu, er solte auszweichen. Der andere schwieg stille vnd fuhrte immer fort. Dieser ruffte wieder: Wirstu nicht auszweichen, soltu wol sehen, was ich thun will. Da wiche der andere beyseits vnd fragte: Lieber, was hettestu gethan, wenn ich dir nicht gewichen were? Dieser antwortet: Werestu nicht gewichen, so were ich gewichen.

Die gleiche Version begegnet in Samuel Gerlachs *Nova Gnomotheca philologico-historico-ethico-politico-theologica* (Leipzig, 1681, Vol. 1, Nr. 707), in Nicolais *Vademecum für lustige Leute* (Vol. 2, Berlin, 1768, p. 70, Nr. 115) und in Karl Julius Webers *Dymokritos oder hinterlassene Papiere eines lachenden Philosophen* (Vol. 2, Stuttgart, 1832, p. 80f.).

Die zweite Fassung erscheint zuerst in Johann Peter Memels *Erneuerter und Vermehrter Lustiger Gesellschaft* (Zippelzerbst im Drömbling, 1657, p. 25, Nr. 29):

> In Italien hat es an den Bergen enge Steige oder Wege, dasz einer dem andern nicht allezeit weichen kan, wo nicht einer von den beyden etwas wieder zurück fähret, bisz

er kompt da er zu weichen Platz findet. Nun begab es sich, daß sich 2 Schaubkärner
einander vff so einem engen Weg begegneten, der eine fieng bald zornig an, sagte:
Fahr mir ausz dem Wege, oder ich thue dir wie ich den vorigen that. Der ander voll
Schreckens, fuhr weit zurück, bisz er kam, da er weichen kundte, wolte da gleichwol
wissen, was der ander jhm hätte thun wollen, sagte derowegen: Was hättestu mir
denn gethuen wollen, wenn ich dir nicht wäre ausz dem Wege gefahren? Der ander
sich voller Zorn stellend, sagte: Ich hätte dir thuen wollen, wie ich den andern that,
den fuhr ich ausz dem Wege.

Varianten dieser Version finden wir fast gleichlautend im *Kurtzweiligen Hansz-
Wurst von Frölichshausen* (s. l. 1718, p. 326), bei Hilarius Sempiternus, *Der
kurtzweilige Polyhistor* (Cosmopoli, 1719, p. 64, Nr. 17), in Johann Laurenz Helbigs
Anatomia Canis Mystica et Moralis (Würzburg, 1720, p. 127), in: *Der in der Ein-
samkeit und in Gesellschaften allzeit fertige schnackische Lustigmacher* von Semper
Lustig (Cosmopoli, 1762, p. 113, Nr. 169), in Joh. Peter Hebels *Schatzkästlein des
Rheinischen Hausfreundes* (Tübingen, 1811) usw. Eine moderne Fassung, die um
1920 gesammelt wurde, bietet etwa Bernd Schmitz, ,,*Wat is de Ape doch 'n spassig
Mensk! segg de Bur*" (Emsdetten in Westfalen, s. a. p. 102). Andere Parallelen
aus unserer Zeit zeigen einige Veränderungen:

In einer niederdeutschen Anekdote begegnen sich ein Bauer mit einem schweren und
ein Landrat mit einem leichten Fuhrwerk. Der Bauer droht: Wenn Sie nicht gleich
ausbiegen, passiert etwas, was ich sonst nicht gerne tue. Der Landrat weicht aus,
aber der Bauer wird ob dieser Drohung vor den Kadi zitiert und gefragt, was er denn
sonst hätte tun wollen. Antwort: Mit dem vollen Wagen wäre er ausgewichen. Das
hätte er wirklich nicht gern getan. Er wird freigesprochen (Hinrich Kruse, *Wat sik
dat Volk vertellt*, Rendsburg, 1953, p. 13).

Man sieht, hier herrscht schon ein moderner sozialkritischer Ton, der in den
früheren Exempeln fehlt. In einigen litauischen Varianten scheint dagegen die
alte Berufung auf des Vaters Beispiel aus der ersten Redaktion wieder aufzutau-
chen, s. Balys, *Motif-Index*, p. 238, Nr. 1564:

"I will do as my father has done before me." "Well, what did your father do?"
"When he was refused the path, he himself withdrew from it."

Einer ganz ähnlichen Geschichte begegnen wir wieder in Podolien:

Der Pan Gutsbesitzer trifft mit seinem Wagen auf engem Wege einen Szlachcic,
einen kleinadligen Bauern, mit schwer beladenem Fuhrwerk. Der Bauer droht: ,,Ich
werde tun, was mein Vater tat!" Der Pan weicht aus und erfährt auf seine Rückfrage,
daß der Vater im gleichen Falle ausgewichen sei (Mykola Levčenko, *Kazky za opovidannja z Podillja*, Kyjiv, 1928, p. 553, Nr. 609).

Auch auf dem Balkan finden wir unsere Anekdote. Salomon Krauss ist es wieder, der in seinem *Zigeunerhumor* (p. 169) ein vermutlich serbisches Beispiel bringt:

> Ein Zigeuner zu Fuß trifft auf einen sechsspännig über Land fahrenden Herrn und bedroht ihn mit einem Knüttel, er solle weichen, sonst tue er, was er auch gestern getan. Der Herr weicht aus und fragt. Antwort: Der Zigeuner wäre selbst gewichen.

Die Vitalität ihres Witzes hat unsere Geschichte schließlich bis nach Nordamerika geführt. Herbert Halpert teilte sie mir mit, und das Hübscheste an diesem Hinweis ist, daß er ihn wiederum seinem zehnjährigen Sohn Nicholas verdankt. Die Anekdote ist hier an den großen amerikanischen Nationalhelden Abraham Lincoln geknüpft:

> In many a prairie cabin by candlelight as the snowdrifts piled, and another crock of apples was passed to those who sat by the wood fire, the tale had been told of Abe Lincoln driving a two-horse team on a road heavy with mud. It was sunset time and Abe had his back to the sunset. And he met another driver with a two-horse wagon. Both knew that whoever turned out would be up to the hubs in mud, almost sure to get stuck in the mud. "Turn out," the other fellow called. "Turn out yourself," called Abe. The other fellow refused. Then Abe, with his back to the sunset, began to rise from his seat in the wagon, rising and rising, his tall shape getting longer and longer against the setting sun, as he was saying: "If you don't turn out I'll tell you what I'll do." And the other fellow hollered: "Don't go any higher. I'll turn out." And after he had struggled through and passed by Lincoln, he called back: "Say, what would you have done if I hadn't turned out?" Lincoln answered: "I'd 've turned out myself" (Carl Sandburg, *Abraham Lincoln: The Prairie Years*, Vol. 2, New York, 1926, p. 287).

Die Geschichte dieser Redaktion ist nicht sehr interessant. Das Hauptverbreitungsgebiet ist Mitteleuropa mit gelegentlichen Ausläufern nach Osteuropa, England und Nordamerika. Die Redaktion ist erst seit dem 17. Jahrhundert bekannt, und ihre Wirkung reicht bis in die mündliche Überlieferung von heute.

III. Die Drohung des Bettlers.

Die älteste Fassung dieser Redaktion (= Thompson K 1771.3) bringt der Perser 'Ubaïd-i-Zākāni in seiner *Herzerfreuenden Schrift*, die er vielleicht um die Mitte des 14. Jahrhunderts verfaßt hat, da er 1370 oder 1371 gestorben ist. Unser Schwank ist von Horn in *Keleti Szemle*, 1,69 und von Christensen in *Acta Orientalia*, 3,17 veröffentlicht. Ich bringe die Inhaltsangabe nach Christensen:

Un derviche arriva à la porte d'un village et y vit une assemblée des anciens du village. Il dit: "Donnez-moi quelque chose, si non je jure par Dieu que je traiterai ce village de la même façon que j'ai traité tel autre village". Les hommes eurent peur et se dirent: "Il est à craindre, qu'il ne soit un sorcier ou un saint et qu'il ne détruise notre village". Ils lui donnèrent donc ce qu'il demandait. Après cela ils lui demandèrent: "Qu'est-ce que tu as fait de l'autre village dont tu parlais?" Le derviche rèpondit: "J'ai demandé l'aumône là, et on ne m'a rien donné, puis je m'en suis allé et je suis arrivé ici. Si vous ne m'aviez rien donné non plus, j'aurais quitté ce village de même pour m'en aller à un autre".

Es ist bekannt, daß Zākāni manche seiner Stoffe aus der arabischen Überlieferung entlehnt hat, so vor allem die Goha-Anekdoten (s. Basset in *Revue des Traditions populaires*, 11, 498; 15, 57 usw.; Horn in *Keleti Szemle*, 1, 222; Wesselski, *Hodscha Nasreddin*, 1, 230; 2, 181; Spies, *Orientalische Stoffe in den KHM der Brüder Grimm*, 1952, p. 38 usw.). Es nimmt daher nicht Wunder, daß unsere Geschichte ziemlich übereinstimmend im 16. Jahrhundert im arabischen *Nuzhat al udaba* auftaucht (s. die Übersetzung Bassets in *Revue des Traditions populaires*, 15, 461). Jedoch begegnet sie schon etwas früher, etwa zwischen 1490 und 1400 aufgezeichnet, auch als italienische Facetie, die Papanti in seiner Ausgabe: *Facezie e motti dei secoli XV e XVI* (Bologna, 1874) als Nr. 1 veröffentlicht hat (deutsche Übersetzung bei Wesselski, *Italienischer Volks- und Herrenwitz*, München 1912, p. 51):

Che in Hispagna a casa sua era stato uno povero, che andava mendicando con un bordone, a capo del quale era un ferro acuto et lungho; e quando chiedeva la limosina ad alcune, gli voltava la punta di decto bordone, come se gli volessi dare con epso, dicendo: Tale, dammi qualche cosa per l'amore di Dio, se no ... Di che seguiva, che molti, cognoscendolo matto et importuno, vendendosi vòlta la punta, et interpretando quello se no: io ti darò con questo bordone; per non havere a chonbatter con lui, gli davano la limosina. Segui un giorno, che, faccendo il decto povero questo acto a un cavaliere, huomo giovane et animoso; trovandosi la spada allato, come costumano in quel paese ciascun portarla; sdegnandosi questo cavaliere, messo mano alla spada, et voltàtosi al povero con epsa: Che se no, o non se no? Il povero incontinenti rispose: Se non, me n'andrò con Dio sanza danari. Et cosi per la più corta si parti.

Das ist natürlich, wenn auch in Einigem geändert, die gleiche Geschichte, wie sie uns in der persischen und in der arabischen Sammlung begegnete. Nur ist hier eingetreten, was schon einmal in der vorigen Redaktion in einer englischen Variante passierte, daß nämlich der Bedrohte nicht nachgibt, sondern wieder droht. Auch beruft sich der Bettler nicht auf das, was er schon einmal getan habe. Und schließlich wird die Drohung durch die Gebärde mit dem eisenbeschlagenen Stock noch verstärkt.

Es fällt schwer, diese Variationen unmittelbar aus der erwähnten orientalischen Überlieferung zu erklären. Vielleicht helfen hier einige Daten. Unsere Facetie ist nämlich gar nicht italienischen sondern spanischen Ursprungs. Der spanische Gesandte beim Papst Innocenz VIII. hat sie im Jahre 1486 dem Sekretär Lorenzos de Medici und einem Beamten der Signoria von Florenz erzählt. Anlaß war die Bedrohung der Florentiner durch den König von Frankreich, der sie gegen Ferrante II., König von Neapel, aufwiegeln wollte. Vielleicht liegt also eine politische Kontrafaktur vor, um den Widerstand der Florentiner durch ein Exempel zu kräftigen. Vielleicht gehen die Änderungen aber auch auf den weiteren Weg einer maurisch-spanischen als auf den direkten einer türkisch-italienischen Tradition zurück. Denn daß die Anekdote orientalischen Ursprungs ist, geht ebenso eindeutig wie aus ihrer älteren so auch aus ihrer neueren Geschichte hervor.

Der chronologischen Folge und dem ethnischen Traditionsbereich entsprechend, begegnet unser Schwank nunmehr recht häufig in dem Erzählkreis um den türkischen Hodscha-Nasreddin. Wesselski hat in der Einleitung zu seiner Nasreddin-Ausgabe klar herausgestellt, daß die Anekdoten um den älteren arabischen Goha und die um den jüngeren türkischen Hodscha seit dem 16. Jahrhundert, sicher aber seit 1631, dem Erscheinungsjahr des ersten, die Schwänke beider „Helden" vereinenden türkischen Volksbuches, durcheinandergehen (s. auch Basset in der Einleitung zu A. Mouliéras, *Les fourberies de Si Djeh'a*, Paris, 1892, p. 7). Das recht häufige Vorkommen unserer Anekdote in den ost- und südeuropäischen Sammlungen des 19. Jahrhunderts mag also mit einigem Recht auf ein höheres Alter innerhalb dieses Traditionskreises gedeutet werden.

Ich bringe aus dem reichen Material, das Wesselski (l. c., 2, p. 217) notiert, hier die Fassung, die Tewfik in der zweiten Hälfte des vorigen Jahrhunderts in der Türkei gesammelt hat und die kurz darauf in deutscher Übersetzung herauskam: Mehemed Tewfik, *Die Schwänke des Nassr-eddin und Buadem* (Leipzig, 1890), p. 55, Nr. 38. Buadem ist eine von Tewfik erfundene Gestalt, die er mit dem Schwankgut aus dem Nasreddin-Goha-Kreise ausgestattet hat (s. Wesselski, l. c., I, p. XLIV):

> Buadem stieg bei einer Hungersnot in das Dorf Kacht hinab und, nachdem er die Bauern beim Ortsvorstand versammelt hatte, sprach er: „Entweder, ihr gebt mir etwas zu essen, oder ich tue diesem Dorf, wie ich dem vorigen getan habe". Die Bauern, die ihn für einen Zauberer hielten, fürchteten sich und gaben ihm zu essen, so viel er wollte; dann baten sie ihn, er möge doch sagen, was er dem vorigen Dorfe angetan habe. Buadem sagte: „Ich bin in das vorige Dorf gekommen und habe eine Kleinigkeit verlangt; sie haben mir nichts gegeben, und da habe ich sie verlassen. Auch diesen Ort würde ich verlassen haben, wenn ihr mir nichts gegeben hättet". Mit diesen Worten entfernte er sich.

Eine sehr ähnliche Fassung teilt Tachmasib 1958 (!) aus der mündlichen Überlieferung Russisch-Aserbeidschans mit, hier wieder auf den Mullah Nasreddin
bezogen:

> Der Mullah kommt hungrig in ein Dorf und befiehlt den auf dem Marktplatz sitzen-
> den Leuten: „Laßt sofort meinem Esel Futter geben und sättigt mich, sonst werde
> ich das tun, was ich im Nachbardorfe getan habe". Die erschrockenen Dorfbewohner
> erfüllen sein Begehren und einer fragt, was er dem Nachbardorf angetan habe. Ant-
> wort: „Sie gaben mir nichts zu essen und da ging ich fort. Wenn ihr mir nichts ge-
> geben hättet, wäre ich sofort in ein anderes Dorf gegangen." An dieser Antwort er-
> kannten die Dorfbewohner den Mullah Nasreddin und behielten ihn für eine Weile
> als Gast (M. G. Taschmasib, *Anekdoty Molly Nasreddina*, Baku, 1958, p. 318f.,
> Anm. 37).

Diese Fassungen ähneln ganz und gar denen bei Zākāni und im *Nuzhat al udaba*.
Jedoch tritt in einer kroatischen Version, die Wesselski übersetzt hat (l. c., Vol. 2,
p. 134, Nr. 450), eine neue Pointierung auf, die nunmehr für den südeuropäischen
Traditionsbereich charakteristisch wird. Der bettelnde und drohende Zigeuner,
um einen solchen handelt es sich nun fast immer, will nicht fortgehen, sondern
etwas tun, was er noch nie getan hat, nämlich arbeiten:

> Einmal ging der Hodscha Nasreddin spazieren; ein junger Zigeuner lief ihm nach
> und bettelte, er solle ihm etwas schenken. Dem Hodscha, der die Zigeuner haßte,
> fiel es nicht ein, sich umzudrehen, geschweige denn ihm etwas zu geben. Plötzlich
> schrie der Zigeuner aus vollem Halse: „Schenk mir etwas, Herr, sonst werde ich et-
> was tun, was ich noch nie getan habe!" Nasreddin drehte sich um, warf ihm einen Para
> zu und fragte ihn, was er zu tun beabsichtigt hätte. Darauf antwortete der Zigeuner:
> „Ja, Herr, hättest du mir nichts geschenkt, so hätte ich arbeiten müssen, und das
> habe ich noch nie getan".

Die gleiche Zigeuneranekdote, allerdings nicht mit dem Hodscha, finden wir in
Jugoslawien (Krauss, *Zigeunerhumor*, p. 186) und in Ungarn (J. Kónyi, *A minden
kor nevetö Democritus*, Vol. 2, Buda, 1815, Nr. 192; *Ethnographia*, 1929, p. 94;
L. György, *A magyar anekdota története és egyetemes kapcsolatai*, Budapest, 1934,
p. 122f., Nr. 67: hier sind noch weitere 16 ungarische Varianten aus der Schwank-
literatur und der oralen Überlieferung verzeichnet.
In einer modernen Variante wird unsere Geschichte wiederum auf den Hodscha
selbst bezogen. Gregor von Rezzori teilt sie uns in seinen *Maghrebinischen Geschichten* (Hamburg, 1958, p. 48) mit:

> Einmal aber, so erzählt man sich, als die Not im Lande so groß geworden war, daß
> niemand mehr dem weisen Hodscha etwas gab, lief er zum Gospodar (das ist: der
> Vertreter des Königs) und drohte: „Herr, gib mir einen Beutel Gold, sonst werde

ich tun, was ich noch nicht getan habe!" Der großmütige Gospodar — damals ein Mitglied des Hauses Kantakukuruz —, erschrocken über diese Drohung, ließ ihm das Geforderte übergeben. „Wahrlich!" sprach der Hodscha, „hättest du mich nicht gehört, o Verwalter des Königs über seine Lande, ich hätte tatsächlich arbeiten müssen".

Eine recht alte, an die östliche Essensbettelform und an die archaische Vaterparallele aus der ersten Redaktion anschließende Version hat sich, wie mir Isidor Levin, Leningrad, mitteilte, wieder bei den Juden Polens und Litauens erhalten:

Der Bettelnde bedroht die Einwohner: wenn er nichts zu essen erhalte, werde er tun, was sein Vater getan habe. Er erhält Essen und auf die Frage, was sein Vater getan habe, antwortet er: „Wenn mein Vater nichts zu essen bekam, ging er eben hungrig fort" (Ch. Bloch, *Hersch Ostropoler, ein jüdischer Eulenspiegel des 18. Jahrhunderts*, Berlin-Wien, 1921, p. 118; H. Lew, *Żydowski humor*, Warszawa, 1895, p. 45).

Eine ganz ähnliche, aber in der Situation noch groteskere Variante bringt Jacob Richman in seinen *Laughs from Jewish Lore* (New York and London, 1926, p. 175f.):

"Anything to eat?" asked the weary traveler of the village innkeeper, arriving late at night. "Sorry, sir," replied the owner of the tavern, "but my wife is already asleep, and I know nothing about the kitchen. I have a room for you, tho, right near mine." An hour later the proprietor of the hostelry was aroused from his slumber by his terrified wife. "Listen, Sam," she whispered in terror and excitement. The guest, who had been assigned to a room adjoining theirs, was heard through the thin wall pacing up and down the room, muttering menacingly: "If I don't get something to eat I'll do the same as my father used to do." The hotelkeeper jumped out of bed and started cautiously for the stranger's room. Timidly he opened the door and peeped in. The hungry guest, with hair disheveled, looked wild. He kept on striding across the room repeating the threat. "Tell me, please, what is it that your father used to do?" finally ventured the host, eyeing the strange patron. "Before I tell you, I must have something to eat," declared the desperate guest. Quickly the woman ran down to the kitchen and prepared supper for the guest. "Well," resumed the host, as the ravenous man had finished the meal, "tell me now what your father used to do." "My father," declared the violent man, "when he got no supper, went to bed hungry."

Das Verbreitungsgebiet dieser Redaktion ist somit ebenso wie die Wanderwege ihrer Varianten klar: Eine alte arabische Goha-Anekdote wird einerseits im 14. Jahrhundert von dem Perser Zākāni aufgegriffen, wandert weiter zu den Türken und von dort nach dem Balkan. Die archaischen, ethno-geographisch isolierten jüdischen Fassungen sind wohl von der einwandernden jüdischen Bevölkerung nach Polen und Litauen mitgenommen worden. Ein früher arabischer Ausläufer wird auch den Weg über das maurische Spanien nach dem Italien des 15. Jahrhunderts genommen haben. Eine ähnliche Fernübertragung (wenn nicht überhaupt nur einfache literarische Lokalisierung vorliegt) scheint bei der Fassung vorzuliegen, die Edmont Guérard, *Dictionnaire encyclopédique d'anecdotes modernes et anciennes, françaises et étrangères* (Paris, 1872, Vol. 2, s. v. Mendiants) nach England verlegt. Es ist die gleiche Version wie in den Varianten vom bettelnden Zigeuner, nur etwas umständlicher erzählt.

Schließlich ist unsere Geschichte wiederum nach Nordamerika gewandert. In einer Fassung, die Melville D. Landon in seinem Buche *Wit and Humor of the Age* ([Chicago], 1883, p. 106) mitteilt, ist sie mit der Frau des reichen Bankiers Vanderbilt in Zusammenhang gebracht worden:

> Equally as modest a man was a beggar who called on Mrs. Vanderbilt and said: "Unless you give me aid, Mrs. Vanderbilt, I am afraid I shall have to resort to something which I greatly dislike to do." Mrs. Vanderbilt handed him a dollar, and asked compassionately: "What is it, poor man, that I have saved you from?" "Work," was the mournful answer.

Ähnliches, nur ohne persönliche Fixierung, weiß endlich Frederick Meier, *The Joke Tellers Joke Book* (Philadelphia, 1944), p. 32 zu berichten.

IV. Die verlorene Reisetasche.

Von dieser nicht bei Thompson verzeichneten Redaktion sind mir nur Nasreddin-Varianten bekannt geworden. Ich gebe die Fassung nach Ignácz Kúnos, *Naszreddin hodsa tréfái* (Budapest, 1899, p. 80, Nr. 138), der sie der schon erwähnten Sammlung und Ausgabe von Tewfik (und zwar der türkischen Fassung) entnommen hat (s. Wesselski l. c., Vol. 2, p. 217, der auch weitere bibliographische Angaben macht):

> Der Hodscha hat seinen Mantelsack verloren. Er gibt bekannt: entweder findet man ihn oder er weiß, was er zu tun hat. Die Dorfbewohner suchen alles gründlich nach, finden den Mantelsack und überreichen ihn dem Hodscha. Neugierig fragt man ihn, was er ihnen denn angetan hätte, wenn der Quersack nicht wieder aufgetaucht wäre. „Ich hätte folgendes getan", antwortet der Hodscha, „zu Hause habe ich einen alten Sack; daraus hätte ich mir einen neuen machen lassen".

Wie mir Andreas Tietze mitteilte, ist dies einer der beliebtesten Schwänke in der Türkei. Tietze teilte mir noch folgende Variante mit: Ahmet Halit Yaşaroğlu, *Nasreddin Hoca* (Istanbul, 1950, p. 62, Nr. 134). Lucien Gerschel, Levallois, wies mich auf Kemaleddine Chukru, *Vie de Nasreddine Hodja* (Verlag Kanaat, Istanbul, s. a., p. 55), Walter Anderson auf *Anekdoty o chodže Nasreddine* (übers. v. V. A. Gordlevskij, 2. Aufl. Moskau 1957, p. 82 Nr. 139) und auf M. G. Tachmasib, *Anekdoty Molly Nasreddina* (Baku 1958) p. 150 (mündl. aus kaukasisch-tatarischer Überlieferung in Russisch-Aserbeidschan). Maja Bošković-Stulli, Zagreb, schließlich machte mich auf eine gleichlautende Variante in *Behar* 6 (Sarajevo 1905/6, p. 106, Nr. 7) aufmerksam.

Die Herkunft aus dem Nasreddin-Volksbuch und damit aus dem regional-ethnischen Bereich des östlichen mediterranen Raumes liegt auf der Hand. Die Redaktion hat jedoch nicht die Verbreitung wie die vorhergehende gefunden.

V. Einzelformen.

Mir sind noch einige singuläre Formen bekannt geworden, in denen das Grundmotiv der schrecklichen Drohung: Entweder...oder...!" besondere Ausgestaltung erfahren hat.

Vielleicht von der dritten Redaktion und zwar von der Zigeunerfassung beeinflußt ist eine niederdeutsche Anekdote, die Fritz Specht, *Niederdeutsche Scherze* (4. Aufl., Hamburg, 1954, p. 45) aufgezeichnet hat:

> Der Gemeindediener eines kleinen Dorfes will nicht mehr für den geringen Lohn, den er erhält, arbeiten. Er droht daher dem Bürgermeister: „Wenn ich nicht mehr Geld kriege, werde ich etwas tun, was ich wirklich nicht gern tue". Der Bürgermeister begütigt ihn, setzt die Lohnforderung im Gemeinderat durch und fragt dann den Amtsdiener, was er vorgehabt und was er nicht gern getan hätte. Antwort: Ich hätte für den alten Lohn weiter arbeiten müssen.

Eine ganz andere Fabel weist eine niederdeutsche Version auf, die von dem schon erwähnten Arend Warmund in seinem *Sassischen Döneken-Bok* (Hamburg, 1829, p. 57, Nr. 42) veröffentlicht worden ist:

> Ein Bauer erhält von seiner Frau, die stärker als er ist, häufig Prügel. Einmal kommt ein Nachbar dazu, der Bauer schämt sich und begehrt auf: „Wenn du mich noch einmal schlägst, sollst du sehen, was ich tue!" „Was willst du tun?" ruft die Frau und geht von neuem auf ihn los. „Es nicht dulden!" sagt der Mann und läuft aus dem Haus.

Diese Anekdote vom verprügelten Hasenfuß muß weiter verbreitet sein, als meine wenigen Belege zeigen, denn wir finden sie, wenn auch in etwas anderer Form, in Rußland wieder, wo sie Afanasjev, *Narodnyja russkija skazki* (Vol. 3, Moskau, 1957, p. 286, Nr. 490) aufgezeichnet und A. N. Andrejev in seinem

Ukazatel' skazočnik sjiuzhetov systeme Aarne (Leningrad, 1929) mit der Nummer
*2071 begabt hat:

> Eines Nachts verprügelt man einen Dummkopf und lacht ihn am anderen Tage oben-
> drein noch aus. Da sagt er: „Dankt Gott, daß die Nacht hell war, sonst hätte ich euch
> einen Tort angetan!" „Was für einen?" „Ich hätte mich versteckt".

• • •

Wie ist die Variabilität der Motive bei gleicher Idee zu erklären? Liegt Polyge-
nese auf Grund gemeinmenschlicher Emotionalität und Mentalität vor? Oder ist
an einmalige Schöpfung zu denken, deren komisches Erzeugnis zu ähnlichen Er-
findungen provozierte? Unser unzureichendes Material wird kaum eine präzise
Antwort auf diese Frage gestatten. Immerhin sind drei unserer Redaktionen
(Nr. 1, 3 und 4), darunter die beiden ältesten, im Orient entstanden. War also die
Idee dort zu Hause? Kam östlicher Geist nicht los von ihr, und gestaltete er sie
in sprudelnder Schöpferlaune zu immer neuen Fabeleien? Und gab er sie dem
Abendland weiter nebst einigen der fertigen Bilder? Wir wissen es nicht. Manches
mag auf Herkunft der einfachen Form, des Leitgedankens, aus dem Osten deuten.
Anderes, die verschiedenen Ansätze und Formwerdungen auch in Europa, weist
auf die Ubiquität der Idee.

Aber wenn dem so ist, wenn dieses „Entweder...oder...!", diese bramarbasi-
rende Droherei, hinter der nichts steckt als hohle Phrase, wenn dieses Menschliche
und Allzumenschliche wirklich der großen gemeinsamen Emotionalschicht ent-
springt (und warum sollte es das eigentlich nicht?), dann muß sich umso eher in
ihren regionalen Formwerdungen, in diesen eigenständigen Fabeleien also, so
etwas wie eine ethnisch bedingte Geistigkeit zeigen. Der Genius der Völker hat
noch immer aus allem Kollektiven das ihm angemessen Originale erwachsen
lassen.

Ist es, in diesem Aspekt gesehen, nicht bezeichnend, daß schon die erste abend-
ländische Aufzeichnung, die des Goten Theodulf, entgleiste und daß die Geschichte
dieser Redaktion bei uns eine fortschreitende Degeneration der ursprünglichen
Form aufweist? Aber fragen wir nach dem Besonderen der europäischen und der
orientalischen Fassungen.

Schon ein erster Blick zeigt, daß die Grundsituation in der einzig für den Vergleich in Betracht kommenden europäischen Version, in der nämlich von den beiden Fuhrleuten, eine entschieden gröbere als in den orientalischen ist. Immer
handelt es sich hier um die fast hautnahe Anrempelei zweier, anfangs jedenfalls
durchaus gleichwertiger Parteien. In den östlichen Formen steht dagegen der
einzelne meist von Anbeginn gegen eine Vielheit, wodurch allein schon das Motiv

von der anmaßenden Drohung an grotesker Substanz gewinnt. Im Westen gebiert sich der Witz aus dem gleichwertig-aktiven Zustand der Handelnden, im Osten dagegen aus rein passivem Eingangsgeschehen: die handelnde Person ist entweder bestohlen worden oder leidet Not. In Europa sind Situation, Handlung und Pointe höchst einfach und gradlinig: daß von zweien einer auf engstem Wege ausweichen muß, liegt notwendig in der Natur der Sache. Im Orient ist die Geschichte viel komplizierter und die angedrohte Alternative vor allem nicht zwangsläufig: Der Derwisch brauchte natürlich seinen Sattel nicht zu schleppen, der Zigeuner nicht zu arbeiten, der bestohlene Hodscha sich nicht eine neue Tasche machen zu lassen. Aber die freie Entscheidung zum angedrohten, banal-lächerlichen Tun macht die Pointe gerade grotesker, brillanter. Es ist durch und durch intellektueller Witz, was hier vorliegt, und nicht bare Situationskomik wie in Europa. Vielleicht korrespondiert daher auch die im Grunde passive Entscheidung beider Teile in den östlichen Redaktionen mehr mit dem Wesen des Orientalen, was wiederum, wenigstens soweit es die bedrohte Partei betrifft, die Kontrafakturen im Englischen und Spanischen hervorgerufen hat: der Bedrohte läßt sich eben nicht einschüchtern. Es ist ja allgemeine Erkenntnis, daß morgenländischer Witz resignierter, abendländischer resoluter ist (s. etwa K. Ranke, *Der Schwank vom Schmaus der Einfältigkeit*, FFC 159, Helsinki, 1955, p. 10). Und es fragt sich nun überhaupt, wenn wir die Grundhaltung des Schwankes aus Gemüts- und Mentalwerten des Orients herleiten wollen, ob die europäische Fassung nicht aufgepfropftes Reis ist.

Ich sprach davon, daß die Geschichte dieser zweiten Redaktion nicht sehr interessant sei. Das stimmt! Aber sie zeigt uns dafür etwas anderes: sie weist uns nämlich ganz eindeutig darauf hin, daß in ihr nicht das Thema, sondern das Motiv, nicht die Drohung also, sondern die Situation das ursprüngliche Element gewesen sein muß. Nicht ihre Geschichte, aber die Vorgeschichte ergibt so einen nicht uninteressanten Beitrag zum Verhältnis von Bild und Idee, Motiv und Thema.

Wir sahen, wie der Orient die gleiche Idee zu immer neuen Bildern gestaltete. Diese spielerische Freude am Thema ist sicher ein Indiz für seine Autogenese im dortigen Volkstum. Wir sehen nun, wie Europa die gleiche Situation zu immer neuen Fabeln formt. Nicht die Idee von der grotesken Drohung, sondern das Motiv von zwei sich auf schmalem Wege oder Stege treffenden Wesen, von denen keines weichen will, hat unseren wie auch ähnliche Schwänke inspiriert. Ich erinnere nur an die ebenso alte wie berühmte Geschichte von Diogenes und Kriton (die im übrigen auch von anderen historischen Persönlichkeiten erzählt wird), die einander auf engem Stege begegnen. „Ich weiche keinem Dummkopf", rief Kriton. „Ich tue das mit Vorliebe", antwortete Diogenes und trat zurück. Oder ich denke an die nicht minder bekannte Fabel des Romulus von den beiden Böcken,

die einander ebenfalls auf einem schmalen Stege gegenüberstehen. Keiner will
weichen, beide fallen beim Zusammenprall ins Wasser (AT 202*, Mot. W 167.1).
Oder ich führe als letztes den Schwank aus dem im Jahre 1630 zuerst veröffentlichten *Banquet of Jests* des Archie Armstrong an (letzte Ausgabe, Edinburgh,
1872, p. 216):

> Two Gentlemen meeting, the one jostled the other from the Wall, and had almost
> made him to measure his length in the channel: who by much adoe recovering him-
> selfe came up close to him, and asked him whether he were in jest, or in earnest? He
> told him plainely, that what he did was in earnest. And I am glad, replies the other,
> that you told me so: for I protest, I love no such jesting: by which words he put off
> the quarell. (s. dazu Mot. K 1771.1).

Wir sehen, der Orient kreist seit frühst um die Komik der Idee und formt sie zu
immer neuen Bildern. Europa kreist seit fast ebenso langer Zeit um die Komik
der Situation und kommt nicht los von ihr. Was liegt also näher als die Annahme,
daß in unserem Falle, also in der zweiten Redaktion, das orientalische Thema von
der schrecklichen Drohung dem älteren europäischen Bilde von der Starrköpfig-
keit zweier sich Begegnender überlegt wurde.

Hier wären Aspekte auf die schöpferischen Dispositionen und Potenzen der
beiden ethnischen Bereiche gegeben, aber sie liegen nicht in den beschränkten
Möglichkeiten dieser bescheidenen Untersuchung, und es bedürfte dazu wohl auch
eines weit umfangreicheren komparativen Studiums.

Wenn ich jedoch mit meinen kleinen Analysen einen Hinweis auf diese Problematik gegeben und Ihnen, lieber Archer Taylor, damit eine kleine Freude bereitet
haben sollte, wäre ihr Zweck vollkommen erfüllt.

Christian Albrechts-Universität, Kiel

AT—FRIEND OF LIBRARIES

STANLEY PARGELLIS

It was in the spring of 1945 that Archer Taylor first came to the Newberry as a Fellow, for three months. A Fellowship then meant that the recipient should spend some of his time in recommending purchases of books in his special field, in occasionally running through a bookdealer's catalogue, in writing perhaps an article for the Library *Bulletin,* and in giving advice now and then to the Librarian on how to be a Librarian. Without stipend save for the too few times he has been back in residence, AT has been a Fellow ever since. His letters to the Librarian, upon which this brief article is based, run into the hundreds, some of them several pages long, some a single line. The Newberry counts it as one of its everlasting blessings that it should have been taken under AT's wing.

The combination in one person of bookman and scholar rarely occurs. A bookman is like a collector, is indeed a collector, in the best sense of that much abused word. He knows what the great and not so great books in his speciality are; he knows their market value; and he is willing to take a chance on some offering which he has not seen before but which sounds, from its title, as if it might be useful. He also knows the books which are of no particular merit. The scholar, making use of the books in a way the bookman does not, distinguishes between editions, knows what has been so well-edited that an expensive early edition is not needed; sees what a volume could contribute in a field little explored but needing exploration, and builds up lists of such desirable unknowns, according to his own standards, from recondite sources usually beyond the bookman's ability to use. When once there were many such scholar-bibliophiles, AT is one of the few to be found in this century.

In most of his letters to the Newberry, AT refers by numbers to a bookdealer's catalogue, and recommends purchases. Sometimes the recommendation is emphatic. "As for the Gesner of 1583, let me say that Adrien Baillet said in 1685–86 that he had never seen a copy and doubted its existence, and Gilles Ménage in commenting on Baillet said that Baillet should have known that the book was never published,—but it *was*. And here it is." And again: "Here's something, really something. Stolle's *Anleitung* is one of the real books. You should grab it... Stolle belongs in the list of the big boys." And writing about Nanus Mirabellius, *Polyanthea*, Savona, 1503: "I know something about this book. This is the first edition. I have striven to find somewhere a copy of the first edition, but in vain. The *Polyanthea* is perhaps the most popular and widely used collection of quotations. It was later revised... Just back your ears and cable for this." Yet again, "... buy the Brühl catalogue. This is one of the big ones. Brühl was a rival of Bünau and competed in the building of a library... The Brühl catalogue is rare because the fourth volume, which is present here, was virtually destroyed in a Dresden fire... Rub the spot where it hurts, you will get over the hurt and the set will be an ornament..." And once again. "Grosius.—There are, Sir, three attempts to make or continue the compilation of the *Messkataloge* before 1610. These are Nicolaus Basse, Grossius (usually with two *s*), and Clessius (*Unius seculi ...elenchus*). I disremember which of these you have. This is *not* a precursor of the *Messkataloge*, which had started in 1564, but a cumulation of them. At any rate, Grossius is much the rarest of the three. I hate to see you spend the money, but considering this and that, the book seems worth buying."

Sometimes a letter consists wholly of a long list of items from a catalogue— "This is a good grist of books"—with brief comments: "This I think you might take"; "I think you could pass this up"; "probably yes but I don't press you"; "definitely yes"; "think about this"; "something tells me you should take this"; "too high for an odd vol."; "if you don't take this, I will." Occasionally, out of the myriad odd bits of knowledge in AT's head, would come a remark such as this on a "dirt-cheap incunabulum": "I think you could wisely pick it up for 2 pounds ten. Incidentally, did you ever hear that 2 pounds ten was a codeword of clerks meaning that shoplifters are about? Two hands, ten fingers."

There are scores and scores of books in the Newberry which once belonged to AT. Most of them came as gifts, because he thought they would feel more at home among others of their kind. Once at least he offered to present a little volume, torn and in wretched condition, provided the Library "would make an honest woman of her." In his sustained effort "to build on Walton Place" a great library of reference and bibliographical works, he would send two volumes bound in one, on condition that one of them be rebound and returned to him. Of the Rivadeneira,

1609, he wrote: "I part with it somewhat regretfully, since it is technically a noble job and might give me occasion for an essay to the effect that bibliography has not greatly improved through the centuries." Writing about a number of Naudé items in a catalogue, he says: "Please take the military bibliography... If you speak sweetly, *and buy the military bibliography*, I'll sell you—although I don't want to do so—the first ed. of Naudé, *Bibliographia politica*, and fill in your collection... Naudé is a real guy, and you have his *Bibliotheca Cordesiana*, and somebody will have to write an essay on Naudé the bibliographer."

It does not take an extremely discerning reader to judge from some of these comments that the Librarian to whom they were addressed was often foolish enough, or impecunious enough, to pass up a recommendation. He has regretted it since. Then would come a word of encouragement: "To cheer you up, there aren't so very many more of these catalogues that seem worth buying to me." "You have taken Moller, *Bibliotheca Septentrionalis*, and I'm glad to know that one more big seventeenth-century bibliog. has found a secure resting place. You are now right on top of the world." "I note with sorrow, anger, and surprise the perpendicular trend in prices... There can be no establishment of a new important library. No purse can buy the books." That last quotation, which was by way of congratulation and cheer, and therefore encouragement, was written in 1948; the Librarian expects to learn shortly from what sources AT will find words to describe prices twelve years later.

In the letter files are three long statements, written by request, which contain AT's philosophy of library-building, specifically directed to the Newberry's needs. He believes in digging deeply into some aspect of a subject rather than spreading one's funds over the whole. Find a subject of importance which is unexploited and where therefore prices are still reasonable, find out what the essential books are, and buy them, in the original if possible, if not, in photo-reproduction. He quotes "the line in Faust to which I so often return: 'In der Beschränkung zeigt sich erst der Meister.'"

What some of those subjects are shall not here be divulged, for AT is still writing letters. How he finds time to write them, sometimes three or four a week if the catalogues contain good pickings, and at the same time to write to other libraries fortunate enough to have gained his approbation, and at the same time to carry on other correspondence, and to produce his books—is a miracle unexplained. During many of these years he and his wife were building, partly with their own hands, the new house by the redwoods high above Napa valley, and his letters are full of the difficulties and the successes, as well as of the problems of marketing Bing cherries and walnuts. It is probably a secret—and one he will not thank me for telling—that AT occasionally thought of relaxing. In a letter of May, 1946,

7*

after writing about the assured publication of 950 riddles from oral tradition, he confesses: "With this and that, I now think of sitting under a tree and watching the world." Then comes a letter of June 4: "Some rare and difficult Turkish riddles have come to hand and I am in an excellent humor." By June 21 he was fussing a bit with Italian local bibliography to 1700, and with other oddments, "but did not accomplish more than to push the frontiers ahead a little in each field." But by mid-July he was skirmishing on the outskirts of a general discussion to be entitled The History of Universal Bibliographies, Handbooks of Bibliography, Guides to Best Books, and Universal Subject Indexes. "I shall probably (in fact, I have) turned up some strange beasts in that jungle. Of this more when I have learned what tricks they can do." Those beasts, along with at least twenty other "oddments," have occupied his time since, and he has not yet conquered all of their tricks. Three volumes have appeared; the fourth is still in process.

Again, AT may not thank me for saying that he, like the rest of us, is concerned about the humanities in the mid-twentieth century. "I was not cheered by my reflections on the state of the humanities. I cannot precisely put my finger on the loose screw, but something is wrong with the whole works and is doing serious damage." He attended a meeting, listened to papers that were "a bit Alexandrine. Just why I think so and just what can or ought to be done forms a dark confused mass in the back of my mind. The papers were good, were better than the run of the mine stuff at the national meeting, but... And yet I believe that all the doctors and chemists and agriculturists are working hard to make life easier for the world in order to give scholars time and opportunity to do their stuff, but... (The leaders are AT's own).

One of the loose screws perhaps is that graduate students are not being encouraged to become Archer Taylors. Some teachers deliberately tell their students to put on blinders when they read books or collections of manuscripts, and to take notes only on material that contributes to their theses. Let loose in a wide, lush meadow, full of every variety of growth, they are told they must pick ragweed only, for that is what they are writing about. No wonder, when and if they become Fellows of a Library, they can recommend only ragweed, without being able to discriminate between varieties, because they have little to compare it with. AT has always had several pots boiling, ragweed in only one, and all of them he stirs. He is always alert for new projects, and is always "cracking nuts," i.e., tough little problems. When he needs to, he asks help in his nut-cracking, from scholars all over the world. Publication, a bugbear which worries young scholars, has never bothered him overmuch. Somehow, somewhere or other, his works get published. He might say that there are not more than four hundred libraries or people who could possibly be interested in one of his books, yet he takes some delight when an edition of double that size sells out within a few months.

What began, in this brief essay, to be a tribute to AT for his help to libraries, and to one in particular, has turned into a plea to scholars to keep their horizons broad. Specialization may be all right for the scientist, though there are doubts on that score; specialization is death for the scholar in the humanities.

The Newberry Library,
Chicago, Illinois

„DIE ZEHNTE TOCHTER"
EINE STUDIE ZU EINER GOTTSCHEER BALLADE

Erich Seemann

Beim Erscheinen von Adolf Hauffens Monographie über *Die deutsche Sprachinsel Gottschee* (1895) war Gelegenheit geboten, eine stattliche Anzahl bisher unbekannter deutscher Volkslieder kennen zu lernen. Zu ihnen rechnet auch eine Ballade, die den Hörer durch die sie beherrschende Gestalt ausnehmend fesselt und die sich ihm irgendwie unverlierbar einprägt.

> Eine Mutter von neun Töchtern betet Tag und Nacht, daß ihr zehntes Kind ein Knabe sei. Aber wiederum wird ihr ein Töchterlein beschert. Als dieses Mogreatizle (Margretlein) sieben Jahre alt ist, zwingen es himmlische Mächte, das Elternhaus zu verlassen und in die weite Welt zu ziehen. Das Kind nimmt den Schicksalsspruch an und kehrt auch dann nicht um, als man es zurückruft, weil die Mutter, die wohl mit ganz besonderer Liebe an ihrer gefährdeten Jüngsten hängt, nach dem Abschied in Ohnmacht gesunken ist.

Das Lied hatte s. Zt. Lehrer Perz in Brunnsee/Studeno, einem Dorf etwa 13 km sö.lich der Stadt Gottschee gelegen, aufgezeichnet (Hauffen S. 322). Späterhin zeichnete Ferdinand Erker im Zuge der Erhebungen für das geplante *Österreichische Volksliedwerk* 4 km nwn.lich von Gottschee, in Windischdorf/Slovenska vas eine weitere Variante auf; eine dritte Fassung wurde 1937 von France Marolt in Nesseltal/Koprivnik, 13 km soo.lich von Gottschee, notiert; sie ist veröffentlicht mit näheren Ausführungen von Marolt 1939 im *Kočevski Zbornik* S. 239ff. Alle drei Fassungen sind also im nächsten Umkreis der Stadt Gottschee zu Tage getreten; aus dem übrigen Teil der Sprachinsel besitzen wir keinerlei Aufzeichnungen des Liedes. Die Fassungen bei Hauffen und Marolt entsprechen sich

102

auf lange Strecken wörtlich; inhaltlich bemerkenswert ist nur, daß die Maroltsche Fassung von der Mutter des Mädchens berichtet, daß sie eine Edelfrau war und ein Schloß mit grünem Garten bewohnte. Die Fassung aus Windischdorf weicht inhaltlich in manchen Zügen von den beiden anderen ab; da sie noch unveröffentlicht ist, teilen wir sie mit.

	Übertragung
's hot a Muet'r neun Teacht'rlein.	Es hat eine Mutter neun Töchterlein.
Benn shi von dan zeh'nt'n shbong'r ischt gebân,	Als sie mit dem zehnten schwanger ist gewesen,
Shi ziehot olle Gottschbage u',	Zog sie auf alle Wallfahrten,
/: 'aß ihr Gott lei gabot a jüngen Shuhn. :/	/: Daß ihr Gott wohl gebe einen jungen Sohn. :/
Gott hot ihr bid'r gab'n a Teacht'rle,	Gott hat ihr wieder gegeben ein Töchterlein,
/: A Teacht'rle, a Mogreatizle. :/	/: Ein Töchterlein, ein Margretlein. :/
/: Shi ziechot's auf in Gottesch Num'. :/	/: Sie zieht es auf in Gottes Namen. :/
Benn ummar hent kahm' de shib'n Juhr,	Als heran sind gekommen die sieben Jahr',
's gianot austreib'n shein Vuet'rsch Guet,	Geht es austreiben seines Vaters Vieh,
's treibet aus shein Vuet'rsch Guet.	Es treibet aus seines Vaters Vieh.
Am Toare hot's vunn' a Zedele.	Am Tore hat's gefunden ein Zettelchen.
Af dan Zedelein schteat's alei asho,	Auf dem Zettelchen steht's wohl nur also,
'aß es müß gian af deu Zahinte.	Daß es muß gehn „auf die Zehnte".
's truget dos Zedele in Vuet'r schian:	Sie trägt das Zettelchen zum Vater schön:
"Sho leshet Ihr dos Zedele!"	„So leset Ihr das Zettelchen!"
/: Ar leshet u' dos Zedele:/	/: Er lieset durch das Zettelchen. :/
Asho du schprichet d'r Vuet'r schian:	Also da spricht der Vater schön:
"Oi Muet'r, Muet'r, du liebeu mein!	„O Mutter, Mutter, du liebe mein,
Sho pochescht du a großes Proat,	So du bäckst ein großes Brot,
Sho tue dos Zedele in deu Mitte hinein,	So tu das Zettelchen in die Mitte hinein,
Sho z'rtoil dos Proat in zeh'n Toile,	So zerteile das Brot in zehn Teile,
In zeh'n Toile, nar olle gleich!"	In zehn Teile wohl alle gleich!"
De Muet'r pochet a großes Proat,	Die Mutter backt ein großes Brot,
's Zedele tut shi in de Mitte hinein.	's Zettelchen tut sie in die Mitte hinein.
Shi z'rtoilet 's Proat in zeh'n Toile schian,	Sie zerteilt das Brot in zehn Teile schön,
/: An ältischt'n, bie an jingischt'n. :/	/: Dem Ältesten wie dem Jüngsten. :/
/: Dos Zedele ischt bid'r kahmen af's Mogreatizle. :/	/: Das Zettelchen ist wieder gekommen auf Margretlein. :/
"Sho pehiet Eu' Gott, Vuet'r lieb'r mein,	„So behüt Euch Gott, lieber Vater mein,
Vuet'r lieb'r mein, Muet'r liebeu mein,	Lieber Vater mein, liebe Mutter mein,
Muet'r liebeu mein, mein Shbescht'rlein!	Liebe Mutter mein, liebe Schwesterlein!
Sho shich i' Eu' heint, doch nimm'rmehr."	So seh' ich Euch heut', doch nimmermehr."

Mogreatizle ziehet an Vuet'rsch Gurt'n aúßin,
Únd noch lafet deu ältischte Shbescht'r mon.
"Gea hint'rshin, Mogreatizle!
Dein Múet'r deu ischt schon gestoarb'n,
De Múet'r dein ischt schon geschtoarb'n,
In Vuet'r zintent schei de Kärzlein schon
     uen."
"Nar shein shei geschtoarb'n in Góttesch
     Num'!
I' múß lei gian af deu Zahinte."

Margretlein zieht an Vaters Garten hinaus,
Und ihm läuft die älteste Schwester nach:
,,Gehe zurück doch, Margretlein!
Deine Mutter die ist schon gestorben,
Die Mutter dein ist schon gestorben
Dem Vater zünden sie schon die Kerzlein an."

,,So seien sie gestorben in Gottes Namen!

Ich muß wohl gehen auf die Zehnte."

Vom Deutschen her gesehen mutet schon das Anfangsmotiv fremdartig an:
Kein deutsches Volkslied erzählt davon, daß eine Mutter der Reihe nach neun
bzw. zehn Töchter zur Welt bringt. Beim südslavischen Volkslied sind aber solche
Angaben keineswegs selten. Einige Beispiele seien genannt, in denen, wie in unse-
rem Gottscheer Liede, die jüngste Tochter nach ihrer Wesensart oder ihrem
Schicksal in Gegensatz tritt zu den übrigen Geschwistern.

Wenn in diesen Liedern ein solcher Töchtersegen gelegentlich als Fluch empfunden wird, so ist dies nicht verwunderlich bei einem Volke, das Jahrhunderte lang
unter türkischer Herrschaft stand oder von ihr bedroht wurde und so allen Grund
hatte, auf die Erhaltung seiner Wehrkraft bedacht zu sein. Aber auch der bäuer-
liche Mensch betrachtet Töchter als Kinder eines ,,fremden Hauses" und sieht
den Ruin seines Besitztums voraus, wenn er nur Töchter hinterlassen wird.[1]

Neun Töchter zieht die Mutter auf, flucht aber der letzten, Janja mit Namen: ,,Mö-
gen Dich die Drachen holen oder die Vilen!" Als Janja zur mannbaren Jungfrau
herangereift ist, hört sie die kranke Mutter reden: ,,Wäre Janja ein Knabe, so würde
sie mir Wasser aus dem Strašivice-Gebirge holen." Sofort ergreift sie einen Eimer.
An der Quelle erblickt sie ein Wunder: Drei Rosen wachsen über ihr, und die dritte
sagt zu ihr: ,,Schöpfe Wasser der Mutter zur Gesundung, doch komme bei Sonnen-
untergang zu uns; wir werden ein gutes Mahl richten." Als die Mutter von der
heimkehrenden Tochter erfährt, was vorgefallen ist, schließt sie Janja im Keller
ein. Als die Sonne sinkt, kommt die Vila angeritten; die Kellertür öffnet sich von
selbst. Die Vila setzt Janja hinter sich aufs Pferd, und diese nimmt von der Mutter
Abschied mit den Worten: ,,Nun begebe ich mich zu dem, dem Du mich geschenkt
hast."[2]

Wir lesen dieses Lied auch bei Vuk Karadžić.[3] Hier hat es mit unserer Gottscheer Ballade noch den Zug gemein, daß die Mutter der neun Töchter, als sie mit

[1] S. z. B.: Српски етнографски зборник 7 (1908), 360; 40 (1927), 272.
[2] *Hrvatske narodne pjesme* (HNP) V (Zagreb 1909), Nr. 19.
[3] Српске народне пјесме I⁴ (Београд 1932) Nr. 732.

dem zehnten Kinde schwanger geht, Gott bittet, daß dieses ein Knabe werde. Hauffen hat auf Grund solcher Ähnlichkeiten geschlossen, daß auch in dem Gottscheer Liede das Mädchen deshalb in die Fremde gehen müsse, weil die Mutter es verflucht habe. Dieser Schluß ist jedoch nicht gerechtfertigt und wird auch von Marolt (S. 246) abgelehnt.

Ein bosnisches Lied erzählt folgendes:

Die Hasan-aganica geht nach der Geburt von neun Mädchen mit dem zehnten Kinde schwanger. Ihr Gatte droht ihr, wenn sie nochmals ein Mädchen zur Welt bringe, solle sie sich an dem Apfelbaum, der über ihrem Hause stehe, erhängen oder sich in die Drina stürzen. In Abwesenheit Hasans gebiert sie nochmals eine Tochter; sie trägt das Kind zur Drina und wirft es mit den Worten: „Bald wird Dir die Mutter folgen" in den Strom. Als sich Hasan einfindet, gibt sie vor, einen Sohn wie einen Falken geboren zu haben; sie habe ihn zum Hodscha gesandt, damit er ihm Amulette schreibe. Während sich nun Hasan zurück zur Moschee begibt, stürzt sie sich in die Drina.[4]

Auch ein bulgarisches Lied singt von einer Mutter, die nach neun Töchtern eine zehnte gebiert. Sie heißt das Kind Dimitra, trägt es in den Wald, fertigt eine Wiege und überläßt das Kind seinem Schicksal. Drei Jahre lang wird es von einer Hirschkuh gesäugt. Schließlich begibt es sich nach dem Dorf, um seine Mutter zu suchen und findet sie auch.[5] In einem anderen bulgarischen Liede ist der Vater ungehalten, daß er neun Töchter, aber keinen Sohn besitzt; aber gerade das jüngste Töchterlein stellt, wie die Ereignisse beweisen, durchaus „ihren Mann". Als für eine Wagenkolonne, die von Stambul nach Probadija rollen soll, Wagen und Begleitpersonal zu stellen sind, flucht Stojan seinen neun Töchtern: „Möchte ich euch im Grabe verscharren können, daß ich keinen Sohn habe, ihn mit der Karawane zu senden!" Aber die neunte Tochter läßt sich die Haare schneiden, kleidet sich als Mann, zieht nach Stambul, lädt die Lasten auf und wird wegen ihrer Tüchtigkeit Befehlshaber über 70 Wagen.[6]

Es gibt nun auch Lieder, die statt der 9 Töchter neun bzw. 10 Söhne ins Spiel bringen. Eines dieser Lieder sei noch angeführt, da es besonders schön das innige Verhältnis der Mutter zum Jüngsten zum Ausdruck bringt und außerdem mit unserer Gottscheer Ballade den Zug gemeinsam besitzt, daß die Mutter den Abschied nicht überwindet, sondern bei ihm tot zu Boden sinkt (vgl. die Fassung aus Windischdorf).

[4] HNP V Nr. 46.
[5] Сборник за народни умотворения [Сб] 42 (София 1936), Nr. 206.
[6] Сб 44 (1949), Nr. 202.

Die Witwe Janja vermählt sich von zehn Söhnen weg, deren jüngster erst ein Jahr alt ist. Nach neun Jahren macht dieser den Vorschlag, die Mutter zu besuchen. Alle zehn reiten los und gelangen auch wohlbehalten am Hof des Ban an, den die Mutter geheiratet hatte. Den Hof finden sie schwarz verhängt, da die Mutter um ihre Söhne trauert. Freudig werden sie empfangen, nur Milivoje, den jüngsten, erkennt die Mutter nicht. Er hat ihr als Geschenk die goldene Wiege mitgebracht, in der ihn die Mutter zurückgelassen hatte. Nach drei Monaten lassen sich die Söhne nicht mehr zurückhalten. Die Mutter begleitet sie noch ein Stück Weges, solange sie die Füße tragen; dann winkt man sich aus der Ferne noch zu. Da sehen sie die Mutter niedersinken, kehren auf Rat Milivojes um und treffen die Mutter tot an. Sie begraben sie.[7]

Wir treffen also im Liedbezirk immerhin auf manche Gebilde, die, wie unsere Ballade aus der Gottschee, ihren Ausgangspunkt davon nehmen, daß in einer Familie keine Söhne, jedoch neun (oder zehn) Töchter vorhanden sind, wobei dann noch Näheres über das Schicksal der jüngsten Tochter berichtet wird. Aber keines dieser Lieder greift hinüber ins Mythische; sofern die neunte Tochter aus der Familie ausscheidet, so geschieht dies mehr aus ökonomischen Gründen und auf Betreiben mindestens des einen Elternteils, und nicht infolge eines unumstößlichen göttlichen Gebots, wie im Gottscheer Lied. Dazuhin sind diese Lieder landschaftlich verhältnismäßig eng begrenzt, nämlich auf den Balkan beschränkt. Beziehen wir jedoch in unsere Untersuchung auch die Sage und den Volksglauben mit ein, so ändert sich das Bild. Wir sehen dann, daß es viele Völker gibt, die sich ihre besonderen Vorstellungen über das letzte Kind einer gleichgeschlechtlichen Geburtenreihe gebildet haben, nur daß es dabei zumeist nicht um das zehnte (bzw. neunte) Kind, sondern um das siebente geht, dem dann, sei es Mädchen oder Knabe, teils dämonische, teils zum mindesten Wunder wirkende Eigenschaften zugeschrieben werden. Wir bringen Beispiele:

In Schleswig-Holstein heißt es: Wenn sieben Knaben oder sieben Mädchen nacheinander geboren werden, so ist eins darunter eine Nachtmähr, die sich zu den Schlafenden begibt und sich auf ihre Brust setzt, sie ängstigt und quält.[8] Denselben Glauben hegt auch das Volk in Mecklenburg[9] und Hannover.[10] Im Jeverlande glaubt man, daß unter sieben Töchtern eines Ehepaars eine „Walriderske" sei,

---

[7] HNP V Nr. 194. In der Variante bei Karadžić I Nr. 740 bringt jeder Sohn der Mutter ein Jäckchen, der jüngste bringt ihr seine Windeln; die Mutter schenkt jedem Sohn ein Pferd und einen Falken, dem jüngsten schenkt sie ein Pferd und ein Mädchen.
[8] K. Müllenhoff, *Sagen, Märchen und Lieder der Herzogtümer Schleswig...* (²1921), S. 259.
[9] K. Bartsch, *Sagen, Märchen und Gebräuche aus Mecklenburg* 2 (1880) S. 41. (Darnach auch bei R. Wossidlo, *Mecklenburgische Sagen* 2 [1939], 410 Nr. 1388).
[10] A. Kuhn und W. Schwarz, *Norddeutsche Sagen* (Leipzig 1848) S. 420 Nr. 198.

unter sieben Söhnen ein Werwolf.[11] Und ähnlich lesen wir in einer handschriftlichen Aufzeichnung aus der Oststeiermark: Wenn in einer Familie zehn Schwestern nacheinander geboren werden, so muß die letzte vom Hause und muß als
„Nachtahnl"-Gespenst umgehen[12]; in einer anderen Sage des nämlichen Nach-
lasses trifft dieses Schicksal die neunte Schwester.[13] Die Zahl „neun" und das
„Aus-dem-Hause-Müssen" bringen diesen auch landschaftlich benachbarten
Sagenbeleg in nähere Beziehung zu unserer Ballade, als dies bei den übrigen angeführten Belegen der Fall ist. Angefügt sei noch, daß in Oberkrain die zehnte
Schwester auch gleichgesetzt wird mit der „Rojenica", jenem mythischen Wesen,
das dem neugeborenen Kinde sein Schicksal zuweist.[14] Ferner ist nach unter-
steirischer Überlieferung die jüngste von zehn Schwestern der Tod, weshalb die
Mutter um ein solches Kind stets in Sorge zu sein pflegt.[15]

Weit verbreitet ist auch der Glaube an besondere Heilkräfte, die ein siebentes
Kind (vor allem ein siebenter Sohn) besitzt. Bereits Agrippa von Nettesheim
spricht davon, daß der siebente Sprößling einer ununterbrochenen Reihe männ-
licher Kinder die Kraft besitze, durch bloße Berührung Kröpfe zu heilen.[16] In
Frankreich heißen diese wundertätigen Ärzte „marcou", vermutlich nach dem
Hlg. Markolf, der die Gabe besessen haben soll, Skrofulöse zu heilen und diese
Gabe auf die französischen Könige übertrug.[17] Auf irgend einem Teile ihres Leibes
tragen diese Wunderärzte das Zeichen der Lilie.[18] Die nämliche Überlieferung
kannte auch England, wo aber im 17ten Jahrhundert gegen solche Kuren durch

---

[11] L. Strackerjan, *Aberglaube und Sagen aus dem Herzogthum Oldenburg* I (1867), 390. Dieser Aberglaube findet sich auch in Portugal, s.: *The Folk-Lore Record* III, I (London 1880) S. 143; S. a.
Grimm, *Mythologie* 2⁴ (1876), 964.

[12] Nach M. Lexer, *Kärntisches Wörterbuch* (1862) ist die Nâchtân·l ein weibliches Gespenst, welches
seine Gestalt vergrößern kann und die Kinder schreckt, der Alp...; letzterer scheint nach Sp. 5
identisch mit dem Hausdrachen zu sein.

[13] L. Kretzenbacher, *Germanische Mythen in der epischen Volksdichtung der Slowenen* (Graz 1941 =
Das Johanneum 3) S. 99.

[14] M. Pleteršnik, *Slovensko-nemški Slovar* I (1894), 51.

[15] P. Schlosser, *Bachern-Sagen* (1956), S. 23 Nr. 16. Angefügt sei, daß sich nach portugiesischem
Aberglauben siebte Söhne samstags in Esel verwandeln (W. G. Black, *Folk-Medicine* [London
1883], S. 122).

[16] *Handwörterbuch des deutschen Aberglaubens* 5, 605. Allgemein wird den siebenten Söhnen einer
durch keine Mädchen unterbrochenen Geburtenreihe besondere sympathetische Kraft zugespro-
chen (Vogtland; s. A. Wuttke, *Der deutsche Volksaberglaube der Gegenwart*, 3. Bearb. [Berlin 1900]
S. 323, Kap. 479). Aus Osterode wird 1788 überliefert, daß der siebente Sohn durch einen Schlag
mit der Hand allerlei Schaden heilen kann (Grimm, *Mythologie* 3⁴ [1878], 462 Nr. 786).

[17] D. H. Kerler, *Die Patronate der Heiligen* (Ulm 1905) S. 337. S. a. S. 221f.

[18] F. Liebrecht, *Zur Volkskunde* (1879), S. 346f. S. a. *Revue des traditions populaires* 9 (1894), 555
und Black, a. a. O. S. 136f.

siebente Söhne seitens der Kirche eingeschritten wurde.[19] Nach gewissen fran-
zösischen Berichten soll die Kur am Karfreitag oder an den Quatembertagen
vorgenommen werden[20]; dabei spielen Kreuzeszeichen und Weihwasser eine
Rolle.[21] In der Normandie wird auch der siebenten Tochter einer und derselben
Mutter die genannte Gabe zu heilen zugeschrieben.[22] Auch nach italienischem
Aberglauben kann der siebente Sohn einer durch keine Tochter unterbrochenen
Geburtenreihe Krankheiten heilen; nur sind es andere, als die für Frankreich
überlieferten, so u. a. gewisse Augenleiden, angehextes Übelbefinden, Brand-
wunden und auch bestimmte Vieherkrankungen. Man gibt dem Kind, damit es
später solche Krankheiten zu heilen vermag, bei der Geburt bestimmte Gegen-
stände in die Hand[23]; oder es wird der Vater zu seinem Neugeborenen gerufen,
damit er bestimme, welche Krankheit zu heilen das Kind im späteren Leben die
Fähigkeit haben solle[24]. Mit den siebenten Söhnen teilen nach dem Aberglauben
der Romagna diese Heilbegabung die Kinder, die mit einer Glückshaube auf die
Welt kommen.[25] Auch in Dänemark herrscht der Glaube an die Heilkräfte, die
ein siebenter Sohn besitzt.[26] Berichte liegen vor allem vor aus Fünen. Hier wird
noch erschwerend gefordert, daß dieses Kind an einem Donnerstag geboren ist.
Solche Heilpraktiker heißen dann „Tordagsdoktor"; ihre Heilkraft ist auf
Donnerstage beschränkt.[27] Besonders gesegnet ist nach dänischem Glauben ein

[19] E. Hull, *Folklore of the British Isles* (1928), S. 286 f. Belege von den Hebriden, s. *Folk-Lore* 11
(London 1900), 448 und *The Folk-Lore Journal* 1 (1883), 59 f. und 397.

[20] *Mélusine* 1 (1878), 555 (Loire inférieure). Nach irischem Aberglauben findet die Konsultation bei
einem siebenten Sohn am günstigsten an Freitagen vor Sonnenaufgang statt. (Black a. a. O.
S. 133).

[21] *Mélusine* 3 (1886/87), 196 (Haute-Bretagne).

[22] Liebrecht a. a. O. S. 347. So auch in Cornwall, s. *The Folk-Lore Journal* 5 (1887), 198. Siebente
Töchter vermochten auch Frostbeulen an den Fersen zu heilen (Frankreich; s. Black a. a. O.
S. 137).

[23] Paolo Toschi, *Romagna tradizionale* (Bologna [1952]), S. 57; s. a. S. 131. 142 und Black a. a. O.
S. 136.

[24] Toschi S. 58. Die Sizilianer nennen den mit Heilkräften begabten siebten Sohn kurz 'Settimu';
nach lombardischem Aberglauben eignen Heilkräfte auch dem Siebenmonatskind ('Settimino'):
The Folk-Lore Journal 7 (1889), 62. Bezüglich Sizilien s. noch Giuseppe Pitrè, *Usi e costumi,
credenze e pregiudizi del popolo Siciliano* 2 (1889), 182 (ohne nähere Ausführungen).

[25] Toschi a. a. O. S. 134. Gelegentlich werden bereits dem fünften Sohne besondere Heilkräfte zugeschrieben (Frankreich; s. Grimm, *Mythologie* 3⁴ [1878], 486 Nr. 22). Besonders wundertätig ist
der 21. Sohn (Black a. a. O. S. 137).

[26] H. F. Feilberg, *Ordbog over jyske almuesmål* 3, 713.

[27] Chr. Reimer, *Nordfynsk bondeliv* (IV, 1919) S. 516 ff. mit ausführlichen Berichten. Verbindung mit
der Forderung des Geborenseins an bestimmten Tagen auch im schottischen Aberglauben: Ein
siebenter Sohn geboren am Vorabend des Osterfestes kann auch drei- und viertägiges Fieber heilen
(Black a. a. O. S. 136).

siebenter Sohn, wenn er am 7. VII. eines Jahres, dessen Zahl einen Siebener enthält, um 7 Uhr geboren ist; er ist dann weiser als Salomon. Was allerdings über
einen solchen berichtet wird, stellt nicht dessen Weisheit, sondern seine magischen
Kräfte unter Beweis:

> Einige Deutsche wollten einen solchen Knaben seinen Eltern abkaufen. Das Land
> sollte nämlich von einer mächtigen Flut überschwemmt werden. Würde man aber
> einen solchen Knaben in seinem siebenten Lebensjahr auffinden und ihn in eine
> schwimmende Tonne setzen, durch die jedoch das Wasser strömen kann, so würde
> das Land so viele Jahre von einer Überschwemmung verschont bleiben, als Stunden
> der Knabe am Leben bleibt. Die Sache kam aber nicht zur Ausführung, da sich die
> Eltern zu dem Handel nicht entschließen konnten.[28]

Weithin wird also dem siebenten Kind einer Knaben- oder Mädchenreihe eine
besondere Stellung eingeräumt, mag es sich dabei um die Anschauung von der
Dämonie ihres Wesens oder um den Glauben an den Besitz wundertätiger Kräfte
handeln. Aber die speziellen Züge, die in der Gottscheer Ballade mit einer solchen
Gestalt verknüpft sind, fehlen den beigebrachten volkstümlichen Überlieferungen; lediglich ein Bericht aus der Steiermark ließ verwandte Töne anklingen. Nun
spielen aber auch in Slovenien solche Gestalten eine nicht unbeträchtliche Rolle;
allerdings sind es hier ebenfalls mit Vorzug die Söhne, u. zw. nicht die siebenten,
sondern, balkanischer Anschauung gemäß, die zehnten, um die das Volk seine
Sagen spinnt, sie zu fast mythischen Gestalten erhebend. So lesen wir bei J. Kelemina[29]: „Gebiert eine Mutter der Reihe nach zehn Söhne, ohne daß eine Tochter
dazwischen ist, so ist der zehnte Bruder ohne rechten Verstand und verläßt Haus
und Hof. Er würde auch nicht bleiben, wenn man sich seiner irgendwo noch so gut
annehmen würde; es würde ihn immer weiter treiben. Wer aber einem zehnten
Bruder kein Almosen gäbe, würde eine große Sünde begehen. Dasselbe gilt auch
für Mädchen." Dieser „Zehnte Bruder" (deseti brat oder desetnik)[30] spielt auch
in der slovenischen Hochliteratur eine beachtliche Rolle. Fran Levstik hatte in
seinem programmatischen Essay „Popotovanje iz Litije do Čateža" für den künf-
tigen slovenischen Roman die Durchflechtung mit volkstümlichen Gestalten, wie
dem deseti brat, gefordert und hatte selbst 1863 in der Zeitschrift *Napreja* ein

[28] E. Tang Kristensen, *Danske Sagn* 4 (1896), 574 Nr. 1780. Angefügt sei aus Ungarn, daß der
kugelfeste König der Riesen von Görgény durch eine Kugel getötet werden kann, die ein siebenter
Sohn bei Neumond in einem Feuer von Weizenstroh gießt (W. H. Jones und L. L. Kropf: *The
Folktales of the Magyars.* London 1889. S. XXX [Publications of the Folk-Lore Society XIII–1886]).
[29] Jakob Kelemina, *Bajke in pripovedke slovenskega ljudstva* (v Celju 1930) S. 239 mit Anmerkungen
S. 400; darunter Verweis auf [J.] Paj[e]k, Črtice [1884].
[30] Pleteršnik a. a. O. 1, 133.

Bruchstück unter diesem Titel veröffentlicht. Angeregt durch solche Ratschläge und geleitet durch Vorbilder wie Walter Scott schrieb Josip Jurčič seinen Roman „Deseti brat", dem 1864 eine „Skizze" (črtež) vorausgegangen war. In diesem Roman, einer Leistung von epochaler Bedeutung, hat Jurčič in Martinek Spak eine Gestalt geschaffen, die unter Wahrung mancher Züge des Volksglaubens doch auch realistische mit diesen verknüpft. Uns interessiert hier, was über die Volks-überlieferungen, die den „Zehnten Bruder" betreffen, im zweiten Kapitel des genannten Romans berichtet wird. Es heißt dort: „In früheren Zeiten traf man doch gelegentlich auf jemand, der als zehnter Sohn seiner Mutter geboren, mit wunderbaren Eigenschaften und Fähigkeiten begabt, infolge göttlichen Rat-schlusses verbannt von Haus zu Haus auf der weiten Welt umherwanderte, Glück profezeite, Schätze aufwies, Lieder sang und Märchen vortrug, wie kein anderer. Die Leute haben ihn geehrt, haben ihn gerne gesehen, haben ihm Speise und Nachtlager gewährt... Nun sind die Leute ungläubig geworden, und auch unsere zehnten Brüder sind nicht mehr dieselben wie ehedem..." Hier ist also das Wandernmüssen durch die weite Welt auf Grund eines göttlichen Gebotes klar herausgestellt, ein Zug, der sich mit den in der Gottscheer Ballade ge-schilderten Vorgängen deckt.

Wir kehren zu Kelemina zurück. Er bringt nach seiner Bemerkung, was von den Knaben gesagt werde, das gelte auch für die Mädchen, eine längere Erzäh-lung, die sich aber bei näherem Zusehen nicht als eine selbständige Sage heraus-stellt, sondern als die Umsetzung eines slovenischen Liedes in Prosa.[31] Auch die Sage, die wir in den von Paul Schlosser herausgegebenen *Bachern-Sagen* unter Nr. 16 lesen, dürfte lediglich die Nacherzählung eines slovenischen Liedes sein. Sie ist in Kötsch lokalisiert und stimmt in ihren Motiven ziemlich genau überein mit einer Liedvariante, wie sie in St. Lavrenc auf dem Draufelde, also in benach-barter Gegend, aufgezeichnet wurde (Glasbeno narodopisni institut in Laibach, Stj. III/1 = DVA K 5043).[32]
Unserer Gottscheer Ballade steht nämlich ein slovenisches Lied mit dem näm-lichen Thema zur Seite; ihm müssen wir uns im folgenden noch zuwenden. Es ist zahlreicher belegt, als die deutsche Form. Sechs Fassungen (D–I) sind bei K. Štrekelj (= Š) unter den Nummern 310–315 abgedruckt[33]; F. Kuhač bringt

---

[31] Siehe K. Štrekelj, *Slovenske narodne pesmi* Bd. 1, Nr. 311.

[32] Die Sage stellt sich zu der unten noch herauszuarbeitenden zweiten Gruppe des slovenischen Liedes. Wie nahe ihre Beziehungen zum Liede sind, sieht man etwa aus den Worten der Sage: „Wenn Du [Mutter] einmal stirbst, werde ich neben Dir stehen und Du wirst mich nicht sehen" im Vergleich zu den Worten des Kindes im Liede (M): "Pod vašoj strehoj stala nem, pro vaši smrti stala bom".

[33] *Slovenske narodne pesmi* 1 (1895–98).

unter Nr. 1521 in seinem Werke „Južnoslovjenske narodne popievke Bd. 4 eine Melodie zu Š 310 (s. a. Kočevski zbornik [1939] S. 239ff.) (= K); vier weitere Aufzeichnungen aus neuerer Zeit (= L–O) bewahrt das Glasbeno narodopisni institut; Abschriften verdanken wir Z. Kumer (= DVA K 5042–5045).

Die slovenische Fassung läßt sich bis 1839 zurückverfolgen; das Lied wird in diesem Jahr sowohl in der Sammlung Korytko als auch in den „Illyrischen Volksliedern" von Vraz mitgeteilt. Die beiden Texte weichen, obwohl sie die nämliche Überlieferung repräsentieren, im Wortlaut mehrfach untereinander ab (Š 310). Š 311 ist im Druck nur um ein Jahr jünger; es gibt von dieser Fassung eine Umarbeitung durch Prešeren.[34] Auch die Fassung Š 312 reicht in jene Jahre zurück (1841), und auch an ihr haben sich redigierende Hände betätigt. Geographisch umfassen die slovenischen Varianten ein viel größeres Gebiet, als die deutschen. Zwar erweist sich Oberkrain als Kernlandschaft; Belege finden sich jedoch auch in der Steiermark bis in die Gegend von Marburg.

Die slovenischen Belege lassen sich klar in zwei Gruppen scheiden. Nach der ersten wandert die „Desetnica" auf ein himmlisches Gebot, das ein Engel oder ein Vögelein überbringt, in die Welt, nachdem die Mutter sie sieben Jahre lang aufgezogen hatte. Wir werden auch über das weitere Schicksal des Mädchens unterrichtet. Nach Š 310/311 nächtigt das Kind, nachdem es die Heimat verlassen hat, im Wald unter einem Baum. Der Baum beginnt zu reden und weist das Kind weiter, da ein Blitzschlag zu erwarten ist. Dies wiederholt sich beim nächsten Baum, und erst unter dem dritten findet das Mädchen Ruhe und Schutz. Nach allen Varianten dieser Gruppe kehrt das Mädchen nach sieben Jahren ins Elternhaus zurück, als die älteste Schwester eben Hochzeit feiert, bittet um Herberge, wird aber zunächst abgewiesen. Nach Š 310/311 stirbt die Mutter erst jetzt beim erneuten Abschied. Nur Š 313 weiß nichts von einer Wiederkehr der Tochter, die erst zurückkehren wird, wenn sie dreimal die Welt umwandert hat und sieben Feiertage einander folgen werden. Diese Fassung ist auch die einzige, bei der der Endreim durchgeführt ist; sie ist offenbar stark bearbeitet.

Die zweite Gruppe, repräsentiert durch H, I, M und O, hebt damit an, daß neun (bis zwölf) Schwestern auf dem Felde mähen. Da geht Maria grüßend vorüber, aber nur die jüngste Schwester erwidert den Gruß. Maria reicht ihr einen Ring, den das Mädchen der Mutter überbringt. Er wird in ein Brot gebacken, fällt aber der Jüngsten wiederum zu, die nun für immer Abschied nimmt (Š 315: das Mädchen wandert gleich mit Maria fort). Eine Mittelstellung nimmt L (aus Gornja Sorica/Oberzarz) ein: Hier bittet, wie in Gruppe 1, die Mutter von neun Töchtern um einen Knaben, gebiert aber nochmals eine Tochter. Beim Brotschneiden weint die Mutter, weil sie weiß, daß dieses ihr jüngstes Kind einst in

[34] Faksimile einer Seite bei J. Glonar, *Stare žalostne* (1939), S. 43.

die Welt wird ziehen müssen, ohne jemals zurückzukehren. Dann aber wendet
sich das Lied der Erzählweise von Gruppe 2 zu: Nach sieben Jahren mähen die
zehn Töchter mit der Mutter. Da kommt eine weiße Frau vorüber mit einem gol-
denen Ring, den sie den Mädchen anzustecken versucht; er paßt nur der Jüngsten. Diese nimmt anderen Morgens Abschied. Auf einer großen Wiese hört sie
eine Stimme vom Himmel: „O nur vorwärts, niemals mehr zurück!"

    Gewisse Züge des slovenischen Liedes lassen sich auch bei anderen slovenischen
Liedern feststellen. Wenn die Desetnica bei ihrer Rückkehr um Herberge bittet,
aber zunächst mit der Begründung abgewiesen wird, daß das Haus mit Gästen
voll belegt sei, so treffen wir diesen Zug u. a. auch in dem Lied vom „Heimkehrenden Ehemann", der ja auch zu Hause eintrifft, als eben Hochzeit gefeiert
wird.[35] Auf die Einleitungsszene der Gruppe 2, die schildert, wie auf einem Feld
Mädchen arbeiten und von einem Vorübergehenden angesprochen werden, treffen
wir auch bei dem Legendenliede „Jezus izdan"[36]; hier sind es 2 (3) Mädchen, die
jäten; der Vorübergehende ist Jesus im weißen Gewande. Mit einer ähnlichen
Szene beginnt auch das Lied vom Trudchen aus Reifnitz („Ribniska Jerica")[37]:
Die in die Türkei entführte Jerca schneidet zusammen mit Türkinnen Weizen
auf dem Felde. Auf dem Wege, der vorbeiführt, kommt ein Reiter geritten, der
Jerca anspricht und frägt, ob sie nicht gerne zurück in ihre Heimat möchte. Es ist
ihr Bruder, der sie auch den Eltern wieder zuführt. Bemerkenswert im Hinblick
auf unsere Ballade ist auch der Schluß dieses Liedes, vor allem in der Fassung
Š 94: Jercas Eltern blicken den Türken, den sie nicht als ihren Sohn erkennen,
finster an; als sie aus einem Lied, das er unter einem von ihm einst im Garten ge-
pflanzten Baum singt, entnehmen, wer der Türke ist und diesen wegsprengen
sehen, rufen sie ihn zurück; er aber antwortet: „Niemals werde ich zurückkehren, dort [in der Türkei] werde ich leben, dort werde ich sterben". Bereits
oben wurde das Lied von den zehn Söhnen herangezogen, die ausziehen, die
Mutter zu besuchen; es teilt mit unserer Ballade den Zug, daß die Mutter beim
Abschied stirbt. Ebenso wurde bereits auf das Lied bei Karadžić I Nr. 732 hingewiesen, in dem sich, wie in unserer Ballade, der Zug findet, daß eine Mutter von
neun Töchtern bittet, ihr zehntes Kind möge ein Knabe sein.

    Inwieweit solche gemeinsamen Züge von allem Anfang an der Desetnica-Ballade
angehörten, oder inwieweit sie erst später auf Grund gewisser Ähnlichkeiten im

[35] Z. B. Štrekelj Nr. 215–217; V. Žganec, *Hrvatske narodne pjesme. Kajkavske.* (1950) S. 150f. Nr. 167;
    S. 335 Nr. 377. Vgl. Das slowakische Lied bei A. Melicherčik, *Slovenský folklór* (Bratislava 1959)
    S. 583ff. *Slovenské spevi* 1, 149.
[36] Štrekelj Nr. 447ff. (Vgl. dazu im Deutschen das Lied bei L. Pinck, *Verklingende Weisen* 2 [1928]
    S. 19 Nr. 4).
[37] Štrekelj Nr. 93f.

Verlauf der Handlung in die slovenischen Fassungen unseres Liedes eingedrungen sind, läßt sich heute nicht mehr entscheiden. Wir vermuten, daß die zweite Gruppe mit ihrem ausgeprägteren legendenhaften Charakter die jüngere ist und die für sie charakteristische Szene der Begegnung Marias mit den Schnitterinnen in Anlehnung an die beiden oben genannten Lieder mit entsprechender Eingangssituation entwickelt hat. Daß die Gottscheer Überlieferung auf der Gruppe I der slovenischen beruht, ist ohne weiteres klar, doch ist bemerkenswert, daß sie mit dem Abschied der Tochter vom Elternhaus schließt und über deren weitere Schicksale nichts mehr berichtet. Ist daraus zu schließen, daß sie als Vorlage eine slovenische Fassung dieser Gruppe benutzte, der wie Š 313 (oder dem zwischen beiden Gruppen stehenden L) diese weiterführenden Züge fehlten, oder waren diese zunächst auch in Gruppe I gar nicht vorhanden und sind hier erst später, im Laufe der Zeit hinzugetreten, so daß die Gottscheer Überlieferung eine ursprünglichere Form dieser Gruppe repräsentieren würde? Sinnvoll erscheint die Weiterspinnung nicht, und man könnte sie höchstens damit erklären, daß mit dem Ausscheiden der ältesten Tochter aus der Familie durch Heirat ein Platz für die jüngste frei wird und damit der Bann von ihr weicht. Aber die sagenhaften Überlieferungen von der zehnten Tochter kennen einen solchen Zug nicht. Und warum zieht sie dann trotzdem erneut in die Ferne? Und warum übersteht die Mutter die erste, doch sicher schwerere Trennung, nicht aber die zweite?

• • •

Wir haben einen weiten Umgang gehalten. Wir sahen, daß bei vielen Völkern Europas dem siebenten Sproß einer gleichgeschlechtigen Geschwisterreihe außergewöhnliche Eigenschaften zugeschrieben werden, ja daß ein solches Kind da und dort für ein dämonisches Wesen gehalten wird. Wir sahen ferner, daß bei den Slaven des Balkans Lieder beliebt sind, die von solchen Geschwisterreihen, seien es Söhne oder Töchter, erzählen, wobei vielfach das letzte einer solchen Reihe gegen die übrigen kontrastiert wird. Nur ist hier das letzte das zehnte, und nicht das siebente Kind. In Slovenien erhielten die Überlieferungen und Anschauungen von solchen zehnten Kindern (desetnik; desetnica) eine eigene Ausprägung, wobei als Grundmotiv neben besonderer seelischer Veranlagung der Zwang, das Elternhaus verlassen und ruhelos wandern zu müssen sich einstellte, ohne daß wir Klarheit darüber gewinnen können, welcherlei Gedankengänge sich hierbei abspielten.[38]

[38] An ein „Zehnt"opfer wird man kaum denken können, das Gott beim zehnten Kind darzubringen wäre. Ob Beobachtungen an Epileptikern hereinspielen? Als „Äquivalent" für ihre Anfälle kann bei ihnen ein im Dämmerzustand sich auswirkender Wandertrieb auftreten (G. Venzmer in *Kosmos* 56 [1960], 19).

Diese Volksanschauungen wurden zu einem Lied geformt, wobei, um es zu runden,
Motive beigefügt wurden wie die Himmelsbotschaft, die Siebenjährigkeit beim
Antritt der Wanderschaft, das Brotorakel; außerdem wurde über das Lied der
Schimmer des Märchenhaften und Legendären ausgebreitet. Das slovenische
Lied entwickelte, z. T. unter dem Einfluß anderer Lieder, Spielformen. Die
Gottscheer übernahmen es von ihrer slavischen Umwelt, wohl auf Grund einer
slovenischen Variante, die nicht nur zeitlich, sondern auch gestaltmäßig älter ist,
als die uns überlieferten Spielformen; es scheint aber, daß sich die deutsche Form
nicht über die nähere Umgebung der Stadt Gottschee hinaus verbreitete. *Eine*
Erfahrung freilich mag sich bei unseren Darlegungen aufgedrängt haben:
Was wir auch anzuführen hatten, unterlag immer wieder der verschiedenartigsten
Umgestaltung, so daß es oft schwer hielt, die verbindende Wegstrecke im Auge zu
behalten und sie nicht zu verlieren. Es wäre für die Untersuchung dienlicher und
überdies für den Leser überzeugender gewesen, wenn wir es mit einem härteren
und starreren Material zu tun gehabt hätten. Aber gerade diese ungemeine
Wandlungsfähigkeit und dies ständige Fließen, das dazu führt, daß uns wie beim
Wandern durch eine reiche Landschaft bei jedem Schritt neue, reizvolle Bilder
vor Augen gezaubert werden, dürfte charakteristisch sein für echte Volksüberlieferung und ein ungehemmt sich entfaltendes Volksgut. Und das Belauschen
solch ständig wirkender schöpferischer Kräfte ist ja auch das Beglückende an
volkskundlicher Forschung.

Deutsches Volksliedarchiv,
Freiburg im Breisgau

SUB VERBO "SINNBILD"

HENRI STEGEMEIER

In checking the many and varied German etymological and historical dictionaries *sub verbo* "Sinnbild," one will not find in them a completely accurate statement as to the original use and appearance of the word in German. The compilers
of these reference works have copied and repeated early, often vague and general
statements, and only occasionally have they elaborated on them as information
increased. The sentence found, for instance, in F. L. K. Weigand, *Deutsches
Wörterbuch*², II (Gießen, 1876), p. 719, is typical of the early statements cited
under the word "Sinnbild": "Bereits 1648 in Harsdörfers poet. Trichter."[1]

Moriz Heyne adds a further reference to the appearance of the word "Sinnbild"
in German in the *Deutsches Wörterbuch*, III (Leipzig, 1895), col. 620: "Verdeut-
schendes Wort des 17. Jh.: emblema... wird nach rechter eigenschaft durch das
teutsche wort sinnbild genugsam ausgetrükket. Schottel. 1105."[2]

---

[1] The reference is to Georg Philipp Harsdörffer, *Poetischen Trichters zweyter Theil* (Nürnberg, 1648),
pp. 68–69, in his discussion in "Die zehende Stund": "Von den Gleichnissen." This discussion is
expanded in the third volume of the "Trichter": *Prob und Lob der Teutschen Wolredenheit. Das ist:
deß Poetischen Trichters Dritter Theil* (Nürnberg, 1653), "die X. Betrachtung": "Von den Bilde-
reyen," pp. 101–111.

[2] The reference is to Justus-Georgius Schottelius, *Ausführliche Arbeit Von der Teutschen Haubt
Sprache... In Fünf Bücher* (Braunschweig, 1663), Liber V, pp. 1105–1107, sections 10–12. Much
of what Schottel writes here he had already written in the preface to a work by Frantz Julius von
dem Knesebeck, *Dreiständige Sinnbilder zu Fruchtbringendem Nutze, und beliebender ergetzlichkeit,
ausgefertiget durch den Geheimen* (Braunschweig, 1643). This discussion by Schottel has apparently
not been noted or cited anywhere before. He also authored an almost unknown collection of
emblems: *Jesu Cristi Nahmens-Ehr, Worin alles auf den süßen Nahmen Gottes und dessen Wort
eingerichtet...* (Wolfenbüttel, 1666).

The most thorough listing of references to German literary works where the
word "Sinnbild" and its allied or variant forms are to be found is, of course, in
Jacob and Wilhelm Grimm, *Deutsches Wörterbuch*, X, 1 (Leipzig, 1905), cols.
1153–1155, 1167–1168. Here are repeated the references to Harsdörffer and
Schottel, found in Weigand and Heyne, but all other references are of a date later
than either of these.[3]

The fifth edition of F. L. K. Weigand's *Deutsches Wörterbuch*, II (Gießen, 1910),
p. 870, adds some new references, one of which is of particular interest as a very
early reference to the use of the word "Sinnebild" in 1626 by Julius Wilhelm
Zincgref: "Sinnbild, n. Bild zur Bezeichnung eines von demselben verschiedenen
sinnlichen oder geistigen Gegenstandes, Emblem, 1648 in Harsdörffers poet.
Trichter, dafür Sinnebild 1626 bei Zincgref Apophth. 1, 163.[4] Sinnenbild 1648 bei
Zesen Ibr. 170."[5]

The "classical" etymological dictionary for most students of German is un-
doubtly Friedrich Kluge's *Etymologisches Wörterbuch der deutschen Sprache*. The
ten editions of this almost monumental work, 1881 to 1924, represent the older
form of Kluge's book, for after his death in 1926, Alfred Götze took over the
editorship and constantly enlarged and improved the work. From the time the
word "Sinnbild" occurred in Götze's eleventh edition of Kluge in 1934 up to the
most recent seventeenth edition printed in Berlin in 1957, no basic change has
been made in the descriptive entry under this word. It reads (p. 710):

[3] E. g. Sigmund von Birken, *Guelfis* (*Nürnberg*, 1669), S. v. Butschky, *Pathmos* (Leipzig, 1677),
C. v. Stieler, *Ballemperie* (1680).

[4] Weigand refers here to Zincgref's (or Zinkgref) *Der Teutschen Scharpfsinnige kluge Sprüch*, I [=
Teutscher Nation Apophthegmata] (Straßburg, 1626), p. 163: "Hertzog Renatus in Lothringen —
Diesem hatte der stoltz Hertzog Carlen auß Burgund alle seine Land biß auff Nansi die Hauptstatt
eingenommen, vnd führte in seinem Fahnen ein Feyreisen vnd Feurstein, sampt zwey Creutzweisse
Holtzspeltern, durch dieses Sinnebild anzeigende, daß er die Mittel hette, die gantze Welt zu vber-
ziehen vnd in Brand zustecken, wie es auch an sich selbst die warheit ware." Zinkgref uses the word
"Sinnebild" here to describe an *impresa* or device rather than an emblem. Zinkgref is not only
known for his popular collection of *Apophthegmata*, but he was also an important member of the
literary group associated with Martin Opitz. Zinkgref published a controversial edition of Opitz's
poems in 1624 in Straßburg (*Opicii teutsche Poemata*) and appended to them an important anthology
of contemporary lyrics. There also exists an important collection of emblems by Zinkgref, *Emblematum Ethico-politicorum* ([Heidelberg] 1619), with an interesting nine-page preface, "Praefatio de
Origine et Usu Emblematum."

[5] I.e., Philipp von Zesen, *Ibrahim* (1648). The name of Zesen is also of interest in connection with
his use of the word "Sinnbild," for he translated the French version (by Marin Le Roy, Sieur de
Gomberville) of Otto van Veen's famous emblem book, *Q. Horati Flacci Emblemata* (Antwerp, 1607),
into German: *Moralia Horatiana: Das ist Die Horatzische Sitten-Lehre Aus der Ernst-sittigen Ge-
selschaft der alten Weise-meister gezogen, und mit 113* [should be only 103] *in kupfer gestochenen
Sinn-bildern*... (Amsterdam, 1656).

"Sinnbild N. 'sinnliches Bild von etwas Abstraktem', Ersatzwort erst für gr.-lat. emblema, dann für symbolum. Zuerst in der Form *Sinnebild* Zinkgref 16126 [*sic*] Apophthegm. 1, 163, als *Sinnenbild* bei Zesen 1648 Ibrahim 170. Die endgültige Form zuerst in Harsdörfers Poet. Trichter, Nürnb. 1648. Nnl. zinnebeelde, dän. sindbillede, schwed. sinnebild sind aus dem Nhd. entlehnt. *Sinnbildlich* 'emblematicus' kaum vor Frisch 1741."

Before commenting on the information given here, it might be interesting to add the very similar difinition given in the latest edition of another dictionary edited by Alfred Götze (— Walter Mitzka), *Trübners Deutsches Wörterbuch*, VI (Berlin, 1955), pp. 371–372:

"Sinnbild ist eine Neubildung des 17. Jh. Zunächst sollte sie das Fremdwort gr.-lat. emblēma ersetzen. Anfänglich findet sich *Sinnebild* [= Zinkgref], dann *Sinnenbild* [= Zesen], später gelegentlich auch *Sinnbildnis* [Abr. a S. Clara, *Reimb dich* (1693), 342], *Sinnbild* zuerst in Nürnberg 1648 [Ph. Harsdörffer, *Poet. Trichter*, b. W.]. Nnl. zinnebeelde, dän. sindbillede, schwed. sinnebild sind aus dem Nhd. entlehnt."

There is another German work which appeared in the same year as Zinkgref's *Apophthegmata* where the Latin word "emblemata" is translated in the title by the word "Sinnenbild," and this book has completely escaped the notice of emblem bibliographers. It is Henrich Hudemann's *Hirrnschleiffer. Das ist*: *Außerlesene teutsche Emblemata, oder Sinnenbilder* (1626).[6] The book contains 150 "naked" (= lacking illustrations) emblems, beginning with one dedicated to the reader, "Von Eigenschafft dieser Sinnenbilder" and ending with one, "Vom Tode." Whereas Zinkgref, in his use of the word "Sinnebild," casually refers to a device (*impresa*) on a nobleman's banner, Hudemann definitely has brought together a rather typical collection of emblems in the tradition of the sixteenth century. Hudemann calls his collection—even if erroneously—the first one to be written in German: "da sie in dieser Sprach niebeuor außkommen seynd."[7] Latin

---

[6] This work is excellently discussed in some detail in an article by Erich Trunz, "Henrich Hudemann und Martin Ruarus, zwei holsteinische Dichter der Opitz-Zeit," *Zeitschrift der Gesellschaft für Schleswig-Holsteinische Geschichte*, 63 (Neumünster in Holstein, 1935), pp. 162–213 (cf. especially pp. 193–200). The book is not to be confused with one with a similar title by Aegidius Albertinus, *Hiren schleifer* (München, [1618]).

[7] A check of German emblem books published a few years prior to Hudemann's *Hirrnschleiffer* reveals that the Latin word "emblemata" simply had not yet been replaced by the German word "Sinnbild," so that Hudemann can be credited with being the first to use the German word in the title of a collection of emblems. Cf.: Daniel Cramer. *Societas Iesu et Roseæ crucis vera ... Das ist, Viertzig Geistliche Emblemata auß der heyligen Schrifft ...* (Francofurti, 1617); Georgette de Montenay, *Stamm Buch, Darinnen Christlicher Tugenden Beyspiel, Einhundert außerlesener Emblemata ...* (Franckfurt am Mayn, 1619); Peter Rollos, *Vita Corneliana emblematibus in aes*

had been, of course, the common language of the Renaissance emblem books, and German collections had appeared only slowly. A German translation of the first collection of emblems, Andrea Alciati's *Emblematum liber* (Augsburg, 1531), had, however, been made already in 1542 by Wolfgang Hunger. In any case, it is clear that the references in the etymological dictionaries are incorrect as to where this form of the word "zuerst" can be found.

Erich Trunz makes it quite clear in his article on Henrich Hudemann that this isolated North German minister's writings could hardly have been influenced by the newly published works of Opitz, Zinkgref, Hübner, and others, but that his ties and influences, as he himself indicates,[8] stemmed rather from the Netherlands. The suspicion arises, then, if Hudemann's use of the word "Sinnenbild"—even Zinkgref's use of "Sinnebild" also—did not perhaps come from Dutch sources, even though the etymological dictionaries indicate quite the contrary: "Nnl. zinnebeelde...aus dem Nhd. entlehnt." If we check the general as well as the specialized Dutch historical dictionaries *sub verbo* "zinnebeeld," we will get no help whatsoever on the problem. A checking of Dutch emblem books, however, will show conclusively that there are Dutch words used for the form "emblemata" that are earlier than the German ones of 1626 in Zinkgref and Hudemann. Here are several titles: Dirck Pietersz Pers, *Bellerophon of Lust tot Wysheyd. Begrijpende Veel zeedighe, stichtlijcke en leerlijcke Sinne-beelden met haere verklaringhen* (Amstel-redam, 1614); Jacob Cats, *Maechden-plicht ofte ampt der ionck-vrouwen, in eerbaer liefde, aen-ghewesen door sinne-beelden* (Middelburgh, 1618); Jacob Cats, *Silenus Alcibiadis, sive Proteus...* (*Eerste* [*Tweede, Derde*] *Deel:* "*Sinne-Beelden*") (Middelburgh, 1618); Zacharias Heyns, *Emblemata, Emblemes Chrestienes, et Morales. Sinne-Beelden streckende Tot Christelicke Bedenckinghe ende Leere der Zedicheyt* (Rotterdam, 1625); Jacob van Zevecote, *Emblemata ofte sinnebeelden met dichten verciert* (Lugd. Batav., 1626). A variation of the word "Sinnebild" was even coined by Roemer Visscher for the title of his collection of emblems, *Sinne-poppen* (Amsterdam, 1614); Dutch dictionaries list Visscher's word as a synonymous form of "Sinnebild." Unfortunately, the great nineteenth-century English scholar on emblems, Henry Green, is not always dependable, but he gives in his

artificose incisa ... *Das ist das gantze Leben Cornelij mit außerlesenen gemelten in Kupfer gestochen* ... (1624); Daniel Meisner, *Thesaurus Philo-Politicus ... Das ist: Außerlesene schöne Emblemata und Moralia so wol Kunst ...* (Franckfurt, 1623–1626); Christoph Maurer, *XL Emblemata miscella nova. Das ist: XL Underschiedliche Außerlesene Newradierte Kunststuck* (Zürych, 1622); Daniel Cramer, *Emblematum Sacrorum Prima Pars. Das ist: Fünfftzig Geistlicher in Kupfer gestochener Emblematum ...* (Franckfurt, 1624).

[8] Among others, Hudemann often praises Daniel Heinsius, himself the author of several very attractive and popular collections of amatory emblems, the earliest dated one being *Emblemata amatoria* (Amsterdam, 1608).

emblem bibliography in *Shakespeare and the Emblem Writers* (London, 1870), p. 98, a unique and very early reference for the word "Sinnebild": "Vaenius, Zinnebeelden der wereldtsche Liefde. (Amstel. 1603). 4to." It has not been possible to verify this title by the famous Dutch emblematist, Otto van Veen, with its early example of the Dutch word, in any contemporary trade or fair catalogues, in any emblem bibliography, or in the holdings of any libraries.

It strikes anyone familiar with emblem literature as unusual that the Dutch word "Sinnebild" or "zinnebeeld"—if it is really being used for the first time by D. P. Pers or others, or if it is in any way an unusual contemporary Dutch word—occurs in the above-cited works without any comment whatsoever. One can almost only infer, then, that the word was already known in learned circles. It is a conjecture worth mentioning that the Dutch word had perhaps already been used in the Rhetorical Chambers ("Rederijker-Kammern" or "Rethoriker-Kammern")[9] in the sixteenth century in the performance of their allegorical plays as well as in their other literary productions and in their internal organization. Of particular significance here are the "Spelen van Sinne" ("Sinnespelen" or "Zinne-spelen"),[10] where the illustrations accompanying the allegorical plays of the various Chambers and of their coats of arms are so emblematic in nature, that it is tempting to refer to the entire collection as an emblem book. Were the personifications of the virtues and the vices et cetera in these plays perhaps already referred to as *"zinnebeeldige* personen"? Jacob Cats, one of Holland's great emblematists, was content once to say only of the word: "The Greeks and Latins have called this type of literature emblems, and I do not have to go into the origin of the word.

---

[9] See E. F. von Monroy, *Embleme und Emblembücher in den Niederlanden 1560–1630* (Freiburg i. Br. dissertation, manuscript, 1942), chapter II, "Die Rederijkeremblematik," pp. 14–30; Henry Green, *Shakespeare and the Emblem Writers* (London, 1870), pp. 81–83; Erich Trunz, *Dichtung und Volks-tum in den Niederlanden im 17. Jahrhundert* (München, 1937), p. 6; I have not seen Prudens van Duyse, *De Rederijkkamers in Nederland* (Gent, 1900); N. Cornelissen, *De l'origine des progrès et de la décadence des Chambres de rhétorique établies en Flandre* (Gand, 1812).

[10] Editions of 1539 (Ghent) and 1561 and 1562 (Antwerp) are listed in J. C. Brunet, *Manuel du Libraire et de l'Amateur de Livres*, V (Paris, 1864), col. 484. I have seen this volume of "Spelen van Sinne" only, found in the Folger Shakespeare Library: *Spelen van sinne vol scoone moralisacien vvtleggingen ende bediedenissen op alle loeflijecke consten vvaer inne men claerlijck ghelijck in eenen spieghel, Figuerlijck, Poetelijck, eñ Retorijckelijck mach aenschouwen hoe nootsakelijck ende dienste-lijck die selue consten allen menschen zijn. Ghespeelt met octroy der Con. Ma. binnen der stadt van Andtwerpen op d'Lant-Juweel by die veerthien cameren van Retorijcken die hen daer ghepresenteert hebben den derden dach Augusti int Jaer ons Heeren. M.DLXI. Op die Questie. VVat den mensch aldermeest tot conste vervvect. Tot groote onderwijsinghe van allen liefhebbers der Poeterie ende Reto-rijcke gheciert met diuersse schoone Figueren.* (Tot Antwerpen by M. Willem Siluius, Drucker der Con. Ma. An. M.CCCCC.LXII). It is interesting to note that an emblem book mentioned above by Zacharias Heyns also contained a section, *Sinne-Spel van de dry hoofdeuchden.*

In our language we think the emblem should be called *Sinnebeelden*. Often one sees the picture in one way on the outside, but inside one sees quite another picture and finds quite another meaning. This manner of writing peculiarly pictures the *Sinnen* (opinions, thoughts) of people, and no word can express it better than *Sinnebeelden*."[11]

The most unfortunate error of omission in the German etymological dictionaries *sub verbo* "Sinnbild," however, is the failure to list Georg Philipp Harsdörffer's eight-volume work, generally referred to as the (*Frauenzimmer*) *Gesprächspiele* (Nürnberg, 1641–1649). Perhaps no other German writer was so concerned with emblematics as Harsdörffer, and all his works are more or less variations on this general theme. Perhaps no other German work is more concerned with defining and illustrating the term "emblem" in all its forms and parts than the *Gespräch-spiele*. It is beyond the scope of this paper to analyze the emblematic content and the import of these volumes and others by Harsdörffer (this I have done elsewhere), but chapter after chapter is devoted to the topic of the "Sinnbild" and its syntactical variations (e.g., "Die Erfindung der Sinnbildkunst," "Gesetze die Sinnbilder betreffend," "Der Gesprächspiele Sinnbild," "Von der Sinnbilder Figur und Obschrifft"). Most of what Schottelius (cf. footnote 2, above) wrote about the "Sinnbild" is actually based on Harsdörffer. Harsdörffer's influence through his membership in the two literary societies, "Die Fruchtbringende Ge-sellschaft" and "Der löbliche Hirten- und Blumen-Orden an der Pegnitz," was so great that the German word "Sinnbild" from this time on almost completely re-places the word "emblemata" in book titles and in discussions. If it had been an aim of the "Fruchtbringende Gesellschaft" to rid the German language of foreign words by replacing them with equivalent, native ones, then this principle is nowhere better illustrated than by the replacing of the word "emblemata" with the German "Sinnbild." No words describe Harsdörffer's interests in the "Sinn-bild" better than a phrase he uses himself in a pseudonymously published work, *Das erneuerte Stamm- und Stechbüchlein* (Nürnberg, 1654), "durch Fabianum Athyrum, der loblichen Sinnkünste Beflißnen."

It seems then, that until our bibliographical knowledge of emblem literature is greater than it still remains today, we shall not be able to write the conclusive entry in our etymological dictionaries *sub verbo* "Sinnbild." It is hoped that this discussion will show, however, how the existing entries can and should be revised.

University of Illinois,

Urbana, Illinois

---

[11] Paraphrased from his "Vorreden Over de Proteus" in *Proteus ofte Minne-beelden Verandert in Sinne-beelden* (Rotterdam, 1627).

GEBÄRDENSPRACHE UND SPRACHGEBÄRDE

LUTZ RÖHRICH

Im 18. Kapitel des 1. Buches von Rabelais Pantagruel kommt ein angeblich bedeutender englischer Gelehrter nach Paris mit der Absicht, Pantagruel kennen zu lernen, von dessen unvergleichlicher Weisheit er gehört hat. Es wird nun eine öffentliche wissenschaftliche Diskussion angesetzt; Thaumastos aber — so heißt der englische Gelehrte — stellt zuvor eine Bedingung; er erklärt nämlich: 'Merke dir die Art, wie ich zu disputieren meine: durch Zeichen nämlich allein, ohn alle Worte, weil es sich um so subtile Materien handelt, daß keine menschliche Sprache imstande ist, sie auszudrücken. So werden wir einander verstehen, unbelästigt von diesem albernen Händegeklatsch, das die Sophisten immer erheben, gerade wenn man bei einem gelehrten Gespräch im besten Argumentieren ist.'

Pantagruel freilich wird es angst und bang vor einer solchen Disputation und es wird darum Panurg vorgeschickt, um die Disputation in der Gebärdensprache zu bestreiten, die nun öffentlich vonstatten geht:

> Während nun alles mäusleinstill umherstand und die Ohren spitzte, erhub der Engländer beide Hände getrennt hoch in die Luft, wobei er alle Spitzen der Finger zusammenkniff und mit den Nägeln der einen viermal gegen die andere schlug. Alsbald erhub Panurg die Rechte, streckte den Daumen ins rechte Nasenloch, hielt die vier Finger ausgestreckt gegen das Nasenbein, wobei er das linke Auge ganz zudrückte, und mit dem rechten blinzelte, so daß die Braue und die Wimper tief heruntergepreßt waren... Aber es schien, als sei Thaumast nicht zufrieden hiemit, denn er legte seinen Daumen an die Nasenspitze und schloß die Finger derselben Hand. Da legte Panurg die zwei Mittelfinger an beide Mundwinkel, zog den Mund, so weit er konnte, auseinander und zeigte sein ganzes Gebiß, wobei er noch mit beiden Daumen die Augenwimpern so tief wie möglich herabdrückte, so daß er nach übereinstimmendem Urteil der Versammelten eine sehr leidige Fratze schnitt.

In dieser Weise geht die stumme Zwiesprache der beiden noch eine ganze Weile hin und her, bis Thaumast sich durch die Gebärdenüberlegenheit Panurgs schließlich geschlagen gibt.

Dieser Gebärdenpassus bei Rabelais bringt nicht nur einen der ersten Frühbelege für die 'Lange Nase', wie unser verehrter Jubilar Archer Taylor in seiner Abhandlung 'The Shanghai Gesture' (S. 9f.) nachgewiesen hat, sondern diese Stelle ist überhaupt ein wichtiges Zeugnis in der entwicklungsgeschichtlichen Dokumentation der Gebärdensprache. Die einzelnen Gebärdenzeichen Panurgs und Thaumasts sind jedenfalls nicht, wie man zunächst annehmen möchte, völlig phantastisch, sondern haben eine bestimmte traditionelle Bedeutung. Der Gebärdenpassus bei Rabelais ist andererseits unserem heutigen Gefühl so unverständlich, daß er in den Übersetzungen und populären Ausgaben in der Regel fehlt oder stark gekürzt ist. Es ist natürlich reine Ironie, wenn bloße Gestikulationen hier als nicht zu überbietende Pointe des wissenschaftlichen Gesprächs ausgegeben werden, und es sind wohl die zeitgenössischen Gelehrten der Sorbonne, über die sich Rabelais lustig macht, indem er ihre Weisheit als bloßes Getue, als Zeichenfechterei um im Grunde belanglose Dinge persifliert. Und doch lassen sich an diesem Beispiel wissenschaftlicher Scharlatanerei einige grundsätzliche Beobachtungen zur Gebärdensprache anknüpfen, Beobachtungen, die 1. den Zeitstil, 2. den Sozialstil, 3. den Nationalstil und 4. den Personalstil gebärdenhaften Verhaltens betreffen.

Panurg und sein englischer Diskussionspartner sind eben so 'gelehrt', daß für die Tiefgründigkeit ihrer Gedankenwelt keine Worte mehr ausreichen. Zieht man alles Ironische und Schwankhafte der Situation ab, so bleibt ein erster Grundsatz, der für jede Gebärdensprache ganz allgemein gilt: Man spricht nämlich in Gebärden, wenn die Sprache der Worte versagt oder wenn sie einem versagt ist, d. h. eine Gebärdensprache gibt es überall dort, wo man sich der Worte nicht bedienen will, nicht bedienen kann oder nicht bedienen darf. Beispiele dafür gibt es genug: Vor allem das Fingeralphabet der Taubstummen, das die Schriftzeichen mit den Fingern nachbildet. Oder: es gibt Mönchsorden mit völligem Redeverbot und sie haben z. T. eine besondere Gebärdensprache entwickelt. Wir sind darüber unterrichtet schon durch mittelalterliche Bilderhandschriften, wie z. B. der des Abtes Wilhelm von Hirsau. Zweckhaft gebunden ist auch die Gebärdensprache naturvölkischer Jäger. Bei der Jagd darf das Wild nicht verscheucht werden und darum sind gebärdenhafte Jagdzeichen entwickelt worden, mit denen man sich über die Art des Wildes verständigt (Abb. 2). Moderne Beispiele lassen sich hinzufügen: Mit Gebärden machen sich verständlich: der Ausländer, der die Landessprache noch nicht beherrscht, der Schauspieler des Stummfilms und der Pantomime, die Arbeiter in einer lärmerfüllten Werkhalle, der Verkehrspolizist im

Straßenlärm, der Schiedsrichter beim Fußballspiel, der Dirigent eines Orchesters. In allen diesen Fällen ist das Wort nicht am Platz oder das Wort allein genügt nicht, so daß an seine Stelle die Gebärde tritt. Aber auch das gesprochene Wort ist oft undenkbar ohne die begleitende Gebärde. Wir sehen dies schon bei einfachen Gebärdenformen des täglichen Lebens. Das bejahende Kopfnicken, die zeigenden Gebärden, die einladende Handbewegung bei der Aufforderung zum Platz nehmen, d. h. Gebärden kommen zum Wort hinzu, wo das Gesagte allein noch nicht genügt, sondern mit Gesten noch unterstrichen wird. Hierher gehören auch einige Gebärden im rituellen und liturgischen Raum, z. B. die Segensgebärde und andere geregelte Gebärden des amtierenden Geistlichen; auf dem Gebiet des Rechtes etwa die Schwurgebärde bei der Eidesleistung. Es gibt bekanntlich im altdeutschen Recht — erhalten in den Bilderhandschriften des *Sachsenspiegels* — genau festgelegte Haltungen und Gebärden, z. B. Zustimmungs- und Ablehnungsgesten (Abb. 26), Befehlsgesten, Gleichgültigkeitsgesten usw.

Mit Gebärden drückt man schließlich auch das aus, was man aus Gründen des Anstands oder des Taktgefühls nicht sagen darf, wo also über dem zu Sagenden irgend ein Worttabu liegt. Wenn z. B. der Arzt mit den Schultern zuckt, muß der Patient annehmen, daß sein Fall bedenklich ist. Oder wir kennen Worttabus im Bereich des Schimpfworts und des Fluches. Beim Gebrauch von Schimpf- und Spottgebärden braucht man nichts zu sagen, kann sich aber sehr viel dabei denken, und dennoch sind die Gebärden unmißverständlich. Aus demselben Grund gibt es auch so viele Gebärden mit obszöner Bedeutung. Dies führt uns zu einer zweiten Beobachtung:

In dem Gebärdendialog Rabelais' begegnet uns eine ganze Reihe sehr unziemlicher, derber und unflätiger Gebärden. Der ganze Passus entspricht durchaus dem grobianischen Gebärdenstil dieser Zeit. Es gibt also 2. einen Zeitstil der Gebärdensprache. Das wird noch deutlicher, wenn wir an gegensätzliche Gebärdenstile denken, etwa an die fast völlige Gebärdenlosigkeit der isländischen Saga, ihre ausgesprochene Scheu, eine Empfindung gestisch sichtbar zu machen, oder an die züchtigen Gebärden des höfischen Stils in den Huldgebärden hochmittelalterlicher Frauen; entgegengesetzt: die Pose, das sich in Positursetzen barocker Denkmäler usw. Wieder einen anderen zeitgebundenen Stil bringen die Gebärden der spätmittelalterlichen Geißlerzüge, die bei ihren Bußübungen durch eigens ersonnene Körperhaltungen oder Handbewegungen sich ihre Hauptsünden zu erkennen gaben. Es gibt ferner deutliche Zeitstile der Grußgebärden: zunächst sehr altertümliche Grußgesten durch Ablegen der Waffen, durch Erheben der Arme und andere Bezeugungen der Waffenlosigkeit als Zeichen friedfertiger Gesinnung. Dann höfliche, d. h. eben höfische Grüße, Demutsgesten der Selbsterniedrigung, der Unterwerfung, des sich Ergebens, die Verbeugung, das Nieder-

knien, die Proskynese. Schließlich militärische Grüße, Faschisten- und Kommu-
nistengrüße usw. Das alles sind Zeitstile gebärdenhaften Verhaltens, und es gibt
dann 3. einen Sozialstil der Gebärde: Ein gut Teil der Komik unseres Grund-
beispiels bei Rabelais liegt in der sozialen Unangemessenheit der Gebärdensprache,
darin nämlich, daß zwei angeblich berühmte Gelehrte in so derber, d. h. eben in
unangemessener Weise diskutieren. Es ziemt sich eben nicht für einen Gelehrten,
wenn er als Zeichen des Nachdenkens in der Nase bohrt oder den Mund breit
zieht. Es gibt also soziale Abstufungen standesgemäßen Sich-Gebarens. Jeder
Stand hat seine ihm zukommende Haltung und seine typischen Gebärden. Das
gilt vom König bis zum Bettler. Von Ludwig XIV. sagt z. B. ein Biograph: 'Er
hatte einen Gang, der nur für ihn und seinen Rang paßte, und der bei jedem
anderen lächerlich gewesen wäre.' Wir unterscheiden das Schreiten geistlicher
Würdenträger oder auch die würdige Haltung des Richters von der Berufshaltung
etwa des Schneiders, der mit untergeschlagenen Beinen auf dem Tisch sitzt, oder
von der gabenheischenden Haltung des Bettlers. Natürlich streckt der Bettler
nicht immer seine Hand aus, und ebenso natürlich sitzt der Schneider nicht immer
mit untergeschlagenen Beinen auf dem Tisch, aber in der jeweiligen berufstypi-
schen Haltung werden die Vertreter einzelner Stände immer wieder dargestellt.
Auch die ganzen Sozialtypen der commedia dell' arte haben ihre spezifischen Gebärden.

Es gibt 4. ethnische Unterschiede der Gebärdensprache. Nicht zufällig unterliegt bei Rabelais der englische Gesprächspartner bei der Gebärden-
diskussion auf französischem Boden, und ebensowenig zufällig hat der berühmte
französische Illustrator Gustave Doré gerade jenen Augenblick des Gebärden-
konfliktes festgehalten, in dem sich der Engländer der überlegenen Gestik Panurgs
geschlagen geben muß und die bis dahin gestikulierenden Arme sinken läßt (Abb.
22). Die gestischen Ausdrucksmöglichkeiten sind eben bei den einzelnen Völkern
verschieden. Die Bevölkerung verschiedener Landschaften und Erdteile sind bekanntlich mit Händen und Füßen verschieden redselig. Die Deutschen beispielsweise sind im allgemeinen nicht sehr gebärdenfreundlich. Es ist in Deutschland
verpönt, zu viel mit den Händen zu reden und volkssprachliche Wendungen
drücken diese Meinung auch aus. Man tadelt: 'Ei gebärd' dich nit so!' oder 'Redt
nit so mit de Händ'!' Man spricht von einem 'unbeherrschten Gebärdenspiel',
und wenn einer 'gestikuliert', wenn jemand 'eine Rede schwingt', so ist das mehr
ein Tadel als ein Lob seiner Rhetorik. Man spricht von einer 'bloßen Geste'.
'Fromme Gesten' sind so viel wie Heuchelei, und ein gebärdenreicher Prediger
wurde prompt als 'Kirchengöbbels' bezeichnet.

Ganz anders bei den südlichen Völkern Europas und Südamerikas! Haltung
und Gebärden der mediterranen Völker sind lebhafter, feuriger, ausdrucksvoller

und überschwänglicher als die der germanischen Völker, und es gibt in Südeuropa einen reichen Katalog eingewurzelter und herkömmlicher Gebärden für Freude, Bewunderung und Wohlgefallen, für Unwilligkeit, Enttäuschung und Feindschaft, für Schlafen und Essen, Gebärden für Viel und Nichts, kein Geld, gestische Aufforderungen zum Reden, zum Schweigen, Gebärden zur Kennzeichnung eines plötzlichen Einfalls usw. usw. (Abb. 1), d. h. es gibt Unterschiede der Gebärdensprache von Volk zu Volk, und je weiter wir gehen, desto größer werden die Unterschiede und desto unverständlicher werden die Gebärden. Gebärden sind also gemeinschaftsgebunden und kulturell bedingt. Die Grußgebärden sind in jedem Kulturkreis wieder andere, oder sogar die Eidgebärde zeigt über die ganze Erde hin sehr verschiedene Formen: Auf Samoa z. B. wird geschworen, indem man die Hand auf die Augen legt, denn nach der dortigen Vorstellung wird der Meineidige blind, und die Schwurgebärde bedeutet also: Blind will ich werden, wenn ich nicht die Wahrheit sage. Mit wachsendem geographischem Abstand fällt es uns zunehmend schwerer, den gestischen Ausdruck zutreffend zu deuten und zu verstehen. Es gibt z. B. im Buddhismus hunderte von verschiedenen Haltungen des Gebetes, von denen jede einzelne ihren eigenen Sinn und Zweck hat. Die Inder etwa haben eine förmliche traditionelle Fingersprache entwickelt. Nicht nur an ihren alten Götterstatuen hat die Fingerhaltung einen bestimmten Sinn (Abb. 3), sondern auch im täglichen Leben wird lebhaft und sinnbildlich mit den Fingern geredet in Gebärden, die uns nicht von selbst verständlich sind. Eine und dieselbe ganz einfache Gebärde kann deshalb in verschiedenen Kulturkreisen ganz unterschiedlich aufgefaßt werden. Gebärden, die in Nordamerika etwa für harmlos gelten, können z. B. in Südamerika als unanständig empfunden werden.

Das Händeklatschen, das bei uns den Beifall bekundet, ruft im Orient und ebenso auch in Spanien den Kellner herbei, und anderorts werden sogar religiöse Tänze von Händeklatschen begleitet. In Japan klatschen die Schintoisten vor dem Gebet zur Begrüßung der Gottheit und in der Absicht, sie auf sich aufmerksam zu machen. Der Bedeutungsinhalt einer Gebärde wird also durch die Situation, durch Ort und Zeit bestimmt. Sogar anscheinend ganz intuitive und allgemeinmenschliche Gefühlsausdrücke des Erstaunens und der Überraschung, von Abscheu und Verachtung sind bei den Völkern nicht einheitlich. So gilt das Herausstrecken der Zunge z. B., das in Europa ein Zeichen schimpflicher Verachtung ist, in Polynesien als Grußgebärde und Zeichen der Ergebenheit. Oder, noch ein weiteres Beispiel: Das Reiben der Hände wird in der Antike — ganz gegen mitteleuropäische Gewohnheit — sonderbarerweise nur dem Betrübten zugeschrieben. Die in Mitteleuropa geläufige Kommgeste wird in Süditalien, auf dem südlichen Balkan, im vorderen Orient und in Nordafrika mit einer geradezu umgekehrten Handhaltung ausgedrückt. Die Hand wird dabei mit der Fläche nach

unten gehalten, so daß ein Mitteleuropäer glaubt, er werde eher weggewiesen als
herangewinkt (Abb. 15). Schon das einfache Nicken oder Schütteln des Kopfes
bei Bejahung oder Verneinung ist keine physisch gegebene Selbstverständlichkeit,
sondern eine kulturell gebundene Überlieferung. Durch Süditalien und mitten
durch den Balkan geht die Grenze zwischen dem Verneinen durch Kopfschütteln
und dem anderen Verneinen, bei dem das Kinn hochgestoßen oder der Kopf zu-
rückgelegt wird (Abb. 16a); und ähnlich ist es mit der Bejahungsgebärde, die in
Bulgarien und im südlichen Jugoslawien durch ein Seitwärtslegen des Kopfes
nach links oder nach rechts zum Ausdruck gebracht wird (Abb. 16b).

Volkskundliche Kulturgrenzen solcher Art werfen immer die Frage nach dem
Alter der Erscheinungen auf. Die Gebärdensprache ist sehr beharrlich und zeigt
eine große Langlebigkeit ihrer Formen. Gemeinsamkeiten in der Gebärdensprache würden also auf alte Kulturzusammenhänge schließen lassen. Die Untersuchungen De Jorio's über die süditalienische, speziell die neapolitanische Gebärdensprache, von Flachskampf über die spanische Gebärdensprache und andererseits die Arbeit von Sittl über die Gebärden der Griechen und Römer haben
erwiesen, daß viele der uns fremden Gebärden Südeuropas direkte Fortsetzungen
antiker Gebärden sind, wie sie in analoger Bedeutung in der antiken Kunst oder
bei antiken Schriftstellern zu finden sind. Der Handkuß, die Umarmung zwischen
Männern, in der Antike geläufig z. B. nach der Rückkehr von einer Reise, bei
Ankunft eines Gastfreundes (Abb. 6), findet sich in romanischen Ländern noch
heute bei besonders feierlichen Anlässen, wie bei Ordensverleihungen, Staats-
besuchen usw. So findet also die stark ausgeprägte Gestik bei den südlichen Völkern Europas zu einem großen Teil eine historische Erklärung. Es wirkt da auch
die rhetorische und forensische Tradition der Antike nach, und wir können hier
immer wieder beobachten, wie bestimmte traditionelle Gebärden von einer
außerordentlichen Langlebigkeit sind. Diese Gebärden sind insofern Gegenstand
volkskundlicher Untersuchung, als sie nicht individuell, sondern eben primär
ethnisch und kulturell gebunden sind. Und damit kommen wir zu dem eigentlich
volkskundlichen Anliegen, um das es bei der Gebärdensprache geht.

Es gibt also 5. individuelle und kollektive Gebärden, und wir müssen diese
beiden Bereiche klar voneinander scheiden, um den spezifisch volkskundlichen
Anteil an der Erforschung der Gebärdensprache deutlich zu machen. Mit den
individuellen Gebärden beschäftigen sich andere Wissenschaften. Nur an bestimmten typischen Gebärden erkennt z. B. der Kunsthistoriker oder der Archäo-
loge bei einem Bildwerk, wen es darstellt. Der theaterwissenschaftlich geschulte
Regisseur achtet auf die Übereinstimmung der Rolle mit der Gestik des Schau-
spielers. Vor allem aber beurteilt natürlich die Ausdruckspsychologie die Menschen
nach ihren Minen, Gesten und Gebärden; sie beobachtet Haltung, Gangart und

Gebärdensprache des einzelnen Menschen und sieht in diesen Gebärden charakteristische Ausdrucksformen eines Individuums. Sie stellt geradezu experimentell fest, mit welcher Mimik und Gestik ein Mensch auf bestimmte Eindrücke reagiert, weil alle diese individuellen Gebärdennuancen das 'gewisse Etwas' einer Person ausmachen. Uns interessiert hier aber nicht so sehr das individuelle Gebaren differenzierter Persönlichkeiten, als vielmehr die Gebärdensprache als Kollektivbesitz einer ethnischen Gruppe.

Gebärden sind weithin überindividuell und traditionell bestimmt, d. h. sie werden zwar von Individuen ausgeführt, jedoch in bereits vorgeformten, von der Überlieferung bestimmten, also nicht individuellen Formen. Hierher gehört z. B. das ausgedehnte und kulturgeschichtlich so interessante Gebiet der Grußgebärden. Solche traditionellen Gebärden gehören ferner zu magischen Abwehrmaßnahmen aller Art, und sie gehören vor allem zum Gebiet der Volkssitte. Es gibt gewisse durch Brauch und Herkommen bestimmte Gebärden und Haltungen z. B. für das Halten des Gesangbuches beim Kirchgang (Abb. 17), für die Braut bei der bäuerlichen Hochzeit, für den Gang zum Abendmahl, für den Hochzeitbitter und Todansager, oder für die Leidtragenden. Wenn z. B. in manchen schwäbischen Dörfern ein Mann als Leichensager zum Pfarrer geht, macht er sich dadurch kenntlich, daß er die rechte Hand vorn im zugeknöpften Rock trägt, ähnlich wie vielerorts die Frauen zum Abendmahl gehen, indem sie die Hände unter einem Taschentuch gefaltet haben. Es gibt brauchmäßig geregelte Fälle, in denen die Hände verborgen werden müssen, wobei sogar eine bestimmte Haltung vorgeschrieben ist. Die Hände werden beim Abendmahl aus Ehrfurcht verhüllt, um dem Verehrungswürdigen nicht mit bloßen Händen zu nahen (Abb. 18). Dieser Ritus der verhüllten Hände hat eine lange Geschichte. Wir kennen ihn von einer großen Zahl altchristlicher Denkmäler her, namentlich bei Darstellungen von Heiligen, wie sie mit verdeckten Händen den Himmelsschlüssel oder die Märtyrerkrone empfangen. Wir finden dann den Ritus der verhüllten Hände im byzantinischen Hofzeremoniell, nach dem Beamte und Gesandte mit verhüllten Händen vor den König treten mußten, und als gebärdenhaftes Relikt hat er sich in den Volksbräuchen bis heute erhalten.

Oder noch ein Beispiel aus dem Jahresbrauch, auf das Leopold Schmidt aufmerksam gemacht hat: In manchen österreichischen Dörfern ist es üblich, daß in den sog. Rauchnächten, das sind die zwölf heiligen Nächte von Weihnachten bis Dreikönig, sich die ganze Familie um einen rauchenden Topf herum versammelt, der in der Mitte der Stube aufgestellt wird. Alle stehen dabei in aufrechter Stellung herum, aber mit gesenktem Kopf. 'So sollen' — sagt man — 'die Halme mit den schweren Ähren zur Erntezeit auf den Feldern stehen.' Das heißt, diese Kopfgebärde des einfachen Kopfsenkens wird direkt mit einer glaubensmäßigen Be-

gründung vollzogen, und zwar im Sinne des Analogieglaubens: Wie die Köpfe,
so auch die Ähren. Die Gedankenverbindung von den sich beugenden Garben zu
dem sich beugenden Menschenhaupt ist an sich alt. Die Analogie ist bekannt aus
Josephs Traum von den Garben seiner Brüder, die sich vor der seinen verneigen,
und noch Shakespeare läßt die Herzogin von Gloucester sagen:

> Warum senkt mein Gemahl das Haupt,
> Wie Korn beschwert von Ceres' überreifer Last?

> *(Heinrich VI., 2. T., I, 2).*

Hier ist die Haltung individuell: Jemand läßt den Kopf hängen. Aber das Spezi-
fische und Interessante an der Brauchübung der Losnächte ist die traditionell
und kollektiv geübte Gebärde. Nicht jede Kopfneigung könnte selbstverständlich diesen Ernteerfolg haben, sondern nur eine brauchtümliche, eben zu der
kultisch-magischen Zeit der 12 Nächte, in der alles Tun prophetisch auf das
kommende Jahr vorauswirkt.

Dies sind gemeinschaftlich ausgeführte Gebärden, Haltungen; doch daneben
gibt es vom Einzelnen ausgeführte, aber dennoch traditionelle Gebärden. Und
genau zu dieser Gruppe gehört der Gebärdenpassus bei Rabelais. Die Gebärden
der beiden Disputanten, die Rabelais für unser heutiges Verständnis fast zu aus-
führlich schildert, weil uns eben diese Gebärden nichts mehr sagen, sind nicht
etwa Phantasieerfindungen des Dichters, sondern es sind tatsächlich geübte Gebärden der Volksüberlieferung, und sie waren den Zeitgenossen noch durchaus
geläufig. Die Komik bei Rabelais liegt gerade darin, daß die beiden Pseudogelehr-
ten nicht individuell, sondern mit traditionellen Gebärden gestikulieren, daß das
Primitive, noch Vorsprachliche der Gebärden pseudowissenschaftlich als Ge-
lehrtensprache ausgegeben wird, und daß es reine Spottgebärden sind, mit denen
Panurg den Engländern überlistet. Und nicht nur die von Rabelais geschilderten
einzelnen Gebärden sind volkstümlicher Art, sondern auch das Ganze des Wett-
kampfes. Wir haben im volkstümlichen Bereich tatsächlich solche Gebärden- und
Grimmassenwettkämpfe. Besonders im alpenländischen Raum hat sich z. B. das
Grimmassenwettschneiden der Sennen erhalten. Ein sehr eindrucksvolles Beispiel
für Grimmassenschneiden um die Wette, das sog. 'Chäs-Zennen' findet sich bei
L. Trenker: *Berge und Heimat*, Berlin 1937 (Abb. 29). Schließlich gibt es einen
über ganz Europa verbreiteten Schwank vom Rededuell eines Mannes mit seinem
streitsüchtigen Weib, das immer das letzte Wort behalten will. Als der Mann
schließlich seines Weibes überdrüssig wird und sie kurzerhand ins Wasser wirft,
da setzt sie, bereits unter Wasser, den Streit der Worte noch mit Gebärden fort
und behält auch hierin das letzte Wort. Der Schwank ist in der *Gartengesellschaft*

des Montanus (1560) wiedergegeben und ist auch sonst in mancherlei Schwank-
sammlungen abgedruckt.

Wir greifen nun einige Spottgebärden heraus und kommen damit vom allgemeinen zum besonderen Teil, indem wir uns einzelne Gebärden etwas näher ansehen wollen. Eine der verbreitetsten Spottgebärden ist die, die man als 'Feige' zu
bezeichnen pflegt. Bei dieser Gebärde wird der Daumen aus der geschlossenen
Faust zwischen Zeige- und Mittelfinger herausgestreckt, wie das etwa schon auf
einer Handzeichnung Dürers dargestellt ist. (Abb. 35). Von Dürer selbst wissen wir
nun allerdings nichts über den Sinn und die Bedeutung dieser Handstellung, aber zu
Dürers Zeit ist sie schon im ganzen Abendland als Hohn- und Spottgebärde bekannt gewesen. Die Hauptverbreitungsgebiete dieser Geste liegen in Italien, und
schon in der Antike wie noch im heutigen Italien und Griechenland, aber auch
sonst weit verbreitet, macht man dieses Zeichen gegen den bösen Blick. Historische und bildliche Quellen für die Feige sind schon deshalb nicht allzuhäufig,
weil die Feige meistens heimlich in der Tasche oder unter dem Tisch gemacht
wird. Wo nun die schriftlichen Nachrichten fehlen, da müssen uns andere Belege
als Quelle dienen. Es gibt z. B. eine ganze Reihe antiker Amulette mit der Gebärde der Feige, und im Mittelalter und noch in der Neuzeit wurde diese Tradition
fortgesetzt. Als Amulett gegen den bösen Blick kommt die Feige also zu fast allen
Zeiten sehr häufig vor (Abb. 32). Auch sonst finden wir die Feige in bildlicher
Darstellung an allen möglichen brauchtümlichen Geräten, z. B. auf Narrenprit-
schen. Die Feige ist nämlich nicht nur ein wichtiges Abwehrmittel, sondern sie ist
schließlich als Zeichen schimpflicher Verachtung bekannt geworden. Wir besitzen
spätmittelalterliche Bildbelege auf Darstellungen der Verspottung Christi. Die
Wendung 'einem die vîgen bieten' ist den Liederdichtern des 14. und 15. Jahrhunderts bekannt, und dieser Wortgebrauch ist noch spürbar in mundartlichen
Versionen, z. B. 'einem den Daumen stecken', oder österreichisch 'Ja Feign!', ein
Zuruf, der einer höhnischen, herausfordernden Verneinung und Abweisung gleich-
kommt. Es gibt schließlich eine obszöne Bedeutung der Feige als Aufforderungs-
und Verständigungsmittel in sexuellen Angelegenheiten.

Das methodische Problem für die Geschichte und Systematik der Gebärdensprache liegt nicht nur in der langen Überlieferung von der Antike bis zur Gegenwart, sondern in der offenkundigen Mehrdeutigkeit dieser Gebärde. Es ist sogar
durchaus eine Ambivalenz der Bedeutung bei ein und derselben Person denkbar:
Ein und derselbe Mensch kann das Feigenamulett als mächtiges Zaubermittel und
Anhängsel an der Uhrkette tragen und zugleich die Feigengebärde zum Spotten
und Schelten verwenden, d. h. es kommt also wieder auf die jeweilige Gebrauchs-
situation an, was eine und dieselbe Gebärde bedeuten kann. Man wird hier auch
nicht von einer eigentlichen Bedeutungsentwicklung sprechen dürfen, sondern

9 Taylor

wahrscheinlich besteht von Anfang an ein Zusammenhang zwischen dem Spottcharakter und dem magischen Charakter. Auf einem von Joh. Bolte publizierten
Kupferstich aus dem Jahre 1650 sieht man eine junge Frau, die auf einer Henne
reitet (Abb. 36). Mit der rechten Hand macht sie die Gebärde der Feige, deutlich in
obszöner Bedeutung, denn aus der Bildunterschrift ergibt sich, daß es sich um eine
Ehebrecherin handelt, die sich eben durch diese Gebärde ausweist. Die Hennenreiterin hat ein männliches Gegenstück, den Hahnrei (Abb. 37). Doch macht der Hahnrei die Spottgebärde der H ö r n e r. Aber eigentlich ist der Hahnrei oder Hörnerträger,
d. h. also der Gatte einer Ehebrecherin, der betrogene Ehemann, selbst das Objekt
dieser Gebärde: Man verspottete ihn, indem man ihm die Hörner wies, d. h. indem man Zeigefinger und kleinen Finger in Form von zwei Hörnern gegen ihn ausstreckte. Das bedeutet also: Du bist nicht der einzige Mann deiner Frau. Her-
leitung, Entstehung und Geschichte der gehörnten Hand sind allerdings kaum zu
erhellen. Im Grimm'schen Wörterbuch hat Moritz Heyne die Redensart vom gehörnten Mann auf eine mittelalterliche Legende zurückführen wollen. Doch wissen
wir heute, daß Gebärde und sprichwörtliche Redensart schon im Altertum
existierten, z. B. auf einem Wandbild in Pompeji, das vermutlich eine Kom-
mödienszene darstellt (Abb. 7), und es gibt ebenfalls schon antike Amulette dieser
Art (Abb. 33).

Beziehen sich nun die zwei Hörner auf die Zweiheit der Männer, oder liegt ein
phallisches Zeichen vor? Bedeuten die Hörner einen Vergleich des betrogenen
Ehemanns mit einem gehörnten Tier, also soviel wie: 'du bist ein Rindvieh!', oder
bedeuten sie, wie Joh. Bolte angenommen hat, daß der Gehörnte unter dem
Sternzeichen des Steinbockes geboren und zu ehelichem Unglück bestimmt ist?
Es ist auch gesagt worden, die Redensart sei aus einer Volksglaubensvorstellung
erwachsen, wonach die Untreue der Frau sich durch ein Horn zeige, das ihrem
Mann aus der Stirn wachse. Aber für alle diese Deutungsversuche fehlen wirklich
überzeugende historische Belege. Wichtiger als die fast unlösbar erscheinende Ur-
sprungsfrage der gehörnten Hand erscheint zunächst wieder die Tatsache der
Mehrdeutigkeit dieser Gebärde. Sie kann sowohl eine Ehrenkränkung mit ero-
tischem Sinn meinen (Abb. 27), wie auch als magisches Abwehrzeichen gegen den
bösen Blick gelten. Es erscheint zweifelhaft, ob die Gebärde der gehörnten Hand
überhaupt eine Art 'Entwicklung' von einer zauberischen Abwehrgebärde zur
Spottgeste durchgemacht hat, denn 1. hat diese Gebärde z. T. bis heute noch den
magischen Abwehrsinn zum Schutz gegen den bösen Blick erhalten, und 2. scheint
die gehörnte Hand andrerseits z. B. schon auf etruskischen Grabmalereien des
6. vorchristlichen Jahrhunderts eine profane, aufs Erotische zielende Bedeutung
gehabt zu haben (Abb. 34).

Abwehrgesten und Spottgesten schließen sich ja nicht aus, sondern erweisen im

Gegenteil immer wieder ihre innere Verwandtschaft. Vielfach haben die Spottgebärden noch eine geschlechtliche Nebenbedeutung. Die sexuelle Komponente
gehört aber keineswegs nur zum spöttischen Teilsinn der Gebärde, sondern vielleicht beruhte gerade hierauf ursprünglich auch ein Teil der magischen Abwehr-
kraft der Gebärde, und vielleicht wollte man ursprünglich die magische Wirkung
der Gebärde gerade durch ihre geschlechtliche Bedeutung hervorrufen. Von der
Abwehr zum Spott ist also nur ein kleiner Schritt und die Doppelbedeutung wird
dann beibehalten.

Das Herausstrecken der Zunge ist eine weitere Spottgeste, die sich in der Kinder-
welt erhalten hat. Damit ist aber nur noch die äußere Form bewahrt geblieben.
Die ursprünglich magische Abwehrbedeutung der Geste zeigt sich mit voller Deut-
lichkeit noch bei Naturvölkern als Abwehrgebärde, etwa aus Angst vor dem
Photographiertwerden; sie zeigt sich ferner bei älteren dinglichen Zeugnissen, an
vielen Hauszeichen, den sogenannten Neidköpfen. Das berümteste Beispiel ist der
sog. Lällekönig in Basel, der dem Deutschen Reich jenseits des Rheines Hohn
bieten sollte (Abb. 30). Durch einen von der Rheinströmung getriebenen Pendel
verdrehte die Fratze fortwährend die Augen in fürchterlichster Weise, während
sie gleichzeitig taktmäßig die Zunge ausstreckte und einzog. Altertümlicher als
diese Hohngeste ist die Vorstellung, man könne böse Geister und schlimme Feinde
durch fratzenhafte Gebärden abschrecken. Das Mittelalter liebte es, derartige
Fratzen an den Tortürmen der alten Festungen anzubringen, und von hier reicht
die Darstellung des Grimmassenkopfes mit der herausgestreckten Zunge über die
Wasserspeier unserer mittelalterlichen Dome zurück bis zu den antiken Gorgonen-
häuptern als Tempelfirstzeichen (Abb. 31). Der Spottcharakter der Gebärde ist
allerdings auch hier nicht erst eine ganz neuzeitliche Entwicklung. Das zeigen
beispielsweise die Spottgebärden der Henkersknechte auf den spätmittelalterlichen Passionsbildern, die, wie wir immer wieder feststellen können, eine wichtige
Quelle für die Geschichte der Spottgebärden darstellen.

Eine Verstärkung der herausgestreckten Zunge ist jene Grimmasse, bei der mit
zwei Fingern die Mundwinkel eingehakt werden. Der Mund wird so zu einer un-
natürlichen Breite auseinandergezogen, wodurch eine ganz scheußliche Fratze
entsteht (Abb. 10). Als Panurg zu dieser Gebärde ausholt, findet sie den besonderen
Beifall der Umstehenden. Aber das gibt es nicht nur im grobianischen Zeitalter in
Frankreich, sondern in Bayern auch noch in der Gegenwart. In Bayern nennt man
diese Gebärde sehr sprechend das 'Gähnmaul'. In Österreich findet sich die volkstümliche Bezeichnung 'blecken', oder auch 'die Lippen recken', und es wird da in
seltenen Fällen auch noch von Erwachsenen gebraucht. Sonst wird diese Gebärde
nur noch von Kindern ausgeübt (Abb. 21). Wir haben aber ganz interessante
historische Belege. Wir finden sie z. B. bei Maskengestalten des 15. und 17. Jahr-

hunderts, wie bei der Teufelsgestalt beim Schembartlauf in Nürnberg aus dem
Jahre 1539, und wir finden das 'Gähnmaul' in der bildenden Kunst derselben Zeit
bei den Darstellungen der Verspottung Jesu (Abb. 25), z. T. verbunden mit noch
einer weiteren Gebärde, bei der das Auge mit den Fingern künstlich weit auf-
gerissen wird. Wir haben übrigens zu diesen bildlichen Belegen, den Darstellungen
der Verspottungsszene nach der Dornenkrönung auch literarische Entsprechungen,
und es kommt auch darin die Verspottung Jesu nicht nur mit Worten, sondern
mit Gebärden zum Ausdruck. In einer solchen Schilderung heißt es z. B.:

> Sie stachen ihm den Narren und Esel.
> Sie stupten ihn mit den Fingern.
> Kruemten über ihn das Maul.
> Zaigten ihm die Feigen.
> Rissen die Augen auff in alle weit.
> Warfen die Zunge auss solang sie kundten.
> Schlugen und paschten ihre blutdürstige Hend nach aller Macht.
> Stosseten ihm zum öfteren die zugedruckten Hendtfäust unter Augen und Nasen.

Das alles sind Spottgebärden, zugleich aber auch Abwehrgebärden des Volksglaubens insbesondere gegen die Dämonie des Blickes. Mit der Bezeichnung 'Böser
Blick' ist man freilich in der Volkskunde immer schnell zur Hand. Gehörnte
Hand und Feige, wie auch das Herausstrecken der Zunge, sie alle gelten als Abwehrmittel gegen den bösen Blick. Aber was ist der böse Blick denn selbst? Wenn
er ein aktives schadenzauberisches Sehen ist, ist er dann nicht selbst gleichfalls
eine Gebärde? Dieses Aufreißen der Augen, das 'Äugl geben', wie es in Österreich
noch redensartlich bezeugt ist, kann im Spanischen direkt bedeuten: 'Jemandem
etwas antun', wodurch diese Gebärde also wirklich in die nächste Nähe des bösen
Blickes rückt. Das Herabziehen des Augenlides, das 'Äugl-geben', könnte einer
der seltenen Fälle sein, wo wir noch eine aktiv wirksame Geste im Sinne des bösen
Blickes vorfinden. Es gibt im südlichen Italien noch eine Geste, die in diese Richtung zu verweisen vermag: Man tippt mit dem Finger unter das Auge und zieht auch
das Unterlid herunter (Abb. 4). Diese Gebärde wird ganz allgemein verstanden und
bedeutet etwa: Ich bin nicht so dumm wie ich aussehe, ich habe dich durchschaut.
Eine Gebärde des Mißtrauens, des den anderen Durchschauthabens. Ebenso ist
diese Gebärde noch in der deutschen Soldatensprache des 2. Weltkriegs mit der
Redensart 'Holzauge sei wachsam!' geläufig gewesen.

Eine Spottgeste mit einem einst viel ernsthafteren Hintergrund ist dann das
sog. 'Rübchenschaben': Mit dem ausgestreckten Zeigefinger der rechten Hand
fährt man dabei über den der Linken, wie beim Schaben einer Rübe. Vor allem
ist diese Hohngebärde wiederum auf spätmittelalterlichen realistischen Bildern
zu sehen, wie z. B. auf einem Altarbild von Hans Holbein dem Älteren (Abb. 23).

Auch hier handelt es sich also um eine Gebärde, die vom Volksbrauch der Erwachsenen bis ins Kinderspiel abgesunken ist, und wieder sind über den Kinderbrauch der Gegenwart hinaus die spätmittelalterlichen Passionsdarstellungen unsere wichtigste Quelle (Abb. 24). Interessant sind auch die redensartlichen Bezeichnungen wie 'Ätsch gäbele', 'Gäbelimachen', 'den Guler stechen', 'Rübchen schaben', und insbesondere die Formel 'schabab'. Nur mehr als sprachliche Formel wird dabei gebraucht, was als wirkliche Gebärde sonst ausgestorben ist. Die schweizerische Mundart kennt 'schabab gsi' in der Bedeutung für 'beschämt, niedergeschlagen sein'. Die geistliche Literatur der Barockzeit kennt die Redensart als Wortsinnbild der Vergänglichkeit, und Abraham a Santa Clara dichtet z. B.:

> Die Blätter fallen ab,
> Und du wirst auch schabab.

Bis ins 20. Jahrh. hinein ist die Redensart 'Schabab' im Volksbrauch die sprachliche Formel für den abgewiesenen Freier, und noch bei Hermann Löns heißt es in einer Strophe:

> Schabab, schabab,
> Einen andern Schatz ich hab.

Eine Spottgebärde, ja, aber nicht nur das. Wichtig ist auch hier wieder ein magischer Bezug der Abwehr, das Überkreuzen. Dieses Fingerkreuzen oder auch Händekreuzen oder Beine-Verschränken ist eine primär abwehrende Gebärde. Hier wird im wörtlichen Sinn die böse Absicht des anderen 'durchkreuzt'. Unsere Abb. 11 zeigt einen Mann, der in die Gewalt von Hexen geraten ist, sich aber dadurch vor dem Zauber schützen kann, daß er seine beiden Unterarme kreuzweise übereinander legt. Schon Plinius gibt in der *naturalis historia* an, daß durch Verschränken der Finger wie auch durch Kreuzen der Beine eine Geburt verhindert werden könne. Diese Gebärden des Durchkreuzens und Verschränkens, die irgend ein Vorhaben 'durchkreuzen' sollen, dürfen nicht mit dem Kreuzeszeichen sakralen Ursprungs verwechselt werden: Durch Fingerverschränken, Beineübereinanderschlagen, Händekreuzen werden nach der Volksmeinung Eidschwüre abgeleitet und ungültig gemacht, Blut gestillt, Geburten verhindert usw. Gerade die Volksmedizin weiß von vielen Gebärdenvorschriften solcher Art. Agrippa von Nettesheim schreibt in seinen magischen Werken: 'Es ist ein Zauber, wenn man die Füße übereinanderschlägt, und es ist deshalb bei den Beratungen der fürstlichen Machthaber verboten als etwas, was allen Handlungen ein Hindernis entgegensetzt.' Die Gebärde hat also als Analogiehandlung selbst eine unmittelbare Wirkkraft. Ein Relikt dieser Vorstellung hat sich übrigens noch im Kinderspiel erhalten, wo das Beinekreuzen als Zeichen der Sicherung vor dem Gefangenwerden, als Asylgebärde, vorkommt. Solche Zusammenhänge von der Kindergebärde über Sitte und Brauch bis zu einem ursprünglichen Abwehrglauben sind nicht selten. Es ist vor allem interessant, wie diese Dinge im Volksglauben noch nachwirken bis in heutige Anstandsgesten hinein. Es gehört sich z. B. auch nicht, beim Essen oder in einer Gesellschaft die Beine übereinander zu schlagen. Die ursprünglich magische Funktion des Beinekreuzens zeigt sich sogar noch deutlich in einer Volksglaubensvorstellung, wonach gekreuzte Beine auf die Unterhaltung hemmend einwirken können. Wenn in einer Gesellschaft plötzliches Schweigen eintritt, fragt man manchmal, ob nicht einer der Anwesenden die Füße übers Kreuz habe. Bei dem, was als nicht schicklich gilt, spielen also vielfach ganz andere Traditionen herein. Vielfach sind wir uns der ursprünglich magischen Wirkung bestimmter Gebärden gar nicht mehr bewußt. Das gilt gerade für manche Anstandsgebärden: Daß man z. B. beim Husten, Niesen oder Gähnen die Hand vor den Mund hält, geschah ursprünglich gewiß nicht aus hygienischen Gründen, sondern es waren magische Schutzmaßnahmen gegen dämonische Einflüsse, die durch den geöffneten Mund ins Körperinnere kommen konnten.

Noch ein anderes Beispiel dieser Art: Es gehört sich z. B. nicht, mit dem Finger auf jemand zu zeigen. 'Man zeigt nicht mit dem nackten Finger auf angezogene Leute!' Das ist eine ziemlich moderne Prägung für eine alte Sache, und auch diese nach der Sitte ungehörige Geste beruht auf einem Tabu, das durch die hinweisende Gebärde schädliche Kraftübertragungen befürchtet. Volksglaubensaufzeichnungen noch des 20. Jahrhunderts verbieten es z. B. mit dem Finger gegen den Himmel zu zeigen, weil man einem Engel sonst die Augen aussteche oder ihn töte, weil sonst der Finger abfaulen oder sonst ein Unglück sich ereignen könnte. Wer mit den Fingern auf ein Gewitter deutet, den erschlägt es. Auch auf eine Hexe darf man nicht zeigen, wenn man nicht ihren bösen Blick auf sich ziehen will.

Ein großer Teil von alten Gebärden, die nur noch als Sprachgebärden, d. h. nur noch redensartlich vorhanden sind, gehören dem alten Rechtsleben an. In die volkskundliche Betrachtung gehören da nicht nur die sog. 'umkehrenden Gebärden' zur Aufhebung eines Eidschwures, die Meineidsgebärden des Volksglaubens, bei denen man mit der linken Hand in der Tasche oder auf dem Rücken dieselbe Gebärde macht, oder auch eine Gebärde, die den Eid wie einen Blitzstrahl ableiten soll, oder wenn die Schwurhand abwehrend mit der Hohlfläche gegen den Richter gehalten wird. Gegenstand der Volkskunde sind vor allem die Fälle, in denen alte Rechtsgebärden im Volksbrauch oder wenigstens in Redensarten nachwirken. Das Schwören beim eigenen Bart, das wir aus mehreren mittelalterlichen Literaturdenkmälern kennen (Heinrich der Löwe, oder auch Otto mit dem Bart schwören: 'sam mir mîn bart'); oder die Redensart 'Hand aufs Herz!' als volkstümliches Zeichen der eidestattlichen Versicherung ist ein Relikt einer tatsächlichen alten Eidgebärde. Besonders Geistliche und Frauen mußten beim Schwur die Hand auf die linke Brust legen.

Die wohl am häufigsten angewandte Gebärde, der alltäglich oft vollzogene Handschlag ist ursprünglich auch eine rechtlich verpflichtende Gebärde. Das Abschließen von Kaufverträgen durch Handschlag ist heute noch nicht ausgestorben und so schließen noch heute die Bauern einen Viehhandel ab: Ein Dritter schlägt die vereinigten Hände durch und bezeugt damit den Geschäftsabschluß (Abb. 19). Vor dem Aufkommen des Schriftverkehrs war dies die einzige Garantie. In den niederdeutschen Ausdrücken für kaufen und handeln 'koopslagen' lebt diese Form fort, redensartlich ist sie auch sonst noch vorhanden in Ausdrücken wie 'durch Handschlag bekräftigen', 'gib die Hand drauf!'. Insbesondere Kinder pflegen diese Art der Versicherung noch als eidesstattliche Verpflichtung. Der Handschlag ist aber in alter Zeit bei allen vertraglichen Verpflichtungen vorgenommen worden. Wir kennen den Handschlag beim Verlöbnis in der Kirche (Abb. 12), das Handgeben beim Kauf, beim Schuldgelöbnis, bei der Wette, beim Versprechen, bei staatlichen Verträgen: 'Si strakten den fride mit ir handen' heißt es im Kudrun-Epos, und von hier wirkt der Handschlag sogar bis in die volkskundlichen Sachgüter hinein: Eine beliebte Schmuckform der Brustspange mit zwei ineinander verschlungenen Händepaaren hieß im Mittelalter 'handtriuwebratze' d. h. also Handtreuebrosche (Abb. 20), oder wir besitzen sog. Verlobungszeichen über dem Wirtshaustisch, wo eben sinnbildlich gemacht wird, daß das durch Handschlag gegebene Versprechen vor dem Auge Gottes besteht und also gültig ist.

Auch der sprachliche Ausdruck 'einem etwas beweisen' ist im altdeutschen Recht tatsächlich mit einer hinweisenden Handgebärde verbunden gewesen.

Es erfordert im Sachsenspiegelrecht eine ausgesprochen demonstrative Hinweisgebärde, nicht bloß in Worten, sondern auch in Gebärden: 'mit hand und mit mund', wie ein Glossator zum Sachsenspiegel hervorhebt. 'In den Wind schlagen' ist ebenfalls nicht nur eine Redensart, sondern primär eine Rechtsgebärde, die beim gerichtlichen Zwiekampf eine Rolle spielte, wenn der Beklagte nicht erschien. Eine rechtssymbolische Handlung ursprünglich, die dann allerdings einen Bedeutungswandel durchgemacht hat.

Auch rechtliche Vermahnungen und Verweise waren ehedem von gebärdenhafter Art. Die Zeugen beim Ohr zu zupfen, wohl zur Auffrischung ihres Gedächtnisses, gehört etwa zu diesen rechtseigentümlichen Gebärden. Luitpold z.B., der erste babenbergische Markgraf, wurde bezeugtermaßen als Zeuge in einem Prozeß nach bayerischem Volksrecht am Ohr gezupft. Man 'zieht also einen Zeugen zu'. In den bayerischen Urkunden ist von 'testes per aures tracti' die Rede. Man denkt dabei an ein Ohrenzupfen, das auch bei Griechen und Römern diesem Zwecke

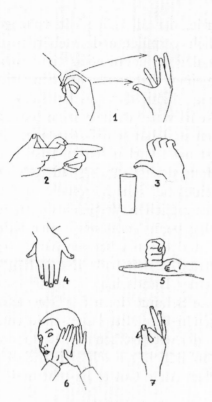

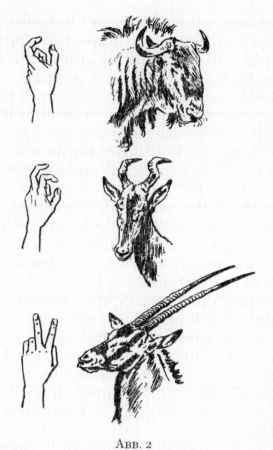

ABB. 1

Spanische Handgebärden
(nach L. Flachskampf)

ABB. 2

Bei der Jagd gebrauchte Handzeichen nord-
amerikanischer Indianer (nach W. Wundt)

ABB. 5

Etruskische Amulettkette mit Handzeichen
(nach S. Seligmann)

ABB. 4

Neapolitanische Gebärde: 'ich habe
dich durchschaut!' (nach A. de Jorio)

ABB. 3

Die 'gehörnte Hand' bei einer indischen
Götterstatue (nach Elworthy)

ABB. 6

Handkuß beim Kaiser. Röm. Relief
(nach K. Sittl)

ABB. 7

Die 'gehörnte Hand'. Wandbild in Pompeji
(nach G. Großmann)

ABB. 8

Antike Gebärden bei der Totenklage (Raufen der
Haare). Schwarzfiguriges Vasenbild im Louvre
(nach K. Sittl)

ABB. 9

'Durch die Finger sehen'. Illustration aus
Sebastian Brants 'Narrenschiff' (1494)

ABB. 10

'Gähnmaul'. Misericordiendarstellung in der
St. Peterskirche zu Löwen (15. Jh.)

ABB. 11

Die 'gekreuzten Hände' im Hexenabwehrzauber.
Holzschnitt um 1500

ABB. 12

Der Handschlag bei der Verlobung in der
Kirche. Holzschnitt von Schäufelein (1520)

ABB. 13

Trauer- und Verzweiflungsgebärden: Ringen
der Hände und Raufen der Haare. Holzschnitt
von Burkmair (1520)

ABB. 14

Illustration aus Sebastian Brants 'Narrenschiff' (1494)

ABB. 16   obere Reihe: 'Nein'-Gebärde in Süditalien und im
Vorderen Orient — untere Reihe: 'Ja'-Gebärde im südlichen
Balkan und im Nahen Osten (nach G. Müller)

ABB. 15   'Komm-Gesten' auf dem Balkan und im Vorderen
Orient (nach G. Müller)

ABB. 17
Kirchgang in Hessen (Schlitzer Tracht)
mit typischer Gesangbuchhaltung
(nach H. Retzlaff — R. Helm)

ABB. 18
Kirchgang im Marburger Land (Hessen)
mit Verhüllen der Hände
(nach H. Retzlaff — R. Helm)

ABB. 19
Handschlag auf einem schlesischen Viehmarkt im 18. Jh.
(nach E. v. Künßberg)

ABB. 20
Handtreuebrosche (Westfalen)

ABB. 21
'Gähnmaul'. Kupferstich von J. Mettenleiter
(1750—1825). München Kupferstichkabinett

ABB. 22
Gustave Doré (1832—83):
Illustration zu Rabelais' Pantagruel

ABB. 23
Ecce homo — Tafel des Dominikaner-
Altares von H. Holbein d.Ä. (1460—
1524). 'Rübchenschaben' als Spottgeste

ABB. 24
'Rübchenschaben'.
Detail aus einer Verspottung Christi

ABB. 25
'Gähnmaul' auf einem Altarbild: Christus vor Kaiphas,
um 1500

ABB. 26
Gleichgültigkeits- oder Verweigerungsgestus.
Heidelberger Bilderhandschrift des Sachsen-
spiegels (nach K. v. Amira)

ABB. 27
Die 'gehörnte Hand'. Bauer und Mohr im
Nürnberger Schembartlauf von 1485

ABB. 28
'Durch die Finger sehen'.
Historisches Kölner Narrenbild

ABB. 29
Grimassen-Wettkampf der Sennen
(nach L. Trenker)

ABB. 30
Der 'Lällekönig'. Basel

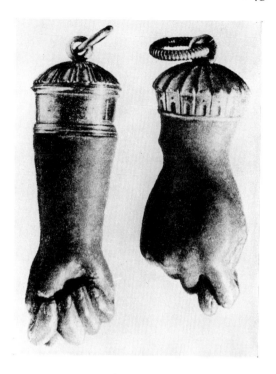

ABB. 31
Gorgonenhaupt auf der Akropolis in Athen
(6. Jh. v. Chr.)

ABB. 32
'Feigen'-Amulette aus dem 18. Jh.
(nach L. Rettenbeck)

ABB. 33
Hand-Amulette der v. Portheim-Stiftung in Heidelberg
(nach G. Großmann)

ABB. 34
Die 'gehörnte Hand'. Etruskische Wandmalerei

ABB. 35
Handgebärden (rechts oben: die 'Feige').
Handzeichnung von Albr. Dürer (1493)

ABB. 36
Hennenreiterin mit der Gebärde der 'Feige'.
Kupferstich um 1650

ABB. 37
Hahnreiter mit der 'Hörner'-Gebärde.
Kupferstich um 1650

diente. Die Handlung ist wohl symbolisch gemeint, d. h. es kam nicht darauf an, daß man sie besonders spürte, sondern nur darauf, daß man erinnert wurde, aufmerksam zu sein, um später Zeugenschaft leisten zu können. Diese Rechtsgebärde spielte im Volksbrauch, z. B. beim Grenzbegang in Bayern bis ins 19. Jahrh. hinein eine Rolle, und die Redensarten 'jemandem beim Ohr nehmen', und besonders 'sich etwas hinter die Ohren schreiben', d. h. eben sich etwas merken, um sich bei rechter Gelegenheit wieder daran zu erinnern, rühren davon her.

Alle diese Gebärden stellen uns vor ein gleichartiges interessantes Problem: es besteht in der Beziehung der Gebärden zum sprachlichen Ausdruck. 'Redensarten als Kontext zur Gebärdensprache' — 'Sprachgebärden statt Gebärdensprache' — das wäre vielleicht ein exakter Ausdruck für das, was mit diesen Ausführungen gemeint ist. Vielfach sind offenbar im Laufe der Zeit aus wirklichen Gebärden bloße Sprachgebärden geworden, d. h. die sprachliche Beschreibung der Gebärde ist an die Stelle der Körperbewegung getreten. Das ist eine sehr wichtige geistige Entwicklung der Aussagemöglichkeiten. Die Redensarten als Ersatz der Geste mochten zunächst noch dieselbe Wirkung wie die Gebärde selbst gehabt haben, sind dann aber mit der Zeit erstarrt und eben nur noch als Redensarten erhalten geblieben. Das gilt für die Gebärden der verschiedensten Art und Herkunft, und es seien zum Schluß noch einige Möglichkeiten kurz angedeutet:

Alte Trauer- und Klagegebärden, z. B. das Raufen des Haares und das Ringen der Hände, als Gebärden der Totenklage aus antiken Schriftstellern und Darstellungen ganz geläufig (Abb. 8), sind auch in Mitteleuropa noch bis in die beginnende Neuzeit in Trauerbräuchen geübt worden. Das zeigt z. B. ein Holzschnitt aus dem Anfang des 16. Jahrh. (Abb. 13). Heute aber sind Ausdrücke wie 'händeringend' usw. nur noch redensartlich erhalten. Ebenso bestimmte Gebärden der Herausforderung, etwa 'einem den kleinen Finger hinhalten'. 'Me brucht im numme e chrumme Finger z'mache', heißt eine Walliser Redensart, die eine geringfügige Herausforderung meint, denn das Krümmen des Fingers bedeutet die Herausforderung zum Häkeln, einem bekannten alpinen Spiel, einer Kraftprobe, bei der einer den anderen am Finger zu sich herüberzuziehen sucht. Die beiden Redensarten 'Ein Auge zudrücken' und 'Durch die Finger sehen' meinen dagegen weder eine Rechtsgebärde, noch eine abergläubische Haltung. Nur die Beschränkung des scharfen Zublicks soll zum Ausdruck gebracht werden (Abb. 9 u. 28). 'Durch die Finger sehen', das meint eben: Nachsicht walten lassen, milde urteilen, eigentlich: nicht mit vollem Blick hinsehen. 'Wir wollen freundlich durch die Finger sehen' verspricht Leonore ihrem Bruder, dem Herzog von Ferrara in Goethes Tasso.

Das 'Daumenhalten', das übrigens schon bei Plinius bezeugt ist, ist dann wieder eine der volksgläubigen Vorstellungen, die auch noch in der modernen Welt mit

Selbstverständlichkeit als Redensart angewendet wird. Man drückt einem den Daumen z. B. für das Bestehen eines Examens. Das Festhalten und Einklemmen des Daumens war ursprünglich wohl eine Art Bindezauber. Auch der Daumen als der kräftigste Finger mag dabei mitspielen. Aber daran denkt man heute nicht mehr. Man *spricht* doch mehr vom Daumenhalten, als daß der Daumen wirklich noch gehalten würde. Und bei anderen sprachlichen Wendungen ist es noch viel deutlicher, daß die Gesten, die sie zum Ausdruck bringen, verloren gegangen sind. Erinnert sei nur an Redensarten wie 'jemand ein Schnippchen schlagen', 'die Nase rümpfen', 'über die Achsel ansehen', 'jemandem geneigtes Gehör schenken', 'sich etwas aus den Fingern saugen', 'sich ins Fäustchen lachen', 'die Faust im Sack machen' (vgl. Abb. 5 mit der geballten Faust als Amulett), 'die Linke kommt von Herzen', wenn man die rechte Hand zur Begrüßung nicht frei hat — auch eine ursprünglich abergläubisch-euphemistische Beschönigung einer gefährlichen Gebärde — oder: 'sich selbst bei der eigenen Nase fassen' — eine sehr interessante Gebärdenredensart, die dann in der barocken Allegorie vom Vogel Selbsterkenntnis eine Bildrealisation gefunden hat.

Dies alles sind Gebärden, die uns überhaupt nur noch in der Form von Redensarten geläufig sind. Oft sind Formeln und Redewendungen erst entstanden, als das Verständnis der ursprünglichen Gebärde schon verloren war. Der reiche Bestand unserer Mundartwörterbücher ist noch nicht auf die gebärdenhaften Redensarten hin untersucht worden, aber gerade bei den mundartlichen Formulierungen treffen wir z. T. noch auf sehr altertümliche Gebärdenrelikte. Nur mehr redensartlich ist z. B. im bayerisch-österreichischen Raum das sog. 'Goderlkratzen' erhalten, das zweifellos mit der bereits bei Homer erwähnten Geste zusammenhängt, bei der der Schutzflehende an das Kinn des Mächtigen faßt. Vielleicht gehören auch unsere Redensarten 'einem um den Bart gehen', 'einem den Bart streicheln', 'einem den Bart kitzeln', d. h. schmeicheln, in denselben Zusammenhang (vgl. Abb. 14). Wie es z. B. die Tochter macht, wenn sie dem Vater um den Bart geht, ist schon im Kudrunepos geschildert:

> in triutlicher wîse, dô was der megede hant
> an ir vater kinne. sie bat in vil sêre...

Wir stehen erst am Anfang einer volkskundlichen Erfassung der Gebärdensprache. Aber diese letzten Beispiele zeigen noch einmal deutlich die methodischen Gesichtspunkte, die dabei zu beachten sind. Zweifellos hat es Epochen gegeben, in denen bestimmte traditionelle Gebärden auch in Mitteleuropa eine wesentlich größere Rolle gespielt haben als heute, d. h. auch Gebärden sind historisch gewordene Erscheinungen, deren Sinn Veränderungen ausgesetzt sein kann. Immer wieder zeigt sich eine Vielschichtigkeit in historischer und geographischer Beziehung. Eine Gebärde kann ihre Bedeutung ändern oder mehrere Bedeutungen nebeneinander aufweisen; sie kann, wie wir es z. B. bei Feige und gehörnter Hand gesehen haben, zugleich der magischen Abwehr, der Verspottung oder einer geheimen sexuellen Zeichengebung dienen. Die quellenmäßige Erschließung der Gesten und Gebärden bewegt sich auf ganz verschiedenen Überlieferungsgebieten: Neben die zeichnerische oder photographische Bestandsaufnahme in der Gegenwart treten als Stütze für Alter und Bedeutungswandel eine Reihe von anderen, teils gegenwärtigen, teils historischen Quellen. Es sind dies:

1. literarische Belege sowie Darstellungen der bildenden Kunst. Unter den bildlichen Quellen nehmen die Amulette einen besonders wichtigen Platz ein, denn um der zauberischen Wirksamkeit einer Gebärde dauernde Wirkung zu verleihen, wurde sie vielfach bildmäßig hergestellt. Amulette als sozusagen erstarrte Gebärden sind eine besonders wichtige und zugleich funktionalistische Quelle.

2. Die zweite Quellengruppe bilden die eigentlich volkskundlichen Belege, besonders aus den Gebieten von Sitte und Brauch, der Anstandsgesten, der Rechtsaltertümer und des Kinderspieles. Vor allem aber besitzen wir eine Gegenwartsquelle von unschätzbarer Bedeutung: Es sind dies unsere Redensarten, die sich als besonders ergiebig erwiesen, da die sprachliche Überlieferung die gestische in den Hintergrund gedrängt hat. Viele Redensarten, die heute nur noch unverstandene sprachliche Wendungen sind, weisen herkunftsmäßig auf früher einmal geübte Gebärden. Es geht also darum, die ehemalige Wirklichkeitsebene der Sprachgebärde, der heutigen bloßen Redensart zu erhellen. Die Gebärden sind jedenfalls gar nicht so völlig tot und verschwunden, wie es zunächst den Anschein hatte, sondern sie sind in der Sprache noch erhalten.

Verzeichnis der benutzten Literatur

Amira, Karl von: *Die Handgebärden in den Bilderhandschriften des Sachsenspiegels* (= Abhandlungen der philos.-philol. Klasse der bayer. Akademie der Wiss. Bd. 23) München 1909, S. 163–263.

Ἀρθριώτης, Ν. Π.: Ἀρχαῖοι καὶ νεοελληνικοὶ μορφασμοὶ καὶ χειρονομίες (=Μορφὲς Θεσσαλονίκη 2, 1947, S. 91 ff.

Darwin, Charles: *Expression of the Emotions in Men and Animals* (1. Aufl. London 1872), New York 1955.

Delling, Hildegard: *Studien über die Gebärdensprache in Dichtkunst und Bildkunst des frühen und hohen Mittelalters*, Diss. Leipzig 1925.

Flachskampf, Ludwig: „Spanische Gebärdensprache", (*Romanische Forschungen*, Bd. 52, 1938, S. 205–258).

Frenzen, Wilhelm: *Klagelieder und Klagegebärden in der deutschen Dichtung des höfischen Mittelalters*, Würzburg 1938.

Frey, Dagobert: *Dämonie des Blickes* (= *Abhandlungen der Mainzer Akademie der Wissenschaften*, Jg. 1953), Wiesbaden 1953.

Grajew, Felix: *Untersuchungen über die Bedeutung der Gebärden in der griechischen Epik*, Diss. Freiburg 1934.

Grimm, Wilhelm: *Über die Bedeutung der deutschen Fingernamen* (= Kleinere Schriften, Bd. 3) Berlin 1883, S. 428 ff.

Grossmann, Grete: „Über die Handamulette der von Portheim-Stiftung in Heidelberg", *Oberdtsch. Zeitschr. f. Vkde.* 5. Jg., 1931, S. 50 ff.

Hayes, Francis: "Should We Have a Dictionary of Gestures?" *Southern Folklore Quarterly*, Vol. IV, 1940, S. 239–245.

————: "Gestures. A Working Bibliography," *Southern Folklore Quarterly*, Vol. XXI, 1957, S. 218–317.

Jorio, Andrea de: *La Mimica degli antichi investigata nel gestire Napoletano*, Neapel 1832.

Jünger, Ernst: *Sprache und Körperbau*, Frankfurt 1949.

Klages, Ludwig: *Grundlegung der Wissenschaft vom Ausdruck* (= 5. Aufl. von: 'Ausdrucksbewegung und Gestaltungskraft'), Leipzig 1936.

Kleinpaul, Rudolf *Das Leben der Sprache und ihre Weltstellung*, Bd. I: Sprache ohne Worte, Leipzig 1893.

Kohlbrugge, Jacob H. F.: *Tier- und Menschenantlitz als Abwehrzauber*, Bonn 1926.

Künssberg, Eberhard Frh. von: *Schwurgebärde und Schwurfingerdeutung* (= *Die Rechtswahrzeichen*, Heft 4), Freiburg 1941.

Lasch, Richard: *Der Eid. Seine Entstehung und Beziehung zu Glaube und Brauch der Naturvölker*, Stuttgart 1908.

Lommatzsch, Eduard: *System der Gebärden, dargestellt auf Grund der mittelalterlichen Literatur Frankreichs*, Diss. Berlin 1910.

Lorenz, K.: *Die angeborenen Formen möglicher Erfahrung* (= *Zeitschrift für Tierpsychologie* Bd. V, 1934).

Mangin, Henri: *Die Hand, ein Sinnbild des Menschen*, Zürich 1952.

Meisen, Karl: „Der böse Blick", (*Rhein. Jahrb. f. Volkskunde* Bd. I, 1950 und Bd. III, 1952).

Mitton, A.: "Le langage par gestes," *Nouvelle Revue Trad. Pop.* I, 1949, S. 138–151.

Moser, Oskar: „Zur Geschichte und Kenntnis der volkstümlichen Gebärden", *Carinthia* I, Jg. 144, 1954, S. 735–774.

Mühle, Günther und Albert Wellek: „Ausdruck, Darstellung, Gestaltung", *Studium Generale*, 5. Jg., Heft 2, 1952, S. 110–130.

Müller, Günter: „Über die geographische Verbreitung einiger Gebärden im östlichen Mittelmeergebiet und dem nahen Osten", *Zeitschr. für Ethnologie* Bd. 71, 1939, S. 99 ff.

Neckel, Gustav: „Über eine allgemeine Geste des Schmerzes", *Archiv für das Studium der neueren Sprachen*, Bd. 167, 1935, S. 64 ff.

Ohm, Thomas: *Die Gebetsgebärden der Völker und das Christentum*, Leiden 1948.

Østrup, J.: *Orientalische Höflichkeit. Formen und Formeln im Islam*, Leipzig 1929.

Rettenbeck, Lenz: *'Feige'. Wort – Gebärde – Amulett*, Diss. München 1951.

Reuschert, E.: *Die Gebärdensprache der Taubstummen und die Ausdrucksbewegungen der Vollsinnigen*, Leipzig 1909.

Prause, K.: *Deutsche Grußformeln in neuhochdeutscher Zeit (Wort und Brauch*, Bd. 19, 1930).

Pritzwald, K. Stegmann von: *Der Sinn einiger Grußformeln im Lichte kulturhistorischer Parallelen (= Wörter und Sachen*, Bd. X).

Schmidt, Leopold: „Wiener Redensarten III. Schabab und Schleckabartl", *Das deutsche Volkslied*, Bd. 43, Wien 1941, S. 119ff.

———: „Der Vogel Selbsterkenntnis. Zwischen Volkskunst und Redensart", (*Österreichische Zeitschr. f. Vkde.*, Kongreßheft 1952, S. 134–144).

———: „Die volkstümlichen Grundlagen der Gebärdensprache", *Beiträge zur sprachlichen Volksüberlieferung*", Berlin 1953, S. 233–249.

Schmitz, G.: „Die Gebärdensprache der Kluniacenser und Hirsauer", *Blätter für Taubstummenbildung*, Bd. 36, 1923, S. 347ff.

Sittl, Karl: *Die Gebärden der Griechen und Römer*, Leipzig 1890.

Stoebe, K.: „Altgermanische Grußformen", *Paul und Braunes Beiträge zur Geschichte d. dtsch. Sprache und Lit.* Bd. 37, S. 173ff.

Strehle, Hermann: *Mienen, Gesten und Gebärden. Analyse des Gebarens*, München 1954.

Taylor, Archer: *The Shanghai Gesture (= FFC 166)* Helsinki 1956.

Villiers, Elisabeth und A. M. Pachinger: *Amulette und Talismane*, München 1927.

Vorwahl, Heinrich: *Die Gebärdensprache im alten Testament*, Diss. Berlin 1932.

Wandruszka, Mario: *Haltung und Gebärde der Romanen (= Beihefte zur Zeitschr. für romanische Philologie*, 96. Heft) Tübingen 1954.

Weise, Georg und Gertrud Otto: *Die religiösen Ausdrucksgebärden des Barock*, Stuttgart 1958.

Wilhelm, *Klagebilder und Klagegebärden in der deutschen Dichtung des höfischen Mittelalters*, Diss. Bonn 1936.

Wilhelmus, Sanctus, Abbas Hirsaugiensis: Constitutiones (= Patrologiae cursus completus, hrsg. v. Migne, Paris 1854, Bd. 150 der 2. Lat. Serie Spalte 890ff.

Wundt, Wilhelm: *Völkerpsychologie*, Bd. I: Die Sprache, 3. Aufl. Leipzig 1911.

Zappert, G.: *Über den Ausdruck des geistigen Schmerzes im Mittelalter (= Denkschriften der philos.-hist. Klasse der Akademie d. Wiss. zu Wien*, Bd. 5, 73) Wien 1854.

Zons, Franz Bernhard: *Von der Auffassung der Gebärde in der mhd. Epik*, Diss. Münster 1934.

Zschietzmann, Willy: *Untersuchungen zur Gebärdensprache in der älteren griechischen Kunst*, Diss. Jena 1924.

Johannes Gutenberg-Universität Mainz

SOME TRACES OF LOST MEDIEVAL
STORY-BOOKS

B. E. PERRY

Codex Laurentianus lvii. 30 in the Medicean Library at Florence, a Greek manuscript written probably in the early sixteenth century, contains on f. 79^r–80^v four fables of unknown origin. One of these, the well-known fable about the donkey who tried to emulate the dog as a playmate to his master, has a counterpart in the ancient collections of Aesopic fables (*Aes.* No. 91),[1] although it is textually and stylistically independent of the latter and somewhat longer.[2] The other three (*Aes.* 419, 420, 421) are stories of a novellistic character which have no equivalents elsewhere in extant Greek literature or in the Aesopic tradition. Their order in the manuscript is *Aes.* 421 (f. 79), 91, 420, 419. The style in which they are written is, in general, much like that of Symeon Seth's *Stephanites and Ichnelates*, which was translated from the Arabic *Kalilah wa Dimnah* near the end of the eleventh century; and certain formulaic expressions in particular, namely *legetai gar hōs*, by which one of the stories is introduced, and the recurring phrase "on one (day) of the days" (*en miā tōn hēmerōn*), are strongly reminiscent of that book, wherein they appear very frequently. Partly for this reason and partly in the light of other considerations, which will be mentioned below, it seems

---

[1] This and similar references below are to the series of Greek and Latin fables published in the writer's *Aesopica*, Vol. I, Urbana, Illinois, 1952.

[2] A. Hausrath, commenting on the text of this fable in *Rheinisches Museum* 87 (1938), 89, cites, as closely parallel to the donkey's soliloquy in the Greek text, the soliloquy of the donkey in No. 115 in the *Dialogus Creaturarum* of Nicolaus Pergamenus (14th cent.) and suggests that N. may have known the *Volksbuch* from which our fable was taken. It is also in Babrius, No. 129.

probable that the three stories, which I am about to describe, were taken from a lost Greek book of stories written in the Near East under the formal influence of *Kalilah and Dimnah*. Since only one of the three stories has, so far as I know, been translated from the Greek, namely the first by Furia into Latin,[3] I will here translate all three.

"The Thief and the Innkeeper" (*Aes.* 419)

A thief put up at a certain inn and remained there several days in the expectation of stealing something, but without being able to do so. Then one day of the days he saw the innkeeper, wearing a beautiful new cloak (for it was festival time), sitting before the gate of his inn; and no one else was around. He went up to the innkeeper, sat down nearby, and began to converse with him. After they had talked together for quite a while the thief began to yawn and, as he did so, at the same time to howl like a wolf. The innkeeper said to him, "Why do you do this?" The thief replied, "I will tell you; but I beg you to look after my clothes, for I shall leave them here. I don't know why it is, Sir, that I yawn like this, whether it befalls me on account of my sins or what the reason is, I don't know; but whenever I yawn three times I become a man-eating wolf." So saying, he yawned for the second time and again howled as before. On hearing this, the innkeeper believed it and was afraid of the thief. He rose up and was on the point of running away, but the thief took hold of him by his cloak and implored him, saying, "Wait, Sir, take my clothes, so I won't lose them." And while he was thus remonstrating, he opened his mouth and began to yawn for the third time. Then the innkeeper, fearing that his guest was about to devour him, left his cloak on the spot and ran to the inn, where he locked himself safely inside. And the thief took the cloak and went off. —This kind of thing is what happens to those who believe what is not true.

Erwin Rohde, in an article in the *Rheinisches Museum* for 1876 (XXXI 628ff. = *Kleine Schriften*, II, 193) called attention to a novella of Franco Sacchetti's, No. 212, which is very similar to our Greek story and is, in fact, the only parallel that I have so far been able to find. Rotunda, in his *Motif-Index of the Italian Novella in Prose*, cites only Sacchetti's version, and the only reference beyond Rotunda given in the new edition of Thompson's *Motif-Index* (K335.0.4.1), is to No. 5 in A. Wesselski's *Die Begebenheiten der beiden Gonnella* (Weimar 1920), a book which is not accessible to me at present. Presumably Wesselski's No. 5 is Sacchetti's No. 212, in which the thief is the buffoon Gonnella; but whether or not Wesselski has cited other versions of the story I do not know. In any case it is noteworthy that for two of the three Greek stories contained in the Florentine

[3] F. Furia, *Fabulae Aesopicae*, Leipzig 1810, No. 423 in Greek and Latin, whence Halm 196.

manuscript, namely, the one of which we have been speaking and that about the sailor and his son which will be given below, the closest parallels are found in Sacchetti. In the Italian version Gonnella is required by King Ruberto of Naples, as a condition of receiving the royal favor, to get something of value away from a very rich and avaricious abbot, either as a gift or by theft. This he does by persuading the abbot, dressed in a fine robe, to hear his confession, in the course of which he pretends to be on the point of becoming a bloodthirsty wolf. The abbot, like the innkeeper in the Greek, is thoroughly frightened and runs away leaving his fine cloak for Gonnella to carry off.

"The Two Adulterers" (*Aes.* 420)

A man used to go secretly at night to visit a certain woman and to commit a-dultery with her. He had given her a sign by which she might recognize him, that when he arrived outside her door he would bark like a little dog, and she would open the door for him. Another fellow, having seen him walking along that street at night, and knowing what mischief he was up to, followed him secretly one night at a distance. Without suspecting anything the adulterer came to the woman's door and performed as usual. The other fellow, following him, saw everything and went home. But on the next night he bestirred himself early and was the first to arrive at the adulterous woman's house. He barked like a little dog and she, being assured that it was her paramour, put out the light lest anyone should see him and opened the door. And he went in and had intercourse with her. Not long afterwards the first paramour arrived and barked as usual. When the man inside heard the one outdoors barking like a little dog, he himself began to bark from within the house in a very loud and vigorous tone, to indicate the presence of a very big dog; and the man out-side, realizing that the one in the house was bigger than himself, went away. (No moral given)

Rohde, who published the Greek text of this story in the article above men-tioned, called attention to its recurrence as No. 54 in the *Nouvelles Recreation et Joyeux Devis* of B. Desperiers, written in the sixteenth century.[4] There the action relates to "une dame d'Orleans qui aymoit un escolier qui faisoit le petit chien à sa porte, et comment le grand chien chassa le petit." After much search-ing, I fail to find any reference to this particular story in Thompson's *Motif-Index*; although the type of story that represents a second paramour as triumphing over the first and humiliating him, as in Chaucer's Miller's Tale (K 1577; cf. Rotunda's *Index*, K 1577.1: "The Pope in Rome" is followed by "The Turk in Constan-tinople," Masuccio No. 5) is broadly similar. A derivative of our Greek story, in

---

[4] Edited by Louis Lacour, Paris 1874, I, 226–229.

which the second paramour, upon the arrival of the first barks like a big dog from within the house, but without any motivation for so doing, since the first paramour does not bark for entrance, is cited by Rohde in the *Cent Nouvelles Nouvelles*, No. 31. Our story, though rare, may have been old in France and Italy; and it seems very probable, as Rohde suggests, that it came from the lost Greek collection from which the stories in the Laurentian codex have been excerpted.

The text of the story which follows, about the Sailor and his Son, is only partially preserved in the manuscript, owing to the loss of a large part of the leaf (f. 79) on which it is written, which is torn off diagonally from top to bottom. Rohde could make nothing of this story, beyond what little is contained in the few lines that are left intact, and he made no attempt to restore conjecturally what is lost. Such an attempt was made for the first time by Hausrath in the article to which we have already referred (n. 2), and his reconstruction of the Greek text appears also as fable No. 306 in his recent *Corpus Fabularum Aesopicarum* I. 2 (Leipzig, 1956). Hausrath's reconstruction is based on the analogy of a very similar story told by Sacchetti, No. 123. This is one of the many forms of the widespread story of carving a chicken and apportioning it to the members of a family in a symbolical fashion, but to the advantage of the carver, who gives himself all of the bird except the extremities. Professor Taylor, in one of his many interesting contributions to folklore, has briefly outlined the history of this story together with references to the literature about it, and with the addition of a new version told by a Dane in Minnesota.[5] Among the principal references are Thompson, *Motif-Index* H 601; R. Köhler, *Kleinere Schriften*, II, 645 ff., Bolte-Polivka, *Anmerkungen...*, II, 360. In Sacchetti, as in our Greek text, the chicken is carved "according to grammar," the carver is a young man whose education has been prolonged at his father's expense, and his claim to the body of the chicken is based on the assertion that he himself is, in a figurative sense, either a *corpo morto* (Sacchetti)[6] or (as probably in the Greek) one whose occupation is with dead or barren things. In these respects, Sacchetti's version is peculiarly close to the Greek; but in respect to the number of persons among whom the chicken is divided—six, including two daughters who get the wings—it differs from the Greek and follows the pattern of the great majority of the other versions, wherein five or more persons are at the table. Hausrath's supplements to the Greek text, which aim to restore the substance of the original, but not its exact words, are such that I can follow them only in part. His restoration gives us almost

---

[5] Archer Taylor in the *Journal of American Folklore*, XXXI (1918), 555 f.

[6] In Sacchetti the young scholar's stepmother, who disapproved of his higher education in law at Bologna, had been in the habit of referring to him as a *corpo morto* on whom his father was wasting his money.

everything except the main point of the story and its wit; for it fails to make the young man explain why there is any analogy between himself and a dead or barren body, and it misses the ironical division into two parts according to rhetoric, which, as it seems to me, is clearly implied in the concluding lines of the story, which are preserved. In the translation of my own conjecturally restored text, which here follows, I print Hausrath's supplements in roman type within the brackets and my own, where they differ, in italics.

"The Sailor and his Son" (*Aes.* 421)

It is said that a sailor, who had a son, wanted him to be educated in grammar. Accordingly he sent him to school, and after spending some time there the young man attained the highest proficiency in grammar. Then he said to his father, "Behold, Father, I have mastered all of grammar thoroughly. Now then, ⟨allow me⟩ to go through the subject of rhetoric." To this his father consented and once more put him in school, where he ⟨became an accomplished⟩ rhetorician. ⟨*One day*⟩ of the days, when the young man was in the house ⟨with his father and mother⟩ and they were eating together, he told ⟨his parents that he was a master⟩ of both grammar and rhetoric, ⟨and the father⟩ said to his son, "Concerning ⟨*grammar*[7] I have heard that it is the key⟩stone of all the arts, ⟨*and that whoso has learned it well*⟩ *writes without making mistakes*.[8] ⟨Come now, give me a sample of the art." The young man⟩ answered and ⟨said, "By dividing this chicken according to the principles⟩ of grammar, ⟨I will show you that in very truth grammar is⟩ superior ⟨to the other arts"⟩ ... And, as he carved the chicken, he said, "To you,⟩ Father, ⟨I shall give the head, because you are the head of the house and give orders to all of us; and to you, Mother, I apportion these feet, because you run back and forth through the house all day, having many⟩ things ⟨to do, and without feet⟩ you are ⟨not⟩ able ⟨to accomplish this; but this *barren* body (psilon sōma)[9] befits me especially, whose⟩ pleasure ⟨*it is to spend my time on barren, empty speeches, owing to my rhetorical*[10] education."

[7] Hausrath's supplement, *rhetorices*, contradicts his own restoration of the passage a sa whole. The keystone of the arts is not rhetoric but grammar; cf. Lucian's epigram 22.

[8] The manuscript reads ἀπτέστος γράφει, which is an orthographical error of a very common kind for ἀπταίστως γ., meaning "writes without blundering"; but Hausrath finds a proper name in the adverb (by changing the accent), and so reconstructs the passage as to read "as the late Aptestos of blessed memory writes." But no one, not even Hausrath, knows any writer by that name, sc. Mr. Impeccable!

[9] Hausrath puts *sōma nekron* (= *corpo morto*) in his text, but suggests *sōma psilon*, which I have adopted, as an alternative.

[10] Hausrath's restoration (whose—education) reads thus: "in whose life there is nothing pleasurable, in order that I may get some profit from my extensive education." In my own Greek text I followed H. in reading ⟨*pollēs dida*⟩*chēs*, extensive education; but I now think that *rhētorices*, which I translate above, is more suitable.

⟨So saying, he began to devour the chicken. But his father, being angered, snatched it away from him and said, *"You divide this bird into three parts according to grammar, but I shall divide it into two, according to rhetoric.*⟩[11] One of these I intend to eat myself, and your mother shall eat the other. You eat what you made with your rhetoric." — This kind of thing is what happens to those who go through life with villainy and trickery.

It will be seen that the story as I have reconstructed it includes an additional motif, serving as the denouement, which is nowhere else connected (so far as I can learn) with the motif of carving the fowl. This additional motif, or something very much like it, is described as follows in the new edition of Thompson's *Motif-Index* under J1539.2: "A scholar, showing his skill in logic, proves that two chickens (or eggs) on the table are really three. His father (or host) takes one chicken for himself, gives the other to the mother, tells son that he can have the third one." This entry was not in the first edition of the *Index*, and the only reference given in the new edition is to an Indiana dissertation by E. W. Baughman dealing with the folktales of England and North America comparatively, which is available only in microfilm and which I have not been able to consult. It was only after I had reconstructed the Greek text, as translated above, that I came across the following story in Joe Miller:[12]

"A rich farmer's son, who had been bred at the University, coming home to visit his father and mother, they being one night at supper on a couple of fowls, he told them that, by Logic and Arithmetic, he could prove those two fowls to be three. Well, let us hear, said the old man. Why this, cried the scholar, is one, and this, continued he, is two; two and one, you know, make three. Since you have made it out so well, answered the old man, your mother shall have the first fowl, I will have the second, and the third you may keep yourself for your great learning."

The lost Greek book from which the foregoing stories were excerpted was probably only one of many story-books which were written in the early middle ages in the Near East and by means of which story-lore was communicated to southern Italy and Spain, and from those regions later to France and northern Europe. This literature was not Byzantine, except in a purely chronological sense, or in a linguistic sense if written in Greek. It stands apart from the main current of Byzantine prose literature, which is highly scholastic, traditional, and uninventive in the transmission of story-lore, whether from later Greek antiquity, as in the Aesopica, or from translations made in Byzantine times of oriental books,

[11] Hausrath: (snatched the bird away from him and said), making it into two portions, "at first I did not care to apportion this bird."
[12] *Joe Miller's Jests, with Copious Additions*, edited by Frank Bellew, New York, 1865, p. 42, No. 208.

10*

as in the case of *Sindbad and the Seven Wise Masters* from the Syriac, and in that of *Stephanites and Ichnelates* from the Arabic *Kalilah wa Dimnah*. In the Byzantine tradition of the two books last mentioned only one new story is added, and the variants throughout some forty or more Greek manuscripts are otherwise all purely verbal, or else they consist in omissions or rearrangements of materials contained in the original translation. The case is similar with the Greek *Life of Aesop* and with the collected fables ascribed to Aesop in over a hundred Byzantine manuscripts. With only one or two possible exceptions, not a single new fable has been added to the repertoire of the ancient collections, which these manuscripts transmit in various combinations and verbal recastings, supplemented in only a few cases by fables drawn from the ancient rhetoricians, from Babrius or Aphthonius, or from some other ancient author. There is no accretion of new fables taken from contemporary folklore or books, oriental or Greek, and the ancient fables are never expanded dramatically beyond their original length.

All this contrasts strongly with the development of medieval story-lore in both the Near East among Persian, Arabic and Armenian writers, and in western Europe among Latin writers. In those regions the ancient fables,—themselves sometimes expanded into little epics, or *extravagantes*, by prolonging the narrative dramatically or by the agglutinative process of stringing together three or four originally independent fables as the adventures of the unfortunate wolf or fox,—are augmented by a large number of other stories of all kinds taken from the great reservoir of popular narrative substance, most of which had always been there in oral circulation, especially in the Near East, but which had not been exploited in literature, except in a very limited way, previous to the early Middle Ages. At that time the canons of literary propriety, which had been much more severe and intellectual throughout the ancient world, and which had approved prose narrative only as historiography in theory or an example subordinated to a context, were relaxed under the pressure of a new and less disciplined culture, and stories came to be written down in books for their own sake as never before. They were based on many sources and combinations of sources, both oral and written, local and foreign, and they were freely elaborated and dramatically prolonged with much fanciful invention. Often what was only a short anecdote summarily told in passing by an ancient writer becomes a real story, as we should say, in a medieval writer. The latter elaborates it and adds much of his own to it, because his object is simply to tell a good story as such, while that of the ancient writer was to illustrate a point or to summarize an action for the sake of its bearing on something else. The proliferation of story-books in the Near East in the time of the 'Abbasid Califate (750–1258 A.D.) was not due to the importation of materials or models from India, as is too often supposed, but to the recognition of prose fiction on its own account as a legitimate form of literature, which came about with the rise of the new Persian-Arabian culture. A new world of ideas and values brought with it new concepts of what could and could not be exploited as literature. In the period of the Arsacidae literature was mainly Greek and more or less under the control of scholastic standards. Many books of fiction were written and circulated in this period by and for the poor-in-spirit; but they were in a sense contraband, frowned upon by the Greek academy. Most of these, the popular Greek romances and other story-books, whether ideal or comic, have perished, because they were disowned by fashion in the Hellenistic world and later in the Byzantine; but it is probable that much of this unhonored Greek story-lore has passed into oriental books, such as the *Arabian Nights*, where it is transformed and combined with other motifs and freely exploited as literature.[13] The greater license accorded to pure fiction by the Persian and Arabic literature, which succeeded the Hellenistic and became dominant in the Near East, so far influenced those who wrote in Greek in that region that some of them were emancipated from the scholastic tradition by which the main current of Byzantine literature was controlled. Under those conditions some Greek story-books were produced in western Asia which did not survive as such; partly because they could not circulate in the Moslem world without being translated into Arabic or Persian, and because the conventions of Byzantine literature were unfavorable to their transmission.

Muhammad b. Ishāq an-Nadim, in his well-known *Fihrist*, completed in the year 987–88 A.D., lists the titles of eleven Greek books under the heading "Names of Greek books containing night-stories (*asmār*) and histories."[14] Among these titles, very few of which are intelligible or can be connected with anything that we know, is the following: "Book of Samsah and Dimna, on the pattern of the book of Kalilah wa Dimnah; and its name in Greek is... (lacuna). It is a frosty composition and repulsive in its makeup. It is said to be the work of some recent writer."[15] Now it must have been a book of just this nature, and it may have been

---

[13] The career of much of this popular Greek lore in the later literature of the Near East is sketched in my recent article on "The Origin of the *Book of Sindbad*," *Fabula*, III (1959), 6–27.

[14] Reference is made to the Arabic text of the *Fihrist* edited by G. Flügel, Leipzig 1871, p. 305, line 25–306.3.

[15] The proper names in the title are very uncertain, and neither the vowels nor the syllabication nor even the consonants s and d (which might be sh and dh respectively) are indicated. It is also uncertain just what the author meant by the adjective 'frosty' (*bārid*), which he applies in a previous passage (304.20) to the Persian *Hazar Afsaneh*, on which the *Arabian Nights* was founded. In that place, where it is coupled with the adjective 'corrupt' (*ghath*), Burton translates it 'cold', in the figurative sense of Greek *psychros*; but Flügel in his notes (p. 148 f.) comments as follows on the possible sense of the word in both passages: "doch kann letzteres (*bārid*) auch ihre Possenhaftigkeit, Scurrilität bezeichnen... wie *bārid* anderwärts erfrischend, gefällig, anmutig, lustig, spaßhaft

the same book, from which the stories in the Laurentian manuscript were excerpted. Another story which may have been taken from the same or a similar
Greek book is that about the young man and the old woman in the fables ascribed
to Syntipas (*Aes.* 410, p. 547 = Synt. 54). This, an amusing but obscene story,
is the only one of its kind in the collection, which is otherwise made up of ordinary
Aesopic fables translated from a Syriac text near the end of the eleventh century,
probably by Andreopulus of Melitene.[16] And it is also the only fable in the collection for which there is no equivalent in the Syriac manuscripts.[17]

In his list of Persian story-books the author of the *Fihirst* (305,6) mentions
one entitled *Book of the Bear and the Fox*. We cannot be sure, of course, what the
contents of this book were; but the analogy of an Armenian fable, No. 96 in the
collection published by Marr, suggests that the story told how the bear denounced
the absent fox for failing to attend upon his majesty the lion during his sickness;
and how the tardy fox, after presenting himself and explaining that he had just
returned from long travels in search of medical advice from the physicians of the
world, saved himself and took vengeance on the bear by prescribing, as a sure
remedy for the lion's illness, the application of the warm skin of a newly-flayed
bear.[18] This is the well-known fable that served as the basis for the epic of *Reynard
the Fox*, except that the fox's opponent in the latter is not the bear, but the wolf.
The bear appears as the victim in the Latin poem of Paulus Diaconus at the end
of the eighth century (*Aes.* 585), and the Armenian fable to which I have referred
is the same in outline as that of Paulus. There must be some historical connection
between these two texts, because they are the only ones, so far as I know, in which
the bear appears in place of the wolf, and the form of the story in which the wolf
is the victim occurs nowhere in the Armenian collections nor in any Greek text
previous to the fourteenth century. In the corpus of 380 Armenian fables published
by Marr, which date mainly from the thirteenth and fourteenth centuries, the
fable in question, No. 96, in the only one in which a bear and a fox are brought
together, and there are only two others in which a bear plays a leading part. For
this reason it seems probable that the Persian *Book of the Bear and the Fox* dealt
with the same story; but the fact that it circulated as a separate book suggests

bedeutet, also mehr ein Lob als einen Tadel ausspricht." Even so, the word is probably derogatory
in the sense that it shows disdain for a trivial kind ot writing, whatever its merits might be as
fiction.

[16] See *Aesopica* I, 517–520.

[17] See *Aesopica* I, 525.

[18] N. Marr, *Sborniki Pritch Vardana*, St. Petersburg 1899, II, 114–116. Four versions of the story
are here printed from different MSS, each about 15 lines long, but the variants are only verbal. This
is one of the 45 Armenian fables translated by J. Saint-Martin in his *Choix de Fables de Vartan*,
Paris 182525., No.

that its contents were not confined to the relation of that one story, which would be, ordinarily, too short for a book. Instead, it seems likely that in this Persian book, as in many others, one story (in this case the story about the bear and the fox) served as a frame into which a number of other stories were introduced. Indeed it is quite possible, depending upon the manner in which the other stories were introduced, whether as episodes of the main story or as independent insertions, that our lost Persian book was a veritable protype of *Reynard*.

Since a large proportion of the Armenian fables come from Greek originals, although supplemented by many eastern folktales, it is probable, as Marr says in discussing this fable about the bear and the fox,[19] that it came from a Greek source. If so, one can understand how it may have come to the knowledge of Paulus Diaconus; he knew Greek and had spent some time in southern Italy at Monte Cassino. That version of the story which features the wolf in place of the bear, as in *Reynard*, is told in the tenth-century *Ecbasis Captivi* and later in *Isengrimus* and other Latin texts; but the only extant Greek fable in which the wolf appears in place of the bear is very late and does not belong among the 'fables of Aesop' which were transmitted from antiquity. The fable to which I refer (*Aes.* 258), is one of eight in a row which Planudes (ca. 1300 A.D.) took from odd sources other than the traditional Aesop and inserted in the middle of his collection (Nos. 72–79 in the Mss.).[20] Three of these come from the tetrastichs of Ignatius Diaconus (ninth century); two are from Aphthonius; one is from the Babrian paraphrase, not elsewhere used by Planudes; and the other two (Nos. 73, 74), including the one with which we are concerned (73 = *Aes.* 258), are new and of unknown origin. Since Planudes was familiar with Latin and went on an embassy to Venice in 1296, it is not unlikely that he found the substance of these two fables in Italy. No. 74 (= *Aes.* 246), telling how a wife, in the hope of reforming her drunkard husband puts him in a sepulchre and makes him believe, when he wakes, that he is dead, is very similar to the central motif in Boccaccio's story of Ferondo (*Dec.* III, 8), except that Ferondo is not a drunkard but a stupid husband, and that there is no adulterous intrigue in the Greek fable.[21] The fable as we have it was certainly composed by Planudes himself, as the style shows, whatever may have been the source of its substance. In the light of this analogy, and of what has been said above concerning the history of the motif, we may infer with much probability that Planudes got his fable about the sick lion, wolf, and fox from a

[19] *Op. cit.* I, 478.
[20] On the sources of these fables and Planudes as their editor, see my *Studies in the Text History of the Life and Fables of Aesop* (1936) 204–228, and especially the analytical table on p. 215.
[21] Cf. *Studies* 225, note 16. The close resemblance of the Planudean fable to the story in Boccaccio was pointed out by Hausrath in 1894, who concluded that its source was Italian.

late Latin text, such as the *Ecbasis Captivi* or the *Isengrimus*. The earliest known form of the Graeco-Armenian fable is that which is given by Paulus Diaconus in the time of Charlemagne; and the form in which the wolf appears as the victim is probably a later development in the Latin literature of the West.[22]

University of Illinois,
Urbana, Illinois

[22] Just the opposite was assumed by L. Sudre in his valuable book on *Les Sources de Roman de Renart*, Paris, 1893, 111, 117; owing to the fact that he supposed the Greek fable (Halm 255) to be ancient.

"DISPLACED" FOLKTALES

Reidar Th. Christiansen

The ever increasing masses of recorded folktales, in itself gratifying evidence of a healthy interest in the subject, offers many new problems to the student. In spite of this interest and in spite of the investigation of folktales from many points of view, there is still considerable resignation concerning the possibility of solving questions of the ultimate origins of tales. In the long run, neither have studies of individual tales, however exhaustive, led to definitive results. The newer approaches in folktale studies, involving the insights of sociology, psychology, in their way are hardly more convincing than earlier efforts to find mythological reminiscences everywhere.[1] More promising, perhaps, is the growing interest in the activity of storytellers, who view their stories as expressions of narrative art, and as a revelation of human personality. In this approach to the folktale through the teller, or by any of the other means of analysis, investigations are seriously imperilled, or even invalidated, when every variant of a tale is deemed of equal value with every other. All too often investigators have lost sight of the various vicissitudes a tale undergoes before it is finally available for study. The prudent worker must always consider the person who told the story in the first place, the field collector who recorded it (at least before fidelity could be achieved through mechanical recording apparatus), and last, but not least, the person who finally edited the tale for publication, for all have a share in the folktale text before us. For these reasons a critical analysis of variants is imperative, and especially so with regard to folktales recorded, say, within the last fifty years.

---

[1] See a paper by Laurits Bødker, "Folkeeventyrenes forskningsproblemer," *Arv*, XII (1956), 69–94 (with a summary in English).

In studying the migration of a folktale the question of the possible influence of books is especially important, and most students have been confronted at one time or another with the unexpected emergence of tales with alien plot elements in some area far removed from its normal habitat.[2] Where such a tale exhibits features contrary to the normal developments within an area, one may properly speak of a "displaced folktale." The subject of the following notes constitutes an intriguing example of a tale that moves somewhat outside the accepted channels of "oral tradition." The tale under discussion does not occur in recurrent patterns, as is the case, for example, with the Cinderella story, but seems to have been recorded in strength only in a very restricted area. On the other hand, single versions appear in places so widely separated that movement by oral transmission is seriously open to question. One is therefore forced to posit the influence of the printed page in carrying this tale so far afield without intermediate developments.

The tale selected for illustration is included in the Aarne-Thompson list of folktale types (FFC 74) as No. 577, and is said to be recorded only in Norway with one version in the Lapp language. The title assigned is "The King's Tasks." The incidents of the tale, as noted in the Aarne-Thompson list, are as follows:

> The King's daughter is promised to the one who is able to perform some difficult tasks, usually to cut down a large oak tree. The three brothers set out, and the youngest is the one who pays attention to certain things they see on their way, or who shows kindness toward an old woman. Accordingly, he receives magic objects; with these and with other information he has, he succeeds where others fail.

Accordingly, the definite central group consists of the Norwegian variants, and these must be the point of departure in trying to account for the appearance of the tale in places as far apart as northern Norway (Lapp [recorded 1879]), Ireland, County Mayo, 1937), and Leslie County, Kentucky, U.S.A. (1955).

The distribution of the Norwegian variants, some twelve in number, present some curious local features. Any folktale, recorded once or twice only, is of course to be regarded as strictly local, but when several variants are found, they are as a rule more widely distributed. In the tale under discussion, apart from a couple of versions derived from printed sources, all variants were recorded in the Telemark districts, that part of Norway, where, thanks to isolation, oral tradition has been best preserved, and where, accordingly, most collectors went a hundred years ago when interest first focused on the ancient oral tradition of that province. The tale was printed in the Norwegian classic collection of Asbjørnsen and Moe,

[2] An interesting case of such literary transplantation is the telling of Grimm tales by Irish storytellers. Cf. L. Mühlhausen, Zehn Irische Volkserzählungen aus Süd-Donegal, Nos. 9 and 10, pp. 144–148.

in the second edition of 1852—the first was never completed—as No. 50. Most of the other tales in the collection have copious notes about other known Norwegian versions, and contain parallel stories from other countries. With tale No. 50, however, the only information given is that it was recorded in western Telemark, and that it was retold by J. Moe. All versions now known were taken down after the publication of the tale in Asbjørnsen and Moe, and to ascertain their relationship to this classic printed text, therefore, these versions will have to be examined. These treatments are also interesting in showing how the various storytellers handled the fairly simple plot, each in his own manner, and each with greater or less success. Somehow all of them managed to achieve a reasonably coherent composition. Want of space prevents the printing of texts, or even summaries, but for reference a short list of versions is added. For further particulars one is referred to my catalogue of Norwegian folktales, *Norske Eventyr*, hereafter referred to as NE.[3]

From the parish Bö in eastern Telemark, M. Moe on his first visit in 1878 recorded two versions: *a.* (NE 2) and *b.* (NE 3). Two years after, on a second visit, he recorded, from new storytellers, two more: *c.* (NE 4) and *d.* (NE 5). From a parish further towards the West, Kviteseid, Sophus Bugge: *e.* (not in NE), probably some time in the 1860's. Another (NE 5) was probably taken down about 1880, and another one *g.* (NE 6) as late as 1891. Still further west, parish Fyresdal, there is a version, *h*, recorded 1875–1880 (NE 7), and still further west, a fragment, *i*, recorded by J. Moe, in Aamli, perhaps the first version recorded, but only a few lines (NE 11). A version, *j*, taken down in southern Norway in 1920, was obviously taken from the printed text, as was also one other version (NE 1). From western Norway, and from the same source two variants are recorded—k. 1. (NE 13, 14).

The obvious introductory incidents involve the presentation of the actors and the problems of the king, but which particular element comes first does not influence the sequel. In the variants the two brothers are not individualized by having personal names, the third, however, has the traditional name: Askefisen, i. e., "Ash-blower," or also Askeladden, as the first was considered too coarse for polite speech. One storyteller, a woman, used Askeladden, but added: "we always used to call him Askefisen" (*g*). The motif, three brothers leaving home to seek their fortune, is a standard opening of many tales, as is also the one of the two eldest brothers refusing to take the third along, as they thought he was a good for nothing. Some variants use it (*a, c*). One version, told by a boy of thirteen years, seems to have a predilection for realistic detail, making the eldest brothers,

---

[3] *Norske Eventyr. En systematisk fortegnelse efter trykte og utrykte kilder*, ved R. Th. Christiansen (Kristiania, 1921), No. 577.

four in this case, miners, probably in the silver mines, like many other young
fellows from their district, because they could be assumed to have had far wider
experience than their stay-at-home brother. The task imposed by the king may
be stated first (c, g), but fit in equally well later, offering a welcome chance for the
lads. The variants mention only the problem of getting rid of the oak tree, and the
character of a difficult test is stressed by the additional clause that it had to be
felled within a single day (c, e, f). Things go according to what might be expected
in keeping with folktale custom—when the three meet somebody, human or animal, that needs their help, and when only the youngest of them is willing to help,
he will naturally be given the implements needed for his success. Two variants
(b, f) feature the incident of an old woman who gives Askeladden a pipe by which
he may summon whatever he wants. The other story (e) has connected the motif
more closely with the present tale, as she gives him the axe he needs, and later on
also the means of delving and of providing water. In the first case it is interesting
to see how the storyteller managed to weave the pipe-incident, which is obviously
borrowed from another tale, "Herding the Hares" (Type 570) into the pattern of
this present tale. The king, reluctant to give his daughter to the winner, imposes
a new task, namely, to herd his hares, and the story even manages to use still
another incident from the other story where the lad in the end is ordered to
"fill the vat with lies" and goes on to describe all the mean tricks employed by the
royal family to get hold of the pipe, forcing the king to call a halt, and declare that
the vat is more than full. In rendering the present tale the additional test is to
fill the vat with water, and his nut comes in handy. The other variant (e) needed
fewer alterations, but also in this case the introduction of the helper-episode led to
the story's deviating into the tale of "The Skilful Companions" (Type 513), and these
companions are used to assist the hero in performing new tasks set by the king.

   The main reason, however, for considering the helper-episode as foreign to the
tale is that it is superfluous and stands in direct contradiction to the point of the
tale, which is the value of the omnipresent curiosity displayed by the third
brother, in spite of all criticism and ridicule.

   He shows this curiosity again after the appearance of the old woman, again
(c) when they were approaching the tall oak, and, quite naturally, on their travels
away from home. Less apt is the statement that they occurred after the two
brothers had miserably failed (g), or even from inside the house where they lived
(k). They heard somebody hewing, and the curious brother found the axe. Then
they heard somebody delving, and the brother found what he needed; then he
followed a brook to see from where it came, and thus found the nut from which
the brook trickled. The order of these things is not constant. Usually, however,
the hewing comes first. He finds an axe—sometimes two (a, f, h)—and he may

even see them at work upon the oak (c). In coming to the episode of the delving, storytellers disagree as to the verb used to describe what he heard, but practically all agree that what he found was a pig's snout, or even two of them, burrowing in the ground. The obvious implement, a spade, is mentioned only in the variants derived from the printed text (i, k). The hero naturally puts a plug of moss into the snouts, imitates the natural procedure when he finds a nut, as he follows the river (a, b, f, h, i, k), or a nutshell (i), and even an eggshell (j). The walnut of the printed text occurs only in the versions dependent upon it, as walnuts were probably not known in the countryside at that time. The ridicule of the brothers, and their impatience with his extra excursions are referred to in a few versions (a, b) only.

On the arrival at the castle of the king, the failure of the two is naturally only briefly mentioned, and the second brother is treated by a "likewise," which it must be pointed out, may result from the recorder's wishing to abbreviate his notes.

The need of some kind of explanation for their failure seems to have been felt at least by some of the storytellers, and an incident is introduced, namely: the king's daughter carries a meal to the workman, and when he leaves something uneaten, she throws what remains on to the oak, which grows whole again (b, e, f, g). The episode is presupposed even in the version when Askeladden is at work (e), and nearly had cut through the oak, while she urged him to finish the meal, and he kept on talking until the oak fell down, and she "went shouting up to the king's house." In the story told by the boy, the two brothers thought it bad manners not to leave anything, and thus themselves caused their failure. Another storyteller solved the problem by providing the lady with some kind of ointment; other narrators in turn, left the failure unexplained, stating that the cutting had no effect at all. As to the punishment for the failure, the variants are strangely silent. Strips of skin were cut off (g), or, more drastically, they were beheaded (h), or sent away to a barren island (j), which is derived from a book. The king—however, sometimes also the princess—is reluctant to let the winner have the reward, and may require further tasks. One storyteller (e) makes Askeladden comment that this was not in the agreement. When he was told to dig up the roots of the oak (a, b, c, e, h) the two pig-snouts came in handy, even if some say (a, b) that it had to be done in a single day. The king then claimed that a channel had to be dug up to his castle, where ships could pass, or a lake. In this latter case the nut provided the water, even in such abundance that the king had to seek a safe place to escape from the flood, and thus be forced to give his consent to the marriage and the wedding. That, according to folktale law, is the inevitable conclusion.

As mentioned, all of these versions were recorded some twenty years after J. Moe's text had been printed, and the survey, I think, has conclusively shown that they are not derived from the book, apart from one or two (*j, k*). One point of difference is in the construction of the pattern. The printed version refers to the king's tasks separately—oak, well, constant water supply—and Askeladden accordingly acquires the implements needed in the same order. The variants mention the oak only, and the digging and delving come in as further tasks set by the king. For digging, the printed text provides Askeladden with the very simple instrument, a spade, while all the variants had the unexpected pig-snouts, which may be said to be in the same general conception as the nut, though not of the axe, but their use conveys a slightly farcical or grotesque character. This deviation was so marked that one could understand the alteration in a version printed for general reading, even a hundred years ago when magic and marvel were more prominent than they are now. The incident of the princess' bringing food Moe did not use, or he might not have known it. The recording he used as his source is not known, and the fragment from his notebook (*i*) had only the final passage, and yields no information. It may perhaps be noted that the incident is reminiscent of a similar situation in the "task story," with the "Mastermaid" (Type 313) bringing food to the man at work, even if she, in that story, came to help him. One may also note that the variant from the parish farthest to the West corresponds most closely with the printed version. As to further additions and changes in this tale, some may be due to the editor, such as the reason why the king wanted to have the oak felled: namely, it kept the light from his windows. The bits of dialogue between the brothers and between Askeladden and the axe, etc., merely indicated in the version, were probably added by J. Moe, as for example, Askeladden on seeing the axe: "So you are standing here hewing all by yourself?" "Yes," said the axe, "I have been standing here for many a long day waiting for you." "Well, here I am," said Askeladden, wrenched the axe from the handle and put it into his bag. Or the final comment: "Peter and Paul were lucky indeed in having their ears cut off, as otherwise they would have heard nothing else but people saying how lucky their brother had been." Truly to appreciate the skilful retelling, one has to bear in mind the attitude of the Norwegian reading public a hundred years ago when the literary diction was closely molded upon Danish literature, and one of the leading literary critics of the period could write about the book of folktales that "the editors had indeed in a remarkable way managed to preserve the coarseness of the native storytellers."

As mentioned, a variant told in the language of the Lapps was taken down in Northern Norway.[4] It was told by a storyteller who knew a fair number of folk-

---

[4] *Lappiske Eventyr og Sagn*, ved J. Qvigstad. Vol. III, 1, No. 72, p. 330. Instituttet for Sammenlignende Kulturforskning, Ser. B. Vol. XIII, 1929. According to the 1929 census there were still some 7,000 Lapps living in the Lyngen district.

tales. In the year of recording (1879), books were not likely to be current in these parts, as the editor points out, but even so this particular story is obviously a very brief retelling, or summary, of the Norwegian printed tale, and was, through one or more intermediaries, taken from J. Moe's text.[5]

Far more puzzling is the occurrence of the tale in a manuscript collection of Irish folktales made in 1937 by a young woman in a parish in Co. Mayo, in Western Ireland. The person who told it, she says, was about ninety years of age, and had heard it told some seventy years ago, i. e., about 1870, from another man about 65, a native of the same parish.[6] The collection in question must, according to several circumstances, be viewed with certain suspicion. All the tales are told in English, while the traditional tales from these districts are generally recited in Irish, and some of the items in the manuscript can not be classed as folktales at all. Accordingly, the dates given concerning her sources can not be implicitly accepted, and the connection with Irish oral tradition of the West is far from close. Some folktales that she has are versions of well-known tales, known in Irish, while others are either obviously from books, and some are local legends.

Tale No. 7 (pp. 155–160) is the tale in question, and bears the title: "The Use of Wondering." With its didactic touch, summarizing the moral of the tale, it is hardly traditional. The correspondence with the Norwegian printed story is far too close to be a mere coincidence, and the Norwegian text was available in English in the translation by G. W. Dasent. The first edition of his *Tales from the Norse* appeared 1858, followed by a second edition in 1859, where on page 380 the tale is called "Boots and his Brothers."[7] The title accordingly is not that of the Irish story, but the names given to the lads are the same. In Irish the third one is

[5] Compare such details as the oak growing close to the windows of the castle. Since walnuts were probably unknown, it is natural that changes should occur in the means used to gain the water supply. He was told to cut a piece from his bag and soak it in the source from which the brook sprang.

[6] Irish Folklore Commission, MS 339, pp. 155–160. The story of "The Poor Man's Lucky Son" is a combination of Tale-Type 461 and 930. "The Giant's Heart" (Type 302) is widely known in Ireland, as is also Type No. 981* ("Why the Killing of Old People Was Discontinued"). Cf. Albert Wesselski, *Märchen des Mittelalters*, p. 237; FFC, No. 121. In "The Golden Bowl," the hero is named Hugo, but it is no folktale, and "The Lonely Lady" is a retelling of a local legend.

[7] As early as 1850 Dasent had published translations of Norwegian stories in *Chambers Edinburgh Magazine* (Vol. XIV, pp. 23 and 123). In his introduction he speaks about the lack of interest in such tales in Britain, noting that in Norway the rising generation was still as busy as ever with fairy lore. Among other things he sticks to the misleading term "fairy tales," and he mentions the "male Cinderella" of the Norwegians, even employing the obscure form "Cinderellus"—probably as a joke, Furthermore, he mentions the common Norwegian nickname given to the third brother, Askefisen, which he correctly renders as Ashblower. The three tales published, together with another one in *Blackwoods Magazine* the next year (1851, p. 595), do not include this particular tale.

called John, but in the sequel he is Jack; the two others are Peter and Paul. The name Boots adopted by Dasent is not very well chosen, transferring the story, as it does, to quite another background, and in "Ashipelt" Dasent would have had the exact counterpart. Word for word the Irish story follows Dasent's translation, and a comparison line by line is quite convincing. What is left out in the Mayo story are the asides, which serve as the editor's comments. The conclusion seems inevitable that the ultimate source of the Mayo version is Dasent's book.[8]

There may be still another trace of the *Popular Tales from the Norse* in the Mayo collection in a story "The Giant's Heart," told by another farmer who had heard it from his father some forty years ago—another man, not he who told the first tale. The tale—type 302 is far more widely spread, both in Norway, and still more in Ireland, where 279 variants are listed in the Archives of the Irish Folklore Commission. The point hinting at a connection is a special type of introduction, found only in the printed version in Norway, and not in the Irish variants accessible in print, with every reservation for those in manuscript. We are told that twelve sons of a king depart to look for suitable brides, one stays at home, and as the couples pass by a hill where lives a giant, they are caught and turned into rocks all round the giant's dwelling. There is also a close similarity as to the place where the giant has hidden his heart. Thus, this tale may also suggest a connection with a Norwegian story, though there were probably intermediaries. How the tale reached Mayo, however, is probably impossible to determine. Books were probably rare in those parts of Ireland around 1870, if the date given by the collector may be relied upon; so probably some paper or magazine may have reprinted the tale. The title, "The Use of Wondering," might suggest such transmission. Since no definite date is given, such a link would be exceedingly difficult to establish, and

[8] Compare, for example, Dasent (hereinafter abbreviated "D") "... just against the king's windows a great oak had sprung up that was so stout and thick that it took away all the light from the king's palace..." with the version from Mayo (abbreviated "M"): "...just near the king's palace a great tree had sprung up that was so big and stout that it let no light in the windows..." For "...cut a *chip* of the oak..." (in D), M has "a *clip*." As for the well: in D: a well that could hold water for a whole year; the same in M. Further, D: "...it might happen that they might get a place somewhere with a good master..."; M: "...they might somewhere happen upon a good master..." Exactly parallel are the dialogues between the third brother and the axe, the spade, and the nut. Both have: "So you stand here alone and hew, do you?" "Yes," said the axe, "I have been hewing here for a long time, waiting for you." "Well, here I am at last." On coming to the brook, both D and M proceed: "They were (D: all) thirsty after their long walk (D: and) so they lay down beside the brook to have a drink." Both use the same verbs, "digging" and "delving," and, of the nut, "trickling" and "running down." The hole in the nut is plugged with a lump of moss, and when the wise brother speculates on the origin of the brook, his words are identical in both tales: "I wonder where the brook comes from...still I have a fancy to see...a rare sight it must have been (brother), it was only a hole it ran out of," etc., etc.

would be of secondary interest only, as there seems to be no reasonable doubt as to the derivation of the Irish version.

Far more puzzling is the appearance of the same story in *Kentucky, U.S.A.*, where it was recorded in 1955 by Leonard Roberts, the well-known collector of folktales and editor of excellent collections of Kentucky tales, with descriptions of countryside and the people. He published this tale in 1957, separately,[9] and it comes as a real surprise to meet the same incidents, in the same sequence, and even to find a faint echo of the diction of J. Moe through the English of Dasent, but retold in a way that suggests several intermediaries. It is told in an individual manner by a practiced and very able storyteller. She introduces three lads, as follows:

Once upon a time there was three boys that lived with their mom and dad way out in the woods. Their names were Jack and Bill and Merrywise who was the youngest. The two agree to leave home, but refuse to take Merrywise along. At last, however, they consent to his coming, saying: "Merrywise, you will have to mind us, and you can't go off on your foolish rambles. You will have to stay with us and act your age." So they went along and sat down to have their lunch, when they heard someone chopping up in the woods, up in the mountains. Merrywise said he would investigate, and did so in spite of his brothers' saying there was no time for that. He found the axe chopping, all by itself, and took it, and when they asked him what it was, he said: "Oh, nothing at all." Further they came to a stream, sat down again and Merrywise was wondering from where the water came. He found a tiny walnut with a hole in it, and the water trickling out of it, but to his brothers he said the water did come out of a rock up there. Walking on, they come to "what looked like a king's territory," and there they saw a big sign: "Any man who can dig and find water to run in the king's well, I will give him the princess in marriage. Any man who tries and does not succeed will be laid down on the chopping block and his ears will be cut off." The brothers decided to have a try, but when Merrywise suggested he also would, they said: "Merrywise, you never could do anything."

They applied to the king, who said: "You know the penalty," but he said: "The whole land is starving for water, and somebody has got to find some purty soon." Jack and Bill failed, and had their ears chopped off, but when Merrywise started digging it was not long before he was out of sight, and he took the walnut out of his pocket, took the moss out of the hole and throwed it down. Then he told them to

[9] *Kentucky Folklore Record*, III (1957), 1–8. The story, "The King's Well," was told to Roberts in 1957 by Jane Muncy, Hyden, Leslie County, Kentucky. The storyteller had learned the story from her grandfather. The editor adds an interesting note: "I have some 25 excellent tales from the same source. Instead of the usually youngest-best being named Jack, he goes under the name of Merrywise in almost a dozen of her tales, almost amounting to a cycle. I have never seen the name elsewhere in folktale tradition." For this reference to the tale recorded by Leonard Roberts I am indebted to Professor Warren Roberts, Indiana University.

> throw a rope, and they throwed him one, and he came up out of there with the water rolling right up behind him, and purty soon the whole well was full with pure, clean water, and the king said: "Well, how did you do it, Merrywise?" He said, "I just dug in the right place."

The storyteller used this story as an introduction to further developments, and her transition to another tale is very well managed.

> So the king like many other fathers, did not like to give up his youngest daughter if he could help it, and he said: "Merrywise, you are a country lad and have just come out of the woods, and you would not suit my daughter. Wouldn't you just as soon have half my kingdom in money, as to have my daughter's hand in marriage?" He said: "I guess I would just as soon have the money," and he went back home, and he built his parents a fine house, and he stayed around with them until he got tired, and wanted to go off on some more adventures. He said to them: "I believe I will go back and see what my brothers are doing there back in the town with their ears cut off."
>
> Going on he sees another sign. This time another king advertised for someone to free his woods from giants. Merrywise still had his axe unused, and handy, and had a series of encounters with the giant, winning in the usual contests in cutting down trees, carrying the wood home, and in eating, and even, by hiding under the bed, escaped when the giant tried to kill him at night, but hit the block. When next morning Merrywise complained that he had been disturbed by the flies, the giant was nobody like you." Then in the end, Merrywise married a princess after all, and took completely overawed and decided to go "to another part of the world where there is over the kingdom, the old king deciding to spend his old days in the castle of the giant.

The sequel, as will be seen, represents another cycle of folktales, well known in many countries (Type 1000 ff.)

It seems evident that the first part of the tale is somehow derived from the Norwegian tale, while it seems impossible to ascertain how the transmission took place. The dependence upon a printed text is, however, far less evident than in the Irish story. The plot has been handled by an able storyteller, and the whole manner is refreshingly realistic, even if in contradiction to folktale custom, when the successful hero prefers "half the kingdom in money" to the marriage with a royal lady. The relationship is startling, and the assumption of a connection rests upon the story itself, and upon the fact that it seems to be recorded in Norway only.[10]

[10] In looking through various catalogues of folktales, one is often reminded of the fact the indexing of tales according to types is by no means an easy task. There is often a confusion between the general heading of a type, and the story itself. To mention an instance of interest to the present paper, in the recently published *Types of the Folktale in Cuba, Puerto Rico, the Dominican Republic,*

The problem of the ultimate origin of the story has not been considered in this brief paper, and the hunt for the source of the Kentucky tale seems hopeless. The point of this case—a perfect instance of a "displaced folktale"—[11]is the evidence of such unexpected transmission and a warning against considering all variants as links in the same chain.

University of Oslo

and *Spanish South America*, by Terrence Leslie Hansen ("Folklore Studies," 8, University of California Press, 1957), there are variants listed under this type, if with a cautious asterisk. In looking up the tales in Andrade's *Folklore of the Dominican Republic*, one can see that tales numbered 204, 205, and 220 do not belong to Mt. 577 at all. True, tasks are mentioned, but they are of a more general sort, freeing a lady from a giant, staying in haunted places, etc., motifs that are not characteristic of any individual type, and certainly not of such a definite pattern as is the story which constitutes the subject of the present paper.

[11] For another strange displacement in a folktale, see Warren Roberts, "A Norwegian Fairy Tale in Jamaica," *Arv*, X (1954), 109–113.

11*

VRIENDEN SIJN GOET BIDEN WEGHE

Matti Kuusi

*We cannot make much use of the fact that proverbs possess peculiarities which
bind them to the soil until we know what those peculiarities are. The first step
is obviously a minute examination of each individual proverb or formula.*

—Archer Taylor

A. Einfache germanische Redaktion

1. *Freunde sind gut am Wege. Proverbia Communia* 775. Peder Låle 1135.
Isländische, norwegische, schwedische, dänische, deutsche und niederländische
Quellen bei Wander I 1183, Reinsberg-Düringsfeld I 504 und Jente 296. Dazu
Ein Vin i Vegen er god aa ganga til. J. Aasen 1881 178. *Det er godt at finde Ven
paa Veie.* Peder Syv 1682 I 346, Grundtvig 1845 108, Molbech 1850 2822, Mau 1879
11300. *Det är godt at have Gud og gode Venner i Ledtog med sig.* J. Meyer 1757 578.

2. *Es ist gut, einen Freund in der Bucht zu haben.* Nur in Schweden: *Godt att
hafva en vän i viken.* Wensell 1863 35, H. Reuterdahl, *Den svenska ordspråks-
boken,* 1865 39, C. Marin 1867 13, G. A. L–n, *Ordspråk sanna språk,* 1889 68. *Gott
ha vän i viken.* Fredrik Ström 1939 134. K. Strömbäck erklärt in seinem Manuskript: ,,Viken war der ehemalige Name von Bohuslän, dessen wilde Bewohner
berühmt wegen ihrer Zuverlässigkeit und Hilfsbereitschaft gegen ihre Freunde
waren.'' Vgl. das finnische Sprichwort: *Hyvä on täti niemennenässä* 'Es ist gut,
eine Tante auf der Spitze der Landzunge zu haben', *Ei ole tätiä tiellä* 'Es gibt
keine Tante am Wege'. A. V. Koskimies, *Kokoelma Suomen kansan sananlaskuja,*
1906 257–259 und 338.

3. Zusammenhang mit der Redaktion unklar: '*Tis good to have a friend in a corner.*' Reinsberg-Düringsfeld 1872 I 504. *Det er godt at have Venner, hvor Mad og Hugg skiftes* 'wo man Essen und Schläge gibt'. Peder Syv 1682 I 476. *It is good to have friends everywhere. Il fait bon d'avoir des amis partout.* H. G. Bohn 1857 21 und 486. *E bene aver amici per tutto. Gli amici son buoni in ogni piazza.* G. Strafforello 1883 I 53. Udgl.

B. Vergleichende westeuropäische Redaktion

1. *Ein Freund am Wege ist so gut wie Geld im Beutel.* Nur in Dänemark: *En Ven paa Vejen er saa god som Penge i Pungen.* Mau 1879 11326, Emil Thomsen, *3400 Ordsprog,* 1919 34.

2. *Besser ist ein Freund am Wege als Geld im Gürtel.* Älteste französische Variante: *Mieus vaut amis en voie que deniers en corroie. Proverbes au vilain,* Ende des 12. Jahrhunderts, N. 68. Zahlreiche altfranzösische Varianten werden von A. Tobler, F. Schepp, E. Ebert, Samuel Singer und Richard Jente zitiert. *Beter vrient ouer wech, dan ghelt in den coffer.* F. Goedthals, *Les proverbes anciens flamengs,* 1568. ...*inden wege beter si Vrient dan gelt.* Heinric van Aken, *Die Rose,* 4798. *A friend on the way is better than a penie in the purse.* 1611 und 1664, siehe Morris Palmer Tilley F 687.

3. *Besser ist ein Freund am Hofe als Geld im Beutel* ∼ *Ein Freund am Hofe ist von gleichem Wert wie Geld im Beutel.* Nach Morris Palmer Tilley 1950 F 687 und Smith-Heseltine-Harvey 1952 227 kommt der Typus *Better is a friend in court than a penny in purse* um 1400, 1509, 1536, 1580, 1597, 1598, 1600, 1611, 1641, 1659, 1664, der Typus *A friend in court is worth a penny in purse* um 1510, 1552, 1616, 1639, 1640, 1659, 1668, 1670, 1721, 1732 vor. Einfacher Typus: *It is good to have friends at court.* Burt Stevenson 1948 901. Zum erstgenannten Typus gehört die wallisische Variante *Gwell car yn llys Nog aur fys* und *A Friend in the Market is better than money in the Chest* von Thomas Fuller, *Gnomologia,* 1732 N. 119. Vgl. *Bon fait avoir ami en cour, car le procès en est plus court.* C. Marin 1863 12.

4. *Besser ist ein Freund am Platze als Geld im Kasten. Más valen amigos en plaza que dineros en arca.* Pedro Vallés, *Libro de refranes,* Zaragoza 1549. Reinsberg-Düringsfeld I 504 und Giuseppe Pitrè, *Proverbi Siciliani* I 98 bringen südfranzösische, spanische, portugiesische und italienische Varianten.

5. *Ein Freund in der Not ist mehr wert als Geld im Beutel.* Reinsberg-Düringsfeld I 505 zitiert lateinische, französische und dänische Varianten. Chr. Grubb 1678 72 kennt eine deutsche Variante: *Besser ein Freund in der Noth als Geldt in der Faust.* Dazu: *Más vale un amigo en el apuro que dineros en el puño.* Luis Martínez Kleiser 1953 3393.

6. *Ein (guter) Freund ist besser als Geld im Beutel.* Deutsche und niederländische Varianten bei G. Henisch 1616 1234, R. Eckart 1893 129, P. J. Harrebomée 1866 II 411. Vgl. *Néha többet használ a jó barát az erszény pénznél* 'Manchmal ist ein guter Freund nützlicher als ein Geldbeutel'. E. Margalits, *Magyar közmondások,* 1897 43. Vgl. das allgemeineuropäische Sprichwort *Gut freund sind vber silber vnd vber gold.* S. Franck 1541 I 9b. G. Pitrè 1880 I 92, 1910 25. V. Dalj 1904 IV 23. Čelakovsky 1852 228. E. Normann, *Valimik Eesti vanasõnu,* 1955 242. F. Ström 1939 133. Aasen 1881 178. Le Roux de Lincy 1859 II 171. Vgl. auch *Besser ohne Geld als ohne Freund.* Wander I 332. Grubb 1678 72. F. Bresemann 1843 16. A. Sutor 1740 19. G. Strafforello 1883 I 457.

C. Vergleichende finnische Redaktion

1. *Gut ist ein Freund am Wege, ein Abstecherhaus im Dorfe, besser der Ranzen im Schlitten.* Henricus Florinus 1702 B 4. *Ystäwä hyfwä kyläsä, tuttu tjelä poikettawa, reppu rèsä parempi* 'Ein Freund ist gut im Dorfe, ein bekanntes Abstecherhaus ist gut am Wege, besser ist der Ranzen im Schlitten'. Handschrift des Erzbischofs K. F. Mennander (vor 1766) im Archiv der Finnischen Literaturgesellschaft. *Hywä tiessä ystäwä, reppu reessä parembi* 'Gut ist ein Freund am Wege, besser der Ranzen im Schlitten'. J. Juteini, *Walittuja Suomalaisten Sananlaskuja,* 1818 25.

2. *Besser ein Ranzen im Schlitten als ein Freund am Wege.* Die frühesten Varianten um 1780. Kuusi *Vanhan kansan sananlaskuviisaus,* 1953 324. Juteini 1818 58. Lönnrot 1842 387. *Parempi reppu reessä kun ystävä kylässä* 'Besser ein Ranzen im Schlitten als ein Freund im Dorfe'. R. E. Nirvi-Lauri Hakulinen, *Suomen kansan sananparsikirja,* 1948 343, vgl. 332. *Parempi reppu reessä kuin täti tien laidassa* 'Besser ein Ranzen im Schlitten als eine Tante am Wegrand'. A. V. Koskimies, *Kokoelma suomalaisia sananlaskuja,* 1906 336. Das Sprichwort ist allgemein in Westfinnland, unbekannt in Ostfinnland. Die einzige schwedische Variante an der Sprachgrenze in Südfinnland aufgezeichnet: *Matsäck i släden är bättre än vän vid vägen* 'Ein Proviantsack im Schlitten ist besser als ein Freund am Wege'. Väinö Solstrand, *Finlands Svenska Folkdiktning* III, 1923 108.

3. *Gut ist ein Freund im Dorfe, in der Familie soll man ihn fürchten.* Nur bei Florinus: *Hywä kyläs ystäwä, perhes peljättäpä.*

· · ·

Das Streben nach Reim, Alliteration und Parallelismus, die Milieudominanz und der Einfluß nahestehender Sprichwörter erklären das übliche Schwanken der Tradition, beispielsweise daß als Aufbewahrungsort des Geldes in Italien *cassa,* in Spanien *caixa, arca, puño*, in Frankreich *courroie, bourse, poing*, in England *purse, pocket, chest*, in den Niederlanden *beurs, koffer*, in Deutschland *Beutel, Tasche, Faust* und in Dänemark *punge, skød* genannt wird. Das französische *courroie* 'Lederriemen, Gürtel, Geldkatze' ist in England, wenn nicht schon in Frankreich mit dem bedeutungsmäßig fernstehenden, aber lautlich nahestehenden *cour, court* 'Hof' assoziiert worden (B3), und noch verständlicher ist, daß man in Schweden, einem alten Seefahrerlande, das Wort *veg* durch *vik* 'Bucht' ersetzt hat (A2). Das Streben nach Erweiterung des Anwendungsgebiets des Sprichworts hat verursacht, daß „am Wege" im Süden durch das unbestimmtere „am Platze" ersetzt (B4) oder völlig weggelassen worden ist (B6). Die stark dominante Vorstellungsverbindung „Freund in der Not" ist bei verschiedenen Völkern auch in den Rahmen dieses Sprichworts eingedrungen (B5). Als Ergebnis einer ähnlichen Kontamination hat „die Tante am Wegrande" (vgl. A2) in einem südfinnischen Gebiet „den Freund am Wege" (C2) verdrängt.

Von tieferem methodischen Interesse ist die Frage, was das Verhältnis zwischen der A-Redaktion („Freunde sind gut am Wege"), der B-Redaktion („Besser ist ein Freund am Wege als Geld im Beutel") und der C-Redaktion („Besser ein Ranzen im Schlitten als ein Freund am Wege") ist. Muß man die einfache A-Redaktion als Verkümmerung eines ursprünglicheren, von den Redaktionen B und C vertretenen Strukturtyps ansehen, oder haben sich B und C getrennt auf der Grundlage von A entwickelt, oder kann man schlußfolgern, daß B aus Westeuropa am skandinavischen A-Gebiet vorbei nach Finnland „gewandert" wäre und sich dort inhaltlich in sein eigenes Gegenteil, in die C-Redaktion, verwandelt hätte?

Eine Analyse der Altersschichten der C-Redaktion bringt Licht in diese Frage. Der Anfangsvers der drei ältesten Varianten „Gut ist ein Freund am Wege im Dorfe" schließt sich seiner Formel nach an die germanische A-Redaktion an. *Ystävä hyvä kylässä* ist ein fehlerloser Kalevala-Vers, dem der regelmäßige Parallelvers *tuttu tiellä poikettava* oder *perehessä peljättävä* folgt. Hingegen läßt sich *reppu reessä parempi* 'Besser ein Ranzen im Schlitten' wohl kaum zu einem Kalevala-Vers rekonstruieren, und hier fehlt auch der Parallelvers. Der Reimversuch *reessä – tiessä* beweist unwiderlegbar, daß der Typ C2 in eine spätere Stilperiode gehört. Das finnische Sprichwort hat die charakteristische Verbreitung eines aus dem Westen entlehnten Sprichworts, und seine Urzelle ist ganz deutlich der einfache A-Vers gewesen, der schon im Mittelalter entweder einen synonymen (C1) oder einen antithetischen (C3) Parallelvers erhalten hat. Die gedrängte Reimformel *Parempi reppu reessä kuin ystävä tiessä* 'Besser ein Ranzen im Schlitten als ein Freund am Wege' gehört frühestens zur Mode des 16. Jahrhunderts; die Dreizeiler bei Florinus und Mennander wirken als Kontamination

dieses Typs und des früheren, im Kalevala-Versmaß gehaltenen. Die Formel
„Besser... als" ist schon im 17. Jahrhundert in Finnland so häufig, daß man zur
Erklärung des Typs C2 durchaus nicht nötig hat, einen Einfluß der westeuropäi-
schen B-Redaktion anzunehmen.

Samuel Singer kommentiert das in der Sammlung „Proverbia rusticorum"
enthaltene Sprichwort *Mieiz vaut amis en voie ke denier en coroie* durch die Behauptung, daß es sich um ein ausschließlich französisches Sprichwort handle und
daß ihm wohl eine antike Sentenz des Publilius Syrus zugrunde liege: *Comes
facundus in via pro vehiculo est*, die Goethe folgendermaßen umgestaltet hat:
„Ein lustiger Gefährte ist ein Rollwagen auf der Wanderschaft."[1] Die ganze
Entwicklungsgeschichte des Sprichworts zeigt, daß man unter dem Freund am
Wege im allgemeinen nicht einen Reisegefährten verstanden hat, sondern einen
am Wege, in einem Dorf oder an einem Fürstenhof wohnenden oder im richtigen
Augenblick sich zufällig einstellenden Freund, zu dem man seine Zuflucht nehmen
kann. Nach Richard Jente liegt dem Sprichwort *Vrienden sijn goet biden weghe*
zugrunde Jesus Sirach 6:15: *Amico fideli nulla est comparatio, et non est digna
ponderatio auri et argenti contra bonitatem fidei illius.*[2] Daraus erklärt sich jedoch
nicht die den Redaktionen A, B und C gemeinsame und deutlich primäre Orts-
bestimmung: am Wege. Die germanische A-Redaktion und die von ihr sich her-
leitende finnische C-Redaktion stehen kaum in einem genetischen Zusammenhang
mit Jesus Sirach. Dagegen ist es möglich, daß die romanische B-Redaktion aus
der A-Redaktion entwickelt worden ist, indem man damit das gemeineuropäische
und vielleicht auf Jesus Sirachs Sinnspruch beruhende Sprichwort „Ein guter
Freund ist mehr wert als Gold und Silber" (B6) kombiniert hat.

Warum hat man das Sprichwort „Freunde sind gut am Wege" gerade in den
romanischen Ländern und ihrer nahen Nachbarschaft durch den Vergleich „besser
als Geld im Beutel" intensiviert, während man sich in Dänemark und England
mit der Gleichung „so gut wie Geld im Beutel" begnügen konnte, und warum ist
man gerade in Finnland zu der entgegengesetzten Einschätzung gelangt: „Besser
ein Ranzen im Schlitten als ein Freund am Wege"?

In verschiedenen Teilen Europas hat man zwar in Form von Sprichwörtern die
Ansicht kristallisiert, daß Freundschaft im Vergleich zu Geld nur wenig wert sei:
in Dänemark *Mange agte de Venner højest, som de bære i Pungen* 'viele achten die
Freunde am höchsten, die sie im Beutel tragen' (Thomsen 1919 35), *Den bedste
Stalbroder paa Rejsen er tit Penge* 'der beste Reisegefährte ist dein Geld' (Syv 1682
I 345); in Ungarn *Jobb egy erszény mint két barát* 'besser ein Beutel als zwei
Freunde' (Margalits 1897 43); in Spanien *Como fiel y seguro, menos vale un amigo*

---

[1] *Sprichwörter des Mittelalters*, II (Bern 1946) 14/15.
[2] *Proverbia Communia* (Bloomington, Indiana 1947) 296.

que un duro 'obgleich treu und zuverlässig, ist ein Freund weniger wert als fünf Peseten' (Martínez Kleiser 1953 2930); in Wales *Goreu cyfaill bathodyn* 'die besten Freunde sind in deinem Beutel' (zitiert nach Otto E. Moll). Derartige Sinnsprüche können sowohl zynische Materialisten als auch ihre idealistischen Gegner angewandt haben. Sehr viele Moralismen haben gleichsam als Negativ ihre paradoxe Antithese.

Die finnische C-Redaktion hat eine ganz andersartige psychologische Grundlage. Wenn man in den umfangreichsten italienischen, spanischen, französischen und deutschen Sprichwortsammlungen blättert, kann man feststellen, daß es in diesen Sprachen sehr reichlich Sprichwörter gibt, die sich auf die Begriffe 'Freund' und 'Freundschaft' beziehen, z. B. bei Martínez Kleiser 650 und bei Wander über 700. Die entsprechenden finnischen Sprichwörter, die vor unserem Jahrhundert aufgezeichnet worden sind, lassen sich dagegen alle hier aufzählen.[3]

1. In der Not erkennt man den Freund.
2. Ein Freund ist nicht, der die Hand gibt, sondern der Hilfe gibt.
3. Besser ein guter Freund als ein Verwandter.
4. Ein alter Freund ist besser als zwei neue.
5. Verlasse nicht deinen besten Freund und die Landstraße.
6. Wenn die Freunde sich erzürnen, werden nicht alle entzückt.
7. Wenn wir Freunde sind, so werden wir uns begegnen.
8. Freunde sind einträchtig, obgleich sie jeder seinen eigenen Kopf haben.
9. Die Zeit vergeht schnell bei Freunden.
10. Besser wenig Freundschaft als viel Streitigkeit.
11. Besser gute Eintracht als böse Freundschaft.
12. Man wird nicht Schwiegersohn mit Gewalt und Freund mit Übermut.
13. Einseitige Freundschaft erhält sich nicht.
14. Wer neun Freunde hat, hat fünf Feinde.
15. Das Gesetz schaut nicht auf Freundschaft.
16. Es ist nicht Platz für alle Freunde bei einem Gastmahl.
17. Wer Bier hat, hat auch Freunde.
18. Wenn es aus der Tonne tröpfelt, sind die Freunde in Bewegung.
19. Mit Butter bekommt man Gäste, mit Bier Freunde.
20. Mit Geld bekommt man Essen, mit Bier Freunde.
21. Mit Geld bekommt man Freunde.
22. Wer einen Geldhaufen hat, hat einen Freundeschober.
23. So lange hat man Freunde, wie man zu geben hat.
24. Auch der Schurke heißt „guter Freund", wenn er Geld hat.

[3] Archiv der Finnischen Literaturgesellschaft in Helsinki.

25. Auch der Reiche ist gern dessen Freund, der Geld hat.

26. Hunger ist des Armen Freund.

27. Komm, Sommer mit den Fliegen, daß auch der Arme Freunde habe.

28. Jemand erzählt etwas seinem Freund, der Freund dem ganzen Dorf.

29. Vertraue nicht dem Freund, er betrügt dich bald.

30. Vertraue nicht deinem Freund, mit dem Schaftende des Badequastes schlägt er dich.

31. Der Freund betrügt seinen Freund, nie der Feind.

Unter den etwa 11 000 Sprichwortvarianten, die sich aus den Jahren 1544–1826 erhalten haben, findet man von den soeben aufgezählten 13 und von diesen nur fünf (Nr. 12, 13, 16, 18 und 28) mehr als einmal.[4] Es ist leicht zu beobachten, wie zahlreiche gemeineuropäische Sprichwörter, die den Wert der Freundschaft hervorheben, entweder vor ihrem Eintreffen in Finnland erfroren sind oder nur kurzfristig in irgendeiner Küstengegend Fuß gefaßt haben. Eine zynische, ironische, warnende oder einfach schweigende Einstellung zur Freundschaft ist vorherrschend.

Die finnische Sonderentwicklung des Sprichwortes ,,Freunde sind gut am Wege" eignet sich als Beispiel dafür, wie ein Lehnsprichwort einen sozialen ,,Klimawechsel" durchmachen kann. Auch in der Form, die der A-Redaktion entspricht, vertrat das Sprichwort eine zu positive Einstellung zu der Beschaffenheit zwischenmenschlicher Beziehungen, denen man im öffentlichen Sprachgebrauch mit kaltem Spott gegenübertreten mußte. Also entstand zuerst die Spielart C3, die den Schwerpunkt des Sprichworts auf die Warnung verlegte: man soll mit einem Außenstehenden nicht so feste Freundschaftsbeziehungen anknüpfen, daß er in den Familienkreis hineinschauen kann. Allgemeinere Beliebtheit erlangte erst die klare Antithese des germanischen Sprichworts: ein Reisender soll sich auf seinen eigenen Speiseranzen verlassen, nicht auf einen am Wege wohnenden Freund. In einem Lande, wo noch in der ersten Hälfte des 19. Jahrhunderts in weiten Gebieten die Mehrheit der Bevölkerung auch in normalen Erntejahren aus Kiefernrinde zubereitetes Notbrot aß, herrschte an den Winterwegen die Brauchtumsvorschrift, daß bei Übernachtung auch im Hause eines Bekannten der Reisende seine Mahlzeiten aus eigenem Proviant bestreiten mußte.[5] Der erste Bischof von Finnland, der heilige Henrik, wurde im Jahr 1156 totgeschlagen, weil er in einem am Wege liegenden Bauernhof ohne Zustimmung der Bauernfamilie Brot, Bier und Hafer für sein Pferd genommen hatte.

[4] Vgl. die Statistik in FFC 172 S. 36–38.

[5] Eino Jutikkala: *Atlas of Finnish History* (Porvoo 1949) N. 48. Ester Uotila in der Zeitschrift "Kotiseutu" 1930 81–88 und 1933 60–70.

Ein eifriger Volkscharakterpsychologe würde sicherlich in dem Obengesagten wertvolles Beweismaterial im Geiste des Tacitus finden: *Fennis mira feritas, foeda paupertas* (Germania 46). In Wirklichkeit bringen dieser und andere *peculiarities* dieser Art in der Volksüberlieferung wohl kaum etwas vom „Charakter" der Völker zum Ausdruck, beispielsweise von ihrer Freundlichkeit oder Unfreundlichkeit. Die Unterschiede spiegeln Gegensätzlichkeiten der Verhaltensnormen wider, besonders der Normen des Sprachgebrauchs. Wenn man das Sprichwortgut der romanischen Völker und der Finnen, das die Liebe zum Gegenstand hat, miteinander verglichе, wäre der Unterschied hinsichtlich der Menge und des Tones noch schroffer. Es gibt jedoch genügend u. a. folkloristische Beweise dafür, daß Liebe und Freundschaft in den nordischen Wäldern ebenso starke Schicksalsmächte gewesen sind wie im Süden. Aber in Finnland verlangte der gute Ton, daß man von Zuneigung zwischen Menschen nicht anders sprach als in umschreibenden Anspielungen oder grob ablehnend. Die Sprichwörter verlangten vom Reisenden, daß er zu seinem eigenen Speiseranzen seine Zuflucht nahm, aber sie forderten andererseits von den Bewohnern des Hauses, daß sie dem Reisenden zu essen gaben: „Der Geizhals füttert das Schwein nicht, der Knauserige speist nicht den Gast", „Man wird nicht reich wenn man Ähren liest, man wird nicht arm wenn man Gäste speist", usw. Der gemeinsame Zweck dieser scheinbar entgegengesetzten Verhaltensnormen ist gleichgerichtet mit dem der „Freundschaftslosigkeit" des alten Sprichwortgutes: einen leicht verletzbaren Wert — die Freundschaft — vor Konflikten zu schützen und vor den Blicken Außenstehender zu verbergen.

Universität Helsinki

WORDS OF WISDOM IN *BEOWULF*

Kemp Malone

Here and there in *Beowulf* one finds words of wisdom based, in all likelihood, on traditional lore. The first passage of this kind in the poem reads,

> 20 Swa sceal [geong g]uma gode gewyrcean,
> fromum feohgiftum on fæder [bea]rme,
> þæt hine on ylde, eft, gewunigen
> wilgesiþas þonne wig cume,
> leode gelæsten. Lofdædum sceal
> in mægþa gehwære man geþeon

> 'So should [a] young man with freehandedness, with handsome goodly gifts in [his] father's lap, bring [it] about that afterwards, in [his] maturity, well-wishing retainers stand by him when war comes, [well-wishing] tribesmen serve [him]. By praiseworthy deeds one may be sure of doing well in every tribe.'

The gifts are said to be in the father's lap—i.e., in his possession—because they properly belong to him, though the son gives them away as if they were his own.[1] Of course the son has the father's leave in so doing: both are thinking of the future, when the father will be dead and the son will need retainers and subjects loyal to him personally.

The passage is one of generalization but falls into two parts, and the second part, 24b–25, is much more general than the first, which properly applies only to kings' sons in their youth. The behavior that the poet commends to them, urges

---

[1] Compare lines 1143–1144, where *him...on bearm dyde* means 'gave into his possession' [i.e. Hnæf gave the sword Hunlafing to Hengest], and line 2404, where *him to bearme cwom* means 'came into his possession.'

upon them indeed, is tied by *swa* to what the poet has just been saying about King Scyld of the Danes and his son Beowulf. Before Scyld became king the Danes had had no ruler for a long time, a time of *fyrenðearf* 'dire need,' and God, by giving Scyld a son, saw to it that the throne would not again become vacant upon the king's death. This son's behavior as a youth was just that which the poet commends to kings' sons generally and brought about the success in later life on which the poet touches when he says,

> 18 Beowulf wæs breme —blæd wide sprang—
> Scyldes eafera Scedelandum in

'Beowulf was famous— [his] glory spread wide—Scyld's heir [was famous] in the Scandinavian lands.'

The late F. Klaeber in his edition of the poem has a note on lines 20ff. in which he glosses *swa* with 'in such a way [as he (Beowulf or, more likely, Scyld) did].' That is, Klaeber, like me, takes the poet's advice to kings' sons to be a generalized statement tied to a specific case in which the course of action that the poet recommends was taken and proved effective. I cannot agree with Klaeber, however, in thinking that the exemplary conduct was "more likely" that of Scyld. On the contrary, it seems to me evident that the son, not the father, was the one who in his youth set for all kings' sons a good example. The story of the father was highly exceptional if not indeed unique and makes no proper basis for the poet's advice to young princes. For one thing, Scyld was a waif and thus had no father's lap to go to for gifts. Again, as founder of a new royal house, taking the throne after a long interregnum, he became king in a most irregular way, whereas the poet's advice presupposes a normal succession and deals only with what a recognized heir ought to do, while yet a youth, to ensure for himself a prosperous reign in later years, after he has succeeded his father on the throne. Beowulf was such an heir; Scyld was not.

One might have expected the poet first to speak of Beowulf's freehandedness as a youth, the loyal following that he built up thereby, and the fame that this following enabled him to win after he became king. The moral for young princes would then be obvious: go ye and do likewise. The poet might have drawn his moral explicitly or he might have left it for his hearers to draw. A modern artist would prefer the latter course. But in fact our poet simply tells us that Beowulf was famous and goes on to words of wisdom aimed at all kings' sons in their youth. We may be sure that Beowulf laid the foundation for his kingly fame by giving freely from his father's hoard as a young man, but we know this only through the poet's *swa*. Even without the *swa*, it is true, we might reasonably have inferred that young Beowulf was openhanded, since otherwise the words of wisdom would be without relation to their context. But *swa* makes the matter certain. The poet speaks clearly but passes over the particular case briefly enough, putting the emphasis where he thinks it belongs: on the words of wisdom. These words fit the case of Beowulf and are set in their proper place but one may legitimately suspect that they, or their like, existed before the poet's day as a piece of traditional wisdom, known to the poet and here used by him to good effect.

The passage we have just looked at may be described as one of worldly wisdom. Our next passage gives us something very different: godly wisdom. It comes after the poet's account of Danish heathendom. He follows this with a general statement about life after death:

183   Wa bið þæm ðe sceal
            þurh sliðne nið sawle bescufan
            in fyres fæþm, frofre ne wenan,
            wihte gewendan. Wel bið þæm þe mot
            æfter deaðdæge drihten secean
            ond to fæder fæþmum freoðo wilnian

'It is ill for him who is fated to thrust [his] soul with cruel hostility into the fire's grasp, [who is fated] not to expect help, [not to expect] to change in any way. It is well for him who after [his] death-day may seek out the Lord and ask for protection at the hands of [his] father.'

This view of man's destiny belongs to Christian tradition, of course. The poet brings it in at just the right point. He might have said nothing about the false religion of the Danes but having brought the subject up, realistically enough, he goes on, with equal realism, to the doom hanging over devil-worshipers and, by contrast, the bliss awaiting worshipers of the true God. The damned man is the enemy of his own soul: with cruel hostility he thrusts it into the flames of hell. It is his fate to do this and to be without hope of help or change. The saved man goes to heaven, where he finds a father's protection. The kingdom of heaven is seen in Germanic terms, with God for king and the righteous for retainers. But heaven was a kingdom for the Christians of the apostolic age too, and the poet's Germanic terms are a coloring that does not hide the Christianity of the picture. The picture of hell that the poet gives may also be colored by native tradition; I have in mind the hopeless heroism of warriors who fight on, faithful to their code of honor, after defeat and death become certain. But no such coloring need be there; the poet's words can readily be explained in strictly Christian terms.

Each of the two passages taken up above ends a larger unit of discourse and has a concluding function. But a wisdom passage may head the unit to which it belongs and have an introductory function. The Danish keeper of the shore begins his second speech thus:

287   Aeghwæþres sceal
       scearp scyldwiga gescad witan,
       worda ond worca, se þe wel þenceð

'The sharp[-minded] fighting-man, he who thinks well [i.e. acutely], ought to be a good judge of each [of two things]: words and deeds.'

We have here a general observation that is given immediate practical application: the speaker proceeds to "size up" Beowulf and his men as friends of the Danish king and to govern himself accordingly. His words of worldly wisdom serve also as self-characterization: by his good judgment in this case he shows himself to be indeed a sharp-minded fighting-man, one who thinks well.

Beowulf's kinsman Wiglaf, like the Danish sentry, begins one of his speeches with words of wisdom, though these are philosophical rather than practical:

3077 Oft sceall eorl monig anes willan
      wræc adreogan

'Oft shall many a man on account of one man's self-will endure misery.'

Here too the generalization is immediately followed by a case in point. The Geatas are now enduring misery because of the self-will of Beowulf, who insisted on fighting the dragon in spite of the protests of his followers and has lost his life in the fight. The misery that the tribesmen endure comes in part from grief, in part from forebodings of disaster, now that their great king is dead. In this passage, then, we have first a general statement of a kind of trouble that is bound to come time after time in bodies made up of a leader and his followers; this is tied to the particular situation in which Wiglaf and his fellows now find themselves. Wiglaf among other things is giving the Geatas company in their misery when he tells them that many a man is destined to have the experience they are now having; the comfort is cold but it is comfort of a kind. He ends, in line 3084, by explaining if not justifying Beowulf's decision to fight the dragon: the hero *heold on heah gesceap* 'held to [his] high fate,' moved by compulsions unknown to lesser men.

In Beowulf's reply to King Hroðgar's lament over the death of Aeschere the words of wisdom come, not indeed at the very beginning, but so near the beginning that they make almost the whole of the introductory passage:

1384 Ne sorga, snotor guma! Selre bið æghwæm
        þæt he his freond wrece þonne he fela murne.
        Ure æghwylc sceal ende gebidan
        worolde lifes; wyrce se þe mote
        domes ær deaþe; þæt bið drihtguman
1389 unlifgendum æfter selest

'Grieve not, wise man! [It] is better for everyone that he avenge his friend than [that] he mourn much. Each of us is destined to come to the end of worldly life; he who may should try to win high repute before death; that is best afterwards for a man [who is] not living.'

These words fall into two parts: lines 1384b–85 and lines 1386–89. The former make the positive counterpart of the negative exhortation with which the passage starts. Their generality is limited by the fact that they apply only to the conduct deemed proper when a friend is killed by a foe. Lines 1386–89 are words of consolation cast in general terms: we are all mortal [and Aeschere has suffered the fate common to man]; everyone who can should try to win for himself the good opinion of his fellows while he lives [and Aeschere was your right-hand man in peace and war and prodigal of good things to all]; that is the best way for a man to keep his name alive after he is dead [and Aeschere's name will long be remembered because of his services to you and his generosity].

Klaeber's note on lines 1386 ff. ends thus: "Of course, a hero's striving for fame would seem to be in no need of explanation or comment." But these lines need both, to bring out the way in which they fit the particular situation. Beowulf's mention of man's mortality needs no gloss in itself, since the application of this truism to the case of Aeschere and the consolatory intent of the utterance are obvious enough. It is hardly otiose, however, to point out that this very obviousness is functional: the poet thereby gives us the key to what follows. Aeschere is an exemplar, one who made a great name for himself, a name that will be remembered by future generations. The king should take comfort: his lamented retainer had done much and gone far; he had won lasting fame before death; he was not untimely cut off.

I have found no other words of wisdom with an introductory function. Further examples with a concluding function are 1838b–39 and 2890b–91, where the wisdom is worldly; 455b, 1002b–08a, 1887b, and 2265b–66, where it is philosophical; and 700b–702a and 2858–59, where it is godly. In 1057b–62 philosophical and godly are blended. We take these examples in the order given. In the first, Beowulf follows up an invitation to King Hroðgar's son Hreðric with a general observation on the benefits of foreign travel:

1838   feorcyþðe beoð
        selran gesohte þæm þe him selfa deah

'For him who himself is worthy, visiting far countries is better [than staying at home].'

In other words, promising young princes like Hreðric need to have the experience of seeing what other countries are like. Our second example, though aimed at retainers, has more general application. Wiglaf ends his denunciation of Beowulf's cowardly followers by saying,

2890   Deað bið sella
        eorla gehwylcum þonne edwitlif

'For every man of rank, death is better than a life of shame.'

After Beowulf has made it known to King Hroðgar that he came to Denmark to rid the Danes of the hall-haunting monster Grendel, he goes on to provide for the possibility that he rather than Grendel will lose the fight. If that happens the monster will eat him and his body will not have to be looked after, but his armor will be left and he asks King Hroðgar to send it back, in such case, to King Hygelac of the Geatas. He ends his speech with words of philosophical wisdom: *Gæð a wyrd swa hio scel* 'Fate always goes as it must' (455b). A fit conclusion indeed! But as things turn out, Grendel is the loser and he flees from the Danish hall, mortally wounded. The certainty of Grendel's death leads the poet to a general statement about mortality:

1002   No þæt yðe byð
        to befleonne, fremme se þe wille,
        ac gesecan sceal sawlberendra,
        nyde genydde, niþða bearna,
        grundbuendra, gearwe stowe,
        þær his lichoma legerbedde fæst
        swefeþ æfter symle

'That [i.e. death] is not easy to flee from, let him try to do [it] who will, but [he who flees] is destined to seek out [i.e., go to, reach] the place made ready for soul-bearers, for children of men, for earthdwellers, [the place] forced [upon them] by necessity, where his body, grave-fast, sleeps after the feast [of life].'

The place made ready for mortals is the grave, and whoever tries, like Grendel, to flee from death actually flees, like Grendel, to his grave. The concluding generalization was inspired by Grendel's hopeless flight and is beautifully integrated with it.

12 Taylor

At leavetaking, Hroðgar gave to Beowulf many rich presents and the band of
Geatas on their way to ship had much to say in praise of the gifts. The poet adds
his own praise of the king:

> 1885   þæt wæs an cyning,
> æghwæs orleahtre, oþ þæt hine yldo benam
> mægenes wynnum, se þe oft manegum scod

'That was a king peerless, in every way faultless, until age took from him the joys of strength,
[age] which has often harmed many.'

Here the last half-line gives us a generalization about old age, a piece of philosophical wisdom grown out of the common experience of mankind.

Our next example ends a lament with which the only one left of a noble house
gives back to earth, before he dies, the hoard that has come down to him:

> 2265   Bealocwealm hafað
> fela feorhcynna forð onsended

'Baleful death has sent on [i.e., sent to the grave] many life-kindreds, [has sent them] forth.'

The generalization proceeds from the particularity of the lament, making what
happened to the speaker's kindred one case among many. These words of wisdom
come properly at the end, of course.

The passage in which the poet contrasts the forebodings of the Geatas [left to
hold the Danish hall against Grendel] with the happy outcome [made certain by
God's help] ends thus:

> 700   Soð is gecyþed
> þæt mihtig God manna cynnes
> weold wideferhð

'The truth is made known that mighty God has always controlled mankind [i.e., guided the
course of events].'

Beowulf's victory over Grendel serves to make this truth known and the half-line
700b makes a link between the particular event and the generalization about
God. The words of godly wisdom are obviously a fitting conclusion to the poet's
pious explanation of Beowulf's triumph.

After Beowulf dies, his kinsman Wiglaf, not yet certain of the hero's death,
tries to bring him back to consciousness but in vain. The poet comments,

2855 Ne meahte he on eorðan, ðeah he uðe wel,
on ðam frumgare feorh gehealdan
ne ðæs wealdendes wiht oncirran.
Wolde dom Godes dædum rædan
gumena gehwylcum, swa he nu gen deð

'He could not, however much he would, keep life on earth in the leader [as opposed to life in heaven] nor arouse the Lord's creature [i.e., Beowulf, now in God's keeping]. God's decision would control doings for every man, as it still does now.'

With the generalization of lines 2858–59 the passage comes to an end.

In our final passage of conclusion the wisdom is both philosophical and godly:

1057   Metod eallum weold
gumena cynnes, swa he nu git deð.
Forþan bið andgit æghwær selest,
ferhðes foreþanc. Fela sceal gebidan
leofes ond laþes se þe longe her
on ðyssum windagum worolde bruceð

'God had power over the race of men, as he still does now. Therefore understanding is everywhere best, forethought of mind. Much of good and ill he must experience who long here, in these hardship-days, brooks the world [i.e., keeps living].'

More commonly words of wisdom do not have either an introductory or a concluding function but come somewhere within the units of discourse to which they belong. The first utterance of wisdom in the poem with such a medial position reads thus:

572   Wyrd oft nereð
unfægne eorl, þonne his ellen deah

'Fate often saves a man not doomed to die, when his valor is good.'

The speaker is Beowulf, in the fliting with Unferð. He has told of the swimming match, the storm that parted the swimmers, and the desperate fight with the sea-monsters and hard-won victory over them. Now the sun rises and the waters become calm, so that he can see the shore. His long ordeal is nearly over and he speaks the words of philosophical wisdom quoted above before going on to tell how many monsters he slew and how he reached land in safety. The words are evidently to the point and stand in their proper place. The thinking that they reflect is far from rigorous but the passage bears witness to the fact that the tradition on which the poet was here drawing had something to say about the

12*

philosophical problem of free will vs. determinism. Klaeber compares the proverbial "Fortune favors the brave" and paraphrases the poet's words with "Fate
does not render manly courage unnecessary."

We must all die but we do not know when, where, or how. The poet expresses
himself on the where of it:

3062   Wundur hwar þonne
            eorl ellenrof ende gefere
            lifgesceafta, þonne leng ne mæg
            mon mid his [ma]gum meduseld buan

'[It is] a mystery where then a man famed for courage reaches the end set by fate for [his]
life, when he cannot longer, the man, dwell in mead-house with his kinsmen [i.e., when his
time has come].'

He goes on to say that so it was with Beowulf, when he sought out the dragon: he did
not know through what his death would come about. From the context we learn
that a curse went with the hoard and at bottom it was this that brought about
the hero's death, the bite of the dragon being instrumental only. Beowulf had
been predestined to die at a particular place, the spot where the hoard lay; if he
had not gone there we would not have died. He knew nothing about this and
heroes in general do not know where they are doomed to die; the place set by fate
for one's death remains a mystery to the last.

The poet puts these words of philosophical wisdom in the middle of a passage
dealing with the spell laid on the hoard. First we learn of the existence and the
potency of the spell [no spell had been mentioned in the earlier passage, lines
2233 ff., telling how the hoard came to be hidden]. The poet tells us next [lines
3058–60a] that that way of doing [i.e., laying a spell on the hoard] did not turn
out well for the one "who wrongly hid treasure inside, under the wall [i.e., within
the cave]." That is, the man who put the hoard in the cave did wrong in hiding
it [a hoard should be given away, not stowed away] and his measures did not
keep the hoard from being found and taken. In four half-lines, 3060b–62a, the
poet now sums up the workings of the spell: the dragon killed Beowulf and was
himself killed. The words of wisdom about death follow. The passage ends with a
fuller account of the spell than had been given at the beginning, where only its
existence and potency are spoken of. By this repetition with variation the poet
rounds out his passage effectively enough. One is reminded of musical composition,
though composers get their circular effects more simply, by mere repetition.

In our next passage philosophical and godly wisdom are blended. The runaway
who stole an ornamented cup from the hoard came too near the sleeping dragon's

head and aroused his sense of smell but got away in safety. The poet before going on with the story draws a moral:

> 2291 Swa mæg unfæge eaðe gedigan
> wean ond wræcsið, se ðe waldendes
> hyldo gehealdeþ

'So can one not doomed to die readily outlive woe and wretchedness, he whom the Lord's friendship shields.'

A like blend of Christianity and native philosophy is to be seen in the poet's generalization,

> 2590   swa sceal æghwylc mon
> alætan lændagas

'so [i.e. like Beowulf] every man is destined to leave transitory days [i.e., to die].'

The traditional theme of man's mortality is here given a Christian coloring by *lændagas*, which implies a contrast between temporal life on earth and eternal life in the world to come.

The next two examples come under the head of godly wisdom. We take up first King Hroðgar's utterance,

> 930   a mæg God wyrcan
> wundur æfter wundre, wuldres hyrde

'God can always work wonder after wonder, heaven's keeper.'

The king's speech, lines 928–56, begins with thanks to God, ends with a prayer to God, and is interspersed with pious expressions, among them the words of wisdom just quoted. These words are especially appropriate here: the victory over Grendel, after twelve years (147a) during which he had haunted the royal hall by night and slain many of the king's best fighters, was a wonder indeed, a miracle wrought by Beowulf *þurh drihtnes miht* 'through the Lord's might' (940a).

The other example of godly wisdom is grammatically parenthetical, though semantically an integral part of the passage in which it occurs. We are told that the hoard was so strongly bespelled that no man could get to it

> 3054   nefne God sylfa,
> sigora soðcyning, sealde þam ðe he wolde
> —he is manna gehyld—hord openian,
> efne swa hwylcum manna swa him gemet ðuhte

'unless God himself, truth-king of victories, should give to him whom he would—he is men's protection—to open the hoard, to whichever man it might seem fit to him.'

In effect this means that God might give protection to a man of his choice, who could then safely disregard the spell and open the hoard. But the poet preferred to put God's protective function in general terms, applicable to humanity in all situations, not merely to the particular case of the bespelled hoard. Hence the parenthetical construction. We are not told that God actually protected anybody against the workings of the spell; certainly he did not protect Beowulf, who lost his life. Lines 3054b–57 have the pious function of assuring the poet's audience that God, if he so chooses, can nullify any spell, however powerful.

All our remaining examples are words of worldly wisdom. In speaking of the raid made by Grendel's mother on the Danish hall the poet says,

> 1282   Wæs se gryre læssa
> efne swa micle swa bið mægþa cræft,
> wiggryre wifes, be wæpnedmen...

'The terribleness [of her attack] was less [compared with that of her son] by just so much as the strength of females, a woman's fighting power, [is less] compared with [that of] a man...'

Here the poet sets up a proportion: the strength of Grendel's mother was to that of Grendel as the strength of a woman is to that of a man. Underlying this proportion, of course, is the generalization that a woman has less physical strength for battle than a man has. The degree of difference is left vague enough, but if we go by what happened in the Danish hall, Grendel was many times as formidable as his mother: he would take thirty victims (123a) before returning to his lair whereas she was content with one (1294b).

Klaeber in his note on these lines says,

The inserted remark...seems at variance with the facts, for the second fight is far more difficult for Beowulf than the first, although he is well armed. It is evidently to be explained as an endeavor to discredit the un-biblical notion of a woman's superiority.

This explanation does injustice to the poet, who is specifically and explicitly comparing what Grendel did in the Danish hall with what his mother did there, and who quite naturally explains in terms of sex the great difference between mother and son as hall-raiders. The mother proves much more formidable, it is true, when she is defending her own home and her mortally wounded son against Beowulf than when she is attacking the Danes in their hall. But this feature is traditional enough and holds for both sexes, witness the added danger implied when we speak of bearding a lion in his den.

Beowulf in the fight with Grendel's mother at the bottom of the mere, finding that she is proof against his sword, throws this down and trusts to his muscular strength alone. The poet before going on with the story of the fight makes this comment:

1534   Swa sceal man don
   þonne he æt guðe gegan þenceð
   longsumne lof; na ymb his lif cearað

'So must one do, when he has [it] in mind to win lasting glory in fight; he cares not at all about his life.'

That is, a hero risks his life as a matter of course. He is fearless because safety as such means nothing to him; glory is all. Only by heroic deeds can one win heroic fame, and a deed is not heroic unless it involves great risks, taken without hesitation. The poet's generalization about a hero's state of mind is traditional enough in thought if not in wording; he brings it in at a point where it beautifully fits the situation.

In the passage about Thrytho the poet expresses his disapproval of her ways in terms applicable to all women of high birth:

1940   Ne bið swylc cwenlic þeaw
   idese to efnanne, þeah ðe hio ænlicu sy,...

'Such is not a queenly way of doing, [such is no way] for a lady to behave, though she be unique [i.e., a law unto herself], ...'

Here the use of *swylc* instead of *þæt*, and that of *bið* instead of *is*, broaden the scope of the judgment and make it timeless. The poet's view of what is right and proper for a woman of rank presumably reflects the one traditional in the society to which he belonged, though we have no reason to think that he inherited the precise form of words in which he passed judgment on Thrytho's conduct. Note that the words of wisdom are negative: we are told not what ladies should do but that they should not behave like Thrytho.

Beowulf in his report to King Hygelac has something to say about the betrothal of Hroðgar's daughter to King Ingeld of the Bards. The Danish king has arranged the match for reasons of state: by giving his daughter to Ingeld he thinks he will settle the feud between Dane and Bard. At this point Beowulf makes a general observation on royal marriages:

2029   Oft seldan hwær
   æfter leodhryre lytle hwile
   bongar bugeð, þeah seo bryd duge

'[it is] always seldom anywhere [that] after man-fall the deadly spear rests long, though the bride be a good one.'

Here *oft* 'often' by meiosis means 'always' and *lytle hwile* 'a little while' by the
same figure of speech means 'long.' Beowulf's point is that after man-fall [i.e.,
fall of men in battle] the losers seldom wait long before taking up arms again;
honor forbids, and a royal marriage is powerless to bring about a lasting peace.
These words of political wisdom serve as comment on King Hroðgar's statecraft.

Beowulf after making his report turned over to Hygelac the presents he had had
of Hroðgar. In so doing Beowulf showed himself a model kinsman and retainer,
and the poet comments,

2166   Swa sceal mæg don,
            nealles inwitnet oðrum bregdon
            dyrnum cræfte, deað ren[ian]
            hondgesteallan

'So ought a kinsman to do, not at all [ought he to] weave a net of evil for the other with
hidden cunning, contrive death for [his] comrade.'

Here the poet sets forth the duty of loyalty to the head of one's house in words
of wisdom both moral and political. He has in mind the murder of kinsmen that
brought the Danish royal family to an untimely end, but his terms are general
and apply to all houses. His wisdom is not his own, of course, but that of the
society to which he belongs and of which he is a spokesman.

Our next passage gives us a very different kind of wisdom: pseudoscientific lore;
more precisely, dragon lore. In lines 2270b–71 we are told that a dragon found a
certain hoard standing open; in lines 2278 ff., that he kept the hoard for 300
years. Between these two statements about a particular dragon comes the lore
about fire-drakes as such:

2272 se ðe byrnende biorgas seceð,
      nacod niðdraca, nihtes fleogeð,
      fyre befangen; hyne foldbuend
      [swiðe ondræ]da[ð]. He gesecean sceall
      [ho]r[d on] hrusan, þær he hæðen gold
      warað wintrum frod; ne byð him wihte ðy sel

'he who, the burning one, seeks out caves, the naked evil-minded dragon, [he who] flies by
night, wrapped in fire; earth-dwellers dread him greatly. It is his way to seek out a hoard in
the earth; there he guards heathen gold, [he] old in years; he is not a bit better off thereby.'

The present-tense forms here are consuetudinal and therefore timeless or, rather,
applicable to all times. In the passage we are told what a fire-drake looks like and
how he behaves. His chief interest and major activity are mentioned last: he

spends his time seeking a hoard and guarding it, once found. The poet ends the passage with a philosophical comment on this way of life: the dragon is old in years but shows none of the wisdom that age should bring, since the hoard does him no good.

We go back to human behavior in our next. The hard-pressed hero needs help against the dragon but his retainers become panic-stricken and flee into the woods, all but one, Beowulf's kinsman Wiglaf:

> 2599   Hiora in anum weoll
> sefa wið sorgum —sibb æfre ne mæg
> wiht onwendan þam ðe wel þenceð—
> Wiglaf wæs haten, Weoxstanes sunu, ...

'In one of them the heart welled with cares—nothing can ever set kinship aside for him who thinks well—he was called Wiglaf, Weohstan's son, ...'

Here the words of wisdom are parenthetical but bear directly and immediately on the situation. Loyalty to his kinsman kept Wiglaf from fleeing with the rest and took him to Beowulf's side, where he fought bravely and effectively. But kinship is probably to be understood in a tribal as well as in a familial sense; compare lines 387 and 729.

Parenthetical, too, is the following:

> 2764   Sinc eaðe mæg,
> gold on grund[e], gumcynnes gehwone
> oferhigian, hyde se ðe wylle

'Treasure, gold in the ground, can easily overstrive [i.e., overcome] each of mankind, let him hide [it] who will.'

This utterance is set within a passage, lines 2756–72, specifying what Wiglaf found in the dragon's cave. The words of wisdom go well with the situation. The hoard by being stowed in the ground [i.e. in the cave] had been both secreted and immobilized, though the objects of which it was composed—weapons, armor, banners, gold ornaments, gold and silver vessels, etc.—were meant for use, with much display and movement. This state of things does violence to the hoard's nature and cannot last forever. The poet says that no matter who hides a hoard, he will be defeated: the hoard will get the better of him [i.e.. somebody will find it]. The hoard and its hider are here thought of as fighting a kind of duel, one in which the hider has the upper hand for a time but loses in the end. For another interpretation see Klaeber's note.

Our last passage is a comment on the ceremonial mourning and praise that made part of Beowulf's funeral rites. The poet says,

3174   swa hit gede[fe] bið
              þæt mon his winedryhten wordum herge,
              ferhðum freoge, þonne he forð scile
              of líchaman [læded] weorðan

'as it is fitting that one praise his friend and lord with words, love [him] heartily [i.e., with all one's heart], when he must be led forth, [led] from the body.

We have here a general statement about propriety at the burial of a king. The proprieties should be observed, but as outward signs of inward feelings, not as mere rituals. Hence the poet's *ferhðum freoge* alongside *wordum herge*.

In this survey of words of wisdom in *Beowulf*, I have tried to bring out not only the traditional character of the thinking but also the appropriateness of thought to setting. Everybody knows that the Beowulf poet, like his fellow poets of Old English times, used an inherited verse-form and an inherited stock of words and phrases thought of as poetical. Klaeber puts the matter thus in his *Beowulf* edition of 1922 (p. lxvii):

... the Beowulfian stylistic apparatus...was to a great extent traditional, deeply rooted in time-honored Germanic, more particularly West Germanic, practice. Its conventional character can hardly be overestimated.

The poet's skill in handling the inherited stylistic features is the measure of his stylistic achievement. But his matter as well as his manner was inherited. In introducing words of wisdom into his narrative, moreover, he was doing nothing new, and the wisdom itself was not original with him. Here as in other aspects of his art his greatness shows itself in the aptness of what he has to say and the rightness of his way of saying it.

The Johns Hopkins University,
Baltimore, Maryland

SOME ORAL GREEK PARALLELS TO ÆSOP'S FABLES

GEORGIOS A. MEGAS

It can be said concerning both folktales and fables that oral tradition preserves the original relationships more intact than does literary tradition.[1] This is especially true of Æsop's tales which, because of their shortness and their moral content, were used in the Schools of Rhetoric for centuries for the practice of students in writing correctly. They thus became linguistic essays whose main virtue was their concise form.[2] The "joy in relating" which is supposed to have attached to the old Æsopic fables, as Otto Keller[3] and Aug. Hausrath[4] rightly say, is not evident from the concise versions of the preserved collections. Of course, it is impossible for us to know how long these tales had survived in oral tradition before Demetrius Phalereus made the first collection of these tales in 316 B.C.

Thus, concerning both folktales and animal tales, the investigator should focus his attention particularly on oral traditions which present an integrity of relationships not found in versions in the literary tradition that have come down to us. I think that a few examples will suffice to prove this contention.

Let me take first the tale of the ,,Snake and the Crab," Halm 346 = Chambry 291, Hausrath 211, Perry 196.

[1] A. Aarne, *Leitfaden der vergleichenden Märchenforschung*, Hamina, 1913 (FFC 13), p. 8 and on.
[2] Bolte-Polívka, *Anmerkungen zu den Kinder- und Hausmärchen der Brüder Grimm*, IV 121. W. Wienert, *Die Typen der griechisch-römischen Fabel*, Helsinki, 1925 (FFC 56), pp. 26–28.
[3] Otto Keller, *Untersuchungen über die Geschichte der griechischen Fabel* (Jahrb. für klass. Phil. Suppl. 4 1862), p. 313.
[4] Aug. Hausrath, S.B. der Heidelberg. Ak. d. Wiss. phil.-hist. Kl. 9,2, p. 43 and 47 (1918). Cf. Wienert, *loc. cit.*, p. 11.

According to the ancient version, the crab advises the snake to improve its manners, and as the snake disregards his advice, the crab lurks while the snake is sleeping, seizes it by the neck with its claws and kills it. Seing now the snake lying straight as a rod in its hole, the crab said: "straight like this you should have been before; if you had been straight you would not have suffered this punishment."

Wienert explains the meaning of the tale thus: „die Schlange kann trotz allen Ermahnungen des Krebses von ihren krummen Wegen nicht lassen."[5] Similarly, Thompson's *Motif-Index* (J 1053) contains the reference: Snake disregards warnings to improve his manners: eaten by crab.[6] But the truth of the moral and practical way of living which underlies the last words of the crab is apparently different: One should be straight and sincere in one's manners; crookedness is punished. Besides, this is the meaning expressed in the moral of the best version: "that those who approach their friends with evil intentions are harmed themselves." But no crookedness is evident on the snake's part against his friend the crab in the text of the tale. According to this, the snake's friend, the crab, kills the snake out of indignation, because the snake does not conform to his advice on morality!

But the story is different in the modern Greek versions of the tale. Here the killing of the snake is justified in the most natural and logical way: the two friends, after the entertainment that the snake received in the crab's nest, lie down to sleep; and then the snake, pretending that it is a habit of snakes to sleep coiled, coils around the crab and starts squeezing him little by little, intending to strangle him. So the crab's deed—killing the snake in his nest—is fully justified because of the necessity to defend himself against the sly intentions of his friend. Here is one of the popular versions of the tale that was written down in 1914, by a priest, Reverend P. Stampolas, in Megara, and published in *The Greek Tales*, 2nd ed., 1956, pp. 27–28, by G. A. Megas.

I. "The Crab and the Snake"

Once upon a time, a snake went down to the seashore and came across a crab and said to him: "My dear crab, I want one of you seafolks to be my pal that I may come down here now and then to eat some seafood, and if my pal wanted he could come over to my nest to eat some tender bits of grass. So what do you say? Do you want to be my pal?" And the crab, after having thought it over, replied: "Let it be so." Then they shook hands and sat down to eat right away.

[5] Wienert, *loc. cit.*, p. 89, ST. 13.

[6] This motif is not in the *Oral Tales of India* and it is missing from the *Types of the Folk-Tale* of Aarne-Thompson. In the Greek Catalog it was included under type No. 276*.

The crab brought some seafood, shrimp and seaweeds for him. When they had finished the snake was in good humor and kept on saying to the poor crab, coiling around him in a way of embrace: "Cheer up friend, cheer up!"

His friend, the crab, was a little ashamed to say anything; yet he said to the snake: "You squeeze me too much, pal." "Yes, but I love you, pal!" answered the snake. And again after a while: "Cheer up, you friend, cheer up!" and the snake kept on squeezing him. "But you squeeze me too much, friend, and I'll blow up." And the snake that did it on purpose, said: I can't help it, pal, I love you!"

"I love you too friend" answered the crab but he saw that things were going too badly. The snake kept on squeezing him all the more and did not loosen his hold at all.

After a while the snake squeezed him again, so much that the crab was desperate and turned around and stuck his claws in the snake's neck and then the snake let him loose at last and stretched out at full length in the crab's nest. Then the crab said to him: "There you are! That's all right now, nice and straight, friend, and not the other way, coiling around me as if you wanted to strangle me."

In some versions of the tale a cat sometimes replaces the crab. Published versions: 1–2 of Peloponnesus. 1. *Anecdotes, Tales, Proverbs*, by F. Chrysanthopoulos (Photakos), Mag. *Evdomas*, Vol. 3, 1886, p. 80 = *Historic Anthology* by Vlachoyannis, Athens, 1927, p. ια΄. The crab pretends that he wants to tell a secret to the snake so that he will be saved from the snake's squeezing. The snake moves its head nearer the crab's mouth and so the crab sticks his claws in its neck and strangles it.[7] 2. Patras. Mag. *Laographia*, 1 (1909), 320: The Crab and the Snake = *Hellen. Laographia*, 1922, p. 255, by St. Kyriakides.[7a] After they have hunted together, they shared their prey in the evening. The snake wanted to eat the crab so that he might eat the crab's share too. But the crab said: "Why don't you lie straight friend?" And the snake answered "We snakes sleep this way" and after the snake had stretched, because of the pain it felt the crab said: "Now you are straight, pal." 3. Cyprus. Cypriot Fables by K. Hadjeioannou. Nicosia, 1948, p. 40, No. 10: "The Cat and the Viper Become Friends." The Viper crawled behind the cat which was walking one or two steps in front of her. The viper crawled now this way and then the other and tried to attack the cat. The cat turned around and said: "Why are you moving this way, friend?" "Mind your own business, friend," answered the viper. "There is nothing to worry about." But then, after a while, the viper started doing the same thing again. Then the cat turned around and struck the viper on the head with his claw and killed him. After he

---

[7] It is mentioned that the hero of the Greek Revolution against the Turks, Theodore Kolocotronis told his men this tale at the beginning of the siege of Tripolis in 1821 in order to portray the crookedness of the Turks.

[7a] Also available for study in *Modern Greek Texts*, by D. Loucatos, Athens 1957, p. 52, No. 13.

had killed him he started dragging him by the head; then he looked behind and saw that the viper was not going crookedly as before. "Now friend," he said, "you are going straight, but what's the use of having you now?"

Unpublished Versions:

4. Kyzikos, Asia Minor. Folklore Archives Mt. 276*, 1: "The Snake and the Crab". This is similar to the version from Megara. The Crab's words at the end are: "I want such a friend, a straight friend. I don't like such a crooked, cross-eyed friend." The antiquity of the tale is attested by its use in a couplet that is attributed to the poet Alcaeus (about 600 B.C.):

Ὁ καρκίνος ὦδ᾽ ἔφα,

χαλᾷ τὸν ὄφιν λαβών·

εὐθὺν χρὴ τὸν ἑταῖρον ἔμμεν

καὶ μὴ σκολιὰ φρονεῖν,

The Crab said thus, having grabbed the snake with its claw; A friend should be straight and not think slyly.[8]

II. The Farmer and the Snake

We have two versions of this tale in Halm 96, which versions were also critically published by Chambry 81, Hausrath 51, I and III.[9] According to the first of these versions, the snake seems to have its hole in the farmer's field, and crawling out kills the farmer's boy without any reason at all. The farmer goes and lurks waiting for the moment the snake will crawl out of its hole so that he can strike it with his axe. But he misses the snake and strikes a stone nearby. According to the second version the snake has its hole under the farmer's threshold. Here also, the axe, having missed the snake, strikes at the opening of the hole and leaves its marks on a stone. In the first version, the attempt of the farmer to be reconciled with the snake is made simply by means of implorations out of fear, lest the snake kill him too. In the second version the farmer does not confine himself to words but puts a piece of bread and some salt by the snake's hole, bread and salt being the symbols of friendship among the modern Greeks in the same way as they are symbols of friendship among the ancient Greeks.[9a]

---

[8] Ad. Koraes, *Collection of Aesop's Tales*, Paris, 1810, p. ιγ′ and p. 315, note 6. See *Athenaeus*, XV p. 695A (Bergk *Poetae lyr. gr.* III 648,16). Cf. Hausrath, Pauly-Wissowa, RE VI,2 (1909), 1707.

[9] Unfortunately it was not possible for me to use the edition of B. E. Perry, *Aesopica*, Vol. I. Greek and Latin Texts, while writing this paper.

[9a] See Martin Nilsson, *Roman and Greek Domestic Cult*, p. 78, n. 1 (*Opuscula Romana* I in Acta Inst. Romani Sueciae XVIII 4° 1954).

Both Chambry 81 and Hausrath 51 II carry in their critical edition a third version of the tale which had been already included in the edition by Koraes 1810 No. 141, p. 338. Here we have no explicit indication about the position of the snake's hole, and if we accept Bolte's correction, the farmer found the snake sunning itself. The main difference in this version from the previous versions lies in the fact that the farmer, having failed to strike the snake's head with his axe, cuts off only the end of the snake's tail, and then, in order to be reconciled to it, he puts some flour and honey by its hole, as flour and honey are usually offered in expiation to demons. That is why the snake's answer to the farmer's invitation refers here not to the marked stone, but to its cut-off tail. Two other versions, the third and the fifth in Chambry do not add anything new to the subject of our story.

Now, it should be noted that all three versions leave some obscure points as regards the subject of the Æsopian tale. There is no explanation (1) of exactly what the friendship between the farmer and the snake consists, so that the farmer wants to restore that friendship even after his boy's death, and (2) the reason the snake, which was so friendly, killed the boy. Concerning the food which the farmer puts by the snake's hole after the boy's death, there is a question whether this is offered only in expiation of the snake or as a symbol of friendship, or whether it represents merely a continuation of the daily offering of food to the snake. If the latter is true, what then was the snake giving in exchange to the farmer for this daily offering, since in folktales all over the world, animals are grateful to their benefactors? All that is obscure in the versions of the literary tradition is explained in the oral tradition of the Greek people in Thrace, Lesbos, Pontos, and the Peloponnesus. I give further the texts of the three popular versions, the first of which was written down in 1890 (it is included in the *Greek Tales* by G. A. Megas 1957, p. 29, No. 7) in the village of Hadjigyrion, Kessanis County, in Eastern Thrace by a priest, Reverend Symeon Manasseides, and was published from a manuscript in the Folklore Archives of the Academy of Athens, Nr. 230, p. 132. The second version was written in the Pontian dialect in 1938 by Petros S. Petrides, a twelve-year-old student living in the village of Anatolikon, Ptolemais County, in Western Macedonia. This student heard the tale from his father who had come from Pontos (Folkl. Arch., Academy of Athens, No. 1202, p. 23). Finally, the third version written in 1938 by a fifteen-year-old girl student named Euphrosyne Eustathiou, comes from the village of Poulitsa, Corinthia County, in the Peloponnesus. She had not read any collection of tales, but she knew the tale, having heard it from her father (Folkl. Arch., No. 1182, p. 23).

III. The Snake and the Shepherd

1. Once upon a time there was a shepherd, and while he was milking his sheep he
saw a snake crawling out of its hole and going about among his sheep. When the
shepherd saw it, he poured some milk in a pot for the snake, and the snake drank it.
The day after he poured some milk in the pot again, he put it near the snake's hole,
and said: "My dear little snake, come out to drink some nice sweet milk," and the
snake came out and drank it. When the shepherd went to get the pot he found a
gold coin beside it, and he was very glad. At noon he put the pot of milk by its hole
again and it came out and drank it, and it left another gold coin for him. And in the
evening he poured some milk in the pot again, and he called it, and the snake came
out and drank the milk. So the snake and the shepherd made friends, and he took
some milk for the snake thrice a day, and it left three gold coins for him each day
till the shepherd got very rich and decided to go to the Holy Grave, and he told his
wife to give the milk to the snake every morning at dawn, every noon and every
evening. Then he started out for the Holy Grave.

The shepherd's wife gave the snake its milk every day. The shepherd had also a
little boy about five or six years old, and one day the boy was walking around among
the sheep petting them and playing with them, but the snake was around too, crawling here and there. The boy did not see it and stepped on its tail, and the boy's pig-
skin shoes that had nails sticking out of their soles, cut off the snake's tail. Then the
snake, hurt as it was, turned its head and bit the boy, and the boy was poisoned and
died. And after the boy had died they buried him. At noon they put the pot of milk
by the snake's hole, but the snake did not come out to drink it. In the evening they
went to pour some more milk in the pot, but they saw that the milk they had poured
at noon had not been drunk. So they did not put the pot of milk there any more, and
the snake did not appear to crawl about in the fold any longer.

Six months went by; the shepherd came back from the Holy Grave and as he did
not see his boy, he asked his wife: "Where's our boy?" "Our boy was bitten by the
snake and died," said his wife. The shepherd did not say anything, he only poured
some milk in the pot and he went to put it by the snake's hole and said to the snake:
"My dear little snake, come out to drink some nice sweet milk!" But the snake
shouted from inside: "Alas! Shepherd! As long as you remember your dead boy
and I turn my head and see my tail cut off, what kind of friendship can exist between
us?" So the friendship between the shepherd and the snake was broken.

• • •

2. In olden times there was a man who went to dig in his vineyard. His wife
brought him a glass of milk. Then the husband said to her: "Leave it here, and go."
When he went to drink the glass of milk he saw that a snake was drinking it. The man
let the snake drink the milk and, in return for his kindness, the snake left a
gold pound for him, and crawled back in its hole. Then the man took the pound and

went home. This continued for two or three years. The man became rich, and one day he decided to go to the Holy Grave. So he took his son and went to the snake's hole and said to the boy: "Take this glass of milk, put it by the hole over there, and whistle for the snake. It will crawl out, drink the milk and will leave a gold pound for you. Then the man went home, and the next day he left for the Holy Grave. In the morning the boy went to the snake's hole, he left the glass of milk there and whistled. Then the snake crawled out, drank the milk and left a gold pound. The boy continued doing this thing for two or three days and then he got tired of it and said: "I'll kill the snake and I'll get all the pounds." In the morning the boy went there and put the glass of milk by the hole and the snake drank the milk and left a gold pound, and while it was crawling into its hole, the boy seized it by the tail, and the snake was pulling, and the boy was pulling at it till the snake's tail was cut off. The day after the boy went to the snake's hole, left the glass of milk, and whistled. The snake crawled out and while it was drinking the milk, it bit the boy and the boy died. When the boy's father came back, he asked where his son was. They said that the snake had bitten him and he died. The man got up in the morning and went to the snake's hole, and put the glass of milk there by its hole, and he whistled and the snake crawled out; it drank the milk, left a pound nearby and said to the man: "You are embittered about your boy, and I am embittered about my tail, and so there can be no friendship between you and me, and from now on you won't come any more; neither will I. So their friendship was broken.

• • •

3.   Once upon a time there were a snake and a shepherd and the shepherd had many sheep; the snake used to go and drink the milk secretely. But every time, before returning to its hole, it left behind a pound. As the snake used to go very often the shepherd saw it and hit it with his stick and cut off its tail. The snake went away and it was very angry; but it waited and found the opportunity it wanted; while one of the shepherd's little boys was sleeping, the snake went and bit him and the boy died. After some time, the shepherd who thought that he had lost both his little boy and the pounds, went to the snake's hole and shouted: "Hey! you snake, come out to talk with me." "O! my friend," said the snake "you miss your boy and I miss my tail, what sort of talk shall we have?"

Other versions of the tale:

Published versions:

4. Mytilene. *Zographios Agon* II, 1896, p. 23, No. 4.

A poor old man who carried firewood on his back from the mountain, gave the meat he had roasted to the snake, which threw to him a pound with its tail. When the old man became rich, he left for the Holy Grave. His son got tired of taking meat to the mountain every day. He thought and planned to kill the snake and take all the pounds together. Having shot the snake, he managed to cut off only its tail, and it bit him and he died. Then the old man made an attempt to be reconciled to the snake by offering it some meat. But the snake said: "As long as I see my tail cut off, and as long as you remember your son, both of us will be sad and angry."

5. Audemion in Thrace. Mag. *Thrakika*, 10 (1938), 321, No. 206 = *Modern Greek Texts* by Loucatos, p. 53, No. 15.

This is like the previous one, but the old woodcutter gives the snake milk instead of meat. His son, striking the snake with his axe, cuts off its tail and so it bites his arm, and his arm has to be cut off. Here the words of the snake are: "As long as you see your son's arm cut off, and as long as I see my tail cut off, we can't be friends any more."

Unpublished versions:

6. Adrianople. Folklore Archives, No. 285*: "The Man and the Snake."

The snake, a big snake said to the man who was digging in his vineyard: "We snakes like milk. Bring me one oke of milk tomorrow. The snake said it would give him a reward of one gold coin a day. The same incident with the son of the vineyard owner: cutting off of the snake's tail and biting of the boy's leg. The snake's words and the moral are: "As long as I see my tail cut off, and as long as you see your son limping, there can be no friendship between us.... The same is now with people: Once there is a dislike between two people, whatever you do to restore their friendship, you do it in vain."

As we can see in the above modern Greek versions, the connection of events is reasonable: the friendship between the man and the snake is based on the animal's gratitude for the offer of milk. It is a common belief that snakes like milk; and the killing of the farmer's son does not take place at the beginning of the tale, and without any reason, as in the ancient texts, but out of revenge toward the farmer's son for the avidity and ungratefulness he had shown toward the snake, which he had tried to kill during his father's absence so that he might gain its treasure. Thus, the man's attempt, after his return, to be reconciled to the snake again, is explained not by his fear "lest the snake kill him too," as is mentioned in some versions of the ancient tale, but by his wish not to be deprived of the reward that the snake used to give him before. This he does by offering the same kind of food that the snake liked from the very beginning—milk.

Offerings of the farmer to the snake are mentioned in the literary tradition also, and these offerings consist either of bread and salt, or of flour and honey. One might think that bread and salt are symbols of friendship, and indeed they have symbolized friendship in the customs and the language of Greece since ancient times. But it is more probable that bread and honey used to be offered to heroes and infernal Gods to calm them. Thus, the snake of the ancient tales falls into the class of these infernal Gods, and it should be thought of as the domestic snake, as is meant by a phrase in some versions: "a snake having its hole under a farmer's threshold." The description of the snake's living in a field should be taken only as a modification of that original form of the snake, so that the killing of the boy might be justified since the domestic snake was considered to be harmless.

My unforgettable teacher N. G. Politis who examined this Æsopian tale[10] considers its original to be a form of the tale that is preserved in the modern Greek tradition, and as taken down by Bernard Schmidt in Zante.[11]

> Eines Tages im Sommer kam eine Hausschlange hervor aus ihrer Wohnung und wand sich zischend an dem Herrn des Hauses, einem Landmann, vorüber, welcher eben mit Graben beschäftigt war. Dieser, nicht wissend, daß dieselbe der Schutzgeist seines Hauses sei, erhob sein Grabscheit und schlug damit auf sie los. Voll Unwillens floh die Schlange zurück in ihre Höhle. Tags darauf — es war ein Sonntag — da der Bauer mit seinem Weib zur Kirche gegangen war, kroch sie in das Haus, zerriß die besten von den Kleidungsstücken, die sie da vorfand, und nahm dann das kleine Kind, welches die Eltern in der Wohnung zurückgelassen, mit sich fort. Einige Frauen aus der Nachbarschaft hatten das mit angesehen und berichteten es dem zurückkehrenden Vater. Da begab sich dieser, den Zorn der Schlange zu besänftigen, mit Brot versehen an den Eingang ihrer Wohnung und rief sie. Daraufhin kam denn auch die Schlange hervor samt dem geraubten Kinde, welches lebend und unversehrt war, und nahm das ihr dargebotene Brot an, sagte aber zugleich dem Bauer, daß er sich fortan hüten möge, sie zu mißhandeln, da sie die Macht besitze, ihn und seine ganze Familie zu verderben.

Politis says that "in this legend we have a reasonable and independent account. The father struck the snake with his pick, having ignored the fact that it was the domestic snake. The snake in turn punished the sacrilegious man by tearing to pieces the best clothes in the house, and kidnapping his boy to its hole. The father, conscious of the snake's action, tried to appease it by offering it some bread. The snake accepted the offer which was a sign of favor, gave back the boy without harming him, and advised the host to respect it from then on because it had the power to ruin both him and his house."

[10] N. G. Politis, *Paradoseis*, Vol. 2, Athens, 1904, pp. 1096–97.
[11] *Das Volksleben der Neugriechen und das Hellenische Altertum*, Leipzig, 1871, p. 186.

13*

According to Politis a later Latin adaptation of the Æsopian tale (Romulus II, 11) is more similar to the popular tradition. Here is the translation from the Latin original:

> A snake used to come into a poor man's house under the table, and be fed upon crumbs. After a while the poor man became richer and, as he began feeling more and more angry with the snake, he hurt it one day with an axe. Some time after he was reduced to poverty again. He understood then that the lucky snake was the cause of what happened, and that it made him rich, before being wounded. He came to it to ask to be forgiven for his crime. The snake answered: "I will forgive you because of your repentance. But don't expect from me complete confidence, until my wound heals. We shall become good friends again on condition that I forget the perfidy of the axe. Suspected must be thus one who has hurt once somebody."[12]

As Marx assumed, as long as the snake frequented his house, the man was prosperous and happy. So the man understood that the snake was the cause of it.[13] It should be noticed that the relation in *Gesta Romanorum* C. 141[14] agrees with the tradition as well as the modern Greek version, Nr. 3, above, from Corinthia, because in this version the host of the house delivers the blow at the snake thoughtlessly. After that the snake takes revenge on him by going and biting his baby while he was sleeping. Evidently, as in the previous versions, it is the domestic snake here too. The shortcomings which this Æsopian tale presents are due, according to Politis, to the fact that "the man who adapted the tale, was not able to fit the elements which he received from the popular tradition to the purpose that the tale should serve and to its character." Also, the tradition from Zante in the writings of Schmidt, as well as the above modern Greek version, No. 3, from Corinthia, "indicates by what kind of changes the folk tales received sometimes the moral and didactic character which prevails in the collection of the Æsopian tales."

The tale of the farmer and the snake is found, as it is known, in the *Pantschatantra*, where it was inserted later. Here it has the same connection and sequence of events as in the modern Greek versions. Bolte and Polívka II 461 f., who included the rest of foreign parallel versions (Kurdish, Serbocroatian, Syriac, Bulgarian, Turkish),[15] mention a version from the *Hist. Nat.*, (10,208), according

---

[12] *Der Lateinische Äsop des Romulus und die Prosa-Fassungen des Phädrus.* Kritischer Text mit Kommentar und einleitenden Untersuchungen von Georg Thiele, Heidelberg, 1910, p. LIII, p. 118–120: "Der arme Mann und die Glücksschlange."

[13] A. Marx, *Griechische Märchen von dankbaren Tieren*, Stuttgart, 1889, p. 104.

[14] Bolte-Polívka, II 461.

[15] Two Turkish parallels should be added Eberhard-Boratav, Type 49, as well as the parallel in Tauschen, *Volksmärchen aus dem Jeyporeland*, No. 4 which is very different in meaning from the previous ones.

to which a viper used to go every day to the table and take its food. Once, having its two young along, it happened that one of the little snakes killed the host's son. After that the viper killed its little one and did not go to the house any more. Pliny took the version from Phylarchos.[15a] This same version we find in the redactions of the Latin tales absolutely unchanged. Therefore, owing to chronological reasons also, Bolte and Polívka[16] accept with Crusius, Marx, and Hausrath, that this tale which has so many versions, originated not in India as Benfey and Keller had asserted, but it is an original Greek tale.[17] At any rate, this tale, which, according to the oral tradition is a reasonable and independent version, and which, being widely diffused, as one can see in the parallel texts adduced by Bolte and Polívka, should be included in the *Types of the Folk-Tale*, by Aarne and Thompson, after Mt. 285.

It is true that all ancient tales do not survive nowadays in the oral tradition of the Greek people; however, those of the modern tales which correspond to ancient ones are more complete. They have a more logical connection of the details, and they do not depend mainly on the formulation of a moral, as is the case with the old tales that have come down to us. Therefore modern tales help us to restore the narrative aspects of the ancient tales. And not only that. There are cases where only hints of the existence of an ancient tale are found, and these hints are often preserved in one or two lines, or even in a proverb; in such a case the modern tales are able to fill the gaps of the ancient tradition. For example a mediaeval Greek proverb, which was preserved by Planoudis Nr. 275, says: "Ποίησόν με ἔνοικον, ἵνα σε ποιήσω ἔξοικον", *Take me in your home so that I will drive you out of it* and in a more concise form Apostolis Nr. 676 Ἔπηλυς τον ἔνοικον *The stranger drives out the tenant.* O. Crusius,[18] having in mind a sixteenth-century tale, narrated by Abraham a Santa Clara, which tells of hedgehog occupying a hare's den,[19]

[15a] Müller, *Fragmenta histor. Graec.* I, 340 fr. 27.

[16] *Loc. cit.*, p. 462.

[17] Cf. Hausrath, RE VI (1909), p. 1726.

[18] *Rhein. Museum f. Philologie*, Vol. 42, pp. 424-425.

[19] The following New Greek tale deals with the expulsion of the hare from its hole by the hedgehog. This tale comes from the village of Xiropigadon, near Naupactos, retold by an old woman. (Greek Folklore Archives, n. 1205 (M35), p. 33).

Once upon a time there was a hare sleeping in his hole. There came a hedgehog and said to him: "Won't you let me sleep beside you, for daybreak has nearly overtaken me?" The hare drew himself aside and left a little place for the hedgehog to be too. And the hedgehog lay beside him and kept on getting closer to the hare so as to get warm. The hare, though unwilling, kept moving over, for the hedgehog with his big spines hurt him every little while. Thus it came about that the hare was thrown out of his den. Then the poor hare understood what had happened to him, and he swore, putting down a cross and seal, never to let anyone sleep in his den again.

concludes that the Greek proverb had been derived from an ancient Greek tale.[19a]
In reality, according to Bolte and Polívka (II, 120), Archilochos, a poet of the 7th
century, had in mind such a tale about a fox and a hedgehog. Here is the verse:
Πόλλ' οἶδ' ἀλώπηξ, ἀλλ' ἐχῖνος ἕν μέγα.[20]

Plutarch refers to this verse as proverb and adds: Προϊούσης γάρ αὐτῆς (δηλ. τῆς.
ἀλώπεκος) ὥς φησιν ὁ Ἴων (fr. 38N = 81Bl) στρόβιλος ἀμφ' ἄκανθαν εἰλίξας δέμας, κεῖται
θιγεῖν τε καὶ δακεῖν ἀμήχανος.[21] That is to say, the fox knows many things, but the
hedgehog knows one important thing, that is, when the fox approaches him, as
Ion (a poet of the 5th century) says, he curls up and makes a ball of spines out
of his body so that the fox will not be able to harm him. The meaning of these
verses is that he who is cunning will come across another person who is more
cunning and will suffer some harm.[22]

The above meaning with a perfect justification of the details, is found in a
modern Greek tale from Patras in Peloponnesus, published in the *Laographia*,
I (1909), 322 = St. Kyriakides, *loc. cit.*, p. 255 = D. Loucatos *loc. cit.*, p. 6, No. 5.

THE HEDGEHOG AND THE FOX

Once upon a time when it was raining and hailing, a hedgehog found himself in
a forest. He did not know where to find a hole so that he might be protected from
the hail. After a while he found a fox hole and tried to enter it, but the fox which
was inside would not let him. He begged her to let him put only his head in, as he
did not mind about his body. After he had begged her very much, the fox let him
put up his head in; but the hedgehog crawled in little by little and when he approach-
ed the fox he put up his spines and started pricking her. What could the fox do? She
shrank into the corner as the hedgehog came further in. So little by little he threw
the fox out of her hole and he remained the only master of it.

A version of this tale is published in *Laographia* 2 (1910), p. 692: The Hedgehog
and the Snake. This version also comes from Patras. The hedgehog who did not
wish to make his den for the winter asked the snake to let him take the plan of
his den. When he entered the snake's hole he prevented the snake from approaching by using his spines.

A second Greek version of the above tale, from Southern Italy, is published in
G. Morosi's *Studi sui dialetti Greci della Terra d'Otranto*, Lecce, 1870, p. 76v =

[19a] N. G. Politis, *Laographia*, I (1909), 328.
[20] Bergk, Poetae lyrici⁴ 2,418 fr. 118. Leutsch and Schneidewin, *Paroemiographi Graeci*, I, p. 147
(Zenob. V 68), 2,619,60. *Camerarius*, Fab. Aesopicae, 1570 p. 297.
[21] Plutarch, "Which of the animals is more prudent." 16, p. 971, and p. 1189,22.
[22] See the corresponding proverbs N. G. Politis, *Proverbs* Vol. I, p. 461, Nr. 37.

Em. Legrand, *Recueil de Contes Pop. Grecs*, Paris, 1881, p. 181: "La chèvre et le renard": The fox and the wolf are afraid of the horns of the goat, which is hiding in the fox's hole. The hedgehog throws her out.

The ancient tradition is completed perfectly by this modern Greek tale, but one more ancient tale can be added in the collection of Aesop's tales. This tale is similar in content to Aa-Th. 105: The cat's only trick (Motif-Index J1662—not 1661—), but it should be classified under an additional number between 105–110. The slyness of the hedgehog is seen in the fact that he enters the hole of the fox, and, pricking up his spines, throws out the fox little by little.[23]

Wienert in his notable study[24] recommends that we make a comparison between the ancient Greek tales and the fable literature of other peoples, as an appropriate method for the restoration of the narrative side of Aesop's tales to their old vividness.

I think it has been made clear by the examples given above, that this comparative research should have as a starting point the relations preserved in the oral tradition of the Greek people, because the Greek people of today have preserved along with their language, many customs of their ancestors and also the oral tradition, which, as it has been made clear already, has preserved the folktales purer than the literary tradition.[25]

University of Athens

[23] The fable Hahn, *Griech. u. alban. Märchen* Nr. 91 is a version of the tale which I have classified under type No. 105**. Here the fox boasts that she has three sacks full of lies but the hedgehog, who is skilful in only one thing, that is to pretend that he is dead, manages to save her from a trap. See the foreign parallels Bolte-Polívka II 120.

[24] Wienert, *loc. cit.*, p. 27.

[25] See the last study by Karl Meuli, "Herkunft und Wesen der Fabel" Basel, 1954, Separatabdruck aus: *Schweizer. Archiv f. Volksk.* Bd. 50 (1954), p. 65 f.

THE LATIN STYLE OF
MICHAEL SCOT IN *DE CELO*

Francis J. Carmody

By linguistic analysis alone one can identify with assurance the Latin translator of a given Arabic work, and thereby determine the date of the Latin and perhaps even that of the original, which in turn may be a translation from the Greek.[1] Through signatures appended to the Latin texts, and through early bibliographies, we may first draw up a list of the translations for example of Gerard of Cremona, and by induction speak of some particular "corpus" with which he worked.[2] By the further test of his language, we may add to his repertory, establish his terminology and syntax, and through these means isolate interpolations and choose between manuscript variants. I propose to search for those linguistic criteria which serve this purpose.

The problem of attributions to Gerard and to Michael Scot has never been examined in this light. Scot's signature is appended to his version of al-Biṭrûjî (dated 1217), and reference is made to this work in a short dedication to Stephen of Provins found in some of the manuscripts of Averroes' *De Celo*.[3] Similar evidence, however fragile the above may be, is wholly lacking for the Latin of Averroes' *De Generatione*, *Metaphysica* and *De Anima*, and no effort has been made to verify the general suspicion that Scot executed them as well. It seems certain that the

---

[1] A good example is the Alexandrian Corpus of minor Greek astronomers and mathematicians prepared by Theon of Alexandria, set into Arabic about A.D. 873, and thence into Latin by Gerard; see my book *The Astronomical Works of Thâbit b. Qurra*, Univ. of Calif. Press, 1960, pt. I,2.

[2] I have documented many attributions to Gerard in my book on Thâbit, *loc. cit.*

[3] For example Paris B. N. lat. 17155; Stephanus was apparently still alive in 1231.

al-Biṭrûjî is Scot's work, for it contains verbatim quotations from Gerard's translation of the *Almagest* (*ca.* 1175).[4] Although several stylistic differences seem to separate *De Celo* from al-Biṭrûjî, the common element is very strong, and this element is basic in the other Latin versions of Averroes just mentioned: we need merely allow a greater measure of linguistic competency, and suppose some differences between the usages of the two Arabic writers, in al Biṭrûjî a free meandering, in Averroes a constant logical correlation of propositions related to his syllogistic method. Indeed, on account of similar differences in the model, Scot's style in *De Celo* varies between the Aristotelian "textus" and Averroes' "commenta" thereon.

For Aristotle's *De Celo*, that is the "textus" in Averroes' book, we have three mediaeval Latin translations, by Gerard (perhaps about 1170), by Scot (perhaps about 1220), and, from the Greek, by William of Moerbeke (about 1265). My analysis of the style is based on a close correlation of Gerard and Scot. The first query concerns the Arabic versions used by Gerard and by Averroes, which I believe could well have been almost identical. According to Averroes (the only source of information I have found), there were three Arabic translations, one by al-Kindî, which he used, a better one by Isḥâq, which he regretted not having, and a third by the Syrian monk Abu 'l-Farâj, which he consulted for a very few details. Since the original of Averroes' *De Celo* (1171) is lost, we can only surmise that his earlier Paraphrase of the same work (1169) was based on the same manuscript of Aristotle, and from it glean a few verbatim quotations. Mere comparison between Gerard and Scot, meanwhile, assures us that each had very much the same text of Aristotle, for both diverge from the Greek at the same spots, in a false term, a wordy amplification, or a substantial interpolation.

The two Latin versions of Aristotle's textus allow without other evidence a searching comparison of the styles of Gerard and of Scot. The ideal for analysis of this kind is precisely such a pair of translations. Thus between the two renditions of al-Farghânî,[5] by Gerard and by John of Seville (the latter dated A.D. 1135), one may set up standard sets of alternates or synonyms such as *centrum*: *cuspis*, *aggregatio*: *differentia*, *stella erratica*: *planeta*, and *igitur*: *-que*. Since the words *differentia* (= chapter) and *cuspis* are peculiar to John, they determine his authorship, while in contrast *aggregatio* was also used by John in other senses. The last example (*igitur*: *-que*) meanwhile has the advantage of independence from the technical subject matter, and hence may be more broadly applied.

A last generalization concerns evolution of style, whether Arabic or Latin. About 830, in the first translations from the Greek, the lack of proper terminology

[4] See my *Al-Biṭrûjî de Motibus Celorum*, Univ. of Calif. Press, 1952, p. 17.
[5] See my edition of John's translation, *Al-Farghânî Differentie*, Berkeley, 1943.

led to the breaking of the word into parts. Thus, considering the *Almagest*, we may establish three styles: that of al-Ḥajjâj, in 829, marked by elaborate circumlocutions faithfully maintained by Gerard, that of al-Ḥunayn (sometime during the next several decades), with far tighter structure eliminating particles (quoted by al-Biṭrûjî, and hence put into Latin by fragments by Scot), and that of aṭ-Ṭûsî (about 1255), rich in participles and substantival adjectives (never translated into Latin).[6] The wordiness of Gerard's *De Celo* indicates an early Arabic type, and Scot's dependence on participles might represent his own manner imposed as it were on a diffuse style. It is then conceivable that Gerard and Scot had before them one and the same Arabic Aristotle, and that it originated in the Baghdad school, whether the work of al-Kindî or of Isḥâq b. Ḥunayn.[7]

By the term style one implies a variety of elements, not always distinguishable. The lexicon, for example, represents an interplay of roots and of inflections. There appears to be no real difference between the verb and its abstract noun if the latter has an active force: *aggregatio* normally indicates the act of collecting, and only a verifiable nuance of the thing collected establishes a true noun, as for example by extension its meaning as "chapter." This alternance may be illustrated by one of the most troublesome words, *opus*, and such sets of correspondences as *opus*: *actus*: *negotium*, or *operare*: *facere*: *negotium*, or *operari*: *investigare*: *agere*: *esse*: *ponere*.[8] Similarly, there is a question regarding the independent status of Scot's many neuter adjectives of the type *grave* (= a heavy thing), which he uses for instance in predication as in *aqua est grave*; finally, there is a similar real difference between the limited repertory of such derivatives as *societas* and the general system of *lapideitas*. Prefixes, if they imply some special nuance of correlation, also represent a system, and such types as *accrescere*, *alligare*, *circumvoluere*, *coattendere*, *coequatio*, etc., are not integral parts of Gerard's and of Scot's usage, though current among their contemporaries. Clearly, the matter of the lexicon can only be treated in extensive lists.

One special type, of limited extension, is the technical term based on a Greek word. *Zodiacus* was well known in the twelfth century, but both John and Gerard prefered *circulus signorum*; John used *planeta*, Gerard clung almost exclusively to *stella erratica*. By 1265, in his translations from Greek, William of Moerbeke extended the Greek vocabulary very freely, but the identical terms also appear in translations from the Arabic and hence presumably as living entities. The following pairs of synonyms, from two translations of Thâbit b. Qurra's *De Figura sectore*,[9]

---

[6] See *The Astronomical Works of Thâbit*, pt. II,2.
[7] See *idem*, pt. I,2, regarding al-Kindî's reputed ignorance of Greek.
[8] See *idem*, appendix II, 4.
[9] See *idem*, partial editions of *De Figura sectore*.

illustrate the fate of this system; the Greek derivatives, created by an unknown hand, precede the corresponding words used by Gerard: *analogia* (*proportio*), *apodixis* (*probatio*), *cathetos* (*perpendicularis*), *ephodos* (*modus*), *periferia* (*arcus*), *theorema* (*exemplum*). Scot forged (or used) a minimum of Greek words, of which most had no current Latin equivalents: *categoricus, cocedron, duodecedron, heptagonus, hexagonus, hipotheticus, icocedron, octocedron, piramis, sillogismus, sinonima, sophisticus.*

As noted above, peculiarities in the choice and use of adverbs constitute an important criterion for authorship. Among adverbs with rhetorical meanings common during the times, Gerard, John and Scot use none of the following: *amplius, deinceps, denique, hactenus, nimirum, nullatenus, pariter, quippe, quotiens, rursum* and *siquidem*. Of these several often open major compound propositions, and serve to punctuate the text. The pattern of greatest importance concerns the choice between initial *Et* and post-initial *igitur*, then further the choice between *igitur, enim, autem, quidem, vero*, etc., and finally the exact definition of "post-initial." Thus, in a proportion of three to two, John prefers either *Et* or *-que* to words of the *igitur* class, while Gerard regularly prefers the latter or, allowing for scribal errors, always prefers it. The *igitur* construction rises simultaneously from Greek, Latin and Arabic usage, being least rich in this last. It operates as follows: the first clause may open with a noun (*Motus igitur est*), but more often with a dependent conjunction (*Quando igitur est*); it is followed by a second clause, marked solely by an initial comma, and frequently the major independent statement. Beyond this second clause, additional statements tend to open with *et, sed, deinde*, etc., except if they are of syllogistic type. The first distinction rises from the particular adverbs most often used, that is *igitur, enim, vero*, etc., in Gerard and Scot, in absolute contrast to *rursus, deinceps* and *utique*, in Hermann of Carinthia and Hugh of Santalla.[10] The second distinction lies in the kind and number of words which can be set before the adverb. Gerard allows only one word, but excepts monosyllabic prefixes (hence his *Non est autem, Ex hoc igitur*), while Scot accepts several initial monosyllabic words and preposes both parts of neuter impersonals (*Non igitur est, Manifestum est igitur*).

In general, possible differences of meaning between *igitur, vero*, etc., are indeterminable, in contrast to adverbs found in other positions and which have emphatic force. The most significant adverbs in this respect are *etiam, autem, ergo*, and *enim*. Scot uses *etiam* post-initially as well as in other positions; it always almost corresponds to Gerard's *iterum* (not post-initial). Thus Scot writers *Et etiam* (but never *Et igitur*) as well as *Et est etiam*, and these correspond to Gerard's *Et dico*

[10] See *idem*, appendix II. I find *Et rursum*, very exceptionally, in *De Generatione* (edit. F. Fobes, 1956, p. 138).

iterum[5], *Dico autem iterum, Tunc iterum* and *ergo*.[11] Despite occasional departures from this set of correspondences (such as Scot's movable *etiam* for Gerard's *autem* or *Iam ergo*), this term is surely emphatic, and requires translation as *also* or *furthermore*, while *igitur* might best be left untranslated. Only in later parts of *De Celo*, and in the commenta, does Scot use *igitur* as an alternate for *enim*, as discussed below. *Autem*, in other translations by Gerard, is emphatic and movable (*Et secundum hoc autem, Scribo hoc autem*), while in his *De Celo* it corresponds to Scot's *autem*,[7] zero[3], *enim, igitur, etiam, vero* and initial *Iam*; in reverse, Scot's *autem* corresponds to Gerard's *autem*[7], *vero* and initial *Et*, and his *Si autem* to Gerard's *Nam si* and *Et*; in our texts, *autem* seems less emphatic than *etiam*, and might often be translated *indeed*. *Ergo* serves two distinct functions in Scot, as a post-initial, and after a comma as the second or third part of a syllogism; the considerable margin of its force may be illustrated by its use in Gerard, which corresponds to Scot's *ergo*[7], *igitur*[3], *etiam*[2], *Cum*[2] and *Quapropter*[2], and in reverse its use by Scot corresponding to Gerard's *ergo nunc*[2], *Iam ergo* and *ergo*, and further in Scot's *Et cum* for Gerard's *Si ergo* and *Cum ergo*, and in Scot's *Si ergo* for Gerard's *Si ergo*[3], *Si igitur* and *Et si*. Briefly, *ergo* may be translated as *therefore* or *as a result of which*. *Enim*, corresponding to Gerard's *Quoniam*[6], *quia*[5], *vero, enim, etiam* and *Et*, has in Scot two distinct functions. Generally, in the Aristotelian *textus*, it belongs to the post-initial class and seems to have no particular force; in contrast, in the commenta, post-initial *enim* calls for a preceding colon, and proposes a known fact or law ("for we know that...," "for the rule is that...").

Initial *Et*, in either Gerard or Scot, raises one further problem. It may represent the minimum copula, implying that the translator or the author did not feel that a major proposition really opened at the point in question, or it might relate to scribal variations in the manuscripts, whether Arabic or Latin. Thus Scot uses *Et* where Gerard uses *autem*[4], *Iam*[3], *Nunc*[2], *ergo, enim* and *vero*, or no term at all where Gerard uses *Tunc*[3], *quidem*[3], *iterum*[2], *autem*[2], *itaque, vero* and *Iterum etiam*. In another sense, such use of *Et* recalls its frequency in al Biṭrûjî, and might be explained as the retention of an earlier manner. Finally, it is important that neither Scot nor Gerard pays any attention to the construction of the very first proposition in a given chapter or major section, and this fact in turn serves to establish the principal parts of a given work. One excellent conglomerate of the above, incorporating the movable adverb *modo*, so common in Scot, will illustrate the workings of the system: *Manifestum est ergo modo etiam quod* for Gerard's *Iam ergo nunc manifestum est iterum quod*.

[11] Initial capitals indicate position after a full pause (end of paragraph or demonstration), superior figures state the number of examples counted in folios 2–7 of the Juntine edition of 1550.

The above usages contrast rather strongly with the system of *De Generatione* and of *De Anima*,[12] in which the number of examples of such adverbs is far smaller, in which one reads *autem* without variation as *in contrast* or *on the contrary*, and *etiam* as *also*, and finds for *enim* the same two values as in *De Celo*, though most often non causal (*to continue, furthermore*). The most striking difference is the apparent lack in these works of *ergo*, replaced by *igitur* to close a paragraph or demonstration, as occasionally in *De Celo*, especially in its later books. I note further the weakness or absence in *De Generatione* and *De Anima* of *unde* and *quare* after a comma (with the approximate force of *ergo*), of *quapropter*, and most strikingly of the movable adverb *modo*. Since in Gerard's usage *ergo* is strong and *etiam* and *igitur* weak, since both he and Scot often use several other such words (*vero, itaque*), and finally since in later parts of *De Celo* Scot tends to use them far less frequently, it would seem that *De Celo* is relatively archaic; the dedication to Stephanus further suggests that *De Celo* may have been Scot's first attempt to render Averroes, and sets its date rather close to that of his al-Biṭrûjî.

In order to illustrate the above arguments, a comparative specimen [SPECIMEN I] is here appended showing one Aristotelian textus in the three Latin translations (Gerard, Scot, and William of Moerbeke), and another in SPECIMEN II (Gerard and Scot) along with its entire though unusually short commentary.[13] The several translations are coordinated by use of the Bekker line numbers of the Greek, and illustrate the general nature of the correspondence, essentially verbatim in William, expanded and sometimes transposed in the others as in their Arabic model. The first sentence of specimen one shows Gerard's manner of evading *predictis* and *circulariter*, and Scot's non-use at this point of *nunc*; it also reveals occasional identity of terms (*gravitas, omnino*), but more generally a fluid set of synonyms.

Collation of Gerard and Scot reveals the nature of the interplay of many other elements of sentence structure. If one were to choose to deal with the former writer as a point of departure, one would find the solution of a wide variety of critical problems in his uses of the genitive, the partitive and the ablative, cultivated almost to a point of obscurity. I shall here arrange the topics according to the usage of Scot. His genitives, in *linearum nulla est perfecta* and *corpus corporum* imitate the Arabic construction, but correspond most frequently to Gerard's partitive (*de lineis non est aliqua completa* and *corpus de corporibus*). In al-Biṭrûjî the partitive is also frequent (*illud de celis quod est sub ipso, aliud simile de corporibus, illud quod videtur de*). But Gerard also uses the genitive in this sense in

---

[12] Edition F. Crawford, 1953.

[13] I quote Gerard from Paris B. N. lat. 17155, William from the Juntine edition of 1550, and Scot from four copies.

other works (*una extremitatum, nullus horum*), and his liking for this case led him to adapt it to multiple nuances which one might call "genitives of reference," representing place at which (*locus sectionis*), manner (*est directi cursus*) and inter-relationship (*orbis declivis orbis signorum*). These are peculiar to Gerard's style, and examples in Scot are rare and surprising (*vidimus ipsam minoris ambiguitatis*).[14]

The genitive also serves to construct the superlative, which may be merely implied (Gerard's *in canone maiore quod* for Scot's *regula est maxima ut*), but normally takes the form of *maior eorum, maior omnium, fortius celorum, maius in quo apparet*, as in general in many writers of this period. The superlative inflection, in Gerard as in al-Biṭrûjî, is limited to a very few words, usually as adverbs such as *maxime* and *certissime*. In contrast, Scot's *De Celo* uses the superlative freely (*gravissimum* for Gerard's *ultimum in gravitate*).

The past participle concerns another critical set of attitudes. We may say that the ablative absolute is foreign to both Scot and Gerard.[15] The abnormality of *the moved body* in English indicates the presence of a problem of usage, logic or clarity; as do we, Gerard prefered to rephrase as *the body that is moved*. Two simple types appear in Scot's *corpora mota* and *aliquod corpus*, where Gerard writes *corpora que moventur* and *aliquod ex corporibus*. Gerard may amplify to a point of apparent futility, developing Scot's *corpora predicta* and *ex propositionibus predictis* as *corpora de quorum rememoratione evacuati sumus* and *propter ea que narravimus ex propositis*; yet this verbiage tends to clarity.

Similar hesitancy rises with respect to adjectives, especially if they retain some participial force or implication of action done. Although on occasion Gerard, like Scot, writes *finitus*, he normally renders the idea by the attributive *est finis ei*, or less often as *habet finem*. His solution for Scot's *eternus* takes the same form (*cui non fit finis*), indicating that his *sempiternus* (for Scot's *stabilis* and *permanere*) was felt as an independent word rather than a derivative. Other examples suggest that this entire system of derivatives was in a state of flux: Scot's *terminus* and *caret fine* correspond to Gerard's *ultimum* and *cui non invenitur ultimum*, and, although both write *motus circularis*, Scot's *naturalis* and *stabilitas* are more modern than Gerard's *per naturam* and *fixio*. An extreme type of alternance appears between Scot's *extrinsecus inter* and Gerard's *tangens extra*. The general trend is however clearly toward synthetic forms.

[14] Scot's genitive here (and *cf.* further *est illius generis*) seems to appear only for wholly abstract nouns, not nouns of motion, etc.

[15] Hence a double difference from Adelard of Bath's common formula for opening a new chapter: *Hiis hactenus explicatis*; in *De Celo* the ablative appears, though very rarely, only with the present participle and apparently for one verb only: *mediante forma* for *if form is involved*.

We may follow the same evolution in the abstractions inherent in neuter adjectives.[16] The older Arabic bearer of adjectives was *shay* or *amr*, meaning *thing*, commonly translated as *res*. Although Scot often uses *res*, he also turns to neuters, especially in *De Celo*: *est idem* (Gerard *est res una*), *totum* (*res tota*), *omne quod* (*omnes res que*), *ex omnibus predictis* (*ex istis rebus quas diximus*), *aliquod homogeneum* (*res sui generis*), and not dissimilarly *secundum totum* (*cum totalitate sua*). Adverbs in *-ter* indicate a comparable movement away from Gerard's ablative: *vadens equaliter* (*procedens incessu equali*), *movetur circulariter* (*movetur motu circulari*), *naturaliter* (*motu naturali*).

The above interplay, although in part a matter of morphology, also depends on purely lexical alternances and hesitations in a language which was seeking precision in new kinds of thought. The lexical problem is far too immense to treat in any brief manner, but a few remarks may help situate Gerard and Scot as representatives of two generations of translators. I here note several types of correspondence. Both writers use, in the same spots, *prioritas, sanitas, perscrutatio, dispositio, generatio, augmentum, habet complementum, non est dubium quin sit*, etc. Different words, apparently true synonyms, correspond to Scot's *similis* (*homogeneus*), *homogeneus* (*sui generis*), *necessario* (*proculdubio*, cf. in al-Biṭrûjî *de necessitate*), *moveri* (*moveri, vadere, incedere*), etc. More particular to Scot are *vicinare* (*sequere*), *distantia* (*longitudo, seiunctio, exeuntia*), *superius* (*nuper*), *ad superius* (*qui est sursum*), *forma* (*habitudo*), *activus* (*imprimens*) and *ens* (*status*), the last term constantly confused by the scribes with *esse* and *existere*.

Scot's use of several prepositions constitutes a useful though elusive test for his work. His *de* implies *regarding, concerning, with respect to, about, through the evidence of* (*curare, credere, dicere, perscrutare, scire* as in al-Biṭrûjî, *loqui* and *consideratio* as in *De Generatione*, *apparere, videri* and *perscrutare* as in the *Metaphysica*). Since the sense of *de* is in itself hardly distinguishable from that of *in* with the ablative and of *secundum*, exactly according to the pattern of al-Biṭrûjî, Scot's choice among these prepositions is no doubt a lexical matter (*diversitas in locis, convenire in ordine, similis in forma, causa in opinione, credere in orbe quod habet*). Similarly, given the strongly aspectual nature of the passive form of the verb, which echoes Arabic usage, it seems vain to try to distinguish between cause, result, agent and instrument, and we have several solutions, with *per* (*accidere per rationem, videre per sensum*), or the ablative (*moveri motibus, declarari ratione, videri visu, comprehendi sensu*), or *ab* (*moveri, sciri, notari, generari*). *Ab* meanwhile may indicate source (*fieri, derivare, exire*), though *ex* is the standard term (*consequi, esse, generari, componi*), but *ex* also implies means through which

---

[16] The neuter adjective is so frequent in *De Celo* that one may suppose its indefinite extension to a wide set of words (*grave, motum, universum*, etc.).

(*declarare, estimare, inducere, intelligere, videri*). Among less common prepositions, *apud* has the almost exclusive force of "opinion" (*est apud me*), in contrast to Gerard's use for a locative or a substitute for *habere*.

Further criteria of comparative nature would no doubt permit more numerous distinctions between the Latin writers, and an extensive study might clarify the obscure points pertinent to a real evolution of usage. It seems that from John through Gerard to Scot, a stylistic stability arose. Scot for example was either less slavish or conscientious than Gerard, or he was making a conscious effort toward clarity; more than Gerard, he seems to have been subject to external stimuli, from contemporary writers, from his model Arabic texts, or from his linguistic assistants, whose own style, Spanish or Italian, may be reflected in the Latin. Editors quite naturally tend to ignore, in already overcharged glossaries, the terms of basic interest, so that even with carefully prepared texts the needed comparisons require tedious experimental sampling and run the risk of the many unknown factors treated above. In these circumstances, linguistic tests can at best assure us of a very high probability of attribution of translations of technical works of the above type.

University of California,
Berkeley, California

SPECIMEN I
Text 17 (269b 18–29)

[*William of Moerbeke, from the Greek*] [18]*Quoniam autem eorum que dicta sunt hec quidem supponuntur, hec autem* [9]*ostensa sunt, manifestum est quod neque levitatem neque gravitatem habet corpus omne.* [20]*Oportet autem supponere quid dicimus grave et leve;* [1]*nunc quidem sufficienter quoad in presentia est opus,* [2]*diligentius autem rursus cum considerabimus de substantia ipsorum.* [3]*Grave igitur sit quod ferri natum est ad medium,* [4]*leve autem quod a medio, gravissimum autem quod omnibus substat* [5]*que deorsum feruntur, levissimum vero quod omnibus supereminet* [6]*que sursum feruntur. Necesse est autem omne quod fertur* [7]*aut deorsum aut sursum, aut levitatem habere aut grivatitem* [8]*aut ambo, non autem ad idem: ad alia enim sunt gravia* [9]*et levia, ut aer ad aquam et ad terram aqua.*

[*Gerard*] [18]*Iam ergo manifestum est nunc propter ea que narravimus ex propositis et per ea que posuimus ex ratiocinationibus* [9]*quod corpus primum mobile, quod movetur motu circulari, non habet gravitatem neque levitatem.* [20]*Convenit ergo nobis ut ostendimus quid intelligamus per grave et leve;* [1]*dico ergo in utrisque nunc sicut indigemus utrisque in hoc loco, [2]inquisitio autem sufficiens de utrisque et demonstratio sufficiens in utrisque erit ex nobis si Deus voluerit in futuro, postquam perscrutati fuerimus substantiam utrorumque. [3]Ponamus ergo nunc grave descendens ad medium [4]et leve ascendens ex medio, et iterum ponamus grave ultimum in gravitate [5]rem subsidentem sub rebus descendentibus omnibus deorsum, et leve ultimum in levitate idem rem [6]superiorem supra res omnes ascendentes sursum. Si ergo est secundum quod diximus...*

[Scot] [18]Manifestum est ergo ex propositionibus predictis et ex hiis demonstrationibus [9]quod primum corpus nobile quod circulariter movetur neque habet gravitatem neque levitatem [20]Quapropter videtur esse rectum declarare grave et leve que sunt, [1]et disserere in eis secundum necessitatem in hoc loco ab eis; [2]demonstratio autem sufficiens et perscrutatio abundans erit in futuro, cum note fuerint substantie eorum. [3]Ponamus ergo quod grave sit descendens ad medium [4]et leve ascendens a medio, et ponamus gravissimum [5]descendens sub omnibus descendentibus ad inferius, et levissimum quod [6]super omnia ascendentia elevatur. Cum igitur ita est, omne ergo corpus [7]procedens ad superius aut inferius necessario habet gravitatem aut levitatem [8]aut ambo insimul, non eodem modo sed in respectu, [9]sicut in respectu aeris ad aquam et aque ad terram.

SPECIMEN II
Text 15 (269b 3–13)

[Gerard] Dico autem iterum quia [3]si est motus circularis naturalis, tunc manifestum est et clarum [4]quia est aliquod ex corporibus simplicibus primis quod movetur motu circulari naturali, [5]sicut est motus ignis sursum, terre deorsum. [6]Si ergo motus corporum que moventur motu circulari non est nisi accidentalis, [7]tunc hoc est mirum et extra rationem omnino [8]ut sit motus accidentalis continuus semper cui non fit finis neque extremitas, [9]cum testificetur visus contrarium illius: quoniam nos videmus res accidentales corrumpi et finiri velociter. [10]Et dico iterum quod si res que movetur motu circulari est ignis, [1]sicut est sermo quorundam hominum, tunc accidentalis ei; [2]quoniam non videmus motus ignis incedere [3]nisi ex medio in sursum incessu equali.

[Scot] Et etiam [3]si motus circularis sit naturalis, manifestum est [4]quod aliquod corporum priorum simplicium movetur motu circulari naturali, [5]sicut motus ignis ad superius et motus terre ad inferius. [6]Si ergo corpora mota motu circulari non moventur nisi accidentaliter, [7]hoc est mirabile et extra rationem omnino, [8]scilicet ut motus accidentalis tantum sit continuus et eternus et infinitus. [9]Sed visus testatur contrarium: videmus enim res accidentales corrumpi et consumi cito. [10]Et etiam si illud quod circulariter movetur est ignis, [1]ut quidam dicunt,

14 Taylor

accidentalis est ei; [2]videmus enim quod motus ignis [3]est ascendere equaliter ad superius. [Comm.] Hec est demonstratio vi aut vii ostendens motum circularem esse naturalem. Et dixit *Et etiam si motus circularis etc.*, id est et hoc manifestum est quoniam omnis motus simplex proprius est corpori simplici; esse autem motum circularem naturalem ipse declarat in hoc loco dicendo *Si igitur corpora mota motu circulari etc.*, id est impossibile est ut iste motus sit accidentalis corpori rotundo: declaratum est enim in libro predicto quod iste motus est continuus et perfectus, et impossibile est continuum perpetuum esse accidentale. Deinde ostendit ipsum esse continuum per sensum, et dixit *Et visus testatur etc.*, id est celum autem non videtur corruptibile neque consumptibile per sensum: hec autem est de propositionibus de quibus dixit Albunasir quod non inducunt ad prime certitudinis ordinem, sed tamen nullus sensus contradicit eis neque ratio. Deinde dixit *Et etiam si illud quod movetur motu circulari etc.*, id est ex hoc apparet quod impossibile est ut hoc corpus quod movetur circulariter sit ignis, quoniam si esset ignis, esset motus circularis ei accidentalis: motus enim ignis naturalis est ascendere superius; et in eodem corpore non sunt duo motus naturales, cum non habeant nisi unam eandem naturam.

DAS WERDEN UND DIE AUFGABEN DER *INTERNATIONALEN VOLKSKUNDLICHEN BIBLIOGRAPHIE*

Robert Wildhaber

In den meisten Disziplinen der Wissenschaft ist das Schrifttum in den letzten Jahren und Jahrzehnten so riesig gewachsen, oft geradezu bedrohlich angeschwollen, daß eine annähernde Kenntnis, geschweige denn ein völliger Überblick kaum mehr möglich sein wird. Wo es sich um ein großes und reiches Forschungszentrum handelt, das sich einen Korrespondentenstab im Ausland leisten kann, wird diese Schwierigkeit einigermaßen zu überbrücken sein durch systematische Exzerption der Fachzeitschriften und Verlegerkataloge. Eine Hilfe bietet auch das Studium des Besprechungsteiles größerer Zeitschriften, vor allem dann, wenn diese versuchen, einen internationalen Raum zu überspannen. Für das Gebiet der „Volkskunde" („cultural anthropology" und „western ethnology") möge in dieser Hinsicht etwa auf die *Österreichische Zeitschrift für Volkskunde*, die *Zeitschrift für Volkskunde* (Westdeutschland), das *Deutsche Jahrbuch für Volkskunde* (Ostdeutschland), das *Schweizerische Archiv für Volkskunde, Anthropos, Arts et Traditions populaires, Bulletin folklorique d'Ile-de-France, Volkskunde* (Amsterdam) und in zunehmendem Maße auf *Journal of American Folklore* verwiesen werden. Ein Zeitschriften-Besprechungsteil wird immer von einer Reihe Zufälligkeiten und subjektiven Bedingtheiten abhängig sein, so daß er nur als Ersatz und als willkommene und kritische Ergänzung einer völligen Übersicht dienen kann. Diese völlige Übersicht zu vermitteln ist Aufgabe einer Bibliographie. Für einen Wissenschaftler, der auf dem Gebiete der Forschung arbeitet (research work) oder der vergleichende Studien betreibt (comparative studies), sind Bibliographien heute unumgänglich, denn sie müssen ihm den Zugang zu Titeln ermöglichen und erleichtern, deren Kenntnis ihm nicht zugemutet werden kann oder die er nur unter einem Aufwand von Zeit und Kosten sich erwirbt, welcher in keinem Verhältnis zum Ergebnis steht. Damit eine Bibliographie ihren Zweck sinngemäß erfüllt, müssen eine Reihe von Anforderungen an sie gestellt werden.

Eine Bibliographie kann sich Beschränkungen auferlegen hinsichtlich des Stoffgebietes, des geographischen, ethnischen und historischen Bereiches und hinsichtlich der Auswahl der Titel für ein bestimmtes Gebiet. Lassen Sie mich dies an einigen Beispielen in aller Kürze aufweisen. Es gibt Bibliographien, welche nur das Volkslied, die Volksmusik, den Jazz erfassen wollen, oder solche, welche der Hausforschung behilflich sind. Eine Reihe von Ländern haben ihre nationalen Bibliographien; daneben gibt es regionale, sogar nur Städte-Bibliographien. Meist sind diese regional begrenzten Zusammenstellungen in ihrem Inhalt dafür mehr oder weniger umfassend. Andere Bibliographien wollen das Schrifttum ethnischer Gruppen erreichen, sagen wir etwa der Lappen oder der Zigeuner. Dann gibt es Bibliographien, die nur auf die Antike oder auf gewisse geschichtliche Zeitepochen beschränkt sind.

Für alle Bibliographien aber stellt sich die Frage nach der Art der Auswahl und der Präsentation der Titel. Es können zum Beispiel nur selbständig erschienene Publikationen aufgenommen werden, daneben aber auch Aufsätze in Zeitschriften, sogar Artikel in Zeitungen. Diese Frage kann theoretisch so gelöst werden, daß man versucht, alle selbständigen und durch das Quellenmaterial, die Problemstellung oder die Ergebnisse wertvollen und anregenden Abhandlungen zu verzeichnen. Bei räumlich umfassenden, vor allem bei internationalen Bibliographien mag als weiteres Desideratum hinzutreten, daß die Zeitschriften oder Zeitungen einigermaßen zugänglich oder in größeren Bibliotheken greifbar seien. Diese beiden Forderungen werden von der *Internationalen Volkskundlichen Bibliographie* gestellt (sie schließt Artikel in Zeitungen irgendwelcher Art gänzlich aus). Die Bedingung der „leichten Zugänglichkeit" ist heute allerdings nicht mehr so nötig wie früher, da Mikrofilme verhältnismäßig gut herzustellen und leicht transportierbar sind. Aus diesem Grunde würde ich auch in Maschinenschrift hergestellte Manuskripte, z. B. Doktordissertationen, unbedenklich in eine Bibliographie mitaufnehmen unter genauer Angabe, von wo eine Photokopie der Arbeit zu beziehen wäre. Die Titelangaben können vollkommen sachlich und neutral sein; sie können auch zusätzliche Bemerkungen enthalten. Diese ergänzenden Angaben mögen sich ebenfalls rein sachlich darauf beschränken, für welche Gebiete die Abhandlung besonders aufschlußreich ist, sofern sich dies nicht schon aus dem Titel ergibt. Insbesondere bei „Heimatbüchern" ist der eigentlich neue und wertvolle Gehalt aus dem Titel nicht immer zu ersehen. Die Titel können ferner mit Angaben über den Wert oder Unwert, die Originalität oder Kompilation, die Einreihung in einen bestimmten Fragenkomplex versehen sein. Damit ergäbe sich dann eine „bibliographie raisonnée". Ob dem Forscher damit in allen Fällen gedient ist, bleibt eine andere Frage. Sie setzt eine riesige Fachkenntnis, Belesenheit und eine unbeirrbare Objektivität voraus. Zudem enthebt sie einen seriösen Forscher keineswegs der Aufgabe, das Material nachzuprüfen und zu sichten. Der Bearbeiter einer Bibliographie kann auch nicht voraussehen, welche Fragestellungen, Ergebnisse und Materialien einem Wissenschaftler für ein ganz bestimmtes Problem und in einem ganz bestimmten Fall wichtig sein mögen. Es scheint mir, der Bearbeiter müsse reine Kompilationen und populäre Auswahlen aus der vorhandenen Literatur zum vornherein ausscheiden, dürfe sich dann aber nicht mehr zu einer „Erteilung von Qualifikationsnoten" verleiten lassen, weil das Kriterium für derartige Noten einfach nicht absolut und objektiv sein kann, sondern immer relativ und subjektiv gefärbt bleiben muß. Wohl sind ergänzende und erläuternde Angaben, die aus dem Titel nicht ersehen werden können, wünschbar. Ein weiteres Problem, welches der Bibliograph zu lösen hat, ist die Frage, ob Buchbesprechungen aufgenommen werden sollen oder nicht. Es mag wünschbar sein, Rezensionen zu kennen, sofern sie den Leser sofort sehen lassen, ob ein Buch für ihn in Frage komme oder nicht, und sofern sie berechtigte und begründete Einwände erheben und Ergänzungen bieten. Ganz praktisch betrachtet, stellt sich sofort die Frage, ob alle irgendwo erschienenen Besprechungen und Anzeigen verzeichnet werden sollen, oder ob irgendwo eine Grenze gezogen werden müsse. Welches ist dann das Kriterium für die Grenzziehung? Ich muß aus meiner eigenen Erfahrung bekennen, daß ich wohl theoretisch eine Antwort konstruieren könnte, daß aber die praktische Anwendbarkeit dieser Konstruktion bisher in den meisten Fällen versagt hat. Zudem gibt es immer und immer wieder Besprechungen, welche sehr verspätet publiziert werden. Muß in einem solchen Fall der Buchtitel um dieser Rezension willen wiederholt werden oder muß die Besprechung, selbst wenn sie wirklich wertvoll wäre, fallen gelassen werden? Die *Internationale Volkskundliche Bibliographie* ist — sehr stark mitbedingt aus finanziellen Erwägungen — dazu übergegangen, Buchbesprechungen fallen zu lassen; nur dann, wenn solche Besprechungen den Charakter von eigenen Aufsätzen annehmen und Neues bieten, werden sie aufgenommen, aber nicht als Buchbesprechungen, sondern als eigene Nummern.

Es gibt Bibliographien, welche einmalig und abgeschlossen sind neben solchen, welche periodisch immer wieder erscheinen: jährlich oder mehr oder weniger regelmäßig und mehr oder weniger große Zeitspannen umfassend. Zur letzten Gruppe ist im gegenwärtigen Moment die *Internationale Volkskundliche Bibliographie* zu zählen.

Schon 1913 gab es einen Ansatz zu einer umfassenden Bibliographie; damals erschien: Die volkskundliche Literatur des Jahres 1911, ein Wegweiser im Auftrage der hessischen Vereinigung für Volkskunde und mit Unterstützung der dem Verband deutscher Vereine für Volkskunde angehörenden Vereine herausgegeben von A. Abt, Leipzig und Berlin 1913.[1] Im *Schweizerischen Archiv für Volkskunde*, das damals noch von E. Hoffmann-Krayer betreut wurde, finden sich ebenfalls während einiger Jahre bibliographische Zusammenstellungen.[2] Systematisch wurde der Plan zu einer einigermaßen international orientierten volkskundlichen Bibliographie von John Meier ausgearbeitet, der als Leiter des Verbandes deutscher Vereine für Volkskunde Hoffmann-Krayer in Basel mit der Redaktion beauftragte.[3] 1919 konnte dann in Straßburg der erste Band der Reihe publiziert werden unter dem Titel *Volkskundliche Bibliographie für das Jahr* 1917.[4] Von da an erschien die Serie ziemlich regelmäßig, manchmal ein Jahr, gelegentlich auch zwei Jahre umfassend; der letzte Band, der das Material für die Jahre 1935 und 1936 enthielt, wurde 1941 publiziert; mit dem Jahr 1931 (Material für 1925 und 1926) übernahm Paul Geiger anstelle von Hoffmann-Krayer die Redaktion. Nach den ersten 13 Bänden brachten die Kriegswirkungen einen längeren Unterbruch. Das Manuskript für die Jahre 1937 und 1938 wurde von Geiger noch zusammengestellt; es kam dann über John Meier und Adolf Spamer an die Deutsche Akademie der Wissenschaften zu Berlin (Ostberlin), wo es endlich 1957 vom Akademie-Verlag in Berlin veröffentlicht wurde, nachdem sich weder die CIAP noch ein westdeutscher Verlag zum Druck bereit erklären konnte. Im Einverständnis mit dem Vorstand des Verbandes deutscher Vereine für Volkskunde übernahm ich die Herausgabe dieses etwas unerfreulichen und nicht gleichmäßig sorgfältig vorbereiteten Bandes, damit die Kontinuität der Herausgabe gewahrt bleibe. Es ergab sich also die gewiß einmalige Situation, daß das Material der stark nationalsozialistisch gefärbten Jahre 1937 und 1938 unter der Herausgabe eines neutralen Schweizers in Ostdeutschland gedruckt und in Ostberlin publiziert wurde.[5] Da auch dieser Band im Laufe der Zeit sicherlich ein interessantes historisches und kulturelles Denkmal sein wird, dessen Inhalt man aus objektiver Per-

---

[1] 115 Seiten, 2259 Nummern.

[2] Vide ,,Gesamtregister" der Schweizerischen Gesellschaft für Volkskunde, S. 452, s.v. Bibliographie.

[3] Kurzer geschichtlicher Überblick bei: Robert Wildhaber, "Die Volkskundliche Bibliographie," in: *Laos* I (1951), 202–204.

[4] XV, 108 Seiten, Verfasser- und Sachregister.

[5] XXXII, 543 Seiten, 7440 Nummern, Verfasser- und Sachregister. Das Vorwort bringt Daten zur ,,Geschichte" des Bandes.

spektive nüchtern beurteilen wird, muß man dem Verlag bestimmt dafür Dank zollen.

Diese erste Reihe der Bibliographie zeigt ein nicht immer klar umrissenes Gesicht. Sie ist herausgegeben vom deutschen Verband und im wesentlichen für deutsche Benützer gedacht. Darüber hinaus versucht sie, in durchaus anerkennenswerter Weise, die Grenzen zu überschreiten und mehr oder weniger international zu werden, was ihr allerdings in keinem einzigen Bande wirklich systematisch befriedigend gelungen ist. Daraus darf ihr aber kein Vorwurf gemacht werden, da sie sich immer nur als „Volkskundliche Bibliographie" bezeichnete; man mochte nun in den Titel hinein interpretieren, was man gerne wünschte. Hoffmann-Krayer erklärte im ersten Band (für 1917), er beschränke sich regional „auf die indogermanischen Völker und die Juden". Damit wären zwar bereits einzelne europäische Gruppen ausgeschlossen geblieben, doch erwies sich die Formulierung als mehr theoretisch. Andererseits wären gewisse Völker Asiens hierher zu zählen gewesen, was wiederum nie konsequent durchgeführt wurde. Geiger hat denn auch in seinem ersten Bande (für 1925 und 1926) die „exotische Völkerkunde" völlig ausgeschieden. Die Ungleichmäßigkeit in den Titeln ist teils der ungenügenden Belieferung durch einzelne Mitarbeiter (die damals, wie heute noch, sich freiwillig und unentgeltlich zur Verfügung stellten) zuzuschreiben, teils aber auch der allzusehr ins Detail gehenden und nur für eine Spezialbibliographie bedeutsamen Angabe von Titeln; dies gilt durchwegs für den Abschnitt „Volkslied", der durch sein mustergültiges Streben nach Vollständigkeit sich völlig von den anderen Abschnitten abhebt und dadurch — unbeabsichtigt — das Gleichmaß etwas zu stark verschiebt. Das von Hoffmann-Krayer ausgearbeitete Einteilungsschema blieb im großen und ganzen beibehalten und erleichterte damit das Aufsuchen der Titel durch die Serie hindurch. Verfasser- und Sachregister erschließen die Titel von anderen Aspekten her, als es aus dem Inhaltsverzeichnis allein möglich wäre. Etwas befremdlich berührt einzig die Art und Weise der Zusammenstellung der exzerpierten Zeitschriften. Daneben konnten die Herausgeber trotz ihrer Bemühungen keine Gleichmäßigkeit in der Wiedergabe der Titel aus den verschiedensten Ländern erreichen. Es finden sich hin und wieder unverständliche und unlösbare Sigel; ich habe einige auch in dem von mir herausgegebenen Band 1937–1938 bemerkt, und ich kann nur hoffen, daß es dem zufälligen Benützer gelingen möge, die Lösung intuitiv zu fühlen; mir wurde die „Erleuchtung" nicht zuteil.

Das war der Ausgangspunkt, mit all der verdienstvollen Vorarbeit und den Mängeln, die sich im Laufe der Jahre zeigten, für die neue Serie der Bibliographie, die völlig andersartige Probleme aufwarf, die auch heute noch nicht alle befriedigend gelöst sind. 1947 faßte die Generalversammlung der CIAP (Commission

internationale des arts et traditions populaires) den Beschluß, die Bibliographie
als *Internationale Volkskundliche Bibliographie* herauszugeben, und zwar unter
den Auspizien des Conseil International de la Philosophie et des Sciences humaines
mit finanzieller Unterstützung der UNESCO. Der erste Band, der 1949 unter der
Redaktion von Paul Geiger herauskam, umfaßt die Jahre 1939–1941; er ist noch
stark nach der alten Serie ausgerichtet. Gefordert war die Verwendung des
Deutschen, Englischen und Französischen nebeneinander. Wie zögernd und un-
sicher diese Forderung in die Praxis umgesetzt wurde, zeigt bereits der Titel, der
in der französischen und englischen Fassung das Wort „international" enthält,
in der deutschen aber die alte Formulierung „Volkskundliche Bibliographie"
beibehält. Mehrere dieser Anomalien sind im folgenden Band ausgemerzt; er erschien 1950 für die Jahre 1942–1947 und wurde von Paul Geiger und dem Schreibenden herausgegeben. Für die nachfolgenden drei Bände[6] übernahm ich die
Herausgabe. Ich wurde unterstützt und beraten durch eine kleine Bibliographie-
Kommission, welche auf meinen Wunsch von der CIAP bei der Konferenz in
Namur 1953[7] ernannt wurde. Für die Gestaltung der Bände verweise ich auf das
Vorwort im Band 1948/49, besonders aber auf die „Richtlinien" im Band 1950/51.
Es sollen danach die drei erwähnten Sprachen als gleichwertig nebeneinander
stehen; weiterhin bleiben italienische, spanische und portugiesische Titel unüber-
setzt. Alle anderen Titel sollten entweder ins Deutsche, Englische oder Französische übersetzt werden. Daß dies gelegentlich ein „frommer Wunsch" bleibt, ist
dem Herausgeber leider nur zu klar.

Das konsequente Durchführen des internationalen Prinzips, demgemäß alle
Länder möglichst vollständig und gleichmäßig vertreten sein sollten, zeigte bald
manche Schwierigkeiten, weil die Terminologie unserer jungen Wissenschaft
nicht für alle Länder einheitlich durchgeführt wird und weil sogar innerhalb eines
Landes unter demselben Wort nicht überall das Gleiche verstanden wird („Volkskunde", „folklore"). Es liegt mir völlig fern, hier eine terminologische Diskussion
heraufzubeschwören; ob der eine Wissenschaftler nun Volkskunde, western
ethnology oder cultural anthropology verwendet, oder der andere Folklore,
Laographie oder géographie humaine bevorzugt, für mich ist wesentlich, daß ich
das Material erhalte und publizieren kann, das gemäß der Inhaltsangabe in
dieser Bibliographie zu finden sein sollte. Es geht also um geistige und materielle
Kultur, um Glauben, religiöse Volkskunde, Volksdichtung, Sitte und Brauch
ebenso wie um Hausforschung, Gerätekunde, Bodenbearbeitung, Nahrung und

[6] 1948–1949, erschienen 1954; 1950–1951, erschienen 1955; 1952–1954, erschienen 1959.
[7] Vide Actes de la Conférence de Namur. Compte-rendu édité par la Commission nationale belge de
   folklore, Bruxelles, 1956.

Kleidung.[8] Es geht darum, daß das Einteilungsschema so gehandhabt wird, daß die rasche Benützbarkeit für möglichst alle Länder gewährleistet ist. Bis jetzt wurde im Prinzip das Hoffmann-Krayer'sche Schema beibehalten, aber möglichst gleichmäßig ausgeglichen und den neuen Richtungen innerhalb der volkskundlichen Wissenschaft angepaßt. Eine völlige Neugestaltung würde die Verwendbarkeit der alten und der neuen Serie nebeneinander über Gebühr erschweren und hätte ein ständiges Umdenken zur notwendigen Folge. Das bedeutet nicht, daß im Laufe der Zeiten gewisse Unklarheiten nicht geklärt werden sollten. Aus seinen Erfahrungen heraus möchte der Schreibende etwa auf folgende Punkte hinweisen: es geraten durcheinander und sind oft nicht sauber zu trennen VI D Landwirtschaft und X B 8 Landwirtschaftbräuche, III C Haus und X B 5 Hausbräuche, IV C 3 Geräte (für den Pflug) und VI D Landwirtschaft, und was dergleichen Fälle mehr sind. Es gibt einen Abschnitt I A Bibliographie, als dessen Konkurrenten die beiden Abschnitte XII A und XVIII A wieder Spezialbibliographien für Volksglaube und Märchen aufweisen (aber nur gerade diese beiden Abschnitte). Die Unterschiede zwischen XVI Volkspoesie, XVIII Märchen, etc. und XX Sonstige Volksliteratur sind zu wenig klar herausgearbeitet. Die beiden Gruppen XVI Volkslied und XVII A Musik sind gelegentlich nur schwer zu trennen und zu unterscheiden.

Weitere Schwierigkeiten haben sich sehr bald bei der Zuteilung zu den „Sprachgebieten" ergeben. Man sehe sich beispielsweise die alte Serie unter X A an (Band 1923/24); da finden sich „Deutschland, Österreich, Schweiz" (im Band 1935/36 „Deutsche Schweiz"), „Frankreich", dem offenbar stillschweigend auch Wallonien, Luxemburg und die französisch-sprechende Schweiz eingegliedert wurden (der Redakteur war Deutsch-Schweizer!), „Italien", dem ebenso unbedenklich die italienisch-sprechende und die rätoromanische Schweiz einverleibt wurden. Der Schreibende, der aus einer deutsch-rätoromanischen Kontaktzone stammt, die ursprünglich rätoromanisch war, seit langer Zeit aber deutschsprechend ist, empfand es immer als stoßend, wenn Werke über die ganze Schweiz regelmäßig beim „Deutschen Sprachgebiet" verzeichnet wurden, nur deshalb weil sie deutsch geschrieben und die Verfasser meist Deutschschweizer waren. Im Band 1935/36 sind die Niederlande und England zu einer Gruppe zusammengefaßt; die Vereinigten Staaten waren dann entweder großzügig unter „England" zu suchen oder sonst, etwas weniger großzügig, unter „Anderweitiges". Daß Schottland und Wales zu „England" gezählt wurden, wird nach den obigen Angaben nicht verwunderlich sein. Der Schreibende hat versucht, diese „Sprachgebiete" nach Rücksprache mit den Fachkollegen der verschiedensten Länder

[8] Vide: Bericht über die „Internationale Volkskundliche Bibliographie" in: *Laos*, 3 (1955), 160–162.

möglichst behutsam, sinngemäß und objektiv zu ordnen, aber auch ihm sind
schon mehrmals schier unüberwindliche Schwierigkeiten erwachsen. Wenn er
daran denkt, wie schwierig zu deuten und „pulvergeladen" das Wort „Mazedo-
nien" ist, wird ihm heute noch angst; er hat in seiner Verzweiflung das Wort einfach aus den „Sprachgebieten" gestrichen!

Sogar selbst was geographisch und sachlich zur „Volkskunde" im Sinne der
Bibliographie zu zählen sei, ist heute eine noch sehr umstrittene Frage, eine Frage
allerdings auch, deren Beantwortung sich leider aus finanziellen Überlegungen
mitergibt. Ist der „Raum" der Bibliographie Europa und die überseeischen Gebiete europäischer Siedler (also Nord- und Südamerika, Afrika, Australien, Neu-
Seeland, Kolonien in Asien)? Wären also die „amerikanisch" gewordenen Neger
und Indianer,[9] ferner die „zivilisierten" Eingeborenen Südamerikas nicht dazu
zu zählen? Wie steht es mit den „Hochkulturen" Indiens, Chinas, Japans,
Koreas? Wie steht es mit der Türkei in ihrem europäischen und asiatischen Raum;
wie steht es überhaupt mit den mohammedanischen und arabischen Ländern
Asiens und Afrikas? Wie steht es mit der Abgrenzung der slavischen und finno-
ugrischen Völker im eurasischen Gebiet? Sind die europäischen Eskimo und
Lappen zur europäischen Volkskunde zu zählen? Man sieht, für eine internationale
Bibliographie ergeben sich Schwierigkeiten, die in einer nationalen Zusammenstellung kaum auftreten. Unglücklicherweise spielen heute Finanzierungs-
schwierigkeiten eine entscheidende Rolle für die Gestaltung unserer Bibliographie. Als Ordnungsprinzip muß im großen und ganzen gelten: Europa und
„weiße" Siedler. Auf Grund dieses Schemas ist zum Beispiel Archer Taylor's
„Annotated Collection of Mongolian Riddles" (1954) nicht aufgeführt. Es tritt
dann öfters der Fall ein, daß derartige Werke in „ethnologischen" Bibliographien
ebensowenig verzeichnet werden, da sie nicht zu den „Primitivkulturen" gehören.
Mehrere Aufsätze, welche im *Journal of American Folklore* publiziert sind oder die
neuerdings in *Fabula* sich befinden, gehören nicht in den Rahmen, welcher der
Bibliographie im jetzigen Zeitpunkt vorgeschrieben ist. In dieser Hinsicht Klarheit, Abgrenzung und neue Möglichkeiten zu schaffen, scheint mir eine dringende
Aufgabe zu sein.

Eine ganze Anzahl von Ländern geben entweder periodisch erscheinende oder
auf einen bestimmten Zeitpunkt abgeschlossene Bibliographien heraus; besonders
zu erwähnen ist hier das *Deutsche Jahrbuch für Volkskunde*, das bereits einer
großen Zahl von zeitlich begrenzten, nationalen Bibliographien seinen Platz zur
Verfügung gestellt hat. Auch belgische, italienische und französische Zeitschriften bringen periodisch derartige, sehr verdienstliche Überblicke. Seit 1938

---

[9] Die Bedeutung der Frage und ihre ganze Problematik wurde mir zum erstenmal klar bei der Lektüre
von Richard M. Dorson, *American Folklore*, Chicago 1959.

gibt R. S. Boggs seine Folklore Bibliographies in *Southern Folklore Quarterly* heraus,[10] seit einigen Jahren erscheint im *Journal of American Folklore* ein Supplementsheft mit einer jährlichen Bibliographie. Diese beiden letzteren Bibliographien beschränken sich nicht auf die nationale oder regionale Erfassung von Arbeiten, sondern sie bringen darüber hinaus eine Auswahl aus europäischen Zeitschriften. Man möge es dem Schreibenden nicht übel nehmen, wenn er sich hierzu eine kritische Bemerkung gestattet.

Eine internationale Bibliographie kann durch ihre notwendige Beschränkung auf Wesentliches nie eine nationale Bibliographie ersetzen; sie kann auch nicht einfach eine Addition nationaler Bibliographien sein; andererseits sollte eine nationale oder regionale Bibliographie möglichste Vollständigkeit anstreben, vielleicht verbunden mit kritischen Würdigungen; sie wird keineswegs „übernational" dadurch, daß sie eine willkürliche Auswahl weiterer Titel vornimmt. Sie kann im Gegenteil damit den falschen Eindruck bei einem Benützer erwecken, es werde ihm nun alles benötigte Material geboten. Eine derartige Auswahl muß Zufallsergebnis, schlecht angebrachter Eklektizismus sein. Es ist mir völlig klar, daß solche Zusammenstellungen sich oft einfach als „Dank" für erhaltene Publikationen erweisen; doch scheint mir, es wäre richtiger, sie in diesem Fall als „Neueingänge" zu verzeichnen, wie es etwa die *Österreichische Zeitschrift für Volkskunde* in völlig einwandfreier Weise tut. Ob nicht die beiden erwähnten amerikanischen Zeitschriften besser daran täten, generell auf die internationale und eventuell nationale Bibliographien hinzuweisen, oder irgendwie eine Zusammenarbeit mit der internationalen Bibliographie zu suchen? Man möge mich, bitte, nicht mißverstehen: es geht mir um eine Anregung und nicht um eine Kritik.

Wenn sich je die Möglichkeit ergäbe, die internationale Bibliographie zu einem mehr oder weniger vollkommenen und, auf jeden Fall, praktischen Handbuch auszuarbeiten, dann müßten als Desiderata angemeldet werden: der vermehrte Gebrauch von ergänzenden Titelangaben und damit verbunden die Verbreiterung des Sachregisters, die dreisprachige Durchführung des Sachregisters, die Einführung eines geographischen Registers und schließlich, bei Gelegenheit, die Durchführung eines „Gesamtregisters" aller bisher erschienenen Bände, welches das lästige Nachschlagen ersparen würde. Ein weiteres Desideratum, auf das ich schon mehrmals hingewiesen habe, wäre die Schaffung einer zentralen Nachweis-Stelle, die Auskunft geben könnte über das Vorhandensein und die Ausleih-

---

[10] Mit Bedauern lasen wir in der Märznummer 1959, daß die Bibliographie für 1958 seine letzte Zusammenstellung sei und er nicht weiterfahren wolle. Die Weiterführung der Boggs'schen Bibliographie ist Américo Paredes, University of Texas, anvertraut worden. Siehe S. 315 unten.—WDH.

möglichkeiten der volkskundlichen Bücher und Zeitschriften in den verschiedenen
Bibliotheken und Instituten der ganzen Welt.[11]

Vielleicht darf ich diese Desiderata voller Zuversicht meinem hochverehrten
Freund Archer Taylor anvertrauen; schon im Vorwort zum Bibliographieband
für 1920 haben John Meier und Hoffmann-Krayer von seinem „nie erlahmenden
Eifer" und der „völlig selbstlosen Weise" seiner Hilfeleistung gesprochen. Ein
herrliches Zeichen für einen Gelehrten, an den 35 Jahre später ein Jüngerer sich
mit der gleichen Bewunderung und der gleichen Dankbarkeit für immer wieder
gebotene Hilfe wenden darf!

Schweizerisches Museum für Volkskunde, Basel

[11] Vide *Laos*, 3 (1955), 162.

"KACHI-KACHI MOUNTAIN" — AN ANIMAL
TALE CYCLE

Hiroko Ikeda

Ninety years ago a system of universal compulsory education was introduced in Japan. Textbooks and readers introduced under the system, edited and published by the Ministry of Education, revised from time to time, were in universal use in schools throughout the country until the end of World War II. Nationwide use of the same textbooks for so extended a period of time had rather interesting results. One is thought to be the establishment of standard Japanese as a means of common communication co-existing with local dialects. A second, relevant to this study, is the prevalence of so-called standard versions of "representative" folktales.

The "Kachi-Kachi Mountain" story, the subject of this paper, is an example of the second. The development of the standard version, of course, dates back earlier than the adoption of uniform textbooks. The earliest printed text appears to be one of the rare seventeenth-century *aka-kohon*, 'little red book,' a Japanese equivalent of a chapbook, published in Kyoto. It already had the features of the standard version, and continued to be printed in the subsequent types of chapbook, *kuro-hon*, 'black book', and *kibyoshi*, 'yellow covers', published in Edo. This literary version is the one adopted for use in the school readers.

The standard version is known to children all over Japan through picture books and school readers. Anthologies of Japanese folktales, whether written in Japanese or foreign languages, never fail to include the tale. Even *Nippon Bungaku Daijiten*,[1] the standard dictionary of Japanese literature, which contains few references to folklore, includes this plot.

[1] Fujimura, Tsukuru (ed.): *Nippon Bungaku Daijiten*, 1950–1952, Tokyo: Shincho-Sha, 8 v. (Revised edition), v. 1, p. 543.

Considering the prevalence of the standard version, it is truly remarkable that local versions are still available to folklore collectors. Eighty-nine versions, collected from various Prefectures, are compiled in *Nippon Mukashi-banashi Shusei*,[2] a source book of Japanese folktale material.

First a translation of the standard version of plot given in the *Nippon Bungaku Daijiten* follows:

> An old man traps a bad badger in the mountain, brings it home and hangs it from the ceiling, tying its legs together. After he has gone to work again, the captive badger persuades the wife to untie the rope. When freed, the badger kills her and makes a soup of her. He disguises himself as the wife, and when the old man comes home, serves him the soup calling it badger soup. The badger taunts the old man that he has eaten his own wife, then flees.
>
> A rabbit comes along while the old man is crying, and promises to seek revenge for him. The rabbit by deception makes the badger carry firewood on his back, and from behind strikes a flint, "Click-Click," to set fire to the firewood. The badger questions the sound, and the rabbit says that there is such a noise here because the place is the Click-Click Mountain.[3] A similar explanation is given for the sound of burning wood on his back, before he realizes that he is afire.
>
> Red-pepper plaster is applied as ointment to the burns by the rabbit. When the burns have finally healed, the rabbit invites the badger for boating. Riding a wooden boat himself, the rabbit provides the badger with a boat of mud, which dissolves in the water and drowns the badger.

Many popular Japanese tales begin with "Once upon a time there was an old man and his wife." So it is with the standard version of the "Kachi-Kachi Mountain" story. Very often the standard version tends to forego the reason why the bad badger had to be trapped, but many local versions explain it.

For convenience in presenting and charting the tale, I have divided the plot into 10 component parts, ordering them in sections from A to K, omitting I. The charts appended at the end show how the component parts Section A-K of 89 versions form 33 different combinations.

A. The old man is sowing seeds in the mountain patch, chanting a charm for good crops:

> "May one seed multiply a thousand-fold!.
> And two seeds ten thousand-fold!"

[2] Seki, Keigo (ed.), 1950–1958, Tokyo: Kadokawa Shoten, 6 v., v. 1, pp. 175–210.
[3] Hence the title *Kachi-Kachi* (the sound of a flint being struck) *Mountain Kachi*, a noun or an adjective, and *katsu*, a verb, also mean 'winning' and 'to win' respectively, and are considered words of good omen. In writing the title in characters, we use the character for 'winning', which then reads "Winning-Winning-Mountain." Here I am observing the custom, frequent in Japan, of choosing words of good omen as titles for contributions to *Festschriften*.

The badger comes and jeers, sitting on a stump near by:

> "One seed will stay one,
> And two seeds will stay two."

Or: the old man is tilling a field. The badger makes fun of his motions with the hoe. On the following day the old man has smeared the stump with pine-resin, bird-lime, or rice-paste. The badger returns and mocks him again, but this time it cannot flee when the old man comes after it. The badger is caught and taken home to be made into soup. The above is *Section A*. Four local versions consist of *Section A* only.

B. *Section B* does not differ from the corresponding part of the standard version. The badger asks the old woman to free him so that he may help her pound wheat. When freed, however, he pounds her head with the pestle, makes her into soup, and serves it to the old man (G61). Then the badger taunts him that he has eaten his wife, and tells him to look at her bones under the sink, and flees back to the mountain. Eleven versions end here.

The motif (G61): "Relative's flesh unwittingly eaten" plus subsequent taunting is widely known among the American Indians as with "The Trickster kills the Children," and "Bear-Woman and Deer-Woman."[4] "The trickster kills the Children" of the Arapaho Indians is a very close counterpart of the "Click-Click Mountain," although the lapse of time has caused the role of the trickster to be divided between the dupe and the hero in the Japanese story.

> Nihansen, the Arapaho trickster, is travelling down a stream, and sees red plums in the water. He dives to get them and realizes that they are only reflections (J 1791).
>
> He comes to where the bear-women live. He offers to watch their babies while they go to get the plums. He cooks the babies and serves them to the family when they come home. Then he taunts: "Ho! Ho! Bear-women, you have eaten your own children."
>
> When the bears realize what has happened, they go after him. Just before he is caught, he finds a hole which extends through a hill, jumps into it, and comes out on the other side. The bear-women are still standing before the entrance. He paints himself with white paint to look like a different person, and goes back to the bear-women (K 1821).
>
> He offers his help to get hold of the rascal Nihansen, and crawls into the hole. He cries out as if hurt, scratches himself bloody, and comes out again. "I cannot drag him out. You go in," he says. The bears all go in. Then he gets brush and grass, and makes a fire at the entrance.
>
> "That sounds like flint striking," one of the bear-women syas.
>
> "The flint birds are flying," says Nihansen.

[4] Stith Thompson. *Tales of the North American Indians.* Cambridge, Mass., 1929, p. 66.

"That sounds like fire," says another.
"The fire birds are flying about."
"That is just like smoke."
"The smoke birds are passing."
The heat follows the smoke into the hole. The bear-women begin to shout.
"Now the heat birds are flying."
Thus the bears are all killed.

In the above, the chase by the angry bears and their attempt at revenge follows immediately after the taunting by the trickster. In the "Kachi-Kachi Mountain," the rabbit, the real hero of the story, comes along where the old man is crying, to ask why and to promise revenge for him. From then on the old man is forgotten.

This switch of characters became necessary because the story had come to follow the popular pattern of opening a tale with the introduction of an old man and his wife. The element of "Culture hero trickster," as found among the American Indians, seems not to have flourished in Japanese folktales. We have only some scattered traces of such.

The result of having the old man and his wife as actors of the tale might have contracted *Section A*. The charm chanted by the old man is in actual use at the New Year's rice planting ritual in agricultural villages to pray for a good crop. A theory in Japan is that *Section A* might be reflecting some local agricultural rites.[5]

The introductory motif J1791: "Reflection in water thought to be the original of the thing reflected" in the American Indian tales is also well known in Japan, although it does not appear in the "Kachi-Kachi Mountain" cycle. The motif is associated in Japan with *yama-uba*, or a mountain ogress, who is the adversary in an Obstacle Flight story (J-Type 327D) and in the Mountain Ogress Coming 'Home' to Children (J-Type 333A).

We have seen in the Arapaho version the explanation of the sound of flint striking and of fire burning given as "flint bird" and "fire bird." Although in Japan the tale is titled "Kachi-Kachi Mountain" because of the explanation given to the badger by the rabbit in the standard version, we have a number of versions all over Japan in which these sounds are explained as "the flint bird is crying," "Kachi-Kachi bird has started to sing," "Kachi-Kachi bird of Kachi-Kachi Mountain," "Click-Click cricket is chirping," and "Mr. Click-Click is passing."[6]

---

[5] Minzokugaku Kenkyujo (ed). *Minzokugaku Jiten* (Dictionary of Japanese Folklore). 1951, Tokyo: Tokyo-Do, p. 108.

[6] The same motif "Kachi-kachi bird, Bo-bo bird" occurs for the ending of *J-Type* 333A, when the mountain ogress is about to be burned to death in the oven.

The method Nihansen, the trickster, uses to kill the bears in the hole is still used in Japan. It is called *aoridashi*,[7] meaning "driving out by smoke," and is used to catch badgers, foxes, etc.

C. In the American Indian tale given above, the bears are killed in the hole and the trickster goes his way. However, in the „Kachi-Kachi Mountain," getting burned is only the beginning of the dupe's ordeal, consisting of *Section C*. In many local versions, the badger is persuaded by the rabbit to go along with him to get some brush or firewood, as in the standard version, but there are about fifteen versions in which the dupe is induced to build a grass shack, thatch the roof with rushes, or help build winter shelter for his own and for the trickster's house. In any case, the dupe is always made to work inside, so that when the fire is set from the outside, he has to accept the rabbit's explanation of Click-Click bird, etc. Only one version in northern Japan[8] is exactly the same as the Arapaho version: the rabbit tricks the dupe into entering the hole before burning him, the dupe being a bear in this case. Some versions of northern Japan which begin with *Section C* retain a more primitive element, for these are the tales of the rabbit and the badger or the bear, the pure trickster-dupe story.

D. In the Arapaho version, the core of which consists of *Sections B and C*, the trickster paints himself white in order to go back to the bears in *Section C* to play further tricks on them. In the South Ute version,[9] the coyote, the trickster, puts piñon tree gum on one eye to change his appearance (K1821). In many of the Japanese versions, the rabbit comes to the burned badger in the guise of a medicine peddler or a doctor (K1825.1.5) to prescribe painful ointment like the paste of red-pepper, mustard, and *tadé* or knot-weed (K1014), which constitutes *Section D*.

However, often in the northern Japanese versions, the rabbit can deceive the badger (bear) only with words, without changing his appearance. The dupe, after getting burned in the Mountain of Rushes, goes on to the Vine Mountain where the rabbit is cutting and gathering vines. The dupe starts to reproach the rabbit, and the latter says, "I am the rabbit of the Vine Mountain. I cannot be responsible for what the rabbit of the Rush Mountain has done to you."

E. The dupe is easily persuaded and wants to know what the rabbit is doing there. Under *Section E* are grouped minor or regional motifs of the rabbit's tricks on the dupe such as the following:

[7] Minzokugaku. Kenkyujo (Inst. of Japanese Folklore Studies) ed. *Sogo Nippon Minzoku Goi* (Encyclopedia of Japanese Folk Terms). 1955–1956, Tokyo: Heibon-Sha, 5 v., v. 1, p. 7.

[8] Akita Prefecture. SEKI, Keigo ed. *Nippon Mukashibanashi Shusei*. 1950–1958, Tokyo, 6 v., v. 1, p. 206.

[9] *Journal of American Folklore*, XXXVII (1924), 58.

1. In order to conjure away the pain which the dupe feels from the burn, the rabbit says that it is necessary to bind him up with the vines. When the badger submits to the bondage, the rabbit delivers him to the old man.
2. The rabbit says that it is fun to bind the hands and feet with the vines and roll down the hill.
3. By blocking the anus with the vines (birch-bark, lacquer), there is no need of eating food through the winter.
4. The rabbit offers to hold the dupe (a monkey) in his arms and run. Telling the dupe to close his eyes at a certain point, he dashes to the old man's house and throws the dupe into boiling water, which the rabbit has told the old man to have ready. This is found only in Tokushima Prefecture in Shikoku.

F. *Section F* is the end of the standard version, and as shown in Chart II, the most common way of winding up the local versions also. The dupe comes to the place where the rabbit is building a wooden boat, and is persuaded to build his with mud. As the standard version has it, the rabbit sometimes does the construction of both boats, the dupe being clumsy. They row out their boats together to fish, but the boat of mud dissolves (J2171.1.3) and the dupe drowns. Thus our standard version consists of Sections B-C-D-F. I am certain that it has had a considerable influence over the oral versions, especially over those of more centrally located districts.

In *A-T Type 43*, the bear is supposed to build a house of wood: the fox of ice. However, in a Russian version translated by A. Gerber,[10] the fox proposes that they build huts, the fox making hers of bark and the wolf using ice for his. When in spring-time the hut of ice melts, the wolf sees that he has been tricked. With the reversal of the building material, the smarter using the bark and the dupe the ice, it is easier to see a possibility of *Section F* being the analogue of *A-T Type 43*.

The versions that go further into *Sections G, H, J, K* are all peripheral, found mostly in the northern part of Japan. There are eleven such versions, and in five cases the dupe is the bear.

G. *Section G*. After the dupe has drowned, the rabbit pulls him out of the water, and goes to a nearby house. The housewife is away. The rabbit borrows a pan from the children, makes the dupe into soup, and eats it all by himself, leaving his droppings in the pan. In two cases he steals *sake* and gets drunk on it.

H. *Section H*. Upon learning what has happened in her (his) absence, the housewife (the man of the house) is very angry. She goes after the rabbit and catches him outside the house. She tells a child to fetch a dagger from under the pillow.

[10] Adolph Gerber. "Great Russian Animal Tales," *Publications of the Modern Language Association of America*, VI (1891), 17.

He brings the pillow (XIII.7). She tells him to get a knife on the cutting-board, and he brings the cutting-board. So she tells the child to hold the rabbit while she gets the weapon. For the motif of misunderstood instructions, the only motif number that I have found so far is XIII.7: Misunderstood words lead to comic results. A similar motif occurs in Japan in connection with *A-T Type 1653A*: The Robber under the Tree: Guarding the Door (K1413).

J. *Section J*. While she is gone, the rabbit asks the child the size of some object. He shows the size with both his hands, and the rabbit escapes. It is clearly the counterpart of *A-T Type 6*, in which the captive makes the captor release his grip by asking him questions.

K. *Section K*. The housewife returns with the knife, in time to throw it at the fleeing rabbit, cutting off its tail. That is why the rabbit's tail is short (A2378.4.1).

Section K is the counterpart of a detail in *A-T Type 3*: Sham Blood and Brains. As the type appears in northern Europe, the fox steals milk at a farmhouse while the housewife is away, getting his head covered with milk. Upon coming back, she finds most of her milk gone. In disgust she throws the remaining milk at the fleeing fox, which accounts for the white tip of the fox's tail. When the bear complains of his hard luck in losing his tail (*A-T Type 2*), the fox shows his milk-covered head and says that he is worse off having been beaten by the housewife so severely as to have his brains knocked out.[11]

The striking parallel of explaining the white tip of the fox's tail and *Section K*: "Why the rabbit's tail is short" leads me to think that our *Section G* in which the rabbit eats the self-cooked bear soup, or steals home-brewed *sake*, is the counterpart of the main body of *A-T Type 3*.

There are two local versions which have *A-T Type 9*: The Unjust Partner, as their introductory part. There is another consisting of *Section C* and *A-T Type 2*: The Tail-Fisher: still another having an episode which suggests *A-T Type 2*.[12]

• • •

What I have tried to show through my analysis is that this animal story, which is one of the five representative tales in Japan, has its distant relatives in amazingly widespread areas, having close parallels with American Indian motifs as well as with the north European animal cycle: the Fox and the Bear.

---

[11] The last part of *A–T Type 3* exists in Japan in another form also. Three animals find three objects. Each takes one, the trickster taking beans. He puts the husks of beans among his fur, and when the others have complained about their gains, he says that he has fared the worst, getting malignant boils from eating beans.

[12] *A–T Types 2 and 9* are extensively known in Japan, as well as occuring as episodes in our "Kachi-Kachi Mountain" Cycle.

15*

Is this cluster of tales—at least the elements found in *Sections B* and *C*—a part of many motifs, which, on their way through Bering Straits to the American Continents, branched off to Japan thousands of years ago? What could be the explanation of so much parallelism between "Kachi-Kachi Mountain" and "The Trickster Kills the Children"? I think that in the investigation of the relationship between the tales of the Old World and the New, this "Kachi-Kachi Mountain" cycle has certainly a full claim to be included.

As for the motifs belonging to the Northern animal cycle which have found their way to Japan, how and when did they come? To my knowledge we have analogues of *A-T Types* 1, 1*, 2, 3, 6, 7, 9, 10**, 15, 43, 47, 49, 57, 61, 101, 103, 111, 112, 120, 121, 123, 124, 130, 154, 156, 160, 210, 221, 222, 228, 234, 245, 275, und 295, in the animal tale section. The earliest record of the above group is the latter half of *A-T Type 228*, a small bird flying into the ear of a deer thus killing him, which appears in *Nihon Shoki*, also known as *Nihongi*, an official Imperial history of Japan, compiled in 720 A.D.

Did these two groups of motifs considered above, one belonging to the Northern animal cycle and the other to the American Indian tales, come their separate ways to Japan and then intermingle in the course of time to form Japanese animal tales, of which the "Kachi-Kachi Mountain" cycle is one? And what was the relationship between the Northern animal cycle and the tales found among the North American Indians before Columbus found them?

In *A-T Type 36–37–43*, which are very often found as a group of episodes, (*A-T Type 43* is represented in the "Kachi-Kachi Mountain" as *Section F*), the fox returns to the dupe again and again to play further tricks, but to avoid later recognition, he covers himself with soot to look like a monk or a priest. What could be the connection between this and the disguise of Nihansen the trickster painting himself white, or posing as a one-eyed man, as seen in the Arapaho and South Ute versions?

Possible pre-Columbian contact of the Northern animal cycle with the American Indian tales is an intriguing problem for future study, if enough material is available.

University of Hawaii, Honolulu

Chart I. The Combination of Component Parts

Sections										Districts
1. A										2, 2, 40, 42
2. A B										1, 14, 32, 33, 35, 40, 41, 41, 42, 43, 43
3. A B C										2, 21
4. A B C D										41
5. A B C DD F										5
6. A B C D F										2, 2, 6, 6, 6, 14, 14, 14, 16, 17, 19, 21, 39, 40, 40, 41
7. A B C E F										2
8. A B C D E F										1, 3
9. A B C E										2
10. A B C F										37, 44
11. A B F										2, 2, 34, 42, 43, 43, 44
12. A B E										37, 37
13. B H J										3
14. B										7, 14, 36
15. B C D E F										7, 7
16. B C F										19
17. B F G										14, 35
18. B F										29, 33
19. B C D F										7, 7, 14, 14, 14, 14, 14, 23, 29
20. B C E F G K										7
21. C (or combined with other motifs)										2, 21, 41, 41, 42
22. C D E F										1, 1
23. C E F										2
24. C F										5
25. C D E F G H J K										1
26. C D E F G J K										7
27. C E D F G H J K										2
28. C D G H J										3
29. EE F G H J K										2
30. C G										21
31. C G H J K										19
32. G H J K										1
33. G										19

CHART II

Versions beginning with A 1, 1, 2, 2, 2, 2, 2, 2, 2, 2, 2, 3, 5, 6, 6, 6, 14, 14, 14, 14,
16, 17, 19, 21, 21, 32, 33, 34, 35, 37, 37, 37, 39, 40,
40, 40, 40, 41, 41, 41, 41, 42, 42, 42, 43, 43, 43, 43,
44, 44

,,   ,,   ,, B 3, 7, 7, 7, 7, 7, 7, 14, 14, 14, 14, 14, 14, 14, 19, 23, 29,
29, 33, 35, 36

,,   ,,   ,, C 1, 1, 1, 2, 2, 2, 3, 5, 7, 19, 21, 21, 41, 41, 42

,,   ,,   ,, E 2

,,   ,,   ,, G 1, 19

Versions ending with B   1, 14, 32, 33, 35, 40, 41, 41, 42, 43, 43

,,   ,,   ,, C   2, 21, 14, 35

,,   ,,   ,, D   41

,,   ,,   ,, E   2, 37, 37

,,   ,,   ,, F   1, 1, 1, 2, 2, 2, 2, 2, 2, 3, 5, 5, 6, 6, 6, 7, 7, 7, 7, 14, 14,
14, 14, 14, 14, 14, 14, 16, 17, 19, 19, 21, 23, 29,
29, 33, 34, 37, 39, 40, 40, 41, 42, 43, 43, 44, 44

,,   ,,   ,, G   21

,,   ,,   ,, J   3, 3

,,   ,,   ,, K   1, 1, 2, 2, 7, 7, 19

Single-episodic A   2, 2, 40, 42

,,   B   7, 14, 36

,,   C   2, 21, 41, 41, 42

,,   G   19

KEY TO DISTRICT NUMBERS

Prefectures of Japan are represented by numerals 1 to 44 from the northern end
of Honshu on down to the southern end of Kyushu.

1 Aomori Prefecture	17 Shizuoka	35 Ehime
2 Iwate	19 Gifu	36 Kochi
3 Akita	21 Ishikawa	37 Tokushima
5 Yamagata	23 Shiga	39 Fukuoka
6 Fukushima	29 Hyogo	40 Nagasaki
7 Niigata	32 Okayama	41 Oita
14 Saitama	33 Hiroshima	42 Saga
16 Yamanashi	34 Yamaguchi	43 Kumamoto
		44 Kagoshima

DAS SLOWENISCHE KETTENMÄRCHEN VOM MÄUSLEIN, DAS DURCH EINEN ZAUN KROCH, AUS DEM GAILTAL IN KÄRNTEN*

(ZUR KLÄRUNG VON MT. 2034A [Z41.4.1])

IVAN GRAFENAUER

Aus meinen Kinderjahren war mir ein Märchen in Erinnerung geblieben vom Mäuslein, das durch einen Zaun kroch, sich das Bäuchlein zerriß und bei einem Schuster Hilfe suchte. Mein mütterlicher Großvater *Janez (Johann) Flaschberger* (1830–1905), Gotthardbauer in Velika ves (Micheldorf) bei Brdo (Egg) im Gailtal (Kärnten, Österreich), hatte es mir unzähligemal erzählt und auch ich selber manchmal meinen Kindern. Dann war mir die Helferkette entfallen und den Enkelkindern konnte ich das Märlein nicht mehr weitergeben. Bei Dialektaufnahmen im Gailtal fahndete ich daher in meiner Heimatgemeinde auch nach diesem Märchen und fand es auch wirklich; zuerst bei einer Ururenkelin meines Großvaters, dann auch zu Hause in einer völlig vergessenen eigenen Aufzeichnung, leider ohne Datum, unter meinen studentischen dialektologischen Notizen aus der Zeit um 1900.

Diese älteste Niederschrift, eine Kurzfassung, ist nicht das Märlein, das mir der Großvater in meinen Kinderjahren erzählt hatte, sondern eine Fassung, möglichst kurz gefaßt und mit tödlichem Ausgang, mit welcher der Erzähler seine kleinen

* Dank den Herren Archer Taylor, Berkeley, California, und Robert Wildhaber, Basel, Schweiz, für Übermittlung von in Jugoslavien unzugänglichen Texten und Nachweisen.

239

Zuhörer manchmal neckte, bevor er zum eigentlichen Erzählen überging. Sie lautet in Übersetzung:

(Brdo 1)[1]

Es war einmal ein Mäuslein, das kroch durch einen Zaun und zerriß sich das Bäuchlein. Und es ging zum Schuster, er möchte ihm das Bäuchlein zusammennähen. Schuster sagte: „Gib mir Fett!" Es ging zur Sau. Die Sau sagte: „Gib mir Mais!" Es ging zum Acker. Acker sagte: „Gib mir Dünger!" Es ging zur Kuh. Die Kuh sagte: „Gib mir zu Essen!" Es ging zur Wiese. Die Wiese sagte: „Gib mir Wasser!" Es ging zur Quelle, Wasser holen, aber es überschlug sich hinein und war hin.

Das Kindermärchen, das mir der Großvater vor mehr als 70 Jahren zu erzählen pflegte, wiederholte mir fast wörtlich seine Ururenkelin *Helga Kopič* (Kopitch), Urenkelin meiner Tante, der Mutterschwester *Neža* (*Agnes*) *Flaschberger*, verehel. *Kopič*. In der Schusterkeusche in Melani (Mellach) bei Brdo (Egg) erzählte und diktierte sie mir das Märchen, wie folgt:[2]

(Brdo 2.3)

Es war einmal ein Mäuslein und es kroch durch einen Zaun und zerriß sich das Bäuchlein. Und dann ging es zum Schuster und bat ihn, ihm das Bäuchlein zusammenzunähen. Aber der Schuster sagte: „Gib mir Fett!" Dann ging es zur Sau und sagte: „Gib mir Fett!" Aber die Sau sagte: „Gib mir Mais!" a) [Und dann ging es zur Maispflanze und sagte: „Gib mir einen Maiskolben!" Die Maispflanze aber sagte: „Du muß mir Dünger geben, daß ich wachse!"] Und es ging zur Kuh und sagte: „Gib mir Dünger!" Aber die Kuh sagte: „Gib mir Futter!" Da nahm es flink eine Sense und ging Futter mähen.

Und es gab der Kuh Futter und die Kuh gab ihm Dünger; b) [den Dünger streute es zur Maispflanze und die Maispflanze gab ihm einen Maiskolben; den Maiskolben gab es der Sau] und die Sau gab ihm Fett; und mit dem Fett lief es zum Schuster und der Schuster nähte ihm das Bäuchlein zusammen.

Hier war des Großvaters Märchen zu Ende. Seine Ururenkelin begann aber wieder von Anfang an:

Aber das Mäuslein lief (schlüpfte!) noch einmal durch den Zaun und zerriß sich noch einmal das Bäuchlein...

---

[1] Velika ves (Micheldorf) bei Brdo (Egg). Erzähler Janez Flaschberger, Gotthardbauer, 70-jährig. Aufgezeichnet von Ivan Grafenauer um 1900. Das Original erscheint im *Slovenski etnograf* XIII (1960).

[2] Melani pri Brdu (Mellach bei Egg). Erzählerin Helga Kopič, Schulmädchen, Schusterhaus. Aufgezeichnet von Ivan Grafenauer am 25. August 1958.

Auch sonst unterschied sich die Erzählung des Großvaters von der seiner Ururenkelin in Kleinigkeiten, vor allem aber an den zwei mit a und b bezeichneten Stellen (vgl. Brdo 1):

a) Und dann ging es zum Acker und sagte: „Gib mir Mais!" Aber der Acker sagte: „Gib mir Dünger!"

b) ... den Dünger streute es auf den Acker und der Acker gab ihm Mais.

Es sind das Fassungen von *Formelmärchen*, wie sie von unserem verehrten Jubilar im *Journal of American Folklore* und im *Handwörterbuch des deutschen Märchens* behandelt worden sind,[3] und zwar gehören sie zu deren wichtigster Gruppe, den *Kettenmärchen*, die mit 23 Punkten neun Zehntel (89,9%) des ganzen Artikels vom „*Formelmärchen*" im *Hdwb. d. M.* einnehmen.[4] Diese Kettenmärchen sind in der slowenischen Volksliteratur recht beliebt. Außer der Gruppe 19, zu der das Mäusleinmärchen gehört,[5] sind das hauptsächlich die folgenden:

5. *Ehod mi jodea* (Eins; wer weiß es? Le dodici parole della verità; Las doce palabras retorneadas).[6] *Slow.* „*Hagada*",[7] meist mit den Eingangsworten „Brüderlein von Ljubljana, Sag an, was ist eins... was ist zwölf?" und mit Antworten, die gut denen der westeuropäischen Fassungen entsprechen.

6. *Lönen hos den rike man* (wie der reiche Mann seinen Diener bezahlt; Mt. 2010 [Z21.3]). *Slow.* „Was ich verdient habe."[8]

13. *Had Gadya*; Der Bauer schickt den Jockel aus = Das Birnli will nit fallen; The Old Woman and Her Pig — mit vielen Variationen.[9] *Slow.* „Ungehorsame Diener" = "Herr und Birnbaum"[10]; „Bodin und Bodina".[11] Das Verhältnis der Kettenglieder zueinander ist in dieser Gruppe unfreundlich.

[3] Archer Taylor, "Classification of Formula Tales," *JAmFl.* XLVI (1933), 77–88. Idem, „Formelmärchen." *Hdwb. d. Märchens* II (1934–40), 164a–191a.

[4] II. „Kettenmärchen" 1–23, *Hdwb. d. Märchens* II, 165a–189b.

[5] 19. *Die Maus, die den Schwanz verlor*, Mt. 2034; Motiv Z41.4. Die Märchentypen (Mt.) sind hier nach Taylors Klassifikation angegeben, die Motive nach der neuen Auflage von Stith Thompson, *Motiv-Index of Folk-Literature* I–VI. Kopenhagen, 1955–1958.

[6] *Hdwb. d. Märchens* II, 171a–174a.

[7] K. Štrekelj, *Slovenske narodne pesmi*—Slowenische Volkslieder I–IV (1895–1923), Nr. 1–8686. SNP III, Nr. 6661–80.

[8] *Hdwb. d. Märchens* II, 174a–175b, Mt. 2010 I, Z21.3 mit Angabe schwedisch-finnischer Literatur, Anm. 53. *SNP* IV, Nr. 7515–32. *Kaj sem zaslužil*—Was ich verdient hab.

[9] *Hdwb. d. Märchens* II, 180a–182a; BP (Bolte-Polívka, *Anmerkungen zu den KHM d. Br. Grimm*) II, Nr. 72a, S. 100–108.

[10] SPN I, Nr. 968–9. *Neposlušne stvari*—Ungehorsame Dinge. Dazu Ms.-e im Institut f. Musikvolkskunde in Ljubljana. Zitiert in BP II, 103.

[11] Bodin in Bodina, *Nar. pripovedke v Soškikh planinah* III, Nr. 15; ²1910, Nr. 21. Zitiert in BP II, 107.

15. *„Die stärksten Dinge"* (ohne Rückkehr zum Anfangsglied).[12] *Slow*. „Über-
wundene Raubtiere": Ein Tier frißt das andere auf, das letzte nimmt der Tod.[13]

Dazu kommt eine Reihe von Kinderliedern verschiedener Art in Form von
Frage und Antwort, wie etwa die folgenden: „Mit den Glocken im Turm
werd ich den Teufel schrecken"[14]: „Ich werde Zwirn kaufen." / „Was wirst
mit dem Zwirn tun?" „Mit dem Zwirn werd ich Säcke nähen." / (Weiter:)
„. . . Eicheln sammeln", „. . . Schweine züchten", „. . . Wagen schmieren",
„. . . Steine fahren", „. . . Turm bauen", „. . . Glocken aufhängen", „. . . Teufel
jagen."

Noch ein Wort zur Reihenfolge der Kettenglieder in diesen Märchen. Sie können entweder nur einmal in der bestimmten Reihenfolge in Erscheinung treten
oder zweimal in entgegengesetzter Reihenfolge, ja auch öfter. *Einmal*, wenn die
Handlung unbehindert zum Ziel kommt, wie im gerade angeführten Kinderlied,
oder wenn der Tod vorzeitig die Handlung abschließt (wie in Brdo 1). Zweimal in
entgegengesetzter Richtung, wenn der Weg zum Endziel behindert ist und erst
die Bedingungen zum Enderfolg geschaffen werden müssen durch einen willigen
Helfer oder durch Selbsthilfe (z. B. das mähende Mäuslein). Öfter, wenn bei jedem
folgenden Kettenglied die bis dahin in Erscheinung getretenen Glieder in umge-
kehrter Reihenfolge kumulativ angeführt werden, immer um ein Glied vermehrt,
bis im letzten Abschnitt (Strophe) alle Glieder aufgereiht sind.[15]

In den Märchenfassungen von Brdo-Egg kommen noch andere Arten von
Formelmärchen vor, z. B. die Form des Rundmärchens (Rounds) in der Fassung
der Helga Kopič, die hier dem Wunsch von Kleinkindern entgegenkommt, immer
wieder dasselbe Märlein zu hören — um es sich einzuprägen — während Kurz-
formen dieser Gattung den Zweck haben, die Zuhörer zu necken.

· · ·

Schon fünf Tage nach der längeren Fassung von Brdo-Egg, erzählt von Helga
Kopič, konnte ich in der östlichen Nachbargemeinde Blače-Vorderberg eine etwas
abweichende Fassung aufzeichnen, die mir am 30. August 1958 von der Schwie-
germutter im Goličhaus (Blače Nr. 44) Maria Miče (Mitsche) erzählt wurde. Ein
Jahr später, am 7. September 1959, nahm Professor Dr. Paul Zablatnik eine

---

[12] *Hdwb. d. Märchens* II, 182a–184b; Punkt 6. Der Typ *Die stärksten Dinge* entartet in Europa. . .
und verliert. . . die charakteristische Rückkehr zum Anfangsglied (S. 184a).

[13] *SPN* I, Nr. 964–7. *Zverina premagana.* Vgl. BP II, Nr. 72a, S. 104f. Anm. 1–2; Zitiert in Anm. 2,
S. 105.

[14] *SNP* IV, Nr. 7448. *Z zvonom v turnu bo vraga strašil.*

[15] Beispiel s. BP II, Nr. 72a, S. 100–101; *SNP* I, Nr. 968–9. *Das Birnli will nit fallen — Neposlušne
stvari — Ungehorsame Dinge.*

weitere Fassung von einer anderen Erzählerin, Neža Anderwald, geb. *Jamrič*, auf Tonband auf. Diese kürzere, altertümlichere Fassung lautet:[16]

(Blače 1)

Ein Mäuslein ging durch einen Zaun und zerriß sich das Schwänzchen. Und es ging zum Schuster, sagte: „Nähe mir das Schwänzchen an. Der Schuster sagte: „Gib mir Fett!" Es ging zur Sau; der Sau sagte es: „Gib mir Fett!" Die Sau sagte: „Gib mir Mehl!" Es ging zum Müller. Dem Müller sagte es: „Gib mir Mehl!" Der Müller sagte: „Gib mir Getreide!" Es ging auf den Acker, sagte zum Acker: „Gib mir Getreide!" Der Acker sagte: „Gib mir Dünger!" Und es schieß auf den Acker und der Acker gab Getreide — das Getreide wuchs heran.

Das Getreide brachte es dem Müller, der Müller gab ihm Mehl; das Mehl gab es der Sau, die Sau gab ihm Fett; das Fett gab es dem Schuster, der Schuster nähte ihm das Schwänzlein zusammen und es war wieder ganz.

Die längere Fassung von Blače-Vorderberg, erzählt von Maria Miče, lautet in der Übersetzung, wie folgt:[17]

(Blače 2)

Ein Mäuslein ging durch einen Zaun und zerriß sich das Schwänzchen. Und dann ging es zum Schuster und sagte: „Würdest du mir das Schwänzchen annähen?" Aber der Schuster sagte: „Gib mir Fett!" Und dann ging es zur Sau und sagte: „Sau, gib mir Fett!" Aber die Sau sagte: „Gib mir Milch!" Und dann ging es zur Kuh und sagte: „Kuh, gib mir Milch!" Aber die Kuh sagte: „Gib mir Futter!" Und es ging zu den Mähern und sagte: „Mäher, gebt mir Futter!" Die Mäher sagten: „Gib uns Krapfen!" Dann ging es zur Hausfrau und sagte: „Hausfrau, gebt mir Krapfen!" Aber die Hausfrau sagte: „Bring mir Mehl!" Und dann ging es zum Müller und sagte: „Gib mir Mehl!" Der Müller sagte: „Bring mir Getreide!" Und dann ging es zum Acker und sagte: „Acker, gib mir Getreide!" Aber der Acker sagte: „Gib mir Dünger!" Und es schieß darauf und das Getreide wuchs heran.

Und das Getreide brachte es dem Müller und der Müller gab ihm Mehl; das Mehl brachte es der Hausfrau, die Hausfrau gab ihm Krapfen; die Krapfen brachte es den Mähern, die Mäher gaben ihm Futter; das Futter brachte es der Kuh, die Kuh gab ihm Milch; die Milch brachte es der Sau, die Sau gab ihm Fett; das Fett brachte es dem Schuster, dieser aber nähte ihm das Schwänzchen an.

Die Zusammenschau der Gailtaler Fassungen von Brdo-Egg und Blače-Vorderberg ergibt Folgendes:

---

[16] Blače Nr. 90. Erzählerin Neža (Agnes) Anderwald, geb. Jamrič. Tonbandaufnahme am 7. Sept. 1959. Das Original erscheint im *Slovenski etnograf* XIII (1960).

[17] Blače, Nr. 44. Erzählerin Maria Miče; Niederschrift von Ivan Grafenauer am 30. August 1958. Das Original erscheint im *Slovenski etnograf* XIII (1960).

A. Betreffs des Eingangs:

Mit dem Kriechen durch den Zaun steht die Verletzung des Bäuchleins in vollem Einklang. Den Zaun haben wir uns geflochten vorzustellen und mit Dornästen verstärkt, wie sie in Gebirgsgegenden noch hie und da zu sehen sind. Das zerrissene Schwänzchen hat aber da keinen rechten Sinn.

B. Betreffs der Helferkette:

Die Glieder der Helferkette sind durchwegs rein agrarischen Charakters; dasselbe gilt auch vom Eingange: die durch einen Zaun kriechende Maus ist keine Hausmaus.

Die beiden Gailtaler Typen des Mäusleinmärchens sind demnach rein bäuerlichen Charakters.

Bevor wir diese zwei Typen in die Gesamtheit der bisher bekannten Typen einreihen, müssen wir uns noch die Fassung des *Slovenski Gospodar* (*Slowenischer Hauswirt*, ein Wochenblatt) in Maribor-Marburg, Jhrg. 63, Nr. 4 (23. Januar 1929), S. 9, ansehen.

Im Abteil „Für Kleinkinder" erschienen, bietet dieses Mäusemärchen zwar keine Angaben über Ort, Zeit, Erzähler und Aufzeichner, trägt auch keine Unterschrift, auch der Stil ist ungelenk und kindisch, gar nicht volkstümlich; aber es ist fast identisch mit dem Stöberschen Märchen "Vom Kätzchen und dem Mäuschen" (*Elsässisches Volksbüchlein*, Straßburg 1842, Nr. 237, S. 95), doch mit Abweichungen, wie *Mehl* statt *Kleie*, *Weizen* statt *Frucht* (= Getreide), nähte *zusammen* statt *flickte* u. a. m. Es könnte die Übersetzung einer ungelenken Bearbeitung für Kinder sein.

Die Fassung lautet in Übersetzung:[18]

(Slov. Gosp.)

Kätzchen und Mäuslein gingen zusammen auf Reisen. Sie kamen an ein großes Wasser und konnten nicht hinüber. Sie nahmen einen Strohhalm und legten ihn übers Wasser. Und das Kätzchen sagte zum Mäuslein: „Mäuslein, geh du zuerst hinüber!" Aber das Mäuslein wagte es nicht und sagte: „Kätzchen, geh du zuallererst!" Da begab sich das Kätzchen auf den Strohhalm. Wie es aber auf dem Halm war, zerbrach(!) er und das Kätzchen fiel ins Wasser. Da lachte das Mäuslein derart, daß ihm das Bäuchlein barst.

Das Mäuslein eilte zum Schuster und bat ihn: „Schusterlein, nähe mir mein Bäuchlein zusammen!" Der Schuster antwortete: „Mäuslein, gib mir Borsten, dann nähe ich dir das Bäuchlein." (S. 10) Darauf schritt das Mäuslein zum Ferkelchen und bat es: „Ferkelchen, gib du mir Borsten, ich die Borsten dem Schusterlein, Schusterlein wird mir das Bäuchlein nähen." Ferkelchen meinte: „Mäuslein, gib mir Mehl!" Dann

---

[18] *Slovenski gospodar*, Jahrg. 63, Nr. 4 (23. Januar 1929), S. 9.

ging Mäuslein zum Müller, sprach: „Müllerchen, du mir Mehl, das Mehl geb ich dem Ferkelchen, Ferkelchen..." Müller sagte: „Mäuslein, gib mir Weizenchen!" Mäuslein eilte aufs Feld und bat: „Feldchen lieb, gib mir Weizenchen für den Müller, er wird mir geben..." Das Feld forderte: „Mäuslein, bring Dünger!" Mäuslein trippelte zum Ochsen und sagte: „Öchslein, gib mir Dünger fürs Feld, es wird mir Weizenchen geben..." Der Ochs forderte: „Mäuslein, gib mir Wässerchen!" Sogleich ging Mäuslein zum Bach und bat ihn: „Bächlein mild, gib mir Wässerchen! Ich geb es dem Öchslein und es gibt mir Dünger. Diesen Dünger geb ich..." — Das Bächlein äußerte sich: „Mäuslein, nimm, soviel du willst!"

Das Mäuslein nahm also, soviel es tragen konnte, und brachte es dem Öchslein. Öchslein gab ihm Dünger. Den Dünger trug es aufs Feld und bekam Weizen. Den Weizen gab es dem Müller, wo es Mehl bekam. Das Mehl war dem Ferkelchen willkommen, das ihm gerne Borsten gab. Mäuslein brachte die Borsten zum Schuster und der nähte ihm das Bäuchlein zusammen. So bekam das Mäuslein endlich doch, was es gewünscht hatte.

Wie stellen sich die slowenischen Mäusleinmärchen zu den bisher bekannten Typen?

Die bisher bekannten Typen des Mäusleinmärchens kennzeichnet Stith Thompson in seinem *Motif-Index of Folklore-Literature*[2] V, (1957), wie folgt:

Z41.4. (V[1] [1935]: Z41.5). *The mouse regains its tail.* The cat bites off the mouse's tail and will return it in exchange for milk. The mouse goes to the cow for milk, the farmer for hay, the butcher for meat, the baker for bread. Other persons mentioned are the locksmith and the miner. *Taylor, *JAmFl.* XLVI, 86, No. 2034, *Hdwb. d. Märchens*, II,185b; *Wesselski, *Hess. Blätter f. Vksk.* XXXII 28; *Newell, *JAmFl.* XVIII (1905), 34, n. 1; BP II,107–8; Basset *Contes Berbères*, No. 45, *Nouveaux Contes Berbères*, No. 168. (V[2]:) England, U.S.: *Baughman.

Z41.4.1. (V[1] [1935]: Z41.5.1). *Mouse bursts open when crossing a stream.* Series of helpers similar to Z41.4. *Taylor, *JAmFl.* XLVI, 86, No. 2034A; *Wesselski, *Hess. Blätter f. Vksk.* XXXII 28; BP II 107–8.

Zu Z41.4 (Mt.2034) stehen in irgendeinem Verhältnis die zwei Märchenfassungen aus Blače-Vorderberg (das zerrissene Schwänzchen). Die Märchenfassung des *Slovenski Gospodar* gehört zum Mt.2034A (Z41.4.1). In irgendeinem Verhältnis zu diesem Typ stehen auch die Fassungen von Brdo-Egg (das zerrissene Bäuchlein), jedenfalls aber auch die Fassungen von Blače-Vorderberg. Mehr über das gegenseitige Verhältnis dieser Typen und ihre Entwicklung kann uns nur eine genauere Analyse ihrer Motive und das Studium ihrer gegenseitigen Einflußnahme bieten.

Grundlegendes über den Märchentyp (Mt.) 2034A (Z41.4.1), „das Mäuschen mit geborstenem Bäuchlein," hat schon Bolte in den *Anmerkungen zu den Kinder-*

und Hausmärchen der Brüder Grimm (BP) ausgesagt, doch nicht an der oben an-
gegebenen Stelle (BP II,107–8). Da (in Nr. 72a. *Das Birnli will nit fallen*) gab er
allerdings als erster eine knappe Charakteristik der beiden Typen des Mäusleinmärchens, vom Mäuslein, dem die Katze den Schwanz abgebissen hat (Mt. 2034)
und vom Mäuslein, das vor Lachen über den Unfall der Katze geborsten ist
(Mt. 2034A). Von weit größerer Bedeutung ist aber die Stelle, die *Bolte*, II,107
bei Sutermeister, Nr. 5 ,,Müsli gang du zerst" nur kurz zitiert (oben I,137), die
aber seine Nachfolger ganz außer acht gelassen haben. Er führt da, ganz wie nur
nebenbei, die Tatsachen an, wie der Mt. 2034A entstanden ist. In Nr. 18, *Strohhalm, Kohle und Bohne* (BP I, 135–137) sagt er auf S. 136f.: In einem lateinischen
Gedicht des Mittelalters (Handschrift des 15. Jahrh. zu Straßburg, Joh. C. 102)
kommt die Fabel von der reisenden *Maus* und *Kohle* mit der Wendung vor, daß
beide ihre Sünden zu beichten in die Kirche wallfahrten, beim Übergang die Kohle
in ein Bächlein fällt, zischt und erlischt und die Maus schilt, das sei schlechter
Weihrauch (es folgen die 8 Disticha dieser Fabel). Eine Maus statt der Bohne tritt
auch bei Sutermeister, Nr. 5 'Müsli gang du zerst' (aus Baselland; dazu Singer 1,
46–54) und in einer bernischen Fassung (Schweiz. Archiv 15,24 'La braise et la
souris') auf; in einer elsässischen Aufzeichnung in Stöbers *Volksbüchlein*, S. 95,
Nr. 237 ist außerdem für die Kohle eine Katze eingetreten, unter deren Gewicht
der als Brücke benutzte Strohhalm zur Freude der Maus bricht. Dazu bemerkt
Bolte in der Anm. 1 (S. 137): An die schweizerischen und die elsässische Fassung
ist ein *Häufungsmärchen* in der Art des Jäckel, der den Hafer schneiden soll
(R. Köhler 3,355) angehängt: die Maus will sich beim Schuhmacher den Pelz
flicken lassen und wird weitergeschickt zur Sau, zum Müller, zum Acker, zur Kuh,
zur Wiese, zum Bach.

Die Bedeutung dieses allmählichen Einsickerns von Motiven des Mäusleinmärchens in das Bohnenmärchen (Mt. 295 [F1025.1]), zuerst der Maus anstatt der
Bohne, dann der Helferkette, zuletzt der Katze anstatt der Kohle, ist auch Bolte
nicht klar geworden, sonst hätte er in BP II,107 wohl mehr zu sagen gehabt als
nur den Hinweis ,,oben S. 137". Jedenfalls fand er dafür im Märchentyp von der
Maus, der die Katze den Schwanz abbeißt (Mt. 2034 [Z41.4], zu wenig klare An-
knüpfungspunkte. Schade nur, daß es Bolte versäumt hat, an dieser Stelle
(BP II, 107–8) die angeführten Fassungen genauer zu kennzeichnen betreffs des
Eingangs (ob geborsten oder des Schwanzes beraubt) und der Helferketten.

Die breit angelegten ,,Kettenmärchenstudien" von *Martti Haavio*[19] bedeuten —
namentlich im Betreff des Mäusleinmärchens — eher einen Rückschritt gegenüber

[19] Martti Haavio, *Kettenmärchenstudien* I (Allgemein und "Was hätte ich sagen sollen), FFC Nr. 88
(1929), 224 S. *Kettenmärchenstudien* II. (Die einzelnen Kettenmärchen "Hahn und Henne",
Märchen und Lied), FFC Nr. 99 (1932), 160 S.

Joh. Bolte als einen Fortschritt. Die Darstellung ist unübersichtlich, oft vor-eingenommen, vielfach lückenhaft und unzuverlässig. Dabei führt er zwar in den von BP übernommenen Fassungen, soweit er sie erfaßt hat, Eingang und Helfer-kette an, doch nicht selten unrichtig.

Albert Wesselski hat zu Haavios zweiter Kettenmärchenstudie in der Abhand-lung vom „Märlein von dem Tode des Hühnchens und anderen Kettenmärchen"[20] eine Reihe von Berichtigungen und Ergänzungen geboten, aber eine durchgrei-fende Ordnung brachten in die Masse der Kettenmärchen erst Stith Thompson[21] und unser Jubilar.[22]

In Archer Taylors Artikel „Formelmärchen" (*Hdwb. d. Märchens* II, 164b–191a) nimmt der Abschnitt II. „Kettenmärchen" (S. 165b–189b) mit 23 Punkten knapp 90% des ganzen Artikels ein. Im Punkt 19 spricht er speziell vom Mäusleinmär-chen (S. 185b–187a). Er scheidet streng die beiden Typen: 1. die Maus verliert den Schwanz, 2. die Maus platzt beim Übergang über einen Bach. Beim ersten Typ betont er die Mannigfaltigkeit der Helferketten; darum „ist es noch nicht möglich, die ursprüngliche Reihe festzustellen". Beim Typus Mt. 2034A (Z41.4.1) spricht er aber folgende Vermutung aus (S. 186a): „Womöglich gehört das Auf-platzen (der Maus) eigentlich zu „Strohhalm, Kohle und Bohne", (KHM Nr. 18; Mt. 295 [F 1025.1]), das sich oft mit unserem Kettenmärchen in Kontamination findet." Dazu führt er Sutermeister, KHM Nr. 5 als Zeugnis an.

Boltes oben verzeichnete Angaben in BP I, 136–7, und die slowenischen Fas-sungen beweisen, daß seine Vermutung buchstäblich das Richtige getroffen hat.

Das Aufplatzen der Katze stammt unweigerlich aus dem Bohnenmärchen. Diese Fassungen sind nicht zahlreich:

1. Elsaß. Aug. Stöber, *Elsässisches Volksbüchlein* (1842) S. 95, Nr. 237 (BP I, 137; II, 107). Kennzeichen (nach Haavio II, S. 9): GG 6. Kätzchen fällt ins Wasser, Mäuschen lacht so, daß ihm der Bauch versprungen ist.

2. *Simrock, Märchen*, Nr. 36 = *Das deutsche Kinderbuch*, Nr. 1031. (Nach Haavio II, 12:) GG 40. Mäuschen lacht, daß ihm das Pänzchen zersprungen ist.

3–4. Zwei französische Fassungen des *Schweiz. Archivs* 15 (1911), 24–26, aus Miécourt, Ajoie im bernischen Jura (BP I, 137; bei Haavio II und Wesselski nicht erwähnt): La braise... tomba dans l'eau... La souris rit tant que sa panse creva (b: sauta).

5. Slowenisch. *Slov. Gospodar* 1929 (s. oben): Mäuslein lacht, daß ihm das Bäuchlein birst.

---

[20] *Hessische Blätter f. Volkskunde*, Bd. XXXII (1933), 1–51.
[21] Aarne-Thompson, *Types of the Folk-Tale*, FFC, Nr. 74 (1928); Stith Thompson, *Motif-Index of Folk-Literature* I–VI.
[22] Siehe Anm. 3.

Das Motiv übertragen auf andere Tiere: 6. Schwaben. Meier, Nr. 80. (Nach
Haavio II, 9:) GG 4. Gockel und Henne. Graben. Hüpfen darüber. Bauch auf-
gesprungen (wem?).

7. Flämisch. *Volkskunde. Tijdschrift voor Nederlandsche Folklore*, Jahrg. 15
(1903), S. 75, Nr. 29. (Haavio II, 13:) GVI. Laus und Floh. Floh fällt in den Fluß.
Laus lacht so, daß ihm sein „achterste" zerspringt.

Ohne klare Angaben: Haavio II, S. 7. RF 10. *Wallonia, Recueil de littérature
orale*, IV (Liège 1896), S. 31: Croque-Noyaux und seine Schwester Souricette...
S. fällt ins Wasser. C.-N. lacht. -?- Schuster, flicke!

Der Pelz der Maus zerrissen oder versprungen:

1. Canton Basel, Schweiz. Sutermeister. *KHM aus d. Schw.*, Nr. 5. (Haavio
II, 9:) GG 2. Müsli und Glüetli gehen über einen Bach. Glüetli fällt ins Wasser.
Müsli lacht, sodaß ihm das Pelzli verspringt.

2. Ems im Turtmannstal, Jegerlehner, *Sagen und Märchen aus Oberwallis*
(1913), S. 142, Nr. 163. Bei Haavio fehlt diese „Schweizer Schnurre", Wesselski,
a. a. O., 25, kennzeichnet sie, wie folgt:[23]

> Die Maus und die Grille, die auf einem Spaziergang an ein Wässerlein kommen,
> überbrücken es mit einem Strohhalm. Als die Grille, die zuerst darüber geht, ins
> Wasser fällt, muß das Mäuslein so lachen, daß es sich das Pelzchen sprengt. Der
> Schuhmacher, der es flicken soll, verlangt Borsten, das Schwein Mehl, der Müller
> Korn, der Acker Mist, den liefert ihm die Maus selber und schließlich flickt ihr der
> Schuster den Pelz.

---

[23] (Auf die Stelle hat mich Archer Taylor aufmerksam gemacht. Dank!). Jegerlehner, *Sagen und
Märchen aus Oberwallis.* (Basel, 1913), Turtmannstal, Nr. 163, S. 142. Der Wichtigkeit dieses
Textes halber führe ich ihn ganz an (Grilli ist wohl eine Verballhornung von Glüetli):

163. Z'Müsi und z'Grilli.

Z'Müsi und z'Grilli hend wolle ne Spaziergang machu. Du schints cho bis anes Wasserli. Da
sig keis Briggelti gsyn. Da sindsch z'rat einig cho, fir e Strohhalm drüber z'tue fir es Briggelti.
Du het selle z'Grilli zersche drüber ga. Das ischt aber derwegu abgheit, und du hets du z'Wasserli
gno. Z'Müsi het e so agfangu lachä, daß z'Belzi zersprängt het. Du isch es zum Schuhmacher
gangu, daß er em z'Belzi biezi (flicke). Der het mu aber gseit, er chönne's nit machu ohni Burscht
(Borsten). Du ischt's zum Schwyn gegangu fir Burscht. Das het mu gseit, es miessi zersch Mähl
ha, daß em z'Burscht wachsi. Du ischt's zum Miller gangu fir Mähl. Der het mu gseit: „I chou
dr nit Mähl gä ohni Choru (Korn)". Ischt z'Müsi zum Acher gangu fir Choru. Der het mu gseit:
„I chou dr nit Choru gä ohni Buw (Mist)". Du het sie z'Müsi umgkehrt und het im e Hufe dar-
gschiessu, du heig em dr Acher schön Chor gä, dermit isch es zem Miller gangu, dr Miller heig im
Mähl gä, das het es em Schwyn gebrungu, du hets vom Schwyn chönne Burscht näh, darmit
isch es zum Schuhmacher gangu, und der het im z'Belzi wieder gebiezt.

> Där wo schi über z'andre schi Schade fröüt,
> chunt gwendli sälber gärn dry.   (Ems)

Woher dieses Motiv des beschädigten Pelzes stammt, darüber kann auf Grund der neuen Fassungen aus dem Gailtal wohl kein Zweifel walten: vom noch nicht klassifizierten Märchentyp der Fassungen von Brdo-Egg vom „Mäuslein, das durch einen Zaun kroch und sich das Bäuchlein zerriß".

Diese Art von Beschädigung steht übrigens nicht vereinzelt da. In einer Reihe von mecklenburgischen Märchen von der Katze und dem Katzmann bleibt der Kater in einem Dorngeäst, Nußbaumgeäst hängen.[24]

Dieselbe Sprache spricht auch die Helferkette in den schweizerisch-elsässischen und slowenischen Varianten. Dies zeigt anschaulich folgende *Tabelle*:

BP I, 137:	: Schuster[a],	Sau,	Müller,	Acker,	Kuh,	Wiese,	Bach
Slov. Gosp.	: Schuster[a],	Sau,	Müller,	Acker,	Ochs,	—	Bach
Brdo-Egg 1	: Schuster,	Sau,	—	Acker,	Kuh,	Wiese,	Quelle
Brdo-Egg 2–3	: Schuster,	Sau,	—	Maispfl. Acker	Kuh,	Mahd[b]	—
Blače-Vdbg. 1	: Schuster,	Sau,	Müller,	Acker gedüngt[c],	—	—	—
Blače-Vdbg. 2	: Schuster,	Sau,	Kuh,	Mäher, Hausfrau, Müller, Acker gedüngt[c]			

(a) Schuster verlangt (Schweins-)Borsten für die Spitze des Schusterdrahtes; sonst wird (Schweins-)Fett verlangt für den Faden. (b) Mäuschen mäht die Wiese selbst. (c) Mäuslein düngt den Acker mit selbsteigenem Dung.

Die Helferkette der schweizerischen und der elsässischen Fassung, wie sie in der ersten Reihe steht, angeführt nach BP II, 137 Anm., stimmt genau mit der Sutermeisterschen Fassung aus dem Baselland und der ersten französischen aus dem Kanton Bern im *Schweiz. Archiv* 15 (1911) überein. In der elsässischen Fassung ist die Wiese entfallen (wie in der Fassung des *Slov. Gospodar*), in der oberwallisischen aus Ems im Turtmannstal reicht dieselbe Helferkette nur bis zur Selbstdüngung des Ackers durch die Maus, genau wie in den Fassungen von Blače-Vorderberg. Die Angaben der Helferketten in Sigeln bei *Martti Haavio*, Kettenmärchen II, FFC 99, S. 9 (GG 2,6, auch sonst) sind ungenau, teils auch falsch.

Die in BP I, 137 angeführte Helferkette der schweizerischen und der elsässischen Fassung — wie sie in der ersten Reihe steht — wird durch Jegerlehners Variante und den Schluß der französischen Variante 1 aus dem Bernischen bestätigt:

La rivière donna de l'eau au pré; le pré donna de foin au boeuf; le boeuf donna du fumier au champ, le champ donna du blé au meunier, le meunier donna du son a la truie; la truie donna de la soie au cordonnier, le cordonnier (appareilla) prépara son poiçon pour recoudre la panse de la souris. Mais en attendant, la souris (était) avait crevé.

[24] *Haavio* II, S. 11.

16 Taylor

Der Tod am Schluß entspricht der Fassung Brdo-Egg 1. Ganz besonders zu betonen ist auch der vollkommene Zusammenklang der Helferkette von Oberwallis und von Blače-Vorderberg samt der Selbsthilfe der Maus durch Düngung des Ackers aus dem eigenen Leib. Bezeichnend ist die Variante aus Ems im Turtmannstal in Oberwallis auch deshalb, weil sie aus jeder Gruppe der slowenischen Fassungen je ein spezifisches Motiv in sich vereinigt: die Schweinsborsten der Fassung des *Slov. Gospodar*, die Selbstdüngung des Ackers der Fassung von Blače-Vorderberg und das Zerreißen des Pelzes der Fassung von Brdo-Egg.

Alles das spricht dafür, daß der Mt. 2034A (Z41.4.1) entstanden ist durch allmähliges Einsickern von Motiven aus dem nicht klassifizierten Typ, dem die Fassungen von Brdo-Egg angehören, in den Mt. 925 (Strohhalm, Kohle und Bohne), zuerst der Maus statt der Bohne, dann der bäuerlichen Helferkette; zuletzt kam in einigen Fassungen auch noch die Katze aus dem Mt. 2034 (Z41.4) hinzu.

Der Typ von Blače-Vorderberg unterscheidet sich vom Typ von Brdo-Egg nur dadurch, daß die Verletzung des Bäuchleins unter dem Einfluß des Mt. 2034 durch die Verletzung des Schwanzes ersetzt wurde.

Die beiden nicht kontaminierten, also die ältesten Typen sind daher der Mt. 2034 (Z41.4), über welchen die slowenischen Fassungen nichts aussagen als dessen Existenz, und der noch nicht klassifizierte Typ von Brdo-Egg.

Slovenska Akademija Znanosti in Umetnosti, Ljubljana

OBSERVATIONS ON ALOISII MARLIANI IN *MARTINUM LUTERUM ORATIO*

JOHN G. KUNSTMANN

[Sincere congratulations and best wishes for a long *otium cum dignitate*. The following lines are meant to provide you with a few minutes of light reading.]

In recent years historians interested in Luther, especially church historians, have investigated *young* Luther either exclusively or with special emphasis. Whether they are right or wrong in their assumptions concerning the relatively greater importance of the Reformer's earlier years, it must be admitted that they have succeeded, in a number of instances, in separating fact from pious legend, and that they, occasionally, have furnished new insights, with the result that we are now fairly well acquainted with the span of Luther's life extending from 1483 to 1525 or 1530 —with at least one conspicuous exception: comparatively little work has been done to date by *literary* historians on Luther's early *Italian* opponents, those who wrote against him in the era of Pope Leo X.

Easily the most important of these men was the distinguished physician-theologian-humanist Aloisius Marlianus. About him and his anti-Luther oration. I shall make a few remarks, in the hope that others may be prompted further to investigate him and his colleagues and their writings, an investigation which, in my opinion, is needed, if only for the sake of *Vollständigkeit*, and which, I am sure, will add considerably to our understanding of the West-European background of the German Reformation and its protagonist, Luther.

Aloisius Marlianus, a relative of the celebrated historian Peter Martyr, was born in Milan, Italy. Having completed his medical studies, he became physician to the son of Emperor Maximilian from his first wife, the Archduke Philip, later known as Philip I, The Beautiful, King of Spain. In 1506, Marlianus accompanied him to Castile. This journey and the death of his royal patron a few months after the arrival there was written up by Marlianus in his *Epistola qua calamitosa Philippi Regis Hispaniae in Hispaniam navigatio describitur*, of which a Johannes Prüss print (Strassburg, 1514) was known to Conrad Gesner and his redactor, Iosias Simler, in 1545 and 1574, respectively.

It is not impossible—as a matter of fact, it is very probable, that the intimate relationship of physician and patient and, moreover, the close association which Marlianus was bound to have had with Philip's mentally deranged queen, Joanna, created between him and the members of the Habsburg family a feeling of belonging together, of trust, and reliance. And so it is not unexpected that Philip's father, Maximilian, and especially the son of Philip and Joanna, Emperor Charles V, should employ Marlianus as their official and unofficial counsellor. Particularly the son, Charles, for whom Marlianus invented the device "Plus ultra," leaned on Marlianus most heavily—so much so that he was fittingly described by Peter Martyr as *Caesaris semi-anima*. Marlianus became even more useful and, incidentally, more powerful as adviser to Charles, after he, being versed in theology and having entered the service of the Church, was made bishop of Túy in Galicia in Spain. This event took place about August, 1516. It is as a native of Milan, as bishop of Túy, and as member of the Privy Council of Charles V that Marlianus appears on the title page of his important anti-Luther oration. It seems unlikely that he spent much time in his bishopric. He accompanied Charles to the Netherlands and to Germany and was at his side during the diet at Worms. And in this city he died, in 1521, during the night of May 10 to May 11. That he was against Luther has been mentioned. But his stand against the Reformer and his anti-Lutheran advice to the Emperor did not automatically make him a favorite of Leo X and his emissaries at the imperial court and during the Diet at Worms. One has but to read the reports sent from Worms to Rome by the papal legate Aleander to learn that Marlianus, indeed, was a staunch defender of the Catholic Church and that he was working zealously and successfully against Luther and the Lutherans. At the same time, it is evident that Aleander was irked by the independence of the all-powerful Marlianus and by the necessity of handling him diplomatically, lest Marlianus proceed counter to the wishes of the Roman Curia. Aleander, understandably, advised the Roman Chancery to bestow a suitable award on Marlianus, to keep him "buttered up." Whether or not, as a result of this recommendation, Leo X actually awarded Marlianus the red hat shortly before the latter's death— this has been claimed—I do not know. One of the reasons why Marlianus may have been suspected by Aleander and other champions of the Curia of having only lukewarm feelings for Rome was, undoubtedly, Marlianus' association with Erasmus, or perhaps Erasmus' association with Marlianus. For it was Erasmus who made an effort to conciliate Marlianus after the latter, having been made a bishop, had become a patron of letters. At the time prior to and during the Diet at Worms, Erasmus was openly attacked by several influential persons as pro-Lutheran, and it was said, explicitly, or by implication, that Erasmus was the real author of writings circulated under the names of Luther and Melanchthon. It is these outspoken attacks and these insinuations against Erasmus which constitute the chief content of the letters exchanged between Marlianus and Erasmus toward the end of 1520 and during the first months of 1521, letters which indicate that Marlianus himself was more than inclined to side with the enemies of Erasmus, even though the correspondence oozes with protestations of mutual esteem. At any rate, Marlianus' association with Erasmus and his letters to him are evidence of still another facet of Marlianus' accomplishments: he was a humanist. His devotion to humanism is exhibited in his interest in the classics, the cultivation of a fine style in his Latin letters, and, very concretely, in the two poems he composed in the humanist tradition (*Silvae fortunae* Brescia, 1503; and *De Bataviae laudibus*, Leyden, 1511) and in the two orations which are preserved: one was composed for Charles' Chapter of the Order of the Golden Fleece in January 1517 (printed in Basel, June 1517, by Pamphilus Gengenbach); the other is the remarkable address against Luther, *In Martinum Luterium Oratio*, which he declamed in Worms prior to November 6, 1520, and which was, I believe, printed in Rome early in 1521.

The *Oratio* is written in the elegant Latin of a veteran humanist. It does not use the violent tone of theological invective which one encounters almost on every hand at that time. On the whole, the *Oratio* is conciliatory. After all, *mit Speck fängt man Mäuse*. Luther is called *vir non omnino malus*—not wholly bad. He is the child of Christian parents, has had a Christian upbringing, and has grown to manhood *non sine magna laude*—with an excellent record. It is not really this *non omnino malus* Luther who is responsible for the turmoil in Germany: rather is it a Luther who was carried away by wrath and passion and, above all, a Luther who was actually the cat's-paw of unscrupulous plotters who are using him as their "front." Easily the worst of these undercover men is Erasmus. To be sure, Erasmus' name is not spelled out with so many letters. Nevertheless, it is he who is meant—Erasmus, the real author of some of the more nefarious works which are passed out as Luther's writings—the same Erasmus in whose acknowledged publications can be found false doctrines of the most pernicious kind. Does Luther realize what his activities entail? The Germans have captured the whole world. Military discipline, all the arts, wisdom, eloquence, have found a home in Germany. No longer is Italy the golden land. But what of it? As long as the Germans do not turn their power and skill against religion! But that is exactly what is being done now, and Luther, who perhaps is not aware of it, is the spiritus rector of this rebellion. By waging war against the city of Rome and the Capitol the Germans are, in truth, waging war against their own altars and flocks. And, thus, by permitting their intellects to fare forth without the proper religious restraints, they are lining up catapults in an attack on the head of the Church. Luther, foolishly, has followed the advice of counsellors who, combining the highest degree of impiousness with the highest degree of shamelessness, directed him to show forth the sins in the personal lives of the popes and the lack of morality of the Holy See. How different from your conduct, o Luther and Lutherans, is the conduct of Him who, when the woman caught in adultery was brought into His presence, stooped down and wrote in the sand the sins of her *accusers*, condemning *them* and *absolving* her, cautioning her to sin no more. (Here Marlianus does not follow the text of John 8.) That is how Jesus dealt with such as accused others of sin! Surely, o Lutherans, to list your own sins, neither an immensely large threshing-floor, nor an entire battlefield would be large enough. One would need a globe—Marlianus knew the earth was not flat—to register just the two categories of your sinful ambition and your desire for notoriety. The Germans, that most pious nation, whose sacred duty it is with arms and with counsel to protect the Catholic religion, should realize that Luther is leading them to revolution and anarchy. Thus they are actually bent on destroying their own Holy Roman Empire. Indeed, Luther is reviving the Hussite heresy and its unhappy after-effects. Now you Germans do not mean to make liars out of the *German* emperor, the *German* princes, and the *German* Council who and which condemned Huss and his followers, do you? – It is, indeed, insanity, o Luther, to insist that you alone are wise. But you *will* be wise, if you listen to me, your best friend.

In the second part of the *Oratio* Marlianus defends against Luther the prayers for the dead, the primacy of the Roman pontifex, and the sacrament of confession. The arguments he advances against Luther and the Lutherans are the traditional ones. Marlianus presents them, however, comparatively calmly and in excellent rhetorical style. Luther is evidently in danger of confusing religion and philosophy, reason and faith, paying more attention to philosophy and reason. His basic attitude is, therefore, one of pride—something very dangerous. In order to save himself, Luther should return to the fold. If you have fallen, o Luther, it simply proves that you are a human being. Admit your mistake. Be no longer proud. Repent, and retract your errors. St. Augustin, your spiritual father, did the same with certain of his writings. And you Lutherans, you should heed the same admonition, lest you find that both God and men turn against you.

Copies of this oration of which I have given only the most saliant points, are today available probably in Pavia and Munich, and certainly in the British Museum and, to mention one American depository, in the Rare Book Room of the University of Chicago Library. I have, so far, investigated two printed 16th-century editions of the *Oratio*. One of them was printed or purports to have been printed in Rome, no date. The other was definitely printed in Vienna, in 1521, by Johannes Singriener. I shall confine myself to a discussion of one problem connected with the Rome edition. There were, to be sure, other 16th-century printings of the *Oratio*. One was probably published by Kaiser in Cologne (no date), and a second and a third one assuredly by Martin Landsberg, also known as Baccalaureus Herbipolensis, in Leipzig. One of the Landsberg editions is dated 1522. The British Museum claims to have "the genuine Rome edition" as distinguished from the one which purports to have been printed in Rome. I confess that this statement of which I have a photostatic copy means nothing to me, at least not now. I, likewise, fail to understand the entry in Olschki, *Choix de Livres...* (Florence, 1923), p. 1996, no. 4816, where a *sine anno et loco* print of the *Oratio* is dated by the compiler "Rome, ca. 1530." The description given by Olschki fits the 1521 Singriener Vienna edition with its "beautiful flower-border" and the five Latin distichs on the verso of the title-page by one Paulus Exorcista. It is, of course, not impossible that we have here a *reprint* of the 1521 Vienna edition of the *Oratio*. The fact, however, that the Olschki-Rome print is adorned by the distinctive Singriener flower-border forces me to doubt, for the time being, the separate existence of this Rome edition. If I have confused you with respect to the existence and identification and dating of the several existing or postulated 16th-century editions of the *Oratio*, then I have succeeded, indeed. At present, there is nothing but confusion apropos of these points, and continued investigation and, especially, autopsy are sorely needed.

A similar state of affairs exists with respect to the literary-historical interpretation and evaluation of the text itself. Only the following have significantly contributed to the study of the *Oratio*: (1) Otto Clemen, in *Beiträge zur Reformationsgeschichte aus Büchern und Handschriften der Zwickauer Ratsschulbibliothek*, III (Berlin, 1903); (2) Friedrich Lauchert, in *Die italienischen literarischen Gegner Luthers* (Freiburg i. B., 1912) [This is *Erläuterungen und Ergänzungen zu Janssens Geschichte des deutschen Volkes*, hg. von Ludwig von Pastor, VIII]; and (3), several notes in the Weimar edition of Luther's Works, *Briefwechsel*, II (1931). More than 50, more than 40, and more than 25 years ago! and in each case only a few pages! Nobody, so far, to the best of my knowledge, has actually compared, line for line and word for word, the various extant editions. It was blithely assumed that we have the text of the *Oratio*. I have compared the text of the purported Rome edition with that of the 1521 Vienna edition and, not counting differences in the appearance of the title-page or simple spelling mistakes or spelling variants, and not counting the presence or absence of the vocatives *Luteri* and *Luteriani* and not counting the accidental or intentional transposition of words, I had to list a considerable number of major differences in the texts of the two editions! This certainly demands an explanation. Most of these differences, both the minor and major ones, in my opinion indicate that the Rome edition was printed in great haste directly from Marlianus' manuscript or from a copy of his original manuscript. This assumption would account for the fairly numerous "boners" in the Rome edition. It would also account for the fact that the Rome edition is, from beginning to end, an *oration* containing an abundance of questions, exclamations, and statements directly addressed to Luther or the Lutherans. The 1521 Vienna edition, on the other hand, seems to be a *revised* version of the Rome edition. True, it is still an oration. But it tones down the rhetorical character of the original: it dispenses with most of the vocatives of the Rome text. It is no longer as faithful a reproduction of the *viva vox* of the orator as printer's ink can make it, but rather the publication of an important *Zeitdokument*. And so the Vienna edition, correctly, ends with the FINIS of the *printer*, while the Rome edition, fittingly, stops with the DIXI of the *speaker*. From my remarks it is obvious that I place the Rome edition *before* the Vienna edition. And since the Vienna edition is clearly dated 1521, I date the Rome edition "beginning of 1521".

According to Goldschmidt, however, the Rome edition was not printed in Rome. "In spite of its explicit, though anonymous, imprint, we cannot believe that it can be a Roman, or even an Italian production" (E. P. Goldschmidt Co., Ltd., London, catalogue 87, n.d., p. 24, No. 90). And Johnson of the British Museum agrees with Goldschmidt: "I agree, the imprint is fictitious and the book certainly printed in Germany, probably Strassburg" (Photostat of letter by Johnson of the British Museum to Goldschmidt, dated Feb. 28, no year).

I disagree. I must admit I have as yet not been able to identify the interesting printer's device on the last leaf. But as long as the imprint clearly states *Impressum Romae apud aedem Divi Marci*, "Printed in Rome near the Church of St. Mark" or "Printed in Rome near the temple of Divus Marcus," i.e., Marcus Aurelius—topographically speaking, there would be little difference—and as long as there is no *proof* to the effect that the imprint is or must be fictitious, I shall assume that the imprint means what it says. The burden of proof is on the other side. In addition, I am able to cite two sets of facts in support of my claim that the Rome edition was actually produced in Rome.

(1) It has been said that there was no such place as "apud aedem Divi Marci" in Rome around 1500. Now the church of San Marco in Rome dates from the Middle Ages. Furthermore, San Marco was one of the titular churches of cardinal priests in the city of Rome. Again, San Marco in Rome is important, since about 1465, in the annals of Renaissance architecture and reconstruction of existing buildings. But this is not all. *Apud aedem Divi Marci* is not *ein falscher und fingierter Druckort*. I have found two other books printed at this address. An incunabulum was printed by Vitus Pücher in Rome "apud Sanctum Marcum," and in 1517 Gabrielis Bononiensus issued a book "Impressum Rome prope Divi Marci." These books are not ghost books. They were examined as late as 1898 and 1864, respectively. I might also mention that the *printer*—yes, the printer—Jean-Philippe La Legname de Messine, in 1470, lived in Rome "in via papae prope S. Marcum." There was, then, such a place in Rome before and after 1500.

(2) It occurred to me to look for the watermark in the paper used in the Rome edition. It was not easy to gain a clear impression of this mark. It happened to be close to the inner margin and it was, consequently, distributed over two leaves. And for obvious reasons I could not take the rare copy of the Rome edition apart. At last, however, I succeeded in tracing a fair copy of the "filigrane." After that it was only a question of time and eye strain to identify the watermark. It is one of the "Sirènes." It is exactly and in every detail the *mermaid* of Briquet, vol. IV, no. 13, 884. The mermaid watermark is of *Italian* provenance. And exactly this particular mermaid watermark, No. 13, 884, turns up for the first time in *Rome*, in 1501, and in Rome, in 1502, and, according to plentiful evidence, was used in Italy throughout the 16th and 17th centuries. Incidentally, my mermaid with her two alluring tails, inscribed in a circle, is one of the most beautiful women I have encountered.

The demonstrated existence of a place "apud aedem Divi Marci" and the fact that the paper on which the *Oratio* was printed was Italian paper do not, of course, constitute 100 per centum mathematical proof that the *Oratio* was printed in Rome. They disprove, however, the assertion that the *Oratio* could not have been printed there. The proof that the Oratio was actually printed, and printed first, in Rome, early in 1521, I shall submit elsewhere.

University of North Carolina,
Chapel Hill, North Carolina

SOME NOAH TALES FROM SWEDEN

Francis Lee Utley

In the late 1930's, spurred on by Archer Taylor who had told me of the treasures in foreign archival collections, I was busy searching for new Noah tales to supplement the core of such material in Oskar Dähnhardt's *Natursagen*.[1] Fresh stories had been pouring in from Oskar Loorits of Estonia, Jonas Balys of Lithuania, and Martti Haavio of Finland. It was natural therefore that I write the four great Swedish collections to see whether they had anything. There was good reason to do so, for there was clear evidence from certain fourteenth-century wall-paintings in Scania and other parts of southern Sweden that the basic story of the Devil in the Ark (Mt. 825) had existed in that area.[2] Art historians, aware of the tendency for such iconographical motifs and styles to travel from England to Sweden, had made much of the correspondence between these paintings and the illuminations in a British Museum manuscript, Queen Mary's Psalter, also of the fourteenth century.[3]

---

[1] (Leipzig and Berlin, 1907–1912), I, 257–314.

[2] See Anna Jean Mill, "Noah's Wife Again," *PMLA*, LXVI (1941), 622–633; Andreas Lindblom, *La Peinture Gothique en Suède et en Norvège* (London, 1916), pp. 210–214, 242, pl. 42; and his "Den Apokrifa Noahsagen i Mideltidens Konst och Litteratur," *Nordisk Tidskrift för Vetanskap, Konst och Industri*, 1917, pp. 358–368. First noted by N. M. Mandelgren, *Monuments Scandinaves du Moyen Age* (Paris, 1862), pl. xiii. The monuments are at Edshult (Småland), Villberga (Uppland), Risinge and Örberga (Östergötland).

[3] Sir George Warner, ed., *Queen Mary's Psalter* (London, 1912), pp. 13–15, 56–57, pl. 9–12. The manuscript is Royal 2. B. vii. The late Philip Souers suggested that I write to the art historian Johnny Roosval, who responded from Alnäs, Stockholm, on May 16, 1939. He believed that Lindblom's conclusion assigning the paintings to French or English influence is correct, so far as artistic style is concerned. But he refused to be dogmatic about the genesis of the folktale, which he admitted might come from the East.

258

But there was certainly a possibility that the tale might have reached Sweden from Eastern Europe, where it is well attested and where it probably originated. In any event, there ought to be modern oral tales to correspond to the medieval icons.

It was to no avail: the archives reported nothing. C. W. von Sydow stated flatly in a letter dated from Lund June 6, 1939: "Li etiofabules pri Noah e su arc ne es conosset ex un sol sved collection scrit o printet." He gave me some comfort: "Ma to ne deve significer que illi ne existe in sved tradition, nam tal un poc despectosi jocant narrationes ne es tro respectat del popul self, e li collectores ne ha demandet les. Si on nu sercha les che li popul, on va forsan trovar les... Yo va misser vor questiones ad omni nor rapportatores in li different districtes e yo espera que li reponses va esser positiv. Yo tamen ne crede que vu posse reciver alquel informationes ante li mense de octobre hoannu."[4] But then intervened the war, and after it von Sydow's death (March 4, 1952), and I assumed that nothing had come of his generous offer.

In the spring of 1955 I had a brief but profitable visit to Sweden, during which I visited the archives at Uppsala and Stockholm directed by Dag Strömbäck and Sigurd Erixon. I asked anyone who would listen my usual question — did anyone know of any Swedish Noah tales? Miss Åsa Nyman of the Uppsala Landsmåls- och Folkminnesarkivet revived my hopes a little. She provided me with the following two fragments of the authentic Mt. 825, from their special file on origin legends:

> When Noah's Ark stopped on the mountain, Noah made a fire. A serpent runs into the fire. Noah throws the ashes around himself. From that come fleas and lice (Ulma 303:170 c, p. 26).

· · ·

> When Noah built the Ark he had a stone as chopping-block. The serpent escaped from the flood through a knot-hole of the Ark (Ulma 736, p. 113, 110).[5]

Here the "serpent" is both the helpful but demanding animal and the Devil. Miss Nyman provided me with even better news, that the Lund Folklivsarkivet had once sent a questionnaire to its collectors containing these items:

10. How the devil came into the Ark and what he did there.
11. How flies, serpents, vermin and the like came into the Ark and what they did there.
12. How the animals helped Noah.

[4] The language, which seems easily comprehensible to any student of modern European languages, is probably Novial.

[5] Ulma is an abbreviation for Uppsala Landsmåls- och Folkminnesarkivet.

13. How Noah's wife appears and what she did.
14. How some animals refused to go into the Ark. (Which, why?)
15. How some animals were thrown out of the Ark.
16. How Noah rescued an ogre.[6]

On the advice of Albert Eskeröd of the Stockholm Outdoor Museum (Nordiska Museet, Skansen), I wrote to Dr. Anna Birgitta Rooth of Folklivsarkivet Lund, who was then in the United States. On her return she sent me microfilm of six responses to the questionnaire: M5965, M6414 : 3, M6504 : 1–26, M10958 : 1, and M10990 : 1–3. Not only were they crammed with tales of Noah, but they clearly were the completion of the promise von Sydow had made to me. On page 9 of M5965 the collector, Carl Viking, remarked: "I have no doubt that the American scholar of this questionnaire has heard far more about Noah and the animals when he travelled in Finland, Estonia, Latvia and England; but in our country the forefathers never liked to joke about the Holy Men of the Bible." This was proof positive that I had been mentioned as the curious inquirer (though I have never been in Latvia), and the mild rebuke to other nations and myself reflects a remark Viking had heard from a cantor of Kråksmåla, the then deceased J. A. Thorsaa: "I have heard (it is certainly an old monkish saga) the following: that when Noah opened the door ot the ark, the animals in pairs walked in according to God's command. The devil managed to drive in several of those animals which he had bewitched but Noah threw them out, because he got wind of it. But... to such medieval superstitions about the Bible we must not give credence, though at times we lend our ears to such tales. For the Bible clearly teaches that all flesh perished."[7] It gives a folklorist such pleasure to hear of himself in such close company to the folk that I humbly accepted the lesson and do once more. For these remarks are revelation of a kind of folk pride which kept such tales out of any former "sved collection scrit o printet," as von Sydow had surmised. The fox was there, but he had to be flushed.

[6] The questions slightly resemble those on p. 548 of Seán ó Súilleabháin, *A Handbook of Irish Folklore* (Wexford: Folklore of Ireland Society, 1942): "The Flood (supposed to have started on the day corresponding to St. Swithin's Day); Noah and the Ark (coloured races descended from Noah's son who mocked his father when making the Ark; noise of the hammer blows heard all the world over); animals in the Ark (no stallion)." O Súilleabháin's debt to von Sydow and other Swedish archivists is generously acknowledged, but his list seems to be an independent one based on Irish materials, a large body of which Séamus ó Duilearga and other members of the Irish Folklore Commission have sent me.

[7] These translations of the handwritten Swedish film have been dictated to me by the kindness of my colleague, Wolfgang Fleischhauer. At times I have paraphrased, to avoid problems raised by dialect and by occasional illegibility, but any unmarked omissions are honorable, I hope. Dr. Rooth has made a number of helpful suggestions on the original typescript.

Of all these responses, Carl Viking's (recorded in 1939) is extremely full, though sometimes questionable. He calls on his "memory" for stories ostensibly gathered from some ten informants.[8] He described himself as sixty-five years old, a simple peasant from the parishes of Älgshult or Kråksmåla in the province of Småland, who lacked the necessary studies to get ahead in the world, but who is pleased that he can in some measure contribute to the collection of folk-memories of the land. His best informants were Susanna Erlandsdotter, his mother's mother, and Nils Jonsson, his father's brother, both of them long dead at the time of the questionnaire, to which he replies directly.

To Question 10 he answers that Susanna Erlandsdotter used to speak of Noah's difficulties in building the Ark. "He had to hire workers, for neither Noah himself nor his sons had any success with the enormous undertaking. Grandma said that at that time they had wretched tools. Those that Noah hired to help him with the task made fun of him and said, 'Fool have you been and fool will you stay. You won't get that thing to sea!' They turned their back on Noah, but he doubled their wages and they returned to the building, and at length the ark was finished. Before Noah entered the ark he wished to bring a sacrifice to God. Just as he was in the middle of it the devil, in the shape of a snake, came and said, 'It is true, Noah, that God protected you and furthered your work; but if I hadn't also been helpful the ark would not have been built, and now I want my share of the sacrifice!' But Noah did not want to hear with that ear, and he took *Brännastaken* and hurled the serpent into the flames. [Viking, probably inventing, remarks that these stakes are pieces of juniper or oak which one stirs with in the glowing embers according to Old Norse custom.] But that was a Holy Fire, and the devil (*fan*) could not escape from the fire. So he changed himself into an enormous cloud of flies, gnats, and wasps, and these were able to escape from the fire without singeing their wings, strangely enough. When I commented on that grandma said, 'You surely understand that the devil can do more than mortals,' and that settled it." Viking begins Question 11 with what appears to be a sequel from grandma, "The flies settled on oxen and cows among other animals, when these went into the ark." His memory is faulty, but we seem to have a fuller version of the sequel in the tales told by Ordgren and Ståhle below.

---

[8] (1) Susanna Erlandsdotter, 1800–1896; (2) Nils Johnsson, 1811–1892; (3) Petter Danielsson, 1810–1901; (4) Mathilda Svensson, 1846—?; (5) Enrika Pettersson, 1844—?; (6) the carpenter Johan Petter Pettersson, 1838–1936; (7) the soldier Carl Johan Augsdahle, 1825–1916; (8) Mina Jansson, 1840–1937; (9) Johan Jonsson, 1841–1939; (10) Albert Svartz, born in 1852. Despite this array of authority, Mrs. Rooth warns me, Viking was probably too helpful, too imaginative. He was later dismissed by the Archive for testimony "too good to be true." Yet, as we see by comparisons, there are many authentic folk-elements scattered throughout his report.

In the Bible Noah's sacrifice comes after the landing of the Ark, not before its
launching. The burning of the helpful snake in the Eastern tales is also a sequel
to the Deluge.[9] The snake had been asked to fill the hole in the Ark which the
Devil had gnawed in it (usually in the form of a mouse). Noah promised him the
blood of one man a day after the flood, but to escape his promise he burned the
snake, with patriarchal superiority to ordinary morality, and the snake's ashes
became flies and gnats and mosquitoes and they still have their blood of one
statistical man per day. (A group of medical faculty to whom I recently told this
story added, with proper scientific credence, "More!") In Viking's version the
devil is identified with the helpful serpent (he is never explicitly so equated in
versions from other lands) and, since Noah had obviously parted from the devil
long before, Viking's tale has to shift the Bible's sacrifice and the serpent's burning
to the period before the deluge begins. Yet in gratitude to both Viking and von
Sydow may it be said that we probably have here a true Swedish *oikotype*, for
the independent fragments from Uppsala quoted above also identify devil with
serpent.[10]

Viking continues with his answer to Question 11. "As a boy I said to my
uncle, informant No. 2, 'Why should God create flies, gnats, ticks, and then
save them in the Ark? They are after all a pest to men and cattle.' Uncle
answered, 'See, such *Yllmark* are the devil's offspring and have hung behind
the end since the Fall of Man [*syndafallet*, not *syndaflod*]; but you should
realize that God created fleas and lice so that lazy people should be forced
to scratch themselves.[11] The gnats were the worst in the Ark, for they have a
Judas-mind, and they say Friend, friend, friend[12] until people are bitten, just
as the Christ-traitor Judas did.'" Uncle refers snakes in general to the story
of Mother Eve.

[9] See, for instance, Dähnhardt, I, 279–283; Thompson motif A 2001.

[10] On oikotypes see C. W. von Sydow, "Märchenforschung und Philologie," *Årsbok* of the Vetenskaps-
Societeten i Lund, 1932, p. 16; and his *Selected Papers on Folklore* (Copenhagen: Rosenkilde and
Bagger, 1948), pp. 212–213 and *passim*. The devil in many tales of the kind is said to be the in-
ventor of such vermin (Dähnhardt, I, 164–170, 173, 189, and for dualistic tales with a possible
Iranian source in general *ibid*. I, 1–205).

[11] The translation is not wholly clear. The tale is probably the common one which attributes insects
to a punishment for the laziness of women of or a neighboring ethnic group. See Thompson A 2005;
Maurits de Meyer, *Les Contes Populaires de la Flandre* (Helsinki [*FFC* No. 37], 1921), p. 89 (no.
125a).

[12] "Vån, vån, vån," an onomatopoeic etiology. Related to the group of tales on "Tierstimmen und
andere Naturlaute," which have a honored place in the Folk Fellows' indexes. See, for instance,
Antti Aarne, *Estnische Märchen und Sagenvarianten* (Hamina [*FFC* No. 25], 1918), pp. 153–156;
Dähnhardt, *Natursagen*, III, 355–404.

A more or less proper version of the hole in the ark story then appears as answer to question twelve on helpful animals. Viking says: "That the animals helped Noah to stop leaks in the ark we have heard of only by chance. Grandma...talked about it's being a stormy night when the ark fastened onto (crashed into?) the Mountain of Ararat. All eight people were lying down and sleeping, but it was a crushing blow when the ark bumped against the mountain,[13] so Noah rushed up on deck with only his shirt on, but he did not find any damage there. Then he went down into the hold and there was a hole in the bottom, but the bear sat down over the hole and prevented the water from coming in. But then a hungry fish watched for his chance to bite off the bear's tail as it was at that time. It was then long, but since that night the bear has had only a stump for a tail." A striking *oikotype*! The bear of the North has significantly replaced the Russian and Asian serpent, and along with himself he has attracted into the story the celebrated animal tale of Tail-Fisher.[14]

Question 13 leads to a rather lengthy story about Noah's wife, which Viking had from his third informant, Petter Danielsson, a neighbor in the village of Krokshult in the parish of Algshult. "When Noah was building the ark, he had only a grey stone (*gråsten*) as chopping-block. He had to be careful not to hit the stone and make the axe dull. The devil envied Noah's building of the ark because he knew it was to be the salvation of Noah and his family. The devil knew also that women were especially susceptible to flattery, and he decided to mislead Noah's wife.... One day he came to her and said, 'You are beautiful, woman, and Noah loves you. But you two don't have much to do with one another. For he stands yonder and builds at his ark and longs for your presence. You ought to go to him, for he is desirous of your love.'" She obeyed and tried to lure Noah to intercourse with "honey-sweet words," but he was preoccupied and paid no attention. "But women can be troublesome. She began to dance before Noah and unnecessarily bared her body." (Dr. Rooth thinks this is Viking's invention.) He was distracted, and the axe hit the stone and became dull. He swore, and the devil was evoked, and offered his help. But Noah sent him away. Yet he owed a task to the devil after calling him up, and he ordered the devil to make sewing-needles from the pubic hairs of his wife. The devil "was going to press them straight with a warm iron, but the more he pressed them the more the hairs curled, so he had to give up." Then, said the old sagaman, "the devil wept."

[13] This recalls a Kurdish tale told in the vicinity of Ararat itself, which explains the two-peaked mountain. See *Sbornik materialov dlia opisania mestnostei i plemen Kavkaza*, I, part 2, pp. 107–108 (translated for me by Professor Justina Epp).

[14] Mt. 2. Antti Aarne and Stith Thompson, *The Types of the Folk-Tale* (Helsinki [FFC 74], 1928), p. 22.

The dulling of the axe on the chopping-block is a true remnant of the Eastern tales,[15] but the accompanying motif, in which Noah's wife gives a devil's potion to Noah to find out the secret of the ark, is almost wholly obscured by substitution. The true sequels, the destruction of the ark by the devil and the entrance of the devil to the ark, are replaced by a primitive-sounding obscenity about sewing-needles from pubic hairs, badly adapted and inconsequential. Yet we may have echoes here of the potion motif in addition to the chopping-block and axe (which, being a sharp instrument, may have attracted the needle into its magnetic field). Nowhere else, so far as I know, was Noah's wife quite so openly seductive, but her potion was a woman's devilish trick, and the calling up of the devil by a misplaced curse ("Come in, you devil!", addressed either to Noah's wife or to the hesitant Ass)[16] is an authentic part of the tradition.

After this story Viking jumps to Question 16, and remarks "That Noah rescued a giant we have not heard, but I will tell a story of Noah's tar-burners as compensation." Here his willingness betrays him, and he somewhat cavalierly attaches a well-known tale, that of Myself or Noman, to the building of the ark, on the strength of Genesis vi. 14, in which God commands Noah to pitch the ark within and without. (He gives the Genesis reference himself.) The story concerns a tar-burner named Self (*Själv*), hired by Noah. Self is tempted by a fallen angel who has turned into a wood-nymph with a hollow back. Sent by Satan, the nymph "came stark naked and sat astride on a pine-branch and swung her legs back and forth and winked at Self." He ignored her, and in revenge she tried to put out his fire; in return he hurled a scoop of hot tar into the hollow place in her back. So she fled, but her loud complaints were not heeded, any more than those of Polyphemus when he cried that Noman had put out his single eye.[17] All of this is presented by Viking with evident humorous relish, including an oblique remark about "very learned scholars," and notably this time with no mention of an informant. One suspects him of pulling our leg. The mention of a naked Noah's wife in the last story may have combined with the pitching of the ark to produce this tale, though of course it is also possible that the rather inconclusive intrusion of a lovely Noah's wife the former tale may owe something to the wood-nymph who tempted Själv.

[15] I have it in a number of Estonian tales collected by Hurt and sent me by Oskar Loorits before the war from the Estonian Archives. It is related to Hungarian examples cited by Dähnhardt, I, 269–271, but none of these contain the motif of the *dulling* of the axe.

[16] See Dähnhardt, I, 258–259; Bernhard Heller, "Nuḥ," *Encyclopaedia of Islam*, ed. M. Th. Houtsma et al. (Leyden and London, 1913–1934), IV, 948.

[17] Mt. 1137; Thompson motif K 602; Johannes Bolte and Georg Polívka, *Anmerkungen zu den Kinder- und Hausmärchen der Brüder Grimm*, 5 vols. (Leipzig, 1913–1931), III, 378 (many Scandinavian versions are attested).

The pitch recalls to Viking another story, about the old man who is reading the Bible aloud. He reads "And Cain knew his wife..." and then turns over more than one leaf and comes out with "And she was three hundred ells long, fifty ells broad, and thirty ells high, and pitched on the inside and out." His wife remarks that people were big and black in those days, and asks if the Negroes are descended from them. This is an old preacher's jest, which can settle on any part of the Bible.[18]

Viking continues with an answer to Question 14, how some animals refused to enter the ark. Sagaman seven, the soldier Carl Johan Augsdahle, told this one. It was the loon (*lommen*) who refused to enter. Satan had created the loon but forgot to create legs for him. God reminded him of his omission, and Lucifer (Satan) then created two legs and threw them after the loon as it was flying. "But the legs got stuck on the stern-end. For that reason when the loon has to go by chance on land he is not able to walk, but he draws himself forward with his bill on the grass." This bit of unnatural natural history has really nothing intrinsically to do with Noah, but Viking's instinct is correct, for it belongs to the *simia Dei* stories of a dualistic nature which Dähnhardt prefaces to our story of the Devil in the Ark.[19]

Now Viking tells the tale of the cantor Thorsaa which he have already quoted in rebuke to inquisitive American scholars. He is answering Question 15, how some animals were ejected from the ark. He continues with an account, from Mina Jansson, of Noah's planting of the vine and his drunkenness. But it has an apocryphal twist. The devil was annoyed at the righteous souls after the Deluge, who were so good that there were no souls to take to hell. "It didn't pay any more to keep fire-masters, and the fires of hell almost went out by themselves." He fermented the grapes that Noah had planted, and misled Noah into drinking the product. From that time on men get roaring drunk, and hell has never been empty of souls. This story I have not encountered elsewhere, but we should recall that the devil's potion of Mt. 825 is often the origin of wine or spirits, and that the devil is said to have created the various stages of drunkenness by telling Noah to

[18] Mr. Grafton Mintz, after hearing in a seminar this paper with my complaint that though I have several times recorded it but could not at the moment locate a reference, told me that it had been a favorite of his father, the Rev. E. G. Mintz (1890?–1946) of Southport, North Carolina. Here it was a North Carolina minister whose eyes were dimming with age. Two mischievous boys copied out the description of the Ark and pasted it after the name of Ruth in the minister's Bible. The minister read it to the congregation next Sunday and said, "I never saw that before, but it's in the Bible and it must be true!"

[19] Dähnhardt, I, 1–105; see note 10. The misplacement of the legs is achieved in a manner similar to that of another part of the anatomy in the tale cited in note 22. The loon was specifically cited in question 9 of the questionnaire, of which Mrs. Rooth has since provided me a full copy.

17 Taylor

fertilize the vine with the blood of sheep, ape, lion, and pig.[20] Viking's last two contributions are remarks about the cloud formation called Noah's Ark, widely known in Scotland, England, and the Baltic regions,[21] and an imperfect story about the creation of Eve by the devil. Here the collector's notes break off.

None of the other informants or collectors are so cooperative as Viking. M6414, recorded by Aug. Let. Ordgren in 1940 (in the parish of Hallaröd, Skåne), tells how, when the ark landed at Ararat, Noah could not get any of the animals to be first to leave the ark. Then he heard a humming sound outside the ark, a sound he had never heard before. It was the horsefly, who flew noisily round the horned cattle. Then Noah opened the door of the ark and the tormented beasts rushed out first, followed by all the other animals. The hare came last, but he sat and looked at the whole affair. He laughed over his freedom and the whole affair, so hard that his lips split, and that is the origin of his hare-lip. Presumably the horse-fly is an answer to question eleven, how vermin got aboard the ark. The hare's lip is a common origin story theme, and it often takes its beginnings from the Flood.[22]

M6448, collected from her mother by Blenda Andersson in 1940, contains a pointless off-color tale about the aspen leaf. The devil tried to carry off a man, but he broke wind, and the *fis* flew up and rested on an aspen leaf. When the devil tried to take the *fis* from the leaf, it began to tremble, and does so still.[23] Miss

---

[20] Dähnhardt, I, 258, 261–265, 298–314.

[21] I have some forty-five references, all limited to the Baltic Area and the British Isles. See, for instance, Henning Feilberg, *Bidrag til en ordbog over Jyske Almuesmål*, 4 vols. (Kjøbenhavn, 1881–1914), I, 30, and Joseph Wright, *The English Dialect Dictionary*, 6 vols. (London, [1898]), I, 70–71, IV, 284.

[22] The following tale, of which I have variants also from Lithuania and from several Moslem sources, was sent me by Martti Haavio from the Finnish Archives. It was collected in Kiikoinen by R. Koivussaari (KRK 30. ii. 1935). "When the Deluge was near God commanded Noah to take a pair of each species of animal into the ark. Noah did as he was commanded. But during the flood the animals began to multiply excessively, so that the ark was much too full. Then Noah castrated all the animals, so that they could not breed. When the flood was over, Noah began to give the animals their testicles back again. But he no longer remembered which belonged to which, and to the hare fell the testicles of the bull. The hare began to laugh, since his were now so large, and he laughed so much that a fissure appeared in his mouth which is still there." A Pashto (Pakistan) version told by Peter Mayne, *The Narrow Smile* (London: John Murray, 1955), pp. 50–52, attributes the exchange of parts to donkey and camel. Noah is forced to hurl the donkey's portion at the indignant camel, in a fashion similar to Lucifer and the loon in the tale reported by Viking from the soldier Augsdahle.

[23] I myself recall from my college days a similar tale about a hoax played on the devil by a wily Irishman. Since at least four of these informants give something about the aspen leaf, the question-naire must have contained an item seeking the well-known tale about the trembling of that tree because it allowed itself to be used as the wood for the Crucifixion. See, for instance, Thompson Z 232.

Andersson, who reports from the parish of Visland in Småland, then tells another brief tale: "When Noah let the dove fly from the ark the first time it collided with a fly which sat on the uppermost part of a high tree. And when the dove returned it was covered with all kinds of vermin, which it took into the ark." I know of no exact parallels to this tale, which Miss Andersson apparently associates with the tale about the aspen leaf in answer to question eleven.

M6504 is the work of J. I. A. Larsson of the parish of Berga, Småland. He is both collector and informant. His contribution, made in 1940, has little for us: an apology for knowing such unbiblical tales, which he connects with the Sin Against the Holy Ghost, a few remarks about the division of the earth among Noah's sons and the resulting colors of men's skins, an aspen leaf story, and an origin tale on the Creation of Småland.

M10958 was recorded by Ellida Ohlsson of the parish of Skurup in Skåne, in 1949. She has apparently heard of the aspen leaf and of Adam's apple sticking in his throat, but that is all. She does not think such stories worth preserving, but admits that she is uneducated and asks forgiveness for her stupidity and for her boldness in making such a comment, which impugns the efforts of scholars interested in such stories.[24]

M10990 is more rewarding. The collector is August Svinningsson, and his informant, who told him the tale in 1949, is Axel Andersson of the parish of Gnosjö, Småland. "When Noah had finished his ark he needed only to open the door and the animals came by themselves and sprang, ran, and crawled into the ark. The tame animals Noah led in himself. Then God opened the windows of heaven and the water streamed down. On the morning after the first night Noah's wife went to milk the cow, and it was discovered that Noah had forgotten to take the milk-pail into the ark with him... Noah's wife was angry and claimed that Noah always had been careless." So Noah took his Sunday hat and pitched it within and without. "He shaped the hat and made it flat in the crown and the brim stiff." This Noah's wife used for the milk-pail, and after the flood Noah had no other hat to use for festive occasions. "This is why the Sunday hat got the shape and color it has today, and could still be used for milking." The milk-pail is new to me, but the animals' entrance to the ark voluntarily or in obedience to God's command is a common motif in Noah stories.[25]

M11331 was collected in 1949 from Svante Ståhle of the parish of Perstorp, Skåne. He has forgotten his informant, for he heard the story over fifty years

---

[24] There are several cases where the blank on the questionnaire sheets for *Upptecknat av* (written down by) is filled out and *Berättat av* (told by) is not. This means, Dr. Rooth informs me, that the collector is his own informant.

[25] See Louis Ginzberg, *The Legends of the Jews*, 7 vols. (Philadelphia, 1912–1938), V, 177.

before from old men. He was a child then and, he remarks, a child only hears scraps of such conversation. One, an account of how Adam and Eve obtained their distinct sexual organs, I will pass over. Adam's apple follows (the last bite of the apple lodged in Adam's throat when Our Lord screamed at him for what he had done), and there is a brief reference to the hare's lip splitting when he laughed at the fox. The aspen's trembling and bloodspots on its leaves are ascribed to the Cruxifixion. Then follow two good Noah stories. "A knot got loose in a bottom plank of the ark and Noah didn't know what to do to stop the hole. He had chanced to get the devil with him in the ark, and for a certain compensation the devil offered to close the hole with his tail. So the devil sat there a good while, but he caught a cold from the icy water splashing against his buttocks. There followed a terrible attack of sneezing, and at the same time he sneezed so strongly that the whole ark, because of the gas-pressure (*gastrycket*), which issued through the hole, flew up onto Mount Ararat." Here the helpful serpent is again identified with the devil, who usually is the cause of the hole rather than the patch for it. The sneezing is new to me. In some tales Ararat is likely to be the source of the hole through collision,[26] rather than the haven reached by this unusual form of jet-propulsion. But the knot-hole in a defective plank is common enough.[27]

Ståhle's final tale would do credit to a Darwin. It is new to me, and one more proof that almost any origin-tale finds the Noah story a congenial setting. "The Giraffe did not want to enter the ark, and when the flood came he was forced to trot up to the highest mountain, where he believed himself safe. There he stayed, but the mountain proved not high enough, and as the water rose he had to stretch his neck more and more. This is the reason it has become rather long." Many antediluvians, Ham or Canaan,[28] a County Kerryman,[29] the donkey, or Noah's wife all refused to enter the ark for one reason or another—some were forced to come aboard, some were drowned, and some were unaccountably saved without the ark, but none of them to my knowledge included this etiological Giraffe.

With that our story ends. It is clear that Sweden has preserved Noah tales, and that there were probably many more of them, missed by collectors because the folk found them embarassing and unchristian, however much sport they may have been for an idle hour. Viking's story of the Devil on the Ark and Noah's

[26] See note 13.

[27] I have it in an Irish version of Mt. 825 provided by James Delargy, with translation by Ciáran Bairéad, from Irish Folklore Commission MS 368, pp. 165–169, and in several Finnish versions provided by Jouko Hautala and Lauri Honko. It is often a nail-hole, a twig or thorn-hole, or a hole where a peg was lacking.

[28] See *Chronique de Abou-Djafar...Tabari*, tr. Herman Zotenberg (Paris, 1867), I, 109.

[29] F. L. Utley, "Conflict and Promise in Folklore," *Journal of American Folklore*, LXV (1952), 118.

Wife, though badly reworked by modern fancy, and the fragmentary tales provided by Ståhle and the Uppsala collection, are evidence that modern lore still remembers the tales told on the walls of medieval Swedish churches.[30] We cannot say for sure these are the medieval tales themselves, for they are far from the fully developed form of Mt. 825, and it is not beyond belief that some of them might have been recreated from the extant wall-paintings as iconographical legends. Whether they were so created, or came from the East as tales borrowed from Russian contact, or from the West either as artist's borrowings from such as source as Queen Mary's Psalter or as folk tradition from Ireland, cannot yet be settled, and may never be. (I hope for some results from my work on over 275 variants of Mt. 825, on which I am now preparing a monograph.) Apart from Jewish and Moslem written sources, stemming originally from Asia Minor, the most prolific harvests of such tales are gathered from Russia and Eire. If Sweden is the bridge to Eire from the originating East, a distinct possibility, folktale evidence may possibly counter the general conclusions of art historians. But, though the contacts between Russia and Eire were not so frequent as they were between Sweden and Russia and Sweden in turn and Eire, the remarkably full development of both Russian and Irish tales may argue something like a leap over the sea avoiding intervening spheres of transmission. Mt. 825 is remarkably rare in the intervening land areas (Germany and the Low Countries), but its absence in archival manuscript or print may be further witness to the untrustworthiness of the *argumentum ex silentio*. The tales uncovered by von Sydow's help change completely the Swedish scene as hitherto known, and provide in addition the reason for the silences—the unwillingness of informants to tell such apocryphal tales without special stimulus.

The Ohio State University,
Columbus, Ohio

[30] The geography fits fairly well. I have checked the locales of the wall-paintings and of the modern tales in *Bonniers Stora Världsatlas* (Stockholm, 1951). The guide numbers locate the place on maps 10–11–12, of southern Sweden, with an inset for Skåne. Proceeding northwards we find these correspondences:

1. Skåne—tales at Perstorp (D8), Hallaröd (E9), and Skurup (I9).

2. Småland—paintings at Edshult (k90); tales at Vislanda (n57) near Ljungsby, Gnosjö (L55), both inland, and at coastal Berga (M64) and Kråksmåla (m63). Edshult lies midway between the inland pair and the coastal pair.

3. Östergötland. Dr. Rooth informs me that the Risinge painting is at Finspränga parish Läns härad, and that Örberga is a parish in Dal's härad. I have not located Örberga on the maps, but Risinge is found at f63.

5. Uppsala län. Paintings at Villberga, which is in Trögd's härad. Perhaps further search would uncover tales in these last two more northerly provinces.

ZWEI BIBLISCHE RÄTSEL

HUGO HEPDING †

Es heißt allerdings Eulen nach Athen tragen, wenn man dem besten Kenner der Rätsel aller Völker ein paar biblische Rätsel zum Geburtstag sendet. Aber ich wollte nicht unter den Gratulanten fehlen. Der Freund weiß ja, wie für mich hier in Gießen seit der Zerstörung unserer Universitätsbibliothek und des größten Teiles meiner eigenen Bücher (1944) alles wissenschaftliche Arbeiten erschwert ist, und wird es entschuldigen, daß ich aus den als Ergänzung zu meinem Aufsatz „Hessische Hausinschriften und byzantinische Rätsel" (*Hess. Blätter f. Volkskunde*, XII (1913), 161 ff.) gesammelten Belegen nur einige Kleinigkeiten für diese Festschrift beisteuern kann. Wahrscheinlich wird wenig darunter sein, was dem Jubilar entgangen ist, denn wie sorgfältig er die Rätsel-Literatur verfolgt, sieht man an seinem Buch "A Bibliography of Riddles" (FFC. 126, Helsinki, 1939), in dem die S. 142 f. den biblischen Rätseln gewidmet sind.

1. *Das Rätsel vom Durchzug der Kinder Israel durchs Rote Meer* habe ich in dem genannten Aufsatz, S. 170 f., und in einem Nachtrag dazu *Hess. Bl.* XXVII, 194 besprochen, und Archer Taylor hat dann in seinem Beitrag "A Seventeenth-Century Collection of Biblical Riddles" zu der *Volkskundlichen Ernte, H. Hepding dargebracht* (Gießen, 1938), S. 241 Nr. 9 das Rätsel aus einer Baseler Handschrift veröffentlicht und S. 247 f. eine umfassende Literatur-Zusammenstellung zu diesem Rätsel vorgelegt. Ich gebe im Folgenden einige Ergänzungen dazu.

Eine schöne lateinische Fassung fand ich noch in Joh. Heid(e)feld, *Sphinx theologico-philosophica* (Ed. VII., Herborn, 1616), S. 259:

> Est sera aquis constans, reserat quam lignea clavis,
> Venator capitur, libera casse fera est.

Zwei österreichische Varianten aus des P. Amand Baumgarten Sammlung werden in *Heimatgaue*, XV (1934) 193 mitgeteilt:

> A hölzerner Schlüssel,
> A wåsseres Schloß,
> D'Jaga san gfånga,
> s'Wildpret is los.

(stimmt fast wörtlich mit der Fassung aus dem Bz. Kempten (*Hess. Bl.* XXVII, 194) überein, nur in Z. 3 heißt's hier im Plural: Die Jäger sind gefangen.)

> Ein gläsernes Haus,
> Ein hölzerner Stab,
> Der Jäger kommt um,
> Das Wild kommt aus.

„Haus" und „Stab" verderben natürlich den Text, aber „Stab" steht auch bei K. Mersch *Die Luxemburger Kinderreime* (1884), S. 189, Nr. 799:

> Ein hölzerner Stab,
> Ein wässernes Schloß,
> Der Jäger wird gefangen,
> Das Wild kommt los.

Vier schwedische Fassungen teilt Fredr. Ström *Svenska folkgåtor* (1937), S. 247 mit, von denen ich mir leider nur die folgende abgeschrieben habe:

> Vattnet var låset,
> trädet var nyckeln,
> jägarn jagade sin rov,
> bytet undkom,
> men jägarn blev fången.

Aus Norwegen kenne ich noch drei Fassungen:
Halldor O. Opedal *Makter og menneske. Folkeminne ifrå Hardanger* III (1937) S. 181 Nr. 188:

> Låset va tå vatn,
> lykilen var tå tre,
> fåren (Var: jagaren) vart burte,
> men fåri gjekk i fred.

Aus Rogaland ("Norske Folkeminnelag," 35 [1935], Nr. 199):

> Laasen var av vatn,
> og lykjelen av tre,
> veidaren i faare
> og dyret i fred.

Aus Gauldal ("Norske Folkeminnelag," 42 [1939], S. 68, Nr. 36):

> Låset va tå vatn
> og nykkjyl'n va tå tre,
> hårrån sprang i gjønom
> og skyttar'n gjekk te.

In Finnland sind die Ägypter Wölfe, die Juden Schafe; s. G. Henssen, *Zeitschr. f. Volksk. N.F.*, V (1933), 79, Nr. 298:

> Ein Schloß aus Wasser,
> Ein Schlüssel aus Holz,
> Die Wölfe ertranken,
> Die Schafe wurden gerettet.

    2. *Das Rätsel von Jonas im Walfisch* (Thompson *Motif-Index*, F911.4; H821) ist ungemein beliebt gewesen (s. R. Wossidlo *Mecklenburgische Volksüberlieferungen*, I, Nr. 412 mit den Anm. S. 304). Ich hatte schon darauf hingewiesen (*Hess. Bl.* XII, 172f.), daß wir in den frühbyzantinischen Gesprächsbüchlein und den frühmittelalterlichen lateinischen Fragensammlungen (wie den "Joca monachorum", H. Leclercq im *Dictionnaire d'archéol. chrét. et de liturgie*, VII, 2569ff.) die Quellen für dieses Rätsel haben, das bis zur Gegenwart lebendig geblieben ist. (Vgl. Rob. Petsch *Das deutsche Volksrätsel* (1917), S. 21ff. u. Archer Taylor in *Volkskundlicher Ernte*, S. 239f., der da S. 242 (16) aus einer Baseler Handschrift des 17. Jahrhunderts die Rätselfrage mitteilt: Welcher hat sein leben 3. tag im Wasser erhalten? Ich hatte mich für dieses Rätsel besonders interessiert, weil ich es bei uns in Hessen oft als Hausinschrift verwendet fand (a. a. O., S. 171), s. a. Adolf Spamer *Hessische Volkskunst* (1939), S. 47, Paul Bender in *Zeitschr. f. d. deutschen Unterricht*, XXVIII (1914), 835f., R. Nies *Das schöne Nassau*, II (1931), S. 181. In seinem Aufsatz „Rätsel als Hausinschriften" in *Heimat im Bild* (Gießen, 1937), S. 9f. bildet v. Baumbach eine solche Hausinschrift aus Kehna in Kurhessen ab (S. 11), 1889 von dem Weißbindermeister Phil. Will aus Lohra in eine Fachwerkfüllung aufgemalt. Von diesem stammt auch die wörtlich übereinstimmende Inschrift in Lohra, die ich S. 171 mitgeteilt habe. Während diese hessischen Varianten wohl alle aus dem 19. Jahrhundert stammen, ist die Verwendung dieses Rätsels auch als Hausinschrift schon für 1715 an einer jetzt abgebrochenen Mühle in Göppingen bezeugt (Wilh. Münch *Schwäbische Spruchkunst* (1937), S. 74, Nr. 234):

> Es lebt ein Mann nicht uff der Erden
> Und nicht in dem Himmel auch nicht fern
> Ißt nicht und trinkt nicht
> Ich frag, wer er ist?
> Such in der Schrift, besinn dich! 1715.

Aus ungefähr derselben Zeit stammt die Sammlung des Linzer Notars J. C. Seyringer, aus der das Rätsel in *Heimatgaue*, XVI (1935), 69, Nr. 9 veröffentlicht wird:

> Es war ein Mann an einem Ort,
> Er saße nit und hört kein Wort,
> Er aß nit und trank nit,
> Er war weder im Himmel noch auf Erden,
> Wer er ist, können wir alle werden,
> Wer er gewesen ist, sind wir alle,
> Lieber, rat mir das zu Gefallen.

Ganz ähnlich ist die Fassung aus Münchenbuchsen, Kt. Bern (*Schweiz. Archiv f. Volksk.*, IX [1905], 103, Nr. 169):

> Es war ein Mann, von dem wir lesen,
> Er war ein Mann wie wir gewesen.
> Er wollte Gott nicht gehorsam sein
> Und wollte leben ohne Pein.
> Er wohnte nicht im Himmel
> Und nicht auf Erden,
> Nicht in der Hölle, nicht in der Luft,
> Sondern in einer tiefen Kluft.

Das letzte Wort sollte wohl heißen ,,Gruft'', s. Simrock, *Das deutsche Rätselbuch* (3. Aufl.), S. 91 (offenbar eine Umdichtung, kein Volksrätsel):

> Ich leb und liege doch im Grabe,
> Ob keine Erd ich auf mir habe,
> Ich leb und schöpfe keine Luft
> In der so wunderbaren Gruft.

Der Vergleich des Walfischs mit einem Grab oder Sarg ist seit den griechischen und lateinischen Fragbüchlein bis heute am beliebtesten in den Jonasrätseln. Er findet sich schon *hebräisch*, s. Sal. Schechter "The Riddles of Salomon in Rabbinic Literature," *Folk-Lore*, I (1890), 355, Nr. 11: "The dead lived, the grave moves, and the dead prays: what is that?" (aus dem 1430 kompilierten *Midrash Hachephez*). Aus dem Arabischen in Palästina kennt Erich Ruoff *Arabische Rätsel* (1933), S. 57, Nr. 7: ,,Das Grab ist lebendig, und sein Bewohner drin ist lebendig.''

Mit dem von mir S. 172 mitgeteilten Rätsel aus Pommern stimmt z. T. fast wörtlich überein der Text bei Joh. Heid(e)feld, *Sphinx theologico-philosophica*, (Ed. VII. 1616), S. 924, s. a. Wilmanns, *Zeitschr. f. dt. Altertum*, XV (1872), 170:

> Begraben lag ein mann gar tief,
> Das grab mit ihm herumer lief,
> Gleichwohl im himmel noch auf erd
> Weder er noch sarck gefunden ward.

(Eine Bearbeitung bei Simrock, a. a. O., S. 91).
Aus Tirol habe ich mir notiert, Renk, *Zeitschr. d. Ver. f. Volksk.* V (1895), 149:

> Fürchterlich begräbt man mich,
> Ich hab mein Grab, bewege mich.
> Zwischen Himmel und Erden
> Wird mein Grab nicht gefunden werden.

Aus Hinterpommern nach v. Baumbach, a. a. O., S. 9:

> Es war einmal ein Mensch,
> Er aß nicht und trank nicht,
> Ihm schien auch keine Sonne [nicht].
> Der Mann lebte,
> Der Sarg schwebte
> Nicht im Himmel, nicht auf Erden
> Und wird auch nicht gefunden werden.

Wie in dem von mir S. 172 zitierten holländischen Text heißt es in Belgien nach Jos. Schrijnen *Nederlandsche Volkskunde*, II, 97:

> De kist, die leefde,
> Die er in zat, beefde,
> De kist, die at,
> Die er in zat, bat.

Dieselben Vergleiche finden wir auch in den skandinavischen Texten, so aus Schweden: Rußwurm, *Zeitschr. f. dt. Mythologie u. Sittenkde.*, III (1855), 347, Nr. 39:

> Kistan swäfwade,
> liket bäfwade;
> kistan åt och drack,
> liket ba' gud bå' dag och natt.

oder bei Fredr. Ström, *Svenska folkgåtor* (1937), S. 249:

> Likkistan svävade,
> liket lag och bävade,
> likkistan åt och fick mat,
> licket lag och bad.

Besonders beliebt ist die von Rußwurm, Ström a. a. O. und P. Aug. Sandén *Gåtor från Norra Vadsbo härad* (1887), S. 33, Nr. 17 bezeugte Form:

> Levande lik i levande kista,
> levande kista i gungande graf (Var.: svallande hav).

Manchmal ist noch eine dritte Zeile hinzugefügt (Ström, a. a. O., S. 250):

> stod upp och predika den heliga lag.

Vgl. aus Västergötland: "Folkminnen och folktankar," XXII (1935), 190, Nr. 21b:

> Ett levande lik i en levande kista
> i en våt grav, och liket det stod upp,
> men kistan blev kvar.

Ganz ähnlich eine Variante in der Zeitschrift *Västerbotten* 1929, S. 107 Nr. 53. Ebenda auch noch eine etwas kürzere Variante.

In Norwegen haben wir dieselben Gedanken, so bei Opedal, a. a. O., III, 181, Nr. 189 aus Hardanger:

> Levande lik og levande kista,
> ikkje i himmel og ikkje på jord.

Ebenda Nr. 190 (vgl. a. Nr. 191):

> Kista svum og svømde,
> liket skalv og bevde,
> kista fekk seg mat,
> men liket låg og bad.

Ganz ähnlich sind die Varianten dieser Form, die ich in "Norsk Folkeminnelag," 39 (1937), 117, Nr. 39; 42 (1939), 68, Nr. 37; 47 (1941), 127; 48 (1942), 31, Nr. 81 gefunden habe.

Aus Irland habe ich nur eine Fassung: *Béaloideas*, IV (1933), 145, Nr. 12:

> As dark, as dismal, as deep as a cave,
> A living man in a living grave.

Aus Finnland nennt Henssen, *Zeitschr. f. Volksk. N. F.* V (1933), 79, Nr. 299, nur:

> Ein lebendes Grab, ein lebender Körper.

Bei den schwedischen Finnen heißt es nach *Budkavlen*, III (1924), 43, Nr. 57:

> Halvdö lik ligger i oroli grav.

Auf Jamaica kennt man nach Martha Warren Beckwith *Jamaica Anansi Stories* (1924), S. 213, Nr. 239 auch das englische Jonas-Rätsel:

> There was a man of Adam's race,
> He had a certain dwelling place;
> He wasn't in earth, heaven or hell, —
> Tell me where that man did dwell.

Das nette Walfischrätsel bei Arthur Huff Fauset *Folk-Lore from Nova Scotia* (1931), S. 165f., Nr. 121 ist zweifellos eine Kunstdichtung.

Zum Schluß mögen hier noch die drei „Conundrums" über Jonas und den Walfisch erwähnt werden, die aus der californischen Zeitschrift *Golden Era* Archer Taylor im *California Folklore Quarterly*, V (1946), 275 veröffentlicht hat, das schönste ist Nr. 33:

> Who was Jonah's tutor? —
> The whale who brought him up.

Universität Gießen

CHIBIABOS, VÄINÄMÖINEN, AND ORPHEUS

Anna Birgitta Rooth

The "Song of Hiawatha" was published by Henry Wadsworth Longfellow in November, 1855. "Hiawatha" was a literary sensation but not wholly a success in the Anglo-Saxon world. Some of the people interested in literature in England and America were shocked by the metre, which was considered offensive to refined taste; the metre was parodied and the poem ridiculed. Others in turn praised Longfellow and gave him credit for having created a new metre. By this uncritical admiration—which was due to lack of knowledge of the runo-metre— Longfellow innocently gained the reputation of being an innovator. This literary praise in its way induced C. T. Porter to show in a couple of newspaper articles[1] that the metre was actually derived from the Finnish runo-metre, and that certain parts of the Finnish epic had served as the basis of some of the poems in "Hiawatha."

The fact that Porter's criticism was well founded is also confirmed by Longfellow's own diaries and letters published by Samuel Longfellow.[2] The poet's diary records make it possible to follow his conception of Hiawatha and to give one an idea of what works inspired and furnished the materials for his epic. On the 5th of June, 1854 he writes: "I am reading with great delight the Finnish Epic, *Kalevala*. It is charming." Again on the 22nd Longfellow records in his diary:

---

[1] *National Intelligencer*, Nov. 26, 1855. The *Mercersburg Quarterly Review*, April 8, 1856, Chambersburg, 1856. The first mentioned paper was not available to me.
[2] *Life of H. W. Longfellow*, I–III, 1886–1887.

I have at length hit upon a plan for a poem on the American Indians, which seems to me the right one, and the only. It is to weave together their beautiful traditions into a whole. I have hit upon a measure, too, which I think the right and only one for such a theme.

25th. I could not help this evening making a beginning of 'Manabozho,' or whatever the poem it to be called. His adventures will form the theme, at all events.

26th. Look over Schoolcraft's great book on the Indians; three huge quartos, ill-digested, and without any index. Write a few lines of the poem.

27th. Begin Manabozho's first adventure and lament for his brother. Interrupted by Mr. Wales, who called with two Cubans,—pleasant young men.

28th. Work at 'Manabozho;' or, as I think I shall call it, 'Hiawatha,'—that being another name for the same personage.[3]

Thus the diary entries show that Longfellow had read the *Kalevala* and Schoolcraft's romantic works, as well as a number of other books about the North American Indians, later referred to in the diary, and that consequently both the Finnish and the Indian mythology had been his sources of inspiration. In view of these facts it is astonishing that Longfellow himself did not consider the *Kalevala* to be of any greater significance for the composition of Hiawatha, whereas in the same breath almost he unreservedly acknowledged the importance of Schoolcraft's works. In December 1855, Longfellow, in a letter to Charles Sumner, expressed his indignation at Porter's criticism:

> This is truly one of the greatest literary outrages I ever heard of. But I think it is done mainly to show the learning of the writer. He will stand finally in the position of a man who makes public assertions which he cannot substantiate. You see what the charge of imitation amounts to, by the extracts given. As to my having "taken many of the most striking incidents of the Finnish Epic and transferred them to the American Indians"—it is absurd. I can give chapter and verse for these legends. Their chief value is that they *are* Indian legends. I know the *Kalevala* very well; and that some of its legends *resemble* the Indian stories preserved by Schoolcraft is very true. But the idea of making me responsible for that is too ludicrous...[4]

Ferdinand Freiligrath, an old friend of Longfellow, also immediately recognized the Finnish runo-metre. It is evident from his letter that they had read Schröter's *Finnische Runen* 13 years earlier at Marienburg, and that at that time the two friends had not found the measure exclusively charming.

[3] *Ibid.*, II, 247–248; cf. also pp. 249 and 250.
[4] *Ibid.*, II, 268.

London, December 7, 1855.

Are you not chuckling over the war which is waging in the [London] Athenæum about the measure of Hiawatha? Of course William Howitt is right; and your trochaic metre is taken from the Finns, not from the Spaniards. The very moment I looked into the book I exclaimed,—

Launawatar, Frau die alte,

and was laughing with you again over the pages of the *Finnische Runen*, as thirteen years ago on the Rhine. The characteristic feature, which shows that you have fetched the metre from the Finns, is the *parallelism* adopted so skilfully and so gracefully in Hiawatha. I wonder that just this decisive circumstance is overlooked by all the combatants. It settles the question at once.[5]

Already thus on his visit to Europe in 1842, Longfellow had become acquainted with the Finnish runic poetry, which may be gathered from the above cited letter from Freiligrath. The source of inspiration was not, as has been suggested, Howitt's anthology which contained several Finnish runic poems. Before 1855, there were not many Finnish runic poems that could be used as sources.

As is well known, Longfellow could read Swedish, and his ambitions had even gone as far as a couple of sporadic lessons in Finnish. The *Kalevala* edition which he read in 1859 may have been Castrén's Swedish edition which was published in 1841 and was found in the library left by Longfellow.[6] Another possibility is Schiefner's edition of 1852,[7] as suggested by Porter.

Even Freiligrath's amicable letter with its cheerfully frank observation caused Longfellow to take slight exception in his diary record of Jan. 11, 1856.

A letter from Freiligrath, and a short article by him on the metre of Hiawatha, which is making some discussion in the English papers. He puts the matter right at once. But he does not seem aware that the parallelism, or repetition, is as much the characteristic of Indian as of Finnish song.[8]

It is interesting to read Hiawatha in comparison with the *Kalevala* and Schoolcraft's books on the Indians in the northeastern part of America. Without hesitation most of the chapters can be traced back to the Indian tradition, a fact to which Longfellow himself called attention.[9] This tradition on which Hiawatha

[5] *Ibid.*, II, 269.
[6] A. Hilen, *Longfellow and Scandinavia*, New Haven, 1947. (Longfellow's Scandinavian Library, p. 170).
[7] Cf. W. F. Kirby, "Hiawatha and the *Kalevala*," *The Archaeological Review*, I (1888), 376.
[8] *Life of H. W. Longfellow*, II, 272.
[9] *The Poetical Works of H. W. Longfellow*, II, Leipzig, 1856. In the notes on p. 315 Longfellow refers to the Indian myths he has used. Unfortunately Schoolcraft's *History, Condition, and Prospects of the Indian Tribes of the United States*, I–III, has not been available to me; neither has C. S. Osborn, Schoolcraft-Longfellow: Hiawatha, Lancaster Pa., 1942.

is founded consists first and foremost of two long, well-known myths. One deals with Manabozho's birth and exploits, and begins with the tale of the Skywoman. This myth is met with in The Four Winds, Hiawatha's Childhood, and in Hiawatha and Mudjekeewis. The other myth is found in Hiawatha's Lamentation. Various isolated Indian myths and tales are added to these. Longfellow has followed up his intention "to weave together their beautiful traditions into a whole." Thus The Peace-Pipe corresponds to Pontiac's tale, of which Schoolcraft has given an account in Paradise opened to the Indians.[10] The song of Hiawatha's Fasting and Wrestling with Mondamin is built upon Schoolcraft's tale of "Mondaw-min; or the origin of Indian corn, An Objibwa tale."[11] In the song of Blessing the Corn-field has the motif, Laughing Water goes naked around the corn-field to secure the fertility of the field, also its equivalent in Schoolcraft's chapter on Cornplanting.[12]

As previously pointed out by Porter, a couple of the songs have their equivalents in the *Kalevala*, although the content was adapted to the North American Indian *milieu*. Thus the Introduction to the Song of Hiawatha is a parallel to the Introduction to the *Kalevala*, which gives an account of the origin of the runo-singing. Furthermore, Hiawatha's Wooing and Wedding-feast correspond to the important runos about the Wooing-journey and Wedding-feast of Ilmarinen. Also in Hiawatha's Sailing—with its canoe-building—and Fishing, influences from the *Kalevala* may have prevailed, even though Longfellow had chosen a well-known North American myth for the fishing-episode itself. To Schoolcraft Chibiabos and Iago as musician and storyteller, seems to have been unknown as well as the description of the wedding-feast of Hiawatha. In a letter to Longfellow Schoolcraft thanks him for a copy of Hiawatha and at the same time sanctions, so to say, those parts of the epic of Hiawatha: "For Hiawatha to collect together this poetic force on the occasion of his wedding, was certainly a most felicitous and eligible method of celebrating his nuptials."

Thus Schoolcraft points out that this was a good idea of Longfellow, and he gives some examples from his own somewhat different experience:

> There are among the Indians persons who are called on at burials to recite the praises of the dead. These men generally cut the hieroglyphics on their wooden graveposts. Others are skilled in songs, which are often of a religious, mystic, or elegiac cast; or are noted as persons who recite legends and stories. I have frequently had these persons at my house during the long winter nights in the North, where the introduction of a good meal has put them in the best humor

[10] H. R. Schoolcraft, *Algic Researches*, I, New York, 1839, p. 239.
[11] *Ibid.*, p. 122ff.
[12] *Ibid.*, The Indian in his Wigwam. Buffalo, 1848, p. 179ff. Cornplanting and its incidents.

possible for whiling away the time in relating their lore. To assemble these on grand occasions, with their rude instruments of music, appears to me the most eligible mode of procuring a correct and pleasing delineation of the picturesque and social scenes and beliefs of aboriginal life.

The rest of this letter which is too long to quote fully is also interesting because it gives Schoolcraft's opinion that Longfellow was the first poet to give a picture of the North American Indian as a "human" being endowed with the same human qualities as the white man, sharing his emotions and passions, responsibilities and pleasures.[13]

Hiawatha's friends Chibiabos and Kwasind also seem to depict features possibly borrowed from two characters in the *Kalevala*, Väinämöinen and Kullervo. Both Chibiabos and Väinämöinen might be described as the best of all musicians," even though Chibiabos appears as a young man and Väinömöinen as an old one. Obviously Longfellow was inspired by Väinämöinen, the great musician who moves nature to tears by his playing and entices the wild animals to gather round him. This is evident from his description of "the gentle Chibiabos, he the best of all musicians" in Hiawatha's Friends:

> When he sang, the village listened;
> All the warriors gathered round him,
> All the women came to hear him;
> Now he stirred their souls to passion,
> Now he melted them to pity.
> From the hollow reeds he fashioned
> Flutes so musical and mellow,
> That the brook, the Sebowisha
> Ceased to murmur in the woodland,
> That the wood-birds ceased from singing,
> And the squirrel, Adjidaumo,
> Ceased his chatter in the oak-tree,
> And the rabbit, the Wabasso,
> Sat upright to look and listen.
> Yes, the brook, the Sebowisha,
> Pausing, said, "O Chibiabos,
> Teach my waves to flow in music,
> Softly as your words in singing!"
> Yes, the blue-bird, the Owaissa,
> Envious, said, "O Chibiabos,
> Teach me tones as wild and wayward,
> Teach me songs as full of frenzy!"

[13] *Life of H. W. Longfellow*, III, 45–46.

18 Taylor

Yes, the Opechee, the robin,
Joyous, said, "O Chibiabos,
Teach me tones as sweet and tender,
Teach me songs as full of gladness!"
And the whippoorwill, Wawonaissa.

. . .

Very dear to Hiawatha
Was the gentle Chibiabos,
He the best of all musicians,
He the sweetest of all singers;

. . .

Animals gathering round the performing musician is a motif unknown in the Indian tradition in the northeastern part of America as well as in other parts of the continent.

The prototype of Chibiabos's playing is, however, to be found in the 41st runo of the *Kalevala*, part of which reads in the translation made by W. F. Kirby:

Played the aged Väinämöinen.
Nothing was there in the forest,
Which upon four feet was running,
Or upon their legs were hopping,
And which came not near to listen,
Came not to rejoice and wonder.
     Gathered round him all the squirrels,
As from branch to branch they clambered,
And the ermines flocked around him,
Laid them down against the fences,
On the plains the deer were springing,
And the lynxes shared the pleasure.
     In the swamp each wolf awakened,
From the heath the bear aroused him,
From his lair among the fir-trees,
And the thickly growing pine-trees,
And the wolves ran lengthy journeys,
And the bears came through the heather,
Till they sat upon the fences,
Side by side against the gateway.
On the rocks the fence fell over,
On the field the gate fell over,

> Then they climbed upon the pine-trees,
> And they ran around the fir-trees,
> Just to listen to the music,
> All rejoicing, and in wonder.[14]

In the same way is described how the different *birds* and the different *fishes* hasten to hear the playing of Väinämöinen.

The connections between these episodes of the playing musician in the *Kalevala* and Hiawatha is particularly obvious. Certainly, we know from the Indian tradition of Northeast America the motif of the mourning animals gathered round their dead master—which Longfellow also uses in Hiawatha's Lamentation. This motif is best known in connection with a notion that in the ethnological literature is called the Lord of Animals. The great musician whose playing also influences nature and the wild animals is a motif alien to the Indian tradition in Northeast America as well as in other parts of the continent. However, the motif is well known in both Europe and Asia. Probably Longfellow derived his inspiration to this passage from the *Kalevala* and likewise that part of the Chibiabos-figure, where he is mentioned as being "the best of all musicians, he the sweetest of all singers."

The imposing figure of Väinämöinen in the *Kalevala* is the object of a study by Martti Haavio, who gives a congenial picture of the great runo-singer.[15] Väinämöinen has been called the Finnish Orpheus as well as Pan and Apollo.

In a special section—Väinämöinen's Kantele Music—Haavio gives several interesting parallels in the classic tradition to the motif of the animals gathering round the great musician. Haavio refers to Simonides who narrates that "the birds gather around his head, the fish come from the waves, the winds die down so as not to disturb his melodies." In the same manner is Orpheus represented in images and pictures surrounded by animals frequenting southern climes. "How enticing it would be to see in all this a prototype of Väinämöinen playing!" Haavio exclaims. And he thinks also that there may very well exist a connection between the classic and the Finnish motif. As an example of the popularity of the motif in Europe in the Middle Ages Haavio mentions Froumund's 10th-century poem about Orpheus from Germany and a 15th-century English poem, Sir Orfeo, the prototype for some Scandinavian ballads. Further Haavio refers to Horandt's singing in the Kudrun epic, where "the animals stop eating, the crawling things their crawling, and the fish their swimming."

[14] W. F. Kirby, *Kalevala the Land of Heroes*, translated from the original Finnish, Vol. 2, London, 1907.
[15] *Väinämöinen Eternal Sage*, FFC 144, Helsinki, 1952.

18*

According to Haavio, this German motif may be a possible prototype for the playing figure around which the animals gather on Olaus Magnus' Carta Marina of 1539. It seems, however, more tempting to connect the picture of Olaus Magnus with Bissucio's miniature illustrating Orpheus in a chronicle of the 15th century (see reproduction page 285), or some other iconographic prototype.

It may be added here that Orpheus playing for the wild animals was a popular motive of Roman as well as Renaissance art. It was used by artists such as Hans Leu il giovane, Francesco del Cossa and Giacomo Bassano.[16] It seems more plausible that Olaus Magnus got the prototype for his musician on the Carta Marina from some contemporary Renaissance iconographs.

What other motifs have been tied to Väinämöinen's playing and the closer connection between the Finnish and the classic Orpheus fall outside the scope of this investigation. Haavio's study has already hinted at a connection between the antique and the Finnish tradition as regards the animals gathering round the great musician, a problem which I cannot enter upon more thoroughly here. My intention has been only to prove the connection between Longfellow's motif and that of Väinämöinen.

It is a statement frequently heard that motifs arise spontaneously—an old statement which was revivified by Jung's doctrine of archetypes. The scope of this investigation has been only to find a demonstrable connection between Longfellow's tale of Chibiabos and Väinämöinen playing for the animals, and in that way historically to connect the three musicians Chibiabos, Väinämöinen, and Orpheus.

Folklivsarkivet, Lund, Sweden

---

[16] *Dizionario letterario Bompiani*, 5, "Orfeo" p. 280ff. Milano 1951.

ORFEVS

"Jean de Calais, ou La Vertu Récompensée." – Image populaire parisienne, de Glémarec rue Saint-Jacques, milieu du XIX° siècle. *Au Musée des arts et traditions populaires, à Paris.* (Photo P. Soulier, cliché ATP). – Cf. ci-dessus pp. 268–269.

JEAN DE CALAIS (MT. 506A) EN FRANCE: TRADITION ECRITE, TRADITION ORALE, IMAGERIE

Marie-Louise Tenèze

"Trop longtemps par leur brigandage,
Les forbans ont souillé ces bords:
Calais gémit sous l'esclavage.
Vengeance, mon père, ou la mort!
C'est en ces termes qu'à son père
Le fils d'un riche négociant
S'exprime en son ardeur altière
Pour obtenir un bâtiment.
Tous les Calaisiens du rivage
Et de leurs remparts foudroyants
Sont témoins du noble courage
Dont il chasse tous ces brigands:
A son nom celui de sa ville
Est joint par acclamation,
Et répété par mille et mille
Jean de Calais devient son nom.
Mais quel terrible coup du sort
Pour le jeune héros s'apprête!
Son vaisseau prêt d'entrer au port,
Essuie une affreuse tempête.
Au calme, enfin, cède l'orage.
Une île est offerte à ses yeux;
Un délicieux paysage
Est l'ornement de ces beaux lieux:

"Vous êtes dans l'Orimanie
Que gouverne un roi généreux:
Sa capitale est Palmanie;"
Lui dit-on d'un air gracieux.
"Ce mont vous en cache la ville,
Et ses fortunés habitants;
Montez-y, là, d'un oeil tranquille
Vous pourrez voir s'ils sont contents!..."
Il descend dans la capitale;
Son regard est partout frappé
De la richesse qu'elle étale;
Il voit qu'on ne l'a point trompé.
Mais arrivé sur la grand'place,
Un cadavre mangé des chiens
S'offre à ses yeux. Son sang se glace...
"Quelles lois, et quels citoyens!..."
Il s'informe; on lui dit qu'en Somme
C'est l'ordinaire châtiment
De tout débiteur, ou tout homme
Qui meurt en ne point s'acquittant.
Alors au port, sûre retraite,
Faisant entrer son bâtiment,
Du mort il acquitte la dette,
Et l'enterre honorablement.

Bonne oeuvre aura sa récompense;
Sur son bord, un soir retournant,
Il voit un vaisseau qui s'avance,
Et près du sien vient se rangeant.
Sur le pont, deux dames navrées
Exhalent leurs vives douleurs:
Si magnifiquement parées,
Devraient-elles verser des pleurs?
Oui! Ces deux dames sont esclaves
Qu'un forban va vendre à l'instant:
Soudain, Jean brise leurs entraves,
Et les rachète à prix d'argent.
Seconde oeuvre de bienfaisance
Dont le ciel lui garde le prix;
Tant l'amour, la reconnaissance
Peuvent tout sur coeurs bien épris!
Le leur, déjà d'intelligence,
A reçu leurs plus doux serments,
L'hymen unit Jean et Constance
Par les plus saints engagements.
Mais, à son retour, par son père,
Cet hymen n'est point confirmé;
Il ne voit qu'une aventurière
Dans l'objet dont il est charmé.
Pressé pourtant par ses amis,
Il fournit un autre équipage,
Avec lequel pourra son fils
Entreprendre un second voyage;
Mais Constance avec son enfant
Sur la poupe y veut être peinte
Afin qu'à Lisbonne abordant,
Ce tableau soit vu de l'enceinte.
Jean de Calais met à la voile,
A sa poupe ayant ce tableau;
Conduit par son heureuse étoile,
De Lisbonne il voit le château.
Il range sous lui son navire
Paré de l'ornement nouveau;
Chacun, le Roi lui-même admire
Et la peinture et le vaisseau.
Tout s'explique. Il embrasse un gendre
Dans le noble libérateur,
Qui lui-même a peine à comprendre
Un si grand excès de bonheur.
Le Roi l'informe que Constance,
Il y a cinq ans se promenant

Avec sa compagne d'enfance
Au bord de l'humide élément,
Fut prise, hélas, par des corsaires,
Et que depuis ce triste jour,
Le sommeil fuit de ses paupières,
Perdant l'objet de son amour.
C'en est fait, une escadre est prête
Pour l'aller chercher; et Don Juan,
Héritier du trône s'apprête,
Pour la ramener avec Jean;
Mais l'amour, que chez lui réveille
La dévorante ambition,
Ronge son coeur, et lui conseille
La plus infâme trahison.
A Calais, cette escadre arrive;
Tous les Calaisiens sont surpris,
Informés qu'ils sont, sur la rive,
Ils remplissent l'air de leurs cris:
"Vive Jean, vive la princesse!"
Alors on vit Jean et don Juan,
Lui marquer respect et tendresse,
Devant elle s'agenouillant.
Don Juan fait mettre à la voile,
Détestant au fond de son coeur
De son rival l'heureuse étoile,
Et sa fortune, et sa faveur.
Dieux! le ciel couvert de nuages,
Les flots et les vents furieux
Battent l'escadre, et de l'orage
L'horreur se répand autour d'eux.
Tremblant pour de si chères têtes,
Sur le pont, implorant le ciel
Pour qu'il enchaîne les tempêtes,
Jean est frappé d'un choc cruel.
L'époux de la tendre Constance,
Par son rival précipité
Dans les flots, n'a plus d'espérance,
O mon Dieu, que dans ta bonté.
La princesse alors qui soupçonne
L'affreuse et triste vérité,
A son désespoir s'abandonne
Aux yeux d'un rival détesté.
Il arrive; alors l'infortune
De Jean de Calais se répand;
La douleur en devient commune;
Le Roi la ressent vivement.

Mais tout soupçon fuit de son âme;
Don Juan est accueilli par lui,
Et Constance sera la femme
Du vil bourreau de son mari...
Mais non: Jean de Calais respire
Dans les cuisines du palais,
Un génie a su l'introduire
Par des chemins sûrs et secrets.
Deux ans d'absence de son âme
N'ont point altéré les ressorts;
Et toujours fidèle à sa femme,
Il en partage les transports.
Le Roi, que lui-même il éclaire
Sur son naufrage et son destin,
Dans Don Juan plus ne considère
Qu'un lâche et qu'un vil assassin.
Enfin, le jour même où pour femme
Le plus digne objet est promis,
Don Juan expirant dans la flamme
De son forfait reçoit le prix.
Vers le milieu d'un grand banquet,
On voit paraître dans la salle
Un homme dont l'air imposait,
Dont la taille à l'air est égale,
S'avançant vers Jean de Calais:
"Reconnaîs, lui dit-il, un être

Qui t'a conduit dans ce palais;
De moi tu te souviens peut-être?
"Tu m'a vu dans l'île où les flots
T'avaient jeté par la tempête;
Tu m'as vu prendre part aux maux
Qui s'accumulaient sur ta tête.
Souviens-toi que tu me promis
La moitié d'un second toi-même;
Je veux la moitié de ton fils,
Pour le prix de mon zèle extrême."
Jean frémit; mais au même instant,
A l'horreur succède la joie:
"Vas, dit le spectre, ton enfant
De la mort ne sera la proie.
D'un corps par les chiens déchiré,
Te souvient-il dans Palmanie?
Ce corps par toi fut enterré,
Et soustrait à l'ignominie.
"Ce fut ma main qui conduisit
Près de toi l'esquif du corsaire,
Dont l'avarice, un jour, ravit
La princesse au plus tendre père.
Ces exemples mis sous tes yeux,
Et qui ne sauraient te déplaire,
Te prouvent qu'un coeur vertueux
Est cher au Ciel comme à la terre."

Le lecteur aura reconnu dans ces vers le thème d'un conte-type international (Aa. Th. 506 A) appartenant au cycle du Mort reconnaissant (*The Grateful Dead*) et caractérisé par la coexistence de l'épisode de l'enterrement du cadavre endetté qui se montrera reconnaissant par la suite, avec l'épisode du rachat de la princesse.

Notre texte encadre, sur trois côtés, une image populaire parisienne. Il résume, sous forme versifiée, l'Histoire de Jean de Calais telle qu'elle naquit, en 1722, sous la plume d'une femme de lettres française; "l'Histoire de Jean de Calais dont la mémoire ne s'éteindra jamais par les actions généreuses qu'il a faites pendant sa vie." Ce "jamais" fut vrai, du moins pendant plus de deux siècles. Renommée suffisante pour mériter qu'on s'y attarde quelque peu, n'est-il pas vrai?

I. JEAN DE CALAIS DANS LA TRADITION ECRITE

"Magdeleine-Angélique Poisson, fille de Paul Poisson, comédien, naquit à Paris, le 22 nov. 1684. Elle épousa Don Gabriel de Gomez, gentilhomme espagnol, peu favorisé de la fortune. Madame de Gomez trouva, dans ses ouvrages, des secours contre l'indigence. Sa plume, plus féconde que correcte, en fit éclore un grand nombre qui furent lus avec avidité..." C'est en ces termes qu'un dictionnaire des Françaises[1] présente, au début du XIX° s., celle qui fut l'auteur, entre autres oeuvres, des *Journées amusantes* dédiées au Roi, vaste récit à cadre paru à Paris, chez G. Saugrain, en 8 volumes in-12, de 1722 à 1731.[2] Et c'est au tome II, pp. 253–317 de cette 1ère. édition, qu'est insérée l'Histoire de Jean de Calais, mise dans la bouche de Camille, l'une des six protagonistes réunis.

Ces *Journées amusantes* furent rééditées de nombreuses fois. C'est ainsi que Reinhold Köhler[3] le premier, nous semble-t-il, à avoir attiré l'attention des folkloristes sur ce texte littéraire et à l'avoir mis en relation avec les traditions du mort reconnaissant, eut en mains, en 1898, la 7ème édition, Amsterdam, 1758. Ces *Journées* furent, très tôt aussi, traduites: dès 1758, semble-t-il, en italien (Venise in-12°), dès 1761 en allemand (Berlin, in-8°).[4]

Cependant, ne nous intéressant ici qu'à la seule Histoire de Jean de Calais et à la longue popularité qui fut la sienne, nous délaisserons les *Journées amusantes* dans leur ensemble et partirons de ce qui est la première parution séparée connue de notre récit: Histoire de Jean de Calais, Par M. xxx. Seconde édition. A Bruxelles, chez Eugène-Henry Fricx, Libraire Imprimeur Rue de la Magdelaine. M.D. CCXXXVIII. in-12°, 119 p.[5]

Cette édition, déjà anonyme, ne diffère du texte contenu dans les *Journées amusantes* que par son début, et par sa fin. Dans les *Journées amusantes*, l'Histoire de Jean de Calais débute par l'alinéa suivant: "Ce que je m'engage à vous conter, est tiré d'un livre qui a pour titre, Histoire fabuleuse de la Maison des Rois de Portugal. Je n'y changerai rien, et ne me piquerai point de vous l'embellir;" puis continue: "Au Nord des Gaules, sur le bord de la Mer, est une ville appellée Calais..." Or, ce premier paragraphe, donnant la prétendue source de l'histoire, manque dans l'édition séparée de Jean de Calais, 1738, qui débute ainsi directement par la phrase "Au Nord des Gaules...". Par contre, elle connaît une phrase finale supplémentaire imprimée en caractères italiques (nous l'avons déjà citée ci-dessus partiellement): "Ainsi finit l'Histoire de Jean de Calais, dont la mémoire ne s'éteindra jamais par les actions généreuses qu'il a faites pendant sa vie."

---

[1] *Dictionnaire historique, littéraire et bibliographique des Françaises...* par Mme Fortunée B. Briquet, Paris, An XII–1804, pp. 157–159.

[2] Cette première édition se trouve à la Bibliothèque Nationale, à Paris.

[3] Reinhold Köhler: *Kleinere Schriften zur Märchenforschung*, Weimar, 1898, I, pp. 5–39, particulièrement p. 12 sq.

[4] Cf. Köhler, *op. cit.* et Bolte-Polivka, *Anmerkungen...*, III, p. 498, n. 1.

[5] Cette édition, sous belle reliure, se trouve à la Bibliothèque de l'Arsenal, à Paris: 14 cm., assez mauvais papier, coquilles, ponctuation relâchée.

Cette phrase additive a son importance. En effet, nous allons la retrouver, presque inchangée, dans la plupart des éditions de colportage du récit de Mme. de Gomez, qui ont fleuri en France, pendant un siècle environ, démontrant ainsi que c'est à l'édition de 1738 que celles-ci remontent.

Il semble bien que c'est à Jean Garnier, Imprimeur-Libraire, rue du Temple, à Troyes, que Jean de Calais est redevable de son entrée dans la littérature de colportage fançaise; le permis d'imprimer est du 18 décembre 1758, datant ainsi la plus ancienne brochure de colportage française de l'Histoire de Jean de Calais que nous connaissions et dont le Musée des Arts et Traditions populaires (A.T.P.) à Paris a la bonne fortune de possèder un exemplaire.

Jean Garnier, toutefois, eut une curieuse initiative: fut-il choqué par la cruauté inhérente à la dernière scène, celle où le sauveur de Jean de l'île déserte vient lui réclamer, conformément à la promesse obtenue, la moitié de ce qu'il a de plus cher... à savoir: la moitié de son fils? Toujours est-il qu'il supprima totalement, de la scène finale, le motif du partage, esquissé cependant seulement, de l'enfant; suppression nettement voulue, puisque, dès la scène entre Jean et son sauveur inconnu dans l'île, est supprimée de même la phrase fatale: "promets moi de me donner la moitié de ce que tu chéris le plus." Bien plus, non content d'avoir ainsi édulcoré le récit et de l'avoir privé d'un ressort dramatique essentiel, il y ajoute une autre suppression: l'inconnu ne se fait pas reconnaître comme étant celui "dont le corps était déchiré par les chiens, lorsque tu entras dans la Ville de Palmanie," celui "dont tu payas les dettes et... à qui tu as donné la sépulture;" toutes ces phrases essentielles de Mme. de Gomez manquent; ainsi aucun lien n'est fait avec le motif de l'enterrement du cadavre endetté du début de l'histoire qui risque d'apparaître au lecteur comme étranger au récit; la boucle n'est plus bouclée dans ce récit bizarrement tronqué.

Ces malheureux coups de ciseaux dans le texte original n'empêchèrent pas Jean de Calais de poursuivre, dans le colportage, une carrière triomphale. Non seulement les éditions se continuèrent à Troyes: chez la citoyenne Garnier (après 1795), chez Garnier (après 1792), chez Baudot (1830–1863)[6]; mais aussi dans d'autres centres: à Lille, cf.: par M xxx, Dixième édition, P. Dumortier, s. d.; Douzième édition, J. Fourray, s. d.; par M. xxx, Treizième édition, Bloquel-Castiaux, s.d.; à Douai, cf. Deregnecourt, s.d.; à Epinal, cf.: Pellerin, 1821, 1825; à Montbéliard, cf.: impr. de Deckherr, s.d., 1824, 1828, (1848); à Rouen, cf.: par M. xxx, Lecrêne-Labbey, 1811; à Toulouse: cf. L. Abadie, s.d.; impr. de L. Dieulafoy, s.d.; impr. d'Antoine Navarre, s.d.[6a] Toutes ces éditions, allant de la fin du

[6] Cf. Pierre Brochon: *Le livre de colportage en France.* Paris 1954, p. 74; cf. aussi planche VI.

[6a] Anatole Le Braz: *La légende de la Mort chez les Bretons armoricains*, annotée par Georges Dottin, 5e ed., Paris, 1928, mentionne dans les commentaires du conte "Jean Carré" (pp. 199–202) l'existence

XVIIIème au milieu du XIXème siècle, sont des brochures in-16 ou in-18, de 32 à 40 pages, intitulées simplement Histoire de Jean de Calais. Elles sont assez souvent ornées de petites gravures sur la couverture ou la page de titre—parfois sans rapport avec le texte—, rarement (chez Deckherr de Montbéliard seulement, semble-t-il) de gravures sur page entière, soit au verso de la couverture, soit dans le cours de l'opuscule. Or il semble bien que toutes ces brochures dérivent de l'une des premières éditions troyennes, dont elles reproduisent les si regrettables suppressions. Elles ne connaissent ainsi pas le motif dramatique de la menace du partage de l'enfant et ne font pas non plus le lien avec l'épisode du cadavre enterré, relaté cependant dans le début du récit. Le sauveur de Jean de Calais reste à tel point inconnu, j'allais dire abstrait, qu'il peut devenir dans deux de ces brochures, à Toulouse chez A. Navarre et chez L. Dieulafoy, "La Sagesse"!

Il n'en est que plus intéressant de constater—face à ces seize éditions de colportage presque rigoureusement identiques que nous avons pu examiner, à la Bibliothèque du Musée ATP et à la Bibliothèque Nationale (B.N.)—l'existence de deux éditions, qui elles, nous ramènent au texte intégral de Mme. de Gomez! Ce sont: Histoire de Jean de Calais, ou La Vertu récompensée (titre intérieur: Histoire de Jean-de-Calais, Roi de Portugal), A Caen, Chez P. Chalopin, rue Froide-Rue, s.d. (B.N.); et: Histoire de Jean-de-Calais, Roi de Portugal, ou La Vertu Récompensée, Limoges, F. Chapoulaud, Imprimeur et Libraire, place des Bancs, s.d. (ATP). Pierre Chalopin a exercé de 1746 à 1786, François Chapoulaud de 1789 à 1840[7]. Ces deux éditions identiques dans leur titre plus circonstancié et dans leur texte qui est bien complet, ignorent par contre toutes deux la fameuse phrase finale, adventice puisqu'elle ne figure pas dans les *Journées amusantes*: "Ainsi finit l'Histoire de Jean de Calais dont la mémoire ne s'éteindra jamais...", phrase que toutes les autres brochures sont unanimes à reproduire. D'autre part, alors que toutes les seize brochures répètent, à la suite des éditions de Bruxelles, 1738, et de Troyes, 1758, une coquille, dans un des derniers alinéas:

d'un "petit volume, de l'impr. J.-M. Corne, à Toulouse, s.d., contenant outre l'histoire de Jean de Calais, nombre d'autres romans d'amour et d'aventures...". Le résumé donné de notre récit montre nettement qu'il s'agit du texte de Mme de Gomez, avec les mêmes suppressions.

[7] L'Histoire de Jean de Calais continua à être imprimée par les successeurs de Pierre Chalopin, et de toutes façons par son petit-fils Théodore Chalopin, qui exerça de 1823 à 1834; en effet le Dr. René Hélot, *La Bibliothèque bleue en Normandie*, Rouen, 1928, cite à la p. 50.
Histoire de Jean-de-Calais, Roi de Portugal, ou la Vertu Récompensée. [Vignette: personnages dans un médaillon]. A Caen, chez T. Chalopin, Imprimeur-Libraire, Rue Froide, n°. 2. s.d., in-16 de 32 p., sans couv.
Les dates d'exercices des Chalopin sont données d'après Hélot, *op. cit.* lxx (= 70) sq.; celle de F. Chapoulaud d'après un fichier manuscrit sur la littérature de colportage (Archives du Musée ATP).

"Apprends par ces *expériences* combien le Ciel chérit les hommes vertueux" là où Mme. de Gomez écrivait dans les *Journées amusantes*: "Apprends par ces *exemples*", nos deux brochures isolées ignorent cette coquille et impriment bien "exemples". On est ainsi amené à conclure que Chalopin de Caen et Chapoulaud de Limoges représentent un courant à part, pur, certainement indépendant de l'édition bruxelloise de 1738 comme aussi des éditions troyennes, remontant—directement ou par un intermédiaire inconnu?—aux *Journées amusantes* elles-mêmes.

Nous n'avons suivi jusqu'à présent qu'un seul des courants de popularité de l'Histoire de Jean de Calais, celui qui, par le truchement de la littérature de colportage, diffusa le récit de Mme. de Gomez dans presque toutes les provinces de France. Le Dr. Hélot ne dit-il pas ainsi, à propos de l'éditeur Lecrêne-Labbey à Rouen que "ses productions étaient tirées à un très grand nombre d'exemplaires: en 1811, il imprima au moins huit mille *Jean de Calais*; je connais deux autorisations données pour un tirage à quatre mille exemplaires, avec la date de 1811."[8]

• • •

Mais, à partir de 1769, un autre courant prend jour, qui, pendant plus d'un siècle, allait répandre Jean de Calais dans des milieux sociaux plus élevés. Il n'y a pas de doute, en effet, que la *Bibliothèque bleue ou Recueil d'histoires singulières et naïves* qui commença à paraître en 1769–1770 chez Lacombe, libraire rue Christine près de la rue Dauphine, et se continua chez Costard, libraire rue Saint-Jean-de-Beauvais[9] se voulait, comme il est dit dans l'Avertissement de l'éditeur, "digne de toute sorte de Lecteurs"; "Il paraîtra sans doute bien singulier qu'on ait pris la peine de rajeunir des ouvrages, qui, depuis plus de deux siècles, sont abandonnés au peuple; des Romans que la plus mince bourgeoise n'oserait se vanter d'avoir lus, non pas à cause du style et du langage, qui les lui rendent... inintelligibles..., mais précisément parce qu'ils ont fait l'amusement de la plus vile populace, qui commence à ne plus les entendre...". Ces mots s'appliquent évidemment moins à Jean de Calais qu'aux autres récits, d'un plus long passé littéraire, contenus dans ce recueil, à savoir: Histoires de Robert le diable duc de Normandie, —de Richard sans peur son fils,—de Pierre de Provence et de la belle Maguelonne,—de Fortunatus et de ses enfants (cette dernière histoire en deux parties distinctes). N'empêche que Jean de Calais a subi ici un traitement sembl-

[8] Hélot, *op. cit.*, p. lxix.
[9] La Bibliothèque Nationale n'en possède que l'Histoire de Robert le Diable; mais le recueil se trouve au complet, à la Bibl. de l'Arsenal, en deux exemplaires, chacun en deux volumes, rassemblant cependant les récits selon un brochage différent.

able à celui infligé aux autres récits, mis par le réfecteur au goût de sa clientèle "en les refondant entièrement et en y ajoutant des situations et des épisodes nouveaux." Aussi bien, cette Histoire de Jean de Calais ici présentée s'appelle-t-elle "sur de nouveaux mémoires".

Le volume de 1769 contient à la suite du Privilège du Roi une déclaration de l'éditeur Lacombe qui mérite d'être reproduite: "Je déclare que le présent Privilège ne peut nuire aux droits et au débit de ceux qui vendent, impriment et distribuent les Livres dits de la *Bibliothèque Bleue*; dont les différens morceaux ont été repris, augmentés et corrigés dans les histoires pour lesquelles le présent Privilège a été accordé..."

On sait en effet que la dénomination *Bibliothèque bleue* désignait couramment la partie récréative de la littérature de colportage (cf. le catalogue de la veuve de Nicolas Oudot intitulé: "Livres récréatifs appelez communément la Bibliothèque bleue"), soit encore, selon la définition de Le Blanc-Hardel: "La Bibliothèque Bleue comprend une collection assez considérable de romans de chevalerie, de contes de fées, d'almanachs, de facéties et de chansons, imprimés autrefois sur mauvais papier, avec des caractères de rebut et vendues à bas prix, en nombre incalculable, dans toutes les foires et dans tous les marchés du pays".[10] Ainsi donc, en 1769, un éditeur parisien reprenait ce titre, à la fois si populaire et si décrié, pour lancer une collection manifestement destinée à un public de niveau social élevé et qui, nous le verrons, sera rééditée, et parfois luxueusement, jusqu'en 1862.

Si ce recueil parut, en 1769 et 1770, sans nom d'auteur, l'éditeur nous avertit cependant qu'il est d'un "critique", d' "un homme de lettres", dont l'anonymat, peut-être, était facile à percer pour les contemporains. Toujours est-il qu'en 1842 Leraux de Lincy[11] nous donne son nom, que nous livre aussi le Dictionnaire des ouvrages anonymes de Barbier.[12] Il s'agit de Jean Castillon, orthographié parfois aussi Castilhon (1718–1799), littérateur, secrétaire-perpétuel des Jeux floraux et de l'Académie des sciences de Toulouse, auteur de trois cents articles dans le supplément de l'Encyclopédie, et de poésies dans l'Almanach des Muses, l'un des continuateurs du Journal encyclopédique de 1769 à 1793, rédacteur aussi, avec son frère, du Journal de Trévoux, pendant les années 1774–1778[13].

[10] Le Blanc-Hardel: *Etude sur la Bibliothèque bleue*, servant d'introduction à la réédition du *Sermon du P. Esprit de Tinchebray*, Caen, 1844, p. 3.
[11] *Nouvelle Bibliothèque Bleue ou Légendes populaires de la France*, éditée par Le Roux de Lincy, Paris, 1842, Introd. par Le Roux de Lincy.
[12] Sous "Histoire de Jean de Calais..."; voir aussi dans le *Supplément* par G. Brunet, Paris, 1889 sous "Bibliothèque bleue..."
[13] Cf. J.-M. Quérard, *France littéraire*, II: C–D, Paris, 1828.

Jean Castillon, réfecteur de l'Histoire de Jean de Calais, a dû, il n'y a pas de doute, se servir non pas de "nouveaux mémoires" comme il l'allègue, mais tout simplement de l'une des brochures de colportage si largement diffusées à la suite de l'édition troyenne de 1758.[14] Aussi, si Jean Castillon relate bien au début l'enterrement du cadavre d'un débiteur insolvable, cet épisode reste en réalité sans lien avec le récit, et le sauveur de Jean de Calais, "homme d'une taille majestueuse et d'une démarche noble et légère" qui à l'avant dernière page, entre dans la salle du festin, non seulement ne réclame du héros aucun partage, mais se fait reconnaître comme étant..." l'Ange tutélaire des Rois"!; celui-ci tient, bien sûr, de sages discours en rapport avec sa charge: "Jean de Calais, lui dit-il, tu n'étais pas né pour le Trône, mais il n'est point d'état sur la terre où la vertu ne puisse élever l'homme. Ta sagesse a mérité les secours dont le ciel t'a comblé par mon ministère, etc., etc." Et l'auteur continue: "Cet être céleste revêtu d'un corps aérien disparut aussitôt, et en se dissipant, laissa dans la salle un parfum délicieux, qu'on y respirait encore plusieurs années après..."!! Cette citation prouve déjà suffisamment que notre histoire racontée somme toute avec une plaisante simplicité par Mme. de Gomez—c'était aussi l'avis de R. Köhler: "die von Mme. de Gomez leidlich schlicht und einfach erzählte Geschichte"—sort absolument alourdie et dénaturée des mains de son trop pédant réfecteur. Dès le début ainsi, celui-ci ne peut s'empêcher de faire allusion au dévouement des bourgeois de Calais, comme aussi, à propos du nom de sa ville accordé par ses concitoyens à notre héros, à un usage semblable des Romains envers leurs généraux victorieux! Le gouvernement de l'Ile heureuse,[15] dans laquelle Jean aborde, est explicité en détail sur près de 9 pages! La si jolie phrase de Mme. de Gomez: "Le roi fit assembler son conseil, et proposa la chose en prince qui souhaitait que l'on fût de son avis" est remplacée par de longs raisonnements! D'une façon générale, des considérations verbeuses alourdissent et ralentissent continuellement le cours du récit. D'autre part, alors que chez Mme. de Gomez, aussi concise en cela qu'un conteur populaire, "le perfide Don Juan fut consumé avant qu'on sût ni le crime, ni la punition", le malheureux Castillon remplace cette phrase si nette et si décisive par une longue histoire compliquée; en plus, il invente en surplus une révolte fomentée par un neveu de Don Juan, Don Alonzo,—péripétie amenée

[14] Il n'est pas impossible qu'il se soit servi précisément de la première éd. troyenne de 1758. En effet c'est la seule, parmi celles que nous avons examinées, qui remplace, au début, le nom de l'état d'Orimanie par celui d'*Ile Heureuse* (changement de dénomination qui n'est d'ailleurs pas maintenu dans le cours du récit, où le nom d'Orimanie reparaît par la suite). Or c'est cette dénomination d'Ile Heureuse que nous trouvons chez Castillon, qui n'en est ainsi pas l'inventeur; elle se maintiendra dans les éditions de colportage dérivant du Jean de Calais remanié de cet auteur.

[15] Cf. note précédente.

semble-t-il pour que l'occasion soit offerte à Jean de Calais de prouver ses vertus guerrières et d'acquérir le titre de duc d'Evora! Et, bien sûr, toute la stratégie de la bataille est minutieusement exposée au lecteur.

Jean Castillon a-t-il rajeuni les autres histoires "singulières et naïves" qui voisinent avec la nôtre d'une aussi déplorable façon? Nous n'avons pas eu le loisir de nous en assurer. Cependant les contemporains ne durent pas partager notre façon de voir. En effet, comme il nous est dit en 1783 lors d'une réédition, "ces Essais hasardés sans aucune prétention réussirent mieux que l'Auteur n'avait osé l'espérer. La première édition, publiée en 1769, in-8°, petit format, fut bientôt épuisée. Peut-être fit-elle naître l'idée de la *Bibliothèque des Romans*."[16] Costard, qui avait acquis le Privilège de la Bibliothèque bleue, en fit, en 1775–1776, une réédition assez luxueuse dite "entièrement refondue et considérablement augmentée", en in-8° de 20 cm., ornée de belles gravures, dessinées par Claude-Louis Desrais, "l'un des illustrateurs les plus courus du dernier tiers du 18ème siècle."[17] Jean de Calais en forme le n° IV, 78 p. et pl. Cette édition resta cependant inachevée, Costard ayant renoncé à la librairie. Elle fut reprise et continuée en 1783 par Fournier, Jean Castillon y ajoutant — encouragé, semble-t-il, par les éloges décernés aux n° parus par le Marquis de Paulmy dans les *Mélanges extraits d'une Grande Bibliothèque*[18] — une réfection, sur d'anciens manuscrits est-il dit, de l'Histoire des quatre fils Aymon. La Bibliothèque bleue, entièrement refondue et considérablement augmentée, Liège, F. J. Desoër, 3 vol. in-12, m'étant restée inaccessible, je ne puis dire si elle reproduit l'édition parisienne de Costard et Fournier.[18a] De toutes façons, d'après Nisard, Jean de Calais fait partie de cette Bibliothèque bleue de Liège; très probablement dans la rédaction de Castillon.[19] Enfin, Garnier, à Paris, publia en 1862, toujours sous le titre "Bibliothèque bleue", 4 vol. in-8° sous couverture bleue, contenant huit récits, soit en plus de ceux déjà nommés et qui sont textuellement repris des éditions antérieures: Geneviève de Brabant. Jean de Calais est au tome II, pp. 109–222: c'est toujours le texte de Jean Castillon.

Là ne s'achève pas la longue fortune de ce Jean de Calais remanié. Car lui aussi est allé au peuple, dans une nouvelle série de brochures de colportage: telles sont:

[16] *La Bibliothèque bleue, Entièrement refondue et considérablement* augmentée, N° VI. Les Quatre Fils d'Aymon. Histoire héroïque. A Paris, chez Fournier, 1783, Avertissement de l'éditeur.

[17] U. Thieme, u. F. Becker, *Allgemeines Lexikon der bildenden Künstler*, 9. Bd., Leipzig, 1913.

[18] Cf. Avertissement de l'éditeur Fournier (cité ci-dessus n. 16), où il est dit: "Voyez ces Mélanges, tome E, pages 178–180".

[18a] Ayant pu, depuis la remise du manuscrit de mon article, consulter cette édition de Liège, je puis affirmer qu'elle reproduit exactement—et les histoires se suivant selon un ordre identique—le texte de la Bibliothèque bleue de Costard et Fournier, 1775–1783.

[19] Charles Nisard: *Histoire des livres populaires...*, Paris, 1864, II, p. 411.

Paris, Libr. popul. des villes et des campagnes, 1848; 1850; Paris, Ruel aîné, 1855; Paris, Renault, (1860); Avignon, Peyri, (1855). Toutes ces brochures in-18º, de 36 p., portent le même titre: "Histoire de Jean de Calais sur de nouveaux mémoires" et offrent le même texte: un texte dérivant incontestablement de celui de Castillon, dont il est le résumé. Ces brochures présentent cependant une innovation: elles rayent entièrement l'épisode du cadavre enterré par Jean de Calais, considéré en bonne logique, par celui qui adapta le texte de Castillon pour le colportage, comme adventice dans un récit qui voyait dans le sauveur de Jean de Calais, non plus du tout un Mort reconnaissant, mais l'Ange protecteur de la royauté!

. . .

Ainsi donc l'Histoire de Jean de Calais s'est-elle propagée dans le colportage à deux (même à trois, cf. ci-dessus) reprises et selon deux modèles littéraires différents; aussi pour la même date de 1848 par exemple, avons-nous deux brochures sensiblement différentes, l'une remontant à Mme. de Gomez (Montbéliard, Deckherr, 1848) et l'autre à Jean Castillon (Paris, Libr. populaire des villes et des campagnes, 1848). Si l'on se reporte au passage où Charles Nisard traite de Jean de Calais,[20] on reconnaît immédiatement qu'il a eu entre les mains une édition de chaque série: Epinal, Pellerin, s.d. et Paris, Libr. popul. des villes et des campagnes, 1849. Et malheureusement aucune des éditions de colportage complètes du texte de Mme. de Gomez, qui semblent bien, il est vrai, d'après notre bref recensement indiqué ci-dessus, avoir été assez rares. Malheureusement aussi Nisard ne s'est-il pas donné la peine de se reporter au texte original: sa référence est d'ailleurs fausse; Jean de Calais n'a jamais fait partie des *Cent nouvelles nouvelles*, 10 vol. in-12º, de Mme. de Gomez, mais bien des *Journées amusantes*. S'il a raison de trouver l'édition d'Epinal "plus courte et plus sensée" que celle de Paris "revue et corrigée par un académicien", il n'en est pas moins injuste pour cette histoire d'un "manque presque absolu d'intérêt" dit-il, alors qu'il ne l'a connue que tronquée et déformée. Et le fait d'émettre que la brochure, "plus elle abrège le texte original, plus elle épargne d'ennui au lecteur", prouve nettement qu'il n'avait pas une vue juste des filiations, telles que nous les avons exposées ci-dessus.

Avant d'en finir avec cette partie retraçant la tradition écrite de notre récit, il nous reste à mentionner que l'Histoire de Jean de Calais de Mme. de Gomez—qui avait d'ailleurs aussi été reprise, sous une forme paraphrasée, dans le nº de

[20] Ch. Nisard, *op. cit.*, II, pp. 407–411.

déc. 1776 de la *Bibliothèque universelle des romans*[21] — fut introduite également par Le Roux de Lincy dans le recueil (1 seul volume) intitulé *Nouvelle Bibliothèque bleue ou Légendes populaires de la France* qu'il fit paraître à Paris en 1842 et pour lequel Charles Nodier écrivit une préface enthousiaste. Dans son introduction, Le Roux de Lincy dit: "Tous les ouvrages qui composent ce volume appartiennent au même genre de littérature: des traditions historiques, des aventures merveilleuses devenues populaires en forment le sujet." Et, rendant hommage à la véritable Bibliothèque bleue, c'est-à-dire à ces modestes brochures "dont les plus anciennes remontent au début du XVII° s. et qui ont obtenu le plus grand des succès, celui de la popularité", il ajoute: "Ce fut donc, suivant moi, une tentative malheureuse que celle qui fut mise à exécution vers 1770, par un nommé Castillon. Il essaya de rajeunir le style de ces anciennes histoires, il crut les rendre *dignes de toutes sortes de lecteurs en les refondant entièrement et en y ajoutant des situations et des épisodes nouveaux*. La simplicité du récit, la naïveté, enfin tout ce qui rappelait l'ancienneté de ces contes et en faisait la valeur, a disparu dans ces maladroites contrefaçons. Bien loin d'imiter Castillon, je me suis appliqué à reproduire les textes de l'ancienne *Bibliothèque bleue*. Il faut respecter cette version admise par le peuple; elle est sacramentelle et nous a conservé la mémoire de nos plus anciennes traditions."

Plus loin, dans la présentation particulière de Jean de Calais, il écrit: "Ce petit roman, en comparaison de quelques-unes des histoires qui composent ce volume, est moderne. La plus ancienne édition que j'ai pu rencontrer est de 1738." Il en donne la référence; c'est celle de l'édition anonyme de Bruxelles, citée par nous dès le début de notre article comme étant la première édition séparée connue de l'Histoire de Jean de Calais et comme reproduisant exactement et intégralement (mis à part l'alinéa d'introduction) le texte de Mme. de Gomez des *Journées amusantes*. Mais c'est là que se place pour moi quelque chose d'assez incompréhensible: alors que Le Roux de Lincy cite cette édition de 1738, édition complète, répétons-le, du texte original, c'est, dans la Nouvelle Bibliothèque bleue, un texte tronqué qu'il reproduit! A savoir ce texte édulcoré qui, à la suite de la première brochure troyenne de 1758, a été celui de beaucoup de livrets de colportage! D'autre part, il se trompe évidemment en croyant, comme il l'écrit, que c'est Castillon qui a fait entrer Jean de Calais dans le colportage.

Si nous ajoutons à ces erreurs d'appréciation de Charles Nisard et de Le Roux de Lincy, celle de Barbier dans son Dictionnaire des ouvrages anonymes qui ne connaît comme auteur de notre histoire que Jean Castillon, et ne se rend pas compte que le Jean de Calais de l'édition anonyme de Bruxelles 1738, celui de

---

[21] Déc. 1776, pp. 134–154.

Castillon de 1770, et celui de Le Roux de Lincy de 1842 sont, finalement, trois textes différents, nous pensons que l'on voudra bien considérer comme justifié le rétablissement des faits que nous venons d'exposer, fut-ce avec quelque longueur.[22]

Cependant, en conclusion de ce périple à travers les textes, nous sommes obligés de constater qu'en dépit d'une bonne fortune littéraire prolongée, notre histoire a, en somme, été très souvent maltraitée, et rarement rendue avec la simplicité dramatique avec laquelle Mme. de Gomez avait su, en 1722, la mettre par écrit.

II. JEAN DE CALAIS DANS LA TRADITION ORALE

Mme. de Gomez nous assure que son récit "est tiré d'un livre qui a pour titre Histoire fabuleuse de la Maison des Rois de Portugal." En réalité—et M. da Camara Cascudo est bien de cet avis aussi[23]—, c'est là certainement pur artifice littéraire de sa part. Son histoire semble bien puisée plutôt—directement ou non—à la tradition orale populaire. Reinhold Köhler ne dit-il pas ainsi, dans son étude déjà citée sur les traditions du mort reconnaissant: "Vergleicht man die von Simrock und soeben von mir beigebrachten Märchen damit, so wird man zugeben, daß in dieser französischen Fassung des Märchens vom Kaufmannssohne und vom dankbaren Toten die echten Elemente vollständig, wie kaum in einer andern Fassung erhalten sind und keine fremden Elemente aus andern Märchen Eingang bekommen haben."[24]

Inversement la nouvelle de Mme. de Gomez a incontestablement influencé, dans une très large mesure, la tradition orale, non seulement française, mais, par l'intermédiaire des traductions et adaptations en plusieurs langues qui en ont été faites,[25] celle de nombreux pays: "Auf die französische, italienische, spanische,

---

[22] Nous nous hâtons d'ajouter que tout n'est pas nouveau dans cette mise au point, encore que nous l'ayons menée presque à terme avant d'avoir pris connaissance, d'un côté de l'article de R. Köhler (cf. n. 3), qui mentionnait déjà à la fois le texte original de Mme de Gomez et, brièvement, l'existence de deux séries différentes de livrets de colportage, de l'autre de l'étude approfondie du savant brésilien Luis da Camara Cascudo: *Cinco Livros do Povo, Introduçao ao Estudo da Novelistica no Brasil, Pesquisas e Notas*: ... *João de Calais*. Rio-de-Janeiro, 1953 (pp. 351–437). M. Cascudo présente à la fois l'auteur, Mme de Gomez, et le réfecteur, Jean Castillon, pour établir que le João de Calais de la "littérature de cordon" encore vivante au Portugal et au Brésil dérive du texte original; aussi reproduit-il intégralement l'Histoire de Jean de Calais d'après la 3ème éd. des *Journées amusantes*, et la fait-il suivre de la traduction en portugais, telle qu'elle a eu cours.

[23] *Op. cit.*, p. 362.

[24] Köhler, *op. cit.*, p. 15.

[25] Cf. Köhler, *op. cit.*, Cascudo, *op. cit.*; voir aussi Luis da Camara Cascudo; *Dicionario de Folclore Brasileiro*, Rio-de-Janeiro, 1954, pp. 330–331: João de Calais.

portugiesische und deutsche Volksüberlieferung hat die Erzählung Einfluß geübt",
écrivent Bolte-Polivka.[26]

Des 32 références de versions, dont six manuscrites, que recense la fiche 506 du
Catalogue du conte français, Paul Delarue estimait qu'une très forte proportion
portait la marque de la nouvelle de Mme. de Gomez.[27] La place limitée impartie
à cette contribution ne nous permet pas d'étudier en détail ces versions orales;
aussi bien le seront-elles dans le deuxième volume, en cours de préparation, du
Catalogue du conte populaire français. Nous en donnons cependant ici les références, classées géographiquement comme elles le seront dans le catalogue:

1. A. Merkelbach-Pinck: Lothringer Volksmärchen, Kassel, 1940, 160–162: *Die
Königstöchter*.
2. Manuscrits A. Millien-P. Delarue: Contes du Nivernais, version A. *Jean de Calais*.
3. ID., ib., vers. B. *Jean de Calais*.
4. ID., ib., vers. C. sans titre.
5. ID., ib., vers. D. *Jean de Bordeaux*.
6. E. Souvestre: Le foyer breton, Nouv. éd., Paris, Lévy frères, 1874, II, 1–21:
L'heureux Mao.
7. F. M. Luzel: Légendes chrétiennes de la Basse-Bretagne, Paris, 1881, II, 40–58:
Cantique spirituel sur la charité admirable que montra St. Corentin...
8. ID, Contes populaires de Basse-Bretagne, Paris, 1887, I, 403–424: *Iouenn Ker-
menou, l'homme de parole*.
9. Revue des Traditions populaires (R. T. P.) XXII (1907), 273–274, Basse-Bretagne
(H. de Kerbeuzec): *Histoire de Jean de Callac*.
10. R. T. P., XXVI (1911), 39–40, B.-Bret. (J. Frison): *Le mort reconnaissant*.
11. R. T. P., XXVII (1912), 387–389, B.-Bret. (H. Genet): *Le fils du roi de Brest*.
12. François Cadic: Contes et légendes de Bretagne avec commentaires explicatifs,
Paris, 1914, 179–187: *Le fils du roi de France et la mort*.
13. Anatole Le Braz: La légende de la mort chez les Bretons armoricains, 5° ed., Paris,
1928, II, 177–199: *Jean Carré*.
14. Paul Sébillot: Contes populaires de la Haute-Bretagne. 3ème série. Contes des
marins, Paris, 1882, 164–171: *Jean de Calais*.
15. R. T. P., IX (1894), 177–178, Hte.-Bret. (P. Sébillot): *Le corps mort reconnaissant*.
16. R. T. P., IX (1894), 178, Hte.-Bret. (P. Sébillot): *Le corps mort reconnaissant*
(résumé).
17. R. T. P., IX (1894), 179–180, Hte.-Bret. (P. Sébillot): *Jean de Bordeaux*
(résumé).
18. Almanach du Phare, 1891, 108 (P. Sébillot): *Jean de Calais*.

[26] Bolte-Polivka, *op. cit.*, III, p. 500.
[27] Paul Delarue: *Le conte populaire français: Catalogue raisonné...* Tome I, Paris, 1957, p. 28.

19. Ariane de Félice: Contes de Haute-Bretagne, Paris, 1954, 121–128, conte X: *Jean de Calais*.

20. Manuscrit Geneviève Massignon, Contes de l'Ouest: *Jean de Calais* (Loire Atlantique).

21. Cenac-Moncaut: Littérature populaire de la Gascogne, Paris, 1868, 5–14: *Rira bien qui rira le dernier*.

22. Jean-François Bladé: Contes populaires de la Gascogne, Paris, 1886, II, 67–91: *Jean de Calais*.

23. Gaston Maugard: Contes des Pyrénées, Paris, 1955, 56–64: *Jean de Calais* (déjà publié *in*: Folklore-Aude, 1938, n° 9, 155–165).

24. Manuscrit Charles Joisten: Contes folkloriques des Hautes-Alpes, n° 37: *Jean de Calais*.

25. James Bruyn Andrews: Contes ligures. Traditions de la Riviéra; 1892, 111–116: *Le mort reconnaissant*.

26. ID., ib., 187–192: *Jean de Calais*.

27. W. Webster: Basque Legends, London, 1877, 146–150: *Juan Dekos* (= Jean d'Ecosse).

28. ID., ib., 151–154: *Juan de Kalais*.

29. Henri Pourrat: Le trésor des contes, II, Paris, 1949, 273–281: *Le conte du marchand de blé* (non localisé).

30. Carmen Roy, Contes populaires canadiens (8ème série), Journal of American Folklore, LXIII (1950), 199–203: *Les sept nègres*.

31. Soeur Marie-Ursule, Civilisation traditionnelle des Lavalois, Québec, 1951, 263–266: *Jean-le-Collet*.

32. Germain Lemieux: Contes populaires franco-ontariens, Sudbury, Ont., 1953, 7–20: *Jean de Calais*.

Me semblent être des versions originales, sans influence de la nouvelle littéraire, les n°s 1, 6, 7, 15, peut-être aussi le n° 16 qui n'est qu'un fragment, et le n° 30. Suivent au contraire de très près le récit de Mme. de Gomez les versions suivantes: n°s 2, 3 (bien que le motif du corps enterré ait disparu), 9, 11, 12, 14, 19, 20, 24, 32. Dans les autres versions aussi l'influence est nette. Le nom de Jean de Calais s'est souvent maintenu, parfois déformé cependant (n° 9: Jean de Callac; n° 13: Jean Carré; n° 31: Jean le Collet) ou remplacé: Jean de Bordeaux (n°s 5, 17), Jean d'Ecosse (n° 27). Les noms des deux jeunes femmes ont été oubliés plus fréquemment, ou parfois intervertis, ou assimilés à des prénoms peut-être plus connus: Constance devient Hortense dans les versions nivernaises A et B, Isabelle y devient Isabeth ou Elisabeth (aussi n° 19). Le traître peut n'avoir pas de nom, mais Don Juan est aussi devenu Don Jean (n° 20) ou, de façon fort amusante, Donjon! (n° 2). Le traître juif dans la version de la Légende de la mort (n° 13) ne s'expliquerait-il pas aussi par la déformation du nom espagnol? Orimanie et Palmanie sont devenus la Lombardie (nº 32), le Portugal peut devenir l'Espagne (nº 12) ou cèder la place à l'Angleterre (nºs 13, 19, 26, 29). La mention "près de deux ans" délimitant le temps passé par Jean de Calais sur son île et aussi le "veuvage" de sa femme—mention banale—devient, dans les versions orales: sept ans (nºs 4, 9, 10, 19, 20, 23, 28), ou plus modestement mais tout aussi folklorique: un an et un jour (nºs 14, 27). Le mort reconnaissant peut apparaître sous forme animale, oiseau (nºs 4, 23, 29: corbeau; nº 5: pie; nº 22: grand oiseau blanc), ou encore renard (nº 17).

Si, reprenant ces 32 versions en mains, nous en écartons le nº 18 (dont nous n'avons pu prendre connaissance), le nº 16 (qui n'est qu'un fragment), et le nº 21 (où le thème est trop altéré pour pouvoir être pris en considération dans ce qui suit), nous constatons que, sur 29 versions, 17 sont des récits complets, c'est à dire comprenant, outre le motif de la fiancée rachetée (rarement conquise d'une autre manière: nºs 6, 7, 15), le motif du cadavre enterré par le héros et celui du partage. Ce sont les nºs 5, 6, 7, 8, 14, 19, 20, 22, 23, 24, 25, 26, 27, 28, 29, 31, 32. Même si l'on objecte que les nºs 6 et 29 sont des versions littérarisées, il demeure un total minimum de 15 contes complets. C'est uniquement dans la version lorraine (nº 1) que les deux motifs, du cadavre et du partage, ne figurent pas. Dans les 11 versions restantes, si le motif du partage manque assez fréquemment, soit dans 9 versions (nºs 2, 4, 9, 10, 11, 12, 13, 15, 30), le motif, plus important, du cadavre enterré ne manque que dans deux versions (nºs 3 et 17), où d'ailleurs celui du partage subsiste.

On remarquera que le conte a été recueilli souvent le long des côtes; mais la versions pyrénéenne (nº 23) est une jolie adaptation terrienne. Chronologiquement ces versions s'étalent sur près d'un siècle, de 1868 (nº 21) à 1958 (nº 20), portant témoignage de la persistance du thème dans la tradition orale.

III. JEAN DE CALAIS DANS L'IMAGERIE POPULAIRE

Jean de Calais, héros d'une double tradition, écrite et orale, s'est assuré au XIXº siècle, un autre moyen de diffusion encore de sa renommée légendaire: l'imagerie populaire. Le Musée ATP a la bonne fortune de posséder, dans son Cabinet des Estampes, trois images de Jean de Calais, toutes trois différentes. Nous avons, d'autre part, retrouvé des formes très voisines de la première image ATP dans d'autres collections, grâce à un bref sondage bibliographique, que nous retraçons ci-dessous à la suite de la fiche signalétique de l'image ATP nº 1.

— I —

Cote ATP: C 54.60.23. Jean de Calais A Lille, chez Castiaux, libraire. 236. Imprimerie de Blocquel.

Bois gravé col. vergé
bois: L. 255 × H. 183 [28]
feuille: L. 367 × H. 230

Sans texte.

Cette image du Musée ATP a été exposée à l'Exposition: *L'Image de Lille*[29]; elle figure dans le catalogue de cette manifestation sous le nº 216 avec les mentions supplémentaires suivantes: "Bois de Chartres. On peut rapprocher cette image de celle de Toulouse."

Consultant la Liste des productions connues de l'imagerie populaire chartraine dressée par M. Adolphe Aynaud en fin de l'étude magistrale de M. Maurice Jusselin sur les "Imagiers et cartiers à Chartres",[30] nous y retrouvons sous le nº 160: Jean de Calais. H. 180; L. 250 Attribué à Fleuret. Semblable à Toulouse. *Album Castiaux et retirage Castiaux* nº 543.

Une notice p. 233 nous apprend que ces deux albums Castiaux (Collection A. Aynaud) nous donnent en retirages les bois de l'Imagerie lilloise ainsi que ceux de Chartres cédés à Castiaux par Garnier-Allabre en 1828."

L'image de Lille est ainsi postérieure à 1828; et certainement antérieure à 1835, l'association Blocquel-Castiaux cessant d'être active à partir de cette date.[31]

"Castiaux réédita en noir et en couleurs, sans texte les bois de Garnier-Allabre", écrit M. Jusselin. Si les deux images, de Lille et de Chartres, sont ainsi identiques quant au bois, il est très probable que l'image chartraine de Jean de Calais contrairement à celle de Lille, s'accompagnait d'un texte.

Le bois de Chartres, antérieur à 1828, est attribué à Fleuret. "En 1822, Garnier retint à son service pendant un an le Parisien un peu bohème Fleuret, et lui fit occasionnellement des commandes à Paris, au moins en 1824 et 1825."[32]

"Semblable à Toulouse", nous apprenaient les catalogues de Lille et de Chartres. Effectivement, voici, au nº 210 du Catalogue "L'estampe toulousaine. L'Imagerie populaire et les graveurs en taille d'épargne de 1660 à 1830"[33]:

[28] Dimensions en millimètres.
[29] Catalogue de l'Exposition *L'Image de Lille*, Lille, Palais des Beaux-Arts, 23 nov. 1957—12 janv. 1958; Paris, Musée des arts et traditions populaires, 13 févr.—14 mai 1958.
[30] Maurice Jusselin: *Imagiers et cartiers à Chartres*... Chartres, 1957.
[31] Cf. Catal. *Image de Lille*, *op. cit.*, pp. XI–XIII et 37–39.
[32] Jusselin, *op. cit.*, p. 173.
[33] Toulouse, Musée Paul-Dupuy, 1952, pp. 96–97.

Jean de Calais. A Toulouse, chez L. Abadie cadet, fabricant de papier-tapisseries, breveté par S. A. R. Madame la Dauphine, rue Pénitens-Gris, n° 32.

178 × 254
Epr. coloriée

Paris, Coll. A. Aynaud.

Cette image toulousaine peut être datée: après 1824; en effet: "Dès 1815, Louis Abadie Cadet est breveté par S. A. R. Madame, duchesse d'Angoulême, privilège dont aucun autre imagier n'a joui... Après l'avènement de Charles X qui faisait de son fils l'héritier présomptif de la couronne, il change le titre de sa protectrice: *breveté par S. A. R. Madame la Dauphine.* Cette modification permet de donner une date aproximative à un certain nombre de pièces qui sont de la sorte antérieures ou posterieures à l'année 1824."[34]

Cette image est reproduite, sans commentaires, dans Duchartre et Saulnier[35], ce qui nous a permis d'en prendre connaissance: bois et texte, ce dernier imprimé sur les deux côtés et au bas du bois.

Consultant "L'imagerie orléanaise" d'A. Martin, nous y avons trouvé:

"Jean de Calais. A Orléans, chez Rabier Boulard, dominotier et marchand de papier,
Rue des Carmes, n° 45

bois: L. 260 × H. 180
feuille: L. 390 × H. 320

L'histoire de Jean de Calais est imprimée sur les deux côtés et au bas du bois".[36]

Cette image orléanaise est antérieure à 1842, Michel Rabier Boulard, né en 1776, ayant cèdé son affaire cette année.[37]

Notre collègue, Melle. Michèle Richet, a eu l'amabilité de nous signaler l'existence, dans la collection de Beauvais, d'un Jean de Calais, exposé à l'exposition "Gravures sur bois éditées à Beauvais au début du XIX° siècle", n° 22 du catalogue; citée aussi par A. Aynaud[38]:

Jean de Calais. A Beauvais, chez Dupont-Diot, rue de la Taillerie, N° 666. (Imp. de Moissand).

bois: L. 260 × H. 175
Feuille: L. 385 × H. 297

[34] *Ibidem*, pp. 84–85.
[35] Pierre-Louis Duchartre et René Saulnier: *L'imagerie populaire*, Paris, 1925, pl. entre pp. 406 et 407.
[36] Auguste Martin: L'Imagerie orléanaise, Paris, 1928, p. 208, notice 310.
[37] *Ibidem*, p. 173.
[38] Adolphe Aynaud: *L'Imagerie de Beauvais.* Extrait du *Vieux Papier*, juillet 1951, 14 p., ici p. 12.

L'image peut être datée entre 1826 — date à laquelle "Diot cède sa maison à son gendre, d'où la firme Dupont-Diot" — et 1828 — date de "la vente des bois à Lacour, de Nancy, qui les cède ensuite à Metz".[39]

La photographie de cette image que nous avons eue à notre disposition montre que le texte est disposé comme à Toulouse et à Orléans.

Si nous avons groupé ces images de Toulouse, d'Orléans et de Beauvais à la suite de notre image ATP de Chartres-Lille, c'est qu'il s'agit incontestablement de bois très semblables; nous n'en sommes pas absolument sûrs pour l'image orléanaise dont nous ne connaissons que la description d'A. Martin, mais pour les trois autres: Chartres-Lille, Toulouse et Beauvais, il n'y a pas de doute possible: on s'est copié sans vergogne.

A. Martin décrit la scène représentée comme suit: "Jean de Calais, en officier de marine, et ayant derrière lui son navire s'entretient avec les deux dames qu'il a délivrées des mains du Corsaire." Cette description s'applique aussi aux trois autres images que nous avons pu confronter. Ajoutons que la scène se passe sur la terrasse d'un château qu'on aperçoit partiellement sur la gauche, et que les deux dames sont en habits de cour, Constance se distinguant d'Isabelle par le port d'une petite couronne.

Les éléments de datation que nous avons donnés ci-dessus pour chaque image ne permettent guère d'établir une filiation. Tout au plus croyons-nous pouvoir avancer que l'image de Beauvais ne doit pas se trouver en fin de chaîne: en effet elle possède des détails particuliers en commun avec Toulouse (tel le collier de Constance; telle aussi la coiffure en mèches de Constance, alors que Chartres la coiffe plutôt en bandeaux) et du moins un autre détail en commun avec Chartres: le collier d'Isabelle, dont la forme, double, n'est pas banale; si l'image de Beauvais se trouvait en fin de la chaîne des filiations, il faudrait supposer que le graveur de Beauvais s'est servi à la fois de deux modèles, supposition qui nous semble à rejeter jusqu'à preuve du contraire.

Réflexions présentées toutefois sous toute réserve: le fait que l'image d'Orléans échappe à la confrontation, et, surtout, le caractère très limité de notre recensement ne peuvent qu'inciter à la plus extrême prudence.

Nous avons pu confronter le texte encadrant l'image de Toulouse et celle de Beauvais. Il est, à quelques tours de phrases près, identique. Il est pris très nettement dans les livrets de colportage de la première série, ceux qui, à la suite des éditions troyennes, reproduisaient le texte de Mme. de Gomez, mais avec des suppressions sur lesquelles nous avons longuement attiré l'attention. Celles-ci vont encore plus loin ici, puisque l'épisode du cadavre endetté est "sauté": on passe tout de suite au rachat des captives. Motif du mort reconnaissant et motif du

[39] *Ibidem*, p. 8.

partage des biens ont complètement disparu. La personnalité du sauveur de Jean n'est pas expliquée. Seule intéresse l'aventure de Jean et de Constance.

Il convient d'attirer l'attention sur le fait que L. Abadie à Toulouse a publié à la fois une brochure de colportage (texte tronqué de Mme. de Gomez) et une image de Jean de Calais. Ce fait est-il suffisant pour étayer l'hypothèse de la primauté de l'image de Toulouse sur les autres? Nous posons la question aux spécialistes de l'imagerie.

— 2 —

Image ATP, cote: C 53.86.3118. Jean de Calais ou la Vertu Recompensée. Paris. – Glémarec, libraire, fabricant d'images, rue Saint Jacques, 29. [en plus petit]: Paris. – Typ. et Lith. Lacour, rue Soufflot, 18. Bois colorié.

bois: L. 265 × H. 190

feuille: L. 382 × H. 291

Si la scène représentée, les personnages, le lieu de l'action (terrasse) sont les mêmes, ils sont traités de façon nettement différente. La façade du château, à gauche a fait place à un mur semblant border un parc et se terminant par une tourelle. A droite devant le navire, qu'on n'aperçoit que partiellement, des caisses sont posées à terre. Les costumes des personnages, qui sont nu-tête, sont entièrement différents: costumes fantaisistes, alliant le drapé à la tunique courte. Jean a toujours l'épée au côté (cf. reproduction ci-après).

Cette image est plus récente que celles examinées au paragraphe précédent. "La plus célèbre des imageries parisiennes du XIXème siècle, celle qui tenta de lutter contre les Lorrains, Pellerin ou Gangel, fut la maison Glémarec... De 1858 à 1860, Glémarec est installé 29, rue St. Jacques, au 1er. étage", lisons-nous dans Duchartre et Saulnier.[40]

Le texte encadrant l'image sur les deux côtés et dans le bas est celui que nous avons reproduit en tête de notre article: vers d'un style détestable, certes, mais retraçant l'histoire de Jean de Calais *au complet*, motifs du mort reconnaissant et du partage compris. Le titre est: "Jean de Calais, ou la Vertu récompensée", ce double titre caractérisant également, on s'en souvient, nos deux brochures de colportage au texte *intégral* de Mme. de Gomez (Caen, P. Chalopin; Limoges, F. Chapoulaud). Il n'y a pas de doute que le texte de cette image parisienne a été versifié d'après une brochure de colportage de ce courant-là, dont nous avons dit la rareté.

A noter que ce texte versifié est entrecoupé de temps en temps (onze fois) d'indications d'airs sur lesquels il est à chanter (nous ne les avons pas reproduites):

---

[40] Duchartre et Saulnier, *op. cit.*, pp. 106 et 108; cf. aussi notice sur Glémarec en fin de l'ouvrage des mêmes auteurs sur *L'Imagerie parisienne*, Paris, 1944.

Peuple Français, peuple de frères — Nous sommes précepteur d'amour — Du Café du Bosquet, etc.

—3—

Image ATP, Cote: C 53.86.3117. Histoire de Jean de Calais. Fabrique de Pellerin, Imprimeur-Libraire, à Epinal. Bois colorié. Signature du graveur: Vanson.

feuille: H. 398 × L. 301

16 petites gravures: H. 80 × L. 68

Légende sous chacune des seize gravures.

Texte et images retracent l'Histoire de Jean de Calais telle que l'a racontée la première série de brochures de colportage, la plus courante: récit inspiré de Mme. de Gomez, maintenant au début (cf. gravures 2 et 3) la découverte du cadavre déchiré par les chiens, dont Jean de Calais paye les dettes et la sépulture—épisode avec lequel pourtant aucun lien n'est fait par la suite, l'histoire se terminant, sans plus, par la réunion des époux et le supplice de Don Juan. Il n'y a même plus de personnage sauveur, Jean de Calais reparaît, après deux ans et "après avoir couru de grands périls", sans autre explication.

• • •

De cet examen d'images populaires de Jean de Calais, deux constatations découlent: d'abord le lien évident entre littérature de colportage et imagerie; tout porte à croire—bien qu'une étude approfondie n'ait pas encore été menée à notre connaissance dans ce sens là—que l'imagerie populaire française—conformément à la théorie de la "fixité littéraire" de l'imagerie mise en avant par M. de Meyer pour l'imagerie flamande, sur la base de quelques exemples bien traités[41]— a eu besoin, elle aussi, en règle générale d'un support littéraire pour mettre en oeuvre des thèmes de notre tradition orale, avec laquelle elle semble ainsi n'être entrée qu'en contact indirect.

Seconde constatation: l'imagerie (mise à part les compositions réunissant plusieurs gravures—dans le cas présent seize sur notre image d'Epinal—sur la même feuille) est obligée de choisir, dans le déroulement du récit, un moment, jugé à tort ou à raison par l'imagier, comme crucial. Ainsi ici de l'entretien entre Jean et les deux jeunes femmes qu'il a libérées.

Ce choix, dans nos images de Jean de Calais, est-il simple hasard? Est-il l'effet de la décision d'un seul auquel les autres ont emboîté le pas? S'explique-t-il par l'influence de la littérature de colportage qui, nous l'avons vu, a toujours maintenu intact l'épisode du rachat des captives, alors qu'elle a, au contraire,

[41] Maurits de Meyer: Le conte populaire dans l'imagerie populaire hollandaise et belge, *Fabula.*, Berlin, I, Heft 3, 1958, pp. 183–192.

souvent malmené, mal compris, voire ignoré, celui du mort reconnaissant? Imagerie et littérature de colportage ont-elles eu le sentiment que c'était là le noyau de l'histoire? Sentiment qui rejoindrait alors celui exprimé par le dernier en date et le plus savant commentateur des contes si complexes du mort reconnaissant, Sven Liljeblad, quand il considère comme "für ihn charakterisches Hauptmotiv... das seine epische Idee bildet" de notre contetype (Type B dans la classification établie par lui des traditions du mort reconnaissant) "das Motiv von dem Loskauf der Prinzessin aus der Gefangenschaft".[42] Sven Liljblad est en effet d'avis que notre conte-type a été raconté primairement sans "Helfermotiv".[43]; ce qu'il commente plus loin, en se plaçant au point de vue de l'unité épique de notre récit: "Besonders in der "Prinzessin in der Sklaverei" (B-Typ) hat man das Gefühl, daß der Tote hier nicht hingehört. Er tritt in dem halb aristokratischen und halb realistisch anspruchsvollen Märchen als das Gespenst aus einer vergangenen Welt auf, das er auch wirklich ist. Episch gesehen hat das Motiv vom Loskauf aus der Sklaverei die Priorität, und man erhält eine vorzügliche Abenteuernovelle, wenn man das Motiv vom toten Helfer wegläßt, das in diesem Zusammenhang bloß ein schwächender Zusatz ist. Die doppelte Tugendhaftigkeit in der Handlung des Märchens, die den Helden gleichzeitig die Schuld des Toten bezahlen und die Prinzessin loskaufen läßt, ist eine bedenkliche epische Schwäche...".[44]

· · ·

Cependant, si nous revenons vers nos versions orales et la statistique rapide que nous en avons dressée, nous constatons que la tradition orale a maintenu, à une assez forte majorité (17 (ou 15) récits complets + 9 récits maintenant le motif du cadavre enterré et ne laissant tomber que le motif du partage) les deux épisodes constitutifs de notre conte-type en un tout cohérent. Face au choix, partial, de l'imagerie et aux inconséquences de la littérature de colportage, cette relative permanence (qui n'exclut pas les variations de détail: on se souvient par exemple que le mort reconnaissant peut être corbeau, pie ou renard), ne porte-t-elle pas témoignage de la vigueur de cette tradition orale?

C'est sur cette conviction, et sur une dernière pensée amicale à Mme. de Gomez qui, en 1722, sut reconnaître le relief dramatique de notre récit et le restituer sans l'altérer, que nous concluerons.

Musée des Arts et Traditions Populaires, Paris

[42] Sven Liljeblad, *Die Tobiasgeschichte und andere Märchen mit toten Helfern*, Lund, 1927, p. 42.
[42] *Ibidem*, p. 97.
[44] *Ib.*, p. 148.

PROBLEMS IN LATIN-AMERICAN
FOLKLORE BIBLIOGRAPHY

R. S. Boggs

The scholar who searches in the bibliography of Latin-American folklore for the materials he needs, encounters a number of problems that make his path of progress rather rugged. I shall try here to review some of these problems, which have plagued me since I began to work in this field some thirty years ago, when Archer Taylor was teaching at the University of Chicago and first inspired in me as a student there such a deep interest in Hispanic folklore that my love for it still endures. Through these years most of my publications have been in this field. I take this opportunity to express my gratitude to him.

My first problem was with libraries. In Latin America, some of the best libraries are private ones, of scholars who take great pride in their personal collections. Frequently they are forced to develop them for lack of public library facilities. Private libraries always present a problem, for one must first find out where they are, and then go there personally to ascertain in detail what they contain. Then one must trust to personal favor to gain repeated access to such libraries. Sometimes the number of hours public libraries are open during the day, and frequent holidays on which they are closed, become irksome factors. They may be poorly cataloged, or have no catalog. In some of the biggest and best libraries of the United States access to materials through catalogues becomes a serious problem to one searching for folklore titles.

Usually folklore is scattered through various divisions of the general classification that governs the subject cataloguing and shelving of library materials. Some libraries now use the Library of Congress classification. Many libraries throughout

309

the New World still use the Dewey system. In any case, university, municipal, and other libraries open to the public are usually general, hence must face the problem of classifying diverse categories of materials, along the lines of broad, logical concepts and large and long established fields of knowledge, or even using more mechanical divisions, such as periodicals and institutional series. Hence one must search for folklore under numerous other headings, such as Music, Art, Indians, etc. Some ten years ago, I spent a summer in the Library of Congress at Washington, combining my humble talents as a folklorist with those of an excellent professional library classifier, and we devised a classification unified for folklore, and tested it against materials in the Library of Congress. It was published in *Folklore Americas* (1948, VIII, Nos. 1–2, pp. 1–65) and in *Southern Folklore Quarterly* (1949, XIII, No. 3, pp. 161–226). But we cannot hope that this Folklore classification, though useful for the folklorist, would ever be adopted by general libraries the folklorist must use.

The persistent folklorist, who overcomes the problems of libraries and classification, and actually lays hand on the folklore items available to him in the average library, is amazed to discover how small is the amount of material he finds on Latin-American folklore. There are several reasons for this situation. The total number of publications in the field is low, and the percentage of this total which is generally available is much lower. Most libraries do not have available a qualified folklorist to guide their purchases in the field. All large universities have professors of literature, history, sciences, etc. Few have professors of folklore. Those that have professors with specialized knowledge of the bibliography of Latin American folklore are rare. The field is not popular in its scientific aspect, either with those who might advise on purchases (or contribute publications of their own) or with those who might wish to study and consult such publications. Hence there is relatively little pressure on libraries to acquire Latin-American folklore publications. Even if there were, the Latin-American booktrade is not as well organized as that, let us say, of Europe; so efficient channels for purchase and information on exactly what is available are not well developed.

Even if an abundance of well organized published materials of scientific interest in the field of Latin-American folklore were at the disposal of folklorists in the United States, for example, the majority of such materials would be in Spanish and Portuguese. And, among those working and interested in folklore in the United States, only a minority can read these languages. Frequently I receive inquiries from folklorists in the United States for bibliographical information concerning problems that interest them in Latin America. When I give them such information, often the question follows: "But what is available *in English*?" The answer must be: "Very little." It is especially desirable in folklore to consult texts and other data in the native language of the informant, for folklore is particularly bound to its local idiom and culture.

It is normal to expect a majority of the scientific publications in Latin-American folklore to be produced by Latin-American folklore scholars. But they are few, hence their publications are few. This field offers little material remuneration, so it does not attract many. Of the few that persist in pursuing it, some are discouraged by lack of public appreciation. They may not be accepted as colleagues by scholars in other fields. The general public, as well as other scholars, often smiles with indulgence at the folklorist, who "wastes" his time dealing with "childish" and "primitive" things, and treating them with scholarly respect. Those few who brave the ridicule or lack of prestige usually must become self-made folklore scholars, educating and training themselves in their field, for folklore professorships and course offerings in folklore in Latin-American universities are perhaps even scarcer than they are in universities of the United States. Those who survive the discouragement of lack of reward and prestige and the rigors of self-training are few.

Even when one of these dedicated few has produced a manuscript, publication frequently is difficult. Two common roads lie open to him, neither of which leads to a very efficient distribution of his publication among his colleagues in other lands, who could profit most by it. One road is that he approaches a local printer and ascertains the cost of printing his manuscript. Then he solicits contributions or orders for his book, accompanied by advanced payments or commitments, among local patrons, any wealthy person he happens to know or to whom he can gain access, his godfather, relatives, friends, etc. If his own resources and the pledges resulting from his personal contacts seem sufficient to the printer, the work is published, often in a lamentably small edition, and distributed among those who have supported the project, with most of the remaining copies mailed out free to people the author happens to know or know about, and the last few are deposited in the printer's shop, a bookshop, or the author's home, for sale or gift, until the entire supply is shortly exhausted. The other road is that of government publication. If the author happens to be working for the government, or to have a good friend or relative with active and influential contacts in the government at the moment he has a manuscript to publish, money may be found in the budget of some governmental department to pay for the printing. In this case, the publication is apt to appear in some governmental series, and is distributed through official channels. The author receives some copies for personal distribution, but the majority is used for publication exchange and is sent to various government offices and to embassies and consulates abroad to be used as cultural propaganda. As can be seen, neither of these methods gets a publication into the hands of the largest possible number of folklore scholars over the world, and in either case the edition is exhausted within a few years.

We have been considering folklore publications which are presumably of scientific interest. Really they form a small portion of the total of so-called folklore publications, of which a majority is largely the product of the creative genius of an author who has found inspiration in folklore materials. Such works range from legends and tales, artistically retold in the diction and style of the author, with some quaint and colorful words and phrases thrown in for a dash of local color, to outright regional novels and literary sketches of customs and types. Often a new folklore publication appears which is a modern literary rendition of some aspects of the cultural heritage of the ancient indigenous population of the author's homeland, perhaps imaginatively vivified for the modern reader. Frequently good folklore data are published with the only indication of their source being that they are from a certain nation, which makes it difficult to fit such data into a pattern of regional variants. On many occasions a European or North American scholar has taken a field trip into some region of Latin America without adequate preparation in the local culture and language, and has worked through an interpreter and innocently incorporated into his report some rather disconcerting errors. While collecting folktales in Puerto Rico in 1926–1927, I discovered the dangers of paying informants, a practice often followed by well intentioned collectors. I was being served up oral renderings of tales gleaned from children's schoolbooks, to increase the quantity of material, and hence the reward. The application of rigid scientific criteria to a Latin-American folklore bibliography of imposing length may reduce enormously its portion of material useful for scholarly purposes.

Latin-American folklore periodicals contain a vast quantity of material that never finds its way into book form. Many Latin-American folklorists are intellectuals who must hold three or four jobs with low pay in order to maintain their families. They must rush about day, and night, teaching classes in this school and in that one, and perhaps spend some hours each day in an office or writing for the local papers. They simply cannot find the time to write a book. But they do find time to commit bits of their knowledge of local folklore to publication in some folklore periodical, often valuable bits which, when pieced together, constitute a rather imposing amount of material. I was sufficiently impressed, for example, with the total value of the large number of small items scattered through the volumes of *Mexican Folkways* to publish a classified and commented bibliography of its articles, with index (in the *Boletín bibliográfico de antropología americana* of Mexico in 1942, VI, Nos. 1–3, pp. 221–265). One of the saddest facts about many of these periodicals is their short life. Some last for several years, but others never survive their first year. Their average life span often is only a few years. A group or society forms, usually led by some vigorous personality. Local or government support is found. Or, some enthusiastic individual secures a position as director of the folklore section in a university, museum, governmental department of fine arts, or other cultural organization. In either case, a folklore periodical may be born. The leader, members of his group, colleagues, and friends, contribute some articles, and others are solicited from famous folklorists elsewhere. A good initial budget is provided, and the periodical is off to a fine start. But the burden of securing a constant flow of manuscripts and money is unceasing, and sooner or later the periodical fails. Enthusiastic readers everywhere ask to be placed on the mailing list, but are slow in sending in their subscriptions, if, indeed, a subscription price is established. Other institutions offer exchange publications but not money. Support from the outside world, as well as locally, proves to be insufficient for continued life. This situation causes endless grief to bibliographers and librarians everywhere. Perhaps by the time they become aware of the existence of such a periodical, it no longer exists. The number of copies was small, they have been distributed, and no more are to be had. Sometimes it seems impossible to ascertain exactly the date and number of the last issue. Those who gave it life may regard its death as only temporary, and for years do not give up hope of resuming publication, hence are reluctant to admit it has definitely ceased to exist. Government or directive personnel may change, and it may indeed be reborn—under another name.

Now that we have surveyed briefly some conditions and problems that prevail in the production and distribution of books and periodicals that appear in Latin-American folklore bibliographies, we can comprehend some ills present in the field, and perhaps even see remedies for a few. I shall try to confine myself to mention of practical remedies, that I myself have tried, or that other folklorists might try with some reasonable hope of success. I shall try to avoid speaking of remedies which may be theoretically correct, but which you and I, individually, or even through our currently existing organizations, could hardly aspire to apply, such as the establishment of folklore professorships in all Latin-American universities, with adequate salaries, so that those occupying them would have time for research, as well as to produce carefully trained students, with scholarships to attract competent young scholars into the field, and with organizational funds secured for long periods, to assure the continuity of publication outlets, etc. Such remedies as these would no doubt improve the quality of the items that constitute Latin-American folklore bibliography, but they fail to take into account various important realities that would profoundly affect their application.

So let us consider more practical remedies and their purposes. A bibliography is merely a list, which means little unless one actually can lay hand on the publications listed, so matters of library cataloguing and channels for borrowing and buying printed matter are of prime importance if a bibliography is to fulfill its useful function of connecting a reader with publications on a topic that interests him. Also of primary concern is the quality of the publications, which depends on those who write them.

When I began to understand the ways of Latin-American folklore publication, the small editions, personally distributed and rapidly exhausted, etc., it became clear that far more important than money for purchases (most Latin-American folklore publications can be bought cheaply at the time and place of publication) was to be in personal contact with an author at the time he publishes something. During these past thirty years, I have managed, not without a considerable investment of time, I admit, to establish personal contact, maintained by correspondence, with a large number of folklorists scattered over Latin America, who, knowing of my interest in their work, often remember to send me copies of their recent folklore publications, sometimes published in places I would never think to look for them (medical or botanical periodicals, almanacs, municipal series, local newspapers, etc.), and to which I probably would not have access, even though I knew where to look for them. This method is effective not for the past but only for the present, but the present is cumulative, and now I have items published twenty to thirty years ago which are impossible to obtain, even though they were easy to get at the moment of their publication. A few large libraries in the United States, which have active bookdealers everywhere obtaining all sorts of current publications for them, by sheer force of quantity acquire many Latin-American folklore publications, but few libraries can afford to maintain such an extensive buying program, and even these large libraries miss valuable items repeatedly because of a lack of direct contact with authors in our specific field. The amount of time required to maintain these contacts is too much to ask of every folklorist who has or may have sometime an interest in this field. But the folklorists and their organizations could form some central agency, in which such an effort could be concentrated. Sometimes Latin-American folklorists have asked me for names of those who might be interested in receiving their publications, which I have sent them, or occasionally they have sent me a number of copies to distribute for them, which I have done, but no one individually has the time actively to develop this sort of public service, as could be done through an agency.

Library and bibliography go together. The best public service I have been able to give has been to publish an annual folklore bibliography, which I maintained without interruption for twenty-two years. Beginning with 1937, I published each year, roughly classified and briefly commented, a list of current books and articles received during the year. These lists have appeared in each March number, of the year following, of *Southern Folklore Quarterly*. At least these bibliographies make known some contributions of Latin-American folklorists to their colleagues over the world, where *Southern Folklore Quarterly* is read, within a short time of their publication. These publications are available for scholarly use here on the campus of the University of Miami (Florida), where my private library is housed for the convenience of colleagues and students. It would be better if some central agency, or several conveniently located regional centers, could be established for similar accumulation of publications in our field, organized for lending and bibliographical service. Copies of the catalogue cards could then be placed in any number of interested libraries. An indispensable function in the maintenance of such a central library organization should be its continuation of annual published bibliographies, and correspondence contacts with those who publish in the field. In my twenty-second bibliography, for 1958 (*SFQ*, XXII, No. 1 [1959], 1–2), my last, I made a farewell statement. I wish to complete a few scholarly projects of my own while there is still time. The 1959 bibliography was sustained on an interim basis. In 1960 Américo Paredes, University of Texas, takes over the bibliography.

After each year's bibliography was published the cards for that year were incorporated into a cumulative file. The convenience of looking in one place instead of twenty-two has caused many colleagues to request publication as a unit of the entire cumulative file to date, but financial support and sponsorship would be needed for such a project.

Another useful and attainable project would be to arrange according to a folklore classification the combined catalogue entries of the folklore holdings already in a number of libraries known to be rich in this field. As has been said, folklore items in general libraries are arranged according to a general classification, like that of Dewey or the Library of Congress, in which things of folklore interest are found in various sections. If all these were arranged in a classification designed specifically for use of folklorists, the scholar's search for materials would be made easier, and he would know exactly where each item might be borrowed.

In libraries generally, books and periodicals are catalogued, but not individual periodical articles. I hesitate to mention the useful but enormous project of going through all periodical files, to compile a bibliography of all articles that deal with some aspect of folklore. The preliminary step of agreeing on a suitable working definition of folklore, to determine what to include, might in itself be difficult. In my annual bibliographies, I cited individual articles, but I had only to agree with myself on what to include.

Besides the bibliographical ills concerned with connecting a reader with publications of interest to him, the other major matter I have mentioned is the quality of publications cited in a bibliography, which depends on those who write them. On a trip around South America in 1940, during which I came to know personally many Latin-American folklorists, and to see the conditions under which they worked, I perceived that in the immediate future, as in the past, many of them will learn about the science of folklore through the reading they have time for. And many of them cannot read English, just as many folklorists in the United States cannot read Spanish. To meet this need, in 1940, I established *Folklore Americas*, which issues two numbers a year. Each number usually contains one essay, in brief form, in Spanish, on some important aspect of folklore. Being for the most part in Spanish, most Latin-American folklorists can read them. Being brief (up to 30 or 40 pages, usually less), they can be read in a short time. Being free, everyone can afford them. Indeed, I have sent them unsolicited to all I believed they might interest. There have appeared essays on major types of folklore, such as the myth, legend, tale, ballad, music, etc.; Spanish translations of the historic letter of Thoms first proposing the word "folklore," and of Krohn's excellent *Folkloristische Arbeitsmethode*; tools of scholarship, like a short bibliography of works that might constitute the basis of a young scholar's library, a folklore classification suitable for arranging materials collected as well as publications in one's library and bibliographical file, and a set of phonetic symbols that can be written on a typewriter, for transcription of textual material; and samples of some types of studies desirable for scholars in Latin America to make, such as a very short account of a project establishing tentatively a folklore map of a country, and a morphological analysis of Hispanic folktales. Also an early number contained a list of names and addresses of folklorists, so they could establish contact with one another. Publications of this sort have proven helpful to those who teach themselves. They should be continued. The greatest authority available in each particular subject useful for the orientation of rising folklore scholars should be invited to compose a short essay on his specialty, with a key bibliography into that part of the field, to be published in Spanish and widely distributed. I am always looking for such articles to publish in *Folklore Americas*. In this way, the quality of items appearing in Latin-American folklore bibliographies can be improved.

Perhaps most of the problems mentioned here are not peculiar to Latin-American folklore bibliography. But peculiar or not, they are problems of this field. If we find them elsewhere, we may find also remedies applicable here. As in many problems, a prime need is a spirit of coöperation and service.

University of Miami,
Coral Gables, Florida, U.S.A.

THE CONCEPTION OF THE NIGHTMARE
IN SWEDEN

CARL-HERMAN TILLHAGEN

The following survey of the conception of the nightmare (Sw. *mara*, pl. *maror*) in Sweden is based on more than 5,000 recordings dealing with the phenomenon which are lodged in the Swedish archives of popular traditions. These recordings, as a rule, were made prior to 1942 and deal with conditions during the middle and latter parts of the 19th century. They have not been made systematically, but form part of the large collections of material concerning supernatural beings, popular medicine, etc., which have been assembled in the course of years as a result of the general inventory made of Swedish popular traditions carried on by the Nordic Museum and other scientific institutions since the 1870's. The printed literature has, of course, also served as a source. The extensive data on the conception of the mara in Swedish Finland, which form part of the large encyclopedia *Finlands svenska folkdiktning* ("Swedish Popular Poetry in Finland")[1] have been of special value.

Belief in the mara has been general all over Sweden.[2] Proofs from historical

---

[1] Wessman, *Mytiska sägner*, Finlands Svenska Folkdiktning II, 3, Helsingfors 1931, pp. 544–555; Forsblom, *Magisk folkmedicin*, Finlands Svenska Folkdiktning VII, 5, Helsingfors 1927, pp. 605–643.

[2] Concerning the conception of the nightmare in Sweden, see Björkqvist, "Om maran i norrländsk folktro" (in *Festskrift till Gunnar Ekholm*, Uppsala 1934, pp. 50–66); Forsblom, "Om mara och marritt i österbottnisk folktro" (in *Folkloristiska och etnografiska studier*, II, Helsingfors 1917, pp. 113 ff.); Heurgren, *Husdjuren i nordisk folktro*, Örebro 1925, pp. 230 ff; Hyltén-Cavallius, *Wärend och Wirdarne*, I, 1863, pp. 260 ff. (ed. 1921); Rietz, *Ordbok öfver Svenska Allmoge-Språket*, Lund 1867, s. v. "Mara"; C. W. von Sydow, "Om maran och varulven" (in *Svenska Landsmål*, Uppsala 1911, pp. 594 ff).

sources go to show that this belief has, on the whole, remained unchanged ever since the 16th century, and data in early Nordic literature would appear to indicate that certain parts of the mara conception at least have retained their character since the 12th century.

The mara "rides" humans and animals, at times trees too. Anybody can be beset by the mara, men perhaps more often than women, however. The risk is especially great if one lies on one's back. The mara usually enters through the key-hole, through a knot-hole, a hole in a window-bar, or it may come down the chimney. It may, as a matter of fact, enter through any kind of round hole, but if the hole is of a different shape it cannot make its way in. Even so window-chinks do not appear to have constituted any obstacle for it.

The mara could be heard coming. There was a click in the lock, there was a patter crossing the floor, there was a sound as if something soft were being hauled across the boards. Sometimes a "sshh, sshh," or some similar indefinite, weak sound could be imagined. But however quick one was there wasn't time after this warning to move before the mara pounced on you. It felt as if a great weight fell over you, most frequently as though rolling on one from down at one's feet. At times it seemed as if someone were trying to stop up one's mouth and nose, sometimes as if one were being squeezed so tight that it was quite impossible to make the slightest movement. A person who was "mar-ridden" became anguished, he groaned, struggled violently but nevertheless could not move a limb, and at last woke up with severe palpitation, and wet with perspiration. Just as the mara let go one might perhaps catch a glimpse of the creature, catch it and strike it to the ground, or make some other movement which gave the victim the impression that he had overcome it.

Here and there certain prophylactic remedies were used for the mara. For one thing, the mara must not be mentioned before bedtime. When the first new moon of the year was seen, this ought to happen under the open sky, for if it were seen through a window or through a crack one would be mar-ridden. Care also had to be taken not to peep through the key-hole before going to bed. If one took home something from the churchyard, such as bones of the dead, earth from a grave and such like,—as often used to be done in popular art of healing,—"One might be squeezed by one of the dead or by the mara," according to one informant.

There are numerous beliefs and statements that the mara could suck or suckle infants. It could also suckle young women and in this way draw forth milk in their breasts.[3]

It was also believed that the mara could ride the domestic animals. This was noticeable from the fact that these animals were found perspiring and tired in the

[3] See Hyltén-Cavallius, *op. cit.*, pp. 261.

mornings, the horses often having a so-called "mar-plait" in their manes. Of all animals it was especially the horse that was the object of the mara's nightly visits. In some quarters it was believed that draught animals only were "ridden" by the mara. It could also ride cows and oxen. There are some few reports testifying to dogs, pigs, and sheep being haunted by the mara.

Only one or two of my accounts state definitely that the mara rode trees.[4] It is indirectly evident, however, that folk-belief bore this out. My material includes hundreds of records of so-called mar-bushes, which are the twiggy excrescences on trees. The belief concerning these was that they were the adventitious growths which resulted from the mara's ride in the trees.

In spite of the fact that the mara by no means is to be seen as a figure every time it besets a person, peasant folks nevertheless have a certain idea of its appearance. The mara can show itself as a human being, animal and object, but it may also be invisible, or, strictly speaking, it may have no figure at all. In human form it most often appears as a woman, then generally as an old, ugly woman. As an animal the mara mostly shows itself as a cat or dog. In a small number of recordings it is said to transform itself into one animal after another, especially in threat of capture. In such cases it can also display obvious rage and cause damage. In the form of objects it most frequently shows itself as a pitchfork (especially in Northern Sweden and in Swedish Finland). Figureless, it turns up sometimes as a ball, a grey skin, something hairy, a feather, etc. A compilation of the data on the appearance of the mara shows the following results:

The mara in human form	Sweden		Swedish Finland	
Human being in general	14		1	
Woman	36		7	
Man	6	56	3	11

The mara in animal form				
Animal in general	19		–	
Ape................................	9		–	
Dog	30		1	
Cat	83		4	
Rat, mouse	10		3	
Bird	7		1	
Other animals	10		7	
Changes form	5	173	–	16

---

[4] See Rietz, op. cit., s. v. "Mara."

The mara resembles objects	Sweden		Swedish Finland	
Ball	7		2	
Feather	3		–	
Ball of fire	2		–	
Pitch-fork	18		19	
Others	2	32	4	25
The mara formless				
Something hairy	13		–	
Something invisible	9		–	
A shadow	1		–	
Others	8	31	–	—
Total		292		52

Notions in popular belief of what the mara really is vary in high degree. The ideas within a certain geographical area regarding the mara as a being are far from logical in their outlines; in fact, they are often contradictory, diffuse, and confused. I believe, however, that I have succeeded in attaining a certain degree of perspicuity as to the conception of the mara as a being by setting down my material in tabular form:

A. *The mara as a human being*

  In general

Not closely characterized	96	
A wicked person	29	
A bewitched person	14	
A somnambulist	15	154

  As a woman

A woman in general	151	
A wicked woman	28	
An erotic woman	33	
A sterile woman	6	
A woman without hair on body	37	
A hairy woman	7	
A red-haired woman	11	
With intergrown eyebrows	21	
Of illegitimate birth	1	
Mother crept through a hole	144	
Bewitched by an animal..............	16	
Bewitched by a human being	10	
With magic power	9	
Born on a black-letter or unlucky day .	6	480

As a man   24   24

B. *The mara as a spirit, thought, soul*
    Shade (Sw. "vård"), soul, spirit 26
    Thoughts of love 12
    Envious thoughts 29
    Resurrected spirits 61   128

C. *The mara as a supernatural being*
    In general 55
    Evil spirit 48
    The devil 24
    Named, supernatural being 17   144

D. *Mar-ride dependent on witchcraft* 23
E. *Mar-ride as a dream* 9
F. *Mar-ride as a sickness* 15
G. *The mara as an animal* 24
H. *Don't know* 9   1,010

My material contains 255 items on how a human being becomes a mara. On going through these we obtain the following results (the figures in parentheses indicate the number of instances).

In the southernmost parts of Sweden there was a very widespread belief that if a pregnant woman crawled naked through a foal's caul she would not suffer the throes of childbirth, but the child to which she gave birth would be a mara, if a girl, and a werewolf if it were a boy. The woman could also for the same purpose and with the same dreadful effect crawl through a hole in a tree trunk (2), a wheel (2), or a horse-collar (7).

If the child were born at a certain, ominous time (certain so-called black-letter days, etc.) it might be a mara. There is proof of this belief only in Swedish Finland (5) and in northernmost Sweden (1).[4] The child also became a mara if a cat ran underneath the cradle or jumped over the cradle before the child was christened (16).

An adult person could be turned into a mara by a person, who had just been delivered from the spell of being a mara, saying: "Now you can be a mara just as long as I have been!" (14). He or she could also be turned into a mara by people with magic powers bewitching the person by magic rites (36). Finally, an adult could become a mara (39) by reason of his own envious or amorous thoughts.

There were several signs by which persons who were regarded as maras could be distinguished. Women without hair on their bodies were generally considered to be maras (37). On the other hand, very hairy and bearded women were maras (7), as were also those with intergrown eyebrows (21); men with intergrown

eyebrows were considered to be werewolves. Red-haired women, especially those
with red hair on their bodies had the reputation of being maras (11), and in
Swedish Finland dark women (4) were strongly suspected. If one wished to find
out who had beset one during the night one should, according to a belief in the
county of Bohus in southwestern Sweden, pass water in a bottle and cork it well.
The woman who was a mara then could not pass her water until she had made
herself known.[5]

There were several ways of releasing a person from the curse of being a mara.
If someone said to such a woman: "You are a mara!", the curse was dispelled and
she no longer needed to act the part (45 cases out of 54). It was therefore possible
to escape from the infliction of the mara by rattling off names quickly. When the
right one was found the mara had to adopt human form and could be relieved by
being spoken to as mentioned above. The mara might also be ordered to return
next day and to ask for the loan of three things one didn't possess.[6] Of the 45 items
21 are of this type; in some of them one invites the mara home to breakfast on the
following day.[6] There is a version from two places that if a child, who had become
a mara because of her mother having crawled through a foal's caul, were again
drawn through a foal's caul, it was released for all future time from the infliction.
From two other places there is a version that the mara had to ride over and kill
some person before she could be relieved of her spell.

There was a widespread popular belief that if it were possible to strike someone
suspected of being a mara a hard enough blow to cause bleeding then you had for
all future time deprived the mara of the power to do anyone harm. This is the same
method that applies in depriving a magician of his "powers," and it is possibly
connected with the fact that the mara was understood to be a person with magic
powers. We shall find below that a protective measure against the mara was to tie
a scythe with edge upwards on the back of the animal beset. The intention
probably was that the mara would cut itself on the scythe and by bleeding lose
its magic power to do harm.

Of the 209 cures mentioned for being mar-ridden only a few are, in our opinion,
rational; the others have a magical bearing. In two cases the sleeper is to be
wakened, in fourteen it is believed that the affected person will get relief if he
can turn on his side. In no fewer than 163 cases the cure is considered to be to
call the mar-ridden person by name.[7] Here the cure in all probability does not have

---

[5] This conception also is common in Germany, cf. Schell, *Bergische Sagen*, Elberfeld 1897, p. 41,
No. 53.

[6] Cf. Meyer, *Badisches Volksleben*, Straßburg 1900, p. 551.
   Common even in the folk belief in Norway, cf. *Maal og Minne* 1924, pp. 159 ff. Concerning the
   same belief in Germany, see Bächtold-Stäubli, *Handwörterbuch des deutschen Aberglaubens*, I, 303.

the significance of simply wakening the person from a nightmare, but the question is of mobilizing the magic power which mentioning the name implies. In many instances stress is laid on the necessity of the Christian name's being pronounced. In four cases prayer is considered to help, whereas in 79 cases remedies adopted are such as are usually applied in popular treatment of afflictions. The mara thus could be warded off by certain magical forms of words (38). One of these is:

Mara, mara, minne!	Mara, mara, mind!
Du får ej bli härinne	Thou may'st not enter here,
förr än du räknat	Until thou counted hast
fåglar i skog,	Birds in wood,
fiskar i flod	Fishes in river,
alla eketrär	All the oak trees,
och Guds ord![8]	And the words of God!

Another cure was to take a little of the mar-ridden person's or beast's hair and attach it in a hole in a gate-post, or in the pole of a fence, etc. (14). The mara would then continue to beset this hair and leave the human being or animal in peace. The mara could also be driven out by magic smoking (6), magic shooting (7), etc.

My material included 2,406 items of magical protective measures against the mara, 651 of which deal with the protection of human beings. A table of these is given below; for the sake of comparison I give the information from Swedish Finland in a separate column.

In studying this table we find that in almost every group one or another of the protective measures dominates. It seems to me justified to place a high value on this specific protection more than others used against the mara, because of the fact that this special protective measure is not used, or at any rate to a very small extent, in other connections when magic protection is needed, e. g., against supernatural beings, against ailments, etc. In the metal group, for example, steel holds a special place, and of steel implements, the practice of tying the scythe above the animal's back, with the edge upwards, seems to predominate. The 256 documentations of this could be increased by another 165 taken from the records of the so-called scythe legend known to the author. A peasant had noticed how his horse stood perspiring and tired out in the stable every morning. He believed that it was mar-ridden and decided to find a remedy. He therefore tied a scythe edge-upwards above the horse's back. On the following morning the peasant himself was found dead in the stable, cut by the scythe. It was the owner who,

[8] From the province of Nerike, the Archives of the Nordic Museum, No. E. U. 786. Several magical forms of words are printed in Forsblom, *op. cit.* pp. 611 ff.

PROTECTIVE MEASURES	HUMAN BEINGS				ANIMALS			
	SWEDEN		SWEDISH FINLAND		SWEDEN		SWEDISH FINLAND	
Word of God								
Calendar	3		1		53		44	
Prayer Book, etc.	42	45	5	6	26	79	28	72
Magic signs								
Crosses	31		3		21		27	
Pentagram	1		–		3		12	
Others	–	32	–	3	–	24	4	43
Metals								
Steel generally	57		21		43		–	
Scythes above victim	7		–		256		9	
Other edged steel	75		–		47		52	
Horse shoes	4		–		30		9	
Other metals	8	151	–	21	3	379	28	98
Parts of plants								
Mar-besom or sheaf	62		–		372		38	
Broom	–		–		6		1	
Others	2	64	–		2	380	18	57
Birds								
Magpies above door	–		–		186		1	
Owls above door	–		–		88		22	
Hawks above door	–		–		35		13	
Others	–		–		21	330	9	45
Clothes								
Garments inside out	8		–		–		–	
Men's trousers, etc.	34		3		–		13	
Women's underclothing	4		1		–		2	
Shrouds	1		2		–		–	
Shoes, toes turned outwards from the bed	156	203	–	6	–	–	–	15
Evil smelling substances		13		1		24		15
Other protective means								
Close all holes	39		–		12		–	
Fire	16		2		–		–	
Stones with holes	–		–		11		–	
Mirror in front of animal	–		–		35		23	
Others	42	97	7	9	55	113	58	81
Total		605		46		1,329		426

unknown to himself, had been the mara. In a number of the versions of the legend it is the stableman, a neighbour, or a neighbour's wife who is found dead. This legend belongs principally to southern Sweden, though only represented by four recorded instances in the province of Scania.

In the group for parts of plants the mar-sheaf[9] is represented very frequently indeed. I do not know of this as a protective measure in any connection other than against the mara. According to folk belief, these growths are supposed to have originated in trees in which the mara rode or rested. These trees were feared in many places, and people spat as they passed trees containing an extreme number of such excrescences, crediting them with attracting the mara. If such a growth was put in the stable the mara entered instead of the horse. In bringing home the mar-sheaf it was important not to cross a road along which a corpse had been carried, for the besom or sheaf then lost all its power. The hoisting of a broom instead of a mar-sheaf must in all probability be ascribed to its similarity to a sheaf.

Another typical precaution against the mara was a bird nailed above the stable door. In Swedish Finland the magpie is unknown as a precaution, but in Sweden it dominates as a protective medium. This is probably not associated with the fact that the magpie is more common and therefore easier to procure, but with the belief which attaches to it in Swedish districts. The magpie is in a high degree an ominous bird, a special disguise (familiar spirit) of witches, and a substitute for the evil one. The resemblance of the magpie's nest to a mar-sheaf may possibly have inspired the popular idea for the belief in the power of the magpie to ward off the mara. Birds of prey do not occupy this position in popular belief. The idea which is behind the use of them as preventive measures is rather that with their sharp beaks and claws they would scare the flying mara. The oldest proof in Scandinavia of a bird of prey as a precaution is to be found in a picture in Olaus Magnus's *Historia de gentibus septentrionalibus*, 1555 (Bk. No. 17, Chap. 12). In it a man is seen grooming his horse, and above the horse's back there hangs a bird of prey, probably as protection against the mara.

Another typical protective medium against the mara is shoes turned with the toes pointing outward, i. e., away from the bed, before retiring for the night. The belief is that before it can beset the sleeper the mara must get into his shoes. If the toes are pointed outwards, however, the mara will not understand (it is often represented as being very stupid) how to get into them, and the sleeper will therefore have no visitation. This is undoubtedly a secondary explanation. It may be imagined in this instance that it is the magic power of the wrong side that

[9] A nightmare-bush, or witch-besom, is a shaggy, twiggy excrescence on branches of trees.

works, exactly as a garment turned inside out serves as a protection against the mara, or breaks the power of the deceptive lady of the woods. Man's trousers or, as a matter of fact, any undergarment as a protective medium, are closely associated with the mara belief.[10] Here it is undoubtedly the contact of these garments with the sexual sphere of the body which creates, in popular imagination, their immanent power to protect. There are, however, parallels in popular medicine as regards the reputed protective and healing power of garments.[11]

As we know, the mara was considered capable of making its way through the finest holes and openings. From this it logically follows that it was desirable to protect oneself against the mara by closing every possible opening into the bedroom. As a rule it is stated that the openings were just to be closed up, but in quite a number of cases it is prescribed that the holes should be closed up with lead, steel, or tar plugs, all of which are substances reputed to possess magic power. The number of documentations for the closing of holes as a protective measure (39) could be augmented by 193 references to a type of legend which might be called "the mar-wife legend." A young man who was permanently tormented by the mara decided to try and catch her. He arranged with a pal to help him. They made wooden pegs and plugs and with them bunged up all the holes but one in the room in which the young man slept. The youth then went to bed, and shortly thereafter his pal, who stood on guard at the remaining hole, noticed that he was mar-ridden. The man on guard promptly plugged the hole, and in the morning a young, beautiful and nude woman stood in the bedroom without knowing how she had got there. The mar-ridden man fell in love with the girl, married her and had several children. On one occasion, however, he was about to show his wife how she had come to him. He pulled out the plug, and the wife disappeared through the hole, never to return. This legend is prevalent in southern Sweden; it is to be found in Norway, is general in Denmark and recorded in several places in Germany.[12]

The mirror is also an interesting protective medium against the mara.[13] This has to be tied up straight in front of the animal which is mar-ridden so that the mara can see herself reflected in it. According to several records she will then be so frightened by her own ugliness that she promptly departs. This of course is a secondary explanation. What undoubtedly is most likely is that the mirror will

[10] Cf. Drechsler, *Sitte, Brauch und Volksglaube in Schlesien*, Leipzig 1903, I, 187.
[11] Cf. Tillhagen, *Folklig läkekonst*, Stockholm 1958, pp. 134, 292.
[12] Cf. Holmström, *Sägnerna om äktenskapet med maran* (in Folkminnen och Folktankar, Malmö 1918, pp. 135ff). See also Reidar Th. Christiansen, *The Migratory Legends*, FFC, No. 175, Helsinki 1958, No. 4010, pp. 60–61.
[13] See Manz, *Volksbrauch und Volksglaube des Sarganserlandes*, Basel 1916, p. 113; Seligmann, *Der böse Blick und Verwandtes*, Berlin 1910, I, 178ff.

make the mara believe that she is known and revealed. It consequently has the same effect as mentioning the mara's name.

It will be seen from the above that the conceptions of the mara we meet with in Swedish folk belief are very heterogeneous. The tables which appear above give a picture of common features of the belief at the close of the 19th century, but they contain few leads as to what was original. The ideas which I have described are—as is always the case when they apply to folk belief—a conglomeration of primary and secondary materials, and it is a most ticklish job to try to delineate between the two. Belief in the mara, however, is undoubtedly very old in Scandinavia. This is evident from several mediaeval references. These instances, however, are too few to give a detailed picture of the changes the belief has undergone in the course of time. I would call attention here to some ancient characteristics which are af special interest.

My material contains 61 instances of the belief that the mara is a resurrected soul. The belief that dead persons reappear and torment the living at nighttime is found repeatedly in ancient Nordic literature.[14] I remember from traditions still current the belief in the ghost that embraces living persons so that they not only become ill but also bear blue marks or other physical injuries. "Mar-ride" can be acquired, according to popular belief, if a person brings something home from the churchyard, belonging to the dead. In the province of Halland in southern Sweden it is said that after many vain attempts to gain protection against the mara flax seed was finally strewn round the farmyard and was immediately efficacious. This medium, employed as a precaution against resurrected souls,[15] has also been used in Denmark.

In 26 of my accounts it is clearly stated that the mara is a human being's shade (Sw. "vård") or soul which leaves the body during sleep and goes off to beset others. From the tables on the nature of the mara further material may be adduced for this belief. Practically all items under groups A and B can be included in this category. The data for the *Scythe Legend* and the *Mar-wife Legend* (in all 358 versions) contain the same ideas, as does also a type of legend in which a woman in the sight of people present rises out of bed, undresses and with the words: "Ugh, cold and raw!" wishes to disappear as a mara, but is awakened and saved (45 examples); then again a type of legend in which a woman disappears at the hour of midnight leaving her clothes (17 examples). Any injury which is done to the figure in which the soul appears also befalls the body to which the soul belongs. This is clearly emphasized in the so-called *Pitchfork Legend* (37 examples). A man

[14] See *Eiriks saga Rauða*, ch. 4; *Svarfdæla saga* (Isl. Fornsögur II), ch. 22; *Fornmanna Sögur*, III, 196; *Grettis saga Asmundarsonar*, ch. 17.

[15] Cf. Hagberg, *När döden gästar*, Stockholm 1937, pp. 626ff.

whose livestock is being ridden by the mara is keen on surprising it, but instead only discovers a wooden fork. In anger he kicks and breaks a prong of the fork. He learns later that his neighbor's wife broke her leg at the same time. The belief that the mara may represent the soul, or even the thought, is consequently widespread. The mara as soul or thought can be brought on by a longing for love, by envy and iniquity, and also by the curse which the mar-ridden person has contracted either through the mother's magic art at the child's birth, or it may be contracted from an ominous animal, or from a human skilled in witchcraft.

These conceptions are very old. Ancient Nordic literature gives us many and clear proofs of the great strength of the belief during the Viking period that the human soul could live a life which was completely independent of its body.[16] According to these beliefs the soul was able to wander off on its own course in a dream and could, as some kind of spirit (Old Sw. *hugr*, *hamr* or *fylgia*) entirely liberated from the body, appear in different forms at places far distant from the body itself. In order to understand the conception of the mara in Nordic countries this creature must obviously be viewed against the background of these extremely ancient beliefs in the various revelations of the soul.

My material contains 23 examples showing that the mar-ride is brought about by magic. Men and women skilled in witchcraft could by means of secret rites force others to "become a mara" (lit. "go mara") in the same way as they cast a spell over men to "go wolf" or "go bear."[17] This conception too is a very ancient one in northern Europe. The *Eidsiva Law* of the 12th century stipulated fines for the woman who was convicted of *"riði manni eða þjónum hans"* (riding a man or his servant), or who appeared as a *"trollriða,"* which is to say, as a mara. It is related in Ch. 16 of the *Eyrbyggja Saga* how the witch Geirid at Måvalid as a mara beset Gunlaug Torbjörnsson so seriously as to cause his death. In Ch. 16 of the *Ynglinga Saga* Snorre Sturlasson tells how Vanlande, king of the Swedes at Uppsala, was ridden to death in Finland by the mara evoked by the witch Huld. In 1863, more than 600 years after Snorre, the Swedish folklorist G. O. Hyltén-Cavallius wrote that the people in Wärend, a district in the province of Småland, still adhered to these old mythical conceptions. According to this the human soul can be bewitched so that it is at times transformed into a mara. The mara is a human being who has been forced in this way, namely by witchcraft, to change his guise for a time, whether merely now and then, every night, or every moonlight night, etc.[18]

[16] Cf. Lid, "Magiske fyrestellingar og bruk" (in *Nordisk kultur* XIX, Oslo 1935, pp. 3ff.); Reichborn-Kjennerud, *Vor gamle Trolldomsmedisin*, I, Oslo 1928, pp. 8ff; Hagberg, *op. cit.*, pp. 531ff.
[17] Concerning "go wolf" and "go bear," see Odstedt, *Varulven i svensk folktradition*, Uppsala 1943, pp. 58ff.
[18] Hyltén-Cavallius, *op. cit.*, p. 260.

In a number of cases, according to the popular belief, the mara is an independent being (55) or an evil being (48), consequently a creature equivalent to other supernatural beings of popular belief. How old can such a conception be? In a manuscript from the 14th century,[19] "Siælinna thrøst" in the Royal Library, Stockholm, we read: "...Thu skalt ey thro oppa maro ellir elfwa oc oppa enga handa spook ellir willo..." (Thou shalt not believe in maras, fairies, or in such spooks or delusions), and in 1767 Olof von Dalin wrote[20]: "A mara, that is a spook, a witch-spirit, which attacks many good souls in their sweet sleep, preferably when they have turned their shoes inwards on retiring to bed, and wants to suffocate them completely, plaiting a lock in their hair, which is called 'Mar-tof'." This conception of the mara as an independent supernatural being would also seem to derive from the Middle Ages.

Finally, certain named supernatural beings act as maras or have much the same effect as a mara. The Evil One is most frequently mentioned. This belief need not necessarily be so deep-rooted. The pains suffered in the mar-ride have no doubt caused many scholars to jump to the hasty conclusion for example, that "the devil himself" is at work, because no other one can cause such great agony. What is even more interesting is the fact that brownies are sometimes thought to take over the mara's work in plaiting the horses' manes. In this office the brownie is thought first to look after the best animals and those of a certain colour. The wood-nymph or lady of the woods (Sw. skogsfrun) too, the trolls and goblins, as well as other creatures of the nether regions (Sw. de underjordiska), were thought to cause the mar-ride.

The Swedish conception of the mara is closely connected with the belief in the mara in Norway,[21] Denmark,[22] and Germany.[23] A more detailed analysis of the conception of the mara in Scandinavia can hardly be carried out until this weird phenomenon has been investigated more thoroughly in other parts of Europe than has yet been done.

The Nordic Museum, Stockholm

[19] *Siælinna thrøst*, ed. Sam. Henning, Uppsala 1954–6, p. 25, lines 25 ff.
[20] Dalin, *Vitterhetsarbeten*, V, Stockholm 1767, p. 50.
[21] See Reichborn-Kjennerud, *op. cit.*, pp. 42 ff.
[22] See H. F. Feilberg, *Ordbog over jyske almuesmål*, København 1894–1904, II, 550 ff; Grundtvig, *Danske Folkesagn*, København 1946, I, 377 ff; Evald Tang Kristensen, *Jyske Folkesagn*, København 1876, No. 103 and 455; *ibid.*, *Danske Sagn*, Århus 1893, II, 241 ff; *ibid.*, Danske Sagn, *Ny række*, København 1929, pp. 154 ff.
[23] See Bächtold-Stäubli, *op. cit.*, I, 282 ff.

EINE OSTELBISCHE KULTURPROVINZ

WILL-ERICH PEUCKERT

Es ist schon öfters ausgesprochen worden, und Laistner hat es in seinem *Rätsel der Sphinx* vor nun sechzig Jahren überdeutlich dargetan, daß sich das nächtliche „Druckerlebnis" zu allen Zeiten und wohl auch bei allen Völkern finde. Wir haben, als wir den „Alb" für unser *Handwörterbuch der Sage* bearbeiteten, versucht, die nordamerikanischen und europäischen Namen für den drückenden Spuk zu erruieren, und aus der Vielzahl der Benennungen wollte es bereits sichtbar werden, daß er bei jedem europäischen Volk, jedoch in kleinen Sonderausgestaltungen, zu Hause sei. Ich habe dann weiter in der Hepding-Festschrift 1958 zeigen wollen, daß — neben den europäischen — deutsche Differenzierungen bestehen und daß im fränkischen Sprachgebiet der Alb zu einer ausfahrenden Seele hatte werden können. Darf ich nun heut an diese kleinräumige Untersuchung — kleinräumig, stellt man sie dem weltweiten Phänomen der nächtlichen Druckangst gegenüber — anknüpfen und einige weitere Sonderungen sichtbar machen, die uns zugleich Datierungen erlauben?

In meiner schlesischen Kinderheimat nahe Liegnitz existierte diese Sage: Die Paten oder Gevattern stehen mit einem zu taufenden Kinde am Sonntag vor der Kirche und warten auf den Pfarrer. Der Küster, der eben vorübergeht, hört, wie sie untereinander sprechen: Wås wull'n mersch denn warn lōn, a Olbla odr a Hexla? (Was wollen wir es denn werden lassen, einen Alb oder eine Hexe?) Das meldet der Küster dem Pfarrer und der schickt die Paten wiederum nach Hause, redet dann mit dem Kindesvater, und dieser bestellt am selben Tage andere Paten, die keinen Zauber bei der Taufe treiben. Der Glaube, daß man ein Kind durch einen bei seiner Taufe gemurmelten Zauberspruch oder durch irgendwelche Zeremonien zu einem Albe oder einer Hexe machen könne, deutet zunächst auf ein

Gemeinsames der beiden üblen Wesen hin, das uns auch sonst bezeugt ist, etwa in den hexerischen Qualitäten der oldenburgischen Walriderske, die schon in ihrer Sonderbezeichnung walriderske der thunrida: Hexe nahe kommt; auch jene Vorstellung, daß aus dem siebenten Kinde in einer Familie ein Alb oder Hexe werde, die skandinavische Behauptung, daß ein Mädchen, das durch ein Fohlen-hemd zu kriechen wage, einen Alb gebäre oder Hexe, die alpenländische Bezeich-nung Trud, die Alb wie Hexe meinen kann, — bereits in diesen termini und Aber-glauben sehen die beiden Gestalten sich sehr ähnlich.

Doch mir ist heute ein Zweites wichtiger und interessanter. Die Sage „Albla oder Hexla" begegnet nur ostwärts der Elbe: in Pommern, Ostpreußen, Schlesien und Wolhynien; wahrscheinlich besaß sie auch das Brandenburgische, doch blaßte sie dort zeitig aus. Die besten Varianten finden sich in Pommern, Schlesien und der Oberlausitz. Westwärts der Elbe kenne ich keinen einzigen Beleg. Es liegt mithin die Frage nahe, ob sie der slavischen Welt (der sorbischen oder polnischen) ent-sprang, oder ob sie auf deutschem Boden, auf welchem ein slavisches Substrat noch wirksam war, erschien. So weit ich sehe, — ich kenne die polnische Über-lieferung freilich nicht sehr gut, — weiß aber der Westslave um die nahen Be-ziehungen zwischen Alb und Hexe nichts; die scheinen viel eher, wie ja skandina-vische Zeugnisse auch vermuten lassen, vorzugsweise den germanischen Völkern zu gehören. Man wird deshalb am ehesten eine Entstehung der Sage in einer slavisch-deutschen Kontaktlandschaft, in der das Deutsche überwog, vermuten müssen.

Für diese Deutung spricht ein Zweites: von allen Belegen sind diejenigen der ehemaligen deutschen Sprachinseln in Wolhynien, wo ja die slavische Umwelt auf das stärkste hat einwirken können, die unklarsten und die schlechtesten: sie schweifen ab, sie mischen durchaus andere Züge ein, so daß man schließen darf, daß sie nicht mehr auf ihrem Wurzelboden stehen. Und das ist sicher auch der Fall: sie stellen Ableger aus den pommerschen Varianten dar. Als in den 1830er Jahren Deutsche in Wolhynien angesiedelt wurden, da waren es pommersche Deutsche, — und die haben ihre heimischen Sagen mitgebracht: die Festigkeit und Klarheit ihrer Erzählungen freilich ließ im Osten nach.

Wenn die soeben besprochene Sage zauberische Züge hat, denn die Verwün-schung zu einem Albe oder einer Hexe ist doch eine Zauberhandlung, so fügen sich die Sagen von den hexerischen Walridersken ihr gut an. Ich darf von einer oldenburgischen Überlieferung ausgehen; es heißt bei Strackerjan (*Aberglaube und Sagen aus dem Herzogtum Oldenburg* I. 1867 Nr. 250): „Als die Heimat der Walridersken wird meist England angegeben. Sie kommen über das Wasser daher gefahren, um ihre Opfer aufzusuchen. Ihr Kahn ist ein Milchsieb, ihre Ruder sind die fächerförmigen Schulterblätter von Tieren oder Menschen, oder Kuhrippen.

21 Taylor

In dem hochgelegenen, schiffbarer Gewässer ermangelnden Kirchspiele Visbek geht die Reise durch die Luft, aber auch hier in einem Siebe", und Strackerjan bemerkt in einem andern Zusammenhange (Nr. 207): „Den Hexen beigezählt werden... manchmal die Walridersken, weil auch diese anderen Leuten Böses zufügen und noch sonst in manchen Punkten mit den Hexen sich berühren". Aber es kommt mir auch hier nicht auf die hexerischen Qualitäten, sondern auf das — freilich sehr stark an die Hexenfahrt erinnernde — Fahren im Siebe an. Im Siebe oder im Siebrande fahren in Oldenburg, in Wagrien wie in Mecklenburg und Pommern Hexe oder Alb. Es sind, sieht man von Oldenburg im nördlichen Westdeutschland ab, ostelbische und zwar dem Niederdeutschen zugehörige Landschaften, die von einem solchen Fahren sprechen. Und da wir wissen, daß die eben genannten Landschaften aus dem Oldenburgischen besiedelt worden sind, so ist die im Ostelbischen von den andern dortigen Gebieten sich abhebende Siebrand-Insel leicht und einfach zu erklären. Sie gibt uns auch ein Datum an die Hand. Die deutsche Besiedlung setzte in diesen Strichen im elften und zwölften Jahrhundert ein; damals erzählte man also im Oldenburgischen von der Fahrt der Walridersken im Siebe, — wie übrigens der terminus Walriderske sich in diesen Gegenden auch erhielt, — und die in das Ostelbische ziehenden Siedler nahmen die Sage in die neue Heimat mit. Als in den 1830er Jahren Mecklenburger und Pommern nach Wolhynien gingen, fand sich in ihrem Reisegepäck die ihnen offenbar sehr wichtige Siebrandsage, und wie die Sammlungen Karaseks erkennen lassen, erhielt sie sich dort bis zum letzten Kriege, ja bis in die 1945er Zeit. Ob sie die 1945 Ausgezogenen wiederum zurück und nach Westdeutschland brachten, läßt sich heut noch nicht ausmachen; möglich wäre es gewiß.

Aber ich wollte weniger von der Siebrand-Sage als von ostelbischen Alb- und Mahrtensagen sprechen. Da ist noch eine dritte, deren hinterpommersche Variante ich nach Otto Knoop (*Volkssagen, Erzählungen, Aberglauben, Gebräuche und Märchen aus dem östlichen Hinterpommern* 1885. Nr. 171) zitiere: „Ein Knecht sah mal auf einem Pferde, das sehr unruhig stand, einen Apfel. Er ging hin, nahm den Apfel und biß hinein, in der Meinung, daß es ein wirklicher Apfel sei. Der schmeckte aber scheußlich sauer, und er warf ihn deshalb auf den Misthaufen. Am Morgen lag da ein häßliches Weibsbild, dem hatte er in der Nacht ein so großes Stück aus der Lende gebissen, daß es nicht hatte nach Hause gehen können." Es ist, obwohl in dieser Variante nur von einem Apfel und von keiner Birne gesprochen wird, die als „Birnfeige" bezeichnete Geschichte. Der Alb sieht nächstens wie ein Apfel oder eine Birne aus; man ißt von ihm auch wie von einer Frucht, er ist im Essen noch ein Apfel, aber einer mit besonderen Eigenschaften, und früh am Morgen wird er rückverwandelt in den täglichen Leib des Menschen; was ihm als Apfel widerfuhr, das wird am Menschenleibe morgens offenbar.

Wir kennen die Sage wiederum aus Ostelbien: aus Mecklenburg und Pommern, aus Schlesien, der brandenburgischen Niederlausitz, endlich aus Ostpreußen, wo sie bei Deutschen und Masuren lebt, und schließlich aus den Sprachinseln in Wolhynien. Darüber hinaus begegnet sie im Warthelande oder der früheren preußischen Provinz Posen. Wir werden summierend sagen dürfen, daß sie im westlichen Deutschland nirgends, im östlichen aber ziemlich häufig sei. Sie zeigt sich in dem vorhin bereits erörterten Kontaktgebiete, das ist, in jenen Landschaften, die vom zwölften Jahrhundert ab von Deutschen angebaut, jedoch von in den Untergrund geratenen slavischen Stämmen noch nicht aufgegeben worden sind. Wir dürfen darüber hinaus als recht gewiß annehmen, daß die bereits erwähnten Deutschen in Wolhynien die Sage aus ihrer Heimat, Mecklenburg und Pommern, nach Wolhynien brachten, daß sie deshalb schon, um daraus auf ihre Zeit zu schließen, schon vor dem neunzehnten Jahrhundert in der pommerschen Welt vorhanden war. Der Westen kennt sie, wie ich vorhin bereits bemerkte, nicht; wahrscheinlich ist sie entweder dort geschwunden und zwar ohne jeden Rest geschwunden, oder sie ist erst nach dem zwölften Jahrhundert, nach der „Siedlungszeit" entstanden.

Entstand die Sage im ostelbischen Deutschland, dann erhebt sich wiederum die Frage, ob sie den deutschen Siedlern oder dem slavischen Substrat gehört. Da wir im westlichen Deutschland keine irgendwie gearteten Anklänge an sie haben, und da im Slavischen grotesk-grausame Züge von verwandter Art bestehen, — daß nämlich der Alb, ehe er den Menschen drückt, den Leib aufschlitzt und seine Eingeweide aus dem Leibe nimmt und irgendwo verwahrt, — so wird man eher als dem Deutschen dem Substrat die Sagen geben wollen. Wir hätten dann einen von den deutschen Siedlern und Erzählern ausgeformten, in seinem Wesen aber aus dem Slavischen kommenden Bericht vor uns.

Wenn ich nach dieser Behauptung das soeben Vorgetragene überblicke, so scheint es mir, — obwohl ich mir der ganzen Gefährlichkeit des Beginnens, aus einem Einzelfall ein Ganzes zu beurteilen, durchaus bewußt bin, — als ob die östlich der Elbe gelegenen Landschaften eine eigene Kulturprovinz gebildet hätten. Sie nahmen vom Westen — siehe die Sage von der Mahrt im Siebrande, der Walriderske, — was ihnen der Westen an Lebendigem und im Augenblicke „Gültigem" bieten konnte; aber sie lebten letztlich aus dem eigenen Leben. So bildete sich eine eigentümliche, mit besonderen Zügen ausgestattete Kulturprovinz. Ich zeigte jüngst, daß sie die Blocksberg-Sage ausgebildet habe; wir werden, wenn unser Sagen-Wörterbuch fortschreitet, weitere Eigenarten zu verzeichnen haben. Dies aus-dem-eigenen-Bestande-leben aber zwingt zu einer nächsten Folgerung: daß diese Landschaft eine in sich ganze und geschlossene gewesen sei. (Und nicht allein erst seit dem zwölften Jahrhundert eigenartig und geschlossen: sie zeichnet

21*

sich schon im vierten Jahrhundert, ja vielleicht schon in den Taciteischen Tagen als ein Eigensein von anderen ab.)

Und um dazu noch eins zu sagen, was weniger die Landschaft als den Menschen angeht, der in ihr im zweiten nachchristlichen Jahrtausend ackert oder werkt: sie war nicht durchaus deutsch, das slavische Substrat hat in ihr Glauben und Vorstellen eingewirkt; sie war nicht slavisch, deutsche Denk- und Glaubenslehren überströmten sie, — sie wurde eine Kontaktlandschaft, eine slavischdeutsche Ehe. Das sind zwar keine Aussagen, wie sie in der gängigen und bequemen Volkskunde üblich sind, sie greifen hinüber in die Völkerschicksale und Geschicke nachbarlicher Stämme, doch es sind Aussagen, denen ein Volkskundiger sich nicht wird entziehen können. Denn wenn Politiker, Parteipolitiker Grenzen ziehen und Völker tauschen und verschieben, — der Volkskundler und nur er allein kann sagen, was am Gemeinsamen oder Bindenden wie am Trennenden vorhanden ist.

Universität Göttingen

THE SUPERNATURAL IN CHINESE FOLKTALES FROM CHÊKIANG

Wolfram Eberhard

The "Great Tradition" of Chinese religion—to use a term coined by R. Redfield—is by now fairly well known; at least, we know the content of the main religious texts and the forms of worship. Parts of the "Little Tradition" are also known. The forms of popular worship, the names of popular deities of different areas have been studied. A number of "secret societies" and their cults have also been analyzed. Yet, the question remains: what are the religious ideas and beliefs which are in the minds of the ordinary farmers—not in the minds of local priests or more or less educated persons. Folktales can be used as *one* source to find out what the common man believed, especially if such folktales do not consist only of the more or less "standardized" tales, but also include local legends or happenings which are supposedly true, but which are told without the official names of the actors and without the name of the place. If personal name and place name are given, a Chinese would regard a story as a historical text of some kind and not as a tale. Of course, a study of tales cannot give us the whole picture; it should be supplemented by other information, especially from life histories.

As the source of the following discussion, I am using a collection of some 500 texts, collected for me by Mr. Ts'ao Sung-yeh in Chin-hua (Chêkiang) in 1934.[1] The stories were collected from school children, with an average age of 12 years. The children came from the surrounding area, from villages and towns and may

[1] The stories are quoted, after a translation made by myself, in 7 parts. The original Chinese texts were in the Berlin Museum of Anthroplogy. It is not known to me whether they still exist. They were also organized in 7 parts with the same numbers.

335

represent a cross-section of the general population. The stories do not contain examples of all Chinese tale types: some tales occur very often, others do not occur at all in this collection. Therefore, to a degree, the collection reflects motifs which occupied the minds of the children most strongly. The material does not render itself to a statistical analysis; yet, in my opinion, some conclusions can be drawn from it.

1. *Gods*:

(a) *The Persons*: Most common is "the Buddha "(2,44; 5,35; 6,86; 7,7), an unspecified deity of Buddhism. Never is any further detail given as to which of the many Buddhas is meant. Next to Buddha, the Earth-God is important (5,8; 6,2c; 6,69). His temple is in every village and town and every child has seen him often. All other deities occur more rarely. There is the highest Taoist God, Yü-huang (6,16; 6,23), the Thunder God (6,64; 6,65); the daughter of the Dragon King (7,27; 7,28), a female Star God (7,39), the God of Pestilence (6,29), a Treasure God (6,57), and a God of Fate (6,58). The Sun occurs once (6,54), but not really as a deity: she has a house and much gold.

(b) *Activities of the Gods*: The Gods live on sacrifices (5,8), have families (7,27), marry (7,28), have the same social values as men (7,27). Some live in caves in luxury and with many concubines (6,87), others play chess (6,58). They get angry when persons kick their statues in the temples (6,2a); they speak out of figures or out of the person which they want to punish (7,7; 2,44), and in general punish the bad or kill them and help the good (6,64; 6,65; 6,69; 6,86; 7,1; 7,7; 6,58).

(c) *Service to Mankind*: Gods also have definite functions and, on occasion, have to serve man. If a man is destined to become an emperor, the Gods show their devotion to him (6,2b; 7,48; 7,49), and if they fail to do so, the future emperor can punish them (6,2f). They protect treasures for the right owner (6,57). If necessary, they marry humans (7,28). Scholars who recite texts can change the intentions and plans of Gods (7,39) and the statues can be used to impress moral teachings upon people, even if a trick has to be used (2,44; 5,35). Gods might even participate in tricks and cheating in order to help a future emperor (6,2c), and they can be cheated by man (5,8). They may make use of an invention made by man, for their own purposes. The thunder was invented by man and used by the Gods (6,23).

Gods, thus, are not much different from human beings. They have more, but not unlimited power. An emperor is more powerful than most of the Gods. Most of these deities are usually regarded as belonging to the Taoist pantheon, but our tales are not much interested in their official character. Often, a God could easily be replaced by another one.

2. *Deified Persons*:

(a) *Origin*: Usually persons who sacrificed themselves for their community became deities or the community built a temple and began to worship them (7,37; 6,21; 7,8; 7,10; 7,11; 7,14; 7,34; 7,35). Sometimes a person who exhibited unusual feats became deified (7,12, a quick captain).

(b) *Activities*: Their most important activity is to help the good (1,2; 1,7; 1,12; 1,14; 1,23; 1,33; 1,41; 2,4). They give children (1,10), but expect that the children later give them sacrifices as a reward (3,27). They continue to help the community by giving rain (7,37; 7,35) chasing away demons (6,21) or by general protection (7,8; 7,10; 7,11; 7,34). They are easily offended and get angry (1,6) and punish persons who are not sincere when they come to worship (1,1; 1,3; 1,6; 1,8; 1,10; 1,31; 1,32; 1,40; 1,42).

These deified persons, then, are much closer to the people. It is with them that people have most often contacts, not with the Gods. Their names and often traits of their life are well known, much better than the Gods are known.

3. *Saints*:

(a) *Origin*: A person may learn the art of becoming a saint from a Taoist (7,23) or his fate may be changed but the change was incomplete so that he did not become a God (7,48; 7,49). Saints can be recognized as they remain young (7,23).

(b) *Activities*: Saints know the future (6,8; 6,51; 6,55), perform miracles (6,79; 6,7c; 7,16) which sometimes are socially valuable, but in most cases have no importance for man. Sometimes they sell good things, but people do not recognize it (6,6). They help good persons who often do not recognize with whom they are dealing (7,49). But normally, they help people (7,16), assist the good and punish the bad (6,5; 6,55; 6,59; 6,62; 6,72; 7,50; 5,66). They are, in general, similar to the deified persons, but they cannot be asked to do something, mainly because they do not have temples where they can be reached. Their use to mankind is limited to their own fancy and cannot be directed.

4. *Ghosts and Demons*:

(a) *Origins*: Most often persons in coffins which have not yet been buried, or not been correctly buried, become demons (6,27; 6,31; 6,32; 6,33; 6,34; 6,38; 6,41; 6,104; 7,9), but also pieces of the coffin itself can become demons (1,4; 3,50; 6,30; 6,35). The hanged often become ghosts (6,28; 6,37; 7,30; 7,31; 7,32; 7,33). Such persons are usually young women who have been forced to commit suicide and who have not lived out their lives. Murdered persons, too, can become ghosts for the same reason (6,63). Finally, all objects which are very old, can come to life (7,2; 7,4; 7,45).

Ghosts are often of female sex (3,50; 6,28; 6,30; 6,36; 6,37; 6,38; 6,44; 7,9; 7,13; 7,29; 7,30; 7,31; 7,32; 7,33), but male ghosts also exist (6,39; 6,42; 6,63). Some ghosts are in animal shape (6,40; 6,84; 6,83). Ghosts are very ugly (1,4), hairy (6,35; 7,47), with short hair (6,36), and have big, black teeth (6,52). Often, they at first look beautiful, but then become really ugly with long tongue and with claws (6,28). They like to transform themselves into frightful shapes with long hair, long tongue, and blood all over (6,30; 6,37; 7,32; 7,33). They emanate a red glow (6,34; 6,35; 6,44) and dress in white, the color of mourning (6,53). When they jump into the water, they make no sound (5,60). In general, their character is bad (1,4; 6,26; 6,83; 6,84), and the more time goes on, the more powerful they become (6,104).

(b) *Their Social Life*: Ghosts, too, have families and like to stay together (6,41); they have sex life among themselves (6,44) or with humans (6,38; 6,83). They even have a king (6,52). They visit the theatre (6,38), talk in groups at night (6,53) and discuss human affairs (6,42). They make tricks just in order to have some fun (6,43). They go to human judges to claim their rights (6,63).

Ghosts collect riches (6,52) and food. Their food may be ordinary food like melons (6,52), but normally it is human flesh (1,4; 3,50; 6,32; 6,33). For this purpose, they go out at night-time (1,4; 3,50; 5,60; 6,27 et al.). Ghosts try to induce people to commit suicide in order to serve as their replacement (6,28; 7,30; 7,31), or to drown themselves for the same purpose (5,60; 4,61)—both interesting ways to explain suicide as actions for which the victim is not really responsible. Ghosts, on the other side, fear spirits of the hanged, because these are powerful (7,31).

(c) *Actions Against Man*: Ghosts and demons are normally harmful and attack people for no reason (6,27; 6,34; 6,40; 7,29), try to frighten people by assuming frightful shapes (6,28; 6,30), or really to kill them by frightening (7,4). They trick people into graves and kill them there (6,30), rob princesses for no reason (6,84), capture girls (7,29) or cut off the pigtail of a man for no reason (6,26). They may catch souls (6,39) and steal (6,83). They try to seduce a man (7,13) or have sexual relations with him (6,38). Usually, they then try to draw his life essence out of him in order to strengthen themselves; the man finally dies of exhaustion. They also can have sexual relations with women (6,83). It is rare that they just play with a man without harming him (7,45).

They revenge themselves if they are cheated (5,60), kill people in order to keep a treasure for the right man (6,56). But very rarely they also do good things, such as protecting a man against another ghost (7,31) or giving food to a man (7,30). People are, therefore, interested in getting rid of ghosts. This can be done by several methods. Ghosts can be tricked by ink (1,4; 3,50; 6,38; 7,47) or by the classical texts (6,27; 6,32). Both methods are favorites among scholars. They also can be eliminated by burning (1,4) or burning of the coffin (7,32), filling of the coffin with dirt (6,33; 6,35; 6,44) or by removing the cover of the coffin (6,27). They die when the sun rises, if they cannot take refuge in their coffins (6,33). Fire-crackers frighten them away (6,36; 7,32; 7,33) or statues of Gods protect against them (6,34). Even dogs may prevent their attacks (6,40). It is also helpful not to talk to them (6,36). If a courageous man can force them to eat rice, they will have to change into human beings (6,38), and some men even have forced ghosts to serve them (7,47). Persons who are drunk meet ghosts more often (7,31; 7,33).

Ghosts and demons seem to play a very important role, though almost always a negative one. They seem to be ordinarily *Wiedergänger*, walking dead, and exhibit a bad, aggressive character. Chinese religious theory would explain that such walking dead are in possession of the "animal soul" but not of the "personal soul." The animal soul does not recognize friends and is by nature bad. But our tales do not go into such speculations. Ghost stories are very common in the short-story literature. Here, too, ghosts have similar traits, but the sexual element is much more underlined than in our tales. It seems to me that this is not only the case because the stories were written by children, but that, on the other side, the writers of short-stories used the concept of a ghost to describe sexual and other emotional events which they could not ordinarily describe because of social taboos.

5. *Animals*

Animals formerly lived in heaven (4,73; 6,17) and sometimes were punished by being made to live on earth for a while or forever (5,73). Some human beings became animals as a result of a bad treatment given to them (6,15), or as a punishment (6,14). Animals can be good or bad: they help man (5,73; 6,60) because man has helped them (6,76; 6,77; 6,78), they punish the bad (2,26) and those who do not believe in them (6,45). They revenge themselves if they are killed by man (7,36). Sometimes, they like to play tricks on man (6,45), but sometimes, they are outright bad (6,76; 6,77; 7,6; 7,45; 7,46). Some may become bad in time (7,5). Their role is quite limited in our tales, and those animals which have a bad character are really demons in animal form, often snakes or dragons.

6. *Magic Things:*

Magic objects are also quite similar to the ghosts and demons: blood (2,17; 3,28; 3,65) or a painting (2,20) can produce magic actions. But in most cases reported in our stories, some craftsmen made small models of objects and enlivened them by magic formulae (1,5; 1,17; 1,20; 1,30; 1,36; 1,37; 1,44; 1,47b). The magic which is produced in this way may work immediately, but often it begins to work after several days or as long as after 3 years (2,9; 2,44). The magic just plainly terrifies people (1,5; 1,17; 1,20; 1,30; 1,36; 1,37; 1,44; 1,47; 1,47b; 3,42; 2,17; 2,20; 3,28; 3,65), but it may also cause harm to them (1,16; 1,21; 1,22; 1,24; 1,25; 1,27; 2,2; 3,5) or may change the whole fate of the family (1,15; 1,19; 1,18; 1,22; 1,28; 1,29; 1,35; 1,43; 1,44; 1,45; 1,46; 1,48; 2,1), or may change the luck in gambling (2,8; 2,13; 2,32). Magic may spoil the bridal night completely (1,30; 1,25; 1,24; 2,30; 3,5), or may only spoil food (2,31). If the magic is discovered in time, its effects turn against the person who made it (1,23; 1,27; 1,22). A bed-pan can avert magic (2,9; 2,31). Magic rarely serves a moral purpose, such as punishing greedy persons (2,13). But it might be said that magic which is started by craftsmen served a social function: the employers were afraid and did, therefore, not dare to mistreat the craftsmen too badly. Magic which is not caused by man, often does not cause any effects.

7. *Geomancy*:

Finally, one typically Chinese belief has to be mentioned: geomancy, or the belief that the place where a house or a tomb is built influences the future life of the owner or his family. It may also be an unusual feature in the landscape which influences the life of the people living nearby. Any action against a future gravesite influences the fate of the future generations (6,98). The right site may make the family rich after generations (6,100). Such a site may provoke fires (8,101) but may still be good (6,102). Bad places should be destroyed (6,103), but the killing of stone animals or figures (6,97) may lead to a loss of good luck. Such figures may have indicated a place where a future emperor was supposed to be born (7,18; 7,20; 7,21), and when they are destroyed, no emperor will be born (*ibid.*, and 7,19). Even a camphor tree may influence the fate of people: when a tree was trimmed, people began to die (4,1).

Conclusion

In popular belief, as expressed in folktales from Chêkiang, deified persons are the main source of good, and ghosts or demons the main source of bad. Deities seem to be aloof and are not as potent and actively interested in human affairs as the deified persons are. Saints are too unreliable to be a real source of good. Animals are not important at all—and in general, Chinese folklore is quite poor in animal tales. Nature has some powers in itself which can be socially useful, if not destroyed, and magic objects have power which can be used for social purposes if they are not detected.

The "Little Tradition" which these folktales exhibit, does not deviate much from what we can also find in collections of short stories written by educated persons. But there seems some difference in weight: less interest in sex, greater fear of the dead, and much more belief in the effectiveness of magic objects. The stories exhibit little real, emotional, religious feelings; the supernatural is regarded as a part of the social world, only with some more powers than the ordinary society has. Man is not helpless against these powers. He can defeat them. The supernatural beings are not ideal pictures of the good, but have character traits pretty much like ordinary beings, if they are not basically bad in character. It is clear from all stories that human society is the real, legal society: the other-worldly powers, although also organized in form of a society, have basically no autocratic rights over human society and have not given laws to nor created human society.

University of California,
Berkeley, California

MR. BEADLE AND THE FOLKLORISTS: POPULAR ELEMENTS IN THE DIME NOVEL

Lawrence S. Thompson

The economics of cheap editions have changed little in the last five centuries. Publishers count on a large volume of business, rapid turnover, and a relatively small margin of profit. In the United States in the last hundred years there have been two significant periods of cheap book publication, in editions ranging from 10,000–25,000 upward.[1] They are generically and somewhat inaccurately known as the dime novel and the pocket book, respectively.

Any editions in these quantities have their effect on the folk-mind simply by virtue of their readership. The dime novel, a genre which depended mainly on the original work of journalistic hacks, is more important as a generator and medium of folk tradition than such reprint series as Reclam's *Universalbibliothek* or the various series of contemporary American "paperbacks." Thus it is important to ascertain to what extent the dime novelists used folk tradition and how authentic it was.

Mr. Johannsen seems to have read most of the Beadle novels for his monumental study of *The House of Beadle and Adams*, and it is doubtful that any other bibliographer, literary historian, or folklorist should ever again subject himself to such a tedious and painful experience. For the purposes of this note, the raw material has been restricted to the sixty-one titles relating to Kentucky[2] (surely a fertile enough source for frontier tradition) and to twenty-eight others set in the

[1] Albert Johannsen, *The House of Beadle and Adams and its Dime and Nickel Novels* (Norman, Okla., 1950; 2 v.), makes several references to the size of editions of individual titles in the Beadle and Adams series.

[2] Listed and annotated in Lawrence S. and Algernon D. Thompson, *The Kentucky Novel* (Lexington, 1953), pp. 137–157. Imprint and series of dime novels listed in this bibliography will not be repeated here.

Ohio Valley, mainly in the pioneer period. Along with the groups dealing with Texas and with the mountain-plains states, this Ohio Valley sample seems to be a potentially greater source of folk tradition than the parlor tales or the exotic romances. In any event, we will have to wait for another scholar with Mr. Johannsen's diligence if the material taken from the Ohio Valley sample is inadequate for the purposes of this paper.

The dime novelists were incurably romantic. Their imagination would have put a modern science-fiction novelist to shame. Most of them, as the biographies in Mr. Johannsen's second volume will show, came from relatively unsophisticated origins. Some, such as Edward Sylvester Ellis, son of the famous Ohio rifle-shot and hunter, Sylvester Ellis, were surely exposed at one time to the current frontier traditions. Major Sam S. Hall (Buckskin Sam) was himself as much of a tradition as his famed buddy, Big Foot Wallace; and Buffalo Bill's literary efforts contributed largely to the creation of his own legend. On the other hand, an Englishman such as Percy Bolingbroke St. John, who translated Oliver Gloux' (Gustav Aimard's) *Prairie Flower* and let an ostrich hunt on the Upper Missouri prairies pass unglossed, was hardly in touch with bonafide American folk traditions.

It would be somewhat short of actual fact to describe the dime novelists as gullible media for the transmission of hoary tradition. Charles B. Lewis ("M. Quad") wrote a charming little satire on the alleged prowess of the hunter and Indian-killer in an article in the Detroit *Free Press* in 1889.[3] Buckskin Sam pokes fun at the supposed diet of the western hardrock when he has Reckless Joe call for a dish of Texas victuals:

> My kingdom for a b'iled mule, and if you haven't that article of food upon yer bill-o'-fare, just sling-a-long a brace of broiled buzzards, a stewed coyote, and a dessert of prickly pears, washed down with a good square drink from Chock-a-late Creek; but mind you, pick out the bugs and singe the buzzards.[4]

He indulges in more flyting, frontier-style, when he tries to persuade his readers that Big Foot Wallace kept a tame panther for a ranch cat to stand guard when he was not in residence, a tale about Big Foot that is still current in Texan oral tradition.

The dime novelist had just enough education to poke fun at the supernatural or at least to provide a physical explanation for apparently supernatural occurrences. The prolific Arthur Livermore Meserve created a bogus spook in *The Indian Spirit*, actually a giant half-witted Indian who used the paws of beasts for moccasins. Again, in *The River Spirit*, Meserve has a medicine man masquerade as a phantom kidnapper who knows enough legerdemain to wreath his canoe in

---

[3] Johannsen, *op. cit.*, II, 180–181, quotes it in full.
[4] *Kit Karson, Jr., the Crack Shot of the West* (New York, 1878; "Beadle's Dime New York Library," v. I, no. 3).

smoke and give the appearance of breathing fire. In *Walking Bear* Meserve creates a title character whose mufti is a bearskin designed to arouse superstitions of both races. Maro Orlando Rolfe plays on the humble settler's belief in ghosts in *Star-Face, the Slayer*, but he lets the reader in on his secret.

Efforts to use supernatural backgrounds are clumsy and not based on authentic popular tradition. The title character of Henry J. Thomas' *Ben Bramble* (based on John Lewis' *Young Kate*) attributes villain Zac Forster's ability to perform simple geometrical problems in surveying to "onnatural powers and gifts." William Osborn's *The Scotch Detective* is aided by the hermit Flintlock, who has strange powers over beasts and has four tame "painters" he sets on hostile redskins. Osborn's tradition is a pale, probably garbled reflection of other more specific qualifications for beast-taming (by a chaste woman, a beautiful woman, or a saint; cf. *Motif-Index*, B 771 *et seq*.). John W. Mackey's *The Shawnee Witch*, starring one Ca-tis-ka, has conjuring scenes about as convincing as the Kentucky alligators that devour the villain at the end. She uses a child's skull, ignited by her own blood, to whip up a vision to help avenge the death of her son. Percy Bolingbroke St. John's *The Big Hunter* has a scene with the Indian Massaquoit using a grotesque ceremonial that would never have passed muster in a genuine Shawnee camp.

There are few examples of balladry or any other type of folk song in the dime novels. Samuel Fletcher plagiarizes some contemporary vaudeville songs in Negro dialect for the Indian-killing title character of his *Black Sampson*. Captain Latham C. Carleton (a pseudonym of Edward S. Ellis) has his comic Negro, Jake, sing two verses of a spiritual in *Spotted Dan*, but nearly all the other dime novels of the Ohio Valley frontier are verseless and tuneless.

Occasionally folk medicine is used to heal grievously wounded heroes. St. John has Massaquoit concoct a poultice of crusted herbs to heal the back of Ned Harris, brutally lacerated in a beating administered by Simon Girty.[5]

The dialect used by the dime novel characters will bear further investigation. Meserve's comic Yankees may use an authentic New England dialect that he himself knew, but the comic Irishmen, Germans, and Negroes speak a language that comes directly from the minstrel show. Whether the grizzled scouts who appear in every dime novel of the Ohio Valley frontier use authentic dialect can be ascertained only when we have detailed historical studies of the speech of this region comparable to Norman E. Eliason's *Tarheel Talk*.

---

[5] The writer owns a fragmentary copy of the second edition of Richard Carter's *Valuable Vegetable Medical Prescriptions* (Versailles, Kentucky, 1825) that has St. John's signature on the fly-leaf. Various vegetable poultices are mentioned in it. D. C. and L. B. Thomas, *Kentucky Superstitions* (Princeton, N. J., 1920), list three poultices (items 1,102, 1,225, and 1,347), one of which involves the use of herbs.

If the dime novelists were not close enough to indigenous folk tradition to use it intelligently in their generally pedestrian work, they were nevertheless responsible for the creation of a popular image of certain folk heroes, notably Daniel Boone, Simon Kenton (and his counterpart in the realm of evil, Simon Girty), Buffalo Bill, Big Foot Wallace, and others of slighter reputation. Boone, Kenton, and Girty are the Roland, Oliver, and Ganelon of mid-American tradition. As creatures of the devil, the Harpe brothers, Big and Little, rivalled Girty. While there is generally a moral attached to the deeds of the good and bad men of the border, the writers and readers of the dime novels were more interested in action of any variety than in didacticism. At least the comparable popularity of books featuring Boone and Kenton on the one hand, and of Girty and the Harpes on the other, would indicate this rather common reaction of the people to a folk hero.[6]

Boone appears in numerous dime novels and dime biographies, e.g., St. John's *Queen of the Woods*, Wehman's *Book on the Adventures of Daniel Boone*, Burke Brentford's (pseudonym of Nathan Dane Urner) *On the Border*, an anonymous biography, *Daniel Boone*, issued as No. 32 of "Ornum and Company's Indian Novels," and Frederick Whittaker's *Boone the Hunter*. A good example of the Kenton-Girty dichotomy appears in A. D. H.'s *The Invisible Scouts*, and John J. Marshall's *The Outlaw Brothers* is perhaps the best known dime novel on the Harpes. The dime novelists used Filson, Marshall, Flint, Collins, McClung and other early historians as their sources; but they in turn became the source for popular novelists of the succeeding generation. Before his death the late Joseph A. Altsheler stated to the writer that he had read only one of the five Ohio Valley historians mentioned above, that he derived most of his information about the frontier from Ellis' "Boone and Kenton Series" (1896–97) and his biography, *Daniel Boone, Hunter of Kentucky* (1861). Several of Ellis' fictions about the age of Boone that appear nowhere else are repeated even by such a distinguished writer as Elizabeth Madox Roberts in *The Great Meadow* (1930). Specific evidence is not available at this time on the direct line of transmission; but when cheap books issued in comparatively large editions are involved, an acceptable guess may be made.

The Boone, Kenton, Girty, and Harpe legends are precisely the type with which Albert Wesselski could operate most effectively.[7] These tales were first given wide currency in the books of the early historians, the newspapers, the Cincinnati magazines, and even some of the more sedate periodicals of the eastern

[6] Cf. remarks at the end of L. F. Werner Boette's article "Helden," *Handwörterbuch des deutschen Aberglaubens* (Berlin, 1927–1942), III, 1701.

[7] See his *Versuch einer Theorie des Märchens* (Reichenberg i. B., 1931).

littoral; and, using these sources as a general point of departure, Mr. Beadle's hacks played freely with the traditions of the west. The alligator-horse has never been allowed to appear in his true light until Arthur Moore published his penetrating study of *The Frontier Mind* in 1957. For this distortion of facts and partial facts into a pseudo-folk tradition we can thank four generations of western story-tellers from Filson to Altsheler.

The most striking folk element in the dime novels is the use of the tall tale. He who is willing to go through the whole corpus will find some rewarding examples, although it will be difficult in nearly all cases to establish the immediate source. A few examples of the tall tale as it is used in the dime novel of the Ohio Valley will give some idea of the available material and how it was used.

Stith Thompson has properly stated that some of the outrageous yarns spun by the American frontiersman often correspond to some well-known European form.[8] Still one may suspect that at times we may find examples of a Sydowian *oikotype* among the unlettered frontier groups of European origin. A further element is the alligator-horse's penchant for humourous insult. For example, I have an undated, unidentified clipping, probably from the *Kentucky Gazette* in the closing years of the eighteenth century in which the Kentuckian expresses his belief in his superiority over his relatives on the other side of the mountains. It seems that Daniel Boone carved the words, "This is the way to Kentucky," on large trees at suitable intervals along the Wilderness Trail, and every Virginian or North Carolinian who could read betook himself to the New Eden in the Bluegrass.

A characteristic tall-tale-teller is Abner Green in *The Brave Boy Hunters of* Kentucky by an anonymous author. Green, a comic New England Yankee, relates a whopper about Uncle Joe Hall, who was fishing from a log in a mill pond in the south. The log began to move, and it turned out to be a snake (*Motif-Index*, X 1321.12). Uncle Joe stood there for an hour as the snake wiggled along, and when he left the tail still wasn't in sight. This story is the *reductio ad absurdum* of the New England sea serpents,[9] none, however, as elongated as the southern reptile. Here is a story which seems to be something that frontier Americans could call their own; and it was an ideal vehicle for the dime novelists' favorite sport, abuse of the readers' credulity in much the same classic backwoods style as that in which John Findley led Daniel Boone on with stories of the abundance of game in Kentucky, or in which Audubon kidded Rafinesque about the "Jack-Devil-Diamond" fish.[10] The frontiersman was not content to tell a twice-told tale. He had to compound it with his peculiar brand of humor.

[8] *The Folktale* (New York, 1946), p. 214 *et seq.*
[9] R. M. Dorson, *Jonathan Draws the Long Bow* (Cambridge, Mass., 1946), pp. 133–137.
[10] Lawrence S. Thompson, *Kentucky Tradition* (Hamden, Conn., 1956), pp. 163–164.

Squint-Eyed Bob, hero of the anonymous dime novel which bears his name, had to tolerate the fabrications of comic Irishman Barney McBride. Barney is not satisfied to recite the herpetocidal feats of St. Patrick. He elaborates on the famous tale to prove that all the snakes driven from the auld sod went to England and became the lineal ancestors of the inhabitants of that realm. The reptilian character of Englishmen, still suspected in parts of the Middle West and in the columns of its largest newspaper, is hardly the direct result of the propaganda of Squint-Eyed Bob's creator; but the dime novelist was able to give a humorous turn to one of the deeply engrained prejudices of the region. He was not content with a simple folk tale as a literary device.

Edward Willett's *The Drummer Sport* has a river character named Si McGumphey, who pulls the leg of a travelling Englishman by telling him the story of a pickaninny who was tossed into the boilers of a river packet to build up more steam. The denizens of the interior valley went to no end of trouble to manufacture tales exaggerating the persecution of the Negro. The most famous example is Joe Mulhattan's Louisiana hoax, or the tale of the cotton-picking monkeys.[11]

Col. Meserve, writing under the pseudonym of L. Augustus Jones, has a tall-tale-telling sub-title character in *The Imps of the Prairie; or, The Slasher of the Cave*. The Slasher, prototype of the story-telling scout, has such fabulous adventures as the one in which he stared down a mad dog in a row boat, of the dying grief-stricken girl whose heart was found split in two upon autopsy, and of Indian cannibalism as part of torture. Cannibalism is not documented in any reputable ethnological studies as a device of torture, and it was practiced solely as ritual. The Slasher's buddy, Grizzly Jake, tells of Indian torturers repelled by the accuracy of a tobacco-chewing victim. Here, except for the dead girl's story, are yarns, that are not likely to have grown up east of Ambrose Light.

The dime novelists were among the most widely read agents who perpetuated the traditions of the frontier hero and the tall tales he and his companions told. They added almost nothing to already recorded folk tradition in these fields; but they preserved it, sometimes in corrupt forms and always in massive editions, for the late nineteenth and early twentieth century. Those elements which have been confused with history have had to be re-evaluated in works such as Moore's *Frontier Mind*. The stories, especially the tall tale, its sources, forms, and corruptions, still need further study.

University of Kentucky,

Lexington, Kentucky

---

[11] James Tandy Ellis, *The Tang of the South* (Lexington, 1924), pp. 78–79.

22 Taylor

"R. B." AND ASBJÖRNSEN

Henning Larsen

Rasmus Björn Anderson Kvelve, known best both to friends and foes as "R. B.", was a pioneer in the movement to keep Norwegian traditions and language alive among immigrants to America. One of Anderson's contributions to this cause, important but now almost forgotten, is a small volume of stories (mostly *eventyr*) published under the title *Julegave* aimed to interest the children in Norwegian literature.[1]

Anderson's purpose in issuing the volume is clearly stated in his preface: "De Ældre læse helst vore norske Digtere, Historikere, og Romanforfattere. Men Börnene maa have Eventyr, mindre fortællinger og Fabler—noget, som er let fattelig og morsomt."

The volume, which is largely made up of selections from Asbjörnsen and Moe, has escaped most bibliographers. It is listed in Halvorsen's *Forfatter-Lexikon*, s. v. "Jörgen Moe," but the entry seems to have escaped the folklorists. My own discovery of the volume comes from articles by Einar Haugen.[2]

There is no mention of the volume in Paul Knaplund's recent article, "Rasmus B. Anderson, Pioneer and Crusader," a superficial and rather inaccurate evaluation of Anderson's work, published in *Norwegian-American Studies and Records*, Vol. 18.

---

[1] *Julegave. Et Udvalg af Eventyr og Fortællinger.* Udgivet af R. B. Andersen (sic!). Chicago, Ill. "Amerikas'" Forlag. 1872. The volume I have used is from the Archives of the Norwegian-American Historical Association. I hereby express my sincere thanks for the loan.

[2] "A Critique and a Bibliography of the Writings of Rasmus B. Anderson," *Wisconsin Magazine of History*, 1937.

Julegave is a collection of twenty-seven stories; all but three are folktales and nineteen are from the collections of Asbjörnsen and Moe. At the time Anderson's volume appeared, Asbjörnsen and Moe had published two collections of *eventyr*, *Norske Folkeeventyr*, 1843–1844, a first edition left unfinished, but completed in a second edition of 1852 (known in Norway as "Fællessamlingen") and *Norske Folkeeventyr, Ny Samling*, 1871, (commonly called "Enesamlingen" because Asbjörnsen alone was responsible for the editing). In the years from 1850 to 1866, Asbjörnsen published four small volumes called *Juletræet*, mostly made up of *eventyr*. Many of these tales were included in the collection of 1871. In the meantime the third and fourth editions of "Fællessamlingen" appeared in 1866 and 1868, respectively.

Anderson obviously had most of these volumes before him. Of the nineteen *eventyr* from Asbjörnsen and Moe, fifteen are from the collection known as "Fællessamlingen"; and textual characteristics make it almost certain that he used the third or fourth edition. The other four stories are found in *Ny Samling*, the edition of 1871 ("Enesamlingen"). These four had already appeared in *Juletræet* from which they were incorporated in the edition of 1871. Variant readings definitely establish that one story, *Guldfuglen*, derives from *Juletræet* of 1850, and two stories, *Goddag Mand!—Øxeskaft* and *Veslefrik med Felen* are from the edition of 1866. .

Anderson's idea of calling his volume *Julegave* may have come from Asbjörnsen's *Juletræet* or from Moe's two collections of poems *At hænge paa Juletræet* (1855) or *En liden Julegave* (1859) or from a combined influence of all.

It is astounding after reading Anderson's Introduction, with its plea for keeping alive Norwegian language and Norwegian literature, to find the volume begin with "Rödhætten" ("Little Red Ridinghood") translated from the German of the Grimms—a story in content and style completely foreign to the Norwegian—and end with three more from Grimm, "Hans, som havde Lykken med sig," "Den tro Johannes," "En Kat og en Mus i Selskab," stories which again add a false note.

Anderson's enthusiasm for Norwegian language and culture was genuine, his sense of a good story was keen, but his sense of style cannot have been dependable. Not only does he include the stories just mentioned, placed at the beginning and end of the volume, but he also adds, without sense of misfit, three modern tales—two excellent, and at that time very popular, stories by Jörgen Moe, "Gamle Hans Grenader" and "Allarm" (from *I Brönnen og i Tjernet*) and "Lille Alvilde," by Mauritz Hansen, a sample of the worst sentimental stuff created in the name of "Children's literature."[3]

[3] I owe the identification to Professor D. A. Seip of the University of Oslo. Personally I knew the story from childhood but could find it in no volume available to me.

22*

Anderson's *Julegave* must have been a real success, for at least eight editions appeared, the last in 1900. Later editions were enlarged to bring the number of stories to thirty-eight. I have reason to believe my own copy, seventh edition, represents the final form.[4]

It adds eleven stories of which ten are from *Norske Folkeeventyr—Ny Samling*, 1871 ("Enesamlingen") and one from H. C. Andersen, "Hvad Fatter gjör, det er altid det Rigtigste." This adds illustrations. Both Andersen's text and the pictures are so thoroughly Danish that they are, in spite of excellent quality, definitely out of harmony with "R. B.'s" plan and purpose—and close the volume on a false note.

University of Illinois,
Urbana, Illinois

[4] *Julegave. Et Udvalg af Eventyr og Fortællinger.* Udgivet af Rasmus B. Anderson, Professor i de Skandinaviske Sprog ved Wisconsin Stats-Universitet. Syvende forögede Oplag. Chicago, Ill. Skandinavens Boghandel, 1890.

THE POLISH PROVERB "THE DOG IN THE WELL"

Julian Krzyżanowski

The proverb about a dog in the well, quite common in Polish and extremely rare in other languages,[1] is rather difficult to explain as far as its origin and development are concerned. The problems that have attached to an understanding of this proverb over the centuries have, of course, influenced its very career in folk tradition. Therefore the parœmiologist who wants to arrive at a correct solution of questions connected with this proverb is bound to master the entire material, namely to examine its Polish forms, and to try to explain the variations that developed on Polish soil under the influence of cultural factors peculiar to its Polish habitat. If solutions suggested here do not prove quite satisfactory, elucidation of some obscure details may at least lead, in course of time, to more positive and satisfactory results.

A. The point of departure of the present investigation is hardly an easy one. In the magnificent *Dictionary of Polish Proverbs* compiled by Samuel Adalberg (1894)[2] the dog-in-the-well proverb is dispersed and must be looked for in several places and under at least nine different catchwords. If collected under a common head, the family tree of this proverb is represented by nine variants: "He is okay —like a dog in the Dominican well" (= Dobrze mu jak psu w dominikańskiej studni); "He revelled like a dog in the well" (= Hulał jak pies w studni); "Bad business to tease (irritate, enrage) a dog in the well" (= źle psa w studni drażnić);

---

[1] The English proverb "There is a dog in the well" meaning There is something amiss (Smith & Heseltine: *The Oxford Dictionary of English Proverbs*, 1952, 151) has nothing in common with problems discussed in this paper.

[2] S. Adalberg: *Księga Przysłów Polskich*, Warszawa 1889–1894, pp. 100, 173, 399, 515, 538, 558, 580, 585.

"To irritate a dog in a narrow place (gorge) is a bad business" (= Psa w cieśni źle drażnić); "To perform one's part like a dog in the well" (= Spisać się jak pies w studni); "Happy like a dog in the well" (= Szczęśliwy jak pies w studni); "He dances like a dog in the well" (=Tańczy jak pies po studni); "He enjoys himself like a dog in the well" (= Używa jak pies w studni), and finally "He ingratiates himself like a little bitch in the well" (= Wdzięczy się jak suczka w studni). A few further items could be added to the list from the typescript collection of the editorial board of the *New Dictionary of Polish Proverbs*, as the new edition of the work of Adalberg will be styled.The number and variety of items cited, however, seems sufficient for the present attempt to solve some of the riddles connected with the dog-in-the-well proverb.

Even a first glance at the Polish material under examination reveals that it consists of two different classes, the serious and the jocular. The first is just a simple warning: "Bad business to enrage a dog in the well (gorge)." The second class, on the other hand, which is much more numerous, is represented by a series of images the sense of which, sometimes tinged with irony, is quite obvious: it introduces an entrapped personage who makes vain efforts to get out of an uncomfortable situation. The very predicates (to revel, to enjoy oneself, to perform one's part, to ingratiate oneself) stress the comic aspect of the series.

The division in two classes finds an additional support in the fact that the first of them is older and that its roots may be traced in the ancient world. In Poland it was inserted in the collections of proverbs of Samuel Rysiński (1618)[3] and of Gregory Cnapius (1632)[4] who were educated humanists and well read not only in the *Adagia* of Erasmus but also in his sources, the works of Greek and Roman writers. Rysiński, who might have heard the dog-in-the-well proverb in the spoken language, rendered it after its Latin model "In puteo cum cane pugnare" i.e., "Bad business to tease a dog in the well." Different was the position of his follower, the Jesuit lexicographer, Cnapius. He was accustomed to instruct his readers to help them solve linguistic puzzles, a fact which seems to account for the circumstance that, although he knew the Latin proverb with the word "well," he preferred another form of it: "To tease a dog in a narrow place is a bad business." Evidently he understood the colloquial and secondary sense of the proverb, for he wrote in his commentary:"In puteo cum cane pugnare—dicitur is, qui cum homine litigioso et rixoso negotium habet, ex quo nec se extricare nec impune urgere

---

[3] S. Rysiński: *Proverbiorum Polonicorum... Centuriae decem et octo*. Lubecae ad Chronum 1618. Its second edition was published under the Polish title: *Przypowieści Polskie*, 1629. Modern reprint: Warsaw 1854.

[4] *Thesauri Polono-Latino-Graeci* Gregorii Cnapii e Societate Jesu *Tomus tertius. Continens ADAGIA POLONICA selecta... Cracoviae Anno MDCXXXII*. p. 984.

potest"; at the same time, however he was not able to understand the literal, (original) significance of the proverb. He did not know what a dog had in common with the well, and therefore he replaced the puzzling word by a "narrow place."

Thanks to the friendly help of my colleagues, Polish professors of Greek philology in the Iagellon and Copernicus Universities in Cracow and Toruń, Mr. Jan Safarewicz and Mr. Stefan Srebrny, I am able to cast some light upon the origin of the proverb under examination. It failed to attract the attention of the great pioneer of modern parœmiology, Erasmus, while in the handbook of Paolo Manuzio it was given only a superficial commentary[5] which was repeated in the work of Cnapius. Now, according to my present-day informants the Greek proverb, ἐν φρέατι κυνομαχεῖν or ἐν φρέατι κυνὶ (κυσὶ) μάχεσθαι, i.e., in Latin "In puteo cum cane (canibus) pugnare," in English, "To fight with a dog (with dogs) in the well" appeared rather late in the compilations of Byzantine scholars, Apostolios, Hesychios, Gregory of Cyprus, Suda (Suidas) and others.[6] I cannot desist from quoting a passage from Professor Srebrny's letter: "The sense of the proverb is clear: it means a difficult and no-way-out state of things, if you have to fight with dogs, confined with them in a well. But it is hardly possible to locate here an actual well." That proves that the modern scholar is exactly as helpless as his 17th-century predecessor, when he tries to penetrate into the fundamental significance of the dog-in-the-well proverb and the cultural circumstances that gave birth to it. And yet, desperate though it seems to be, the situation is not quite hopeless.

Analytical examination of the structure of the proverb leaves no doubt whatever, that the well, one of its basic elements, is a symbol of a trap or pitfall of some sort or other, as in the ancient popular saying quoted by Plato (in *Theaitetos* B 165).[7] From this standpoint the solution of the trap-well and the fighters in it seems much easier. Anybody who has had the experience of climbing rocky mountains is aware of the treacherous holes which are easy to enter but extremely difficult to get out of. And Greece is the very land of mountains, gorges and pits. Moreover, at the bottom of rocky "cauldrons" one often comes across springs of water welling up and attracting all sorts of thirsty animals. To encounter in a place like that a stray and enraged dog and to tease him would imply serious danger, the consequences of which are expressed in the warning sense of our proverb. One may add another detail. The springs in the mountains in ancient Greece were often consecrated to various gods and goddesses (like the famous Castalian

---

[5] P. Manutii: *Adagia Optimorum Scriptorum Omnia*, Ursellis 1603, p. 414.

[6] *Corpus Paroemiographorum Graecorum*, ed. Leutsch, Schneidewin & Ludow (Göttingen 1839, 1859), passim.

[7] Cf. "*Les Belles Lettres*," *Platon*, éd. A. Diès, Paris 1924, v. VIII, 2.

or Hippocrene); they were protected by all sorts of cunning devices to keep off undesired quadruped visitors, and one may easily imagine that stray dogs were not welcome in fenced and narrow places. This was the geographic and cultural background of the Greek dog-in-the-well proverb. The background fell into oblivion, but the image which formed the nucleus of the proverb and the warning attached to it survived and, in course of time, passed to other nations, inter alia to the Poles. The proverb was easy to understand and remember in its secondary, allegorical meaning, and people who adopted it, did not care about its original significance, unless, of course, they were learned hairsplitters like the reverend Father Gregory Cnapius.

B. The expressive and picturesque form of the dog-in-the-well proverb was sufficiently attractive to insure its popularity among people who adopted it in Poland and developed its comic varieties as quoted above. Their number may be enlarged if one remembers two more variants: "He enjoys himself like a dog in the dry well" and "He enjoys himself like a dog in the Dominican well," the latter meaning evidently the same as the proverb about "the little bitch in (the Dominican) well." But as a result the Polish variants compel us to face a new problem, that of the Dominican well and monastery lore. Why Dominican?

An expert student of the history of the Dominican cloisters might be able to solve the riddle of their wells. The point is that the big church festivals held on various days of the patron-saints, attracted pilgrims who were used to come hungry and thirsty and gathered round the local fountains to get water. Steps must have been taken to prevent disasters. It seems very probable, too, that the Black Friars held some architectural secrets regarding the construction of their wells. There is a Polish proverb that sounds like an admission of that sort: "He seems to have entered a Dominican well—neither can he drink it up, nor get out of it."[8] In fact, the proverb in question is nothing other than a variation of the Latin saying: "Ventus neque manere sinit, neque navigare"; still there must have been some reason why it referred to Dominicans.[9]

For the time being a tentative explanation may be found in the history of the Polish Dominicans. At the very close of the 17th century a "miraculous" event was recorded in their monastic annals. On the confines of the provinces of Volhynia and Little Poland, not very far from the town of Lwow, stood the celebrated monastery in Podkamień. It drew to its famous walls thousands of pilgrims for years and was in a position to supply them with food but had no water for the visiting crowds, although it was situated in an area where there were springs of many rivers. Finally in November 1690 the monks encouraged by what was con-

[8] Adalberg, o. c., p. 363 (s.v. Osiąść).
[9] P. Manutius, o. c., p. 606.

sidered a miraculous omen, undertook a painstaking enterprise. They celebrated the festive day of St. Clement to whom they prayed for help, and suddenly they saw a stork which, in the uncommon season of the year, came from a distant wood, flew in circles round the cloister and landed on a certain spot. Here they started digging into the rocky hill and after eighteen years of unceasing efforts they discovered a big cave with a cascade of crystalline water forming an abundant underground rivulet. In this way the monastic miracle was completed in the year 1708.

The simple and charming local legend of Podkamień is worth reading in its Latin garb.[10]

> In festo s. Clementis papae et martyris, post solemnem celebratam missam et absolutas ferventes supplicationes, in conspectu omnium ciconia ex silvis advolante atque deambulante in loco nunc existentis putei... inchoatus est hic puteus, finitus autem post 18 integros annos in festo purificationis Deiparae.

> Expensa sunt omnino triginta millia florenorum in eruendo hoc puteo, tam longo tempore operariis extra dies dominicos et festos, omni parte anni, aliis de die, aliis de nocte continuo ad lumen laternarum laborantibus atque chalybe et igne duritiem rupis nonnunquam quasi silicis frangentibus ac in ipsa serena meridie stellas in coelo videntibus.

> In ipso putei fundo est candidissima arenula, per quam assidue labitur profundior rivus limpidissimus a parte meridionali ex rupe profluens et in cavernam a natura paratam versus occidentem descendens. Vasa uti magna dolia in puteum hunc demittuntur et plena extrahuntur continuo.

The story told by the pious chronicler of the Podkamień monastery constitutes an excellent illustration to elucidate the proverb of the Dominican trap-fountain which cannot be drunk up and offers no way out, unless one takes recourse to buckets hanging on long chains. Tales like that spread by the preachers and retold by pilgrims after they reached their homes, might have produced the proverb concerned, provided, of course, that it was coined in Poland and was not earlier than the end of the 17th century. Unfortunately Adalberg's dictionary furnishes no details as to its origin.

The moral of the present essay, however, is quite clear. The investigation of the dog-in-the-well proverb, insufficient though it is, runs across lands distant in space and time, ancient Greece, the Middle Ages and Poland in the 17th century; the track of its history is picturesque enough to attract the scholar's attention. This would seem to confirm the opinion that it seems worthy of further digging into the well of the folklore tradition.

University of Warsaw

[10] Text from the manuscript *Liber Memorabilium*, quoted by Sadok Barącz in his history of the Polish Dominicans: *Rys Zakonu Kaznodziejskiego w Polsce*, Lwow 1861, v. 2, p. 479.

BIBLIOGRAPHY OF THE WRITINGS
OF ARCHER TAYLOR

COMPILED BY C. GRANT LOOMIS*

1916 "A Parallel to the *Rosengarten* Theme," *Modern Language Notes*, XXXI (1916), 248–250.

1917 "OHG. quëcbrunno," *Modern Language Notes*, XXXII (1917), 48–50.

"Dane Hew, Munk of Leicestre," *Modern Philology*, XV (1917) 221–246.

The Loathly Lady in the Wolfdietrich Epics, "Washington University Studies," IV, ii, 175–189.

Three Birds of Ill Omen, "Washington University Studies," IV, ii, 151–173.

1918 "Notes on the Wandering Jew," *Modern Language Notes*, XXXIII (1918), 394–398.

"An Old-World Tale from Minnesota," *Journal of American Folklore*, XXXI (1918), 555–556.

"The Motif of the Vacant Stake in Folk-Lore," *Romanic Review*, IX (1918), 21–28.

Reviews:

R. M. Dawkins, *Modern Greek in Asia Minor*: *Modern Philology*, XV (1917–1918), 735–737.

Adolf Taylor Starck, *Der Alraun*: *Journal of American Folklore*, XXXI (1918), 561–563.

1919 "Schrätel und Wasserbär," *Modern Philology*, XVII (1919), 305–324.

Judas Iscariot in Charms and Incantations, "Washington University Studies," Humanistic Series, VIII, 3–17.

1920 "'O du armer Judas'," *Journal of English and Germanic Philology*, XIX (1920), 318–339.

* After this bibliography had already been set, Elli Kaija Köngäs kindly made available to the Editors a bibliography of Professor Taylor's writings which she had prepared for a graduate seminar at Indiana University. To her, and to her instructor, Professor Richard M. Dorson, hearty thanks are expressed for helping track down several items that otherwise might have been missed.

1921 "The Devil and the Advocate," *Publications of the Modern Language Association*, XXXVI (1921), 35–59.

"Notes on the Mandrake," *Journal of American Folklore*, XXXIV (1921), 323–327.

"'In the Evening Praise the Day'," *Modern Language Notes*, XXXVI (1921), 115–118.

"The Death of Qrvar Oddr," *Modern Philology*, XIX (1921), 93–106.

"Arthur and the Wild Hunt," *Romanic Review*, XII (1921), 286–289.

"The Judas Curse," *American Journal of Philology*, XLII (1921), 234–252.

"The Mandrake: A Bibliographical Note," *Journal of American Folklore*, XXXIV (1921), 323–327.

"The 'Dream-Bread' Story Once More," *Journal of American Folklore*, XXXIV (1921), 327–328.

1922 *Northern Parallels to the Death of Pan*, "Washington University Studies," Humanistic Series, X (1922), 3–102.

"The Three Sins of the Hermit," *Modern Philology*, XX (1922), 61–94.

The Gallows of Judas Iscariot, "Washington University Studies," Humanistic Series, IX, 135–156.

"Der tote Pan in der Volkssage?" *Schweizer Volkskunde*, XII (1922), 29.

1923 "Ein Diebszauber," *Hessische Blätter für Volkskunde*, XXII (1923), 59–63.

"The Three Hundred and Sixty-Five Children," *Notes and Queries*, 12th Ser., XII (1923), 96.

The Burning of Judas, "Washington University Studies," Humanistic Series, XI, i, 159–186.

1924 *Proverbia Britannica*, "Washington University Studies," Humanistic Series, XI, 409–423.

1925 *Reviews*:
Albert Wesselski, *Märchen des Mittelalters*: *Modern Philology*, XXIII (1925–26), 493–494.

E. Hoffmann-Krayer, *Volkskundliche Bibliographie*: *Modern Philology*, XXIV (1926–27), 124–127.

A. C. L. Brown, *The Grail and the English "Sir Perceval"*: *Philological Quarterly*, V (1926), 287.

1926 "Sunt tria damna domus," *Hessische Blätter für Volkskunde*, XXIV (1926), 130–146.

Reviews:
Andreas Heusler, *Altgermanische Dichtung*: *Modern Philology*, XXIV (1926–1927), 373–374.

Wilhelm Kosch, *Deutsches Literatur-Lexikon*: *Modern Philology*, XXIV (1926–1927), 499–500.

Lutz Mackensen, *Der singende Knochen*: *Modern Philology*, XXIV (1926–1927), 486–489.

Jahrbuch für historische Volkskunde: *Modern Philology*, XXIV (1926–1927), 372–373.

"Fourth Report of the Folksong Committee of the Federation of German Folksong Societies," *Modern Philology*, XXIV (1926–1927), 380–382.

1927 "Thomas Frederick Crane, 1844–1927," *Modern Philology*, XXV (1927–1928), 503–504.

"Das Schloß in Oesterreich," *Modern Language Notes*, XLII (1927) 222–228.

The Black Ox, "FF Communications," 70 (Helsinki, 1927). Pp. 91.

"The Emperor's New Clothes," *Modern Philology*, XXV (1927–1928), 17–27.

"Precursors of the Finnish Method of Folk-Lore Study," *Modern Philology*, XXV (1927–1928), 481–491.

Reviews:

"Das deutsche Volkslied": *Germanic Review*, II (1927), 264.

Kaarle Krohn, *Die folkloristische Arbeitsmethode*: *Modern Language Notes*, XLII (1927), 260–263.

John Meier, *Deutsche Volkskunde*: *Journal of English and Germanic Philology*, XXVI (1927), 593–595.

Count de Montessus de Ballore, *Ethnographie seismique*: *Modern Philology*, XXV (1927–28), 509.

1928   *Reviews:*

A. H. Krappe, *Balor with the Evil Eye*: *Modern Philology*, XXVI (1928–1929), 233–234.

(with Leonhard Bloomfield) *Festskrift til Hjalmar Falk*: *Modern Philology*, XXVI (1928–1929), 367–369.

A. P. Hudson, *Specimens of Mississippi Folk-Lore*: *Modern Philology*, XXVI (1928–1929), 378.

Jan de Vries, *Volks-Verhalen uit Oost-Indië*: *Modern Philology* XXVI (1928–1929), 378.

C. A. Williams, *Oriental Affinities of the Legend of the Hairy Anchorite*: *Modern Language Notes*, XLIII (1928), 271–273.

1929   "The Semantics of 'Child,'" *Modern Language Notes*, XLIV (1929), 309–314.

"The English, Scottish, and American Versions of 'The Twa Sisters,'" *Journal of American Folklore*, XLII (1929), 238–246.

Reviews:

L. C. Wimberly, *Folklore in the English and Scottish Ballads*: *Modern Philology*, XXVI (1928–1929), 357–359.

Carl Diesch, *Bibliographie der germanistischen Zeitschriften*: *Modern Philology*, XXVII (1929–1930), 117–119.

Sächsisches Volkstum: *Modern Philology*, XXVII (1929–30), 244.

Arthur Dickson, *Valentine and Orson*: *Modern Language Notes*, XLIV (1929), 412–413.

1930   "The Texts of 'Edward' in Percy's Reliques and Motherwell's Minstrelsy," *Modern Language Notes*, XLV (1930), 225–227.

Articles in *Handwörterbuch des deutschen Aberglaubens*: "Elster," II, cols. 796–802; "Ente," cols. 849–851; "Eule," cols. 1073–1079; "Feder," cols. 1282–1285; "Gans," III, cols. 290–295; "Gänseei," III, col. 296; "Gänsefett," cols. 296–297; "Gänsefüßig," cols. 297–298; "Gänserich," col. 298; "Gansreiten," cols. 298–299.

"Der rihter und der teufel," *Studies in Honor of Hermann Collitz* (Baltimore, 1930), pp. 248–251.

"The Proverbial Formula 'Man soll,'" *Zeitschrift für Volkskunde*, neue Folge, II (1930), 152–156.

"Aboriginal Poetry" Folk-Say, II (1930), 411–412.

Reviews:

J. Bolte and G. Polívka, *Anmerkungen zu den Kinder- und Hausmärchen*: *Modern Philology*, XXVIII (1930–1931) 122–123.

Hermann Urtel, *Beiträge zur portugiesischen Volkskunde*: *Modern Philology*, XXVIII (1930–1931), 256.

Andreas Müller, *Märchen*: *Germanic Review*, V, (1930), 398–399.

1931 "Anordnungsprincipien," *Handwörterbuch des deutschen Märchens*, I (Berlin, 1930–1933), 73–79.

"Habicht," *Handwörterbuch des deutschen Aberglaubens*, III, cols. 1295–1296.

"Aussetzung im Boot," *Handwörterbuch des deutschen Märchens*, I, 155–156.

Edward and Sven i Rosengård. A Study in the Dissemination of a Ballad. Chicago, 1931. Pp. xi, 111.

"A Contamination in 'Lord Randal,'" *Modern Philology*, XXIX (1931), 105–107.

The Proverb. Harvard University Press. Cambridge, Mass., 1931. Pp. xi, 223.

"A Theory of Indo-European Märchen," *Journal of American Folklore*, XLIV, (1931), 54–60.

Reviews:

Valerie Höttges, *Die Sage vom Riesenspielzeug*: *Modern Philology*, XXIX (1931–1932), 511–512.

Jan de Vries, *De germaansche oudheid*: *Modern Philology*, XXIX (1931–1932), 235–236.

Jean Thomas, *Devil's Ditties*: *Modern Philology*, XXIX, 511.

Jan de Vries, *Contributions to the Study of Othin*: *Modern Philology*, XXIX, 246–247.

Henning Larsen, *An Old Icelandic Medical Miscellany*: *Modern Philology*, XIX (1931–1932), 376.

Ellen Breede: *Studien zu den lateinischen und deutschsprachlichen Totentanztexten des 13. bis 17. Jahrhunderts*: *Modern Philology*, XXIX (1931–1932), 505–506.

Albert Wesselski, *Versuch einer Theorie des Märchens*: *Hessische Blätter für Volkskunde*, XXX-XXXI, 297–299.

Walter Anderson, *Der Schwank vom alten Hildebrand*: *Hessische Blätter für Volkskunde*, XXX–XXXI, 312–313.

Walter Anderson, *Das Lied von den zwei Königskindern*: *Hessische Blätter für Volkskunde*, XXX–XXXI, 326–327.

1932 "The Pertinacious Cobold," *Journal of English and Germanic Philology*, XXXI (1932), 1–9.

"Die zwei Brüder," *Handwörterbuch des deutschen Märchens*, I, 338–340.

"Käfig," *Handwörterbuch des deutschen Aberglaubens*, IV, cols. 912–913.

"Kranich," *Handwörterbuch des deutschen Aberglaubens*, V, cols. 376–377.

"An Introductory Bibliography for the Study of Proverbs," *Modern Philology*, XXX (1931), 195–210.

(with Mary Isabelle O'Sullivan and Arthur P. Coleman) "American Bibliography for 1932. General Section," *Publications of the Modern Language Association*, XLVII (1932), 1206–1212.

Reviews:

E. E. Burriss, *Taboo, Magic, Spirits*: *Journal of Religion*, XII (1932). 268–269.

G. H. Gerould, *The Ballad of Tradition*: *Modern Philology*, XXX (1932–1933), 435–438.

Maximilian Rudwin, *The Devil in Legend and Literature*: *Modern Philology*, XXX (1932–1933), 237–238.

Jethro Bithell, *Germany: A Companion to German Studies*: *Modern Philology*, XXX (1932–1933), 450.

Florence Warren, *The Dance of Death*: *Modern Philology*, XXX (1932–1933), 325–328.

"Harvard Studies and Notes in Philology," XIII: *Modern Philology*, XXX (1932–1933), 345.

E. Windler, ed., *Das Bremer mittelniederdeutsche Arzneibuch des Arnoldus Doneldey*: *Modern Philology*, XXX (1932–1933), 451–452.

F. B. Gummere, *Germanic Origins* (ed. F. P. Magoun, Jr., as Founders of England): *Modern Philology*, XXX, 346–347.

Sverker Ek, *Studier til den svenska folkvisans historia*: *Journal of American Folklore*, XLV (1932), 270–272.

1933 "A Classification of Formula Tales," *Journal of American Folklore*, XLVI (1933), 77–88.

"Erbsenprobe," *Handwörterbuch des deutschen Märchens*, I, 575–576.

"Erraten des Lausfells," *ibid*., pp. 599–600.

"Lerche," *Handwörterbuch des deutschen Aberglaubens*, V, cols. 1219–1221.

"Lerchenfegen," *ibid*., col. 1221.

"American Bibliography for 1933: General Section," *PMLA*, XLVIII (1933), 1296–1301.

Reviews:

S. B. Hustvedt, *Ballad Books and Ballad Men*: *Journal of American Folklore*, XLVI (1933), 95–96; *Modern Philology*, XXXI (1933–1934), 97–98.

Sister Mary of the Incarnation Byrne, *The Tradition of the Nun in Medieval England*: *Modern Philology*, XXXI (1933–1934), 103.

G. G. Fox, *The Medieval Sciences in the Works of John Gower*: *Modern Philology*, XXXI (1933–1934), 104–105.

E. Golenistcheff-Koutouzoff, *L'Histoire de Griseldis en France*: *Modern Philology*, XXXI (1933–1934), 105.

R. B. Roulston, ed., C. F. Meyer, *Huttens letzte Tage*: *Modern Philology*, XXXI (1933–1934), 110–111.

R. D. Jameson, *Three Lectures on Chinese Folklore*: *Modern Philology*, XXXI (1933–1934), 111.

Else Enäjärvi-Haavio, *The Game of Rich and Poor*: *Modern Philology*, XXXI (1933–1934), 111–112.

Fritz Loewenthal, *Bibliographisches Handbuch zur deutschen Philologie*: *Modern Philology*, XXXI (1933–1934), 203–205.

M. Marti, ed., *Wolframs von Eschenbach Parzival*; *Modern Philology*, XXXI (1933–1934), 209–210.

J. R. Caldwell, ed., *Eger and Grime*: *Modern Philology*, XXXI (1933–1934), 323–324.

R. Dähne, *Die Lieder der Maumariée seit dem Mittelalter*: *Modern Philology*, XXXI (1933–1934), 324–325.

W. Gottschalk, *Die sprichwörtlichen Redensarten der französischen Sprache*: *Modern Philology*, XXXI (1933–1934), 334–335.

J. A. Macculloch, *Eddic Mythology*: *Modern Philology*, XXXI (1933–1934), 436–438.

W. P. Jones, *The Pastourelle*: *Journal of American Folklore*, XLVI (1933), 296.

1934 "Meise," *Handwörterbuch des deutschen Aberglaubens*, VI (Berlin, 1934), col. 124.

"Muriceps," *ibid.*, col. 628.

"Problems in the Study of Proverbs," *Journal of American Folklore*, XLVII (1934), 1–21.

"Finger," *Handwörterbuch des deutschen Märchens*, II (Berlin, 1934–1940), 121–123; "Fisch," II, 124–128; "Fleischpfand," II, 153–154; "Glasberg," II, 621–627.

An Index to 'The Proverb', "FF Communications," 113 (Helsinki, 1934), Pp. 105.

"'On Tib's Eve, Neither Before Nor After Christmas,'" *Studia germanica tillägnade E. A. Kock* (Lund, 1934), pp. 385–386.

"'Niemals' in einem historischen Schweizer Volkslied," *Volkskundliche Gaben John Meier...dargebracht* (Berlin, 1934), pp. 280–281.

"American Bibliography for 1934: General Section," *PMLA*, XLIX (1934), 1206–1211.

Reviews:

"Harvard Studies and Notes," XV: *Modern Philology*, XXXII (1934), 105.

W. Hartmann, ed., *Salomon und Markolf: das Spruchgedicht*: *Modern Philology*, XXXII (1934), 106.

Johannes Siebert, *Der Dichter Tannhäuser*: *Modern Philology*, XXXII (1934), 108–109.

Arnold van Gennep, *Le Folklore du Dauphiné*: *Modern Philology*, XXXII (1934), 110–111.

B. J. Whiting, *Chaucer's Use of Proverbs*: *Modern Philology*, XXXII (1934), 431–432.

M. Willinsky, *Bischof Percy's Bearbeitung der Volksballaden* (and another work): *Modern Philology*, XXXII (1934), 433.

Friedrich Ranke, *Volkssage: Modern Philology*, XXXII (1934), 437–439.

Stith Thompson, *Motif-Index*: *Modern Philology*, XXXII (1934), 439; *American Literature*, VII (1935), 359–360.

H. Menhardt, ed., *Das St. Trudperter Hohe Lied*: *Modern Philology*, XXXII (1934), 331–332.

J. R. Caldwell, ed., *Eger and Grime*: *Journal of American Folklore*, XLVII (1934), 265–266.

E. B. Reed, *Christmas Carols Printed in the Sixteenth Century*: *Journal of American Folklore*, XLVI, (1933), 422–424; *Modern Philology*, XXXII, 315–318.

1935 "The überlange Töne in Meistergesang," *Modern Philology*, XXXII (1935), 225–231.

"Parix," *Handwörterbuch des deutschen Aberglaubens*, VI (Berlin, 1935), col. 1460, "Pelikan," cols. 1476–1477. "Phönix," VII (Berlin, 1935–1936), col. 18. "Schwalbe," cols. 1391–1399. "Schwalbennest," cols. 1399–1400.

"Formelmärchen," *Handwörterbuch des deutschen Märchens*, II 164–191.

Reviews:

N. M. Penzer, *The Pentamerone of Giambattista Basile*: *Journal of American Folklore*, XLVIII (1935), 200–201.

A. H. Fox-Strangways and Maud Karpeles, *Cecil Sharp*: *Journal of American Folklore*, XLVIII, 201–202.

Jan de Vries, *Altgermanische Religionsgeschichte*: *Modern Philology*, XXXIII (1935), 212.

G. D. Kelchner, *Dreams in Old Norse Literature*: *Modern Philology*, XXXIII (1935), 212–213.

A. W. Read, *Lexical Evidence from Folk Epigraphy*: Modern Philology, XXXIII (1935), 220.

F. J. Schneider, *Deutsche Textproben für literaturwissenschaftliche Übungen*: Modern Philology, XXXIII (1935–1936), 437.

H. L. Stoltenberg, *Deutsche Weisheitssprache*: Germanic Review, X (1935), 52.

1936 "Benedict von Watt's 'Was zu einem schönen Haus gehöre,'" *Modern Language Notes*, LI (1936), 241–243.

"What Goes Through Water and Is Not Wet?," *Modern Language Notes*, LI (1936), 86–90.

"A Collection of Swedish Legal Riddles," *Zeitschrift für Volkskunde*, VIII (1936–1937), 179–184.

"Vogel," *Handwörterbuch des deutschen Aberglaubens*, VIII (Berlin, 1936–1937), cols. 1673–1679; "Vogelfrei," col. 1679; "Vogelgestaltig," col. 1679; "Vogelmist," cols. 1681–1682; "Vogelnest," col. 1682; "Vogelschießen," cols. 1682–1683; "Vogelsprache," cols. 1683–1684; "Singvogel," cols. 5–6.

(with Frances H. Ellis) *A Bibliography of Meistergesang*. "Indiana University Studies," 113 (Bloomington, Indiana). Pp. 92.

Reviews:

John Meier, *Deutsche Volkslieder*, I–III: Modern Language Notes, LI (1936), 126–127, 564; LIII (1938), 316–317; LVII (1942), 77.

Arthur Haberlandt, *Die deutsche Volkskunde*: Modern Philology, XXXIV (1936–1937), 104–105.

H. Gombel, *Die Fabel vom Magen und den Gliedern*: Modern Philology, XXXIV (1936–1937), 105.

Otto Andersson, *Den äldre folkvisan*: Modern Philology, XXXIV (1936–1937), 105–106.

J. Müller-Blattau, *Zur Erforschung des ostpreußischen Volksliedes*: Modern Philology, XXXIV (1936–1937), 106–107.

Walter Gottschalk, *Die bildhaften Sprichwörter der Romanen*: Modern Philology, XXXIV (1936–1937), 107.

R. L. Green, *The Early English Carols*: Modern Philology, XXXIV, 200–202.

W. G. Smith, *The Oxford Dictionary of English Proverbs*: Modern Philology, XXXIV (1936–1937), 202–204.

C. A. Williams, *The German Legends of the Hairy Anchorite*: Modern Language Notes, LI (1936), 259–260.

1937 "A Finding-List of American Song," *Southern Folklore Quarterly*, I, No. 3, pp. 17–23.

"What Goes Through Water and is Not Wet?" *Modern Language Notes*, LI (1937), 86–90.

"Philip Schuyler Allen, 1871–1937," *Modern Philology*, XXXV (1937–1938), 113–114.

The Literary History of Meistergesang. New York, 1937. Pp. x, 134.

Reviews:

E. Weekley, *Surnames*: Modern Philology, XXXV (1937–1938), 217–219.

A. Menner, *Die altfranzösische Bertasage*: Modern Philology, XXXV (1937–1938), 99–100.

A. G. Krüger, *Die Quellen der Schwanritterdichtungen*: Modern Philology, XXXV (1937–1938), 100–101.

H. Caplan, *Mediaeval 'Artes praedicandi'*: Modern Philology XXXV (1937–1938), 101–102.

E. G. Gudde, *Social Conflicts in Medieval German Poetry*: Modern Philology, XXXV (1937–1938), 104.

G. Bianquis, *Histoire de la littérature allemande*: Modern Philology, XXXV (1937–1938), 104–105.

Eberhard Freiherr von Künssberg, *Rechtliche Volkskunde*: Modern Philology, XXXV (1937–1938), 110.

John Meier, *Balladen*: Journal of American Folklore, L (1937), 103–104.

Carl von Stern, *Estnische Volkssagen*: Journal of American Folklore, L, 104–105.

F. A. Redlich, *Sitte und Brauch des livländischen Kaufmanns*: Journal of American Folklore, L, 194.

W. Gottschalk, *Die bildhaften Sprichwörter der Romanen*: Journal of American Folklore, L, 194.

Gisela Piachewski, *Der Wechselbalg*: Journal of American Folklore, L, 296.

Jonas Balys, *Motif-Index of Lithuanian Narrative Folklore*: Journal of American Folklore, L, 409–410.

1938 "Ze künis erbent ouch diu wip und niht die man," *Modern Language Notes*, LIII (1938), 509.

"Riddles Dealing with Family Relationships," *Journal of American Folklore*, LI (1938), 25–37.

"A Seventeenth-Century Collection of Biblical Riddles," *Gießener Beiträge zur deutschen Philologie*, LX (1938), 239–249.

"Problems in the Study of Riddles," *Southern Folklore Quarterly*, II (1938), 1–9.

"Zugvögel," *Handwörterbuch des deutschen Aberglaubens*, IX (Berlin, 1938–1941), cols. 954–955.

(with William A. Nitze) "Some Recent Arthurian Studies," *Modern Philology*, XXXVI (1938–1939), 307–312.

Reviews:

(with C. A. Bevans) Grace Frank, ed., *Proverbes en rimes*; C. D. Brenner, *Le Développement du proverbe dramatique*: Modern Philology, XXXVI (1938–1939), 73–74.

A. Leitzmann, *Der kleine Benecke*: Modern Philology, XXXVI (1938–1939), 99.

B. J. Whiting, *Proverbs in the Earlier English Drama*: Modern Philology, XXXVI (1938–1939), 102–103.

Friedrich Ranke, *Volkssagenforschungen*: Modern Philology, XXXVI (1938–1939), 107–108.

(See also the review of John Meier's *Deutsche Volkslieder* 1936]).

1939 *A Bibliography of Riddles*, "FF Communications," 126 (Helsinki, 1939). Pp. 173.

Problems in German Literary History of the Fifteenth and Sixteenth Centuries. New York, 1939. Pp. xviii, 211.

(with B. J. Whiting, Francis W. Bradley, Richard Jente, M. P. Tilley) "The Study of Proverbs," *Modern Language Forum*, XXIV (1939), 57–83.

Review:

Freda Kretschmar, *Hundestammvater und Kerberos*: Journal of American Folklore, LII (1939), 213–214.

Marcel Françon, *Notes sur l'esthétique de la femme au XVIᵉ siècle*: Modern Philology, XXXVII (1939–1940), 320–321.

James V. Rice, *Gabriel Naudé, 1600–1653*: *Modern Philology*, XXXVII (1939–1940), 433–434.

1940 "The Themes Common to English and German Balladry," *Modern Language Quarterly*, I (1940), 23–35.

"Some Trends and Problems in Studies of the Folk-Tale," *Studies in Philology*, XXXVII (1940), 1–25.

"The Carol of the Twelve Numbers Once More," *Southern Folklore Quarterly*, IV (1940), 161.

Reviews:

H. K. Schuchard, *Der Minnesänger Otto von Botenlauben*: *Germanic Review*, XV (1940), 300.

Albert Wesselski, *Deutsche Märchen vor Grimm*: *Journal of American Folklore*, LIII (1940), 81.

H. Tampere, *Vana Kannel*: *Journal of American Folklore*, LIII (1940), 81–82.

H. C. Lea, *Materials Toward a History of Witchcraft*: *Journal of American Folklore*, LIII (1940), 280–283.

Julius Petersen, *Die Wissenschaft von der Dichtung*: *Modern Language Notes*, LV (1940), 65–67.

1941 "Zwischen Pfingsten und Straßburg," *Studies in Honor of John Albrecht Walz* (Lancaster, Pa., 1941), pp. 21–30.

"The Friar's Tale," Germaine Dempster and W. F. Bryan, eds. *Sources and and Analogues of Chaucer's Canterbury Tales* (Chicago, 1941), pp. 269–274.

Renaissance Reference Books. A Checklist of Some Bibliographies Published before 1700. (Renaissance Bibliographies and Checklists, I, Berkeley and Los Angeles, 1941), Pp. 24.

"The Proverb 'The black ox has not trod on his foot' in Renaissance Literature," *Philological Quarterly*, XX (1941), 266–278.

(with Gustave O. Arlt) *Printing and Progress. Two Lectures.* Berkeley and Los Angeles, 1941. Pp. 67.

"Twenty-Three Telugu Riddles from Nellore," *Journal of American Folklore*, LIV, 72–75.

"A Metaphor of the Human Body, in Literature and Tradition," *Corona* (Durham, North Carolina, 1941), pp. 3–7.

Reviews:

J. G. McKay, *More West Highland Tales*: *Journal of American Folklore*, LIV, 217–218.

T. A. Rompelmann, ed., *Der Wartburgkrieg*: *Modern Philology*, XXXIX (1941–1942), 100–101.

1942 (with Vernam Hull). *A Collection of Welsh Riddles*, "University of California Publications in Modern Philology," XXVI, No. 3. Pp. viii, 225–326.

"An Armenian Riddle of an Eggplant," *California Folklore Quarterly*, I, 97–98.

Reviews:

Ray Woods, *The American Mother Goose*: *Journal of American Folklore*, LV, 261–262.

F. H. Wagman, *Magic and Natural Science in German Baroque Literature*: *Modern Philology*, XL (1942–1943), 291–292.

W. de Vreese and Jan de Vries, eds., *Dat Dialogus...tusschen...Salomon ende Marcolphus*: *Modern Language Notes*, LVII (1942), 162.

(See also the review of John Meier's *Deutsche Volkslieder* [1936].)

1943 "The Riddle," *California Folklore Quarterly*, II, 129–147.

(with A. G. Brodeur) "The Man, the Horse, and the Canary," *California Folklore Quarterly*, II, 271–278.

"Grete's Bad Name," *Modern Language Notes*, LVIII, 452–454.

"Attila and Modern Riddles," *Journal of American Folklore*, LVI, 136–137.

"California Folklore Society," *Journal of American Folklore*, LVI (1943), 164-166.

Reviews:

A. M. Aurand, *The Realness of Witchcraft in America*: California Folklore Quarterly, II, 54.

Sister Mary Catherine O'Connor, *The Art of Dying Well*: Modern Philology, XLI (1943–1944), 60–61.

L. Deutsch, *A Treasury of the World's Finest Folk Song*: California Folklore Quarterly, II, 229–230.

1944 "Little Red Riding Hood," *California Folklore Quarterly*, III, 318.

"The Rebuke," *California Folklore Quarterly*, III, 319.

"A Riddle for the Sun, Sky, and Stars," *California Folklore Quarterly*, III, 222–231.

"The Tarbaby Once More," *Journal of the American Oriental Society*, LXIV, 4–7.

"American Indian Riddles," *Journal of American Folklore*, LVII, 1–15.

"The Riddle of Morning-Spring," *Southern Folklore Quarterly*, VIII, 23–25.

(with Vance Randolph) "Riddles in the Ozarks," *Southern Folklore Quarterly*, VIII, 1–10.

"Another Story of Buried Gold," *California Folklore Quarterly*, III, 61–62.

"Poe, Dr. Lardner, and 'Three Sundays in a Week,'" *American Notes and Queries*, III, 153–155.

"The Permanent Values of Civilization: The Older Germans and Scandinavians," *The University Review* (Kansas City), X, 160–170.

Reviews:

Seán Ó Súilleabháin, *A Handbook of Irish Folklore*: California Folklore Quarterly, III, 256–257.

Frances Alexander, *Mother Goose on the Rio Grande*: California Folklore Quarterly, III, 347–348.

Theodore Besterman, *The Beginnings of Systematic Bibliography*: Modern Philology, XLII (1944–1945), 191–193.

Hilda R. Ellis, *The Road to Hel*: Journal of American Folklore, LVII (1944), 290.

1945 "An Allusion to a Riddle in Suetonius," *American Journal of Philology*, LXVI, 408–410.

(with M. B. Emeneau) "Annamese, Arabic, and Panjabi Riddles, *Journal of American Folklore*, LVIII, 12–20.

"Valentin Ernst Loescher's 'Literator Celta,'" *Modern Philology*, XLIII (1945), 40–43.

"A Historical Sketch of German Bibliography to 1700," *Monatshefte für deutschen Unterricht*, XXXVII (1945), 185–191.

"A Tall Tale of Cherry Picking," *California Folklore Quarterly*, IV (1945), 418.

Renaissance Guides to Books. An Inventory and Some Conclusions. (Berkeley & Los Angeles, 1945). Pp. ii, 130.

23*

"Death Valley Legend," *California Folklore Quarterly*, IV (1945), IV, 87.

"The Rebuke," *California Folklore Quarterly*, IV (1945), IV, 178–179.

1946 "Superstitions of Publishing Houses," *California Folklore Quarterly*, V, 400–401.

"Biblical Conundrums in the 'Golden Era'," *California Folklore Quarterly*, V, 273–276.

"The Problems of Folklore," *Journal of American Folklore*, LIX, 101–107.

"A Lithuanian Formula Tale," *Journal of American Folklore*, LIX, 194.

Reviews:

Luis da Câmara Cascudo, *Os melhores contos de Portugal*: *California Folklore Quarterly*, V (1946), 219–220.

Anon., *Mother Goose's Melody*: *California Folklore Quarterly*, V (1946), 126–127.

B. C. Forbes, *499 Scottish Stories for the Price of 500*: *Journal of American Folklore*, LIX (1946), 213–214.

O. Zoff, *Riddles Around the World*: *California Folklore Quarterly*, V (1946), 409–410.

Maurits de Meyer, *Vlaamsche Sprookjesthemas*: *Modern Philology*, XLIV (1946–1947), 196.

Samuel Singer, *Sprichwörter des Mittelalters*: *Modern Language Notes*, LXI (1946), 576.

1947 "Pedro!," *Western Folklore*, VI (1947), 85–86.

"Riddles in the *Emigrants' Penny Magazine*," *Southern Folklore Quarterly*, XI (1947), 139–140.

"Ainu Riddles," *Western Folklore*, VI (1947), 163–173.

"Traditional Names for Cats Once More," *Journal of American Folklore*, LX (1947), 86.

"Pedro! Pedro!" *Western Folklore*, VI (1947), 228–231.

"Release from Execution at a Woman's Request or by Marriage to Her," *Journal of American Folklore*, LX (1947), 185.

"Riddles and Poetry," *Southern Folklore Quarterly*, XI (1947), 245–247.

Reviews:

C. H. Tillhagen, *Taikon berättar*: *Journal of American Folklore*, LX (1947), 191–192.

Stith Thompson, *The Folktale*: *Journal of English and Germanic Philology*, XLVI (1947), 429–431.

C. Grönland, *Studien zu Peter Probst*: *Journal of English and Germanic Philology*, XLVI (1947), 215–216.

Vance Randolph, *Ozark Folksongs*, I: *Western Folklore*, VI (1947), 289–290.

Evelyn Faye Wilson, *The 'Stella Maris' of John of Garland*: *Speculum*, XXII (1947), 272–275.

1948 "Locutions for 'Never,'" *Romance Philology*, II (1948–1949), 103–134.

"An Ordnance-Map of Feminine Charms," *Modern Language Notes*, LXIII (1948), 61.

"Folklore and the Student of Literature," *The Pacific Spectator*, II (1948), 216–223.

"A. H. Krappe, 1894–1947," *Journal of American Folklore*, LXI (1948), 201.

"Straparola's Riddle of Pero and Cimon and Its Parallels," *Romance Philology*, I (1948), 297–303.

"Some Recent Books on the Folktale," *Journal of English and Germanic Philology*, XLVII (1948), 403–405.

The Literary Riddle before 1600. Berkeley, 1948. Pp. 131.

"What is 'Mother Goose'?" *New Mexico Folklore Record*, II (1947–1948), 7–13.

"An Early Form of Baseball in Iceland," *Western Folklore*, VII (1948), 389.

Reviews:

M. V. Emrich and G. Korson, *The Child's Book of Folklore*: *Western Folklore*, VII (1948), 94–95.

Studia Norvegica Ethnologica & Folkloristica: *Journal of English and Germanic Philology*, XLVII (1948), 191–192.

E. Linderholm, *Signelser ock besvärjelser*: *Journal of English and Germanic Philology*, XLVII (1948), 192–193.

Helmer Olsson, *Svenska gåtor*: *Journal of American Folklore*, LXI, 95–96.

Alphonse de Marneffe, *Fables des animaux du Congo*: *Journal of American Folklore*, LXI (1948), 101–102.

A. M. Espinosa, *Cuentos populares españoles*: *Western Folklore*, VII (1948), 204–205; *Journal of American Folklore*, LXI (1948), 218–220.

C. E. Funk, *A Hog on Ice*: *American Speech*, XXIII (1948), 135–136.

C. Kruyskamp, *Apologische Spreekwoorden*: *Western Folklore*, VII (1948), 316–317.

Vance Randolph, *Ozark Folksongs*, II: *Western Folklore*, VII (1948), 319–320.

Wolfram Eberhard and P. N. Boratav, *Sechzig türkische Tiermärchen*: *Journal of American Folklore*, LXI (1948), 225–226.

Max Lüthi, *Das europäische Volksmärchen*, *Modern Language Notes*, LXIII (1948), 422–423.

1949 "'Dignitas' in Otfrid, 'Ad Liutbertum,'" *Modern Language Notes*, LXIV (1949), 144.

"The Varieties of Riddles," *Philologica: The Malone Anniversary Studies* (Baltimore, 1949), pp. 1–8.

"Zwei niederdeutsche Rätsel," *Archiv für Literatur und Volksdichtung*, I (1949), 269.

"Wellerisms in Colombia," *Western Folklore*, VIII (1949), 266–267.

"Polish Riddles from Michigan," *Journal of American Folklore*, LXII (1949), 189.

"The Scope of Folklore," *Journal of American Folklore*, LXII (1949), 186.

"Folklore," in *Standard Dictionary of Folklore, Mythology and Legend*, ed. Maria Leach, New York, 1949, I, 402–403; "Germanic Folklore," pp. 445–451.

Reviews:

Maung Htin Aung, *Burmese Folk Tales*: *Journal of the American Oriental Society*, LXIX (1949), 184.

Iona and Peter Opie, *I Saw Esau*: *Journal of American Folklore*, LXII (1949), 77–78.

Norah and W. Montgomerie, *Scottish Nursery Rhymes*: *Journal of American Folklore*, LXII (1949), 214.

Ruth C. Seeger, *American Folksongs for Children*: *Western Folklore*, VIII (1949), 294.

Vance Randolph, *Ozark Folksongs*, III: *Western Folklore*, VIII (1949), 291–293.

C. H. Tillhagen, *Taikon erzählt*: *Journal of American Folklore*, LXII (1949), 455–456.

W. E. Peuckert, *Die große Wende*: *Journal of English and Germanic Philology*, XLVIII (1949), 607–609.

Verissimo de Mélo, *Adivinhas*: *Journal of American Folklore*, LXII (1949), 334.

1950 "'Or est venuz qui aunera' and the English Proverbial Phrase 'To take his measure,'" *Modern Language Notes*, LXV (1950), 344–345.

"Die Sonne tanzt am Ostermorgen," *Hessische Blätter für Volkskunde*, XLI (1950), 195.

"Proverb," in *Standard Dictionary of Folklore, Mythology and Legend*, II, 902–905; "Proverbial Phrase," II, 906; "Quotations and Winged Words (*Geflügelte Worte*), II, 916; "Wellerisms," II, 1169–1170.

Reviews:

E. C. Beck, *Lore of the Lumber Camps*: *Western Folklore*, IX (1950), 88–89.

W. G. Smith and Janet Heseltine, *The Oxford Dictionary of English Proverbs*, 2d ed.: *Journal of American Folklore*, LXIII (1950), 113–114.

Burton E. Stevenson, *The Home Book of Proverbs*: *Journal of American Folklore*, LXIII (1950), 484–485.

Verrier Elwin, *Myths of Middle India*: *Journal of the American Oriental Society*, LXX (1950), 129.

M. Joos and F. Whitesell, *Middle High German Courtly Reader*: *Journal of English and Germanic Philology*, XLIX (1950), 394–395.

C. W. von Sydow, *Selected Papers on Folklore*: *Journal of English and Germanic Philology*, XLIX (1950), 97–98.

Eliza M. Butler, *Ritual Magic*: *Speculum*, XXV (1950), 258–259.

Gerhard Eis, *Mittelhochdeutsche Lieder*; W. Stammler, *Gottsuchende Seelen*: *Modern Language Notes*, LXV (1950), 573.

Hector Lee, *The Three Nephites*: *Western Folklore*, IX (1950), 279–281.

Y. M. Sokolov, *Russian Folklore*: *Western Folklore*, IX (1950), 392–394.

Vance Randolph, *Ozark Folksongs*, IV: *Western Folklore*, IX (1950), 401–402.

1951 *English Riddles from Oral Tradition*. Berkeley, 1951. Pp. xxxi, 959.

(with F. J. Mosher) *The Bibliographical History of Anonyma and Pseudonyma*. Chicago, 1951. Pp. ix, 289.

"Shakespeare's Wellerisms," *Southern Folklore Quarterly*, XV (1951), 170.

Reviews:

James M. Clark, *The Dance of Death*: *Speculum*, XXVI (1951), 151–152.

John Meier, *Untersuchungen zur deutschen Volkskunde und Rechtsgeschichte*: *Speculum*, XXVI, 401.

G. Zink, *Les Légendes héroïques de Dietrich et d'Ermrich*: *Modern Language Notes*, LXVI (1951), 425–426.

V. E. V. Wessman, *Gåtor*: *Journal of American Folklore*, LXIV (1951), 248.

Katharine Luomala, *Maui-of-a-Thousand-Tricks*: *Journal of American Folklore*, LXIV (1951), 140–141.

M. P. Tilley, *A Dictionary of Proverbs in England in the Sixteenth and Seventeenth Centuries*: *Journal of American Folklore*, LXIV (1951), 428–429.

C. H. Tillhagen and Nils Dencker, *Svenska folklekar och danser*: *Journal of American Folklore*, LXIV (1951), 443–444.

Richard Winsted, ed., *Malay Proverbs*: *Journal of American Folklore*, LXIV (1951), 235–236.

R. M. Dawkins, *Forty-Five Tales from the Dodekanese*: *Western Folklore*, X (1951), 184–185.

Waldemar Liungman, *Sveriges samtliga folksagor*, I, II: *Western Folklore*, X (1951), 185–186.

William A. Owens, *Texas Folk Songs*: *Western Folklore*, X (1951), 258.

Ruth C. Seeger, *Animal Folk Songs for Children*: *Western Folklore*, X (1951), 258–259.

Tristram P. Coffin, *The British Traditional Ballad in North America*; G. M. Laws, *Native American Balladry*: *Western Folklore*, X (1951), 335–337.

1952 "'God's Acre' Once More," *Modern Language Notes*, LXVII (1952), 341.

"Tom Peete Cross, 1879–1951," *Journal of American Folklore*, LXV (1952), 138.

(with Thomas A. Sebeok and others), "Addenda to 'Studies in Cheremis Folklore,' Volume I," *Journal of American Folklore*, LXV (1952), 167–177 (especially pp. 175–177: Riddles).

"Investigations of English Proverbs, Proverbial and Conventional Phrases, Oaths, and Clichés," *Journal of American Folklore*, LXV (1952), 255–265.

"A Bibliographical Note on Wellerisms," *Journal of American Folklore*, LXV (1952), 420–421.

"'A nao Catarineta' in India," *Romance Philology*, VI (1952–1953) 304–305.

"Dutch in Proverbial and Conventional Use," *Western Folklore*, XI (1952), 219.

"Riddles," in the *Frank C. Brown Collection of North Carolina Folklore*. 7 vols., Durham, N. C., 1952 ff., I, 283–328.

"The Place of Folklore" (Presidential Address of the Modern Language Association of America), *PMLA*, LXVII (1952), 59–66.

Reviews:

Anna Birgitta Rooth, *The Cinderella Cycle*: *Western Folklore*, XI (1952), 68–69.

Journal of the International Folk Music Council, III; *Jahrbuch für Volksliedforschung*, VIII: *Western Folklore*, XI (1952), 145–146.

W. E. Peuckert, and Otto Lauffer, *Volkskunde, Quellen und Forschungen seit 1930*: *Western Folklore*, XI (1952), 231.

Erhard Lommatzsch, *Beiträge zur älteren italienischen Volksdichtung*: *Romance Philology*, VI (1952–1953), 69–70, VII (1953–1954), 256–257.

Jaarboek, Nationale Commissie voor Folklore, II–III (1940–1950): *Journal of American Folklore*, LXV (1952), 432.

1953 "Riddles in Dialogue," *Proceedings of the American Philosophical Society*, XCVII (1953), 61–68.

"Trends in the Study of Folksong," *Southern Folklore Quarterly*, XVII (1953), 97–113.

"Richard Jente, 1888–1952," *Journal of American Folklore*, LXVI (1953), 200.

Reviews:

Théo Brandão, *Trovas populares de Alagoas*: *Journal of American Folklore*, LXVI (1953), 275–276.

Gianfranco d'Aronco, *Guida bibliografica allo studio dello strambotto*: *Romance Philology*, VII (1953–1954), 400–401.

Eliza M. Butler, *The Fortunes of Faust*: *Western Folklore*, XII (1953), 58–59.

Journal of the International Folk Music Council, IV: *Western Folklore*, XII (1953), 63.

Paul G. Brewster, *American Nonsinging Games*: *Western Folklore*, XII (1953), 220.

Ray Wood, *Fun in American Folk Rhymes*: *Western Folklore*, XII (1953), 222–223.

Linda Sadnik, *Südosteuropäische Rätselstudien*: *Hessische Blätter für Volkskunde*, XLIV (1953), 199–201.

Arno Schirokauer, *Texte zur Geschichte der altdeutschen Tierfabel*: *Modern Language Notes*, LXVIII (1953), 213–214.

Paul Christophersen, *The Ballad of Sir Aldingar*: *Southern Folklore Quarterly*, XVII (1953), 193–195.

1954 "An Annotated Collection of Mongolian Riddles," *Transactions of the American Philosophical Society*, 44, No. 3, pp. 319–425.

Proverbial Comparisons and Similes from California, Folklore Studies, 3, (Berkeley & Los Angeles). Pp. 97.

"Pink Elephants Again," *Journal of American Folklore*, LXVII (1954), 238.

Reviews:

Waldemar Liungman, *Varifrån Kommer Våra Sagor*: *Journal of American Folklore*, LXVII, 92–94.

P. P. Bourboulis, *Studies in the History of Modern Greek Story-Motives*: *Journal of American Folklore*, LXVII (1954), 94.

Gianfranco d'Aronco, *Indice delle fiabe toscane*: *Romance Philology*, VIII (1954–1955), 240–241.

C. Rostaing, ed., *'Constant du Hamel'*: *Romance Philology*, VIII (1954–1955), 165.

Ingeborg Weber-Kellermann and Wolfgang Steinitz, *Beiträge zur sprachlichen Volksüberlieferung*: *Romance Philology*, VIII (1954–1955), 64–65.

A. Götze and L. E. Schmitt, Die 12 Artikel der Bauern (and another work): *Journal of English and Germanic Philology*, LIII (1954), 239.

Carlos Vega, *Las danzas populares Argentinas*: *Journal of American Folklore*, LXVII (1954), 98.

Hilding Celander, Stjärngossarna: *Journal of American Folklore*, LXVII (1954), 221–222.

Wolfram Eberhard and Pertev N. Boratav, *Typen türkischer Volksmärchen*: *Southern Folklore Quarterly*, XVIII (1954), 202.

Giuseppe Cocchiara, *Storia del folklore in Europa*; Inger M. Boberg, *Folkemindeforskningens Historia i Mellem- og Nordeuropa*; J. A. Carrizo, *Historia del folklore Argentino*: *Journal of American Folklore*, LXVII (1954), 407–408.

Four Symposia on Folklore: *Western Folklore*, XIII (1954), 144.

1955 Pappity Stampoy, *A Collection of Scotch Proverbs* (1663), "The Augustan Reprint Society," 52 (Los Angeles). Pp. vi, 58.

(with Vernam Hull) *A Collection of Irish Riddles*, "Folklore Studies," 6 (Berkeley & Los Angeles). Pp. xiv, 129.

A History of Bibliographies of Bibliographies. New Brunswick, N. J. Pp. ix, 147.

"A Riddle for Ashes," *Western Folklore*, XIV (1955), 282.

"'An Old Friend Is the Best Friend,'" *Romance Philology*, IX (1955–1956), 201–205.

"Sigurd Bernhard Hustvedt (1882–1954)," *Western Folklore*, XIV (1955), 1–2.

Reviews:

David Kin, *Dictionary of American Proverbs*: *Western Folklore*, XIV (1955), 292.

Achille Millien and Paul Delarue, *Contes du Nivernais et du Morvan*: *Journal of American Folklore*, LXVIII (1955), 102.

G. Massignon, *Contes de l'Ouest*: *Journal of American Folklore*, LXVIII (1955), 240.

F. de Castro Pires de Lima, *A Sereia na Historia e na Lenda*: *Journal of American Folklore*, LXVIII (1955), 366.

Karl Haiding, *Oesterreichs Märchenschatz*: *Journal of American Folklore*, LXVIII (1955), 374–375.

Hans Sachs, *Sämtliche Fabeln*, I: *Journal of English and Germanic Philology*, LIV (1955), 280–281.

Wolfgang Steinitz, *Deutsche Volkslieder demokratischen Charakters*, I: *Journal of English and Germanic Philology*, LIV (1955), 401–402.

Milman Parry and A. B. Lord, *Serbocroatian Heroic Songs* (and other works): *Modern Language Notes*, LXX (1955), 388–392.

Ricardo de Bury, *Philobiblon*: *Speculum*, XXX (1955), 255.

1956 "Raw Head and Bloody Bones," *Journal of American Folklore*, LXIX (1956), 114, 175.

"Some Japanese Proverbial Comparisons," *Western Folklore*, XV (1956), 59–60.

"Proverbial Materials in Two Novels by Harry Harrison Kroll," *Bulletin of the Tennessee Folklore Society*, XXII (1956), 39–52.

"Proverbial Materials in Two More Novels by Harry Harrison Kroll," *Bulletin of the Tennessee Folklore Society*, XXII (1956), 73–84.

"Schmulowitz Collection of Jestbooks," *Western Folklore*, XV (1956), 282–284.

The Shanghai Gesture, "FF Communications," 166 (Helsinki, 1956). Pp. 76.

"Una Comparación Tentativa de Temas de Baladas Inglesas y Españolas," *Folklore Americano* (Lima, Peru) IV, No. 4 pp. 5–27.

"The Nursery Rhyme of Solomon Grundy," *Journal of American Folklore*, LXIX (1956), 356.

Reviews:

Kurt Ranke, *Schleswig-Holsteinische Volksmärchen*, I: *Journal of American Folklore*, LXIX (1956), 392–393.

Giuseppe Vátova, *Saggio sui proverbi istriani*: *Journal of American Folklore*, LXIX (1956), 403.

Tadao Yamamoto, *Growth and System of the Language* of Charles Dickens: *Journal of American Folklore*, LXIX (1956), 405–406.

Rudolf Glutz, *Miracles de Nostre Dame*: *Speculum*, XXXI (1956), 377–379.

Walther Suchier, *Das mittellateinische Gespräch 'Adrian und Epictetus,'*: *Speculum*, XXXI (1956), 413–414.

L. A. Triebel, *Rasser of Alsace*: *Journal of English and Germanic Philology*, LV (1956), 140.

Christian Nielssen, ed. *De gamle vijses exempler oc hoffsprock*: *Journal of American Folklore*, LXIX (1956), 192.

P. N. Boratav, *Contes turcs*: *Journal of American Folklore*, LXIX (1956), 188.

Antonin Perbosc, *Contes de Gascogne*: *Journal of American Folklore*, LXIX (1956), 187–188.

Deutsches Jahrbuch für Volkskunde, I: *Journal of American Folklore*, LXIX (1956), 187.

Jaarboek, Nationale Commissie voor Folklore: *Journal of American Folklore*, LXIX (1956), 89.

R. M. Dawkins, *More Greek Folktales*: *Southern Folklore Quarterly*, XX (1956), 93–95.

Jan-Öjvind Swahn, *The Tale of Cupid and Psyche*: *Southern Folklore Quarterly*, XX (1956), 92–93.

Patricia Evans, *Hopscotch*; Patricia Evans, *Jacks*: *Western Folklore*, XV (1956), 300–301.

Jahrbuch für Volkskunde der Heimatvertriebenen, I; *Württembergisches Jahrbuch für Volkskunde*, I: *Western Folklore*, XV (1956), 296–297.

Marion Kingston, "A Folksong Chapbook": *Western Folklore*, XV (1956), 214–215.

E. P. Kremer, *German Proverbs and Proverbial Phrases*: *Western Folklore*, XV (1956), 142–143.

1957 *Book Catalogues: Their Varieties and Uses*. Chicago, 1957. Pp. xii, 284.

"'American Bottom,' 'Quarteroon,' and 'True Grit,'" *American Speech*, XXXII (1957), 159.

"'No House Is Big Enough for Two Women,'" *Western Folklore*, XVI (1957), 121–124.

"More Examples of an Obscure Manner of Riddling," *Western Folklore*, XVI (1957), 131–132.

"A Long-Sought Parallel Comes to Light," *Western Folklore*, XVI (1957), 48.

"'No Soap,'" *Western Folklore*, XVI (1957), 198–200.

"'Audi, Vide, Tace' and the Three Monkeys," *Fabula*, I (1957), 26–31.

"Proverbial Comparisons in the Plays of Beaumont and Fletcher," *Journal of American Folklore*, LXX (1957), 25–36.

"Paul Delarue, 1889–1956," *Journal of American Folklore*, LXX (1957), 262–263.

"Proverbial Phrases in the Plays of Beaumont and Fletcher," *Bulletin of the Tennessee Folklore Society*, XXIII (1957), 39–59.

"Proverbial Materials in Tobias Smollett, 'The Adventures of Sir Launcelot Greaves,'" *Southern Folklore Quarterly*, XXI (1957), 85–92.

"Some Recent Studies in Folksongs: A Review Article," *Midwest Folklore*, VII (1957), 229–236.

"Proverbs in the Plays of William Wycherley," *Southern Folklore Quarterly*, XXI (1957), 213–217.

"Das Ei im europäischen Volksrätsel," *Schweizerisches Archiv für Volkskunde*, LIII (1957), 194–198.

Reviews:

Charles Joisten, *Contes folkloriques des Hautes-Alpes*; Ariane de Felice, *Contes de Haute-Bretagne*: *Journal of American Folklore*, LXX (1957), 77–78.

Dimitrios Pétropoulos, *La Comparison dans la Chanson populaire grecque*; Israel Cohen, *Parallel Proverbs in English, German and Hebrew*; V. H. Collins, *A Book of English Idioms with Explanations*: *Journal of American Folklore*, LXX, 80–81.

Hellmut Rosenfeld, *Der mittelalterliche Totentanz*: *Speculum*, XXXII (1957), 394–396.

Lutz Röhrich, *Märchen und Wirklichkeit*: *Fabula*, I (1957), 177–179.

Patricia Evans, *Who's It?*: *Western Folklore*, XVI (1957), 146–147.

Erik Dal, *Nordisk folkeviseforskning siden 1800*: *Journal of American Folklore*, LXX (1957), 378.

Cadernos de Folclore, No. 1: *Poesias e Adivinhas*: *Journal of American Folklore*, LXX (1957), 374.

Nikolaus Poppe, *Mongolische Volksdichtung*: *Journal of American Folklore*, LXX (1957), 370–371.

1958 "'Svend i Rosengård' og 'Edward'," *Danske Studier*, 1958, Pp. 105–107.

(with Bartlett Jere Whiting) *A Dictionary of American Proverbs and Proverbial Phrases 1820–1880*. Cambridge, Mass., 1958. Pp. xxii, 418.

"'Vogel federlos' Once more," *Hessische Blätter für Volkskunde*, XLIX–L (1958), 277–294.

"The Predestined Wife (Mt. 930*)," *Fabula. Journal of Folktale Studies*, II (1958), 45–82.

Catalogues of Rare Books. A Chapter in Bibliographical History. "University of Kansas Publications." Library Series, 5. Lawrence, Kansas, 1958. Pp. iii, 65.

"'Tom, Dick, and Harry,'" *Names*, VI (1958), 51–54.

"Dante, A German Incantation, and an Apocryphal Gospel," *76th Annual Report of the Dante Society*, pp. 37–38.

"'All Is Not Gold That Glitters' and *Rolandslied*, 1956," *Romance Philology*, XI (1958), 370–371.

(with Wolfram Eberhard). "Turkish Riddles from the Taurus Mountains," *Western Folklore*, XVII (1958), 249–256.

"Feed a Cold and Starve a Fever," *Journal of American Folklore*, LXX (1958), 190.

"Proverbs and Proverbial Phrases in the Writings of Mary N. Murfree (Charles Egbert Craddock)," *Tennessee Folklore Society Bulletin*, XXIV (1958), 11–50.

"'One for the Cutworm'," *Western Folklore*, XVII (1958), 52–53.

"More Proverbial Comparisons from California," *Western Folklore*, XVII (1958), 12–20.

"'Sop-gravy'," *Western Folklore*, XVII (1958), 126–127.

"'The Customer Is Always Right'," *Western Folklore*, XVII (1958), 54–55.

"Snakes in Virginia," *Western Folklore*, XVII (1958), 277.

"Americanisms Current in 1845," *Western Folklore*, XVII (1958), 280–281.

Reviews:

Kurt Ranke, *Schleswig-Holsteinische Volksmärchen*, Vol. II: *Western Folklore*, XVII (1958), 293.

Paul Nedo, *Sorbische Volksmärchen*: *Midwest Folklore*, VIII (1958), 227–228.

Vance Randolph, *The Talking Turtle and Other Ozark Folk Tales*: *Southern Folklore Quarterly*, XXII (1958), 108–109.

Thomas A. Sebeok, ed. *Studies in Cheremis*, 6; Paul G. Brewster, *Games*. "Indian University Publications," Folklore Series, 11. *The Slavic and East European Journal*, XVI (1958), 360–361.

Volkskundliche Bibliographie für die Jahre 1937 und 1938: Journal of American Folklore, LXXI (1958), 591–592.

Roger Pinon, *La Nouvelle Lyre Malmédienne ou la vie en Wallonie reflété dans la chanson folklorique: Western Folklore*, XVII (1958), 67–69.

Juan B. Rael, *Cuentos Españoles de Colorado y Nuevo Méjico: Western Folklore*, XVII (1958), 134–135.

1959 "German Folksongs in Spain," *Hispanic Review*, XXVII (1959), 49–55.

"The Use of Proper Names in Wellerisms and Folk Tales," *Western Folklore*, XVIII (1959), 287–293.

"The Place of Portuguese Balladry," *Actas do Colóquio de Estudos Etnográficos "Dr. José Leite de Vasconcelos,"* 2 vols., Porto, 1959–1960, II, 125–132.

"The Blind Man, the Lame Man, and the Naked Man," *Western Folklore*, XVIII (1959), 250.

"Zu Fabula 2, 181," *Fabula*, II (1959), 272.

Reviews:

V. Propp, *Morphology of the Folktale: The Slavic and East European Journal*, XVII (1959), 187–189.

[of bibliographical works]. Hans Ruppert, ed. *Goethes Bibliothek Katalog: Library Quarterly*, XXIX (1959), 146–147.

Emilio Rodríguez Demorizi. Seudónimos dominicanos: *Library Quarterly*, XXIX (1959), 213–214.

L. N. Malclès, *Les Sources du travail bibliographique*, Vol. III: *The Library Quarterly*, XXIX (1959), 268–269.

Curt Faber du Faur, *German Baroque Literature: Library Quarterly*, XXIX (1959), 57–59.

Annuaire, I (1939), VI (1953): *Journal of American Folklore*, LXXII (1959), 86–87.

Studies in Honor of Distinguished Service Professor Stith Thompson, ed. W. Edson Richmond: *Journal of American Folklore*, LXXII (1959), 67–68.

L. Burgstaller, *Brauchtumsgebäcke und Weihnachtsspeisen: Journal of American Folklore*, LXXII (1959), 87.

1960 "'High Spots' in Italian Bibliographical History," *Romance Philology*, XIII (1960), 218–241.

"Wellerisms and Riddles," *Western Folklore*, XIX (1960), 55–56.

"'Gringo'," *Western Folklore*, XIX (1960), 58.

"'Crack Shot'," *Western Folklore*, XIX (1960), 130.

Reviews:

Agnes Kovács, *Magyar állatmesék típusmutatója: The Slavic and East European Journal*, New Series, IV (XVIII [1960]), 71–72.

Oskar Loorits, *Estnische Volkserzählungen: The Slavic and East European Journal*, New Series, IV (XVIII [1960]), 69–71.

Ernst Burgstaller, *Oesterreichisches Festtagsgebäck: Western Folklore*, XIX (1960), 141–142.

University of California, Berkeley